MICROECONOMIC THEORY

MICROECONOMIC THEORY

P. R. G. Layard
The London School of Economics

A. A. Walters
The Johns Hopkins University
Baltimore, Maryland

McGraw-Hill Book Company, New York, New York

McGraw-Hill Book (U.K.), Ltd., Maidenhead, Great Britain

St. Louis   San Francisco   Auckland   Beirut   Bogotá   Düsseldorf
Johannesburg   Lisbon   Lucerne   Madrid   Mexico   Montreal   New Delhi   Panama
Paris   San Juan   São Paulo   Singapore   Sydney   Tokyo   Toronto

A McGraw-Hill Publication

MICROECONOMIC THEORY

2 3 4 5 6 7 8 9 0 FGRFGR 7 8 3 2 1 0 9

This book was set in Times Roman.
The editors were J. S. Dietrich and James W. Bradley;
the cover was designed by John Hite;
the production supervisor was Dominick Petrellese.
The drawings were done by J & R Services, Inc.
Fairfield Graphics was printer and binder.

Library of Congress Cataloging in Publication Data

Layard, Richard.
    Microeconomic theory.

    Bibliography: p.
    Includes indexes.
    1. Microeconomics.   I. Walters, Alan A., joint author.   II. Title.
HB171.L39   330   77-21628
ISBN 0-07-036786-8

To Paddie and Pam

CONTENTS

Part 4   Production and Factor Demand

Part 5   Factor Supply

Part 6   Uncertainty

PREFACE

This book is based on the final-year graduate course in microeconomics that we have been giving at the London School of Economics. The drafts of the book, including the problems, have been tried out on two vintages of students, who have provided many useful comments. In addition, some students have gone systematically through the material page by page and provided detailed comments on obscurities in the text and in the problems. With their help we have, we hope, improved the clarity of the book. Among our students, we want to thank in particular M. Ahmed, C. Bellringer, M. Farmer, M. Foley, D. Grubb, A. Nisaruddin, P. Read, and D. Stanitsky. D. Grubb contributed substantially to Chapters 5 and 6, while A. Nisaruddin was responsible for checking the whole book and producing the index.

We should also like to thank the publisher's reviewers, M. J. Boskin, R. A. Dulaney, E. Foster, J. M. Henderson, W. L. Holahan, R. E. Quandt, and J. P. Quirk for their helpful and enthusiastic comments. In addition many of our colleagues have generously commented on one or more chapters: P. S. Dasgupta, C. R. S. Dougherty, P. R. Fallon, W. M. Gorman, B. V. Hindley, R. A. Jackman, H. G. Johnson, J. Muellbauer, S. J. Nickell, A. K. Sen, M. A. M. Smith, J. E. Whalley, P. J. Wiles, and B. S. Yamey. We are extremely grateful to them and for the atmosphere in the L. S. E. Economics Department, which makes such things possible. The book was superbly typed by S. Brewer, B. Jory, and P. Mounsey.

As regards our own roles, the structure of the course was designed by Alan Walters, who also prepared an initial set of lecture notes. The book was written by Richard Layard.

P. R. G. Layard
A. A. Walters

INTRODUCTION

Economics is meant to be useful. At any rate, most students hope it will help them to think better about public policy or about business or personal matters. This book tries to meet their needs. We have concentrated on those parts of economic theory which are now regularly used in trying to solve real-world problems. This is no low-brow exercise, for the mark of progress in economics is that so much theory is now used in practical analysis. We have not found any textbook which assembles most of the useful theory together in one place and presents it at a level suitable for regular graduate and advanced undergraduate students. Some primarily mathematical texts do indeed cover much of the theory; but, because they concentrate on formal rigour, students often fail to appreciate the real-world relevance of the ideas. We try to illustrate the many imaginative applications of these ideas, partly by using a more intuitive (though, we intend, correct) style of text and also by including practical exercises with every section.

Exercises

These exercises (labelled **Q1-1**, and so on) are an intrinsic part of the text. The pedagogic reason for them is that students often fail to learn from reading because they are not immediately challenged to test their understanding of what they have read. That is why the exercises come with every section. You should be able to answer most of the unstarred questions on the basis of what you have just read. Outline answers are included at the back and, if you have trouble with many exercises, it suggests you should reread the section. The starred questions are more difficult and invite you to intellectual adventure. But even the unstarred questions are likely to take as much time as reading the text.

Content

So much for the method of the book. Its content is also somewhat novel. Economics consists of *positive* theory (about how the world is) and *normative* theory (about what should be done). When discussing positive theory, one often wants to allude to its policy implications. So for many purposes it is best to establish the rules of normative analysis first. By treating welfare economics in the first chapter (rather than the last, as is usual), we hope to make explicit the types of value judgment that have to be made before policies can be properly advocated. Most important of all, the discussion of the welfare basis of normative economics provides a strong motivation for the student and a useful frame of reference for much of what follows.

We next proceed, again unusually, to a treatment of general equilibrium (the two-sector model) before we have discussed in detail the behaviour of consumers and producers. This has many advantages. First, it follows naturally from the welfare economics analysis of the optimality or otherwise of the market system. Second, it encourages from the start a real, as opposed to monetary, approach to the concepts of cost and value. Third, it leads naturally to the interesting topics of tax incidence and international trade, which can be treated effectively within the relatively simple framework of the two-sector model. And finally it focuses one's mind on the importance of certain parameters, such as the elasticity of substitution, which are treated more formally later.

However, tackling general equilibrium this early in the book will be unsuitable for some students. It requires tools they will not have, unless they have completed an intermediate course. And some will in any case prefer to start with the more advanced analysis of individual behaviour and leave the question of general equilibrium to the end. The book has therefore been written flexibly so that the chapters can also be read in the order 1, 5–13, 2–4 or in the order 5–13, 1–4.

Chapters 5 and thereafter proceed in a fairly conventional order, taking the different economic agents in turn. First we consider the equilibrium of the consumer, and then we apply utility theory to public pricing policy. Next we examine the producer, and the properties of competitive and uncompetitive markets, mainly for products. Finally, we turn to factor markets, treating first demand and then supply. The book ends by introducing uncertainty and seeing what difference it makes.

The mathematics needed is nothing more than differential calculus (and the elementary idea of an integral). The book has no separate glossary, but we have tried to write it so that the meaning of terms can be easily looked up through the index. We also include a list of further reading. We hope you will enjoy the book.

WELFARE ECONOMICS AND GENERAL EQUILIBRIUM

WELFARE ECONOMICS

Economics is about making the best of things. In other words, it is about choice subject to constraints. The approach is the same whether we are explaining what actually happens in the world or saying what ought to happen. In the first case, which is a matter of "positive" social science, we assume that individuals are consistently pursuing their chosen objectives. From this we predict various features of behaviour. In the second case, which is a "normative" issue, we assume some ethical objective. From this we deduce what ought to be done, given the facts of life. Whichever problem we consider, the formal approach is the same: optimisation subject to constraint.

Most of this book is about positive economics. But, as we explain in the Introduction, one purpose of positive economics is to discover facts relevant to public policy. To draw policy conclusions from these facts, normative theory is needed. So we start by considering normative, or "welfare," economics.

This deals with three main questions. The first is very ambitious and asks: How should a particular society's resources ideally be used, and what social organisation (capitalism, socialism, or whatever) is best for bringing this allocation about? We deal with this major issue in Secs. 1-1 to 1-4. However, in practice, the world is less than ideal. So it is useful to ask a second, less enormous but in many ways more important question: How can we tell whether any change we make is for the better? This is treated in Secs. 1-5 and 1-6. To answer both questions in any specific way, one must of course use some specific ethical welfare function to evaluate the alternatives being compared. So the third issue, discussed in the last section, is: What would be the properties of an acceptable welfare function? This is ultimately a matter of personal value judgment, since as David Hume pointed out 200 years ago, you cannot get an "ought" from an "is." But the question can still be fruitfully discussed.

1-1 SOCIETY'S ECONOMIC PROBLEM

We begin by examining the ideal configuration of the economy, given any particular welfare function. A society is endowed with resources of all kinds: land, capital, and, above all, the time of its citizens. These can be used in alternative ways to generate benefits for the members of society. Many resources can produce benefits without being used for what is normally called production. For example, people can enjoy spending time in the countryside or any other form of rewarding experience you may care to think of. However, provided we define production in a wide way that does not confine it to what happens in a factory, we can say that resources (or "factors" of production) are always used to produce "products." So the first issue is:

1. How should factors be allocated among products? This will determine both the quantity of each product and the technique by which it is produced, as reflected in its mix of inputs (factors).

But a second question then arises:

2. How should the products be distributed among the different citizens?

Much ink and feeling have been spent on the question of whether these two issues can be treated separately. However, unless special assumptions are made, it is fairly obvious that the two must be solved simultaneously.

This emerges clearly if we set up the problem formally, in order to determine what conditions must be satisfied if an economy is ideally organised. For concreteness we shall assume a very simple closed economy with two people: A (Robinson Crusoe?) and B (Man Friday?). The economy is endowed with two factors, which we shall call capital K and labour time L. This is purely for illustration.† We assume these are available in fixed quantities $\bar{K}$ and $\bar{L}$. (Later in the book we relax the assumption of fixed factor supplies, but it remains true that the ultimate resources of the community, properly defined, are at any one moment given.) Our two factors are homogeneous and perfectly divisible‡ and can be used to produce two equally homogeneous and

---

† We discuss the problems that arise in the measurement of capital (and labour) in Chapter 12.

‡ A factor or good is homogeneous if all units of it have identical qualities. It is perfectly divisible if it can be divided in any way whatsoever; for example, 1 lb of sugar can be readily divided into ounces or similar units, but this is more difficult to do with cars.

divisible outputs: x (wheat) and y (fish). So if K^x indicates capital allocated to producing x, and so on, the allocation of factors is constrained by

$$\bar{K} = K^x + K^y \qquad \bar{L} = L^x + L^y$$

Once allocated, these factors generate outputs. The production function specifies for each product the maximum output that can be produced with any particular set of inputs. We suppose the production functions of x and y are

$$x = x(K^x, L^x) \qquad y = y(K^y, L^y)$$

where more of any factor leads to more output. These outputs in turn must be allocated between Crusoe and his friend. So, if x^A is the amount of x allocated to A and so on, then

$$x = x^A + x^B \qquad y = y^A + y^B$$

We shall suppose that the happiness of A depends only on how much x and y he gets. If he were altruistic, his happiness would also vary directly with what B got; if he were envious, it would vary inversely with what B got. Adding such interdependences does not alter the basic structure of the problem, but for simplicity we omit them. Thus A has a happiness, or *utility*, function u that tells us how well off he is, depending on his consumption of products x and y; so does B:†

$$u^A = u^A(x^A, y^A) \qquad u^B = u^B(x^B, y^B)$$

Once again more of x or y leads to more happiness.

These remarks define the constraints within which the society operates: factor endowments are limited, technology limits the goods that can be produced by given factors, and tastes limit the happiness that can be produced by given goods. What configuration of the economy is optimal depends on one's personal value judgments, embodied in one's own ethical welfare function. In particular, people differ in the importance that they attach to equality as against efficiency, and this will be reflected in their welfare functions. So, if we follow custom and call this function the *social welfare function*, we are not implying that there is any agreement in society about what is desirable. We shall, however, assume that the only variables that are to count towards welfare are the happinesses of the individuals in society. Apart from this, we need not commit ourselves yet to any exact specification of the function, since mathematics enables us to sit on the fence and simply write the welfare function as $W(u^A, u^B)$. The problem is thus:

$$\max W = W(u^A, u^B)$$

---

† As we shall show in the last section, it is necessary, for any satisfactory form of normative economics, to assume that the happiness of an individual is a cardinal entity; e.g., if there are three states of the world, it must make sense to say of a given individual that $u^1 - u^2 = u^2 - u^3$, where u^i is utility (or happiness) in state i. For positive economics no such assumption of cardinality is necessary (see Chapter 5).

subject to

$$\bar{K} = K^x + K^y \qquad \bar{L} = L^x + L^y \qquad \text{(endowments)}$$

$$x^A + x^B = x(K^x, L^x) \qquad y^A + y^B = y(K^y, L^y) \qquad \text{(technology)}$$

$$u^A = u^A(x^A, y^A) \qquad u^B = u^B(x^B, y^B) \qquad \text{(tastes)}$$

The solution involves, besides the six constraints, four other first-order conditions.† These four equations are fundamental to welfare economics and are often called the optimality conditions. We shall discuss their meaning at length in the next two sections. However, it is convenient to list them all here, together with the names we shall give them. Note that throughout the book we denote partial derivatives by suffixes; for example, the marginal product of labour in the x industry $(\partial x/\partial L)$ is written as x_L or, since it depends on K^x and L^x, as $x_L(K^x, L^x)$.‡ Our four equations are then:

1. Efficient consumption

$$\frac{u_x^A(x^A, y^A)}{u_y^A(x^A, y^A)} = \frac{u_x^B(x^B, y^B)}{u_y^B(x^B, y^B)} \qquad \text{or in brief} \qquad \left(\frac{u_x}{u_y}\right)^A = \left(\frac{u_x}{u_y}\right)^B$$

2. Efficient production

$$\frac{x_L(K^x, L^x)}{x_K(K^x, L^x)} = \frac{y_L(K^y, L^y)}{y_K(K^y, L^y)} \qquad \text{or in brief} \qquad \frac{x_L}{x_K} = \frac{y_L}{y_K}$$

3. Efficient product-mix

$$\frac{u_x^A(x^A, y^A)}{u_y^A(x^A, y^A)} = \frac{y_K(K^y, L^y)}{x_K(K^x, L^x)} \qquad \text{or in brief} \qquad \left(\frac{u_x}{u_y}\right)^A = \frac{y_K}{x_K}$$

---

† The solution is derived in Appendix 2 on page 396. Note that we are assuming there is a regular interior solution to the problem, i.e., one that is characterised by the relevant marginal equalities rather than by the inequalities that characterise corner solutions. Sufficient (but not necessary) conditions to generate this are that

(i) All functions are strictly quasi-concave (see definitions in Appendix 1 on page 391).

(ii) All functions are twice differentiable; i.e., if the function is $f(z_1, \dots, z_n)$, $\partial^2 f/\partial z_i \partial z_j$ is defined everywhere for all i, j.

(iii) In each function all variables are "indispensible," i.e., for any pair i, j, $-(\partial f/\partial z_j)/(\partial f/\partial z_i)$ tends to infinity as z_i tends to zero and z_j is adjusted to hold f constant.

We make these assumptions throughout this chapter. Conditions (i) and (iii) guarantee that every variable takes a nonzero value, while condition (ii) guarantees well-defined derivatives. To guarantee, in addition, that any point that is a local optimum is also a global optimum, it is sufficient to make the utility and production functions strictly concave, rather than strictly quasi-concave (see Appendix 1).

‡ There is an annex on notation on page 419. Since derivatives are denoted by suffixes, we use suffixes for as few other purposes as possible.

4. Social justice

$$\frac{u_x^A(x^A, y^A)}{u_x^B(x^B, y^B)} = \frac{W_{u^B}(u^A, u^B)}{W_{u^A}(u^A, u^B)} \qquad \text{or in brief} \qquad \frac{u_x^A}{u_x^B} = \frac{W_{u^B}}{W_{u^A}}$$

where W_{u^A} and W_{u^B} indicate the partial effects on W of u^A and u^B. With these four equations and six constraints we can solve for the 10 unknowns (not counting W) in the original problem.†

1-2 THREE CONDITIONS FOR EFFICIENCY

What does all this mean? Though the original problem has to be solved in one simultaneous operation, it can be thought of in various parts. The first distinction is between efficiency and equity (or social justice). Whatever one thinks of the relative social value of A's and B's happiness (i.e., whatever one's social welfare function), most people would agree that if we could make A happier without making B less happy, we should do so. This is still a value judgment, but is implicit in any benevolent social welfare function in which welfare is held to rise with individual happiness. One part of our objective, therefore, is to reach a position where it is no longer possible to make A happier except by making B less happy. This is the property of a social state that is *efficient*. Since this definition of efficiency owes much to the economist Pareto, an efficient social state is often called Pareto-optimal.

A situation is efficient, *or* Pareto-optimal, *if it is impossible to make one person better off except by making someone else worse off.*

To be in such a position is simply to avoid wasting an opportunity of getting something for nothing. Any other position we call wasteful or inefficient. The three conditions necessary for efficiency are those set out in our first three optimality conditions. Let us take them one by one.

1 Efficient Consumption

First, suppose that the outputs of x and y are given at x^0 and y^0. (Crusoe and Friday have moved to a wilderness where manna and quails fall from heaven.) The only problem is to achieve an efficient pattern of consumption. For an efficient allocation of x and y it must be impossible to make A better off without making B worse off. As we shall show, this requires that both A and B place the same relative value on x and y.

The concept of value often raises difficulty, and is even considered inhuman

---

† The unknowns are K^x, K^y, L^x, L^y, x^A, x^B, y^A, y^B, u^A, u^B.

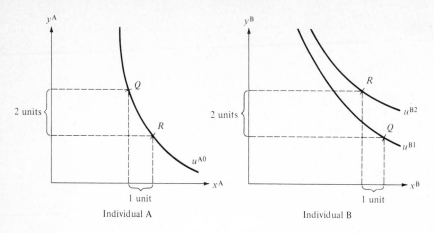

Figure 1-1 Gains from trade.

by some. But it is quite simple. If we say, "I really value having a church on my street," the test of how much we value it is how much we are willing to sacrifice for it.† Accordingly, the value of x is the amount of y a person is willing to give up for it.

Suppose then that A and B place different relative values on x and y. Say A is just willing to sacrifice 2 units of y for an extra unit of x, and vice versa. However, B values x less highly, and is willing to sacrifice only 1 unit of y for 1 unit of x, and vice versa. If A gives B 2 units of y in exchange for 1 unit of x, his welfare is unaffected. But at the same time B is made better off, because he gets 2 units of y in exchange for his x, whereas he only required 1 unit to be just as well off as before. So the original position was inefficient, and the situation has been improved by the exchange: one person has gained, and the other has not lost. This simple example conveys the basic idea of the gains from trade.

To carry the story further it is useful to use indifference curves (see Figure 1-1). For any particular individual an indifference curve shows all combinations of x and y which make him or her equally happy. Thus the curve labelled u^{A0} in Figure 1-1 corresponds to the equation

$$u^{A0} = u^A(x^A, y^A)$$

where u^{A0} is a particular fixed level of utility for A. (In our notation numerical superscripts will always indicate some fixed value of the variable in question.)

---

† This is his private valuation of x. In competitive equilibrium everyone places the same private value on x. This does not mean that the social value of an additional unit of x for a poor person is the same as for a rich person: social value involves the social welfare function.

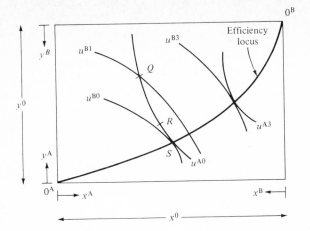

Figure 1-2 Efficient consumption: product space.

The indifference curves are assumed to be strictly convex towards the origin.†
This implies that, as A gets more x (and less y) he values additional x less and
less. In the move from Q to R he valued x at 2 units of y. However, if he were
to continue giving up y he would be willing to give up less and less y for
each unit of x as he moved southeast along his indifference curve. Now
consider individual B. He gained in the move from Q to R, since this moved
him on to an indifference curve further from the origin and corresponding to a
higher level of utility. However, the more he surrenders x in exchange for y,
the more highly he values x and the more y he will need to compensate himself
for each unit of x he gives up. So, as exchange proceeds, A values x less and
less and B values it more and more. Provided that the indifference curves are
smoothly curved (rather than kinked),‡ there will come a point where A and B
both place the same value on x relative to y. This is an efficient point.

The process can be illustrated more generally in the Edgeworth box in
Figure 1-2. The dimensions of the box are the total quantity of x in the
economy, measured along the horizontal axis, and the total quantity of y,
measured along the vertical axis. So if we make the bottom left-hand corner the
origin of measurement for A's allocations of x and y and the top right-hand
corner the origin for B's allocations, any point in the box represents a division
of the total x into x^A and x^B, and likewise for y. All we have done in fact is to
rotate B's part of Figure 1-1 through 180° and add it onto A's part of the
figure. It turns out that, if we keep A's utility constant and continue the process
of exchange until A's and B's relative values are equal, we arrive at S, where each
values x at about $1\frac{1}{2}$ units of y. At this point the indifference curves of A and B
must, of course, be tangential to each other since they have the same slope.

---

† Reasons for assuming this are given in Chapter 5. This corresponds to assumption (i) in
footnote † to page 6.
‡ This corresponds to assumption (ii) in footnote † to page 6.

However, S is only one of many allocations of x^0 and y^0 at which tangencies occur. All of these points are efficient, since at each it is impossible to raise u^A without reducing u^B, and vice versa. The locus of these points is the *efficiency locus*.

Along the efficiency locus, the value of x (in terms of y) is the same for both individuals. We have so far thought of the value of x as the amount of y the person is willing to sacrifice for one more unit of x. But, for small changes, we could equally well ask: How much extra y would the individual need to compensate him for having one less unit of x? This latter is naturally called the *marginal rate of substitution* of y for x (MRS_{yx}). So the efficiency condition becomes

$$\mathrm{MRS}^A_{yx} = \mathrm{MRS}^B_{yx}$$

Efficient consumption requires that all individuals place the same relative value on all products (value being assessed at the margin).[†]

What mathematical relationship describes this? The indifference curve of a given individual for specified utility u^0 is

$$u^0 = u(x, y)$$

Taking total differentials of both sides,[‡] we obtain

$$0 = u_x\, dx + u_y\, dy$$

So the slope of the indifference curve is

$$-\frac{dy}{dx} = \frac{u_x}{u_y} = \mathrm{MRS}_{yx}$$

(There are some responses that are useful to learn in a ratlike fashion. One of these is that the absolute slope $|dy/dx|$ is the marginal utility of x relative to that of y.) If

$$\mathrm{MRS}^A_{yx} = \mathrm{MRS}^B_{yx}$$

then

$$\left(\frac{u_x}{u_y}\right)^A = \left(\frac{u_x}{u_y}\right)^B \tag{1}$$

[†] Note that this equality condition assumes all goods are infinitely divisible. If there are indivisibilities, it needs to be replaced by a more complex expression involving inequalities.

[‡] When taking the total differentials of a given equation, one allows all those variables which can vary to do so (by a small amount). The resulting equation states the relationships that must hold between the changes in all the variables that have changed. If $u = u(x, y)$, the change in u is $(\partial u/\partial x)\, dx + (\partial u/\partial y)\, dy$. This gives the right-hand side of our equation. The left-hand side is zero, since u^0, being a fixed number, cannot change. So the equation describes those changes in x and y which keep us on the indifference curve.

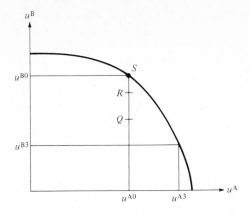

Figure 1-3 The utility frontier for $x = x^0$, $y = y^0$: utility space.

This is the first of our three necessary conditions for social efficiency, set out in Sec. 1-1.

Needless to say, it is not a sufficient condition for a social optimum. For along the efficiency locus there is an infinite number of combinations (u^A, u^B) which are all efficient (but are not all equitable). We can plot these combinations in "utility space" in Figure 1-3 (Figure 1-2 was in "product space"). For example we know from Figure 1-2 that if $u^A = u^{A0}$, the maximum of u^B is u^{B0}. Another pair of efficient points is (u^{A3}, u^{B3}). To choose the best of all points we should need to bring in the social welfare function, and to select that point on the utility frontier for which social welfare is highest.

Q1-1 Suppose the supply of quails and manna is given, such that Crusoe values 1 unit of manna at three quails, and Friday says he is just willing to give up four quails in return for 2 units of manna. Which of them values quails more highly, and in which direction should reallocation proceed between them so as to make both better off?

2 Efficient Production

Efficient consumption, which we have just considered, is about the allocation of given goods between individuals. It therefore ignores the production side of the economy. Efficient production is about the allocation of given factors between the production of different goods and ignores the pattern of human wants. The criterion for productive efficiency is simply that, for a given production of y, the output of x should be the maximum possible. Formally, therefore, the structure of the problem is identical to that of efficient consumption. In the production problem scarce factors have to be allocated as inputs in producing goods; in the consumption problem scarce goods have to be allocated as inputs in producing utilities. And, in both cases, the allocation has to ensure that one "product" cannot be expanded without reducing the other. The formal identity between the problems is brought out in the first two columns in the table on page 12.

Problem	Scarce inputs	Outputs	Efficiency condition
Efficient consumption	x, y	$u^A = u^A(x^A, y^A)$ $u^B = u^B(x^B, y^B)$	$\text{MRS}^A_{yx} = \text{MRS}^B_{yx}$ i.e., $(u_x/u_y)^A = (u_x/u_y)^B$
Efficient production	K, L	$x = x(K^x, L^x)$ $y = y(K^y, L^y)$	$\text{MRS}^x_{KL} = \text{MRS}^y_{KL}$ i.e., $x_L/x_K = y_L/y_K$

Since the problem is similar, so is the solution. For any output an isoquant defines the combinations of capital and labour which can produce a given quantity of output. So the isoquant for $x = x^0$ is given by

$$x^0 = x(K^x, L^x)$$

Efficiency clearly requires that the isoquants for x and y have the same slope. This is illustrated in the Edgeworth box in Figure 1-4. The dimensions of the box are now the quantities of K and L ($\bar{K}$ and $\bar{L}$) to be allocated between the two industries: the diagram is thus in factor space, rather than in product space as is Figure 1-2. Any point in the box represents an allocation. Point P is inefficient (check this by finding a different allocation where $x > x^0$ and $y > y^2$). But there is again an efficiency locus where x can only be increased by cutting back on y.

If we call the slope of an isoquant the *marginal rate of substitution* between K and L (MRS_{KL}), efficiency then requires that this be equal in both industries:

$$\text{MRS}^x_{KL} = \text{MRS}^y_{KL}$$

Efficient production requires that the marginal rate of substitution between factors be the same in all industries.

To find the slope of an x isoquant, we totally differentiate

$$x^0 = x(K^x, L^x)$$

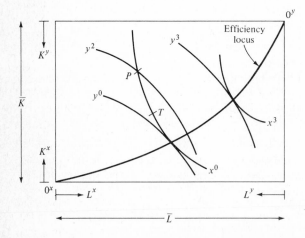

Figure 1-4 Efficient production: factor space.

therefore,

$$0 = x_K \, dK^x + x_L \, dL^x$$

Consequently, the slope of an isoquant is

$$-\frac{dK^x}{dL^x} = \frac{x_L}{x_K} = \mathrm{MRS}^x_{KL}$$

Thus if

$$\mathrm{MRS}^x_{KL} = \mathrm{MRS}^y_{KL}$$

then

$$\frac{x_L}{x_K} = \frac{y_L}{y_K} \qquad (2)$$

which is the second of our three necessary efficiency conditions for a social optimum.

To see the inner meaning of this, consider the inefficient allocation at T, where the factors are being used in the same proportions in both industries. What is wrong with this? We know that

$$\mathrm{MRS}^x_{KL} > \mathrm{MRS}^y_{KL}$$

So

$$\frac{x_L}{x_K} > \frac{y_L}{y_K}$$

Hence

$$\frac{x_L}{y_L} > \frac{x_K}{y_K}$$

The ratio of the marginal product of labour in x to labour in y is higher than the corresponding ratio for capital. In other words, labour has comparative advantage in producing x: it is relatively more efficient at producing x than capital is. But if the factors are employed in the same ratios in both industries, this difference in comparative advantage is not exploited. To exploit it we allocate more labour to x and more capital to y, each factor being allocated towards the industry in which it has comparative advantage.† For the same reason one hopes that you (and we) are best employed doing economics, even though we might be better at driving than the average taxi driver and might find economics difficult.‡ The point is that our *relative* advantage (or relative marginal product)

---

† A similar argument applies in consumption. If people have differing tastes, some may have comparative advantage as consumers of wheat (vegetarians) and some as consumers of fish.

‡ Max Planck, the originator of quantum theory, once told Keynes that in early life he had thought of studying economics but had found it too difficult. (There is no record of which famous economists had thought of studying physics but found it too difficult.)

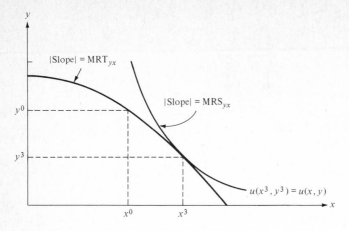

Figure 1-5 The transformation curve: product space.

is higher in the economics industry. Efficient production requires that we exploit differences in comparative advantage and allocate inputs differentially towards those outputs where they have comparative advantage.

Of course efficient production is not sufficient for an optimum. The efficiency locus in factor space traces out a sequence of combinations of x and y which can be plotted in product space in Figure 1-5. This curve is formally analogous to the utility frontier. It has been given many names: the production frontier, the production possibility curve, the transformation curve. We will often use the last of these, because we intend to refer to the absolute slope of the curve as the *marginal rate of transformation* of y into x (MRT_{yx}). This slope measures, of course, the cost in terms of y of one additional unit of x, efficiently produced, or the *marginal cost* of x.

Q1-2 Suppose the production functions of wheat x and fish y are as follows:

$$x = K^{1/3}L^{2/3} \qquad y = K^{2/3}L^{1/3}$$

Currently one-half the total capital $\bar{K}$ and one-half the total labour time $\bar{L}$ is allocated to each output. In which direction should factors be reallocated if both outputs are to be increased?

3. Product-Mix Efficiency

To choose between the different feasible combinations of x and y we need to bring in the pattern of human wants. Suppose, for a moment, there were only one person in this economy (Robinson Crusoe), with $u = u(x, y)$. Then clearly social welfare would be maximised when he had reached the highest point on his utility function consistent with remaining within the production frontier. We can picture him climbing the hill of happiness until he reaches the frontier and then travelling along it till he has reached the highest point. When he is at this point he must be walking along a level contour of the hill. Nevertheless, he is also walking along the frontier. Accordingly, the utility contour is tangential to the production frontier, as at (x^3, y^3) in Figure 1-5. At this point

$$\text{MRS}_{yx} = \text{MRT}_{yx}$$

But MRS_{yx} is the amount of y that Crusoe is willing to sacrifice for a unit of x and MRT_{yx} is the amount he has to sacrifice. So long as he is *willing* to sacrifice more than he *has* to, he ought to produce more x, stopping only when the two measures are equal.

Product-mix efficiency requires that the subjective value of x in terms of y should equal its marginal cost.

But how do we measure the marginal cost of x in terms of y? One way of increasing x is to shift 1 unit of capital from y to x. This increases x by x_K and decreases y by y_K. The amount of y lost per additional unit of x is y_K/x_K, and so the slope of the transformation curve is†

$$-\frac{dy}{dx} = \frac{y_K}{x_K} = \text{MRT}_{yx}$$

If

$$\text{MRS}_{yx} = \text{MRT}_{yx}$$

---

† Though one way of increasing y at the expense of x is to shift only one factor (here K) between them, it is not obvious that this is as good a way of increasing y as to shift some of both factors. However, for small changes the two cost the same. Let both factors vary, and totally differentiate the two production functions $y = y(K^y, L^y)$ and $x = x(\bar{K} - K^y, \bar{L} - L^y)$:

$$dy = y_K\, dK^y + y_L\, dL^y \qquad\qquad (A)$$

$$dx = -x_K\, dK^y - x_L\, dL^y \qquad\qquad (B)$$

From (B) we have

$$dK^y = -\frac{dx}{x_K} - \frac{x_L}{x_K}\, dL^y$$

Substituting in (A), we find

$$dy = -dx\,\frac{y_K}{x_K} - \left(y_K\,\frac{x_L}{x_K} - y_L\right) dL^y$$

But efficiency requires that

$$\frac{x_L}{x_K} - \frac{y_L}{y_K} = 0$$

Therefore

$$-\frac{dy}{dx} = \frac{y_K}{x_K}$$

then

$$\frac{u_x}{u_y} = \frac{y_K}{x_K} \tag{3}$$

which is our third efficiency condition. One way of viewing this result is to notice, from cross multiplying, that it is impossible by shifting capital to increase utility. Needless to say, the condition could equally well be expressed in terms of labour, since Equation (2) tells us that $y_L/x_L = y_K/x_K$. Finally, we can introduce a second person, but this raises no problem since from Equation (1)

$$\left(\frac{u_x}{u_y}\right)^A = \left(\frac{u_x}{u_y}\right)^B$$

If we are at a position where

$$\text{MRS}^A_{yx} = \text{MRS}^B_{yx} > \text{MRT}_{yx}$$

then it must be possible to make both individuals better off by producing more x, since both individuals are willing to make the necessary sacrifice.

Q1-3 Suppose that the transformation curve is given by $x^2 + y^2 = 20$ and that Crusoe's and Friday's utility functions are, respectively $u^A = x^A y^A$ and $u^B = x^B y^B$. Production and consumption is

	x	y
Crusoe	1	2
Friday	1	2
Both	2	4

What is the value of x in terms of y and what is its marginal cost? In what direction must production shift if both Crusoe and Friday are to become better off?

Q1-4 Suppose Crusoe is on his own, with $u = xy$ and production functions as in Q1-2. How should he allocate his total resources of capital $\bar{K}$ and labour time $\bar{L}$ between x and y?

Q1-5 Suppose there are two goods (wheat and lamb) and two perfectly divisible fields, K (hilly) and L (flat), each of 100 acres. Output per acre is as follows and requires no labour or capital input.

Good	Hilly field (K)	Flat field (L)
Wheat (x)	1.5	5
Lamb (y)	1	2

Derive the transformation curve. (Warning: it is not smooth but kinked.) If Crusoe has $u = xy$, how should the fields be allocated?

Q1-6 This is a simpler question, to revise the simplest form of the equimarginal principle. Suppose there is only one good x and two fields A and B. Crusoe has a given amount of time $\bar{L}$ to divide between the fields. Output is given by

$$x^A = aL^{A^{2/3}}$$
$$x^B = bL^{B^{2/3}} \qquad a > b$$

What proportion of his time should Crusoe spend in each field?

1-3 SOCIAL JUSTICE AND THE SOCIAL OPTIMUM

So far we have only worried about efficiency. However, there are a whole host of efficient configurations of the economy. We can easily see how the utility frontier of the economy is constructed. We simply take each feasible output mix from Figure 1-5 and construct its utility frontier, just as we constructed the utility frontier for (x^0, y^0) in Figure 1-3. This gives us a family of utility frontiers. The overall utility frontier is then the outer envelope of all these frontiers (see Figure 1-6).

To find the social optimum (or constrained "bliss point") we use the social welfare function to pick the preferred utility mix. At the optimum the slope of the isowelfare curve equals the slope of the utility frontier. The isowelfare function has the equation

$$W^0 = W(u^A, u^B)$$

so its slope is

$$\frac{\partial W/\partial u^A}{\partial W/\partial u^B} = \frac{W_{u^A}}{W_{u^B}}$$

But what is the slope of the utility frontier? To think about this, remember

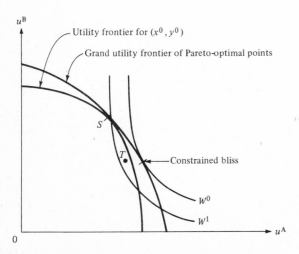

Figure 1-6 The social optimum: utility space.

that at the optimum some given (x, y) mix is being produced. So, locally, the grand utility frontier has the slope of the utility frontier for that particular output mix. Now suppose that, with those outputs given, we transfer one unit of x from A to B. The utility of B goes up by u_x^B and that of A goes down by u_x^A. So the slope of the utility frontier is u_x^B/u_x^A and social justice requires

$$\frac{u_x^B}{u_x^A} = \frac{W_{u^A}}{W_{u^B}} \tag{4}$$

This was our fourth optimality condition.† As you can see by cross multiplying, it says simply that the social value of giving an extra unit of x to A must be the same as the social value of giving it to B.

Once we have picked the bliss point we have solved all our economic problems, for this point corresponds to a unique product-mix (x, y),‡ which corresponds to

1. A unique allocation of factors between goods (K^x, K^y, L^x, L^y)—this solves the problem of what shall be produced and how
2. A unique allocation of goods between people (x^A, x^B, y^A, y^B)—this solves the problem of "for whom"

There is one other crucial point. Suppose for some reason we are prevented from producing the ideal output. There are many inefficient points (like T) which are preferable to efficient points like S. Thus efficiency is only unambiguously desirable if equity is also fully satisfied, in other words, if the distribution of income is also right.

A final word on terminology. We have distinguished between efficiency and equity (or justice). Others distinguish between problems of allocation and distribution to refer to the same dichotomy. However, the distinction dates back to the time when it was thought possible to solve the economic problem in two stages:

1. Maximise the value of the social product by correctly allocating resources, i.e., factors of production.
2. Ensure an equitable distribution by a fair allocation of the product.

As we have seen, it is not possible to solve the problem in a step by step (or recursive) manner like this. The distinction, therefore, needs to be used with care.

---

† Notice the similarity between Equations (3) and (4). This is because the following problems are formally identical:
(3) max $u(x, y)$, subject to $x = x(K^x, L^x)$, $y = y(\overline{K} - K^x, \overline{L} - L^x)$
(4) max $W(u^A, u^B)$ subject to $u^A = u^A(x^A, y^A)$, $u^B = u^B(x^0 - x^A, y^0 - y^A)$
‡ This depends on the assumptions listed on page 6.

Q1-7 Suppose

$$x^2 + y^2 = 50 \qquad u^A = x^A y^A \qquad u^B = x^B y^B \qquad W = u^A u^B$$

How much x and y should be produced and how should it be distributed?

Q1-8 "Any allocation of resources and goods from which it is impossible to make one person better off without making another worse off is preferable to all allocations for which this is not the case." True or false?

1-4 CAPITALISM, MARKET FAILURE, AND ALTERNATIVE ECONOMIC SYSTEMS

So far, we have said nothing about the system of economic organisation. We have simply described the technical conditions which must hold at the optimum. Now the question is: What form of organisation will bring us nearest to the optimum? If it had all the information, a computer could, in principle, solve the problem we have posed. In a centrally planned economy the government, if it had the power, could then implement the solution. That is one approach. But how would a freely functioning capitalist economy perform? Remarkably well, if we make four sweeping assumptions, which we shall cite in a few pages. The key assumption is that in every market there are so many buyers and sellers that all behave as though their actions individually cannot affect the price, or, in other words, that we have perfect competition.

Under perfect competition all agents behave as price takers.

Consequently, we need to modify our previous example to include many consumers and many producers. Otherwise, we can continue to use it to illustrate the optimality properties of capitalism. First we show how a perfectly competitive economy can satisfy the three conditions for efficiency, and after that we bring in questions of equity.

To provide the relevant framework, let us rewrite the efficiency conditions (1) to (3) with suitable gaps, which the reader can fill in as we proceed.

1. Efficient consumption

$$\left(\frac{u_x}{u_y}\right)^A = \qquad = \left(\frac{u_x}{u_y}\right)^B \tag{1}$$

2. Efficient production

$$\frac{x_L}{x_K} = \qquad = \frac{y_L}{y_K} \tag{2}$$

3. Efficient product-mix

$$\frac{u_x}{u_y} = \qquad = \qquad = \frac{y_K}{x_K} \tag{3}$$

$$\uparrow \qquad\qquad \uparrow$$
$$\text{consumers} \qquad \text{producers}$$

Let us start with consumption. Suppose there are very many consumers of type A, each with identical tastes and the same factor endowments, and the same number of consumers of type B, likewise identical to each other. Each consumer i is maximising utility $u^i(x^i, y^i)$ subject to budget constraint $p_x x^i + p_y y^i = m^{i0}$, where m^{i0} is money income and p_x and p_y are the respective product prices. Consumption is adjusted until the marginal rate of substitution between y and x is equal to the y cost of an extra unit of x.† This latter cost is the money cost of x divided by the money cost of y. So

$$\frac{u_x^i}{u_y^i} = \frac{p_x}{p_y} \tag{1'}$$

But all consumers face the same prices. Thus the price mechanism ensures that the relative values of x and y get equated among all citizens. This settles Equation (1):‡ consumer's gains from trade are fully exploited.

As for producers, a firm i having the production function $x(K^i, L^i)$ will always want to produce as much as it can for any given money cost C^{i0}. If w_K and w_L are the respective factor prices, then $w_K K^i + w_L L^i = C^{i0}$. Constrained output maximisation requires that the marginal rate of substitution between K and L be equated to the relative factor prices w_L/w_K :

$$\frac{x_{L^i}}{x_{K^i}} = \frac{w_L}{w_K} \tag{2'}$$

The problem is formally identical to that faced by the consumer, and so is the solution.§ Alternatively, we could pose the firm with the more interesting problem: minimise the cost of producing x^{i0}. The first-order conditions are again (2'), so it is useful to think of these as the conditions for cost minimisation. Since a similar equation to (2') holds in the y industry, cost minimisation guarantees that marginal rates of substitution are equated in all industries. In our example this settles Equation (2), apart from one point. Equation (2) shows relative marginal products in the x

† Diagramatically, the consumer's equilibrium is described by the left-hand diagram. Similarly, the producer's cost-minimising equilibrium is described by the right-hand diagram.

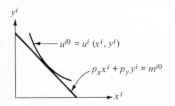
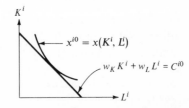

‡ We must, of course, now interpret $u^A(x^A, y^A)$ as describing the utility level of each consumer A when the group as a whole are consuming x^A, y^A and each member of the group is consuming a fraction $1/n$ of each, assuming the group has n members. Similarly, $W(u^A, u^B)$ must rank social states according to the welfare of the representative consumer of each type.

§ See footnote † above.

industry as depending on the total inputs to that industry summed over all firms, whereas our present discussion shows them depending on the inputs to the individual firm. This is all right, provided that we assume that each firm in the industry is producing at constant returns to scale, and likewise in the y industry.[†] From now on, we shall make this assumption. But, even without it, it can be proved that perfect competition ensures productive efficiency.

Finally, what about Equation (3)? If a firm maximises profits, it expands output until the marginal cost of output has risen to equal its price. But what is the marginal cost? Suppose a firm with a production function $x(K^i, L^i)$ employs one more unit of capital. Its costs rise by w_K and its output of x by x_{K^i}. So its additional cost per unit of additional output is w_K/x_{K^i}. That is the marginal cost (MC_x) of x. If all firms in the x industry produce at constant returns to scale, they all have the same marginal products and we can suppress the index i:

$$p_x = MC_x = \frac{w_K}{x_K} \qquad p_y = MC_y = \frac{w_K}{y_K} \qquad (3')$$

By inserting these profit-maximising conditions into (3), you will find that the equality postulated there holds.

Thus the market economy has produced an efficient allocation of resources.[‡] Does it follow that it maximises the ethical social welfare function? Obviously not, since this must also depend on whether the ownership of the factors of production is fairly distributed. However, there must be some distribution of factor ownership which would make capitalism equitable as well as efficient, so that it maximised social welfare. We can, in fact, see in our example how this distribution would be computed. We need to find one or more fair ways of allocating K and L between A and B, in such a way that a free market would lead to the same configuration of output and consumption as maximises social welfare. From Sec. 1-1 we know the desirable allocation of factors (i.e., the values of K^x, K^y, L^x, L^y) and of products (i.e., the values of x^A, x^B, y^A, y^B). From them we can determine the implicit structure of relative prices.[§] For example,

1. x^A and y^A tell us u_x^A/u_y^A and thus p_x/p_y [from Equation (1')].
2. K^x and L^x tell us x_L/x_K and thus w_L/w_K [from Equation (2')].
3. K^x and L^x also tell us x_K and thus w_K/p_x [from Equation (3')].

Since there are only four prices, knowing three relative prices means we can compute any other relative price. It is usually convenient to measure all prices in terms of one numeraire, say y, so that we have p_x/p_y, w_K/p_y, and w_L/p_y.

---

† If there are constant returns to scale, an equiproportional increase in all inputs produces an equiproportional rise in all outputs. In this case marginal products depend only on relative factor proportions (see Appendix 3). Since all firms in an industry will employ the same factor proportions, their marginal products can be written as functions of industry inputs. As regards the assumption that returns are constant at equilibrium, this is not as artificial as it may first seem (see Chapter 7).

‡ This depends on three key assumptions still to be made explicit.

§ These correspond to the "shadow prices" given by the values of the Lagrangian multipliers $(\lambda_1, \lambda_2, \lambda_3, \text{ and } \lambda_4)$ in the solution of the welfare maximisation problem (see Appendix 2).

We can now ask how we can make sure that group A and group B can consume the quantities of output which maximum welfare requires they should have. To do this, we look at A's budget equation. His expenditure on the goods he needs to buy must be matched by his income from the factors he owns:

$$\frac{p_x}{p_y} x^A + y^A = \frac{w_K}{p_y} K^A + \frac{w_L}{p_y} L^A$$

The prices are given and so are x^A and y^A. Consequently, A's needs can just be satisfied by any combination of K^A and L^A which satisfies the equation. The smaller his labour power, the more capital income he will need to buy the given set of goods.

In the economy as a whole, constant returns to scale guarantee that the value of output will exactly equal the value of input:

$$\frac{p_x}{p_y} x + y = \frac{w_K}{p_y} \overline{K} + \frac{w_L}{p_y} \overline{L}$$

If A's equation is subtracted from this one, it is clear that any K^A, L^A allocation that satisfies A's equation will also enable B to buy what he should have. But the assumption of constant returns to scale, though needed for our computation in this particular example, is not necessary for the general proposition that if the distribution of factor ownership is right, a free-market economy can maximise the social welfare.

Market Failure

Let us now look more closely at what assumptions *are* necessary for this proposition to hold. There are four. Where these assumptions do not hold, a pure free-market economy is not optimal, and government intervention is normally suggested.† Thus what follows provides us with a framework for considering the proper role of the state in a mixed economy.

1 No increasing returns to scale As we have seen, the crucial mechanism by which free markets produce efficiency is by facing all agents with prices which they take as fixed. If there are increasing returns to scale, this property is lost. For if returns to scale are increasing, an equiproportional increase in all inputs leads to a more than proportional increase in output. This implies that the average cost of output falls as output rises, so that a larger firm can always undercut a smaller one. Therefore, increasing returns lead to monopoly (one seller) and a noncompetitive economy; for monopolists are price setters, not price takers.

---

† In any particular case one must of course consider also whether governmental institutions in fact have the capacity to do better than the free market. To say that the latter is nonoptimal when compared to an ideal standard does not of itself prove that anything better can be arranged.

If the x industry were monopolised, a profit-maximising producer of x would set prices such that†

$$MC_x = \text{marginal revenue}_x = p_x\left(1 - \frac{1}{|\varepsilon|}\right)$$

where ε is the elasticity of demand for x. So, in equilibrium, $p_x > MC_x$, and the marginal rate of substitution p_x/p_y exceeds the marginal rate of transformation (MC_x/MC_y). Thus, less x is produced than ought to be. (Use Figure 1-5 to verify that this is what happens if $MRS_{yx} > MRT_{yx}$.) The basic problem is that the monopolist is exploiting the public by setting the price higher than is optimal. There are only two possible solutions to this problem (in terms of the present formal theory). One is for the state to regulate the price, such that the optimal quantity of x is produced.‡ The alternative is for the state to nationalise the industry. It would then offer whatever it produced at a price equal to its marginal cost and adjust output until there was neither excess demand nor supply.§ In either case, the enterprise would need subsidising. For price will equal marginal cost; but increasing returns to scale imply that average cost exceeds marginal cost and hence exceeds price. So losses are made. We return again to these problems in Chapter 6. For the moment the key point is this:

> 1. *For a free-market economy to be efficient, increasing returns to scale within the firm must be exhausted before equilibrium levels of output are reached.*

2 No technological external effects The preceding assumption is needed to ensure that every agent is a price taker. But, in addition, the prices which he takes must be relevant. This requires that there be no technological external effects. Such effects arise if one agent's decisions directly affect the utility or output of other agents, over and above any indirect effects they may have through their effects on relative prices.¶ If there are such direct effects, the decision maker is not fully charged for any costs his actions impose on other people nor rewarded for any benefits he may confer; so the prices which are faced are irrelevant.

So far in our example we have ruled this out by not including any external effects in the utility or production functions. But now let us introduce one. Suppose that A and B belong to a competitive society where each is jealous of visible expenditures of the other (e.g., on the car) but indifferent to the invisible expenditures of the other (e.g., on quiet time). If x represents visible goods and y invisible goods, this means that

$$u^A = u^A(x^A, y^A, x^B)$$

† Marginal revenue $= \dfrac{d}{dx}(p_x x) = p_x + x\dfrac{dp_x}{dx} = p_x\left(1 + \dfrac{x}{p_x}\dfrac{dp_x}{dx}\right).$

‡ If the monopolised industry is subject to increasing marginal cost, there is still, strictly speaking, a problem associated with the monopolist's choice of factor proportions (see Chapter 8).

§ If there is inefficiency elsewhere in the economy, then marginal cost pricing may not be efficient (see Chapter 6). We then need to find a second-best optimum price.

¶ Such indirect effects are called *pecuniary*. Chapter 7 explains why they pose no problem.

where $u_{x^A}^A$, $u_{y^A}^A > 0$ (as usual) and $u_{x^B}^A < 0$ (a negative external effect). Similar effects operate for B. Efficiency requires that the amount of x^B be determined so that the amount of y which those affected would be willing to sacrifice for a unit increase in x^B be equal to the amount of y which they have to sacrifice. Thus the efficient solution now requires

B's willingness to sacrifice + A's willingness to sacrifice = MRT_{yx}

Therefore,

$$\left(\frac{u_{x^B}}{u_y}\right)^B + \left(\frac{u_{x^B}}{u_y}\right)^A = \frac{y_K}{x_K} \tag{3''}$$

In deciding on his expenditures on x, B actually only takes into account his own evaluation of them (unless A and B can negotiate about the matter). So in a free-market economy he equates

$$\left(\frac{u_{x^B}}{u_y}\right)^B = \frac{p_x}{p_y} = \frac{y_K}{x_K}$$

Since $(u_{x^B}/u_y)^A$ is negative,

$$\left(\frac{u_{x^B}}{u_y}\right)^B > \left(\frac{u_{x^B}}{u_y}\right)^B + \left(\frac{u_{x^B}}{u_y}\right)^A$$

so that the free-market value of y_K/x_K is too high. And too high a marginal cost of a competitively produced good means that too much of it is being produced. So too many visible goods x are made.

The standard answer to an externality problem is a tax equal to *minus* the algebraic value of the external effect. This faces decision makers with the true effects of their decisions,[†] and brings about the efficient outcome. For example, in the present case we should set a tax T on x^B such that

$$T = -\left(\frac{u_{x^B}}{u_y}\right)^A$$

Then, since B would choose x^B such that

$$\left(\frac{u_{x^B}}{u_y}\right)^B - T = \frac{y_K}{x_K}$$

he would in fact be choosing condition (3''). However, as we show in Chapter 6, taxes are inappropriate where costless negotiation between the parties is possible. For the moment the key point is this:

2. For a free market to be efficient, there must be no technological external effects (unless costless negotiation is possible between the parties concerned).

---

† If the externality is positive, we get a negative tax, i.e., subsidy, which gives a reward for the benefits conferred on others.

There are three main possible classes of externality:

1. Effects of one person's consumption on another's utility; e.g., my consumption of visibles makes you feel bad
2. Effects of one person's production on another's utility; e.g., my factory extension pours smoke onto your washing line
3. Effects of one person's production on another's production; e.g., my factory extension jams the road near your factory with traffic

The example we have given in each case is of a negative externality (pollution), but one can also think of positive externalities (external benefits) in each category. While taxation or subsidy may be a suitable remedy in some cases, in others regulations will be administratively simpler. In addition, when one considers psychic externalities, policies relating to social institutions may be necessary.

One of the most important and most difficult problems in economics is the problem of taste formation. Economists are often criticised by other social scientists for taking tastes as given (the "immaculate conception" of the indifference curve, as Boulding has called it).[†] In fact, tastes are largely acquired from nonmarket interactions with other members of society. In principle changes in taste induced by such interactions can be thought of as external effects in consumption; the past or present activities of others enter as variables in the utility function and affect the happiness obtained from any particular bundle of goods which the individual purchases. A change in taste may or may not alter the individual's preference pattern for purchased goods; it could leave the indifference curves unchanged but lead to more or less happiness being associated with each curve. In either case the matter is difficult to study in a scientific way and requires the help of other social scientists. The fact that the question is difficult does not mean we can pretend it does not arise.

3 No market failure connected with uncertainty Even if conditions 1 and 2 are breached, markets will still exist for all goods, though in the jargon we should say these markets were characterised by *market failure*, i.e., failure of markets to do their job. More serious problems arise, however, when we allow for the prevalence of uncertainty and inadequate information in human life. Given this, many markets which might be desirable may not exist at all. This is a complex subject, which we shall leave until Chapter 13. For the present we need only record its importance.

   3. For a free market to be efficient, there must be no market failure connected with uncertainty.[‡]

---

† K. E. Boulding, "Economics as a Moral Science," *American Economic Review*, vol. 59, pp. 1–12, March 1969; see also T. Scitovsky, *The Joyless Economy*, Oxford, New York, 1976.

‡ Some economists would add the absence of "merit wants," i.e. of items which can satisfy people but whose power to satisfy they do not fully recognise. This case is, however, an information problem.

Provided conditions 1 to 3 are satisfied, capitalism can produce a Pareto-efficient allocation of resources. This proposition is usually referred to as the *first optimality theorem.*†

> *First optimality theorem. Resource allocation is Pareto-optimal, if there is perfect competition, no technological externalities, and no market failure connected with uncertainty.*

However, this does not say that free markets can maximise social welfare. This depends on the idea that any particular feasible configuration of the economy can always be brought about by free markets, provided the ownership of factors is appropriately arranged.

> *Second optimality theorem. Any specified Pareto-optimal resource allocation that is technically feasible can be achieved by establishing free markets and an appropriate pattern of factor ownership, if there are no increasing returns, no technological externalities, and no market failures connected with uncertainty.*

To ensure that capitalism actually does maximise social welfare we need to be sure that the ownership of factors *is* right.

> 4. *For a free-market equilibrium to be socially optimal, the distribution of factor ownership must be such that each consumer can buy the consumption bundle which corresponds to the welfare-maximising configuration of the economy.*

Thus the pursuit of distributional justice provides a fourth reason for state intervention in the mixed economy.

Q1-9 Suppose the transformation curve is

$$y = a - bx + cx^2 \qquad (b, c > 0; \; b^2 > 4ac)$$

where x is steel, and utility functions are such that, regardless of the income distribution and the output of y, we have

$$\mathrm{MRS}_{yx} = e - fx \qquad (f > 2c; \; e > b)$$

What is the optimum output of x, and what output will result, in an unregulated free-enterprise economy?

Q1-10 Suppose Crusoe can make car journeys x. When he drives he gets pleasure from doing so according to the function

$$\mathrm{MRS}_{yx}^{\Lambda} = e - fx$$

---

† We have only illustrated this for the particular case of all variables divisible and indispensible, where conditions (i) to (iii) listed in footnote † on page 6 plus concavity of the production functions are sufficient to generate an interior equilibrium with all variables nonzero. A more general proof of the efficiency of the market is offered in Appendix 4. To prove the second optimality theorem, topological methods are needed (see, for example, K. J. Arrow and F. H. Hahn, *General Competitive Analysis.* Oliver and Boyd, Edinburgh, 1971, chap. 5).

At the same time Friday suffers from pollution an amount g per journey (measured in units of y). The direct cost of journeys is given by the transformation curve

$$y = a - bx$$

   (i) What is the optimum number of journeys?
   (ii) How many will Crusoe make if he and Friday are unable to negotiate?
   (iii) How many will he make if they can negotiate?
   (iv) If no negotiation is possible, what driving tax should the Governor General impose?

Q1-11 Suppose

Production functions	$x = K^{1/3}L^{2/3}$	$y = K^{2/3}L^{1/3}$
Utility functions	$u^A = x^A y^A$	$u^B = x^B y^B$
Welfare function	$W = u^A u^B$	

Friday, being rather handicapped, is endowed with only one-third of the total efficiency units of labour. In a competitive market economy what proportion of the capital should be owned by him if social welfare is to be maximised?

Noncapitalist Alternatives

Although the mixed economy may be able to do the job, so may other forms of organisation. Before the Second World War, Oskar Lange, a Polish socialist working in Chicago, showed that decentralised socialism could have the same formal properties of optimality.[†] Under this system, the state would own all capital and would rent it out to bureaucratically managed enterprises whose managers would be instructed to maximise the profits of their enterprises. There would be freely functioning labour markets, with competitively determined wage levels. The state, as owner of capital, would receive all the income of each enterprise, net of wages and raw material costs. It could then distribute some of this to households to supplement their labour incomes up to the desired level.

If there were constant returns to scale, prices could be left to be determined freely in the market. Alternatively, the state could fix them on the basis of signals observed in the market: if there were excess demand, prices would be raised, and, if excess supply, they would be lowered. Given increasing returns to scale, the state would (as under capitalism) have to regulate prices or instruct enterprises to set prices at marginal cost.[‡]

Even so, the outcome is only necessarily optimal if the supply of capital is taken as given. In fact the rate of saving would have to be determined by the state. So there would be no automatic mechanism by which aggregate saving reflected the preferences of the existing members of society. It may be that

---

[†] O. Lange, "On The Economic Theory of Socialism," *Review of Economic Studies*, vol. 3, 1936–1937.

[‡] If optimal output occurred where marginal cost was constant or rising, it would be sufficient for the state to set prices and leave the enterprises to maximise their profits (even though these would be negative). But if optimal output occurred where marginal cost was falling and the price was fixed at the demand price for that output, enterprises would have to be told to minimise their profits, if they were to produce the required output. Since it is not reasonable to ask enterprises to do this, they would instead be instructed to set prices at marginal cost and adjust output till supply equalled demand.

saving should not reflect these preferences, but if it should not, we enter into a new range of difficult issues.†

The Lange solution, which has only been adopted in a very limited form in Eastern Europe, has one obvious problem, that the state has to be responsible for the initial establishment of an enterprise and the appointment of its manager. A more decentralised system is the Yugoslav arrangement, whereby any group of people can in principle establish an enterprise. The enterprise is worker-managed, in the sense that the workers appoint the managers, and the net income of the enterprise is the workers' wages.‡ But workers do not own capital, which is ultimately owned by the community as a whole. This system too can be shown to have the same optimality properties as Lange's version of socialism.§

Centralised socialism, too, could in principle have these properties, as we have seen. However, it suffers from two obvious problems: of information and incentive. The main problems of information concern tastes, technology, and endowments. Nearly all societies, except the Israeli *kibbutzim* and the religious orders, recognise the problems raised by differences in tastes and therefore provide incomes in the form of general purchasing power (cash) rather than in kind. It is less universal, though general, in most socialist countries for people to be allowed to choose their own jobs, on the grounds that they know best what suits them. Turning to production functions, centralised socialism assumes that the centre can know where and how each good is most efficiently produced. One reason for the growth of decentralisation in socialist economies has been the failure of this assumption.¶ As for endowments, clearly it is not easy for the state to have a detailed list of the talents of its citizens and the stock of its machines and natural resources. This has proved to be another argument against the direction of labour.

If the price system is used, it provides the information that coordinates the actions of the different agents. Goods prices tell producers which goods consumers want and they tell consumers what sacrifices are involved in consuming different goods. Factor prices tell producers the value of the alternative uses of the factors they employ and ensure that they are not wasted. Whether the growing power of computers to process data will overcome the informational problems of

---

† In particular, current savings preferences may give insufficient weight to the ethical claims of further generations. For an introduction to these issues see E. S. Phelps, *Fiscal Neutrality Towards Economic Growth*, McGraw-Hill, New York, 1965 or R. Layard (ed.), *Cost-Benefit Analysis*, Penguin, London, 1972, pp. 35–40.

‡ In the actual Yugoslav system a part may be allocated to investment, but this introduces complications.

§ See J. E. Meade, "The Theory of Labour Managed Firms and of Profit Sharing," *Economic Journal*, vol. 82, no. 325, suppl., pp. 402–428, March 1972.

¶ Various theoretical decentralisation procedures have been developed whereby centralised allocation of resources could be made consistent with information not directly available to the central government. Producers would be invited to state their production plans under an initial set of prices, and prices would then be adjusted until all plans were consistent. Such procedures have never been used.

centralism one can only guess. One must also not forget the success of the Western economies in wartime, when they were subject to detailed physical controls.

However, this brings us to the second problem: incentive. Even a state socialist government with wide powers of compulsion cannot realise its plans without rewarding those who implement them. For this reason the pattern of wage differentials is not as different as one might expect from that in capitalist countries. This may ensure reasonable utilisation of labour. But it is more difficult to devise incentives for the efficient use of capital, where this is not privately owned. If citizens are socially responsible, as in wartime, this may come about, but it is difficult to maintain this type of social discipline without continuous attempts at moral uplift like the Great Leap Forward and the Cultural Revolution.

In choosing between alternative forms of social organisation, at least two other very important considerations are relevant, which are even less amenable to economic analysis. First, the form of organisation will itself influence peoples' tastes. If one form of organisation makes people feel happier with the same consumption bundle, it is, other things being equal, preferable. This is in a sense a problem of psychic externality, but on a mammoth scale. Socialists claim, for example, that people who are brought up with ideas of fraternity get more satisfaction from the welfare of others. By contrast, economic liberals claim that people are happier when allocation is done by impersonal market forces rather than by the exercise of political power by one person over another. Each claim is difficult to test scientifically, but one has to form a view. Second, any plan to change the system must be cast in a dynamic form and take into account the cost of change. With these few remarks we end our skimpy review of alternative economic systems, and henceforth confine ourselves to the mixed economy. In such a context government activity has always to be justified either on efficiency grounds, by market failure due to increasing returns, externality or imperfect information, or on equity grounds by the need to correct the distribution of purchasing power.

1-5 CRITERIA FOR A WELFARE IMPROVEMENT

We have so far discussed only the social optimum. But we often need to compare different economic states, none of which may be optimal. For example, if one is doing a cost-benefit analysis of a public motorway project, one wants to compare social welfare in two "states of the world": state 0, where the motorway is not built, and state 1, where the motorway is built and the money to build it is raised in some specified fashion. This is called *cost-benefit analysis* because in comparing state 0 with state 1 we want to assess the additional benefits generated by the project minus the alternative benefits which would have been available but have been lost due to the project (i.e., the costs of the project). In principle one can do a cost-benefit evaluation of the effects of any action, be it private (getting married?) or public (subsidising food?). How?

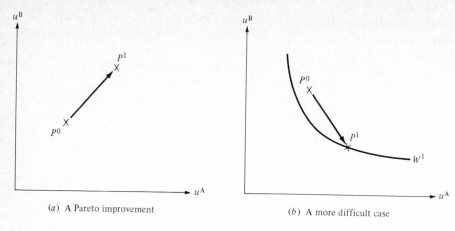

(a) A Pareto improvement   (b) A more difficult case

Figure 1-7 Welfare changes.

The action of shifting from state 0 to state 1 is to be judged by its effects on the happiness of all those affected. One can imagine two main possible types of outcome:

1. Someone gains and no one loses (or no one gains and someone loses).
2. Someone gains but someone else loses.

The Pareto Criterion

Case 1 is illustrated by the move from P^0 to P^1 Figure 1-7a. Whatever one's social welfare function (provided it is benevolent), this must be an improvement. The jargon describes such a change as a *Pareto improvement.*

> *A Pareto improvement is a social change from which at least one person gains and nobody loses, i.e., $\Delta u^i > 0$ (some i) and $\Delta u^i \geq 0$ (all i).*

If the move from P^0 to P^1 is a Pareto improvement, we can say that P^1 is Pareto superior to P^0. Notice the relation between the concept of Pareto improvement, which describes a change from one state to another, and the concept of Pareto optimality, which describes a state. We can formulate the relation as follows.

> *A Pareto-optimal state is one from which no Pareto improvement is possible.*

A General Criterion

Unfortunately in the real world most changes hurt someone (case 2), and if we were only willing to undertake Pareto improvements we should spend much of our time in suspended animation. For the Pareto criterion does not provide a complete ranking of all states, but only orders states in which one utility bundle dominates the other. It says nothing for example about the choices in Figure 1-7*b*. Is A's gain of sufficient importance to outweigh B's loss (perhaps B is a dangerous criminal who would be locked up if the move to P^1 were made)? To get a complete ordering of social states we have to invoke our welfare function $W(u^A, u^B)$ and this speedily tells us that in Figure 1-7*b*, P^0 is to be preferred.

Since $W = W(u^A, u^B)$ we have

$$\Delta W = W_{u^A} \Delta u^A + W_{u^B} \Delta u^B \qquad \text{approximately}$$

The change is an improvement if $\Delta W > 0$. (Put like this, a Pareto improvement is a special case where ΔW must be positive because both Δu^A and Δu^B are nonnegative and one of them is positive.) If enough points like P^0 and P^1 were compared and a move made whenever $\Delta W > 0$, we should ultimately reach the optimum, or bliss point.

However, the approach is not operational so far. For practical policy purposes we need to measure the changes in individual welfare not in units of utility but in units of some numeraire good, and then to attach social value to increments in the numeraire good accruing to different members of society. For this purpose we multiply and divide each term on the right-hand side by the marginal utility of the numeraire good (y) to the individual concerned, so that we obtain

$$\Delta W = W_{u^A} u_y^A \frac{\Delta u^A}{u_y^A} + W_{u^B} u_y^B \frac{\Delta u^B}{u_y^B} \qquad (5)$$

We now have for each individual the following two terms:

1. $\Delta u / u_y$ measures his actual change in utility divided by the change in utility that would be produced by one extra unit of y. It thus indicates approximately how many units of y would have produced the same change in utility as he actually experienced. It also indicates approximately how many units of y he might be willing to pay to bring about the change from state 0 to state 1. For the present we shall leave the question of exact measures of individual welfare change to Chapter 5 and simply assume that all measures give the same answer, which we shall denote by Δy.
2. $W_{u^A} u_y^A$ (or $W_{u^B} u_y^B$) measures the social value of an extra unit of y accruing to A (or B), or what one may call the Weight attaching to a marginal unit of his y.

For any action we then simply tabulate Δy for each of the individuals affected and then assign our own ethical weights to each individual's income (or leave this to the politicians). Suppose the value were as follows:

Person	Δy^i	Weight^i
A (rich)	200	1
B (poor)	− 100	3

The change would be undesirable since, using the previous formula,

$$\Delta W = 1(200) + 3(-100) = -100 < 0$$

The Kaldor Criterion

Here a purist might leave the matter. However, one might well ask: Why not pursue this project and at the same time make A give to B 100 units of y? Then you would have a Pareto improvement. The answer is of course that, if the policy consisted of the project *plus* compensation, the table above would not represent the policy. Instead we should have:

Person	Δy^i
A	100
B	0

and this would pass the test. But if compensation is not actually going to be paid, we can only claim that the project offers a *potential* Pareto improvement. There is no ethical basis for the notion that a project should be done if and only if it leads to a potential Pareto improvement. However, this test has great importance in drawing attention to the waste that can result if productive projects have to be rejected on equity grounds, and we shall therefore discuss the test at some length. It was originally proposed by Kaldor, and we shall refer to it as the *Kaldor criterion*.†

> *A Kaldor improvement is a change from a given output-mix distributed in a given way to another output-mix which would enable the gainers to compensate the losers while continuing to gain themselves. Since the compensation need only be hypothetical, a Kaldor improvement offers only a potential Pareto improvement.*

One should note straightaway that the criterion is explicitly more limited than the general approach offered by the ethical welfare function. For example, if a costless transfer were made between a rich person and a poor one, there would be neither an improvement nor otherwise on the Kaldor criterion. For the criterion is only meant to be used to judge between output mixes. The argument is that we should think separately about production and distribution. Production decisions should maximise the size of the cake, and distributional policy should ensure that it is divided fairly. But the two types of decision should be taken independently. The argument is wrong for at least three reasons.

---

† N. Kaldor, "Welfare Propositions of Economics and Interpersonal Comparisons of Utility," *Economic Journal*, vol. 49, pp. 549–551, September 1939. A slightly different criterion was later proposed by J. R. Hicks, "The Valuation of the Social Income," *Economica*, vol. 7, pp. 105–124, May 1940.

Critique of the Kaldor Criterion

First, the concept of cake is not clear if there is more than one type of cake. One may not be able to decide which of two output mixes is efficient unless one simultaneously settles the question of distribution. In Figure 1-5 we showed how the efficient output mix is chosen by a single person, using his indifference map and setting his marginal rate of substitution (MRS) equal to the marginal rate of transformation (MRT). By analogy, in the many-person case we might be able to do the same thing using a community indifference map. Each community indifference curve (CIC) would show the locus of (x, y) combinations which could maintain all individuals at fixed levels of utility, assuming always that any given (x, y) bundle was efficiently consumed. However, normally there will be more than one community indifference curve through each point in (x, y) space. Consider, for example, point (x^2, y^2) in Figure 1-8. Many different efficient utility mixes (u^A, u^B) can be obtained from that bundle of goods, depending on the distribution of income. Further, the locus of the community indifference curve will depend on which utility mix we take. Take, for example, the utility mix (u^{A0}, u^{B0}), corresponding to the distribution of (x^2, y^2) shown at S. We now want to find all the other (x, y) combinations which are just able to yield (u^{A0}, u^{B0}). To do this we can imagine ourselves holding 0^A steady and thus holding steady A's indifference curve for u^{A0}. At the same time we move 0^B, thus shifting B's indifference map; but we do this in such a way that B's indifference curve for u^{B0} remains tangential to A's indifference curve for u^{A0}. This takes 0^B, for example, to a point such as (x^0, y^0) This point is another point on the community indifference curve for (u^{A0}, u^{B0}). It is intuitively clear that the slope of the community indifference curve at (x^2, y^2) equals the slope of the individual indifference curves at S, where (x^2, y^2) was allocated between the two consumers. The reason is that if one starts to move 0^B along the community indifference curve towards (x^0, y^0), the direction in which 0^B moves is governed by and equal

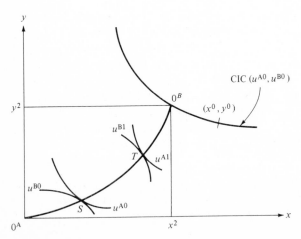

Figure 1-8 The community in-difference curve: product space.

to the slope of the individual indifference curves which are being held tangential to each other.†

A community indifference curve is a locus of (x, y) *points which make it just possible to achieve a given utility bundle* (u^{A0}, u^{B0}). *The slope of the curve equals the marginal rate of substitution of y for x (which is the same for all citizens).*

Clearly more than one community indifference curve can pass through a given point (x^2, y^2). Suppose we redistribute this output mix in favour of A. Let us move to point T with utilities (u^{A1}, u^{B1}). At this point in our particular example the relative value of x is much higher. If we now drew a community indifference curve for (u^{A1}, u^{B1}), it would pass through (x^2, y^2) all right but would have a much steeper slope than the previous community indifference curve. These two intersecting curves are shown in Figure 1-9. In such a case there is no unambiguous ranking of the social output, independent of distribution.

For the same reason, the Kaldor criterion can yield the paradoxical result that a move from state 0 to state 1 is an improvement, and so is a move from state 1 to state 0. Suppose in Figure 1-9 we start at (x^0, y^0) distributed to generate (u^{A0}, u^{B0}). We then move in state 1 to outputs (x^1, y^1) and utilities (u^{A1}, u^{B1}). The move is a Kaldor improvement if (x^1, y^1) can give the original utilities (u^{A0}, u^{B0}), for, if so, it must be possible for the gainers from the move to compensate the losers. Thus the test is whether (x^1, y^1) lies to the northeast of the original community indifference curve. If it does, compensation can be effected, with some of x and/or y left over to make the gainers better off. In Figure 1-9 this criterion is satisfied. But having reached state 1, we now ask if state 0 was not better. A move from state 1 to state 0 is a Kaldor improvement if (x^0, y^0) is sufficient to provide (u^{A1}, u^{B1}). It is. Consequently, moves in both directions

---

† Mathematically, the slope of the community indifference curve is

$$\frac{d(y^A + y^B)}{d(x^A + x^B)} = \frac{dy^A + dy^B}{dx^A + dx^B}$$

But, since the indifference curves of A and B have the same slope,

$$\frac{dy^A}{dx^A} = \frac{dy^B}{dx^B}$$

So

$$dy^A dx^B = dx^A dy^B$$

giving

$$dy^A dx^B + dy^B dx^B = dx^A dy^B + dy^B dx^B \qquad \text{(from adding } dy^B dx^B\text{)}$$

Hence

$$\frac{dy^A + dy^B}{dx^A + dx^B} = \frac{dy^B}{dx^B} = \frac{dy^A}{dx^A}$$

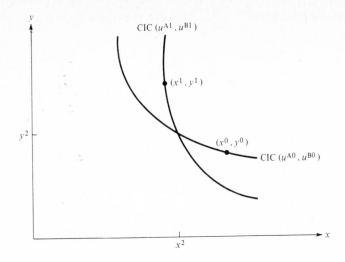

Figure 1-9 Kaldor improvements galore.

are Kaldor improvements. The attempt to separate production issues from distributional issues has failed.†

How serious is this problem? It would not arise if redistribution of a given output mix (x^2, y^2) produced no change in the relative value of x and y. Suppose we start from S in Figure 1-8. We are in a money economy, and each consumer is maximising utility subject to a money budget constraint. We now increase the money income of A and reduce that of B by the same amount, while we hold prices constant. Suppose that out of each additional dollar A buys α units of x and β units of y, and also that for each dollar that B loses B reduces consumption of x by α units and of y by β units. Then, as income is transferred from B to A there is no need for any change in relative prices to ensure that the total supply of x and y is demanded. So the efficiency locus must be a straight line and the marginal rate of substitution remains constant as we move along it. In this case the slope of the community indifference curve does not change as redistribution proceeds. So the condition for a unique set of community indifference curves is that the marginal propensity to buy each good out of additional income must be the same for all individuals at any given set of relative prices. For many limited problems such as a cost-benefit analysis of a motorway, this may be a reasonable working assumption, though for the analysis of large tax changes and so on, the problems may be more serious.

---

† As a partial attempt to salvage the criterion, Scitovsky proposed that state 1 should be counted superior to state 0 only if the move from 0 to 1 was a Kaldor improvement *and* the move from 1 to 0 was not a Kaldor improvement. If this double test was not satisfied and if the corresponding double test for the superiority of 0 over 1 was also not satisfied, the states could not be compared (see T. Scitovsky, "A Note on Welfare Propositions in Economics," *Review of Economic Studies*, vol. 9, pp. 77–88, 1941).

This brings us to a second and more fundamental objection to the Kaldor approach. The reasoning behind the criterion is this: If the optimality conditions are satisfied, the social value of each person's dollar will be equal. This is indicated by Equation (4), which shows that expenditure on x (or y) by A has the same social value as expenditure on x (or y) by B:

$$W_{u^A} u_y^A = W_{u^B} u_y^B$$

Therefore our general welfare criterion, Equation (5), simplifies to

$$\Delta W^* = \frac{\Delta u^A}{u_y^A} + \frac{\Delta u^B}{u_y^B} = \Delta y^A + \Delta y^B$$

However, this only holds if optimality can be achieved. In practice optimality cannot be achieved for one overwhelming reason: We cannot redistribute the ownership of the means of production in the manner described on page 22. The assumption there was that we could identify the labour power of every individual. We would then give him whatever capital he should have. We would transfer capital from those who had more than they should have to those who had less. In the process of transfer there would be no change in the total quantity of factors of production available, for the tax collector would descend unexpectedly, and the taxpayer would have no opportunity to modify behaviour in response to the tax. The transfer would be costless. Such a transfer is sometimes called a *lump-sum transfer*.

A lump-sum transfer is one in which neither the loser nor the gainer can affect the size of the transfer by modifying his behaviour.

But lump-sum transfers are impossible. We cannot identify the original labour power which an individual possesses. Let us suppose the tax collector can only observe an individual's earnings. He then either taxes them if they are high or subsidises them if they are low. But this will induce a substitution effect away from work. And that is the fundamental problem of redistribution, which we discuss in Chapter 11. More redistribution requires higher marginal rates of tax, and higher marginal tax rates imply ever-increasing efficiency losses. After a point the gain in equity from increasing the tax rate will be more than offset by the efficiency cost. At that point we have the optimal tax structure, and it will not embody a 100 percent marginal tax rate. So inequality will remain. And, on the assumptions we discuss in Sec. 1-7, this means that the social value of a dollar given to a rich person will be less than the social value of a dollar given to a poor one (weight^{rich} < weight^{poor}). This is so, even though the distribution of income is the best we can make it, given the constraint that lump-sum transfers are impossible and transfers are effected via the income tax.

If lump-sum transfers are impossible and social welfare is maximised through an optimal income tax, the social value of each person's dollar will not be identical.

If we now have a project which confers benefits in lump-sum form, it might not be worth doing even if it benefitted the rich more than it hurt the poor (e.g., building a motorway through a slum). But it would still be important to notice the cost (in terms of the unweighted $\Sigma \, \Delta y^i$) of not being able to make lump-sum transfers.

So far we have assumed that society is already arranged so as to maximise the project evaluator's ethical welfare function. A third case against using the Kaldor approach would arise when the evaluator did not agree with the welfare function implicit in the existing distribution of income. It will often happen in any state, however monolithic, that individuals (or local governments) can influence actions in directions that are inconsistent with the values of the central government. If they do not agree with the central government, they should presumably pursue what they believe in.†

Q1-12 Consider the following economic states:

	x^A	x^B	Total x	y^A	y^B	Total y
State 0	10	10	20	10	10	20
State 1	9	13	22	13	9	22
State 2	9	13	22	9	13	22

Suppose $u^A = x^A y^A \qquad u^B = x^B y^B$
What can you say about the ranking of the states?

Q1-13 Suppose a move from state 0 to state 1 satisfies the Kaldor criterion and likewise does a move from state 1 to state 0. Draw a diagram in *utility* space to represent this. It should indicate (u^{A0}, u^{B0}), (u^{A1}, u^{B1}), and the utility frontiers for (x^0, y^0) and (x^1, y^1).

Q1-14 Consider the following economic states:

	x^A	x^B	Total x	y^A	y^B	Total y
State 0	9	14	23	9	14	23
State 1			16			36

Suppose $u^A = x^A y^A \qquad u^B = x^B y^B$
Is a move from state 0 to 1 a Kaldor improvement?

---

† On the problems of the individual decision maker in a world where he does not control all policy variables, see A. K. Sen, "Control Areas and Accounting Prices: An Approach to Economic Evaluation," *Economic Journal*, vol. 82, no. 325 suppl., pp. 486–501, March 1972.

1-6 THE MEASUREMENT OF WELFARE COST

Despite the shortcomings of the Kaldor criterion, it is often useful to measure the effects of a change in the total value of output, independently of the distribution of output. One reason is that it is often difficult to know exactly who the gainers and losers are. Even if we do, we can always think of our final choice as depending on the trade-off between effects on total output and on inequality (see Sec. 1-7).‡

So how are we to measure the effect of a policy on total output (measured in terms of y), i.e., on the unweighted sum of Δy^i? Suppose, for example, that in Figure 1-10 we started at P^0, i.e., (x^0, y^0) and then introduced a subsidy on x

† On the measurement of welfare cost see A. C. Harberger, "Three Basic Postulates for Applied Welfare Economics," *Journal of Economic Literature*, vol. 9, no. 3, pp. 785–797, September 1971.

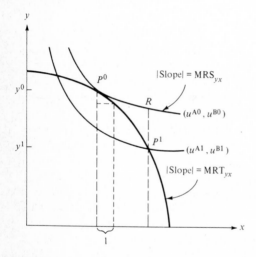

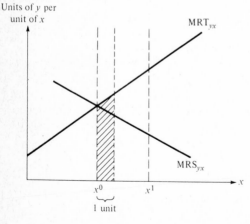

Figure 1-10 Welfare cost of a subsidy.

matched by an equal yield tax on y. This would move us to P^1, i.e., (x^1, y^1). What is the net cost of the move in terms of y? There are two natural questions to ask:

1. If we start from (x^0, y^0), what loss of y would have the same effect on utility as the actual move to (x^1, y^1)?
2. If we start from (x^1, y^1), what gain in y would have the same effect on utility as returning to (x^0, y^0)?

To simplify matters we shall make an assumption that ensures that the answer to both questions is the same. (We relax this assumption in Chapter 5.) The assumption is that x is a good for which, at any particular set of prices, each consumer demands a given amount that does not vary with income. In other words, the income elasticity of demand for the good is zero. This means that for any particular individual the indifference curves are vertically parallel. Once we know his consumption of x, we know his MRS_{yx}, since this depends only on x and does not vary with y. The assumption also means that, since both individuals have the same marginal propensity to consume x out of additional income (a propensity of zero), community indifference curves are unambiguously defined and are vertically parallel to each other.[†] So what is the net cost of moving from P^0 to P^1 in Figure 1-10? Clearly it is the distance P^1R, since with this much more y both consumers could be restored to their original utility.

Exactly the same analysis can be presented in terms of an alternative diagram, in which x is on the horizontal axis as before, but the vertical axis has, not total units of y, but units of y per unit of x. This is in fact the familiar diagram of supply and demand, except that the vertical axis has units of a numeraire good y per unit of x rather than units of money per unit of x. It is vital to understand the relation between this "per-unit" diagram and the "total" diagram above it.

Consider first the transformation curve in the total diagram. Its slope measures MRT_{yx}. In the per-unit diagram MRT_{yx} is measured by a distance above the horizontal axis. Since the transformation curve becomes absolutely steeper as x increases, the height of MRT_{yx} in the per-unit diagram rises with x.

Suppose now that we want to evaluate the absolute change in y along the transformation curve, as x increases from x^0 to x^1. If we use the total diagram, we take the difference in the vertical heights of P^0 and of P^1; i.e., we take $(y^0 - y^1)$. If we use the per-unit diagram, we take the area under the MRT_{yx} curve between x^0 and x^1. To see this, revert to the total diagram. Starting at P^0, commence the descent of the hill towards P^1. First move one unit in the horizontal direction, i.e., from x^0 to $x^0 + 1$. How far have you moved down in the vertical plane?

[†] At any given p_x/p_y, the total demand for x from A and B is given irrespective of their incomes. Thus there is a unique relation of MRS_{yx} and x.

Clearly, $-dy/dx$; so the slope measures the descent per unit movement in a horizontal direction. Now move on one more unit in the horizontal direction. Again you descend $-dy/dx$. Each time the slope must, of course, be evaluated at the point where you are. The total loss of height between P^0 and P^1 is the sum of all the short slopes you have traversed. So, if x were a discrete variable taking only integer values, we should have a loss of height of

$$|\Delta y| = \sum_{x=x^0}^{x^1} \text{MRT}_{yx}(x)$$

where $\text{MRT}_{yx} = -dy/dx$. This expression has a clear counterpart in the per-unit diagram. The loss of y as x rises from x^0 to $x^0 + 1$ is shown by the shaded area under the MRT curve. As x rises from x^0 to x^1 the loss of y is the whole area under the curve from x^0 to x^1. We, of course, expect quantities of y to be measured by areas in the per-unit diagram, since this diagram has dimensions of y/x on the vertical axis and x on the horizontal axis: the product of the two is thus in units of y.

Let us get back to economics. We are saying nothing more than that the cost of increasing x from x^0 to x^1 is the sum of the marginal cost of each unit from x^0 to x^1. Since x is not in fact a discrete variable, a more satisfactory expression is the integral† that corresponds to our earlier summation

$$|\Delta y| = \int_{x^0}^{x^1} \text{MRT}_{yx}(x)\, dx = \text{cost of } x^1 \text{ over and above } x^0$$

This tells us the amount of y that has to be given up if x is increased from x^0 to x^1.

But how much y are people willing to give up? In the total diagram this is measured by the difference in the vertical heights of P^0 and of R. In the per-unit diagram, MRS_{yx} measures the absolute slope of the community indifference curve. As x rises, it falls, since the indifference curve becomes flatter—the relative value of x falls. For reasons identical to those given on the cost side, the vertical difference between P^0 and R in the total diagram is by definition equal to the area under the MRS_{yx} curve in the per-unit diagram:

$$|\Delta y| = \int_{x^0}^{x^1} \text{MRS}_{yx}(x)\, dx = \text{willingness to sacrifice for } x^1 \text{ over and above } x^0$$

The welfare loss resulting from the move is the difference between the actual cost of the move and the cost people are willing to bear:

$$\text{Welfare loss} = \int_{x^0}^{x^1} [\text{MRT}_{yx}(x) - \text{MRS}_{yx}(x)]\, dx$$

This formula is perfectly general.

---

† This corresponds to the following identity, when $y = f(x)$:

$$f(x^0) - f(x^1) \equiv \int_{x^0}^{x^1} - f'(x)\, dx$$

But let us remind ourselves of what it measures. The welfare cost is the sum of individual net losses (losses minus gains). By converse, the sum of net gains could be called the "welfare gain." How does this relate to our previous measurement of welfare change:

$$\Delta W = \text{weight}^A \, \Delta y^A + \text{weight}^B \, \Delta y^B$$

Quite simply it is the same, provided $\text{weight}^A = \text{weight}^B = 1$. When economists talk about "welfare costs and gains," they are making this assumption more often than not. The reader must decide whether they are doing so by reference to the context.

The welfare cost of a move from x^0 *to* x^1 *is*

$$\int_{x^0}^{x^1} [\text{MRT}_{yx}(x) - \text{MRS}_{yx}(x)] \, dx$$

This may be positive or negative. A negative welfare cost implies a potential Pareto improvement; and a positive cost, the reverse. The welfare cost is the unweighted sum of individual losses (gains being negative losses).

Talking loosely, one might say that, if moving from x^0 to x^1 involves a welfare cost, x^1 is a less efficient output than x^0, though strictly, an output mix is either efficient or not and it is a figure of speech to say that one output mix is less efficient than another, if neither is efficient.

In a competitive economy with no technological externalities MRT_{yx} is given by the supply price of x and MRS_{yx} by the demand price of x. However, if there are income effects in supply or demand for x, we should need to measure welfare change using the "compensated" demand and supply curves described in Chapter 5.†

In a full analysis, however, we should always want to allow for the fact that a policy with positive net losses may still help someone. This type of question we examine in Chapter 3, where we show, for example, that food subsidies financed by taxes on manufactures will benefit landowners in a closed economy. Even though the landowners could not compensate the other members of society for their losses, the change might be considered desirable in a country of small peasant proprietors. It could never be as good a way of supporting landowners as a lump-sum tax-transfer, nor (if all factors are in fixed supply) as an income tax-transfer. But it might yet be better than competitive equilibrium, even though the welfare cost appears as positive. To decide this we need to use some specific welfare function rather than the completely general one used so far.

Q1-15 Suppose the transformation curve is

$$y = a - bx - cx^2$$

---

† If there are distortions in the economy, the measurement of welfare cost is complicated by problems of second best, discussed in Chapter 6.

and utility functions are such that, regardless of the income distribution and the output of y,

$$\text{MRS}_{yx} = e - fx$$

(i) A tax of t per unit is imposed on the consumption of x, tax proceeds being handed out to consumers in lump-sum gifts of y. What is the welfare cost of the tax if we ignore income distributional weightings?

(ii) Suppose that, instead, a subsidy of t per unit were given for the consumption of x, financed by lump-sum taxes. What is the welfare cost of the subsidy?

Q1-16 The government of a poor country is considering building a dam to be financed by a foreign loan. Debt service on the loan would be 500 m rupees per year for ever, but the government expects to recoup 250 m rupees per year in water charges. If the dam were built, wheat output would rise by 1 m tons and the price of wheat would fall from 1000 to 900 rupees per ton. The cost of inputs (other than water) is 500 rupees per additional ton of wheat. Should the dam be built?

1-7 THE SOCIAL WELFARE FUNCTION AND THE EQUITY-EFFICENCY TRADE-OFF

What, if anything, can we say about the desirable properties of a social welfare function such as $W(u^A, u^B)$? This is really a philosophical problem, but economists cannot avoid philosophical problems if they want to think about normative issues.[†]

First, a word about individual utility. As we shall show in Chapter 5, for the positive problem of explaining individual behaviour, it is sufficient to assume that an individual has a preference ordering over all possible "states of the world." Suppose we use the vector $\mathbf{x}^i$ to describe the level of all relevant variables in state i. If individual A can rank all vectors $\mathbf{x}^i$, we can represent his or her preference ordering by a utility function $u^A(\mathbf{x})$.[‡] Any utility function will do, so long as, whenever A prefers i to j, we have

$$u^A(\mathbf{x}^i) > u^A(\mathbf{x}^j)$$

So if one specific function which does the trick is $v(\mathbf{x})$, any strictly increasing monotonic transformation of v must also do the trick. In other words, let $f(\ )$ be a function of a single variable which increases as that variable increases. Then $f[v(\mathbf{x})]$ will be as satisfactory a utility indicator as $v(\mathbf{x})$, because it maintains the same ranking of the various bundles $\mathbf{x}$. This is what is meant by saying that the utility function is purely "ordinal"—it simply provides a numerical representation of the preference ordering.

Does such information on preferences provide enough information for making policy prescriptions? It would be very surprising if one could say whether one situation was better than another, just from knowing the preferences of each individual for the two states. For example, if a cake were to be divided between

[†] The best introduction to the issues discussed in this section is A. K. Sen, *Collective Choice and Social Welfare*, Oliver and Boyd, Edinburgh, 1970.

[‡] This assumes his ordering is not lexicographic, see page 125.

A and B, A might prefer the division whereby A gets three-quarters of the cake to the division whereby A only gets one-half; but B might have the opposite ordering. We could hardly expect to say which situation was actually preferable unless we could in some way compare the needs of A and B.

Arrow's Impossibility Theorem

This idea is obvious from common sense, but it has been made familiar to economists as a result of the work of Arrow, who asked: Can there exist sensible rules which would tell us how to rank different states of the world from an ethical point of view if the only information we have relates to individual preferences? Suppose there are three possible states of the world, 1, 2, and 3 and three people, A, B, and C, and we know the order in which the states lie in each individual's preferences. For example A's ordering might be (from highest to lowest) states 1, 2, 3; B's might be states 2, 3, 1; and C's might be states 3, 1, 2. Thus in tabular form we could write the ordering over vectors x^i as

	Person		
Order	A	B	C
1	x^1	x^2	x^3
2	x^2	x^3	x^1
3	x^3	x^1	x^2

The question then is: What is the ethical ordering of x^1, x^2, and x^3? This is a special case of a wider question: Is there any general rule which can rank social states and is based only on the way these states are ranked by individual members of society?

In answer to this wider question Arrow showed that there could be no such rule which would also satisfy four eminently reasonable requirements.†

1. *Pareto rule.* If everyone prefers x^1 to x^2, then x^1 is preferable.‡ Similarly for any other pair (x^i, x^j).
2. *Independence of irrelevant alternatives.* Whether society is better off with x^1 or x^2 should depend only on individual preferences as between x^1 and x^2

---

† K. J. Arrow, *Social Choice and Individual Values*, Oliver and Boyd, Edinburgh, 1970, 2d ed. See also A. K. Sen, "On Weights and Measures," *Econometrica*, 1977. Sen shows that a similar result holds even if individual preferences are already known, as in the table above, and as is assumed in the so-called Bergson-Samuelson welfare function. Thus, given similar assumptions to Arrow's, a Bergson-Samuelson welfare function based only on individual orderings is impossible.

‡ This is weaker than the normal version of the Pareto criterion by which x^1 is preferred to x^2 if at least someone prefers x^1 and no one prefers x^2.

and not also on individual preferences for some other vector, for example, $\mathbf{x}^3$. Similarly for any other pair $(\mathbf{x}^i, \mathbf{x}^j)$.
3. *Unrestricted domain.* The rule must hold for all logically possible sets of preferences.
4. *Nondictatorship.* We do not allow a rule whereby the ethical ordering is automatically taken to be the same as one particular individual's preferences, irrespective of the preferences of the others.

To put the matter another way, the only rule which satisfies 1 to 3 is the rule which makes one person a dictator.

A famous example of an ethical rule which does not work is the principle of majority voting. For example, given the above preferences, a vote between the states of the world 1 and 2 would give $W(\mathbf{x}^1) > W(\mathbf{x}^2)$ since A and C would vote for 1 and only B would vote for 2. Similarly, $W(\mathbf{x}^2) > W(\mathbf{x}^3)$ and $W(\mathbf{x}^3) > W(\mathbf{x}^1)$. The social ordering is thus:

$$\mathbf{x}^1$$
$$\mathbf{x}^2$$
$$\mathbf{x}^3$$
$$\mathbf{x}^1$$

This, of course, is not a social ordering at all: it does not satisfy the basic need for *transitivity*, that if $\mathbf{x}^1$ is preferred to $\mathbf{x}^2$ and $\mathbf{x}^2$ to $\mathbf{x}^3$, then $\mathbf{x}^1$ is preferred to $\mathbf{x}^3$. The reason for this circularity in the outcome of the voting is of course that there is too much diversity of preferences among the voters. However, Arrow's analysis went much further than this particular example, and he was able to show that no rule could exist that would satisfy the four criteria and produce a social ordering based solely on individual orderings.

So, to make ethical judgments, we need more information. In fact, we must be able in some way to compare the experiences (utilities) of different people: our welfare function must contain independent variables that are comparable. In addition these variables must enter into the function in a way that is symmetrical. Let us first look more closely at the question of symmetry and then return to comparability.

Symmetry

A fundamental principle of most modern ethical systems is the principle of impartiality (or anonymity). "Do as you would be done by" means that, in judging what A ought to do in a situation affecting A and B, it ought to make no difference if one is A or B. Thus the welfare function should have the property that welfare is the same whether $u^A = 10$ and $u^B = 20$ *or* $u^A = 20$ and $u^B = 10$. In other words, in a two-person world the welfare function must have the property that $W(10, 20) = W(20, 10)$. Such a function is called *symmetric*: all the variables enter into it in the same way, so that the function value is invariant when individual values are permuted.

Comparability of Levels of Utility

We now return to comparability. What degree of comparability is needed? This depends on our answer to the following question. Suppose we know who is the most miserable person alive and we have a policy that will benefit that person but make millions of others less happy (say, releasing from prison a notorious rapist). Would we necessarily support such a policy? According to the Harvard philosopher Rawls, the answer is yes.† If we agree with him, we evaluate every policy by the welfare of the most miserable person. In terms of information, this policy requires only that we can compare the *levels* of utility of different people in different situations.‡

Comparability of Unit Changes in Utility

However, most people would only be willing to see millions suffer if there were some substantial gain to the most miserable person. And we agree with them. In other words, we consider there is some ethical trade-off between more happiness for some and less happiness for others. To resolve policy problems, we must therefore be able to measure in a comparable way the changes in happiness accruing to different people. *A fortiori* we must, for a given individual, be able to compare the magnitude of that person's change in happiness in moving from state 1 to state 2 with the change in happiness in moving from state 2 to state 3. This property is equivalent to saying that an individual's happiness can be measured on a *cardinal* scale.§ So, to repeat, we need measures of changes in utility that are both cardinal and interpersonally comparable.

The Trade-off Between A's Happiness and B's

But there remains the question of the trade-off between the gains in happiness accruing to some and the losses accruing to others. Bentham, whose utilitarianism provided the initial impetus to utility theory, believed that the changes in happiness should simply be added up. If the net gain was positive, the policy should be followed. Thus according to him

$$W = u^A + u^B$$

and

$$\Delta W = \Delta u^A + \Delta u^B$$

A policy is good if the simple sum of happiness is increased. To Bentham it made no difference whether the gainer was already happier than the loser, provided that his gain was bigger than the loser's loss.

---

† J. Rawls, *A Theory of Justice*, Oxford University Press, New York, 1971.

‡ The most miserable person is not a dictator since we do not know in advance who will be the most miserable.

§ We leave until Chapter 5 a fuller discussion of cardinality.

This approach had some fundamental implications. Imagine a two-person, one-good world with a total y^0 that can be distributed in any way without affecting its total (an unrealistic assumption, as we have said earlier). Suppose too that everybody has the same utility of income function $u(y)$ and that the marginal utility of income diminishes with income. The Benthamite problem is now

$$\max W = u(y^A) + u(y^0 - y^A) \qquad u' > 0 \qquad u'' < 0$$

and the solution $u'(y^A) = u'(y^B)$ implies that $y^A = y^B$. This argument has been regularly used in support of equality.

However, additive utilitarianism has another implication less attractive to egalitarians. Suppose B is a cripple and from any given amount of y obtains half the happiness A would get from the same y. In other words, if $u^A = u(y^A)$, then $u^B = \frac{1}{2}u(y^B)$.

We now have

$$\max W = u(y^A) + \tfrac{1}{2}u(y^0 - y^A)$$

The solution is indicated in Figure 1-11. The cripple is an inefficient happiness machine and gets less y than A does and even less happiness.

This seems hardly fair. So we want a social welfare function in which less value is given to additional units of happiness the higher the original level of happiness. In other words, we need a symmetric welfare function $W(u^A, u^B)$ that is strictly quasi-concave in the individual utilities, so that the happier A is relative to B, the less socially valuable is an addition to A's happiness compared with an addition to B's.† Fairly obviously, this approach cannot be applied in any very exact way. We do not know individual utility functions. But where one knows the people concerned well, one would usually be willing to make judgments about "how upset" or "how pleased" they would be by particular events and how much "it matters" if they are helped or disadvantaged. However, there are other cases when we simply cannot resolve these questions, but, even so, it is important to be clear about how we should proceed if we could.

---

† For the definition of quasi-concavity, see Appendix 1. Quasi-concavity guarantees isowelfare curves convex to the origin, and symmetry guarantees that they cross the 45° line from the origin at right angles: thus

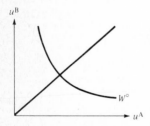

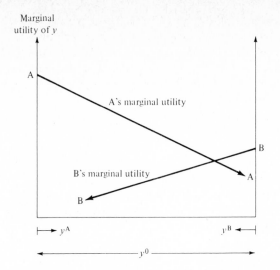

Figure **1-11** The additive utilitarian division of y^0.

Economic Inequality and the Equity-Efficiency Trade-off

Economic policy usually affects so many people that some fairly crude assumptions are needed. For many purposes it may be adequate to assume that everybody has the same utility of income function $u(y)$. If this utility function is concave (diminishing marginal utility of income), then the new welfare function $W(y^A, y^B)$ is symmetric and strictly quasi-concave.† (See Figure 1-12.) Thus if A is richer than B, any transfer of income from A to B (with total income constant) raises welfare. This condition is known as the *principle of transfer* and seems a reasonable

† This follows from the symmetry and strict quasi-concavity of the original welfare function, which specified welfare in terms of the individual utilities.

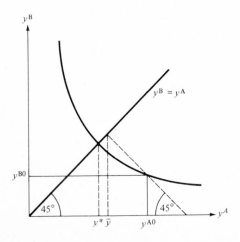

Figure **1-12** The Atkinson measure of equality.

requirement of any welfare function. The more egalitarian one is, the more the isowelfare curves of the function approach right angles. By contrast, if one is indifferent to distribution, the curves are straight lines ($W = y^A + y^B$) and one simply maximises the gross national product, i.e., follows the Kaldor criterion.

It would be convenient to be able to distinguish between the equity and efficiency effects of a policy in a way that embodied an explicit trade-off between equity and efficiency. Atkinson's equality measure provides such an approach.[†] Let equally-distributed-equivalent income (y^*) be that income which, if everybody had it, would generate the same level of welfare as the present distribution of income. So, by the definition of y^*,

$$W(y^*, y^*) = W(y^A, y^B) = W$$

y^* is shown on Figure 1-12 and must be less than the average income $\bar{y}$, unless there is complete equality. The equality measure is now defined as

$$E = \frac{y^*}{\bar{y}}$$

Now clearly social welfare increases if y^* increases. But

$$y^* = E\bar{y}$$

So we have defined equality E in such a way that social welfare increases if $\bar{y}$ increases proportionately more than E falls or vice versa. An increase in $\bar{y}$ is of course a potential Pareto improvement, but we have now derived a framework for saying whether such an improvement is big enough to outweigh any adverse distributional effects. We can also say whether an inefficient policy of equalisation is justified.[‡]

To make any of this operational, we must be willing to use some specific welfare function satisfying the preceding criteria. That most commonly used is[§]

$$W = \frac{1}{\alpha} y^{A\alpha} + \frac{1}{\alpha} y^{B\alpha} = \frac{1}{\alpha} \sum_{i=A,B} y^{i\alpha} \qquad \alpha < 1 \qquad \alpha \neq 0$$

If $\alpha < 0$, W is negative, but it still rises as y^A or y^B rises. The smaller α, the more egalitarian the criterion. As $\alpha \to -\infty$, social welfare comes to depend solely on the income of the poorest person, as Rawls argues it does. In other words, the isowelfare curves become right angles. By contrast, if $\alpha = 1$, we are indifferent to distribution and measure social welfare by the simple sum of y^A and y^B.

[†] A. B. Atkinson, "On the Measurement of Inequality," *Journal of Economic Theory*, vol. 2, pp. 244–263, 1970.

[‡] In a more general model changes in individual incomes ought to be measured in terms of compensating variation. These should include welfare changes induced not only by income changes but also by changes in liberty or fraternity accompanying any enforced increase in economic equality (see page 29).

[§] As $\alpha \to 0$ the function tends to

$$W = \log_e y^A + \log_e y^B$$

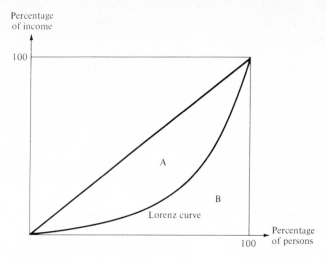

Figure 1-13 The Lorenz curve.

The corresponding equality measure is then, if n is the number of people,

$$E = \frac{\left(\sum_i y^{i^\alpha}/n\right)^{1/\alpha}}{\bar{y}}$$

As a measure of inequality we can take $1 - E$, which, being explicitly related to a social welfare function, is probably preferable to the more traditional Gini coefficient. The latter is half the absolute mean difference in incomes between each pair of individuals, relative to mean income.† It can be graphed by plotting a Lorenz curve, showing on the y axis the percentage of total earnings earned by each poorest x percent of the population (see Figure 1-13). The Gini coefficient is then the area A divided by the area A + B.

When a dollar is transferred from a richer person to a poorer one, the Lorenz curve shifts upwards,‡ so the Gini coefficient falls. Thus the Gini coefficient (like the Atkinson index) satisfies the principle of transfer applied to equality measures: distribution 2 is more equal than distribution 1 if it can be arrived at by starting with distribution 1 and then transferring money income from rich to poor. In fact, for a given total income, any Lorenz curve that lies wholly inside

---

† That is,

$$\frac{1}{2n^2\bar{y}} \sum_{i=1}^{n} \sum_{j=1}^{n} |y^i - y^j|$$

Note that each person's income enters into $2n$ pairs of incomes, n times when the individual appears as i and n times when he appears as j.

‡ If the recipient is at the ith percentile and the donor at the jth percentile, the curve shifts up over the range between the ith percentile and the jth percentile on the horizontal axis.

or along another can be got from the first by a process of transfer from richer to poorer. Thus, of two nonintersecting Lorenz curves distributing a given total income, we prefer that lying to the northwest of the other. (This is saying no more than that such a distribution is preferable, given *any* strictly quasi-concave and symmetric welfare function.)

However, in practice Lorenz curves often cross each other. In such cases the Atkinson index is to be preferred to the Gini coefficient since the latter is not based on a satisfactory social welfare function.† However, the Atkinson index depends crucially on the value assumed for α. Values typically taken vary between $-\frac{1}{2}$ and -2, but they can have no fully scientific basis, since they embody personal ethical assumptions. Their merit is that they do this in a systematic way.

So, briefly, what have we learned in this chapter? It is impossible to judge between two alternative economic states without using an ethical welfare function. For any particular welfare function there is an allocation of resources which maximises welfare for given tastes, technology, and endowments. On certain assumptions this allocation will be reached by the free-market mechanism, provided that the distribution of income is made right by lump-sum transfers. If this is done, other economic policies can, for practical purposes, be judged in terms of efficiency without reference to their distributional effects, by using the Kaldor criterion. However, in fact, lump-sum transfers are impossible, so that at the welfare maximum the social value of a poor person's dollar will exceed that of a rich one's. Thus the equity aspects of policies have always to be considered as well as their efficiency aspects. This explains why we shall focus so frequently in the next chapters on the factors which influence the distribution of income.

Q1-17 Consider the following states of the world, where the utilities are cardinal and comparable:

	u^A	u^B
State 1	1	5
State 2	2	2

Which do you consider preferable?

† The Gini coefficient can also be written

$$G = 1 + \frac{1}{n} - \frac{2}{n^2 \bar{y}} (y_1 + 2y_2 + \cdots + ny_n)$$

where y_1 is the income of the richest person, y_2 of the next richest, and so on. Thus it corresponds to a welfare function in which the weights attaching to individual incomes depend only on the ranking of incomes and not their size.

Q1-18 Consider the following ways in which a given national income of 12 units might be divided between A, B, and C:

	y^A	y^B	y^C
State 1	2	2	8
State 2	1	3	8
State 3	1	5	6

Which do you consider the most equal and which the least equal?

Q1-19 If factors are elastically supplied, most distributional policies change total output as well. How would you evaluate the following:

	y^A	y^B
State 1	1	5
State 2	2	2

Q1-20 Suppose that A and B differ in capacity for enjoyment, one having utility given by y^{i^α} (where y^i is individual income) and the other given by $\frac{1}{2}y^{i^\alpha}$ $(1 > \alpha > 0)$. Policy makers do not know which person has which utility function and consider each alternative equally likely. Suppose social welfare is $W = u^{A^\beta} + u^{B^\beta}$ $(1 > \beta > 0)$. What allocation of a given total $\bar{y}$ between A and B will maximise expected welfare?

TWO

GENERAL EQUILIBRIUM

We turn now to positive economic theory. Its main purpose is to provide a framework for predicting the effects of particular causes and for detecting the causes of particular effects. We might, for example, want to know how immigration would affect relative prices and thus affect the welfare of different classes among existing residents. Or we might wish to predict the effects of some proposed tax, or of an import quota. A full analysis of any of these questions would require a model with many industrial sectors (products), many types of labour, and so on. However, a model with only two products and two factors provides a great deal of insight into many of the basic forces determining the welfare consequences of economic change. We, therefore, confine ourselves, for the moment, to the two-sector model, developing it in this chapter and applying it in Chapters 3 and 4 to problems of public finance and international trade.

If the framework is to be used, it must be checked for consistency. It claims to explain what we observe, i.e., a price system in which relative prices are fairly stable and only change if circumstances change. We need to check this claim. For policy purposes, we also need to know whether the equilibrium of the system is unique, for, if it has more than one equilibrium, only one of them will be the solution to the welfare-maximising problem with which we began.

So this chapter has two interrelated purposes:

1. We prove the existence and stability of general competitive equilibrium and consider whether it is unique. This question is the main focus of Secs. 2-1 and 2-4.

2. We show how the distribution of income is determined and how it would change with changes in factor supplies (due, for example, to immigration) or in international prices. This is the main focus of Secs. 2-2 and 2-3.

It is convenient to stick to the same analytical sequence that we followed in Sec. 1-2. So we first consider the case of consumption without production (Sec. 2-1), then that of production without consumption (Secs. 2-2 and 2-3), and finally the general equilibrium in which both are determined together (Sec. 2-4).

2-1 CONSUMPTION WITHOUT PRODUCTION (PURE EXCHANGE)

Bargaining

We start with a two-person economy. Manna (x) and quails (y) rain down from heaven, most of the total $\bar{y}$ falling into the possession of A and most of the total $\bar{x}$ into the possession of B. So the initial endowment is at E in the Edgeworth box in Figure 2-1. The same endowment arrives every day and has to be consumed the same day. If A consumed his endowment, his utility would be u^{A1} and B's would be u^{B0}. But on this diet A values x more highly than B does, as can be seen from their respective marginal rates of substitution. (Remember that B's marginal rate of substitution, like A's, is measured by the slope of his indifference curve with respect to the x axis, i.e. by $-dy/dx$, even though his consumption bundle is measured by its distance south and west of 0^B.) Thus

$$\text{MRS}^A_{yx} > \text{MRS}^B_{yx}$$

and there is an opportunity for fruitful trade in which A gets more x in return for y. By consuming at any point in the shaded area, both A and B could be

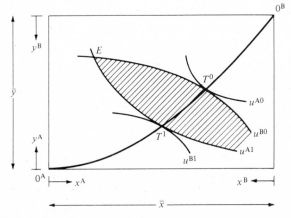

Figure 2-1 Pure exchange.

better off than at E—in this sense all these points "dominate" E. But trade will only occur as the individuals learn something about each other's preferences. At first they may not realise how great the difference is between their valuations, and consumption may occur quite near E. But then further gains from trade will be available, and eventually trade will settle down at some point on the efficiency locus of the economy where neither one can become better off without the other becoming worse off. Clearly this point must make both of them better off than at E, so it must lie on $T^0 T^1$, which is called the *contract curve*. But where exactly it lies on this curve depends on the bargaining strength of the two parties. If Crusoe (A) is able to push Friday (B) to the limit, they end up at T^0, and in the opposite case at T^1. But whatever the point, at least one of the parties will be better off than he would be with no trade. The indeterminacy of the final solution here arises from the fact that we are dealing with bilateral monopoly, where there is a single seller *and* a single buyer.

Existence of Equilibrium

Now assume instead that we move to a competitive market. A now consists of a large number of identical consumers with identical utility functions and identical endowments. The indifference map for A now shows the rate of substitution for each consumer when total consumption of group A is at each particular point in (x, y) space. Similarly for group B. Now what happens? For expositional purposes we introduce at this point a fictional character, though he is dropped later. This man is a kind of experimental social scientist, usually called an "auctioneer." His job is to call out the day's price (p_x/p_y). For convenience we shall call this p. There are three questions that interest him:

1. Is there any price that will clear the market; i.e., does equilibrium exist?
2. Is there more than one such price; i.e., is equilibrium unique?
3. Will the equilibrium be stable?

To tackle these questions he calls out a series of prices on successive days. Suppose he happens to start with the price p^0, corresponding to the slope of ET^0. As Figure 2-2 shows, A indicates that he would like to consume at C^A, so that he would be buying GC^A of x on the market, financing this by the sale of GE of y. (This construction is sometimes called his *trading triangle*.) By contrast, B wishes to consume at C^B, selling only FC^B of x and buying FE of y. So there is excess demand for x. This can be seen in two ways. Viewing the matter in terms of quantities traded, we find that *market* demand GC^A exceeds market supply FC^B. Alternatively, we could assess the *total* demand for x by referring the desired consumption levels at C^A and C^B to their respective origins, and then compare this to the total available supply. The two procedures are equivalent. They reveal net excess demand for x and excess supply of y.

These two phenomena are closely related. For any good z let us call the

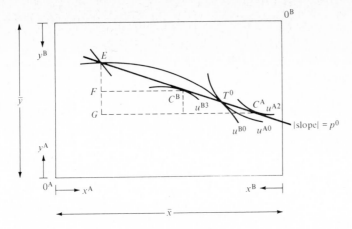

Figure 2-2 A's and B's offers at $(p_x/p_y) = p^0$.

difference between the ith person's desired consumption z^i and his original endowment $\bar{z}^i$ his *excess demand* for z (ED^{z^i}):

$$ED^{z^i} = z^i - \bar{z}^i$$

If this is positive, it measures his market demand for z; if it is negative, it measures his market supply. For any individual the sum of his excess demands, weighted by the prices of the goods, must equal zero. This follows directly from his budget equation, which requires that the value of his market demands must equal the value of his market supplies. So†

$$p_x(x^A - \bar{x}^A) + p_y(y^A - \bar{y}^A) = 0$$

and

$$p_x(x^B - \bar{x}^B) + p_y(y^B - \bar{y}^B) = 0$$

Adding them, we obtain

$$p_x \sum_i ED^{x^i} + p_y \sum_i ED^{y^i} = 0$$

or

$$p_x ED^x + p_y ED^y = 0$$

What holds for all individuals holds for the nation. This is *Walras' Law.*

> *Walras' Law. The sum of price-weighted excess demands, summed over all markets, must be zero. So if one market has positive excess demand, another must have excess supply; and if all but one are in balance, so is that one.*

† Whenever we write an absolute price, as here, rather than a relative price, the units of money should be thought of only as units of account. There is no store of money in this book.

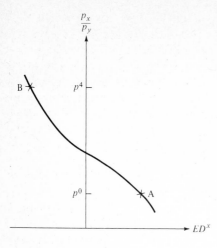

Figure 2-3 The existence of an equilibrium relative price. Note that $ED^x(p^0)$ equals $GC^A - FC^B$ in Figure 2-2.

This makes the analysis quite simple. For if we have only two markets, excess demand in one implies excess supply in the other, as we saw in Figure 2-2. Equally, once we have established equilibrium in one market, we have also established it in the other. Let us concentrate on the market for x and resume our story. At price p^0 the market is not cleared, so the auctioneer declares all existing offers to be void and tries another price. If he has any sense, he will choose a higher price (p_x/p_y) in the hope of choking off some of the excess demand for x. Suppose he chooses p^4, equal to the slope of ET^1 in Figure 2-1. Now he finds excess supply of x, i.e., negative excess demand. (The reader can check why.) So, turning to Figure 2-3, we have now established two observations on the relationship between price and excess demand: at one price excess demand is positive and at another negative. It follows that, if the relationship is expressed by a continuous function linking points A and B, there must be some price at which excess demand is zero. In other words, reverting to Figure 2-1, as we rotate the price line from the slope of ET^0 to that of ET^1 there is some point where A's wishes and B's coincide and an equilibrium price exists. At that point the indifference curves are both tangential to the price line at the same point. They are therefore tangential to each other, and the point is on the contract curve.

Accordingly, an equilibrium price exists.† But how is the auctioneer to reach it? He could of course go on calling out prices at random, but he would then only

---

† Strictly, we should have allowed for the possibility that equilibrium occurs at $p_x/p_y = 0$ or at $p_y/p_x = 0$. If so, that is fine: an equilibrium exists. If not, excess demand for y at $p_y/p_x = 0$ implies, by continuity, excess demand for y at $p_y/p_x = \varepsilon$(small), and, by Walras' Law, excess supply of x. So we have excess supply of x at very high values of p_x/p_y and excess demand at $p_x/p_y = 0$. So the argument in the text stands.

On a different issue, readers may wish to satisfy themselves that if there are more than two goods, there are enough equations to determine the structure of relative prices. If so, they can turn to Appendix 5.

hit on a solution by chance. Alternatively, he could adopt a system. *If excess demand for a commodity was positive, he would raise its relative price; and if negative, reduce it.* In this way, whatever his initial price, he would be bound ultimately to converge on an equilibrium price. In proceeding like this, he would be operating in the manner of an automatic control system. Excess demand is his "target (or signal) variable" and price his "instrument variable." His "response function," which governs the response of the instrument to the state of the target variable, is (to repeat) the following: if excess demand is positive, raise price and vice versa. (That this is an appropriate response function can be checked by seeing what would happen if the opposite rule were followed.)

So the time has come to sack the auctioneer. We have shown that his job can be done quite well without him, provided that there is an automatic response of the kind specified. And the evidence of history suggests that competitive markets do indeed respond in this way. This mechanism, whereby the first response to disequilibrium is a change in price rather than quantities, is that posited by Walras, who was among the first to formulate the theory of general equilibrium at the end of the last century. He also showed how, by the process of *tâtonnement* (or groping), a market clearing price would eventually be found.

Stability of Equilibrium

This raises the problem, will equilibrium be stable? By this we mean: if something temporarily disturbs the equilibrium, will the underlying forces tend to restore equilibrium or to produce further disequilibrium? (Note that a ball resting inside a U-shaped bowl is in a stable equilibrium; but if the bowl is upside down and the ball is perched upon it, the ball's equilibrium is unstable.) The question can be swiftly answered: The control mechanism which brought about equilibrium in the first place will restore it, if it is disturbed.

Uniqueness of Equilibrium

So an equilibrium exists that is stable. But will there be only one such equilibrium? Nothing we have said so far rules out multiple equilibria, for we can perfectly well trace out a path from A to B in Figure 2-4 that gives zero excess demand at more than one price. In our particular example, there are three equilibrium prices. Clearly the number must be odd. Moreover, every alternate equilibrium price, like p^2, will be unstable. (Check why.) But there is no reason why the economy should find itself at p^2, provided that the economy had ever experienced any kind of disturbance. So we can still be sure that the equilibrium will be stable—at p^1 or p^3. Which of these prices will rule depends on where the system started from, as with all dynamic questions.

But how likely are there to be multiple equilibria, as in this example? To

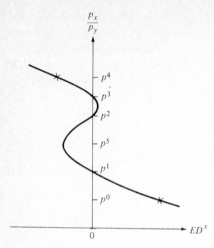

Figure 2-4 Multiple equilibria.

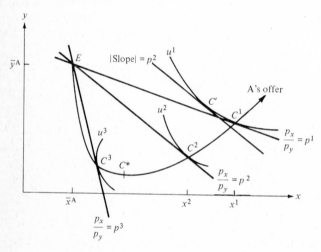

Figure 2-5 A's offer curve.

investigate the question, we need to introduce a new geometrical device (see Figure 2-5).† The *price consumption line* traces the locus of quantities (x, y) which an individual A endowed with $(\bar{x}^A, \bar{y}^A)$ will consume at each relative price p_x/p_y. If we treat E as the origin, we may call the line his *offer curve*, the coordinates measuring his excess demand for each good. Notice again that if his excess demand for one good is positive (he demands it in the market), his excess demand for the other must be negative (he supplies it in the market).

---

† For simplicity the exposition in the next few paragraphs proceeds as though A and B were single individuals, even though the markets in which they trade is competitive.

Now let us see how his market demand (for x) and supply (of y) vary as p_x/p_y rises. At p^1 he desires x^1 of x. When the price rises to p^2, he desires x^2, which is less than x^1. So his demand falls. This change can be thought of as the sum of two effects, if we make the following experiment. When p rises, the individual who is buying x becomes worse off. So let us give him enough extra y (Δy) to enable him to maintain his original level of utility u^1, but at the new price p^2. He will now consume at C'. The change in x as we move from C^1 to C' is called the *substitution effect*. Now take away from him the income compensation Δy. This shifts him from C' to C^2: this change in x is called the *income effect*. The total effect of the price rise is thus the sum of the substitution effect and the income effect:

$$\text{Total effect} = \text{substitution effect} + \text{income effect}$$

As we show in Chapter 5, the substitution effect of a price rise must be negative (or zero). The income effect of a price rise will also be negative if, and only if, the good is *normal*, i.e., it is one for which demand falls when income falls and vice versa. However, even if the income effect is positive, the "total" effect will be negative, unless the income effect is absolutely larger than the substitution effect. This so-called Giffen case is extremely rare, and we shall ignore it. So, in Figure 2-5, as p rises the demand for x falls continuously. The supply of y is more complicated: supply is always more complicated and liable to be backward-bending, as we shall see. This time we shall ask what happens as p_x/p_y falls, i.e., as p_y/p_x rises. At first, as p_x/p_y falls towards p^3, the consumption of y falls so that supply ($\bar{y}^A - y$) rises. But, after a point, the demand for x may become inelastic:† the increased quantity of x demanded when p_x/p_y falls then involves the payment of less y in return. This happens at point C^* in Figure 2-5. Beyond here the supply of y is now reduced when p_x/p_y falls (or in other words when p_y/p_x rises). Thus, as the relative price of y rises. A's supply curve of y is first rising and then backward-bending. Whenever the offer curve is U-shaped, this is implied.

But what has this to do with the uniqueness of general equilibrium? Everything. For an equilibrium exists wherever the offer curves of A and B cross. Now suppose that neither A nor B have U-shaped offer curves. Then the curves can only cross once, so there must be a unique equilibrium. This is illustrated in Figure 2-6. The curve of B is similar in form to that of A, as you can see by looking through the paper at Figure 2-6 from behind, with 0^B in the bottom left-hand corner. At the equilibrium price, the consumption demands of A, at C, are consistent with the consumption demands of B, which are also at C. So demand and supply of both goods are in balance. But now suppose that both offer curves are U-shaped (as in Figure 2-7).‡ A's offer curve is the same as the one we derived

---

† Demand for x is inelastic if, when p falls the proportional rise in x is less than the proportional fall in price, so that total expenditure (px) falls.

‡ By drawing a simple supply and demand diagram for x one might think that multiple equilibria were possible if only the supply curve of x were backward-bending and the supply curve of y were not. However, Figure 2-7 makes it clear that both are necessary.

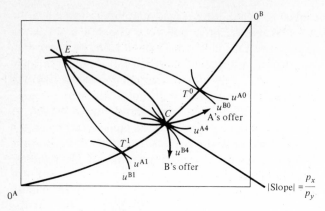

Figure 2-6 A unique equilibrium.

in Figure 2-5. And the two offer curves cross each other at three different prices p^1, p^2, and p^3. At each of these prices, demand and supply of x are in balance, as in Figure 2-4.

But how likely is such a situation? If wherever there is equilibrium it is stable, there can only be one equilibrium (see Figure 2-4). And the test of stability is that a rise of p_x/p_y brings forth an excess supply of x. What determines whether it does? When p_x/p_y rises, the change in demand for x is as follows:

1. For both A and B there is a substitution effect away from x. Demand is reduced.
2. A becomes worse off, so that his income effect also leads to reduced demand, if x is normal for him.
3. B is better off, so that his income effect leads to increased demand, if x is normal for him.

So we cannot say unambiguously whether the demand for x falls. However, the

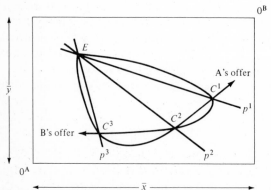

Figure 2-7 Multiple equilibria.

income loss of A (his Δy referred to above) is approximately equal to the income gain of B. So, provided that A and B have similar marginal propensities to spend on x out of additional income, the two income effects (2 and 3 above) more or less cancel out, leaving the negative substitution effect dominant. So for multiple equilibria to occur, there must be markedly different income effects for A and B and one of the income effects must be substantial.

It is important to know whether multiple equilibria occur in the real world, for if they do we might be able to improve social welfare by shifting the economy from one equilibrium to another. We should have positive evidence of multiple equilibria if we observed sudden jumps in the economy over time. For example, suppose that the excess demand function of the economy were initially as shown in Figure 2-4 and the equilibrium price were p^1. Then people progressively acquire a stronger taste for x, so the excess demand function shifts steadily to the right. (Try shifting it over.) At first price rises slowly and smoothly until it reaches p^5. Then suddenly it leaps to above p^3. There are no well-documented cases of such discontinuities and we can probably sleep safely without worrying about multiple equilibria.

Coalitions and Monopoly

This does not mean, however, that the equilibrium which actually comes about will necessarily be a competitive one—it merely says that, if individuals act as price takers, a competitive equilibrium will result. But it is generally not in the interests of any one group of individuals to act as price takers, as any steelworkers' union leader will tell you. In our example group A, who are buyers of x, would like as low a price of x as they can get. Similarly group B, who sell x, would like as high a price as possible. Suppose that all members of group B live close to each other and can organise themselves collectively, while group A members are dispersed. Then there is no reason why group B (the OPEC countries) should behave as price takers. Instead, they can agree among themselves on the price at which they are willing to sell (oil) and on the quantities of x each one of them shall be allowed to exchange for y.

How will they settle the optimum price? They could not, of course, force group A to consume off A's offer curve. But they could choose p_x/p_y so that A voluntarily consumed at that point on A's offer curve that maximised the welfare of B, that is, they could choose a point where A's offer curve was tangential to one of B's indifference curves. In Figure 2-8 this point is at Q. The relative price of x is much higher than the free-market price, given by the slope of ER.

Point Q is not on the contract curve since

$$\text{MRS}^A_{yx} = \frac{p_x}{p_y} > \text{MRS}^B_{yx}$$

So it is inefficient. But of course it may or may not be ethically superior to point R depending on the needs of the two groups A and B. If it is ethically superior, it may not be a sufficient argument against it to say that an even better state could

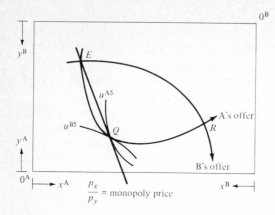

Figure 2-8 B's monopoly price.

be achieved by lump-sum transfers or by taxes and transfers, if these would not, in fact, happen.

However, there are two obvious problems with actions of this kind in restraint of trade, be they "optimal tariffs," union bargaining, or whatever. First they may encourage retaliation, so that in the end both parties end up worse off. Second, there is the basic problem of carving up the gains accruing to the colluding group (B) among its members. At the high, "monopoly," price of x all members would like to sell more x than is being sold at point Q, for the tangency between the price line and one of B's indifference curves occurs to the southeast of Q. So quotas will have to be allocated within the group. If the gains cannot be distributed equally, some members of group B may suffer. This is the kind of problem that arises with a minimum wage, whether imposed by unions or by government. Those who continue in work gain, but others may lose from the reduced amount of labour (here x) being bought.

Clearly, if groups of people can gain by forming coalitions, we should expect to find such collusive behaviour (sometimes called "cooperative" behaviour) occurring on a wide scale. If it does not, this must be because the costs of cooperation between members exceed the benefits they obtain. We have already seen how some of the costs arise: energy needs to be expended in arranging the carve up. We shall revert to imperfect competition in Chapter 8. For the moment we simply note that perfect competition will only be found where the transactions costs of collusion exceed the gains from collusion or where the law is very strong.

Of course, even if there are no coalitions, we need not observe perfect competition. One individual may be a natural monopolist. Suppose for example that B consists of only one individual and A of many individuals. Then if B was endowed with all the x in the economy, he would insist on a price exactly analogous to that set by a coalition of individuals who collectively owned all of x. So our preceding analysis covers the case of monopoly. But from now on we shall assume perfect competition.

Q2-1 Suppose consumers of type A are endowed with the total supply of $\bar{x}$ and consumers of type B with the total supply of $\bar{y}$. $u^A = x^A y^A$, $u^B = x^B y^B$. In a competitive market what is an equilibrium relative price of x? Is this equilibrium (i) unique, (ii) stable?

Q2-2 Suppose that in the above case consumers of type A could agree among themselves on a price at which they would sell x (but consumers of type B could not collude). What price would they set?

2-2 PRODUCTION WITHOUT CONSUMPTION: ONE-SECTOR MODEL

We turn now to the production side of the economy, where we can again learn important lessons, this time without bringing in demand. From now on we shall dispense with individuals A and B and imagine a world peopled by many identical workers, each owning 1 unit of L, and many capitalists, each owning 1 unit of K. Clearly the welfare of both groups depends on their incomes and the prices of the things they live on.

Before tackling the two-sector case, we shall start with an even simpler model in order to develop some elementary ideas about the influence of relative factor supplies on the distribution of income. Suppose there is only one good (corn, y), with price p_y. Clearly the amount of corn that a labourer can buy is his money wage w_L divided by the price of corn. This is w_L/p_y—the real wage. Similarly the real income of a capitalist will be w_K/p_y.

In the one-sector model these prices are determined in the simplest possible way. Suppose the factors are supplied in fixed quantities $(\bar{K}, \bar{L})$. Output is produced by very many firms, each having identical production functions and constant returns to scale at its equilibrium level of output. This assumption does not mean that the firms do not experience increasing returns over some initial range of output—it is hard to think of any real firm that does not. The question is: Would we expect to observe firms actually producing at such low levels of output? If returns to scale are increasing, average costs are falling. So any firm that is a price taker will expand its output (or not produce at all). In fact, it might well expand production to a point at which it had decreasing returns to scale. But at this point average cost would be rising, so that marginal cost would exceed average cost. Therefore, if marginal cost also equals price (as profit-maximising behaviour requires), price must exceed average cost. So profits are made. This tempts new firms to set up in business and, if all potential firms are identical, drives profits down to zero. So price, marginal cost, and average cost all become equal. But the equality between the last two implies constant returns to scale.† We can safely disregard all features of the production function except those which describe it in the neighbourhood of equilibrium, and so we shall in Chapters 2 to 4 treat each firm as having constant returns to scale.

† This point is discussed more fully in Chapter 7, and so are alternative assumptions.

Homogeneous Functions

To understand the implications of this for the distribution of income we must pause for a moment to set out the mathematical properties of such functions (they are proved in Appendix 3). Constant returns to scale functions belong to a wider class of *homogeneous* functions, which have the property that increasing all inputs by a multiple λ increases output by a multiple λ^ρ, where ρ is the degree of homogeneity. If the function has constant returns to scale, it is homogeneous of degree 1 ($\rho = 1$); so doubling all inputs doubles output. If there were increasing returns to scale, say with $\rho = 1.1$, doubling all inputs would change output by a multiple of just over 2.2. Returning to constant returns to scale, the input mixes at points P^0 and P^1 in Figure 2-9a both produce $y = 1$. If we double either of these input vectors, we raise output to $y = 2$. So the $y = 2$ isoquant cuts all rays from the origin twice as far out as the $y = 1$ isoquant does. Thus the two isoquants must be parallel along any ray. If the function had possessed increasing returns to scale ($\rho = 1.1$), the diagram would have looked exactly the same except that the outer isoquant would have been labelled ($y \simeq 2.2$). So our first property is as follows:

> 1. *For any homogeneous function $y(K, L)$ the marginal rate of substitution between inputs y_L/y_K depends only on the input proportions K/L.*

As Figure 2-9a shows, y_L/y_K rises with K/L.

However, if we restrict ourselves to constant returns to scale we obtain a stronger result:

> 2. *For any function $y = y(K, L)$ that is homogeneous of degree 1 the absolute level of each marginal product y_L and y_K depends only on the input proportions K/L. The same is true of the average products y/K and y/L, but this is less important.*

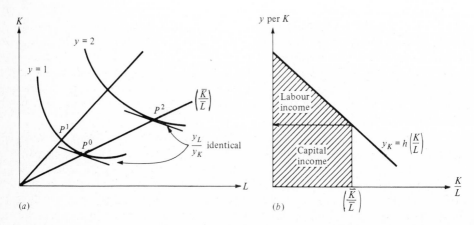

Figure 2-9 (a) The relation of y_L/y_K and K/L. (b) The relation of y_K and K/L.

So constant returns to scale have the key virtue that *scale does not matter*. All the variables that affect welfare depend only on the factor proportions. This logical deduction is sometimes called the *law of variable proportions*. Naturally, y_L rises with K/L, and y_K falls with K/L. So, to repeat:

$$y_K = h\left(\frac{K}{L}\right) \qquad h' < 0 \qquad y_L = j\left(\frac{K}{L}\right) \qquad j' > 0$$

The first of these relationships is illustrated in Figure 2-9b. This makes it clear that the marginal product of capital must be the same at, for example, points P^0 and P^2 in Figure 2-9a. In the later sections of this chapter we do not show the relationship between marginal products and factor proportions in any diagrams. Instead we rely on the reader to keep these in mind. In other words, you must remember that the marginal product of labour is higher at P^1 than at P^0 and the marginal product of capital is lower.

Our final property is an adding-up property known as *Euler's theorem*:

3. *Euler's theorem. If, and only if, the function* $y = y(K, L)$ *is homogeneous of degree 1, then*

$$y_K K + y_L L = y(K, L) = y \qquad \text{all } K, L > 0$$

So if each factor is paid an amount equal to the value of its marginal product, the factor payments are

$$p_y y_K K + p_y y_L L$$

By Euler's theorem this exactly equals the value of the product $p_y y$ if, and only if, there are constant returns to scale. If returns to scale are decreasing or increasing but the function is homogeneous of degree ρ, a more general form of Euler's theorem states

$$y_K K + y_L L = \rho y$$

where $\rho > 1$ for increasing returns and $\rho < 1$ for decreasing returns. Thus, with decreasing returns, marginal productivity payments will underexhaust the product and leave an entrepreneurial excess profit. This can be thought of, if you like, as a return to a factor in fixed supply, the "true" production function, with the entrepreneurial input treated as a variable, exhibiting constant returns to scale. The case of decreasing returns thus poses no difficulties for our competitive theory and our model loses little by overlooking such cases for the time being.

However, under increasing returns to scale, as Euler's theorem shows, if factors of production were paid the value of their marginal product, they would be paid more than the total income of the firm. But, under increasing returns, factors will not be paid the value of their marginal product because the product market will be uncompetitive. Instead, they will be paid their marginal physical product *times* the marginal revenue per unit of output (which is less than the product price). So if some firms do produce with locally increasing returns to scale, this is contrary to the spirit of our analysis, which can then only be justified on the grounds that some simplification is needed to capture the more important aspects of reality—and, in particular, to do policy-relevant comparative statics.

Income Distribution

Let us see where this leads us. We have reached the point where each firm i is producing with the same constant returns to scale production function $y^i = y(K^i, L^i)$.† Each firm faces the same factor prices, so each will choose the same factor proportions K^i/L^i (due to homogeneity). Given this and constant returns we can clearly describe the output of the y industry by an aggregate production function:

$$y = y\left(\sum_i K^i, \sum_i L^i\right) = y(K, L)$$

and use this also to compute the marginal products of each factor. This will be our standard practice throughout this part of the book.

So what can we say about real factor incomes? In perfect competition a firm will hire each factor until its real wage (in units of product) equals its real marginal product. Assuming that both $\bar{K}$ and $\bar{L}$ are fully employed, it follows that

$$\frac{w_K}{p_y} = y_K(\bar{K}, \bar{L}) = h\left(\frac{\bar{K}}{\bar{L}}\right)$$

and

$$\frac{w_L}{p_y} = y_L(\bar{K}, \bar{L}) = j\left(\frac{\bar{K}}{\bar{L}}\right)$$

The solution for w_K/p_y is illustrated in Figure 2-9b. So this is the one-sector theory of distribution.‡

In order to see the relative shares of labour and capital in the total product, let us imagine that, when specifying the production function we had chosen to measure L in units such that the total labour supply $\bar{L}$ consisted of 1 unit of labour. Thus the horizontal axis of Figure 2-9b measures $K/1$, i.e., K. The total national product is the area under the marginal product curve for capital y_K integrated between $K = 0$ and $K = \bar{K}$, in other words, the total shaded area in the figure. But the bottom rectangle is the absolute real income of capital $y_K \bar{K}$. So the top triangle must be the absolute real income of labour. Both are measured in units of product. If we had not fiddled with the units of measurement, the areas would not correspond to the absolute shares, but the ratios of the areas would still be a valid measure of the relative shares. This whole analysis was developed by J. B. Clark at the end of the last century.

---

† We shall assume it is twice-differentiable so that marginal products are well-defined at all points in (K, L) space.

‡ We express some reservations about this model in Chapter 12.

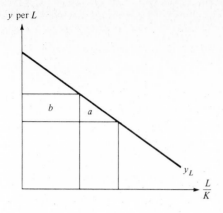

y per *L*

b

a

y_L

$\dfrac{L}{K}$

Figure 2-10 The relation of y_L and L/K.

We can equally, of course, portray the same information with L/K as the dependent variable (see Figure 2-10). The marginal product of labour falls as L/K rises. This diagram provides a whole range of immediate insights. Why, for example, is the real wage y_L and the standard of living y/L lower in India than Europe? Because K/L is lower. Or, how would immigration of labour affect the welfare of capitalists and native workers in a country? Capitalists would gain and resident workers lose, capitalists gaining more (areas $a + b$) than native workers lost (area b).† (To check this, assume $K = \overline{K} = 1$.)

There are, in fact, three main questions that arise in considering the distributional effects of increasing one factor (say L), the other factor being held constant (at $\overline{K}$).

1. How will real factor incomes change? We have already seen that y_L falls and y_K rises.
2. How do relative shares change, i.e., what happens to $(y_L/y_K)(L/K)$? Clearly as the ratio of labour to capital rises, two opposite forces are at work. L/K rises, but y_L/y_K falls (see Figure 2-9a). Whether the relative labour share rises depends on whether the proportional increase in L/K exceeds the proportional fall in y_L/y_K. The ratio of these proportions is called the *elasticity of substitution, s.* So if this exceeds unity, the share of the increased factor rises. We shall discuss the elasticity of substitution more fully in Chapter 9, but clearly the less curved the isoquant, the higher the elasticity of substitution.
3. What happens to the total income of labour, $y_L L$? Since y_K rises, $y_K \overline{K}$ rises. Thus even if $y_L L/y_K \overline{K}$ falls, $y_L L$ may still rise. The condition for this turns out to be that $s > y_K \overline{K}/y$ (see Chapter 9).

---

† This holds if (i) there are constant returns to scale and (ii) we only distinguish between two factors of production. In Chapter 9 we use two types of labour and point out that labour complementary to immigrant labour will gain from immigration.

Q2-3 If $y = 100\ K^{1/2}L^{1/2}$, where y is output per year (millions of dollars), K is the capital stock (millions of dollars), and L is man-years (millions), what is the real wage and output per worker in the following countries:

Country	K	L	
1	9,000,000	100	(say, USA)
2	200,000	20	(say, UK)
3	5,000	200	(say, India)

Q2-4 If $y = K^{1/4}L^{3/4}$ and the labour force is constant at $\bar{L}$, how does capital accumulation (from $\bar{K}$ to $\bar{K}'$) affect

(i) The real wage and real capital rental
(ii) The relative shares of national income
(iii) The absolute share of capital

(Since we have not yet given a formula for s, solve the question algebraically by computing actual answers.)

2-3 PRODUCTION WITHOUT CONSUMPTION: TWO-SECTOR MODEL

We can now move on to a more realistic model with two productive sectors x and y. The interest of this arises because one sector may be more capital-intensive than another and the fortunes of factor owners become bound up with the fortunes of different industries. We shall assume throughout that x is more labour-intensive than y, meaning by this that at any given set of factor prices, x will have a lower K/L ratio than y, whatever the set of prices is. (x might be clothing and y cars.) The welfare of factor owners now depends on the price of both products relative to their own factor incomes. Thus for example w_K/p_x determines the maximum amount of x an owner of one unit of capital can buy if he spends his whole income on x, and w_K/p_y specifies the maximum amount of y. So these two numbers determine the location of his budget line and thus the maximum utility he can get. If we henceforth use u^K to refer to the *maximum* utility available to a capitalist, we can write

$$u^K = f\left(\frac{w_K}{p_x}, \frac{w_K}{p_y}\right)$$

If both w_K/p_x and w_K/p_y rise, capitalists are unambiguously better off; and, if both fall, they are worse off. But if w_K/p_y rises and w_K/p_x falls, the effect on capitalists' welfare depends on their utility functions. Similarly for workers. But how are these prices determined in competitive equilibrium?

In a closed economy we cannot answer the question without bringing in demand (i.e., preferences as between x and y). However, we can do two things. First we can establish a remarkable one-to-one relationship between the relative prices of products and the welfare of workers and capitalists. This is useful as a building block in the general equilibrium of a closed economy. It also provides us with a complete theory of income distribution for an open economy in which all product prices are determined by world trade. Secondly, we can confirm that in a closed economy the welfare effects of changes in factor supply are the same as in the one-sector model.

The Relation of Relative Product Prices to Real Factor Prices

Our first proposition is this.

> *Stolper-Samuelson theorem. In any particular country a rise in the relative (producer) price of the labour-intensive good will make labour better off and capital worse off, and vice versa, provided that some of each good is being produced.*†

The proof is simple. We need to establish a one-to-one correspondence between changes in factor prices and in product prices. For convenience, we shall first think of the causation as running from factor prices to product prices.

Suppose the relative price of labour rises. Two consequences follow.

1. Since x employs a higher ratio of labour to capital than y, the price of x must rise relative to that of y, for labour costs are a higher fraction of the costs of x.
2. At the same time, the capital-labour ratio in each industry is increased in response to the now higher relative price of labour. So the marginal product of labour rises and the marginal product of capital falls.

But

$$\frac{w_K}{p_x} = x_K \qquad \frac{w_K}{p_y} = y_K \qquad \frac{w_L}{p_x} = x_L \qquad \frac{w_L}{p_y} = y_L$$

The first two of these fall, and the second two rise. So the utility of capitalists unambiguously falls and that of workers rises.

The story is illustrated in the "Lerner-Pearce" diagram in Figure 2-11. Since there is constant returns to scale, the price of each good equals the cost of producing 1 unit of it. For convenience we choose units of x and y such that at the initial relative price of the factors (w_L/w_K), $p_x = p_y$. This is indicated by the fact that the initial cost line PQ is the same for 1 unit of x and for 1 unit of y. Measured in units of K, the original price of each is measured by the distance $0P$.

---

† See W. F. Stolper and P. A. Samuelson, "Protection and Real Wages," *Review of Economic Studies*, vol. 9, pp. 58–73, 1941 [also in J. Bhagwati (ed.), *International Trade*, Penguin, London, 1969, pp. 245–267], and P. A. Samuelson, "International Factor Price Equalisation Once Again," *Economic Journal*, vol. 59, pp. 181–197, 1949. The proposition, as we have stated it, is only necessarily true if prices change exogenously (and not due to changes in taxes).

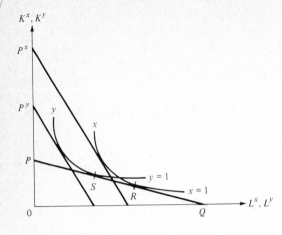

Figure 2-11 The effect of factor prices on product prices.

You can check this is by noting that the cost per unit of x divided by the price of capital is

$$\frac{w_K K^x + w_L L^x}{w_K} = K^x + \frac{w_L}{w_K} L^x = 0P$$

Now we let w_L/w_K rise and trace out our two consequences:

1. The prices of x and y measured in units of K both rise. Now

$$\frac{p_x}{w_K} = 0P^x \qquad \frac{p_y}{w_K} = 0P^y$$

Though both prices have risen in terms of K,† p_x has risen more than p_y. (In terms of L, both prices have fallen but p_x has fallen less than p_y.) The basic reason for this is that a revaluation of the original factor inputs for y (at S) and x (at R) raises the cost of the inputs to x more than of those to y.
2. At the same time we have the change in factor proportions resulting from the new relative factor prices. This raises the K/L ratio in both industries, making capitalists worse off and workers better off (assuming full employment of all factors of production).

So there is a one-to-one relationship between relative product prices and the welfare of the owners of the two factors. This can be usefully illustrated in Figure 2-12. We start with a low w_L/w_K. We now raise the relative price of labour.

1. In the right-hand panel we observe a rise in the relative price of x.
2. In the left-hand panel we observe the change in factor proportions in the

---

† This is because of the increase in the price of labour in terms of K.

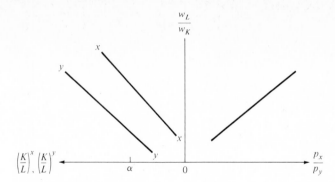

Figure 2-12 The product price/factor price relation: simple version.

two industries. In both of them the capital-labour ratio rises, which brings about the welfare changes we have described. Since the y industry is unambiguously more capital-intensive than the x industry, its capital-labour ratio is always higher, no matter what the relative factor price.

The functional relationship between relative product price and all other variables follows simply from the requirement that the relative price p_x/p_y must equal the relative marginal costs of x and y, whether these are expressed in terms of capital or labour. So

$$\frac{p_x}{p_y} = \frac{y_K}{x_K} \qquad\qquad \frac{p_x}{p_y} = \frac{y_L}{x_L}$$

But each marginal product is a function of the relevant K/L ratio. Writing these functions in a general notation, we obtain from the two preceding equations

$$\frac{p_x}{p_y} = \frac{f^1(K^y/L^y)}{f^2(K^x/L^x)} \qquad\qquad \frac{p_x}{p_y} = \frac{f^3(K^y/L^y)}{f^4(K^x/L^x)}$$

For given p_x/p_y this gives us two equations in the two unknowns, K^x/L^x and K^y/L^y. Having solved for these, we know the whole structure of real marginal products and relative factor prices.

There is, however, one caveat. We have assumed that there is only one set of $(K/L)^x$ and $(K/L)^y$ consistent with a given set of relative product prices. If y is unambiguously more capital-intensive than x, this must be so, for the experiments of Figure 2-11 proved that in such cases w_L/w_K is monotonically related to both p_x/p_y and to the K/L ratios. However, suppose that at a low relative price of labour y is indeed the capital-intensive good, but that, at higher values of w_L/w_K, x becomes capital-intensive. This situation is illustrated in the left-hand panel of Figure 2-13. Suppose we start with low $(w_L/w_K)^0$. This is consistent with prices $(p_x/p_y)^0$. We now raise the relative price of labour. As before, the relative price of x rises. But if we continue to raise the price of labour, a time comes when x is no longer the labour-intensive good, so its relative price begins to fall. This

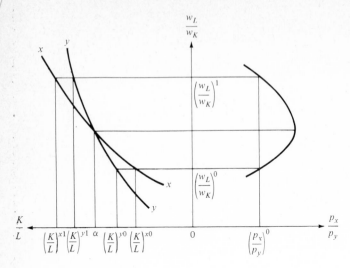

Figure 2-13 A factor-intensity reversal.

is shown in the right-hand panel. As the relative price of labour continues to rise, p_x/p_y eventually falls to its original value and beyond. So a given product price is consistent with two sets of relative factor prices, capital-labour ratios and welfare levels of workers and capitalists.

In the case of "factor-intensity" reversals, a given relative product price is consistent with more than one relative factor price, but a given relative factor price implies a unique relative product price.

The Lerner-Pearce diagram in Figure 2-14 tells the same story. We start with relative factor prices $(w_L/w_K)^0$. At these prices $(p_x/p_y)^0 = 1$. The equilibrium capital-labour ratio is lower in x than in y. We now raise the relative price discontinuously to $(w_L/w_K)^1$. At this relative price we find, not that p_x/p_y has risen, but that it is again unity. But in the meantime the factor intensities have been reversed, and x now has a higher K/L than y. The reason is of course that the capital-labour ratio responds more to relative factor prices in the x industry than it does in the y industry. In other words, the elasticity of substitution is higher.

How serious a problem is all this? It matters considerably if we wish to compare countries engaged in international trade. But if we take any particular country with given factor supplies, it causes no problem. The reason is simple. In the economy as a whole the overall capital-labour ratio is given (at $\overline{K}/\overline{L}$). But, if factors are fully employed, their overall ratio must equal a weighted average of the ratio in the two industries, from the identity

$$\frac{\overline{K}}{\overline{L}} \equiv \frac{K^x}{L^x} \frac{L^x}{\overline{L}} + \frac{K^y}{L^y} \frac{L^y}{\overline{L}}$$

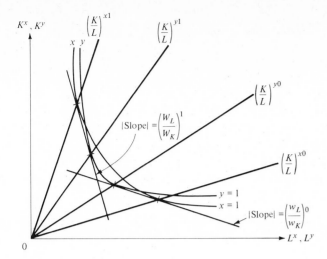

Figure 2-14 A factor-intensity reversal.

But in any particular economy $(K/L)^x$ and $(K/L)^y$ are determined by the same factor prices. So, from Figure 2-13, either both of them exceed the number α or both are less than α. It is impossible for both $(K/L)^x$ and $(K/L)^y$ to exceed α and for their weighted average to be less than α, or vice versa. So if $(\bar{K}/\bar{L})$ is greater than α, so are $(K/L)^x$ and $(K/L)^y$. And in this case x is the capital-intensive good. Equally, if $(\bar{K}/\bar{L}) < \alpha$, y is the capital-intensive good. From now on we shall assume that, in our particular country, the latter holds and x is the labour-intensive good. It follows that if the relative price of x rises, it will benefit workers and hurt capitalists. This will be so if x is a trading nation and the world price of x rises, or if x is a closed economy and peoples' tastes change in favour of x.

The Relation of the Output Mix to Real Factor Prices

The preceding analysis proves the Stolper-Samuelson theorem. However, it does not bring out how the pattern of output is changing as prices change. The Edgeworth box provides the best way of showing this. It also enables us to prove that the transformation curve is convex-outwards.

Figure 2-15 repeats the Edgeworth box in input space. Let us consider a move between two points on the efficiency locus, say from P^0 to P^1. At P^1 more x is produced than at P^0 and less y. But how do relative factor prices alter? For the time being we must not rely on any of the geometrical properties of the drawing. Instead consider the familiar identity:

$$\frac{\bar{K}}{\bar{L}} = \left(\frac{K}{L}\right)^x \frac{L^x}{L} + \left(\frac{K}{L}\right)^y \frac{L^y}{L} \tag{1}$$
$$\text{(low)} \uparrow \quad \text{(high)} \downarrow$$

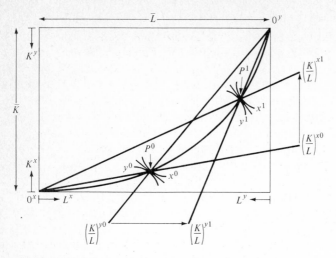

Figure 2-15 The relation of capital intensities and output mix.

If more x is produced at P^1 than P^0, L^x will be higher and L^y will be lower.† But $(K/L)^x < (K/L)^y$. So a higher weight is now being attached to the lower K/L. This will reduce the right-hand side of the equation, unless, to maintain full employment of $\bar{K}$ and $\bar{L}$, either $(K/L)^x$ or $(K/L)^y$ or both rise. Which of these will happen? Since both industries face the same factor prices, $(K/L)^x$ and $(K/L)^y$ will move in the same direction, i.e., they will both rise. (This is how they have been drawn in Figure 2-15.) And since both capital-labour ratios rise, the relative price of labour must rise.

> *So, as x rises and y falls, the relative price of the factor in which x is intensive rises.*

This accords with elementary common sense. If the labour-intensive output expands, a shortage of labour must emerge, followed by a general reduction in the labour intensity of production and a rise in the scarcity price of labour. But we also know that as w_L/w_K rises, p_x/p_y rises. So it follows that, as x rises and y falls, p_x/p_y rises:

> *The transformation curve is convex-outwards.*

Before leaving Figure 2-15, we should note some properties of the efficiency locus. Since $(K/L)^x$ rises as L^x rises, the curve is convex-downwards. If x were

---

† An alert reader may question this and suggest that the extra x could be produced entirely by raising K^x. By rewriting (1) with K and L reversed one can check that the argument which follows in the text applies equally well if K^x is raised. So any discrete increase in x will involve an increase in $(K/L)^x$ and $(K/L)^y$, which implies an increase in L^x and K^x (see Figure 2-15).

capital-intensive, the curve would of course be convex-upwards. But it could never have points of inflection. Still less could it cross the diagonal. The reason for this is obvious. Suppose there were a point on the diagonal which belonged to the efficiency locus. Then at that K/L the marginal rates of substitution between capital and labour must be the same in both industries. But since (by constant returns to scale) the rate of substitution in any industry depends only on its K/L, the rates of substitution must in any one industry be the same at all points on the diagonal. So if the rates in the two industries are equal at *some* point on the diagonal, they must be equal at *all* points on the diagonal. Thus if the efficiency locus touches the diagonal at all, it must lie entirely along it, and at the prevailing factor prices the two industries are both equally capital-intensive. In this case, of course, the transformation curve is straight, since any move of a given distance up the efficiency locus increases x by a constant amount and decreases y by a constant amount (due to constant returns to scale).

If, however, the industries differ in capital intensity, the transformation curve cannot be straight. Figure 2-16 provides the relevant pair of diagrams in factor space and output space. The maximum output of x is x^{max} and of y is y^{max}. In the top diagram the output mix at 0^y is thus $(x^{\mathrm{max}}, 0)$ and at 0^x it is $(0, y^{\mathrm{max}})$. By the properties of constant returns to scale, output at point P, half-way along the diagonal, is $(\frac{1}{2}x^{\mathrm{max}}, \frac{1}{2}y^{\mathrm{max}})$. But on the efficiency locus, the maximum output of y, if $x = \frac{1}{2}x^{\mathrm{max}}$, exceeds $\frac{1}{2}y^{\mathrm{max}}$. So the transformation curve lies outside a straight line in output space joining x^{max} and y^{max}. This is consistent with the proposition we have already proved, that the transformation curve is in fact convex-outwards.†

Finally let us return to Figure 2-12. Suppose the world price of x rises continuously. More and more x is produced. The relative price of labour rises. Eventually all the economy's resources go into producing x. Suppose the overall endowment of the economy is $\overline{K}/\overline{L} = \alpha$. When only x is being produced, $(K/L)^x = \alpha$. Suppose now that the world price of x rises still further. Nothing can alter the marginal products of labour and capital in terms of x. So, while p_x/p_y rises, w_L/w_K remains constant. This breaks the general Stolper-Samuelson relation and is the reason why their proposition is qualified by the remark that "some of each good must be produced."

Effect of Changes in Factor Supply in a Closed Economy

Finally we can revert to the closed economy, and reapproach the question about immigration which we originally asked in the context of the one-sector model. Suppose that K remains at $\overline{K}$ but L rises from $\overline{L}$ to $\overline{L}'$ and that this is not enough to produce a factor-intensity reversal. What is the effect on income distribution?

---

† Our geometry only illustrates that proposition. A geometrical proof is necessarily laborious. See H. G. Johnson, *The Two-Sector Model of General Equilibrium*, Allen and Unwin, London, 1971, pp. 25–26.

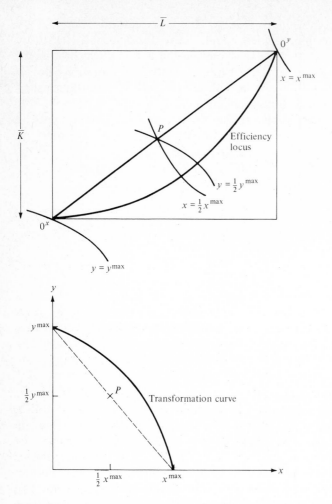

Figure 2-16 Why the transformation curve is not straight if capital intensities differ.

We can now follow a standard procedure which we shall use time and time again in comparing static equilibria (i.e., in what is called *comparative statics*). First assume all prices unchanged. Infer the pattern of supply and demand that would follow. If these patterns are inconsistent, infer the required direction of change of prices. So, holding prices constant, we first examine the effect of the immigration on the supply of x and y. Since factor prices are constant, factor proportions in each industry are unchanged. In Figure 2-17 $(K/L)^x$ is represented by the slope of $0^x P$ and $(K/L)^y$ by the slope of $0^y P$. Now the supply of labour rises from $\bar{L}$ to $\bar{L}'$. We can represent this by a shift of 0^y to $0^{y'}$, 0^x held put. However, factor proportions in the y industry have to remain constant, so output of y must occur along a line through $0^{y'}$ having the slope of $0^y P$. For full

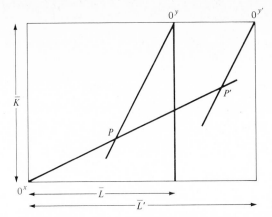

Figure 2-17 The Rybczynski theorem.

employment, production must occur at P'. So the output of x has risen and that of y fallen.

> *Rybczynski theorem. If product prices are held constant, an increase in the supply of factor L will lead to an increase in output of the L-intensive good and a fall in output of the other good.*

The striking point of the theorem is that y falls.

Now let us examine the demand for y. If factor and product prices are constant and there are now more owners of some factors, more of each good will be demanded. But, as we saw, less of y will be supplied. Therefore, to clear the market, p_x/p_y must fall and this will reduce w_L/w_K. A fall in this reduces the welfare of workers and improves that of capitalists. This is the same conclusion as we reached with the one-sector model. As regards the relative and absolute shares of the two factors, we should now need to take into account not only the elasticity of substitution in both industries but also the elasticity of substitution in consumption, another topic treated in later chapters.

Q2-5 How would you rank the welfare of workers in the following states of the world:

	w_L	p_x	p_y
State 1	1	1	1
State 2	2	3	3
State 3	2	1	4

Assume first (i) below, and then (ii):
    (i) You do not know workers' utility functions.
    (ii) $u = xy$.

Q2-6 Are workers rational to lobby for tariffs on labour-intensive imports?

Q2-7 Suppose $x = K^{x^{2/3}} L^{x^{1/3}}$, $y = K^{y^{1/3}} L^{y^{2/3}}$, and the economy is endowed with $\overline{K}$ and $\overline{L}$ measured in units such that $\overline{K} = \overline{L} = 1$.

(i) What are the values of x and y on the transformation curve corresponding to first (a) below and then (b):

(a) $K^x = K^y$

(b) $L^x = L^y$

(Do not evaluate cube roots further than is needed to see what is happening.)

(ii) Evaluate the following at points (a) and (b) above:

$$\frac{w_K}{p_x} \qquad \frac{w_K}{p_y} \qquad \frac{w_L}{p_x} \qquad \frac{w_L}{p_y} \qquad \frac{w_L}{w_K} \qquad \frac{p_x}{p_y}$$

At which point is labour better off?

Q2-8 Same as Question 2-7, but with $y = 2K^{y^{2/3}} L^{y^{1/3}}$ and everything else as before.

Q2-9 Suppose that with production functions as in Question 2-8 we evaluate x and y such that

$$K^x = \tfrac{1}{2}K^y \qquad L^x = \tfrac{1}{2}L^y$$

How does the welfare of workers and capitalists compare with that found in Question 2-8?

2-4 PRODUCTION AND CONSUMPTION

We are now ready to bring together consumption and production in a more general way. The moment of truth can be reached quite quickly. Once again we are asking: Is there an equilibrium set of prices; and is this equilibrium unique?

The first question can be answered by following the same general approach as in Sec. 2-1, except that output is no longer given. As before, Walras' Law guarantees that if there is zero excess demand for x, there is zero excess demand for y (assuming factor markets clear). So we can concentrate on looking at the state of the market for x as the price p_x/p_y varies. We first take two extreme cases, as before. Suppose we start with a very low relative price of x; no x will be produced, only y. But some x will be demanded. So there will be excess demand for x. At the other extreme if the price is high enough, no y is produced, only x. But some y will be demanded, so there will be excess demand for y and (by Walras' Law) excess supply of x. Provided that, as we vary p_x/p_y from very high to very low, excess demand varies in a continuous manner, there must be some price for which excess demand is zero. This is a point of equilibrium.†

But will there be multiple equilibria? As we have seen, this is the same question as: is equilibrium stable? To examine this, bear in mind that the relative price p_x/p_y determines both the pattern of output supplied and the pattern of output demanded. There will be a unique equilibrium provided that at equilibrium a rise in p_x/p_y reduces excess demand for x. Since a rise in p_x/p_y always increases the supply of x, excess demand for x will fall so long as demand does not increase. So, as in Sec. 2-1, we shall focus on the change in demand for x as p_x/p_y varies.

---

† The reader who wishes to check that, in the n-commodity case, there are enough equations to solve for the $n-1$ relative prices can find satisfaction in Appendix 5.

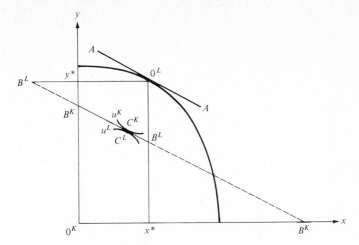

Figure 2-18 General equilibrium

How can we picture the demand for x? Clearly it depends on the opportunities open to capitalists (defined by w_K/p_x and w_K/p_y) and to workers (defined by w_L/p_x and w_L/p_y). But these in turn, as we have seen, are determined by the pattern of output. So some geometry is helpful. Suppose we have an equilibrium with outputs (x^*, y^*) in Figure 2-18. Since the payments to factors exhaust the total product, labour and capital taken together must between them be able to buy the whole product. So the budget line for their combined incomes, with 0^K taken as origin, must be the line AA. But we are interested in the separate budget lines of K and L. Suppose we measure K's budget line from 0^K, but measure L's budget line inwards from (x^*, y^*). Then some line must be able to serve as the common budget line for K (referred to 0^K) and for L (referred to 0^L). In the diagram $B^K B^K$ is K's budget line and $B^L B^L$ is L's budget line. Over the range where both are consuming nonnegative quantities of each good the lines coincide. If we are in equilibrium, the amount of x demanded by K (shown at C^K) plus the amount demanded by L (shown at C^L) must add up to the total output of x. In other words C^K and C^L must occur at the same point, so that the total outputs (x^*, y^*) are demanded. Happily this is so in Figure 2-18.

Now what happens if p_x/p_y rises? Output shifts to (x^1, y^1)—more of labour-intensive x and less of y (see Figure 2-19). So, as we know, the potential welfare of capitalists goes down; w_K/p_x and w_K/p_y fall, so their budget line moves in towards 0^K at both its ends. Similarly the potential welfare of workers rises: their new line is further from the new 0^L at both its ends.

What happens to the demand for x as a result of this rise in its price?

1. The substitution effects of both K and L lead to a reduced demand for x.
2. The income effect of K also leads to a reduced demand, assuming x is a normal good. So far all is simple. But
3. The income effect of L leads to an increased demand.

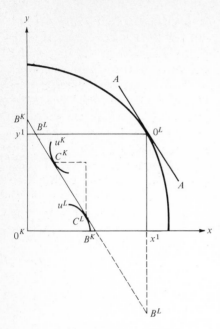

Figure 2-19 Disequilibrium, unless there is foreign trade.

So, as in the case of pure exchange, we cannot say unambiguously that the demand for x falls. But once again it is highly likely. Moreover, even if the demand for x rises, it is unlikely to rise as much as supply. Thus multiple equilibria are unlikely, and much less likely in the case of production and consumption than in the case of pure exchange, since a rise in price now induces an increase in supply that is likely to exceed any possible increase in demand.

This completes our analysis of the equilibrium of a closed economy. But we can also use the same apparatus to see how the economy will respond, if opened to world trade, assuming the country is a price taker. If the world price equalled the equilibrium price at (x^*, y^*), no trade would occur. But suppose the world price equals the higher slope of AA in Figure 2-19. Production would shift to (x^1, y^1) with higher output of x. But on normal assumptions the demand for x falls. So there is excess supply of x. This is illustrated in Figure 2-19, where the sum of K's demands for x (at C^K) and Ls demands (at C^L) do not add up to total output. This excess supply of x is what the country is willing to export; in return it needs to import y of equivalent value in order to satisfy the excess domestic demand for y indicated by the "trading triangle" shown in the figure. Equally, if we had a world price lower than at (x^*, y^*) we should import x and export y. That is what we shall assume in Chapter 4. In addition we shall make our normal assumptions about excess demand, so that the import demand for x increases continually as its relative price falls.

So we end this chapter on the same issue as we began. We have found that in the two-good case there will exist an equilibrium set of prices that will clear all markets. Equilibrium will be stable and is likely, but not certain, to be unique. The two-good approach has also helped us to see what forces determine real factor incomes. In a closed economy, the higher the capital-labour ratio of the economy, the higher the real income of workers. Workers also gain, the stronger is the public's preference for labour-intensive goods. In an open economy, workers gain the higher the relative world price of labour-intensive goods. Thus fairly clear-cut remarks can be made about comparative statics in a two-good, two-factor world. If it is necessary, as it often is, to take into account more than two goods or factors, there are few general propositions available. Instead one must compute the general equilibrium values corresponding to each set of data. Powerful routines now exist for doing this.† But the two-good case is still important for developing one's intuitions about what kind of results to expect. For this reason in the next chapter we use the results obtained so far to throw light on the effect of public policy upon the distribution of income. General equilibrium theory itself is rather dry—it exists for the sake of its applications.

Q2-10 Suppose

$$x = K^x + L^x$$
$$y = 2K^y + L^y$$
$$\bar{K} = \bar{L} = 1$$

What in general equilibrium are

$\dfrac{w_K}{p_x}$	$\dfrac{w_K}{p_y}$	$\dfrac{w_L}{p_x}$	$\dfrac{w_L}{p_y}$	$\dfrac{w_L}{w_K}$	$\dfrac{p_x}{p_y}$

(i) if $u^K = x^{K^{3/4}} y^K$ $u^L = x^{L^{3/4}} y^L$
(ii) if $u^K = x^K y^{K^{3/4}}$ $u^L = x^L y^{L^{3/4}}$

Q2-11 To produce 1 unit of x requires 1 unit of L and 2 units of K. To produce 1 unit of y requires 1 unit of L and 1 unit of K. Suppose $u = xy$. Will there be full employment of labour, and what is the structure of prices
    (i) In a rich country with $\bar{K} = 1.8,$ $\bar{L} = 1$
    (ii) In a less rich country with $\bar{K} = 1.4,$ $\bar{L} = 1$
    (iii) In a poor country with $\bar{K} = 0.5,$ $\bar{L} = 1.$

Q2-12 Suppose a minimum wage is imposed in one industry (x), the wage in y being uncontrolled. The minimum is expressed in terms of w_L/p_x and is above the equilibrium level. Will such a wage necessarily make workers who cannot get jobs in the x industry worse off? (The x industry may be capital-intensive or labour-intensive.)

† H. Scarf, *The Computation of Economic Equilibria*, Cowles Foundation for Research in Economics, Monograph 24, Yale University Press, New Haven, 1973.

THREE

APPLICATIONS TO PUBLIC FINANCE

Who really pays the payroll tax? or, What is the efficiency cost of agricultural subsidies? These are among the questions which general equilibrium theory was invented to answer. For suppose we ask: how will some particular change in public policy affect the welfare of different groups of citizens and the overall efficiency of the economy? Clearly we should look not only at the superficial results of the change but at the overall result when the system has adjusted to it. In this chapter we shall derive some of the basic propositions about the effects of taxes, starting simply and working up to those that require general equilibrium theory. We are here concerned essentially with questions of positive economics: with how to predict the effect of particular policies, without making any judgment about whether they are good.† We leave until Chapters 6 and 11 more normative issues of optimal taxation.

Assumptions

To predict the effects of a fiscal policy change, we must always make certain it is fully specified. For example, if government expenditure is to be increased, we must know how the expenditure is to be financed (or what other expenditure

---

† Some of the inferences we draw about welfare changes are not strictly observable, but we make no normative analysis of the kind involved in maximising some welfare function.

is to be cut). It is totally meaningless to say that increased food subsidies will reduce interpersonal inequality: we must also know how they are financed. Similarly, if there is to be a tax increase, we must know what it is to be spent on (or what other taxes are to be cut). We shall assume throughout that all government expenditure changes are matched by equal changes in taxes, and vice versa. We shall also, in this chapter, assume no saving, so that changes in private income are exactly matched by changes in private spending on goods and services. Since prices are flexible and there is no uncertainty, there is always full employment.

The Purposes of Taxation

Given this, taxes may be levied for three broad purposes:

1. To finance the subsidisation of goods subject to increasing returns to scale (including public goods)†
2. To offset external technological diseconomies, subsidies being handed out where there are external economies
3. To correct the distribution of income, subsidies being handed out to the deserving

Notice how these purposes mirror the reasons for government action given in Chapter 1.‡

Except in case 2 the function of the tax is to drive a wedge between the value of what a factor produces and what the factor can consume. In this way the factor is prevented from consuming its full product, and the difference is made available to pay for worthy causes. This is so whether the tax is levied in the factor market or the goods market. In case 1 the government wishes to pay for factor services and must therefore levy positive net taxes on the private sector. In a free-market economy this is the only way the government can get a claim over real resources and thus pay for public goods.§ In socialist countries explicit taxes are often lower than in capitalist countries (in particular, income taxes are low), but socialist countries drive a similar wedge between the marginal productivity and purchasing power of a factor by fixing prices that are suitably marked-up over cost. Similarly, in case 3 the government subsidises the poor so that they can buy more than they produce, and taxes the rich so that they can buy less than they produce. In case 2 the aim of the tax is to ensure that the private costs (or returns) faced by a decision maker are the same as the social costs (or returns). But, even so, the tax releases resources for government use. There is, of course, no question of particular taxes being linked to particular

---

† These are defined in Chapter 6.

‡ Government intervention can of course also take the forms of regulation or public production (not necessarily subsidised). An important issue, in any particular instance when intervention is required, is which mode of intervention is most appropriate: fiscal activity, regulation, or public production.

§ This assumes the government owns no property.

expenditures. The only requirement for a consistent policy change, as we have defined it, is that the sum of net tax changes equals the sum of expenditure changes.

Agenda

In what follows it is convenient to think of one particular type of policy change: a tax increase designed to finance an increase in government expenditure on public goods. With many public goods (like defence) it is very difficult to detect their impact on the welfare of the different sections of the community. So we shall not discuss the distribution of benefits. But, in assessing the efficiency effects of the tax, we need to make some assumption about the total value of the way the tax proceeds are spent. Here we shall make the usual neutral assumption that the total benefit from the spending of the tax equals the total amount of the numeraire good which the tax proceeds could have bought. So our aim is to answer the following questions for each of the main types of tax available to a government in a closed economy:

1. How does the tax affect the welfare of different groups, outside of any benefits citizens may obtain from expenditure financed by the tax? This is the *incidence* of the tax.
2. What is the efficiency cost of the tax? This is the sum of the welfare losses to taxpayers due to the tax (as in 1) *minus* the benefits it yields, as measured by the tax yield. Being the total burden minus the tax yield, this is often called the *excess burden* of the tax.

3-1 THREE GENERAL PRINCIPLES

The Irrelevance of Who Pays

Before looking at particular taxes, we must first consider three elementary general principles, the first of which is normally overlooked by politicians, journalists, and the world at large:

> *1. If a market is in competitive equilibrium throughout, the effect of a tax upon relative prices and upon quantities is identical whether the tax is levied on the buyers or the sellers.*

For example, the welfare of workers will suffer identically from a social security tax of T paid by each worker and from a social security tax of T per worker levied on the employer. The reason is easy to see. The buyer's price of a commodity measures the cost of a unit of the commodity to the buyer; the

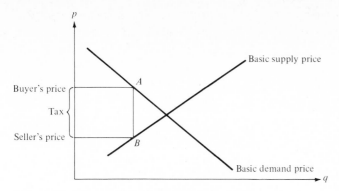

Figure 3-1 Symmetry of a tax on a buyer and a seller.

seller's price measures the benefit to the seller from selling a unit. From these definitions it follows that

$$\text{Buyer's price} \equiv \text{seller's price} + \text{tax}$$

For example, the cost of labour to an employer must exceed the labourer's reward by the amount of the tax, whether the tax is levied on the employer or the employee. But in competitive conditions there is a demand relation $p^D(x)$ which shows the cost which buyers are willing to incur to get an extra unit, when they are already getting x units. Call this the *basic demand price*. Similarly, there is a supply relation $p^S(x)$ which shows the amount that sellers require to receive in return for supplying an extra unit, when they are already supplying x units.† Call this the *basic supply price*. If the market is in equilibrium, buyers are paying what they are just willing to pay for the prevailing x and sellers are receiving what they are just willing to receive. So the actual buyer's price *is* the basic demand price and the seller's price is the basic supply price. Therefore,

$$p^D(x) = p^S(x) + T$$

This determines x. Yet we have said nothing about who is paying the tax money to the tax collector.

This is illustrated in Figure 3-1. It is not really as mysterious as it seems. For suppose the tax is levied on the buyers. Then the amount that they are willing to pay to sellers is less than the final amount that they are willing to pay, the difference being the amount that they have to pay to the tax collector. So we now have a schedule of market demand prices which lies below the schedule of basic demand prices shown in the diagram. Try drawing this in and verify that it produces an equilibrium market price equal to the seller's price shown in the diagram. Now suppose the tax is levied on the sellers and not on the buyers. Then the amount they

---

† If the supply is backward-bending, a different interpretation of the supply curve is needed (see Chapter 7), but it is easy to check that the principle we are proving still holds.

require to be paid by buyers exceeds the final amount they require to receive, since they also have to pay the tax collector. So, we now have a schedule of market supply prices which lies above the schedule of basic supply prices shown in the diagram. Try drawing this in and verify that it produces an equilibrium market price that is now equal to the buyer's price shown in the diagram. The market price, however, is of no real interest. What matters is the benefit to sellers and the cost to buyers. For this reason we shall never specify on which side of the market a tax is formally levied.

The main confusion over this subject arises from the multiplicity of price concepts. However, there are only two sets of prices that are really important in an economy: the seller's prices of factors and the buyer's prices of goods. For the welfare of a factor owner depends on the ratio of the price he gets for selling his factors to the price he has to pay for the products he buys. So we shall henceforth use our symbol w to mean the seller's price of a factor, and our symbol p to mean the buyer's price for a product.

Q3-1 Suppose a tax of T per unit is imposed on labour. Market prices are sticky and do not adjust fully to produce a new equilibrium. Compare the welfare of workers when
   (i) The tax is levied on employers.
   (ii) The tax is levied on workers.
(Assume the supply curve of labour is upward-sloping.)

Incidence

The second elementary principle follows directly from inspection of Figure 3-1.

2. Incidence. A given tax will raise the buyer's price more (and reduce the seller's price less), the less elastic the demand and the more elastic the supply of the commodity.

To check this, first try pivoting the demand curve around point A (holding the supply curve constant), and then pivot the supply curve around point B (holding the demand curve constant). All this is rather mechanical, but the underlying reality is of profound importance. If a commodity is in inelastic demand, buyers have no close substitute for it. So they cannot easily escape a tax. The same applies to sellers. If the supply of a commodity is very inelastic, there can be no good alternative activity available to sellers and so they cannot easily escape the tax. The general principle is thus: the more difficult it is for agents on any particular side of a market to substitute one activity for another in response to a tax, the more likely they are to be adversely affected by the tax. This theme will recur in our ensuing discussion.

The preceding partial equilibrium principle gives us some feeling for the factors that affect the incidence of a tax, incidence being for the moment measured by the change in price which buyers and sellers experience. For example, it suggests that if we are considering a factor market and the factor is taxed, it will suffer

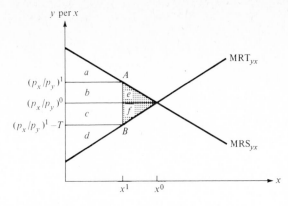

Figure 3-2 The welfare cost of an excise tax.

more the more inelastic its supply. However, suppose we are considering a product market, and a good is taxed. Its price to the sellers falls. But who really loses? After all, in perfect competition, no seller is making excess profits. So the ultimate effect is on factor owners. To sort out who actually gains and who loses we need general equilibrum theory, as we shall show in a moment.

Q3-2 Suppose a small tax of T per unit were levied in the U.S. on the following commodities: salt, hotel rooms in Miami, yellow shirts. Suppose also that equilibrium price and quantity were the same for all three commodities. In which case would the buyer's price per unit rise most and in which case least?

Excess Burden

However, the framework of Figure 3-1 also enables us to say something useful about the excess burden of a tax. We have already seen in Chapter 1 how to measure the welfare cost of a product subsidy, and the approach for a product tax is analogous. If we assume, as in Chapter 1, that there is no income effect in the demand for x, then the marginal rate of substitution of y for x is defined independently of the distribution of income and independently of consumption of y. This schedule is shown in Figure 3-2, together with the marginal rate of transformation.

A per-unit tax of T is now imposed on x, where T equals the distance BA. Output of x falls from x^0 to x^1. The welfare cost is (as in Chapter 1)

$$\text{Welfare cost} = \int_{x^0}^{x^1} [\text{MRT}_{yx}(x) - \text{MRS}_{yx}(x)]\, dx$$

In Figure 3-2 this is measured by the area $e + f$. (Figure 3-3 shows the corresponding information in the total diagram.) From Figure 3-2 one can see that if supply and demand curves are locally straight, then the welfare cost is

$$\text{Welfare cost} = -\tfrac{1}{2}T\,\Delta x$$

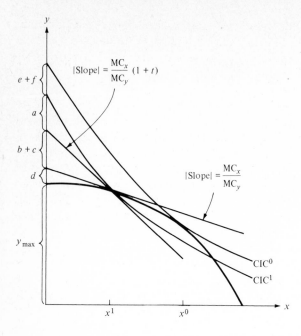

Figure 3-3 The welfare effects of an excise tax.

So, for any given T, the welfare cost is greater, the greater the change in x. And the change in x is greater the more elastic the supply and demand curves. This suggests

> 3. *Excess burden. The efficiency cost of a given per-unit tax on a given commodity is greater the more elastic the demand and supply of the taxed commodity.*

You can check this approximately by again pivoting the curves around points A and B.† Though we have expounded the principle in relation to an excise tax, it applies equally to any tax, as does the method of measuring welfare cost. So the greater the possibilities of substitution in the economy, the greater the welfare cost of a given price distortion. Those who are worried about the distorting effects of taxes must therefore believe that the economy is rife with possibilities of substitution. By contrast, left-wing economists tend to stress the fixity of proportions and to play down the costs of distorted pricing policies. Instead they stress the costs of *quantity* distortions (due, for example, to disequilibrium). These are higher the less elastic the supply and demand curves. (Check this too.)

Going on, we can use Figure 3-2 to provide a commonly used breakdown of the incidence effects of a tax which splits them, not between the two factors of production, but between households viewed first as consumers and then as

---

† Strictly we ought to compare the effects of the tax starting from a given pretax equilibrium. For a more general approach to the issue under discussion, see Q3-3 (ii).

income-earning factors of production. The total welfare change, including the benefits from the tax proceeds, thus has three parts: losses to consumers, losses to producers, and gains to taxpayers. Let us look at the three elements more closely.

1. *Loss of consumers' surplus.* Even if the purchasing power of their incomes in terms of y were constant, consumers would lose from the rise in p_x/p_y. Let us measure this loss, assuming consumers' command over y is unchanged. In the example the price has risen from $(p_x/p_y)^0$ to $(p_x/p_y)^1$. We can compare consumers' welfare in the two positions by comparing the surplus which they obtain in each situation by being able to buy x at the stated price rather than not being able to buy it at all. At $(p_x/p_y)^0$ consumers buy x^0. Their welfare gain from purchasing x^0 as opposed to no x is the sum of the difference between the value and the cost of each unit bought.†

$$\text{Welfare gain} = \int_0^{x^0} \left[\text{MRS}_{yx}(x) - \left(\frac{p_x}{p_y} \right)^0 \right] dx$$

So they would be willing to pay $a + b + e$ more for x^0 than they do. Similarly at $(p_x/p_y)^1$ consumers buy x^1. Their surplus is now only a, So they have lost $b + e$ of surplus.

2. *Loss of producers' surplus.* In fact the purchasing power of consumers over y has not been constant. For factor owners (who are consumers under another hat) have experienced a fall in their income measured in terms of y. This can again be viewed as a difference between surpluses: if x^0 is produced, producers' incomes will buy $c + d + f$ more of y than the amount they could buy if $x = 0$, while, if x^1 is produced, producers' incomes will only buy d more of y than if $x = 0$. So producers have lost $c + f$ of surplus.

3. Taxpayers are now gaining $b + c$ in tax proceeds spent on their behalf.

Putting the three categories together, we find

Consumers	$-b$	$-e$		
Producers			$-c$	$-f$
Taxpayers	$+b$		$+c$	
Society		$-e$		$-f$

Using the Kaldor criterion, we add up the welfare changes of the different parties, and find a social loss of $e + f$, as before. This is the excess burden of the tax, since consumers and producers taken together lose $e + f$ more than the tax that is paid.

---

† To consumers, viewed as consumers, the rate at which they sacrifice y for x (i.e., *their* rate of transformation) is p_x/p_y.

In the case of a tax on a small competitive industry, the breakdown of incidence between consumers (the general public) and the owners of factors of production is very useful. For the main effect of the tax upon total factor incomes (in terms of some numeraire) will be limited to the factors previously employed in this industry. But in the general equilibrium context of a large industry, a release of factors from one industry will alter the pattern of rewards in other industries. So it is less easy to interpret which factor owners are being affected, and a general equilibrium approach is needed. However, even in the general equilibrium context, the breakdown into consumers' and producers' surplus is often a useful step in measuring total welfare costs, as we shall see in the next chapter.

Q3-3 (i) Suppose that the equilibrium price and quantity per annum were the same for yellow shirts and hotel room bookings in Miami. Which, on efficiency grounds, would it be better to tax to get a given revenue?

*(ii) Develop a formula which expresses the welfare cost of a small per-unit tax T as a function of T, x, p, and the elasticities of demand and supply. [Hint: Totally differentiate the relation $p^D(x) = p^S(x) + \text{tax}$ and then set $\Delta \text{ tax} = T$.] Then show that this cost, as a fraction of the tax yield, depends only on the elasticities of demand and supply and the proportional tax rate T/p.

(iii) Check that you understand the relation of Figures 3-2 and 3-3. After the tax is imposed and its proceeds handed back in lump-sum form to consumers, what distances in Figure 3-3 measure (in terms of y)

    (a) The value of national income to consumers

    (b) The national income at market prices

    (c) The national income at factor cost (i.e., the amount of y which can be purchased by factor incomes)

3-2 A GENERAL TAX

In a two-good, two-factor world we can classify any tax (or subsidy) into one of four logically possible categories:

1. A general tax on all factors or products (e.g., a value-added tax)
2. A tax on one factor (e.g., a payroll tax)
3. A tax on one product (e.g., a tax on cigarettes)
4. A tax on one factor when it is employed in producing one product (e.g., a tax on capital in the corporate sector)

We can examine the first two taxes using the one-sector model.

We start with the simplest tax of all, a general (equiproportional) tax on all factors or products. This can be illustrated using the simplest production function, with one good y produced at constant returns to scale by one factor L:

$$y = aL = y_L L$$

The supply of labour is given. The government wants to consume a fraction $t/(1 + t)$ of what is produced, leaving a fraction $1/(1 + t)$ for the workers.

How can this be achieved? Taxes can be levied in either the goods market or the factor market, but in either case the government has to ensure that each worker can only buy a fraction $1/(1 + t)$ of what he produces. So we require

$$\frac{w_L}{p_y} = \frac{y_L}{1 + t}$$

How can this be brought about? Suppose there were a tax on output levied at a proportional rate t on the net-of-tax price.† Then output will be sold at a buyer's price equal to marginal cost times $1 + t$, assuming no other taxes are in force. So

$$p_y = \frac{w_L}{y_L}(1 + t) \qquad \text{and thus} \qquad \frac{w_L}{p_y} = \frac{y_L}{1 + t}$$

Alternatively, suppose there were no tax on output, but a tax were levied on gross factor incomes equal to a proportion t of the net-of-tax wage.‡ Then the gross-of-tax wage of each worker would be the value of his marginal product $p_y y_L$, and he would receive net of tax

$$w_L = p_y y_L\left(1 - \frac{t}{1 + t}\right) \qquad \text{so that} \qquad \frac{w_L}{p_y} = \frac{y_L}{1 + t}$$

The result in each case is the same. In the first case the government obtains command over resources by ensuring that the national product at market prices exceeds that at factor cost. In the second case it ensures that, though these two measures of national product are identical,§ the factors cannot buy the national product so valued.

We have discussed this so far in a model with only one good and one factor. But the following proposition should be intuitively clear and will be demonstrated later in the two-factor, two-product case:

4. *A general tax levied at an equal proportional rate on all products has effects identical to a tax at the same rate on all factors.*

3-3 A TAX ON ONE FACTOR

Suppose now there are two factors, so that $y = y(K, L)$ and factors are supplied in given quantities $\bar{K}$ and $\bar{L}$. The government wants to buy some y for its own use

---

† This is the normal way in which product taxes are expressed. But it makes no practical difference whether we levy a tax of $\frac{1}{10}$ on the net-of-tax price or a tax of $\frac{1}{11}$ on the gross-of-tax price.

‡ In the case of factor taxes paid by households, the rate is more commonly computed as a proportion of gross-of-tax income. If t^* is the rate computed on this basis, $t^* = t/(1 + t)$. However it is convenient to adopt the same approach to factor taxes and product taxes and compute all rates as a proportion of the net-of-tax price.

§ National product at factor cost measures firms' costs of production, inclusive of factor taxes levied on both households and firms.

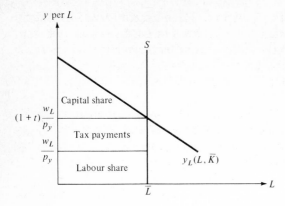

Figure 3-4 A tax on one factor.

and to do this by a tax on labour only. The solution is simple. Competition ensures that each factor is paid an amount gross of tax equal to the value of its marginal product. But labour receives net of tax the value of its marginal product divided by $1 + t$, where t is the tax rate computed as a proportion of its net-of-tax price. So

$$\frac{w_K}{p_y} = y_K \qquad \frac{w_L}{p_y} = \frac{y_L}{1 + t}$$

The tax is borne by labour only.

The result is illustrated in Figure 3-4. The curve shown indicates the marginal product of labour. Since the supply of labour is given, we shall only have full employment if the real cost of labour to the employer equals the marginal product of labour when $L = \bar{L}$. But the real cost of labour is the real wage of the sellers of labour *plus* the real value of the tax per worker. So in equilibrium we have

$$y_L(\bar{L}, \bar{K}) = \frac{w_L}{p_y}(1 + t)$$

When we go on to the two-sector model, we shall find that the preceding approach remains basically valid. If a tax is levied on one factor only, provided that the government spends the tax proceeds in the same way as the owners of the factor would have spent that part of their income, the gross price of the factor in terms of each good is the same after the tax as before. The whole structure of gross prices is unaltered, and the tax is borne by the taxed factor alone. The allocation of factors is also unchanged. If we move on to a wider model where other factors are in variable supply, then the preceding conclusion only holds good if the changes in income produced by the tax do not alter the supply of other factors.

However, even if prices and resource allocation are affected, a tax on a fixed factor cannot involve any efficiency cost, since the wedge that it drives between the social and private returns to the factor does not affect any choice which the factor owners make about their supply of the factor. Henry George's classic case for taxing land rent rested on this proposition, that land is in completely inelastic supply (apart from the results of reclamation). The argument would be entirely sound, if it were possible to disentangle the return to ground space as such from the return to resources invested in maintaining and improving the quality of the land, and provided that the tax did not drive any land out of use.

We can therefore draw the following conclusions:

> 5. *A tax on a factor that is in fixed supply will have no efficiency cost. The allocation of resources will be unaffected, and the tax will be borne entirely by the taxed factor, unless the tax alters the relative demand for products or the supply of other factors that are in variable supply.*

The proposition is perfectly general and therefore applies also to a general tax where *all* factors are in fixed supply.

The underlying concept here is that of economic "rent." If *n* units of a factor are being supplied, the economic rent is the difference between what the factor owners are paid and the minimum they would be willing to accept for supplying *n* units rather than no units. So the rent is the difference between the factor's earnings and the area below its supply curve. If the supply is totally given, then the whole of the factor's income is rent: none of it is needed to induce the factor to become available. And whenever an income is a pure rent there can be no efficiency cost in taxing it away, since behaviour cannot be modified so as to escape the tax.

Q3-4 Suppose the government wants to buy one-tenth of the national product. $y = K^{1/4}L^{3/4}$ and factor supplies are $\overline{K}$ and $\overline{L}$. What tax rate (computed on the net-of-tax price) would it use in the following cases:
  (i) The tax is a product tax.
  (ii) The tax is a tax on capital.
  (iii) The tax is at an equal rate on labour and capital.

Q3-5 "A subsidy to capital will encourage the use of capital-intensive methods of production, even if the supply of capital is fixed." True or false?

Q3-6 Suppose there is a small increase in local property taxes ("rates" in Britain) and that these are levied on tenants. Who will bear this tax, landlords or tenants:
  (i) If market rents are market-determined?
  (ii) If market rents are regulated well below the equilibrium level?

3-4 A TAX ON ONE PRODUCT (AN EXCISE TAX)

We now introduce a second good (*x*). This makes it possible to discuss two more kinds of tax:

1. A tax on one good only (e.g., an excise tax on cigarettes)
2. A tax on one factor when employed in one industry only (e.g., the corporation tax, which is for simplified purposes a tax on capital in the corporate sector)

Since neither x nor y is in fixed supply, each of these taxes will involve efficiency losses and alter the allocation of resources. To look at this (and to check propositions 4 and 5) it is convenient at this stage to make one simplifying assumption. We shall assume that, although taxes redistribute income, they do not affect the relative demand for different goods, because the marginal propensities to consume x and y out of additional income are the same for all consumers and for the government. There is then a unique set of community indifference curves which can be represented by a utility function $u(x, y)$ which will correctly predict the equilibrium relative price p_x/p_y for any particular (x, y) mix. We can now write down the equilibrium conditions of the economy using the following symbols:

p_x, p_y	Product prices to households (gross of tax)
w_K, w_L	Factor prices to households (net of tax)
t_x, t_y	Product taxes (rates as proportions of net-of-tax price)
t_{Kx}, t_{Ky}	Taxes on capital in x and y industries (rates as proportions of net-of-tax price)
t_{Lx}, t_{Ly}	Taxes on labour in x and y industries (rates as proportion of net-of-tax price)
MC_x, MC_y	Marginal cost to producers

Since producers are in equilibrium, the relative marginal costs of x and y must be the same, whether additional output is produced by more capital or more labour. In the presence of taxes, these marginal costs are given by Equations (1) and (2):

$$\frac{MC_x}{MC_y} = \frac{w_K(1 + t_{Kx})}{x_K(K^x, L^x)} \bigg/ \frac{w_K(1 + t_{Ky})}{y_K(K^y, L^y)} = \frac{y_K(K^y, L^y)}{x_K(K^x, L^x)} \cdot \frac{1 + t_{Kx}}{1 + t_{Ky}} \tag{1}$$

and

$$\frac{MC_x}{MC_y} = \frac{w_L(1 + t_{Lx})}{x_L(K^x, L^x)} \bigg/ \frac{w_L(1 + t_{Ly})}{y_L(K^y, L^y)} = \frac{y_L(K^y, L^y)}{x_L(K^x, L^x)} \cdot \frac{1 + t_{Lx}}{1 + t_{Ly}} \tag{2}$$

Note that if there were no taxes, (1) and (2) taken together would give us the production efficiency condition of Chapter 1. We also need an equation to determine the product mix:

$$\frac{u_x[x(K^x, L^x), y(K^y, L^y)]}{u_y[x(K^x, L^x), y(K^y, L^y)]} = \frac{p_x}{p_y} = \frac{MC_x(1 + t_x)}{MC_y(1 + t_y)} \tag{3}$$

Note that if there were no taxes, (1) and (3) would give us our product-mix efficiency condition of Chapter 1. Since we are assuming unambiguous community indifference curves, we do not need equations for the behaviour of the different consumers in order to determine the allocation of resources. However, we do need to tie the system down with endowment constraints:

$$K^x + K^y = \bar{K} \tag{4}$$

$$L^x + L^y = \bar{L} \tag{5}$$

Taking the equality of the left- and right-hand terms in Equations (1) to (3), together with (4) and (5), we have five equations and five unknowns (K^x, K^y,

L^x, L^y, and MC_x/MC_y). We shall assume there is a unique solution which determines all quantities and relative prices.

We can first use this framework to check proposition 4. Suppose we impose a general product tax at rate t, so that $t_x = t_y = t$, all other taxes being set at zero rates. This has the same effect as if we imposed a general factor tax of t $(t_{Kx} = t_{Ky} = t_{Lx} = t_{Ly} = t)$.† And in neither case is the allocation of resources (K^x, K^y, L^x, L^y) altered, given our assumption that income changes do not affect the pattern of demand. Moving to proposition 5, suppose we impose a tax on labour in both industries at a rate t $(t_{Lx} = t_{Ly} = t)$. On our assumptions, this again has no effect on the allocation of resources, all marginal products remaining unaltered.

However suppose we impose a product tax on x $(t_x = t)$. This at once alters the equilibrium of the system. (The same effect would follow if $t_{Kx} = t_{Lx} = t$). Output remains on the transformation curve, since from Equations (1) and (2) productive efficiency is maintained. But the product mix is changed, as shown in Figure 3-3. The tax drives a wedge between the rate of transformation between y and x and the rate of substitution. Consumers equate their rates of substitution to the relative price which they face, which exceeds the relative marginal costs. So, as Equation (3) shows,

$$\text{MRS}_{yx} = \frac{p_x}{p_y} > \frac{MC_x}{MC_y} = \text{MRT}_{yx}$$

To determine the incidence of the tax, we shall start by assuming that, when x is taxed, the final effect is a fall in the output and consumption of x. (This follows automatically if all marginal propensities to consume x are identical.) As a result of the increased output of capital-intensive y it follows that the capital intensity of production falls in both industries, as we saw in the last chapter. So the real marginal product of labour falls in both industries, and the real marginal product of capital rises. However since x is taxed, neither factor can buy its marginal product in the x industry. It follows that labour is unambiguously worse off. But capital may or may not be. This depends on whether or not its ability to purchase x has been reduced and, if so, by how much. Clearly, the higher the share of its expenditure that capital devotes to the taxed good (x), the more likely it is to be worse off.

We can thus summarise the incidence of a tax on L-intensive x:

$\dfrac{w_K}{p_x}$	$\dfrac{w_K}{p_y}$	u^K	$\dfrac{w_L}{p_x}$	$\dfrac{w_L}{p_y}$	u^L
?	↑	?	↓	↓	↓

† This would hold even without our special assumption of no effects of income changes on the pattern of demand.

Note that these evaluations of the welfare of capital and labour exclude the welfare gain to them from increased public expenditure. They also assume that the production of x falls.

We now stop assuming this and ask: Could the output of x rise? To answer this, we follow the standard procedure of examining the impact effect of the tax to see if it generates excess demand or supply of x. Thus assume all prices constant, except p_x, which rises by a factor $1 + t$. So long as the government has a marginal propensity to spend on x (per unit of additional income) that is no higher than the relevant weighted average for the private sector, a transfer of funds from the private sector to the public sector cannot increase the demand for x. For the combined income effects will in this case not be positive, and at the same time the tax will induce a negative substitution effect away from x.

But what if the government does have a higher marginal propensity to spend on x than the private sector? Even if the government spends all the tax proceeds on x, production of x must fall if the private sector consumes more y than before. The condition for the private sector to buy more y when the price of x rises is of course that it spends less on x—in other words that the price elasticity of demand for x exceeds unity. So long as this is the case we can be sure that, whatever the government does, output of x will fall. Our conclusion is therefore as follows.

> 6. *An excise tax on a labour-intensive product will normally make labour worse off and may or may not make capital worse off. It is not efficient.*

Q3-7 x and y are produced at constant returns by K and L in fixed supply. y is labour-intensive. Labour has a relatively strong preference for x. What are the probable effects on the welfare of L and K of an excise tax on y, the proceeds of which are spent on government purchases of x? Does labour necessarily lose?

Q3-8 (i) Suppose a closed economy has as factors only land and labour, with agriculture more land-intensive than manufacturing. A food subsidy is introduced that is financed by a proportional tax on all factor incomes. Must labour necessarily lose?

(ii) The British Government publishes an annual analysis of the incidence of taxes and subsidies.† This assumes that product taxes are "passed on to the consumer" and factor taxes are borne by the factor being taxed. This assumption is often criticised on the grounds that it implies that the supply of factors is perfectly inelastic and the supply of products perfectly elastic, and that these two are incompatible propositions. Evaluate the logic of this criticism.

3-5 TAX ON ONE FACTOR IN ONE INDUSTRY

Finally we look at a tax on one factor in one industry. Suppose the tax is on labour in the labour-intensive industry x—like Britain's Selective Employment Tax which was limited to labour-intensive service industries. Our analysis, as before, is restricted to the case of perfect competition. Such a tax introduces two

---

† United Kingdom Central Statistical Office, *Economic Trends.*

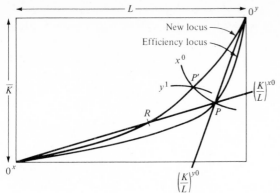

Figure 3-5 A tax on labour in x.

distortions. First, production does not occur on the efficient transformation curve. For competition ensures that

$$\frac{x_L}{x_K} = \frac{w_L}{w_K}(1 + t_{Lx}) > \frac{w_L}{w_K} = \frac{y_L}{y_K}.$$

So the marginal rate of substitution is not equal in the two industries, and we have production inefficiency (as at P' in Figure 3-5). Production does not occur along the efficiency locus in factor space. So the new transformation curve lies inside the efficient transformation curve, except where this touches the x axis and the y axis. On top of this, relative product prices do not correctly reflect the rate of transformation along the new (and distorted) transformation curve. As before, if the government has no more propensity to consume x than the private sector or if the elasticity of demand for x is over unity, we can be certain that x falls. We shall assume it does. The consequences are as follows. Pretax production is at P. Due to the tax, production occurs on the new locus between 0^x and P'. So $(K/L)^y$ falls to something less than the slope of 0^yP (its original level). This raises y_K and lowers y_L. But what happens to the capital intensity of the x industry? There are two possible cases:

1. x falls only a little, and production occurs in the range RP'. In this case $(K/L)^x$ rises, x_K falls, and x_L rises. So capital may lose from the tax. However, labour cannot gain. For labour does not receive its full marginal product in the industry in which it is taxed, and we can prove that in fact the income of labour will buy less x than it would before, even if its marginal product has risen. For

$$\frac{w_L}{p_x} = \frac{w_L}{p_y}\frac{p_y}{p_x}$$

and both fractions on the right-hand side have fallen.

Table 3-1 The welfare effects of taxes

	$\dfrac{w_K}{p_x}$		$\dfrac{w_K}{p_y}$		u^K	$\dfrac{w_L}{p_x}$		$\dfrac{w_L}{p_y}$		u^L
No tax	x_K		y_K			x_L		y_L		
General factor tax	$x_K/(1+t)$	↓	$y_K/(1+t)$	↓	↓	$x_L/(1+t)$	↓	$y_L/(1+t)$	↓	↓
Factor tax on L	x_K	—	y_K	—	—	$x_L/(1+t_L)$	↓	$y_L/(1+t_L)$	↓	↓
Product tax on x	$x_K/(1+t_x)$	?	y_K	↑	?	$x_L/(1+t_x)$	↓	y_L		↓
Tax on										
$\quad L$ in x	x_K	?	y_K	↑	?	$x_L/(1+t_{Lx})$	↓	y_L		↓
$\quad K$ in x										

Note: x is L-intensive.

2. x falls a great deal and production occurs in the range $0^x R$. In this case $(K/L)^x$ falls, x_K rises, and x_L falls. So capital gains, due to the greatly increased quantity of capital-intensive y that is demanded. And, as before, labour loses.

The qualitative conclusion of the analysis is thus the same as for an excise tax. Labour must lose and capital may or may not. This is indicated in Table 3-1, which brings together our results. It shows the value of each relative price relevant to welfare, and, next to it, an arrow indicating how this value compares with its pretax value. (x is labour-intensive, and all marginal propensities to consume x and y out of additional income are assumed the same.) One row is left vacant—the case of a tax on capital in the labour-intensive industry. The conclusion in that case is even less definitive, but the reader is invited to complete the table for himself (see Question 3-9).

To resolve the uncertainties that emerge from qualitative analysis, we need to know the relevant utility functions and production functions, which are discussed later in the book. Happily, more and more information is now becoming available on these, and at the same time powerful computing routines have been developed which make it possible to determine the general equilibrium of complex systems under different tax regimes.†

All the discussion has been cast in terms of a change in budgetary scale, but it is relatively easy to see how it could be altered to cover a switch from one tax to another with public expenditure constant. A subsidy is simply a negative tax, and our preceding discussion applies equally to subsidies and taxes.

Q3-9 Complete Table 3-1.

† See J. B. Shoven and J. Whalley, "A General Equilibrium Calculation of the Effects of Differential Taxation of Income from Capital in the U.S.," *Journal of Public Economics*, vol. 1, pp. 281–321, November 1972.

Q3-10 Suppose one industry becomes unionised, and as a result the money wage in that industry is raised to 15 percent above that in other industries. Assume that employment in each industry is determined by demand at the prevailing relative wages. Use Table 3-1 to predict the effects on the welfare of unionised and nonunionised workers

    (i) If the unionised industry is labour-intensive

    (ii) If it is capital-intensive

*Q3-11 Suppose that for capital, labour, and government $u^i = x^i y^i$. In the economy as a whole

$$x = K^{x^{1\,3}} L^{x^{2\,3}} \qquad y = K^{y^{2\,3}} L^{y^{1\,3}}$$

K and L are in fixed supply with $\overline{K} = \overline{L} = 1$. First a tax is levied on x at 10 percent of the net-of-tax price. Then this tax is replaced by a tax on labour employed in x, levied at a rate giving the government the same share of money national income as the previous tax. Compare u^K and u^L under each of these taxes and under no tax. (Prices can be conveniently looked at in the form of fractions and powers, but to assess u^K and u^L it is easiest to use logs.)

3-6 A FACTOR TAX WITH VARIABLE FACTOR SUPPLIES

The whole of our analysis in Secs. 3-2 to 3-5 has assumed that factors are in given supply. However, the supply of labour and capital do respond to some extent to their returns. This means that there *is* an efficiency cost to any tax affecting labour or capital. However, the excise tax analysis of Figure 3-3 can be readily adapted to these problems. For conformity with the usual geometrical presentation we redraw this here to represent a tax on y (see Figure 3-6). The tax is at rate t. Now suppose we take a tax on labour income. Then we consider our two commodities to be leisure x and goods y. A tax on earned income is a tax on goods but not on leisure. It means that the rate at which people can increase their personal consumption of goods by sacrificing leisure is reduced below the rate at which they can actually produce goods. So we have $\mathrm{MRS}_{yx} < \mathrm{MRT}_{yx}$. This, assuming we remain on the transformation curve, produces a shift to more leisure. We shall examine this case again more fully in Chapter 11. Similarly, consider a tax on capital. We now make our two commodities stand for consumption

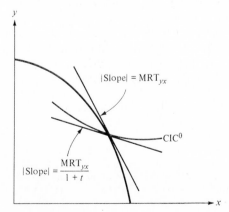

Figure 3-6 A tax on y.

today x and consumption tomorrow y. A tax on capital reduces the amount by which consumers can increase their personal future consumption by abstaining from present consumption. This rate now becomes less than the rate at which society's future consumption can in fact be increased by present saving. Once again $MRS_{yx} < MRT_{yx}$. So saving is discouraged, and present consumption is increased. To determine the incidence of taxes on labour and capital incomes when supplies are variable would require a more explicit model than we wish to develop here. At this stage our only point is that, whenever individuals respond to changes in the terms on which they can operate, there are costs involved in altering those terms in such a way that private returns differ from social returns. One may wish to incur some costs of this kind for the sake of redistribution; how much cost is an issue to which we return in Chapter 11.

3-7 INTERPERSONAL REDISTRIBUTION

Our analysis in Secs. 3-2 to 3-5 was concerned only with the effect of taxes on the *functional* distribution of income (as between factors of production). This helps one to think about the principles involved. But to evaluate any change of budgetary scale in the real world, we want to know how it would affect the *interpersonal* distribution of income, and of course the level of total output. This would require three extensions of the analysis

1. We should include the distribution between individuals of the benefits from any government expenditure.
2. We should recognise that there are many more than two factors of production; in particular there are workers with many different levels of skill.
3. We should allow for the fact that individuals often own both labour and capital, not just one or the other.

Suppose we knew all these things. We might then ask whether a proposed policy change is progressive or regressive. In other words is it equalising or disequalising? The only general test of this is to calculate an inequality measure for the pre- and post-policy income distributions and to compare them. Such measures were discussed in Chapter 1.

However there are many policies where net benefits either rise or fall continuously with individual income. If the net benefits fall continuously as income rises, then the policy is equalising.† The poor gain, and the rich lose.

If a policy confers net benefits that fall continuously as income rises, the policy is progressive.

---

† This only holds as a universal proposition if total income is constant. In this case the condition guarantees that the new Lorenz curve lies wholey inside the old one (see page 49), and the new distribution is more equal than the old using any symmetric and strictly quasi-concave social welfare function with individual incomes as the arguments.

Most policies can be thought of in two parts: a part that confers benefits B (either by subsidies or government expenditures) and a part that imposes costs C (like taxes). A sufficient condition for progressivity is, then, that for all values of y

$$\frac{d}{dy}(B - C) = \frac{dB}{dy} - \frac{dC}{dy} < 0$$

A policy can clearly be progressive even if it benefits the rich more than the poor, provided it imposes even greater differential costs on the rich.

Another unambiguous situation arises if the elasticities of benefits and of costs with respect to income are both constant. Should the cost elasticity exceed the benefit elasticity, the policy is progressive, and vice versa.† A special case of this occurs when the benefits rise proportionately less than income (benefit elasticity < 1) and where the costs rise proportionately more (cost elasticity > 1).

If benefits rise proportionately faster than income, they are called regressive, *and if costs rise proportionately faster they are called* progressive.

If benefits and costs are both regressive, so is the package; and if benefits and costs are both progressive, so is the package. But if one is regressive and the other progressive, the outcome for the package depends on the relative strength of the effects. Thus, a subsidy on food financed by a poll tax is regressive if food is a normal good. For the size of subsidy rises with income while the tax does not. So the regressive tax costs outweigh the benefits, which are progressive since they rise proportionately less fast than income. Much confusion exists on these matters especially among politicians. The essential point is that policy changes must be evaluated in the context of consistent packages, which is where we began our story. The chapter needs no summary since we have already highlighted the main findings. Perhaps the main moral is that, in matters of tax, things often ain't what they seem to be.

Q3-12 Are the following progressive, regressive, or neutral?

(i) A subsidy to a good with income elasticity of 2 financed by a progressive income tax of the form $T = ay^{1.5}$, where T is total tax.

(ii) All students in higher education receive the same subsidy and the following statistics hold:

	Family income		
	$0–10,000	$10,000–20,000	Over $20,000
Children per family getting higher education (av.)	0.2	0.7	1.0
Tax payments per family (av.), ($)	1000	4000	6000

† This is again only universally valid if total income is constant. Write the functions in the relevant range as $B = ay^{\alpha}$, $C = by^{\beta}$. If $\alpha < \beta$, $\Sigma B = \Sigma C$, and $B(y_{min}) > C(y_{min})$, then the new Lorenz curve must lie inside the old one.

Q3-13 "Suppose that people are either rich (with incomes of exactly y_R each) or poor (with incomes of y_P each). A higher proportion of whites than blacks are rich. It follows that if a sum of $1 is given to every white person and this is financed by a proportional tax on whites and blacks, this is regressive." True or false?

FOUR

APPLICATIONS TO INTERNATIONAL TRADE

We can now extend our ideas to include open economies. What, we may ask, are the effects of a tariff (a tax on importing a good)? Who gains and who loses, and do the gains outweigh the losses? Or, what determines the pattern of world trade?

We begin by analysing the effects of a tariff. This depends crucially on whether the country imposing it is "small" or "large." If it is small, we mean that the behaviour of its citizens cannot affect the structure of world prices: the country is a price taker. For example, what happens in Britain (even a record drought) has little effect on the world price of wheat. But if the country figures large in the market for the good (either as a buyer or seller), its actions can affect world prices. For example, if the U.S. imposed import restrictions on coffee, this would inevitably reduce the relative price of coffee in world markets. So the "large" country has variable *terms of trade*, meaning a variable ratio between the price of its export good(s) and the price of its import good(s). In this case a tariff may be more advantageous to a country than in the small country case.

So we first analyse the effects of a tariff imposed by a small country. Then we do the same for a country where the terms of trade are variable. This requires us to develop a theory of how world prices are determined, which in turn leads to some interesting propositions about the pattern of world trade and world income distribution.

4-1 ONE COUNTRY'S GAINS FROM TRADE: WORLD PRICES CONSTANT

Suppose a small country was originally isolated from world trade and was in equilibrium at point P, where it both produced and consumed (see Figure 4-1).

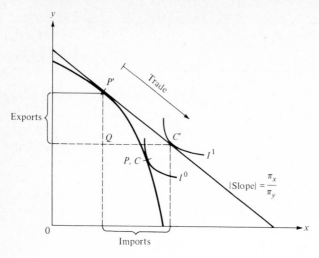

Figure 4-1 Gains from trade.

It then becomes able to trade abroad at relative world prices (π_x/π_y). This expands the consumption possibility set of the economy, which was previously bounded by the production frontier. For if domestic production moves to P', it is then possible to exchange y for x at the rate π_x/π_y given in the world market. So the new consumption frontier of the economy is the line through P' with slope π_x/π_y. However, this will only come about if production does move to P', where the domestic rate of transformation (MRT) is equal to the world price ratio, i.e., to the rate of transformation through foreign trade (MRT^f). So for an open economy we have a fourth efficiency condition

$$\text{MRT} = \frac{\pi_x}{\pi_y} = \text{MRT}^f$$

In other words, production must be organised so as to maximise the value of GNP at world prices. In an undistorted economy this comes about as domestic prices adjust to an equality with world prices:

$$\text{MRT} = \frac{p_x}{p_y} = \frac{\pi_x}{\pi_y} = \text{MRT}^f$$

Notice that in the move from P to P', the country, which previously produced y relatively more cheaply than it was produced abroad, has taken advantage of its comparative advantage in the y industry and increased production in that line.

How does consumption react? This depends on what happens to the distribution of income during the changeover. Clearly the change makes it *possible* for the welfare of both labour and capital to be improved. For suppose that at P, the welfare levels were (u^{K0}, u^{L0}), corresponding to the community indifference curve I^0. Then there must, for example, be some $u^{K1} > u^{K0}$ such that the community indifference curve $\left(u^{K1}, u^{L0}\right)$ is tangential to the new consumption frontier. This tangency is illustrated at point C'. At this point

$$\text{MRS} = \frac{p_x}{p_y} = \frac{\pi_x}{\pi_y} = \text{MRT}^f$$

So, provided world trade prices differ from no-trade prices, a move from no trade to free trade offers a potential Pareto improvement for the country. But will it produce an *actual* Pareto improvement? Without government intervention, no. For, according to the Stolper-Samuelson theorem, the correspondence between factor prices and goods prices means that, if x is imported because it is cheap, this lowers the domestic price of x (p_x/p_y) and the welfare of the factor (L) in which x is intensive.† However, we proved above that it is *possible* for labour to be compensated for this change in its market price. The natural method of compensation would be a negative tax (subsidy) on L financed by a positive one on K, which would have no efficiency cost if factors were in fixed supply.

Q4-1 "When a country is opened to foreign trade, it experiences a potential Pareto improvement whether world relative prices are higher than domestic no-trade prices, lower, or the same." True or false?

Q4-2 (i) After the opening of the American prairies, the relative price of land in England fell. Why?

(ii) In 1832 the British Reform Bill extended the vote to the non-land-owning classes; in 1846 free trade in corn was introduced. Could the first event help to explain the second? How?

4-2 THE EFFECTS OF A TARIFF: WORLD PRICES CONSTANT

However, efficient compensation for the beneficial effects of economic change is comparatively rare in human history. It is more common for disadvantaged groups to seek inefficient ways of protecting their interests. Thus groups damaged by trade usually clamour for a tariff. The effect of a tariff on x is to raise the domestic relative price p_x/p_y above the relative world price π_x/π_y by the amount of the tariff:

$$\frac{p_x}{p_y} = \frac{\pi_x}{\pi_y}(1 + t)$$

where t is the rate of the tariff. This makes x more profitable and (in Figure 4-2) production shifts to P' (more x, less y). At this point

$$\text{MRT} = \frac{p_x}{p_y} = \frac{\pi_x}{\pi_y}(1 + t) > \text{MRT}^f$$

So we have production inefficiency.

† Throughout the chapter we talk in terms of a labour-intensive import good. The corresponding proposition for the case where the import good is capital-intensive can be readily inferred.

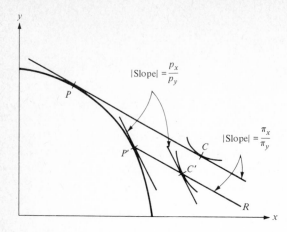

Figure 4-2 Effects of a tariff.

From point P', trade takes place at the prevailing world prices, i.e., along the line $P'R$. But consumers do not equate their rate of substitution to the relative world price, since the prices they face are the domestic prices. Thus equilibrium consumption occurs at a point such as C', where

$$\text{MRS} = \frac{p_x}{p_y} = \frac{\pi_x}{\pi_y}(1 + t) > \text{MRT}^f$$

So we also have an inefficiency in consumption.

We have thus introduced two types of inefficiency. The first relates to the product mix. In moving from P to P', we are producing additional units of x at a greater cost (in terms of y) than is involved if they are got through international trade (i.e., $\text{MRT} \neq \text{MRT}^f$). The second relates to the consumption mix: at C' we are not consuming efficiently, since consumers value additional x more than it costs to provide it through foreign trade. These two sources of waste can be seen clearly in the per-unit diagram (Figure 4-3). D is the total domestic demand curve for x, whether imported or produced at home. This is drawn on the assumption that there are no income effects in the demand for x. S is the domestic supply curve, while S^f is the foreign supply curve. Before the tariff, $0C$ is consumed; $0P$ is produced at home, leaving PC to be imported. After the tariff, less is consumed and more produced at home. The welfare changes are†

Consumers	$-a$	$-b$	$-c$	$-d$
Producers	a			
Taxpayers			c	
Total		$-b$		$-d$

† Throughout the chapter we assume there are no other distortions in the economy (i.e., no problem of second best). But if there are distortions, these should if possible be tackled directly, rather than indirectly (see Question 4-4). We also assume that the tariff proceeds are handed back to consumers in lump-sum form.

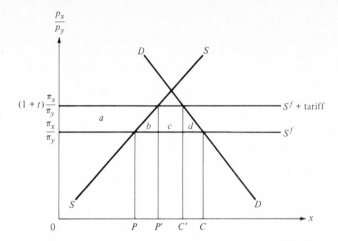

Figure 4-3 Effects of a tariff.

The area b measures the production inefficiency from producing PP' units more expensively at home than abroad; while the area d measures the consumption inefficiency from consuming $C'C$ units less than people would choose to consume at the world price.

So are there any arguments in favour of a tariff? Is there an equity argument? Since x is labour-intensive, any rise in p_x/p_y makes capital worse off and labour better off (both factors can buy their marginal products in both industries). It follows that, even if the whole tariff proceeds were handed over to capital, capital would still lose at least $b + d$ in welfare. However, suppose this did not worry us, since we were particularly keen to raise the welfare of labour. Could this constitute an argument for a tariff? The answer is no, if other instruments are available. Factor taxes and transfers would be a completely costless way to transfer income, if factors are in fixed supply.

Alternatively, it might be argued that the tariff was needed to encourage the development of the x industry, either on infant-industry or defence grounds or as an object of national pride, like the aircraft industry in Britain or France. Suppose we grant that the x industry ought to be operated at a certain minimum level, represented by $0P'$ in Figure 4-3. Could this justify a tariff? Once again, no, if alternative instruments are politically feasible. For it will be more efficient to achieve this by means of a production subsidy than a tariff. Suppose we introduce a subsidy for producing x, and this raises the producers' relative price of x to $(1 + t)\,\pi_x/\pi_y$. Domestic production will rise to $0P'$. But the price to consumers will remain π_x/π_y and consumption will not be reduced. The intended production inefficiency of the tariff will be there, but the unintended consumption inefficiency from the tariff (measured by area d) will not. So, compared to a tariff, this is a preferable way of building up an industry.

Tariffs have also been used to keep down consumption of undesirable luxuries which are largely imported, like air-conditioners in India. However, once again this can be done better by a policy aimed directly at the problem in question, in this case by a consumption tax on x. This would raise the consumers' relative price p_x/p_y to $(\pi_x/\pi_y)(1 + t)$, reducing consumption to $0C'$. But the producers' price would remain at π_x/π_y. So the intended consumption inefficiency would be there, but the unintended production inefficiency of the tariff would be avoided.

Our discussion has concentrated on tariffs (import taxes) because they are more common than export taxes. This is probably because export taxes appear to *hurt* one sectional group (factors specialised in the export industry), whereas tariffs appear to *help* one sectional group (factors specialised in the import industry). However, as we have seen, helping one group implies hurting the other and vice versa. So it is not surprising that in a two-good model an export tax of rate t has exactly the same effect as an import tax of rate t.† If an export tax is imposed, it cannot change world prices. So it must lower the domestic relative price of the export good, since

$$\frac{\pi_x}{\pi_y} = \frac{p_x}{p_y(1 + t)}$$

Otherwise exporters will not find it worthwhile exporting. Thus if p_x/p_y is to be raised by a proportion t, this can be done equally well by a tariff at rate t or an export tax at rate t. In both cases the aim is to reduce trade, and this naturally requires a tax on trade.

Q4-3 In a closed economy a tax of T per unit on the consumption of x has the same effect as a tax of T per unit on the production of x. Compare the welfare loss resulting from these two taxes in an open economy. What determines which is the greater?

Q4-4 "If there is already a tax at the proportional rate t_y on the consumption of y, a new tariff at the same rate on x will restore Pareto optimality." True or false?

Q4-5 "An export subsidy has a different effect from an import subsidy because the latter affects domestic prices, while the former does not." True or false?

Q4-6 You have to advise a poor country whether to build a steel mill and are given the following data:

Domestic price of steel	£150 per ton
Tariff on steel	£ 50 per ton
World price of steel	£100 per ton
Cost of steel on the project	£120 per ton

What is your advice, assuming the government is determined to maintain the tariff and there are no other distortions in the economy?

---

† This assumes that, as usual, we ignore any income effects on demand arising from the disposal of the tax proceeds.

Q4-7 "A country is opened to trade, but a prohibitive tariff is put on L-intensive x (i.e., a tariff so high that no x is imported). This will raise the income of L above its original level." True or false?

Q4-8 Country A can produce x at a constant cost (in terms of ₽) of 10. Comparable figures for two other countries are:

Country B   4
Country C   5

(their production functions are different). Country A has a general tariff on x of 3 per unit. But it now considers a "customs union" (or common market) with country C, under which both countries would impose a common external tariff of 3 per unit but would drop all tariffs between themselves.

    (i) Under what circumstances would country A gain by the change? (Hint: Think about changes in the volume of trade as well as about changes in the cost of imports.)

    (ii) Are there any circumstances when country A could gain more by making the customs union than by dropping *all* tariffs (e.g., by joining a free-trade area)?

4-3 THE DETERMINATION OF WORLD PRICES

We turn now to the case of variable terms of trade. Small countries without special natural resources may not be able to affect their terms of trade, but even little countries that produce a major fraction of the world's tin or coffee or diamonds may be able to have a significant effect on their relative price, and so of course may large countries which import a major proportion of any good. Looking at the matter from the selfish position of one country, we must therefore ask how the terms of trade are affected by commercial policy (i.e., policy on tariffs, export subsidies, and the like).

For this we need a theory of how world prices are determined. As a start we shall refresh our minds about the case of pure exchange. Figure 4-4 is a more or less direct copy of Figure 2-6, except that it is turned upside down to suit the conventions of trade theorists. In addition, the main box only includes that part of the original box relevant to trade, i.e., the part south and east of E in Figure 2-6,

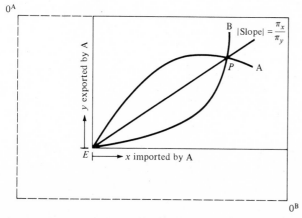

Figure 4-4 Trade under pure exchange.

and north and east of E here. Thus the axes measure not the quantities of x and y consumed but the quantities exchanged: the horizontal axis measures the x *bought* by country A and the vertical axis the y *sold* by country A. As before p_x/p_y is represented by the slope of a line through E, and each point on country A's offer curve EA shows how much x it would buy (import) and how much y it would sell (export) at the corresponding p_x/p_y. Similarly, each point on B's offer curve shows how much x it would export and how much y it would import.† The curves of Figure 2-6 were drawn on the assumption that A and B had fixed endowments of goods. However, we have already seen how to derive the offer curve of an economy when production varies in response to price changes. This was discussed in relation to Figure 2-19 and we can now suppose that the curves of Figure 4-4 do in fact represent the true foreign trade offer curves of each country. As drawn, they bring about a unique equilibrium set of prices and quantities at point P.

But is the equilibrium of world trade necessarily unique? In other words, does a rise in the relative world price of x (π_x/π_y) always decrease world excess demand for x in the neighborhood of equilibrium? The analysis here is formally identical to that for a closed economy. The effects of a rise in π_x/π_y on demand are twofold. First, there is a substitution effect away from x in both countries. Then there is a redistribution of income effect. In the neighbourhood of equilibrium the income gains to gainers approximately equal the income losses to losers. So, unless there are sharp differences in marginal propensities to consume x, the demand effects of these income changes are likely to roughly cancel out. Finally there is an increase in the supply of x. So it is highly likely that excess demand for x falls.

Q4-9 (i) Derive the shape of the offer curve of the following country (A) by showing how exports and imports vary with p_x/p_y:

$$\begin{array}{ll} \text{Transformation curve} & x_P^2 + y_P^2 = k^2 \\ \text{Utility function} & u = x_C y_C \end{array}$$

where x_P, y_P indicate quantities produced and x_C, y_C quantities consumed.

(ii) Suppose there was another country B with the same transformation curve and utility function. Would you expect them to trade?

(iii) If the other country B had

$$\text{Transformation curve} \qquad x_P^2 + (y_P - b)^2 = k^2$$

and the same tastes, in which direction would trade occur?

Q4-10 Suppose the offer curves of two countries are

$$\begin{array}{llll} \text{Country A} & y = Ax^\alpha & 0 < \alpha < 1 & A > 0 \\ \text{Country B} & y = Bx^\beta & \beta > 1 & B > 0 \end{array}$$

(i) Find for each country the relation between x and p_x/p_y. Which country is the importer of x?

(ii) Find the equilibrium world price and quantities of x and y.

---

† To remember which curve belongs to which country, note that when p_x/p_y is very high, it is the country *buying* x that *buys* very little x. So this country's offer curve is the one that is concave from below.

4-4 THE OPTIMUM TARIFF: WORLD PRICES VARIABLE

In this context, neither country is a price taker. Each acting on its own can do better by imposing a tariff (or an export tax), assuming the other does not retaliate. The aim is, of course, to lower the relative world price of your import good. The optimum tariff can be illustrated using either the general equilibrium or the per-unit apparatus. Figure 4-5 reproduces the offer curve diagram of Figure 4-4. If, when a country faces given prices π_x/π_y, it chooses to trade at a given point, we can represent this choice by a tangency between the price line and a "trade indifference curve."† T^{A0} shows the trade indifference curve on which A would be consuming if world prices were determined by free trade. T^{A1} is the highest possible indifference curve which A could attain while B remains on its offer curve (which it cannot be forced off).‡ So the best that A can do is to bring about trade at R, with a world price equal to the slope of $0R$. At R the relative value which domestic consumers place on x is $(p_x/p_y)^1$. So the optimum tariff is the difference between this and the world price:

$$\left(\frac{p_x}{p_y}\right)^1 = (1+t)\left(\frac{\pi_x}{\pi_y}\right)^1$$

The same story is told in Figure 4-6.§ Country A faces a rising supply curve of imports (and a falling demand curve for its exports) and can improve its

† A trade indifference curve shows the combinations of x (imported) and y (exported) which make it possible to keep the community on a given community indifference curve, given efficient domestic allocation.

‡ The analysis here repeats and extends the more general analysis of Figure 2-8.

§ It is best to think of the demand and supply prices of Figure 4-6 as being defined as x varies along B's offer curve $0B$ in Figure 4-5.

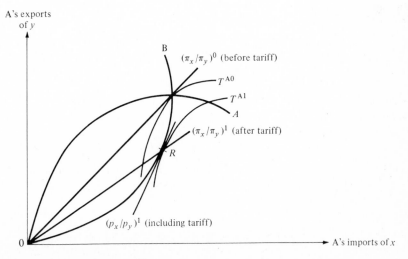

Figure 4-5 The optimum tariff.

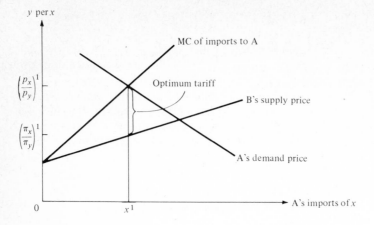

Figure 4-6 The optimum tariff.

position by means of a tariff (or an export tax). Thus an individual importer who buys more imports forces up the price faced by other importers. This externality can be overcome by the government imposing a tax on imports. The social cost of imports is πM, where $\pi = \pi_x/\pi_y$ and M is imports of x. So the marginal cost is

$$\frac{d}{dM}(\pi M) = \pi + M\frac{d\pi}{dM} = \pi\left(1 + \frac{1}{\eta^s}\right)$$

where η^s is the supply elasticity of imports. Since the individual importer pays π per unit to the foreigner, the optimal proportional rate of tariff is $1/\eta^s$. (If the country is a price taker, the optimal tariff is thus zero, as we have already discovered.) As the diagram shows, the country as a whole is behaving like a monopsonist, equating the marginal cost of imports to their marginal value. When the tariff is imposed, foreign suppliers of A's imports are forced back down their supply curves and foreign buyers of A's exports are forced back up their demand curves. So the relative world price of A's import good falls.

The tariff will normally raise the real wage of the factor in which the import is intensive (labour in our case) and will lower the real wage of the other factor.† But whereas, with given terms of trade, the loser loses more than the gainer gains, the reverse is true with variable terms of trade, provided that the optimum tariff is charged. Though other countries will lose more than the country imposing the tariff gains, tariffs or export taxes imposed by poor countries might be justified on equity grounds. Equity arguments, however, provide a clearer case *against* rich-country tariffs on poor-country exports. For the greatest danger with any country imposing a tariff is that it will provoke retaliation, so that world trade contracts further; all countries may end up worse off.

---

† An exception is the so-called Metzler case, where the supply of imports is backward-bending (see Question 4-14).

Q4-11 Draw a diagram like Figure 4-5 showing both countries worse off as a result of a tariff war. For simplicity assume the final π_x/π_y is the same as the original one.

Q4-12 "Suppose a quantitative limit is imposed on the volume of imports (an import quota). If the country has variable terms of trade and the quota is only slightly less than the free-trade quantity, the country must experience a potential Pareto improvement." True or false?

Q4-13 Before Britain joined the European Common Market it protected farmers' incomes by a system of production subsidies. Now this is done through the European Economic Community's common external tariff on foodstuffs. Assuming Britain were given all tariff proceeds levied on British imports, which system would be in Britain's interest?

Q4-14 Suppose the foreign supply curve of imported x is backward-bending. Assuming no income effects on the demand for imports, what is the effect of a tariff on x on p_x/p_y, π_x/π_y, and the welfare of labour?

4-5 WORLD INCOME DISTRIBUTION AND TRADE PATTERNS: THE FACTOR-PRICE EQUALISATION AND HECKSCHER-OHLIN THEOREMS

We have so far looked at trade mainly from the point of view of one country. It is time to widen our horizon. How far can economic theory explain the pattern of world trade and income distribution, and what can it say about the welfare implications of free trade and international migration?

We shall develop three linked theorems applying to the two-good, two-factor case and based on five assumptions (and later a sixth):

1. Technology (production functions) the same in both countries
2. Constant returns to scale
3. Perfect competition
4. No factor-intensity reversals between x and y
5. No specialisation (i.e., each country produces some of each good)

As we saw in Chapter 2, these assumptions imply a unique correspondence between relative product prices and the marginal products of capital and labour in each industry. But under free trade both countries have the same relative product prices. From this follows the *factor-price equalisation theorem*:

> 1. *Under free trade, the prices of factors (in terms of goods) will be the same in every country, given assumptions 1 to 5.*

This remarkable proposition implies that, if the assumptions hold, free migration of labour and mobility of capital are not necessary for efficiency in the world economy. The movement of goods can perform the same function of equating the value of the marginal product of a given factor in all its worldwide uses.

Going on, once factor prices are given, they determine K/L in each industry. And, if the overall capital-labour ratio of the country $(\overline{K/L})$ is given, this determines the product mix. For we always require that the following familiar identity holds:

$$\frac{\overline{K}}{\overline{L}} = \left(\frac{K}{L}\right)^x \frac{L^x}{\overline{L}} + \left(\frac{K}{L}\right)^y \frac{L^y}{\overline{L}}$$

But, if x is L-intensive, the internationally determined $(K/L)^x$ is less than $(K/L)^y$. It follows that in a country where $\overline{K}/\overline{L}$ is low, $L^x/\overline{L}$ is high, and therefore x/y is high. A labour-abundant country will produce relatively more of the labour-intensive good. This is the *weak version of the Heckscher-Ohlin theorem*:

> 2. *Under free trade and given assumptions 1 to 5, the capital-rich country will produce relatively more of the capital-intensive good and vice versa.*

However, this says nothing about what each country will export and import. For suppose country A, though capital-rich, had a strong taste for capital-intensive y, which was not felt by the inhabitants of country B. It might end up importing y.

To rule out the influence of tastes on trade patterns, we clearly have to make some explicit assumption (assumption 6). An apparently neutral, though unrealistic, one is that at any given set of prices all countries spend the same proportions of their total income on the consumption of each good. This would be the case if all countries had identical and homothetic utility functions.† Using this assumption, we arrive at the *strong version of the Heckscher-Ohlin theorem*:

> 3. *Given free trade, assumptions 1 to 5 and identical homothetic tastes in both countries, the capital-rich country will export the capital-intensive good and vice versa.*

The last two principles are illustrated in Figure 4-7, which depicts an equilibrium configuration of world production (at P) and consumption (at C). The construction of the figure is fairly obvious. It puts together the transformation curves of B (upside down) and of A, in such a way that their rates of transformation are equalised, as they will be by free foreign trade. (Make sure you know why.) The levels of production are however affected by demand, for we require that at the prevailing world prices, the demands of each country (given their purchasing powers) add up to the total of world output. In the diagram they do, consumption in both countries occurring at C.

The diagram illustrates both our principles 2 and 3. The ratio of capital-intensive y to x is higher in capital-abundant A than in labour-abundant B. This is in fact a special case of the more general principle of comparative advantage. For suppose we knew nothing about how the transformation curves of A and B were determined, but only their shape. We should still expect that y/x would be higher in A than in B. For suppose instead that y/x were the same in A and B, say at the overall world level of y/x in the equilibrium prevailing in Figure 4-7.

---

† A homothetic function is a transformation of a homogeneous function. For example, if $f(x, y)$ is homogeneous, $g[f(x, y)]$ is homothetic. This means that the isoquant map (indifference map) is the same for the transformation as for the original function, but the function values associated with each isoquant differ. If a homothetic utility function is a strictly increasing function of x and y, it can be regarded as a strictly increasing transformation of an increasing homogeneous function. To check that under homogeneity the shares of expenditure on x and y are independent of scale, see Appendix 3.

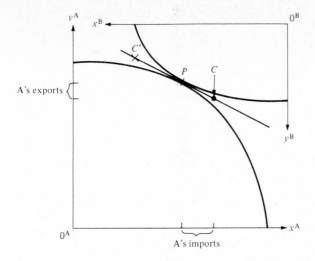

Figure 4-7 World production and trade.

Then the marginal rate of transformation (MRT_{yx}) in A would be much higher than in B: country A can produce more y (for a given sacrifice of x) than B can. So A should increase its production of y, in which it has comparative advantage. And free trade brings this about. Notice that we have said, and need to say, nothing about absolute advantage. For the present argument it is immaterial whether output per unit of input is higher or lower in A (say Britain) or in B (say Germany). There must, by definition, be goods in which Britain has comparative advantage.

Going on, until we have specified tastes, we can say nothing about the pattern of trade. For example, one could imagine sets of tastes where production could occur at P and consumption at C', if A liked y particularly strongly. However, if we assume identical homothetic preferences, the y/x mix in both countries must be the same and consumption must occur on the line 0^A0^B. This guarantees that A exports the good intensive in A's abundant factor.

Finally, what does the theory say about the optimality of free trade? Clearly, even without our special assumptions, any competitive world equilibrium would be fully efficient, if all agents were free to do the best for themselves given their endowments and world prices.† However, there are often international barriers to migration of labour and, sometimes, capital. This is where our theory comes in. Even with these obstacles, our assumptions 1 to 5 guarantee the Pareto efficiency of the world economy under free trade. For they ensure that the real marginal product of a given factor is the same in all countries.

But how realistic is all this? We have so far stated theorems 1 to 3 as tautologies. However, they are often put forward as positive propositions about the world, i.e., it is asserted that assumptions 1 to 5 approximate reality. Let us

---

† This assumes, as usual, no externality nor information problems.

ask first how the strong version of the Heckscher-Ohlin theorem stands up to the facts. Do countries export the good which is intensive in their abundant factor? Needless to say, Ohlin believed they did.† Taking land and labour as the two relevant factors, one would expect densely populated countries to import grain from sparsely populated countries. He found that they do. Similarly, reverting to capital and labour, one might expect that the United States would export capital-intensive goods. However, Leontief calculated the capital-labour ratio for U.S. exports and found it about 25 percent lower than for U.S. import-competing goods.‡ This "Leontief paradox" has provoked much scholarly activity. One weakness of the Leontief analysis is the concentration on only two factors. One factor omitted is, of course, natural resources, but these are extraordinarily difficult to specify and measure; moreover, as far as manufactures are concerned, there is no overriding reason why a country should use minerals extracted in the same country. A second problem is heterogeneity of labour. So recent work has concentrated on distinguishing between skilled and unskilled labour, and has tended to dispel the paradox by showing that U.S. exports are more skill-intensive than U.S. imports.§ However, many of the patterns of international trade remain somewhat mysterious. The evidence in support of the factor-price equalisation theorem is even weaker: the real wage of a given quality of labour is higher in capital-rich countries, as those of us who choose to live in Britain often notice.

These phenomena may be due to the possible failure of any of the assumptions we have been making. We shall relax each of these in turn, starting with the last two, in order to see what difference it makes in relation to income distribution, trade patterns, and welfare. First, we relax the assumption about factor-intensity reversals. There is good evidence that such reversals do occur; for example, when compared with other sectors, agriculture is labour-intensive at low relative wages and capital-intensive at high relative wages. This could mean that at given relative world product prices, relative factor prices differ between countries (see Figure 2-13 on page 72). In the country with the higher $\overline{K}/\overline{L}$, the capital-labour ratio in both industries would then be higher than in the labour-abundant country. So the real wage of labour would be higher and real rentals lower in the capital-abundant country. This of course is what the closed-economy model also predicts. And what about the pattern of trade? In the K-abundant country x is the K-intensive good and would, according to the Heckscher-Ohlin theorem be exported. But at the same time in the L-abundant country x is its L-intensive good: so x would also be exported by this country. Both countries cannot export the same good, so the theory breaks down; or perhaps we should say it becomes meaningless, since no one good is unambiguously capital-intensive. In the

† B. Ohlin, *Interregional and International Trade*, Harvard, Cambridge, Mass., 1933.

‡ W. W. Leontief, "Domestic Production and Foreign Trade: The American Capital Position Re-examined," *Economia Internazionale*, vol. 7, pp. 9–45, February 1954.

§ R. E. Baldwin, "Determinants of the Commodity Structure of U.S. Trade," *American Economic Review*, vol. 61, pp. 126–146, March 1971.

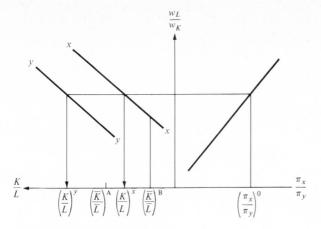

Figure 4-8 Country B specialises in x.

process, of course, an inefficiency has come about: real wages and rentals are not equal in the two countries.

Inefficiency will also result if either country specialises entirely in either of the goods. Suppose for example that x is unambiguously L-intensive but that world prices are as shown in Figure 4-8. For any country like A whose overall $\overline{K}/\overline{L}$ lies between $(K/L)^x$ and $(K/L)^y$, these will be the capital-labour ratios chosen in the x and y industries. But suppose country B is so starved of capital that its overall ratio is $(\overline{K}/\overline{L})^B$. This country will specialise in the labour-intensive good (x). But it will produce this with a lower K/L ratio than is used in the x industry in country A. So the real wage will be lower in capital-poor country B. And what about trade patterns? These will conform quite satisfactorily to the Heckscher-Ohlin prediction: labour-abundant B will be exporting labour-intensive x.

So if assumption 4 or 5 fails, real wages may be higher in one country than another. This will clearly set up pressures from labour wishing to migrate into the capital-rich country. If migration is allowed, the inefficiencies we have just discovered can be eliminated. But the very fact that unsatisfied migration pressures exist suggests that free trade in goods is not sufficient to produce efficiency in the actual world we inhabit.

So far we have assumed that trade arises wholly from different endowments, tastes and technology being held constant. We can now relax these assumptions in turn. If tastes differ (or if expenditure patterns differ with income), we may get different patterns of trade from those predicted by Heckscher-Ohlin (as we have seen). But the income distribution predictions and efficiency implications of the theory would be unaffected.

Allowing variation in technology can make more difference. One country might excel over others in all industries or only in some. Suppose the Swiss could produce 25 percent more than others with any given input bundle in either industry $(x$ or $y)$. This would not alter the shape of the Swiss transformation curve: it

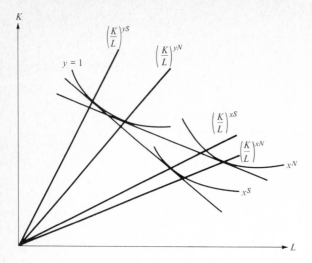

Figure 4-9 Efficiency differences in x (S more efficient).

would push it out along every ray from the origin to a point 25 percent beyond that occupied by another country with the same endowments. So production patterns would follow the Heckscher-Ohlin predictions. But the real marginal products of all factors would be 25 percent higher in Switzerland than elsewhere. But suppose that Switzerland were 25 percent better at (labour-intensive) watch-making only. This would alter their pattern of comparative advantage from that of countries with similar endowments. We shall suppose the superiority is "Hicks-neutral." This means that the isoquant map for watches is the same as elsewhere but each isoquant corresponds to a higher output. This is shown in Figure 4-9, where x^S indicates the Swiss isoquant for that amount of x which fetches the same price as a unit of y, and x^N is the non-Swiss isoquant for the same amount of x. As the diagram shows, the Swiss use higher K/L in both industries, implying higher real wages than in other countries. Given the higher K/L, they must also employ a higher fraction of both factors of production in labour-intensive watchmaking than would another country endowed with the same factor proportions. Since they are also more efficient at making watches, they must produce a substantially higher ratio of watches to other goods. Thus, if we assume identical homothetic tastes between the countries, they will export watches.

Our other assumptions, constant returns to scale and perfect competition, can be dealt with briefly. Increasing returns to scale certainly help to explain the fact of some intercountry specialisation in production. But, assuming the scale economies are the same for all countries, they do not explain which country concentrates on which products. The country that will actually reap the economies of scale in a particular industry will be the one that has comparative advantage in it due to its endowments or its relative technical superiority. As regards imperfect competition, it is extremely difficult to predict its effects on the pattern of trade.

Accordingly, our original model is at best an approximation to reality. But some morals do emerge. World output *is* increased if countries produce disproportionate quantities of those goods in which they have comparative advantage, either because of favourable factor endowments or especially superior production functions. Though some pairs of goods may be subject to factor-intensity reversals, there are many which are not. Thus comparative advantage suggests that labour-rich countries should tend to produce labour-intensive goods, and vice versa.† A tariff or export tax reduces the gains from trade that result when each country exploits its comparative advantage (up to the point where no further marginal advantage is left). But maximising world output may not be in the interests of any one country on its own. If the country is a price taker, it has nothing to gain from a tariff. But if it faces variable terms of trade, a tariff might be morally defensible if the country were poor and retaliation was not to be expected.

Q4-15 Suppose that there are two countries A and B. Which good (if any) will A import in each of the following five situations?

	Country	Endowments K	L	Technology x	y	Tastes u
(i)	A	1	1	$= K^{2/3} L^{1/3}$	$= K^{1/3} L^{2/3}$	$= xy$
	B	2	4			$= xy$
(ii)	A	as above		$= \min(K, L)$	$= \min(K, L/2)$	as above
	B					
(iii)	A	1	1	$= K^{2/3} L^{1/3}$	$= K^{1/3} L^{2/3}$	as above
	B	2	2	$= 1.1\, K^{2/3} L^{1/3}$	$= K^{1/3} L^{2/3}$	
(iv)	A	as above		$= K^{2/3} L^{1/3}$	$= K^{1/3} L^{2/3}$	$= xy^{1/2}$
	B					$= xy$
(v)	A	1	1	$= \min(K, L)$	$= \min(K, L/2)$	as above
	B	2	4			

Q4-16 "Two countries use the same constant-returns production functions under perfect competition and have the same nonhomothetic utility functions. Under free trade, the (unambiguously) labour-intensive good is imported by the poorer country." Suggest a necessary condition for this to occur. (Hint: Think about what factor would generate different expenditure patterns in the two countries.)

(ii) If the assumptions of the factor-price equalisation theorem held, how would the share of capital in national income vary with income per worker?

† This assumes labour-rich countries do not have relative technical advantage in the technology of capital-intensive industries; this assumption is plausible.

TWO

CONSUMER DEMAND

UTILITY AND CONSUMER DEMAND

We have now finished our broad sweep of the general equilibrium of the economy. The time has come to get out the microscope and to examine the behaviour of the different economic agents in more detail and with more rigour. For most of the time now we are concerned with partial equilibrium analysis—in other words, with how to derive the demand and supply curves for particular consumer goods or factor services, other prices usually being assumed constant. We begin with the market for consumer goods, starting with demand. In principle, we ought to be concerned with *market* demand, for example the total demand for tomatoes from all consumers in California. But in practice we shall concentrate on the demands of an individual consumer, and not worry about the problems of aggregating the many individual demands into a single market demand function.

What properties would we expect of the individual demand function? To answer this, we develop a theory of consistent choice, which indicates at least four restrictions which demand functions must satisfy. This general theory also provides a framework for the exact measurement of welfare change and of the ever-topical cost of living. However, for empirical work and for much applied theory, further specific restrictions need to be introduced. So we end the chapter by looking at various possible forms of utility function and asking how plausible they are. We also try to allow for the effect of household size on the pattern of family expenditure.

5-1 PREFERENCE AND CHOICE

Our basic theory assumes first that, for all the alternative consumption bundles he could conceivably face, the individual has a preference ordering. This reflects his *tastes*. At any particular time only some of these bundles are open to him because of his limited income and the terms on which he can use this to buy goods. This constraint defines his *opportunities*. Our theory then says that from the bundles that are open to him he chooses the one that ranks highest in his ordering.† In other words, from the opportunities available to him he does the best he can, best being defined according to his tastes. The approach seems almost banal, and yet, with the aid of a few other undemanding assumptions, it leads to a surprising number of powerful statements about the laws of demand. The key idea which lies behind all of these is the idea of consistency (or rationality): the *same* ordering is used to make choices in all manner of different situations.

Ordering

To clarify the concept of an "ordering" consider for example the ordering provided by the results of an examination: Paul is first, Kenneth and Milton equal second, Bob fourth, and so on. The only important difference between this ordering and the type we are considering arises from our general assumption that all goods are infinitely divisible. This means that there are an infinite number of items (bundles) to be ordered, rather than just the finite number of candidates in an examination. So we cannot quite describe the ordering as a list of items in order, since the list would never end. Instead we can formulate the matter in terms of comparisons between pairs of bundles.

1. (i) Assumption of comparability. For every pair of technically feasible consumption bundles, denoted by the vectors $\mathbf{x}^0$ and $\mathbf{x}^1$, one and only one of the following must be true:

$$\mathbf{x}^0 \text{ is preferred to } \mathbf{x}^1$$
$$\mathbf{x}^1 \text{ is preferred to } \mathbf{x}^0$$
$$\mathbf{x}^0 \text{ and } \mathbf{x}^1 \text{ are equally desirable}$$

(ii) Assumption of transitivity. If $\mathbf{x}^2$ is at least as good as $\mathbf{x}^1$, and $\mathbf{x}^1$ is at least as good as $\mathbf{x}^0$, then $\mathbf{x}^2$ is at least as good as $\mathbf{x}^0$.‡

For convenience we shall also assume that it is not technically feasible for any good i in the bundle to take any negative value ($x_i \geq 0$, all i).

---

† If two or more bundles are equally desirable but better than any others, he chooses any one of them. If we only allowed "strong" orderings, in which indifference was not permitted, we would not have this problem but would have other, worse, ones.

‡ We ought also, for formal completeness, to assume explicitly that x^1 is at least as good as itself (assumption of reflexivity). Our assumptions imply, in addition, transitivity of the relation "is preferred" and of the relation "is equally desirable as."

The Utility Function

If we wanted, we could of course assign a number to each bundle, making sure that we gave the same number to all bundles that were equally desirable—and, where one bundle was preferable to another, making sure it had a higher number. (This is in fact what examiners do.) By assigning a number, or utility index $u(\mathbf{x})$, to each bundle $\mathbf{x}$ we should be saying neither more nor less than was implied before in the preference ordering. To say that $u(\mathbf{x}^i) > u(\mathbf{x}^j)$ means simply that $\mathbf{x}^i$ is preferred to $\mathbf{x}^j$, and $u(\mathbf{x}^i) = u(\mathbf{x}^j)$ means the consumer is indifferent between them.† The indifference curve is thus a line joining all vectors $\mathbf{x}$ which have the property that

$$u(\mathbf{x}) = \text{const}$$

For example, if there are only two goods, so that $\mathbf{x} = (x_1, x_2)$, the equation of the indifference curve is

$$u(x_1, x_2) = \text{const}$$

It obviously makes no difference what numbers we assign to each bundle (or to each indifference curve) provided that, where one bundle is preferred to another, it gets a higher number. Thus, if we start with any system of numbering $u(\mathbf{x})$, we can equally well use any other system $w(\mathbf{x})$, provided that, if u is higher for one bundle than another, w is also higher. For this to be so, we need only ensure that $w = f(u)$, where f is a strictly increasing function (or strictly increasing "transformation") of u.‡

A much more stringent requirement would be that the relative magnitude of the intervals between different levels of utility have some definite meaning. For example, we might want to say that $u^1 - u^0 = u^2 - u^1$: the gain in happiness in moving from state 0 to state 1 equals the gain in moving from state 1 to state 2. Then, if we also wanted to use w as an equivalent utility indicator, we would need to ensure that $w^1 - w^0 = w^2 - w^1$. If $f(u)$ were *any* increasing transformation of u, this requirement would not be met. Instead we would need to restrict $f(u)$ to be a *linear* increasing transformation so that

$$w = a + bu$$

---

† For a preference ordering to be representable by a utility function, one further assumption is needed. The aim of this is to rule out the so-called "lexicographic ordering," of which the following is a two-good example: "$\mathbf{x}^0$ is preferred to $\mathbf{x}^1$ if it provides more beer irrespective of how much bread; but if it provides the same beer, it is preferred if it provides more bread." To rule out jumps of this kind, we need a *continuity assumption* as follows. Consider the set of all bundles $\mathbf{x}$ which are at least as good as any given bundle $\mathbf{x}^0$. This set is closed (i.e., it includes all points on its boundary). Now consider the set of all bundles $\mathbf{x}$ such that the same bundle $\mathbf{x}^0$ is at least as good as them. This set too is closed. And the assumption holds for any bundle $\mathbf{x}^0$ that one may consider.

‡ $f(u)$ is an increasing function if $f'(u) \geq 0$ for all u, but a "strictly" increasing function only if $f'(u) > 0$. In whatever context it is used, the adverb "strictly" rules out the possibility of equality. An increasing function is "monotonic" (as is a decreasing function).

where a and b can take any finite values $(b > 0)$.† We would now be insisting that u is *cardinal*. If we do not make this requirement, the utility function only tells us about the ordering of bundles and not about the distance between them in terms of desirability: the utility function is purely *ordinal*.

> *A utility function is ordinal if it can be replaced by any strictly increasing transformation of itself, and cardinal if it can be replaced only by an increasing* linear *transformation of itself.*

To check that you have grasped this important point confirm that the transformation $w = \log u$ does not satisfy the requirement for cardinality that if $u^1 - u^0 = u^2 - u^1$, then $w^1 - w^0 = w^2 - w^1$. Check too that $w = a + bu$ does satisfy the requirement. (Is temperature cardinal or ordinal: What transformation takes you from Celsius to Fahrenheit?)

There is no need for cardinal measurement of utility in order to explain behaviour on our theory, since all we are concerned with is preference orderings. So even if utility *is* a cardinal variable (like temperature), which is impossible to prove scientifically, we can forget about this for purposes of positive economics. Though normative analysis is difficult without guesses about cardinal utility (see Sec. 1-7), for positive economics we restrict the concept of utility to an indicator of order, that can be subjected to any increasing transformation.

Goods Are Good

We now make one more assumption, from which we can deduce, with no further aid, one of the fundamental laws of demand: that the (compensated) demand curve is downward-sloping. The assumption is eminently reasonable. We simply assume that more of a good thing does you good. Put this way it appears like a tautology. In fact all that is ruled out is satiation. For nothing is said about what things are good. Some people may like silence, some dislike it. All we assume is that those who like silence prefer more silence to less, and those who like noise prefer more noise to less. In the second case, noise is a "good," and in the first case, its negative (i.e., minus it) is a "good." In reality, of course, some things, like leisure, are good up to a point, but may become a burden if you have too much. But we assume that locally every commodity is a good or its negative is a good.

Clearly we are in no way assuming that people are materialistic or selfish. Someone else's welfare may be a good for me, be it that of famine victims in Africa or bureaucrats in Bengal. We are simply assuming the following. {Notice that we are using subscripts to denote particular goods (for example x_1 = quantity of beer), while superscripts are used to indicate particular values either of x_1 (such as x_1^0) or of the vector $\mathbf{x}$ [such as $\mathbf{x}^0 = (x_1^0, x_2^0)$].}

---

† Mathematicians sometimes restrict the term "linear" transformation to proportional transformations of the form $w = bu$, and refer to the transformation $w = a + bu$ as "affine."

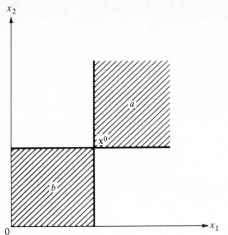

Figure 5-1 The indifference curve slopes down.

2. *Assumption of dominance (goods are good). If* $\mathbf{x} = (x_1, x_2)$ *and* x_1 *and* x_2
are goods, $\mathbf{x}^0$ *is preferred to* $\mathbf{x}'$ *if*

$$either \quad x_1^0 > x_1' \quad and \quad x_2^0 \geq x_2'$$
$$or \quad x_2^0 > x_2' \quad and \quad x_1^0 \geq x_1'$$

(In either case $\mathbf{x}^0$ *dominates* $\mathbf{x}'$.) *In utility terms* $u(x_1^0, x_2^0) > u(x_1', x_2')$ *if these
conditions are satisfied.*

From this we know at once that the consumer will spend his whole income,
provided some good involves him in positive marginal costs. (This does not of
course rule out saving, which for this purpose could be regarded as a good.)

This assumption gives us our first information on the shape of the indifference
curve. Consider the bundle $\mathbf{x}^0$ in Figure 5-1. Clearly all points in area a are
better than $\mathbf{x}^0$ and those in area b are worse than it. So what is the slope of the
indifference curve through $\mathbf{x}^0$? It cannot go through a or b and must therefore
slope from northwest to southeast. You may care to draw it in. It can, for the
moment, wiggle as much as it likes, provided it always slopes down.

The indifference curve slopes down.

The Substitution Effect is Nonpositive

But we know more than this. For suppose we concern ourselves only with an
individual buying goods in a normal market,† where he can buy an unlimited

† We shall usually take a normal market to include one where the consumer can buy an unlimited
quantity of a good x_i at a constant marginal cost to himself (fixed standing charges are not ruled
out). As we shall see, in certain other circumstances consumers may be faced with situations in
which the marginal cost they face either rises or falls with the quantity consumed.

quantity of each good at a fixed price per unit. The individual has a given money income. How will he respond to a rise in the price of x_1 (i.e., in p_1), accompanied by an increase in income just sufficient to preserve his original level of satisfaction?

We start from his original position (see Figure 5-2). His economically feasible consumption set is the shaded triangle $0AB$. We know from assumption 2 (goods are good) that he will consume on AB—at $\mathbf{x}^0$ let us suppose. Now p_1 rises a very little, but the consumer's income is compensated so that he is as well off as before. If his consumption of x_1 changes only a little, the compensation needed will be just sufficient to allow him to buy his original bundle, and this is how we have drawn it.† So his new budget line is $A'B'$. Where on this line is his new optimum?

Consistency requires that it lie on the segment $\mathbf{x}^0 B'$. For previously the consumer could consume anywhere along AB and chose $\mathbf{x}^0$, which must therefore be at least as good as anywhere else on AB. In the new situation, positions along $\mathbf{x}^0 A$ are no longer available, except for the point $\mathbf{x}^0$ itself; while $\mathbf{x}^0 B$ is dominated by $\mathbf{x}^0 B'$. So consumption must occur between $\mathbf{x}^0$ and B', or, exceptionally, at $\mathbf{x}^0$ itself (or B'). In other words the income-compensated effect of the rise in p_1 is to produce a fall in x_1, or otherwise no change. ‡

for the most effect of compensated rise in p₁

---

† If he were to reduce x_1 considerably, he would not need so much compensation and his new budget line would lie to the left of x^0. But the argument would be unaffected. (Figure 5-4 illustrates a case in which x_1 changes considerably in response to a small change in p_1.)

‡ This can be proved formally by the following substitution theorem. Make the following assumptions:

(i) The consumer is indifferent between $\mathbf{x}^0$ and $\mathbf{x}'$: $u(\mathbf{x}^0) = u(\mathbf{x}')$
(ii) He chooses $\mathbf{x}^0$ when prices are $\mathbf{p}^0$ and his income is $\mathbf{p}^0\mathbf{x}^0$
(iii) He chooses $\mathbf{x}'$ when prices are $\mathbf{p}'$ and his income is $\mathbf{p}'\mathbf{x}'$

From (ii) we can infer that when prices are $\mathbf{p}^0$, $\mathbf{x}'$ must be at least as expensive as $\mathbf{x}^0$, since, if it were cheaper, he would have chosen it rather than $\mathbf{x}'$. So

$$\sum p_i^0 x_i^0 \leq \sum p_i^0 x_i'$$

Thus

$$\sum - p_i^0(x_i' - x_i^0) \leq 0$$

From (iii) we can infer that when prices are $\mathbf{p}'$, $\mathbf{x}^0$ must be at least as expensive as $\mathbf{x}'$, since, if it were cheaper, he would have chosen it rather than $\mathbf{x}'$. So

$$\sum p_i' x_i' \leq \sum p_i' x_i^0$$

Thus

$$\sum p_i'(x_i' - x_i^0) \leq 0$$

Therefore, adding our second and fourth equations, we find that

$$\sum (p_i' - p_i^0)(x_i' - x_i^0) \leq 0$$

If only p_1 has changed it follows that

$$(p_1' - p_1^0)(x_1' - x_1^0) \leq 0$$

So if p_1 has risen, x_1 has either fallen or remained constant.

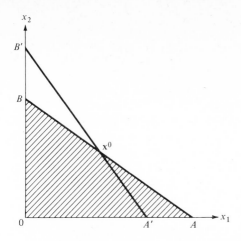

Figure 5-2 Revealed preference and the non-positive substitution effect.

The substitution effect (if any) of an income-compensated increase in p_1 is a negative change in x_1.

Or equivalently,

The compensated demand curve, which traces out the demand for x_1 as p_1 varies, utility held constant, is downward-sloping (or vertical or horizontal).

We have proved this without making any arbitrary assumptions about the shape of the indifference curve. But what in fact does it *tell* us about the shape of the indifference curve? The compensated demand curve is the locus of demands for x_1 traced out, as p_1 changes, by a budget line drawn tangential to an indifference curve. This relationship is drawn in Figure 5-3, which makes it clear that the compensated demand curve diagram is simply the per-unit diagram corresponding to the indifference curves presented in the total diagram.† Figure 5-3 presents the case where the indifference curve (1) is strictly convex to the origin (i.e., is convex and has no straight-line segments in it), and (2) has well-defined derivatives at all points (i.e., has no kinks in it). But one can imagine indifference curves that lack both these properties but could yet generate compensated demand curves that were downward-sloping.

One example is provided in Figure 5-4. Here the indifference curve is in places concave to the origin. However, the individual behaves as though it were convex to the origin. He will not be found consuming at anywhere (such as $\mathbf{x}^4$) that is both in the interior of the technically feasible set ($x_i > 0$, all i) and has locally nonconvex indifference curves. To check this try drawing a budget line tangential to u^0 at $\mathbf{x}^4$ plus a few more indifference curves. So, simply from assumptions 1 and 2, plus the notion of consistent choice, we can infer the following.

At any point where consumption occurs, indifference curves must be convex to

† On the relation of per-unit and total diagrams see p. 39.

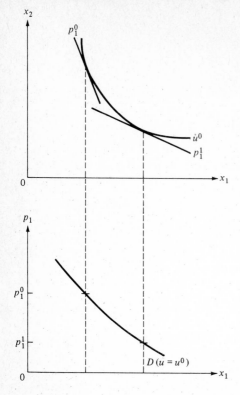

Figure 5-3 A smooth indifference curve and its compensated demand curve.

the origin, except for (i) consumption at boundary points where either x_1 or x_2 equals zero (concavity to the origin is possible in that case), and (ii) consumption in other than normal markets.

This is confirmed later by the second-order conditions for utility maximisation.

Strict Convexity of the Indifference Curve

However, we are still left with a problem, as Figure 5-4 makes clear: at p_1^1 demand is indeterminate. To rule this out and impose differentiability on the demand function, we assume that the indifference curve is strictly convex to the origin at all points.

3. Assumption of strict convexity of the indifference curve. Indifference curves are strictly convex to the origin everywhere. In other words, for all $\mathbf{x}^0$, $\mathbf{x}'$ for which $u(\mathbf{x}^0) = u(\mathbf{x}')$,

$$u[\lambda\mathbf{x}^0 + (1 - \lambda)\mathbf{x}'] > u(\mathbf{x}^0) = u(\mathbf{x}')$$

for any λ $(0 < \lambda < 1)$. Such a utility function is called strictly quasi-concave (see Appendix 1).

This may seem plausible from introspection: the more water one has, the fewer

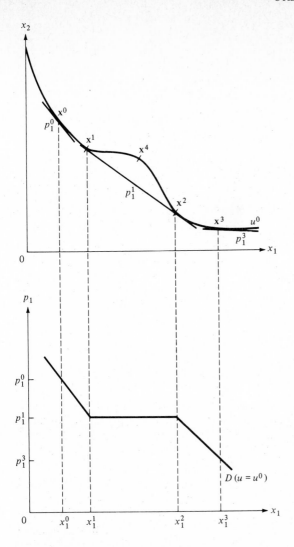

Figure 5-4 An indifference curve not strictly convex to the origin.

diamonds one is willing to sacrifice for the sake of more water. However, it is not difficult to think of off-beat cases in which it might not be true (see Question 5-5).

Differentiability of the Indifference Curve

We still have the problem of kinks in the indifference curve. In Figure 5-5 a kink makes the demand price at x^1 indeterminate. To eliminate such possibilities we add our final assumption.

4. Assumption of differentiability. The utility function has well-defined first and second derivatives (is "twice-differentiable").

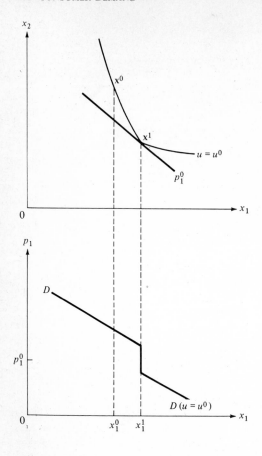

Figure 5-5 A kinky indifference curve.

Q5-1 Can indifference curves cross? If not, which assumptions rule this out?

Q5-2 (i) A householder can buy x_1 and x_2 only. $p_2 = 1$. In situations A and B he behaves as follows. Is his behaviour consistent?

Situation	Income	p_1	x_1 purchased
A	40	1	20
B	60	2	25

(ii) Another householder behaves as follows. (Again $p_2 = 1$.)

Situation	Income	p_1	x_1 purchased
A	40	1	20
B	61	2	15

Is he consistent? Can you say in which situation he is better off?

Q5-3 By drawing the indifference curves, show how the rational consumer might consume at a boundary point (say $x_1 = 0$) where indifference curves were nonconvex.

Q5-4 (i) By drawing the indifference curves, show how he might consume at any interior point where indifference curves were nonconvex if he were faced with a rising marginal cost of x_1 in terms of x_2.

  (ii) What first- and second-order conditions apply at this point?

  *(iii) What market situation is this person likely to be in?

Q5-5 (i) Which of the following types of remark corresponds to nonconvex indifference curves:

  A: "I would rather spend all my time in the country or all in the town, rather than divide myself between the two."

  B: "I prefer a mixture of town and country life to being restricted to one or the other."

  (ii) Which type of preferences will produce a more stable economy?

5-2 THE LAWS OF DEMAND

We can now investigate the properties of demand curves which our assumptions imply. We shall confine ourselves to normal markets in which the individual can buy unlimited quantities of each good at a fixed price. His problem (assuming two goods only) is

$$\max u(x_1, x_2)$$

subject to

$$p_1 x_1 + p_2 x_2 = m$$

where m is a given money income. This is sketched in Figure 5-6. In terms of a map, he mounts the hill of pleasure to its highest possible point while travelling along the fence provided by his budget constraint. We shall assume both here and throughout that the solution is interior.† Forming the Lagrangian expression

$$L = u(x_1, x_2) + \lambda(m - p_1 x_1 - p_2 x_2)$$

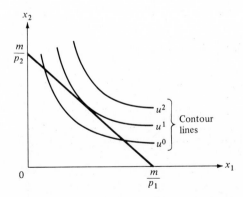

Figure 5-6 Utility maximisation.

† For corner solutions the first-order conditions are provided by the Kuhn-Tucker theorem, which also applies to interior solutions. On this see, for example, W. J. Baumol, *Economic Theory and Operations Analysis*, Prentice-Hall, Englewood Cliffs, N.J., 1972, 3d ed., pp. 151–171.

we obtain first-order conditions for an interior solution

$$u_1(x_1, x_2) = \lambda p_1$$
$$u_2(x_1, x_2) = \lambda p_2 \qquad (1)$$
$$p_1 x_1 + p_2 x_2 = m$$

On the assumptions that we have made, this will have a unique solution for x_1, x_2, and λ. From Equations (1), λ measures the marginal utility of each good divided by its price, i.e., the marginal utility per dollar spent on each good, i.e., the marginal utility of money. The natural way to solve (1) is of course to eliminate λ so as to obtain the following two equations:

$$p_1 x_1 + p_2 x_2 = m$$

$$\frac{u_1(x_1, x_2)}{u_2(x_1, x_2)} = \frac{p_1}{p_2}$$

The first of these requires that we shall be on the fence, and the second requires that at its highest point the fence shall be travelling along a contour of the hill. The second-order conditions are†

$$d^2 u = u_{11} dx_1 dx_1 + 2u_{12} dx_1 dx_2 + u_{22} dx_2 dx_2 < 0$$

subject to

$$0 = p_1 dx_1 + p_2 dx_2 \qquad \text{(for all } dx_1, dx_2 \neq 0 \text{ together)}$$

In other words, any movement along the fence away from the optimum must lead downhill. The condition for the above to hold is‡

$$\begin{vmatrix} u_{11} & u_{12} & -p_1 \\ u_{21} & u_{22} & -p_2 \\ -p_1 & -p_2 & 0 \end{vmatrix} > 0$$

This is nothing other than the requirement of strict quasi-concavity of the utility function which we made in assumption 3. (Try proving this: see Question 5-8 below.)

The system of Equations (1) provides the solution to one particular problem, with given prices and income. But we are mainly interested in how demand varies with these latter. Since the solution to (1) depends only on prices, income, and the utility function, we have, for a given utility function, the demand functions

$$x_1 = f^1(p_1, p_2, m)$$
$$x_2 = f^2(p_1, p_2, m)$$
$$[\lambda = f^3(p_1, p_2, m)]$$

† If we put $d^2 U \leq 0$, we should be allowing for the possibility of more than one local optimum, which we have ruled out by assumption 3.

‡ If we have n goods $(n > 2)$, the equivalent condition requires the principal minors to alternate in sign: the third principal minor (as here) positive, the fourth negative, and so on.

Given our assumptions, these are well-defined and continuous functions. The main question is what properties must they have, given that they arise from utility maximisation. Suppose in empirical work one wanted to use a particular form of demand function (or a system of such functions), what restrictions need be satisfied for consistency with utility maximisation? We discover four restrictions by examining how demand must respond to: (1) a simultaneous change in all prices and income, (2) a change in income only, (3) a change in own-price only, and (4) a change in other prices.

1 Homogeneity of Degree Zero

First, suppose we double all prices and income. A glance at Figure 5-6 shows that the budget constraint does not move, since $2m/2p_1 = m/p_1$, and likewise for the vertical intercept. It follows that demand cannot change: money illusion is ruled out by the assumption of consistency.

> 1. *Demand functions are homogeneous of degree zero in prices and income.*†

Thus if we take a general demand function

$$x_i = f(p_1, \ldots, p_n, m)$$

it follows from Euler's theorem that

$$0 = \sum_j \frac{\partial x_i}{\partial p_j} p_j + \frac{\partial x_i}{\partial m} m$$

Dividing by x_i, we obtain the first of three useful elasticities formulae:

$$\sum_j \varepsilon_{ij} + \eta_{im} = 0 \qquad \text{(E-1)}$$

where ε_{ij} is the price elasticity of x_i with respect to p_j and η_{im} is the income elasticity of x_i with respect to m.

So suppose we take the demand curve

$$x_1 = p_1^{\alpha_1} p_2^{\alpha_2} m^{\beta}$$

What restrictions need to be imposed on the coefficients? (See Question 5-9 below.)

2 Income Effects Must Add Up (the Adding-up Property)

Now suppose we let only income vary; but we have a system of demand equations. What limitations affect the responses of the different quantities demanded to changes in income? Clearly the limit comes from the budget identity. If

$$\sum p_i x_i = m$$

---

† For the definition of homogeneity and a proof of Euler's theorem see Appendix 3.

and prices are held constant, then

$$\sum p_i \frac{\partial x_i}{\partial m} = 1$$

Multiply and divide each term by x_i/m, and we have

$$\sum \frac{p_i x_i}{m} \frac{\partial x_i}{\partial m} \frac{m}{x_i} = 1$$

or

$$\sum_i v_i \eta_{im} = 1 \qquad\qquad (\text{E-2})$$

where v_i is the relative share of good i in total expenditure.

2. The weighted average of income elasticities of demand is unity, the weights being the relative shares of each good in total expenditure.

From this it follows that if some goods (like food) have income elasticities less than unity, some other goods (like opera) must have income elasticities greater than unity.

Goods with income elasticities less than unity are often called *necessities*, and those with elasticities greater than unity, *luxuries*. The reason is clear: as income rises, goods on which spending grows relatively faster than income will occupy a rising share of income. So, if we compare the expenditure patterns of different people, such goods will form higher proportions of the expenditure of the rich than of the poor and are thus naturally called luxuries. This can be checked in Figure 5-7 (left-hand panel). (Which good is a luxury and which a necessity?)

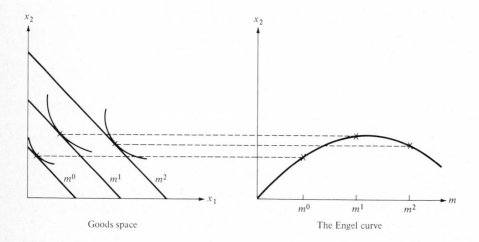

Figure 5-7 The Engel curve (or income-consumption line).

Goods can also be classified according to whether their income elasticities exceed zero, rather than unity as in our previous distinction. Goods where demand falls as income rises are called *inferior* goods, and other goods *normal*. So we have the following classes of goods:

η_{im}	Good
> 1	Normal luxury
$0-1$	Normal necessity
< 0	Inferior necessity

In Figure 5-7, x_1 is a luxury throughout and x_2 is a normal necessity for m less than m^1 and an inferior necessity for higher m.

The relationship between any good and income, holding prices constant, is called the Engel curve (or income-consumption curve). The Engel curve for x_2 is shown in Figure 5-7 (right-hand panel). Clearly such a curve can most easily be observed in cross-sectional studies of household budgets, since at a point in time most people face the same prices. Remarkably similar patterns are observed in many countries, with food always a normal necessity and clothing and shelter often having elasticities around unity.

Q5-6 Derive the demand curves for x_1, x_2 assuming
    (i) $u = x_1 x_2$
    (ii) $u = x_1^{z_1} x_2^{z_2}$
What are the price and income elasticities?

Q5-7 (i) Prove that the utility maximising quantities x_1 and x_2 are the same whether we maximise $u(x_1, x_2)$ or $w = f[u(x_1, x_2)]$, where f is a strictly increasing function of u.
    (ii) "The marginal utility of an inferior good is negative, which is why demand falls with income." True or false?

*Q5-8 Prove that the condition on the determinant on page 134 is equivalent to the condition that the indifference curve be convex, i.e., that

$$\frac{d}{dx_1}\left(\frac{dx_2}{dx_1}\right) > 0$$

subject to

$$\frac{dx_2}{dx_1} = -\frac{u_1}{u_2}$$

Q5-9 (i) If $x_1 = p_1^{\alpha_1} p_2^{\alpha_2} m^{\beta}$, what are the values of $\varepsilon_{11}, \varepsilon_{12}$, and η_{im}? What restrictions must govern the magnitudes of α_1, α_2, and β to satisfy law 1?
    (ii) Is this function (and a similar one for x_2) necessarily consistent with law 2?

Q5-10 We have estimates for British working class families of the income elasticities of demand for the following goods: rice, condensed milk, butter, margarine, tea, coffee, drink (alcoholic and soft), carpets, theatre visits.
    (i) Which goods would you expect to be luxuries, which inferior, and which noninferior non-luxuries? (What is a better name for this category?)

(ii) If you wished to distribute a given amount of money in subsidies to these goods, so as to benefit the poor as much as possible, which goods would you subsidise and why?

(iii) Prove that a subsidy to a necessity, financed by a proportional tax, is progressive.

3 Negative Substitution Effect

The most important of the laws of demand is the law of the downward-sloping compensated demand curve, which we have already established.

> 3. If p_1 rises and m is simultaneously adjusted in order to keep u constant, x_1 falls.†

This does not of course mean that the ordinary demand curve, holding m rather than u constant, necessarily slopes down. For we can think of the "gross" effect of a price rise (along the "ordinary" demand curve) as consisting of two parts— the effect when compensation has been paid *plus* the effect of removing the compensation. The first part is the substitution effect and the second the income effect. The income effect can be further broken down. For it must equal the change in income when the compensation is removed *times* the change in demand for x_1 per unit change in income. How much compensation is needed? If I am buying x_1 units and the price of good 1 goes up by \$1, then I need \$$x_1$ to enable me to go on buying my original bundle (x_1, x_2). So

> *The utility-preserving compensation needed for a unit increase in p_1 is approximately x_1.‡ Thus the income effect of a unit increase in p_1 is $(-x_1)(\partial x_1/\partial m)$. The Hicks-Slutsky decomposition of the gross effect of a price change is consequently*
>
> $$\frac{\partial x_1}{\partial p_1} = \left(\frac{\partial x_1}{\partial p_1}\right)_{u \text{ const}} - x_1 \frac{\partial x_1}{\partial m}$$
>
> *or more generally*
>
> $$\frac{\partial x_i}{\partial p_j} = \left(\frac{\partial x_i}{\partial p_j}\right)_{u \text{ const}} - x_j \frac{\partial x_i}{\partial m}$$

The latter is the general Slutsky equation. Notice that the compensation term equals the quantity of the good *whose price has changed*. In the own-price case the absolute slope of the ordinary demand curve must be less than that of the compensated demand curve for any normal good $(\partial x_1/\partial m > 0)$. For many purposes, it is useful to formulate the Slutsky equation in terms of elasticities.

---

† We deduced from assumptions 1 and 2 in Sec. 5-1 that x_1 falls or is constant. Assumption 4 ensures that it is not constant.

‡ The approximation is due to the fact that if I now buy less x_1 than before, I need slightly less compensation than x_1. But as $\Delta p_1 \to 0$ the required compensation per unit change in price tends to x_1. This is illustrated on page 146.

Multiply through by p_j/x_i and multiply and divide the last term by m:

$$\frac{\partial x_i}{\partial p_j}\frac{p_j}{x_i} = \left(\frac{\partial x_i}{\partial p_j}\right)_u \frac{p_j}{x_i} - \frac{p_j x_j}{m}\frac{\partial x_i}{\partial m}\frac{m}{x_i}$$

Thus
$$\varepsilon_{ij} = \varepsilon_{ij}^* - v_j \eta_{im}$$

where * indicates (as henceforth) the compensated effect.

The preceding decomposition can also be obtained by totally differentiating the first-order equilibrium conditions [Equations (1)], i.e., by the standard method of comparative statics. This gives us

$$\begin{pmatrix} u_{11} & u_{12} & -p_1 \\ u_{21} & u_{22} & -p_2 \\ -p_1 & -p_2 & 0 \end{pmatrix}\begin{pmatrix} dx_1 \\ dx_2 \\ d\lambda \end{pmatrix} = \begin{pmatrix} \lambda dp_1 \\ \lambda dp_2 \\ -dm + x_1 dp_1 + x_2 dp_2 \end{pmatrix} \tag{2}$$

Using D to denote the determinant of the matrix and D_{ij} to denote the cofactor of the element in the ith row and jth column, we learn from Cramer's rule that

$$dx_1 = \lambda dp_1 \frac{D_{11}}{D} + \lambda dp_2 \frac{D_{21}}{D} + (-dm + x_1 dp_1 + x_2 dp_2)\frac{D_{31}}{D} \tag{3}$$

By setting $dp_1 = dp_2 = 0$, we find

$$\frac{\partial x_1}{\partial m} = -\frac{D_{31}}{D}$$

Now suppose we hold p_2 constant and let p_1 vary but in such a way that compensation is effected, i.e., so that

$$-dm + x_1 dp_1 = 0$$

Since in addition $dp_2 = 0$, the term in parentheses in (3) is equal to zero. So

$$\left(\frac{\partial x_1}{\partial p_1}\right)_{u\ const} = \frac{\lambda D_{11}}{D}$$

Therefore, reverting to the gross effect of a change in p_1,

$$\frac{\partial x_1}{\partial p_1} = \lambda\frac{D_{11}}{D} + x_1\frac{D_{31}}{D}$$

$$= \left(\frac{\partial x_1}{\partial p_1}\right)_{u\ const} - x_1\frac{\partial x_1}{\partial m}$$

which is the Slutsky equation for the own-price effect.

We can straightaway confirm the negative sign of the compensated effect,† since, from the second-order conditions,

$$D > 0$$

---

† Note that, however many goods there are, the minor D_{11} must be of opposite sign to D for the second-order conditions to hold (see footnote to page 134).

while
$$D_{11} = -p_2^2 < 0$$

and
$$\lambda = \frac{u_i}{p_i} > 0$$

Hence,
$$\frac{\lambda D_{11}}{D} < 0$$

But the gross effect $(\partial x_1/\partial p_1)$ could of course be positive if the term $-x_1(\partial x_1/\partial m)$ was not only positive but also large enough to outweigh the negative substitution effect. This "Giffen" case is illustrated in the following well-known diagram (Figure 5-8), which traces out the demand curve in the standard fashion. The substitution effect of the price rise is from A to B, but the income effect is from B to C. That such cases are extremely unlikely can be seen from looking at the own-price version of the Slutsky equation:

$$\varepsilon_{ii} = \varepsilon_{ii}^* - v_i \eta_{im}$$

For ε_{ii} to be positive, we must have $|\varepsilon_{ii}^*| < v_i|\eta_{im}|$. Thus a good with an income

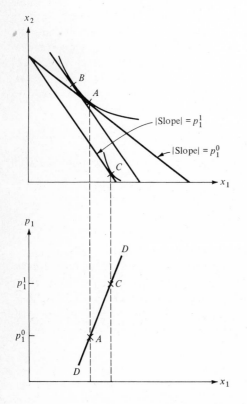

Figure 5-8 A Giffen good.

elasticity of -1 would need an (absolute) compensated price elasticity less than its share of the budget to be a Giffen good. This is most unlikely.

The compensated elasticity cannot of course be directly observed. But, since it is required to be negative, this imposes an obvious restriction on the observable own-price elasticities and income elasticities, which the reader can compute for himself from the preceding equation.

4 Symmetrical Cross Effects

The framework we have just developed also lets us examine the pattern of "cross effects" implied. Setting $1 = i$ and $2 = j$, we find

$$\frac{\partial x_i}{\partial p_j} = \frac{\lambda D_{ji}}{D} - x_j \frac{\partial x_i}{\partial m} = \left(\frac{\partial x_i}{\partial p_j}\right)_{u \text{ const}} - x_j \frac{\partial x_i}{\partial m}$$

But, since $u_{ij} = u_{ji}$, the matrix in (2) is symmetric, from which it follows that $D_{ij} = D_{ji}$. This implies the following remarkable result:

$$\left(\frac{\partial x_i}{\partial p_j}\right)_{u \text{ const}} = \left(\frac{\partial x_j}{\partial p_i}\right)_{u \text{ const}}$$

The matrix with elements $(\partial x_i / \partial p)_{u \text{ const}}$ is known as the Slutsky matrix; it has to be symmetric. These symmetrical cross-substitution effects are not, of course, directly observable, but they have the following clear implication for the structure of ordinary demand functions.

4. Symmetry of cross-substitution effects. Since

$$\left(\frac{\partial x_i}{\partial p_j}\right)_{u \text{ const}} = \left(\frac{\partial x_j}{\partial p_i}\right)_{u \text{ const}}$$

and the relevant Slutsky equation holds for each of these terms, ordinary demand curves have the property that

$$\frac{\partial x_i}{\partial p_j} + x_j \frac{\partial x_i}{\partial m} = \frac{\partial x_j}{\partial p_i} + x_i \frac{\partial x_j}{\partial m}$$

Any pair of goods (i, j) for which $\partial x_i / \partial p_j > 0$ are called *substitutes* and any pair for which the opposite holds, *complements*. If we are concerned with the cross effects in the ordinary demand function, we refer to *gross* substitutes or complements. If we are concerned with compensated cross effects, we refer to *Hicks-Allen* substitutes or complements. It is logically possible for either or both of a pair of Hicks-Allen substitutes to be gross complements, as the elasticity version of the general Slutsky relation makes clear:

$$\varepsilon_{ij} = \varepsilon_{ij}^* - v_j \eta_{im}$$

From this equation we can obtain the following, by summing the effects of all price changes on the demand for good x_i :

$$\sum_j \varepsilon_{ij} = \sum_j \varepsilon_{ij}^* - \sum_j v_j \eta_{im}$$

$$= \sum_j \varepsilon_{ij}^* - \eta_{im} \qquad \left(\text{since } \sum_j v_j = 1\right)$$

So

$$\sum_j \varepsilon_{ij}^* = \sum_j \varepsilon_{ij} + \eta_{im}$$

Therefore, using (E-1) (homogeneity of degree zero), we obtain

$$\sum_j \varepsilon_{ij}^* = 0 \qquad\qquad \text{(E-3)}$$

This is our third elasticities formula: the compensated demand curve is homogeneous of degree zero in prices. If all prices are changed equiproportionately, while income is changed (equiproportionately) to maintain utility constant, the demand for each good i is unaffected. This is hardly surprising: try doubling p_1, p_2, and m in Figure 5-6. Since $\varepsilon_{ii}^* < 0$, it follows that for at least one $j \neq i$, $\varepsilon_{ij}^* > 0$. Every good must have at least one Hicks-Allen substitute, but may have no complements. This is easy to see by taking the two-good case, where the two goods *have* to be substitutes: to preserve utility, x_2 has to rise when a rise in p_1 reduces x_1.

It is often useful when comparing pairs of goods to be able to say not only *whether* they are substitutes or complements, but how strongly they are the one or the other. Presumably, though tea and sugar may be complements, right shoes and left shoes are better ones. To compare strengths of substitutability we want measures that are unit-free—that do not change according to whether tea is measured in pounds or kilos. This is the point of elasticities, but the cross-price elasticity does not give us what we want, since

$$\varepsilon_{ij}^* = \left(\frac{\partial x_i}{\partial p_j}\right)_u \frac{p_j}{x_i} \neq \left(\frac{\partial x_j}{\partial p_i}\right)_u \frac{p_i}{x_j} = \varepsilon_{ji}^*$$

Allen's elasticity of substitution is a relatively useful measure here. It is defined as

$$\sigma_{ij} = \frac{\varepsilon_{ij}^*}{v_j}$$

This may seem a somewhat arbitrary definition. However

$$\frac{\varepsilon_{ij}^*}{v_j} = \left(\frac{\partial x_i}{\partial p_j}\right)_u \frac{p_j}{x_i} \frac{m}{p_j x_j} = \left(\frac{\partial x_i}{\partial p_j}\right)_u \frac{m}{x_i x_j}$$

$$= \left(\frac{\partial x_j}{\partial p_i}\right)_u \frac{p_i}{x_j} \frac{m}{p_i x_i} = \left(\frac{\varepsilon_{ji}^*}{v_i}\right) = \sigma_{ji}$$

So $\sigma_{ij} = \sigma_{ji}$. We have found a measure of the strength of the substitution relationship between x_i and x_j which is independent of which good we happen to mention first. If there are only two goods, this measures the inverse of the curvature of the isoquant; high σ_{ij} implies nearly straight isoquants.† To disentangle the actual structure of real-world demand relationships, it is often necessary to impose restrictions on the pattern of possible cross effects. We shall return to this in Sec. 5-4 when we discuss possible functional forms of the utility function.

Q5-11 (i) Suppose the gross price elasticity for a good is -1, its income elasticity 2, and its income share $\frac{1}{4}$. What is its compensated price elasticity?

(ii) Suppose that in some country the effect of a 1 percent rise in the price of oil is to reduce the demand for scooters by 0.1 percent. The following data are available:

	Oil	Scooters
v_i	5%	1%
η_{im}	2	3

Are oil and scooters Hicks-Allen substitutes or complements? Can you think of any explanation for this result? How would a rise in scooter prices affect the demand for oil?

Q5-12 "If two goods (x_i, x_j) are Hicks-Allen substitutes, the gross cross effect $(\partial x_i/\partial p_j)$ must be positive provided x_j is a necessity." True or false?

*Q5-13 The following additional elasticities formulae also hold:

$$\sum_i v_i \varepsilon_{ij} = -v_j \tag{E-4}$$

$$\sum_i v_i \varepsilon_{ij}^* = 0 \tag{E-5}$$

They are not independent of (E-1) to (E-3).

(i) Prove (E-4) (the so-called Cournot aggregation condition) by differentiating the budget equation.

(ii) Prove (E-5) by differentiating the budget equation and adjusting m to hold u constant.

*(iii) Prove (E-5) by starting from (E-3) and using the property that

$$\left(\frac{\partial x_i}{\partial p_j}\right)_u = \left(\frac{\partial x_j}{\partial p_i}\right)_u$$

5-3 DUALITY AND WELFARE CHANGE

Though the preceding approach is, for many purposes, adequate, another approach is also useful. This is based on the idea that any given equilibrium position of the consumer can equally well be explained on the assumption that he has (1) maximised utility subject to a cost constraint (the primal problem) or (2) minimised cost subject to a utility constraint (the dual of the specified primal problem).

---

† We shall leave further discussion of the elasticity of substitution until Chapter 9, where we discuss it in the context of production.

The second approach is the more useful if we want to measure changes in the cost of living and in real income. It is also useful in ordinary demand analysis, but we shall concentrate mainly on its application to the measurement of welfare change.†

Duality

We begin with the concept of the "indirect utility function," which we have already used in Chapter 2. If $u(x_1, x_2)$ is maximised subject to $\sum p_i x_i = m$, we find that the maximum utility is a function of income m and the price vector $\mathbf{p}$.

The indirect utility function indicates the maximum utility attainable at given prices and income:

$$u = u(\mathbf{p}, m)$$

Since this relation must hold for all u and m, we can also write it in the following form:

$$m = m(\mathbf{p}, u)$$

where m indicates the minimum money cost at which it is possible to achieve a given utility at given prices. To make clear that m corresponds to the minimum cost we shall use the symbol C to describe the function.

The consumer cost function indicates the minimum money cost at which a given utility can be obtained at given prices:

$$C = C(\mathbf{p}, u)$$

The indirect utility function must be decreasing in p and increasing in m.‡ It is also homogeneous of degree zero in prices and income taken together (if everything goes up, real income is unchanged). It is also, fairly clearly, quasi-concave in p: the lower p_1, the more p_2 has to rise to compensate you for a further fall in p_1. The consumer cost function is increasing in p and increasing in u. It is homogeneous of degree 1 in prices: if all prices double, the income needed for a given utility doubles.

We can rapidly develop three extremely useful properties of these functions. First, it is intuitively clear that, if p_1 rises by one (small) unit, the cost to the consumer of maintaining his original utility is x_1: this compensation will just enable him to buy his original bundle. So

$$\frac{\partial C}{\partial p_1}(p_1, p_2^0, u^0) = x_1$$

---

† For a survey of the uses of duality see W. M. Gorman, "Tricks with Utility Functions," in *Essays in Economic Analysis*, M. J. Artis and A. R. Nobay (eds.), Cambridge University Press, London, 1976, pp. 211–244. This also surveys various approaches to separability, an issue discussed in our Sec. 5-4.

‡ I.e. u falls when p rises and rises when m rises.

At a stroke we have obtained the equation of the compensated demand curve for x_1, holding constant p_2 and u.

1. *The compensated demand curve is*

$$x_1(p_1, p_2^0, u^0) = \frac{\partial C(p_1, p_2^0, u^0)}{\partial p_1}$$

Going on, we can immediately discover the cross-substitution effect, by differentiating the compensated demand curve for x_1 with respect to p_2 :

$$\left(\frac{\partial x_1}{\partial p_2}\right)_u = \frac{\partial^2 C}{\partial p_1 \partial p_2}$$

But, as with all cross-partial derivatives,

$$\frac{\partial^2 C}{\partial p_1 \partial p_2} = \frac{\partial^2 C}{\partial p_2 \partial p_1}$$

So

$$\left(\frac{\partial x_1}{\partial p_2}\right)_u = \left(\frac{\partial x_2}{\partial p_1}\right)_u$$

2. *Duality provides a simple proof of the symmetry of the cross-substitution effect.*

Finally, we can also derive uncompensated demand functions from the duality approach. This is a little more tricky. First take the indirect utility function

$$u = u(p_1, p_2, m)$$

Hold u and p_2 constant and totally differentiate:

$$0 = \frac{\partial u}{\partial p_1} dp_1 + \frac{\partial u}{\partial m} dm$$

But if utility is constant, our standard relation must hold between dm and dp_1:

$$dm = x_1 dp_1$$

Income must be increased by x_1 times the change in its price (p_1). Bringing these two equations together, we find that

$$x_1 = - \frac{\partial u(p_1, p_2, m)}{\partial p_1} \bigg/ \frac{\partial u(p_1, p_2, m)}{\partial m}$$

This is known as *Roy's identity* and enables us to find the ordinary demand curve, if we know the indirect utility function. We can confirm that it gives us the ordinary demand curve, rather than the compensated demand curve, by noting that it gives us x_1 as a function of m, rather than of u (as with the compensated demand curve).

3. *Roy's identity. The ordinary demand curve for x_1 is*

$$x_1(p_1, p_2, m) = -\frac{\partial u}{\partial p_1}\bigg/\frac{\partial u}{\partial m}$$

Welfare Change and Price Indices

What is the use of all this? In theoretical and empirical work it is often more convenient to work from the indirect utility function (with utility a function of prices rather than quantities)—and to make assumptions about its functional form, rather than about the form of the direct utility function. However, in this chapter we shall concentrate on the consumer cost function and use it to sweep away the cobwebs surrounding the measurement of welfare change. The argument is unbelievably simple.

Suppose p_1 rises from p_1^0 to p_1^1, other prices remaining constant. How much compensation is needed to make the consumer as well off as before (i.e., to hold u at u^0)? Obviously, an amount equal to the change in the cost of securing u^0: i.e.,

$$C(p_1^1, p_2^0, u^0) - C(p_1^0, p_2^0, u^0)$$

This is a natural measure of welfare change, except that, since welfare has decreased, we naturally measure the welfare change by the negative of this cost difference. This measure is known as the *compensating variation* (CV).† By the definition of an integral, the CV is therefore

$$C(p_1^0, p_2^0, u^0) - C(p_1^1, p_2^0, u^0) = \int_{p_1^1}^{p_1^0} \frac{\partial C}{\partial p_1}(p_1, p_2^0, u^0)\, dp_1$$

Thus
$$CV = \int_{p_1^1}^{p_1^0} x_1(p_1, p_2^0, u^0)\, dp_1 \tag{4}$$

So the CV and the compensated demand curve are directly linked, and the preceding formula holds whether the price has risen or fallen.

> *The compensating variation for a single price change (in p_1) is the change in the area between the compensated demand curve for x_1 and the price line (p_1).*

This is illustrated in Figure 5-9. If $p_1^1 > p_1^0$ (as in our example), the area above the price line is reduced, so the welfare change is negative. And so is the value of the integral (above) from p_1^1 to p_1^0. In cost benefit, the standard approach is the one we have just described. If we assume the demand curve is locally straight, the compensating variation is

$$CV = -[\text{area } (a + b) - \text{area } b]$$

$$= -[\Delta p_1 x_1^0 + \tfrac{1}{2}\Delta p_1(\Delta x_1)_u]$$

$$= -\Delta p_1\left[x_1^0 + \frac{1}{2}\left(\frac{\partial x_1}{\partial p_1}\right)_u \Delta p_1\right]$$

† We discuss the relative merits of the compensating variation and other measures of welfare change later in the section.

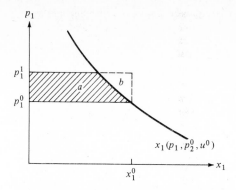

Figure 5-9 The compensated demand curve and the compensating variation.

The slope of the compensated demand curve is of course obtained from the ordinary demand curve, by using the Slutsky equation:

$$\left(\frac{\partial x_1}{\partial p_1}\right)_u = \frac{\partial x_1}{\partial p_1} + x_1 \frac{\partial x_1}{\partial m}$$

And what if two prices changed simultaneously? Suppose, for example, a government research project could reduce the price of televisions (p_1) which in turn, by reducing the demand for movie visits, would reduce the price of movies (p_2). In this process both compensated demand curves have shifted left, since both goods are Hicks-Allen substitutes: $(\partial x_i/\partial p_j)_u > 0$ (see Figure 5-10). How should the change be evaluated? Should we do both evaluations under the original demand curve, or one under the original and the other under the final curve (as illustrated in Figure 5-10). And, if so, which good should be evaluated under which curve?

To resolve this we need to go back to fundamentals. If we consider the consumer cost function $C(p_1, p_2, u^0)$, the relevant compensating variation for a change in p_1 and p_2 is clearly $C(p_1^0, p_2^0, u^0) - C(p_1^1, p_2^1, u^0)$. We can obtain

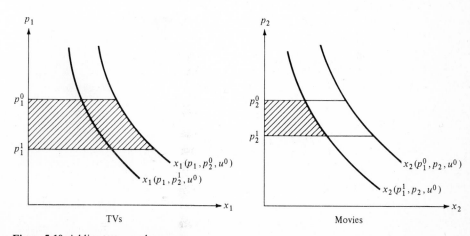

Figure 5-10 Adding areas under curves.

this difference by first holding $p_1 = p_1^1$ and integrating $\partial C/\partial p_2$ between p_2^1 and p_2^0 and then holding p_2 at p_2^0 and integrating $\partial C/\partial p_1$ between p_1^1 and p_1^0.† This gives us the two shaded areas in Figure 5-10. But equally clearly we could proceed in the opposite sequence, first holding $p_2 = p_2^1$. Whichever way the journey is made, the same destination must be reached (see footnote).

> *The compensating variation (CV) is independent of the path of prices chosen when integrating under compensated demand curves.*

Suppose next that we wished to derive a price index to measure the ratio of prices in period 1 to those in period 0. In other words, we want a cost-of-living index. To derive this we must specify what standard of living we want to "cost." Suppose it is u^0. Then if we normalise the cost of living to be unity in period 0, the cost of living in period i is

$$\text{Cost of living index in period } i = \frac{C(p_1^i, p_2^i, u^0)}{C(p_1^0, p_2^0, u^0)}$$

This completes our discussion of the fundamental ideas involved in measuring welfare change. In the next few pages we shall show how these ideas relate to other possible alternative approaches.

Q5-14 Suppose $u = xy$. x is wheat. Find the consumer cost function, if $p_y = 1$. Suppose income is \$100 and the price of wheat, p, falls from \$1 to \$0.25 due to the success of the Indus Valley Project. Evaluate consumers' gains in terms of CV. What is the price index (for $u = u^0$) after the project (setting the preproject price index at unity)?

Q5-15 If $u = xy$, $p_y = 1$, $m = 100$, derive the compensated demand curve for x and compare its slope with the ordinary demand curve. Suppose p falls from 1 to 0.25. Use the method of integration to obtain the CV. Confirm that the result is the same as you obtained in Question 5-14.

Q5-16 Suppose that at the same time as the change in Question 5-14 occurred, the price of y had risen to \$2.25. Is this sufficient to cancel out the advantages of the fall in the price of x? What is the CV for the two price changes and what is the new price index?

† In the first case, in the space p_1, p_2 we proceed from p_1^1, p_2^1 to p_1^0, p_2^0 by the route shown by the solid arrows. For each step we compute the increase in the corresponding value of C, and the sum is the total change in C. But we could equally well follow the path of the dotted arrows.

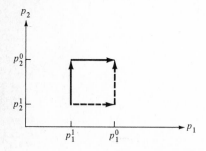

Consumer's Surplus

In considering other approaches to measuring welfare change, our aim is not only to examine these for their own sakes, but also to develop some intuition for what is going on. The old-fashioned geometry is often useful for this purpose. The question is how to measure the effects of an economic change upon a consumer's welfare? We begin by measuring the welfare effect of the following change: initially, the consumer was only able to buy good y, at a price of \$1 per unit, but now he can also buy good x in unlimited quantities at a price p per unit. His money income, and thus his income in terms of y, is unchanged. After the change he buys x^1 units of x (see Figure 5-11). How much better off is he? There are a number of possible answers corresponding to different formulations of the question.

We might ask: What is the maximum amount of money he would have been willing to pay to get x^1 *minus* the amount he actually paid? He actually paid $m - y^1$. But how much would he have been willing to pay? In other words, suppose the world's most skilful blackmailer had wanted to sell him x^1; what is the maximum he could have made the consumer pay by making him the following all-or-nothing offer: You can either buy x^1 for this amount of y, or you can buy no x. The answer is $m - y^2$. For if he had consumed (x^1, y^2), the consumer would have been just as well off as with $(0, m)$. So the maximum he would be willing to pay for x^1 is $m - y^2$. Thus the consumer's gain on this approach is $y^1 - y^2$. This is called the *consumer's surplus*.

> *The consumer's surplus on a good x is the difference between the maximum a consumer would be willing to pay for his current consumption of it and the amount he actually pays. It is measured (in terms of y) by*

$$\int_0^{x^1} [\mathrm{MRS}_{yx}(x, u^0) - p]\, dx$$

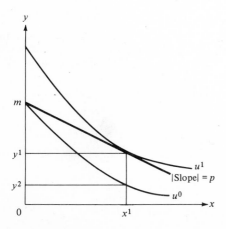

Figure 5-11 Consumer's surplus.

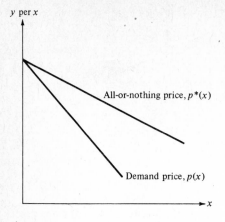

y per *x*

All-or-nothing price, $p^*(x)$

Demand price, $p(x)$

Figure 5-12 The all-or-nothing demand price. Note that for any x, $p^*(x) \cdot x =$ area under the curve of the demand price.

It could not be larger than his whole income and would only equal this if x were indispensable.

This approach introduces us to another useful concept, the all-or-nothing demand curve. For x^1, the most the individual would be willing to pay per unit is $(m - y^2)/x^1$. This is the all-or-nothing demand price. We could now take different values of x and compute for each of them the all-or-nothing price. So, if we write $p(x) = \text{MRS}_{yx}(x, u^0)$, the all-or-nothing price is

$$p^*(x) = \frac{1}{x} \int_0^x p(q)dq$$

Since $p(x)$ falls with x, it follows that $p^*(x) > p(x)$, as in Figure 5-12.†

So consumer's surplus is one measure of the individual's gain when x becomes available at price p. But, though intuitively simple, it is probably not the most useful measure. Two others suggest themselves, which also have the merit of greater generality.

Compensating and Equivalent Variations

We might ask: How much would the individual be willing to pay for the privilege of buying *unlimited* quantities at price p (not just for the privilege of buying x^1 at that price)? This is clearly the same as the question: If we let him buy at p, what is the maximum we can take away from him without making him worse off than before? A glance at Figure 5-13 reveals that this quantity is

---

† Differentiating the expression in the text, we find that

$$p(x) = \frac{d}{dx} p^*(x) x$$

In the jargon, the curve $p(x)$ is marginal to the curve $p^*(x)$.

larger than the consumer's surplus, since being able to buy *any* quantity is a greater privilege than buying a constrained quantity, x^1. The amount we could take from him is in fact $m - c$. For a welfare gain this is clearly finite. It is in fact the compensating variation. We shall now define this term in a way that is applicable to any economic change.

The compensating variation (CV) is the amount of money we can take away from an individual after an economic change, while leaving him as well off as he was before it. (For a welfare gain, it is the amount he would be willing to pay for the change. For a welfare loss, it is minus *the amount he would need to receive as compensation for the change.)*

An alternative question we might ask is: If the market is not opened up, how much would we need to give the individual to make him as well off as if it had been? This is $e - m$, which could clearly be infinite. It is called the equivalent variation and is in some ways the easiest of all the concepts to follow.

The equivalent variation (EV) is the amount of money we would need to give an individual, if an economic change did not happen, to make him as well off as if it did. (For a welfare gain, it is the compensation he would need to forego the change. For a welfare loss, it is the amount he would be willing to pay to avert the change.)

Note that the CV and EV have the same sign as the direction of the change in welfare: for a welfare gain both are positive.

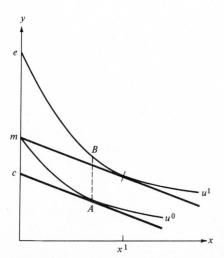

Figure 5-13 The compensating and equivalent variations due to access to a market.

The difference between the concepts is probably seen clearest in terms of the consumer cost function. In each case we are concerned with a move from state 0 to state 1.

1. The CV is the actual income *minus* the income needed to just achieve u^0 after prices have changed from their level $\mathbf{p}^0$ in state 0 to their level $\mathbf{p}^1$ in state 1. But actual income is $C(\mathbf{p}^0, u^0)$, and the new amount of money needed is $C(\mathbf{p}^1, u^0)$. So, as we have already seen,

$$CV = C(\mathbf{p}^0, u^0) - C(\mathbf{p}^1, u^0)$$

If prices have fallen, $\mathbf{p}^0 > \mathbf{p}^1$, so that CV > 0.

2. By contrast, the EV is the income needed to just achieve u^1 when prices are at their original level $\mathbf{p}^0$ *minus* actual income. The former is $C(\mathbf{p}^0, u^1)$ and the latter $C(\mathbf{p}^1, u^1)$. So

$$EV = C(\mathbf{p}^0, u^1) - C(\mathbf{p}^1, u^1)$$

So the only difference between the two concepts is the level of utility at which the cost difference due to the price change is measured, the CV being concerned with the *original* utility level and the EV with the *final* utility level.

It follows that there is a particular symmetry between the two concepts. The compensating variation assumes there has been a move from state 0 to state 1 and asks what money should be withdrawn from the individual to restore him to u^0. The equivalent variation assumes there has been *no* move from state 0 to state 1 and asks what money should be given to the individual to *shift* him to u^1. Now suppose instead that we consider the move from state 1 to state 0. The equivalent variation must be the amount of money to be given to an individual in state 1 to move him to u^0. But this is the same absolute magnitude as the compensating variation for a move from state 0 to state 1 (see the definition of it we have just given). It follows that

CV of move from 0 to 1 equals minus *EV of move from 1 to 0.*

To check this using the consumer cost function, we note that, for the move back from state 1 to state 0,

$$CV = C(\mathbf{p}^1, u^1) - C(\mathbf{p}^0, u^1)$$
$$EV = C(\mathbf{p}^1, u^0) - C(\mathbf{p}^0, u^0)$$

This confirms what we have just said. As we have seen, the CV for a welfare gain must be finite. Therefore the EV for a welfare loss must be finite. Similarly the EV for a welfare gain may be infinite, and so may the CV for a welfare loss.

Q5-17 Suppose in Figure 5-13 that access to the market is withdrawn. What is the CV? EV? Is the remark in the preceding inset correct?

What is the relative size of the CV and EV? This depends on the nature of good x. If the only price which changes is that of a normal good, EV > CV in algebraic terms, whether the change in welfare is positive or negative. This is due to the fact that, holding x constant, the only way to hold the MRS equal to a constant price as income rises, is by increasing not only y but also x. So $\partial \text{MRS}_{yx}(y, x)/\partial y > 0$: for any given x the MRS is higher, the higher the level of utility. In consequence if we take any pair of indifference curves u^0 and u^1, the vertical distance between them rises as x falls. This enables us to prove that EV > CV in our particular case. In Figure 5-13 construct point B vertically above A. Now

$$\text{EV} = e - m > AB \qquad \text{(since } x \text{ is normal)}$$

and $\qquad\qquad AB > m - c = \text{CV}$

For a welfare loss, such as the closure of this market, it is still true that EV > CV since $\text{EV} = -(m - c) > -AB > -(e - m) = \text{CV}$. The CV is greater in absolute magnitude, but both CV and EV are negative.

For normal goods EV > CV and for inferior goods the reverse is true. For goods which have no income effect EV and CV are equal (and equal to the consumer's surplus). That is why we made the simplifying assumption of no income effect in Chapter 1.

Clearly our measures of welfare change can deal with changes in external circumstances other than price changes. For example suppose that the variable d takes the value 1 when your child is alive and 0 when she is run over, and your utility function is $u(x, y, d)$. Your cost function is $C(\mathbf{p}, d, u)$.

The question naturally arises of which measure (CV or EV) is best. To this there is no real answer. If one accepts the approach of Chapter 1, the ultimate problems of social choice can only be solved in principle by allowing for distributional judgments, and it is neither easier nor more difficult to make these in relation to EV or CV. But if the Kaldor criterion were to be used, this would be equivalent to the criterion that

$$\sum \text{CV} > 0$$

provided that the act of hypothetical compensation, if actually undertaken, did not alter the structure of relative prices (see Question 5-21 below). This equivalence arises because the CV (unlike the EV) is defined with reference to the original level of utility, as is the Kaldor criterion. For this reason it has been preferred by economists and we shall concentrate on it henceforth rather than on the EV.

Q5-18 (i) If your utility function was $u(x, y, d)$, what expression indicates how much you would need to be paid to compensate you for your child being run over? Is this the CV or EV or what? What is its maximum value?

(ii) The government is considering building an office block outside a householder's back window. Two economists propose different approaches to evaluating the householder's loss of daylight. A says: Ask him how much he would pay us not to build. B says: Ask him how much we should have to give him before he would agree to our building (assuming he had the right to stop us).

(a) Which question would produce the bigger answer. Why?

(b) Which economist do you think is right?

Q5-19 Return to Question 5-14. What is the EV? Is it larger than the CV?

Q5-20 (i) Suppose $m = 100$, $p_y = 1$, and p_x falls from 1 to 0.25.

$$u = 2x - \tfrac{1}{2}x^2 + y$$

Compute CV and EV. What do you notice? Why does this happen?

(ii) Suppose that the reason for the price fall is a subsidy of $0.75 per unit of x and that the marginal cost of x in terms of y is constant. What is the welfare cost of the subsidy?

(iii) What is the all-or-nothing demand curve for x? Prove that the ordinary demand curve is marginal to it.

*****Q5-21** Suppose a two-good, two-person world inhabited by persons A and B. A new government policy would shift production from (x^0, y^0) to (x^1, y^1) but it so happens that (x^1, y^1) could be distributed in such a way that u^{A0} and u^{B0} were just maintained (i.e., the Kaldor criterion is satisfied). In fact however, x^1 and y^1 will be distributed so that $u^{A1} > u^{A0}$ and $u^{B1} < u^{B0}$. If, starting from x^{A1}, x^{B1}, y^{A1}, y^{B1} compensation were effected, relative prices would change. Suppose that we compute CV^A and CV^B in the standard way at x^{A1}, x^{B1}, y^{A1}, y^{B1}, is the sum $(CV^A + CV^B)$ greater or less than zero?

Laspeyres and Paasche Measures of Welfare Change

The trouble with the compensating and equivalent variations is that you cannot compute them without information about demand curves. So cruder measures are sometimes favoured. We shall illustrate these for the case where the price of x falls from p^0 to p^1, the price of y being constant at $1 (see Figure 5-14 where, as usual, areas in the per-unit diagram correspond to distances in the total diagram).

When the price of x falls the consumer shifts his consumption from A to C: via a substitution effect from A to B and an income effect from B to C. How has his welfare changed? A crude measure would be to say that it has changed by $p^0 - p^1$ times the quantity x^0 he was originally consuming, since on each unit he saves $p^0 - p^1$. This change is measured absolutely by $(m - l)$ in the top diagram and by the area a in the bottom one. It is known as the Laspeyres measure of welfare change. Quite generally, we have

> *The Laspeyres measure of welfare change is* minus *the change in the cost of buying the original bundle:*
>
> $$L = -\Delta p \cdot x^0 = (p^0 - p^1)x^0$$
>
> [*Correspondingly the Paasche measure is* minus *the change in the cost of buying the final bundle*
>
> $$P = (p^0 - p^1)x^1$$
>
> *For a non-Giffen good* P > L.]

Let us revert to our particular consumer who buys only two goods (x, y). If only the Laspeyres cost difference was taken from him, he would be better off than before the price fell. For he could still buy the original bundle A, but since

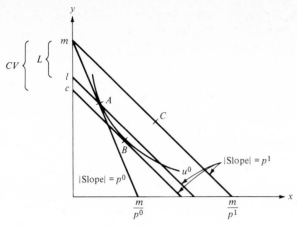

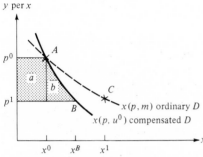

Figure 5-14 Laspeyres and compensating variations.

the price of x has fallen, he may prefer to buy more x and less y. So the Laspeyres measure underestimates his gain. In fact, to reduce him to u^0, we should have to take away his whole compensating variation $m - c$ and reduce his income to c. In this case he would buy bundle B which gives him the same utility as bundle A. So†

$$CV > L$$

To compute the CV note that

$$CV = L + (CV - L) = (p^0 - p^1)x^0 + CV - L$$

But for reasons explained in Chapter 1, the vertical distance corresponding to $CV - L$ is

$$CV - L = \int_{x^0}^{x^B} [MRS_{yx}(x, u^0) - p^1]\, dx$$

Hence,

$$CV = (p^0 - p^1)x^0 + \int_{x^0}^{x^B} [MRS_{yx}(x, u^0) - p^1]\, dx$$

But $MRS\,(x, u^0)$ is the demand price for x on the compensated demand curve for

† Correspondingly, $P > EV$.

x, given $u = u^0$. So, looking at the bottom diagram, the compensating variation is the Laspeyres cost difference *plus* the area between the compensated demand curve AB and the new price line, integrated over the range x^0 to x^B.

$$\text{CV} = \text{area } a + \text{area } b$$

In other words, the compensating variation for a price change is the change in the area between the compensated demand curve and the price line.

We previously derived this proposition from the *assumption* that, for a small unit change in price (p), the required compensation equalled the quantity of the good currently purchased (x). But Figure 5-14 has proved the proposition without making any assumptions. It follows that the original assumption was correct. For if

$$\text{CV} = \int_{p^1}^{p^0} x(p, u^0)\, dp \tag{4'}$$

then, by differentiation,

$$\frac{\partial \text{CV}}{\partial p} = x(p, u^0)$$

And this was the assumption we originally made.† Geometrically the argument is that, as Δp tends to zero, the area b tends to zero faster than the area a, and $\text{CV}/\Delta p$ tends to x. In other words, for small enough price changes, the Laspeyres and compensating variations are the same (and equal to the EV and the Paasche measures).

Q5-22 (i) "To maintain my present standard of living at existing prices I need $5000 per annum. Since I currently buy 100 bottles of whisky a year, an increase in whisky prices of $2.50 per bottle would mean that I need at least $5250 to maintain my standard of living." True or false?
   (ii) Suppose the world price of oil is $12 per barrel and Britain becomes able to produce 1 billion barrels a year of North Sea oil at a cost of $6 per barrel. What is the annual gain to Britain? Is this an approximate or exact measure?

Q5-23 (i) What are the relative sizes of P and EV. Why?
   (ii) Does it matter whether the good is Giffen for purposes of (i).
   (iii) Derive a measure of EV compared with that just given for CV.

Q5-24 Suppose $u = xy$, $m = 100$, and $p_y = 1$. The price of x rises from $0.25 to $1. Calculate L, P, CV, and EV and check that they have the correct relative sizes.

Cost-of-Living Indices

Finally we revert to the cost of living, though implicitly it has been with us for some time. The index most commonly used is the Laspeyres price index (**L**). Assume from now on that there are n goods and write $\sum_{i=1}^{n} p_i^k x_i^k$ as $\mathbf{p}^k \mathbf{x}^k$, where

† We then used the assumption to obtain (4) by integration.

k is the kth time period. Then the Laspeyres price index in year 1 (taking the index for year 0 as unity) is

$$L = \frac{\mathbf{p}^1 \mathbf{x}^0}{\mathbf{p}^0 \mathbf{x}^0}$$

The Laspeyres price index weights the prices by quantities in the base year.

It is, of course, closely related to the Laspeyres measure of welfare change (L): if prices have gone up by a proportion α, welfare (money income constant) would have been calculated to have gone down by a proportion α.

$$L - 1 = \frac{(\mathbf{p}^1 - \mathbf{p}^0)\mathbf{x}^0}{\mathbf{p}^0 \mathbf{x}^0} = -\frac{L}{\mathbf{p}^0 \mathbf{x}^0}$$

Similarly the Paasche price index $\mathbf{P}$ is

$$P = \frac{\mathbf{p}^1 \mathbf{x}^1}{\mathbf{p}^0 \mathbf{x}^1}$$

The Paasche price index weights the prices by quantities in the final year.

Which of these indices is right? The answer of course is neither, for neither corresponds to an accurate measure of welfare change. As we have seen, the Laspeyres measure of welfare change underestimates the welfare gain resulting from a price change (L < CV < EV). If compensation is made on the basis of the Laspeyres price index, the consumer would be guaranteed an income in year 1 equal to his income in year 0 times the price index in year 1. So he would get

$$\mathbf{p}^0 \mathbf{x}^0 \cdot \frac{\mathbf{p}^1 \mathbf{x}^0}{\mathbf{p}^0 \mathbf{x}^0}$$

This would enable him to consume his original bundle. But at the new price structure he can reach a higher level of welfare by consuming some other bundle and so be better off.

The Laspeyres price index overestimates the rise in the cost of the original standard of living. The Paasche price index underestimates it.

A correct cost-of-living index does just what its name suggests: it measures the cost of living at some particular standard (utility). The standard must of course be stated. Two natural standards are u^0 and u^1, u^0 corresponding to the CV approach and u^1 to the EV approach. Taking u^0 as our standard, the cost of living in year 1 (taking the index in year 0 as unity) is

$$\text{True price index for } u^0 = \frac{C(\mathbf{p}^1, u^0)}{C(\mathbf{p}^0, u^0)}$$

This lies between the Laspeyres and Paasche indices.

It is somewhat irritating that a true cost-of-living index should be dependent on the level of utility. The only case where this is not true is when the utility function is homothetic. We can then choose to measure utility using an index which is homogeneous of degree 1 in the quantities consumed: call this index V. But it is a property of constant returns to scale that unit costs depend only on the prices of the things that contribute to output/utility, and not on the scale of output/utility.† So we can write

$$C = f(\mathbf{p})V$$

From this it would follow that the true cost-of-living index would be independent of the utility level V at which costs were measured. However, we know that homotheticity is not a very plausible assumption.

How serious is all this? If we are only using the indices to compare adjacent years, it may not matter too much, provided prices do not change much.‡ For as we have seen, in the limit (as $\Delta \mathbf{p}$ tends to zero)

$$C(\mathbf{p}^1, u^0) - C(\mathbf{p}^0, u^0) \to (\mathbf{p}^1 - p^0)\mathbf{x}^0$$

Hence,
$$\frac{C(\mathbf{p}^1, u^0)}{C(\mathbf{p}^0, u^0)} - 1 \to \frac{\sum \mathbf{p}^1\mathbf{x}^0}{\sum \mathbf{p}^0\mathbf{x}^0} - 1$$

since
$$C(\mathbf{p}^0, u^0) = \mathbf{p}^0\mathbf{x}^0$$

The true index tends to the Laspeyres index. The problem with the Laspeyres index arises if, as often happens with consumer price indices, the same weights are used over a number of years, say for up to 10 years. Suppose the index is based on year 0. Then if we compare the Laspeyres cost-of-living index in year 9 ($\mathbf{L}^9$) with that in year 8 ($\mathbf{L}^8$) we find

$$\frac{\mathbf{L}^9}{\mathbf{L}^8} = \frac{\mathbf{p}^9\mathbf{x}^0}{\mathbf{p}^8\mathbf{x}^0}$$

It would be pure coincidence if this measured the ratio of the costs of producing any level of utility at prices $\mathbf{p}^9$ and $\mathbf{p}^8$, for the quantity weights have become totally irrelevant.§

A preferable approach to cost-of-living indices is to start by ensuring that

---

† This follows from the fact that the expansion path is along a ray, with total costs proportional to distance along the ray and output/utility also proportional to that distance (see pages 64 and 269).

‡ It will also not matter if all prices change fast but at the same rate and money income also changes at the same rate, for then the consumption bundle will not change.

§ The corresponding measure of real income in period 9 relative to that in period 8 is equally bizarre. This is

$$\frac{m^9/m^8}{L^9/L^8} = \frac{\mathbf{p}^9\mathbf{x}^9/\mathbf{p}^9\mathbf{x}^0}{\mathbf{p}^8\mathbf{x}^8/\mathbf{p}^8\mathbf{x}^0}$$

the comparison of each pair of adjacent years is meaningful. This leads to the use of a chain-linked index (call it D). For year 1 the index is the same as the Laspeyres index:†

$$D^1 = \frac{\mathbf{p}^1 \mathbf{x}^0}{\mathbf{p}^0 \mathbf{x}^0}$$

And in year 2 the index is such that D^2/D^1 is the Laspeyres index for year 2 using year 1 as base. Thus

$$D^2 = D^1 \frac{\mathbf{p}^2 \mathbf{x}^1}{\mathbf{p}^1 \mathbf{x}^1} = \frac{\mathbf{p}^1 \mathbf{x}^0}{\mathbf{p}^0 \mathbf{x}^0} \cdot \frac{\mathbf{p}^2 \mathbf{x}^1}{\mathbf{p}^1 \mathbf{x}^1} \neq \frac{\mathbf{p}^2 \mathbf{x}^0}{\mathbf{p}^0 \mathbf{x}^0} = \mathbf{L}^2$$

The only problem with a chain-linked index is that it is not necessarily path-independent, in the sense that if we started with $\mathbf{p}^0$ and returned in period 2 to the original set of prices we would find $D^2 = 1$, regardless of prices in period 1. We would, however, find $D^2 = 1$ if the utility function was homothetic. For then we would have for each adjacent pair of years i, j that in the limit

$$\frac{D^j}{D^i} = \frac{C(\mathbf{p}^j, u^i)}{C(\mathbf{p}^i, u^i)}$$

But with homotheticity $C(\mathbf{p}^j, u^i) = f(\mathbf{p}^j)V^i$. So

$$D^1 = \frac{f(\mathbf{p}^1)}{f(\mathbf{p}^0)}$$

and

$$D^2 = D^1 \frac{f(\mathbf{p}^2)}{f(\mathbf{p}^1)} = \frac{f(\mathbf{p}^1)}{f(\mathbf{p}^0)} \cdot \frac{f(\mathbf{p}^2)}{f(\mathbf{p}^1)} = 1 \qquad (\text{since } \mathbf{p}^2 = \mathbf{p}^0)$$

When, as is particularly common in production theory, constant returns are appropriate, chain-linked indices are peculiarly useful. But they are probably the best we have in any case, and deserve wider use.‡

---

† The chain-linked index for discrete periods is an approximation to a Divisia index, which is formulated in continuous time such that at any instant

$$d \log D = \sum v_i \, d \log p_i = \frac{\sum\limits_i p_i x_i \, d \log p_i}{\sum\limits_i p_i x_i}$$

In the discrete period case a closer approximation to a Divisia index would be got by computing

$$D^1 = \sum_i \left(\frac{1}{2} \frac{p_i^0 x_i^0}{\sum p_i^0 x_i^0} + \frac{1}{2} \frac{p_i^1 x_i^1}{\sum p_i^1 x_i^1} \right) \frac{p_i^1}{p_i^0}$$

rather than (as in the text)

$$D^1 = \sum \frac{p_i^0 x_i^0}{\sum p_i^0 x_i^0} \frac{p_i^1}{p_i^0}$$

‡ The U.K. Retail Price Index is an annually chain-linked Laspeyres index.

Q5-25 "The following data show that the poor were better off in 1971 than in 1965." True or false? (Assume the data relate to the poor, who only consume these two goods.)

	Expenditure per head per week ($)		Price index	
Year	1965	1971	1965	1971
Food	25	30	1	1.3
Other	50	80	1	1.1

Q5-26 Suppose a Laspeyres price index is used to construct an index of real income by dividing it into an index of money income. What are the price weights in the resulting measure of real income? (Assume you are comparing adjacent years.)

*Q5-27 Laspeyres price indices (and any others) are normally computed for a group of people whose expenditure patterns vary. The weights used are the shares of each good in the expenditure of the whole group.

(i) Is the group index a simple average of the indices for each individual?

(ii) If not, which goods have their price changes reflected more heavily in the index than if the index were such a simple average?

(iii) Does this mean that the index necessarily underestimates the inflation experienced by the poor?

(iv) If the linear expenditure system is correct, what is the income level of the "representative" consumer to whom the published price index relates? (Before attempting this, read the next section.)

5-4 THE STRUCTURE OF THE UTILITY FUNCTION

We can now revert to the positive study of demand. We have already seen that any demand function (or system of functions) must satisfy a number of restrictions. But there may be many mathematical functions which satisfy these restrictions and, to make empirical work more feasible, further assumptions are worth exploring. Assumptions can be made about the indirect utility function or the direct utility function. We shall confine ourselves to the direct utility function and explore the implications of various assumptions about its structure—assumptions of homotheticity, additivity, and general separability. Finally, we shall discuss how to allow for differences in household size.

Homothetic Utility Functions

As we have already explained, an increasing homothetic function is any increasing transformation of a linear homogeneous function. For any homothetic function the locus of tangencies to a budget line of constant slope lies along a ray from the origin, since u_1/u_2 depends only on x_1/x_2 (see Figure 5-15 and Appendix 3). It follows that, for given relative prices, the relative shares of expenditure going on x_1 and x_2 are constant. For p_1x_1/p_2x_2 is constant if p_1 and p_2 are constant and so is x_1/x_2. By the same token, for someone of given tastes, the share of each

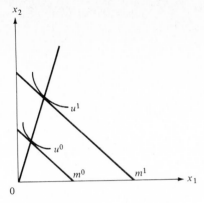

Figure 5-15 A homothetic function.

good in his total expenditure is independent of his income and depends only on relative prices. Hence, if α_i is a function of p_1/p_2,

$$\frac{p_i x_i}{m} = \alpha_i\left(\frac{p_1}{p_2}\right)$$

and

$$p_i x_i = \alpha_i\left(\frac{p_1}{p_2}\right) m$$

A special case of this is the Cobb-Douglas utility function

$$u = x_1^{\alpha_1} x_2^{\alpha_2}$$

where you can check that the expenditure shares of x_1 and x_2 are α_1 and α_2, respectively, provided these add to unity. The expenditure shares are thus for this function independent of prices as well as income.†

Reverting to homotheticity in general, two propositions follow directly from the equation before last:

1. The marginal propensity to spend on x_i out of additional income $[\partial(p_i x_i)/\partial m]$ is independent of income. In other words the Engel curve is straight.
2. Since $\partial \log x_i/\partial \log m = 1$, the income elasticity of demand is unity. The Engel curve goes through the origin.

But we know empirically, from time-series and cross-section data, that income elasticities are not unity. In fact, the share of expenditure on food falls rapidly with income: proposition 2 is false. However, proposition 1, if true, would be extremely useful for many purposes. For suppose we ask the question: "Under what circumstances is the demand for x_i independent of the distribution of income?" The answer must be: "If, when I take one dollar of income from any person A and give it to any person B, A's reduced demand for x_i is exactly

† This is because the elasticity of substitution is unity (see Chapter 9).

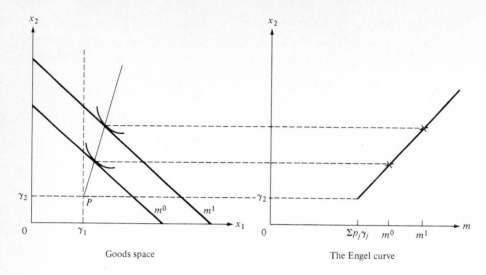

Goods space   The Engel curve

Figure 5-16 The Stone-Geary function.

equal to B's increased demand." In other words, the marginal propensities to spend on x_i must be the same for A and B, even though their incomes differ.

Stone-Geary Utility Functions

So how can we preserve linear Engel curves without tying ourselves to homotheticity and constant expenditure shares? Presumably by keeping a linear expansion path but making it come from somewhere other than the origin. In Figure 5-16 (left-hand panel) the linear expansion path has been drawn to come from point P, where $x_1 = \gamma_1$ and $x_2 = \gamma_2$. Since the expansion path is linear from this point, this implies that the utility function with point P as origin is homothetic. If we assume in fact that the utility function with origin P is Cobb-Douglas, we obtain the Stone-Geary utility function

$$u = (x_1 - \gamma_1)^{\alpha_1}(x_2 - \gamma_2)^{\alpha_2} \qquad 1 > \alpha_i > 0 \qquad \sum \alpha_i = 1$$

We could rationalise such a function by supposing that γ_1 and γ_2 are the subsistence requirements for x_1 and x_2. These are met before any structure of preferences comes into play. So $\sum p_j \gamma_j$ of income is always spent on subsistence. The rest of income $(m - \sum p_j \gamma_j)$ is then divided up in above-subsistence expenditures on x_1 and x_2 in the ratio $\alpha_1 : \alpha_2$.[†] It follows that the demand function is

$$x_i = \gamma_i + \alpha_i \frac{m - \sum p_j \gamma_j}{p_i}$$

[†] If we wanted, we could modify the function to make α_1 and α_2 depend on prices.

This is illustrated for x_2 in the right-hand panel of Figure 5-16. As can be seen, the Engel curve is straight. These demand curves, like the utility function itself, are only defined for $x_i > \gamma_i$ (all i). For the same reason we can only say that demand is independent of income distribution so long as each member of society is consuming at least γ_i of each good i (i.e., he has an income greater than $\sum p_j \gamma_j$). The system of demand equations of the form described is called the *linear expenditure system*, because expenditure on good x_i is a linear function of m, p_i, and all other prices.

Q5-28 A question on the linear expenditure system.
    (i) Can there be inferior goods in it?
    (ii) What distinguishes necessities from luxuries?
    *(iii) If γ_i is positive (which is not required in principle but found for most goods in practice), is x_i price-elastic or -inelastic?
    (iv) If all γ_i are positive, are any goods gross complements? All goods?

Additive Utility Functions

The linear expenditure system is one of the most commonly estimated systems of demand equations. But the corresponding Stone-Geary utility function has a drawback, which it shares with all other utility functions in which utility is treated as the sum of the utility derived from each separate commodity. Such functions can be written in general form as

$$u = f[u^1(x_1) + u^2(x_2) + \cdots]$$

For example, the Stone-Geary function, as we have written it, is

$$u = e^{\alpha_1 \log(x_1 - \gamma_1) + \alpha_2 \log(x_2 - \gamma_2)}$$

$$= e^{u^1(x_1) + u^2(x_2)}$$

However, since we can subject any utility function to any increasing transformation without affecting its ability to explain the world, we can equally well write any additive function as

$$u = u^1(x_1) + u^2(x_2) + \cdots$$

This makes clear that, for all substantive purposes, the marginal utility of each good is independent of the quantity of any other good; for example, the effect of food is independent of how many clothes one has. The assumption is thus of "independence of wants." This has two implications, provided all goods account for sufficiently small proportions of expenditure. First, as you might expect from "want-independence," there are no cross-substitution effects. Second, and more remarkable, the ratio of own-price elasticity to income elasticity is the same for every good.

    The proof is as follows. For any good i we know from Equations (1) on page 134 that

$$\frac{\partial u}{\partial x_i} = \lambda p_i$$

where λ is the marginal utility of money. So, taking logs, we find that

$$\log \frac{\partial u}{\partial x_i} = \log \lambda + \log p_i$$

However, in the present case $\partial u / \partial x_i$ is a function of x_i only: call it $u'_i(x_i)$. So

$$\log u'_i(x_i) = \log \lambda + \log p_i$$

Now we do our comparative statics. First we differentiate by $\log p_i$, then by $\log p_j$ $(j \neq i)$, and then by $\log m$:

$$\frac{\partial \log u'_i}{\partial \log x_i} \frac{\partial \log x_i}{\partial \log p_i} = \frac{\partial \log \lambda}{\partial \log p_i} + 1 \qquad (5)$$

$$\frac{\partial \log u'_i}{\partial \log x_i} \frac{\partial \log x_i}{\partial \log p_j} = \frac{\partial \log \lambda}{\partial \log p_j} \qquad (j \neq i) \qquad (6)$$

$$\frac{\partial \log u'_i}{\partial \log x_i} \frac{\partial \log x_i}{\partial \log m} = \frac{\partial \log \lambda}{\partial \log m} \qquad (7)$$

In (5) and (6), provided the goods whose prices have changed involve a smallish share of expenditure, λ can be taken as approximately constant when p_i or p_j change. So

$$\frac{\partial \log \lambda}{\partial \log p_i} \simeq 0 \qquad \frac{\partial \log \lambda}{\partial \log p_j} \simeq 0$$

Thus there are no cross effects $(\partial \log x_i / \partial \log p_j = 0)$.[†] More strikingly, by dividing (5) by (7), we obtain

$$\frac{\partial \log x_i}{\partial \log p_i} \bigg/ \frac{\partial \log x_i}{\partial \log m} = 1 \bigg/ \frac{\partial \log \lambda}{\partial \log m}$$

Hence

$$\frac{\varepsilon_{ii}}{\eta_{im}} = 1 \bigg/ \frac{\partial \log \lambda}{\partial \log m}$$

So for every good i the ratio of own-price elasticity to income elasticity will be the same as for every other good. Goods with low income elasticities (food) will have low price elasticities (food) and vice versa. So long as we know one price elasticity, we can infer all the others from the income elasticities. If we assume all income elasticities are the same for all individuals at all income levels, we can estimate income elasticities from cross-sectional data without any actual variation in prices. From this plus one (constant) price elasticity we could then infer all the other price elasticities.[‡] However, to avoid relying so heavily on cross-sectional

---

[†] This follows from (6), since strict quasi-concavity requires $\partial \log u'_i / \partial \log x_i$ to be negative rather than equal to zero.

[‡] It is sometimes also suggested that the implied $\partial \log \lambda / \partial \log m$ could be taken as an estimate of the rate at which the *cardinal* marginal utility of income falls with income. However, even if preferences could be represented by an additive utility function, $u^1(x_1) + u^2(x_2)$, there is no reason why *true* cardinal utility might not correspond to some *nonproportional* transformation of this function.

estimates of income elasticities, the linear expenditure system has normally been estimated on time series, where prices also vary. But there is always the suspicion that the estimated price effects may be largely forced to be consistent with the better-measured income effects.

Moreover, direct tests of the additivity assumption have often suggested that it is not satisfied. It is clearly more plausible, the broader the category of goods included in any one variable. For the wants for butter and margarine can clearly not be independent, but those for food and clothing might be.

Separable Utility Functions

A more reasonable assumption is that goods fall naturally into groups, in such a way that there is more independence in some forms of decision making than in others. For example, choices about how to divide a given food expenditure between bread and cheese can be made independently of decisions about how to divide given clothing expenditures between shoes and pants. For this to be possible the utility function must be separable, in the sense that it can be written†

$$u = u[f^r(x_1, x_2), f^s(x_3, x_4), \ldots]$$

The fundamental implication of separability is that if goods i and j are separable from all other goods, then

$$\frac{\partial}{\partial x_k} \left(\frac{u_i}{u_j} \right) = 0 \qquad \text{all } k \neq i, j$$

The idea of separability is of fundamental importance in economics, and many problems become completely intractable unless one assumes that they have a two-stage structure, whereby some decisions have aspects that can be analysed independently of other decisions.

Within the context of demand theory, separability implies some specific restrictions on the possible pattern of cross-substitution effects $\partial x_i / \partial p_j$. This is because, if good i belongs to group r, the demand for good i can be expressed in either of two ways. The usual way would be to write it as a function of m and the whole price vector $\mathbf{p}$:

$$x_i = f(\mathbf{p}, m)$$

However, it could also be expressed as a function of expenditure on its own group r (m_r) and of the price vector of the goods in group r only ($\mathbf{p}_r$). We then have

$$x_i = g(\mathbf{p}_r, m_r) \tag{8}$$

† Strictly, this type of function is called "weakly separable," "strong separability" requiring

$$u = u[f^r(x_1, x_2) + f^s(x_3, x_4) + \cdots]$$

From this we can infer that the cross effects $\partial x_i/\partial p_j$, where i belongs to group r, and j to group s, will have a certain simplicity. If prices in group r are constant but price j in some other group changes, then from (8) the uncompensated price effect is

$$\frac{\partial x_i}{\partial p_j} = \frac{\partial x_i}{\partial m_r}\frac{\partial m_r}{\partial p_j}$$

$$= \frac{\partial x_i}{\partial m_r}\chi^{rj} \quad \left(\text{writing } \frac{\partial m_r}{\partial p_j} = \chi^{rj}\right)$$

So a change in p_j will affect all goods in group r in a way that is proportional to their response to expenditure in group r. The factor of proportionality is χ^{rj}. As for the compensated price effects, these are even neater, namely,

$$\left(\frac{\partial x_i}{\partial p_j}\right)_u = \frac{\partial x_i}{\partial m_r}\frac{\partial x_j}{\partial m_s}\lambda^{rs}$$

where λ^{rs} is a common term applying to all goods in r and s.† The compensated cross-substitution effect is thus a given substitution term between r and s times the responses of each good to expenditure on its own group.

From these formulae it is easy to infer exact expressions, involving no approximation, for the cross-effects with an additive utility function. For, since good i does not belong to any particular group (nor does good j), the group subscripts can be dropped. So

$$\frac{\partial x_i}{\partial p_j} = \frac{\partial x_i}{\partial m}\chi^j$$

† The proof is as follows. By the Slutsky symmetry condition we have

$$\left(\frac{\partial x_i}{\partial p_j}\right)_u = \left(\frac{\partial x_j}{\partial p_i}\right)_u$$

Therefore, applying our previous approach to each of these terms, we obtain

$$\frac{\partial x_i}{\partial m_r}\left(\frac{\partial m_r}{\partial p_j}\right)_u = \frac{\partial x_j}{\partial m_s}\left(\frac{\partial m_s}{\partial p_i}\right)_u$$

Thus

$$\left(\frac{\partial m_r}{\partial p_j}\right)_u\bigg/\frac{\partial x_j}{\partial m_s} = \left(\frac{\partial m_s}{\partial p_i}\right)_u\bigg/\frac{\partial x_i}{\partial m_r}$$

But this equation must hold whichever goods i and j are considered. Therefore each side of the equation equals a constant term relating only to r and s. Call this λ^{rs}, and write it in. Therefore, cross-multiplying, we get

$$\left(\frac{\partial m_r}{\partial p_j}\right)_u = \lambda^{rs}\frac{\partial x_j}{\partial m_s}$$

But

$$\left(\frac{\partial x_i}{\partial p_j}\right)_u = \frac{\partial x_i}{\partial m_r}\left(\frac{\partial m_r}{\partial p_j}\right)_u = \frac{\partial x_i}{\partial m_r}\frac{\partial x_j}{\partial m_s}\lambda^{rs}$$

and
$$\left(\frac{\partial x_i}{\partial p_j}\right)_u = \frac{\partial x_i}{\partial m}\frac{\partial x_j}{\partial m}\lambda$$

Q5-29 (i) People commonly save a part of their incomes. Yet we commonly analyse the demand for a good as a function only of expenditure (i.e., income minus saving). What are we implicitly assuming about the position of saving in the utility function?

*(ii) In the case of an additive utility function the exact expressions for the various effects are

$$\frac{\varepsilon_{ii}^*}{\eta_{im}} = \frac{1 - w_i\,\eta_{im}}{f}$$

$$\frac{\varepsilon_{ij}^*}{\eta_{im}} = \frac{-w_j\,\eta_{jm}}{f} \qquad i \neq j$$

where $f = \partial \log \lambda / \partial \log m$, the "income flexibility of the marginal utility of income." Prove these formulae starting from Equations (5) to (7) and using relations (E-2) and (E-4). Some manipulation is required.

Household Composition and Equivalence Scales

We turn now to a rather different problem. Consumption occurs within households and is influenced by the size of the household. A household with a given income is likely to spend more on food, the more mouths it has to feed. It must correspondingly spend less on something else. Thus household size ought to appear as a variable in functions which purport to explain household demand. Equally, if we are interested in welfare comparisons between families of different sizes, we need to know how to measure their real incomes after allowing for household composition. For example, if we want to abolish poverty, we want to know at what income families of different sizes would be at the same minimum acceptable level of utility.

This raises obvious problems in comparing the utility levels of different types of family. However, it does not seem unreasonable to explain the fact that, at a given income level, larger families spend a higher proportion of their income on food by saying that their real income is lower and food is a necessity. Thus one possible approach is as follows. Utility is a function of the consumption of each good divided by the number of equivalent adults in the household. For simplicity we shall assume that the way in which children are converted into equivalent adults is the same in relation to each type of good, which implies for example that a child's food consumption relative to an adult's is the same as his or her space requirement relative to an adult's, and so on. Thus, if h is the number of equivalent adults in a household,

$$u = u\left(\frac{x_1}{h}, \frac{x_2}{h}\right)$$

This is maximised subject to

$$p_1 x_1 + p_2 x_2 = m$$

or, dividing by h, subject to

$$p_1 \frac{x_1}{h} + p_2 \frac{x_2}{h} = \frac{m}{h}$$

From this it is clear that the correct measure of a household's real income is m/h, since this provides the constraint on the items which affect utility. The problem is how to estimate h for a given household type. This can be done by turning to the demand curve. Since the variables x_i/h appear as arguments in the utility function and in the budget equation (second version), the demand function must be of the form

$$\frac{x_i}{h} = f\left(p_1, p_2, \frac{m}{h}\right)$$

which gives us an Engel curve relation, holding prices constant, of the form

$$\frac{x_i}{h} = g\left(\frac{m}{h}\right)$$

Clearly h depends on the number of members of the family (n_j) of each specific type j (adults, children aged under 2, children 2–4, 5–7, etc.). Suppose that the relationship is linear, with no economies of scale. Then we have

$$h = \sum a_j n_j \qquad (a_{\text{adult}} = 1)$$

where a_j is the adult-equivalent weight attaching to a family member in the jth category. Hence

$$\frac{x_i}{\sum a_j n_j} = g\left(\frac{m}{\sum a_j n_j}\right)$$

If some functional form is assumed for g, the weights a_j can be estimated by first guessing values $\bar{a}_j$ and estimating the parameters of the g function, and then taking the predicted value of g for each household and regressing $x_i/g(m/\sum \bar{a}_j n_j)$ on $\sum a_j n_j$ to reestimate the values a_j. A more subtle approach could allow the a_j to be different for each good.†

This ends a long chapter. The basic idea is that people behave consistently, i.e., they have an ordering, and from given opportunities they will always make the same choice. Mathematically, this assumption is represented by utility maximisation. From it follow four basic laws of demand. The theory provides a powerful framework for analysing changes in welfare and also for the positive study of demand behaviour. But, for empirical work, it is often necessary to make further specific assumptions about the underlying structure of the utility function.

As is obvious, utility functions show how goods "produce" utility, while production functions show how factors produce output. So similar functional

---

† For the implications of this see J. Muellbauer, "Household Composition, Engel Curves and Welfare Comparisons Between Households," *European Economic Review*, vol. 2, pp. 103–122, August 1974.

forms may be useful for either. We have discussed some possible ones in this chapter and will look at one other, the Constant-Elasticity-of-Substitution (CES) function, in Chapter 9. By the same token, the substitution properties of demand systems are identical, whether they relate to the demand for goods or for factors. We have discussed the basic definitions and properties in this chapter (the negative own-price substitution effect and the symmetric cross-substitution effect). In Chapter 9 we shall discuss more fully the concepts of complementarity and substitution.

Q5-30 What values a_j would you expect in Britain? Take a single adult as the numeraire (with $a = 1$) and guess values for children aged 0–1, 2–4, 5–7, 8–10, 11–12, 13–15, 16–18, and additional adults (we allow economies of scale in the pairing of adults but not in the rearing of children).

Q5-31 Suppose that ordinary Engel curves have been run for (i) single adult households and (ii) households of type k, yielding estimates of

    (i) $x_i = c_{i1} m^{b_i}$ for a single adult

    (ii) $x_i = c_{ik} m^{b_i}$ for households of type k

(Note that a common income elasticity has been imposed on both groups.) What is your estimate of h_k? What condition determines whether, given m, x_i is higher or lower for households of type k, assuming $h_k > 1$?

SIX

EFFICIENT PRICING WITH INCREASING RETURNS TO SCALE AND EXTERNALITY

Utility theory provides the indispensable framework for public policy analysis. Suppose we ask questions like: Should railroads be subsidised, or What should be done about pollution? These must ultimately be answered in relation to the value which citizens place on railroad travel or an unpolluted environment. The matter is complicated if distributional considerations are brought in, and for the sake of clarity we shall exclude them from this chapter. Given this, railway travel should be encouraged so long as people collectively would be willing to pay the costs involved. Similarly, pollution should be controlled so long as people collectively would be willing to meet the cost.

Put this way, one might suppose the matter could be left to the free market. But there are problems. Industries like railroads may be subject to increasing returns to scale, with heavy fixed overheads. This means that, if privately operated, they are prone to monopoly, and they are therefore often placed under public control or ownership.† But this makes their pricing policy a matter of public decision. As we have already seen, Pareto optimality requires that the relative prices of commodities correspond to their relative marginal costs (to ensure that MRS = MRT). But if marginal cost pricing is applied in increasing returns industries, subsidies are inevitable. We discuss this issue in Sec. 6-1.

With pollution, the problem arises not from increasing returns to scale but from technological externality: one man's actions affect others without his being

---

† Such industries may also produce at zero output, if privately operated, even though a positive output is socially desirable. See Question 6-1, page 174.

forced by the price mechanism to take these effects into account. The socially efficient level of output of a polluting good would be where the amount which all individuals i collectively were willing to pay when an extra unit was produced equalled the cost of producing it (Σ MRS = MRT). But whether the free market brings this about depends on whether the costs of negotiation between the various individuals concerned are too high or not. If people cannot negotiate among themselves to bring about Pareto optimality, it may be better for the government to act on their behalf. This is the theme of Sec. 6-3.

However, in any particular policy problem it is often unrealistic to pretend that the rest of the economy is Pareto-optimal. In fact, it is full of monopoly, irrational taxes, and so on. So policies cannot be made on the first-best assumption that the rest of the garden is lovely. Instead, they must be made in the face of given imperfections. An optimum that takes these constraints into account is necessarily second best. We discuss some important problems of second best in Sec. 6-2.

These are all problems of the price mechanism. But even in capitalist countries, nonprice methods of allocation are sometimes practised (queues and rationing in particular). We conclude the chapter with a look at these.

6-1 FIRST-BEST PRICING AND INVESTMENT

We shall start by looking at the problem of pricing and investment in a typical increasing-returns industry. An example will give us a feel for the issues. Suppose there is a bridge which would cost (per period) f units of y to build,† and is able to provide up to g uncongested crossings per period. The demand curve (compensated and uncompensated) for crossings is $p = a - bx$ ($a/b < g$), where p is the price per crossing (in units of y) and x is the number of crossings per period (see Figure 6-1a). Should the bridge be built and what price should be charged per crossing?

These questions must be answered in one specific order. For the social value of the bridge (to consumers and taxpayers taken together) depends on how much the bridge is used, and this depends, in turn, on the price that is charged. The decision-making sequence is thus:

1. Determine the optimal price, if the bridge is built.
2. Decide whether it is worth building, given the price that is charged.

First consider step 1. For a given distribution of income, there is only one efficient number of crossings, given that the bridge is built. This is the number at which the amount of y that people are willing to sacrifice for an extra crossing (MRS_{yx}) equals the amount that society has to sacrifice (MRT_{yx}). In

---

† f is the once-for-all capital cost converted into an equivalent cost per period to make it comparable with the other information which is on a per-period basis (see Chapter 12).

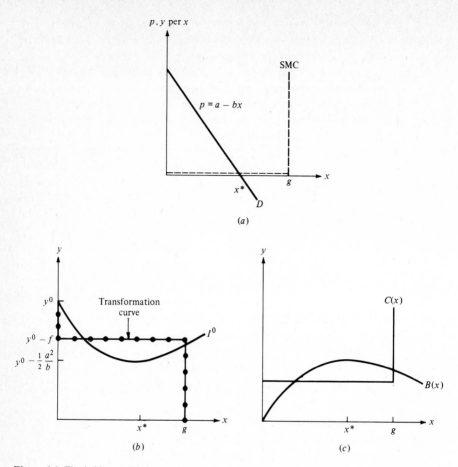

Figure 6-1 The bridge problem.

Figure 6-1a this is x^*, and the marginal cost of crossings at this optimal number is zero. Since it costs nothing to let more people cross, they should be allowed to cross for nothing. But the general pricing rule is our third efficiency condition: Solve

$$\mathrm{MRS}_{yx}(x) = \mathrm{MRT}_{yx}(x, f) \tag{1}$$

for x and then set the private price at $\mathrm{MRT}_{yx}(x^*, f)$, where x^* is the solution value of (1). In our example $x^* = a/b$.

We now need (step 2) to decide whether the bridge should be built. This requires us to compute the net welfare gain from building it and using it for the projected number of crossings. This welfare gain is the difference between the amount of y people would be willing to sacrifice for the project and the amount they have to sacrifice.†

---

† See Sec. 1-6.

The first of these corresponds to the benefits from the project, and the second corresponds to the costs. To secure x^* crossings rather than zero, the amount of y which people would be willing to forego is measured by

$$\text{Benefits} = \int_0^{x^*} \text{MRS}_{yx}(x)\, dx$$

But against this must be set the cost, which, including any fixed cost f, is

$$\text{Cost} = \int_0^{x^*} \text{MRT}_{yx}(x, f)\, dx + f$$

The project should be done if benefits exceed costs, in other words if net benefits are positive. In the present case these are

$$\text{Benefits} - \text{Costs} = \int_0^{a/b} (a - bx)\, dx - f$$

$$= \frac{1}{2}\frac{a^2}{b} - f$$

In the two equivalent total diagrams in Figures 6-1b and 6-1c, this net benefit is positive. Figure 6-1b is familiar, Figure 6-1c is less so but in many ways more useful: it shows the benefits and costs. The costs $C(x)$ are obvious, and the benefits are got from Figure 6-1b by taking the community indifference curve I^0 and for each x reading off the corresponding value of $y^0 - y$. The net benefit is the benefits minus the costs.

The cost-benefit terminology suggests a useful general way of looking at the joint pricing-cum-investment decision. The objective is simply to maximise net benefits $B(x) - C(x)$ with respect to x over the domain from zero to infinity. Method:

1. Suppose x is positive (the bridge is built). To ensure optimum utilisation find x^* such that $B'(x^*) = C'(x^*)$, and then price at $C'(x^*)\,[= B'(x^*)]$ to ensure that x^* is consumed. The optimal price is the marginal cost of x^* *and* its demand price (which equals its marginal benefit).
2. Evaluate $B(x^*) - C(x^*)$ and build if this is positive. In our case it is.

The important point is that the price being charged at x^* is the *short-run marginal cost* (SMC)—it includes no allowance for the capital cost of the bridge. For the consumer of an extra unit ought only to be confronted with those costs which could be *escaped* if he did not consume that unit. Adding in an allowance for capital costs would lead to underutilisation of the available plant. But you might say, Will we not get excessive consumption of a good if we include no allowance for its capital cost in the price? The answer is: No, provided we never expand capacity more than the cost-benefit calculus, outlined above, indicates. If we *have* overexpanded, we should not on that account underutilise the plant we have.

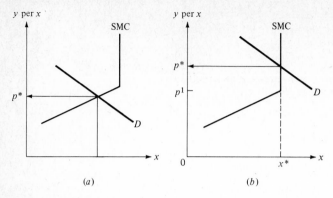

Figure 6-2 Pricing with fixed capacity output.

The general approach is thus:

> The pricing rule is:† Find that output which, for the existing plant, equates the demand price to the marginal cost; then charge the marginal cost (and demand price) for that output. The investment rule is: Do all investments whose benefits (given the prices that will be charged) exceed their costs.

This completes our discussion of the principles of first-best marginal-cost pricing, subject to one minor amplification. If there is a facility with a fixed capacity, and optimal output equals full capacity output, then the optimal price is the demand price for the full capacity output. This is illustrated in Figure 6-2. In Figure 6-2a we illustrate the normal case of a good with nonzero SMC (say, coal); the optimal price is the SMC. In Figure 6-2b we present the same cost curve but with a higher demand curve, such that optimal output is capacity output. The optimal price is the demand price for capacity output, though in a sense it can also be called the marginal cost since at x^* the marginal cost is anything between p^1 and infinity. Notice that in both cases the optimal price equals the demand price for the output being consumed, since this ensures that the available quantity is allocated to those who value it most highly.

Q6-1 A bridge could be built across a river. The cost per week (in terms of interest charges on a permanent loan to finance the construction) is $800. The bridge has a capacity of 2500 crossings per week and is uncongested up to that point. The (compensated) demand curve for crossings per week is

$$x = 2000 - 2000\,p$$

where p is measured in dollars.

---

† An alternative formulation is to say that price should always equal the marginal cost of the *existing* (rather than the optimal) output, but that output should be increased if there is excess demand and vice versa.

(i) What is the optimal price?

(ii) Should the bridge be built?

(iii) What price would maximise revenue?

(iv) Would a private entrepreneur be willing to build the bridge?

(v) If the revenue-maximising price were charged, should the bridge be built?

(vi) Suppose capacity were only 1500 crossings. What would be the optimal price?

Deficits and Surpluses

This is nearly all that needs to be said about first-best pricing. However, the crucial question arises of whether the marginal-cost pricing rule will generate a financial surplus or deficit for the agency which applies it. For this may in fact determine whether it is possible to apply the rule in all its rigour (see next section). The question is easy to answer where the technology provides an infinitely large number of different sizes of plant. For in such a case, if plant size is optimal for a given output, the short-run marginal cost is the same as the long-run marginal cost.† And, if there are increasing returns to scale, long-run marginal cost is less than long-run average cost.‡ So, if prices are set equal to short-run marginal cost, which equals long-run marginal cost, which is less than long-run average cost, losses will result.

Deficits will result from marginal-cost pricing under increasing returns to scale, and surpluses under decreasing returns.

But in many industries (like the provision of roads) there are sharp discontinuities in size of plant, and generalisation becomes more difficult. For example, consider the following problem. Only two sizes of bridge are possible: a one-lane bridge with a capacity of 10 crossings per period and costing $50 per period and a two-lane bridge with a capacity of 20 crossings per period and costing $75. The demand curve is

$$p = 20 - x$$

where x is the crossings per period and p is the price per crossing in dollars. Thus the optimal price is $10 per crossing on the smaller bridge, and zero for the larger bridge. But the larger bridge should be built. For the benefits from each bridge are

$$B(x) = \int_0^x (20 - q)\, dq = 20x - \tfrac{1}{2}x^2$$

---

† This is proved in Chapter 7.

‡ The production function $y = f(z)$ has increasing returns to scale if

$$\frac{dy}{dz}\frac{z}{y} > 1 \quad \text{i.e.} \quad MC = \frac{w_z}{dy/dz} < \frac{w_z}{y/z} = \text{average cost}$$

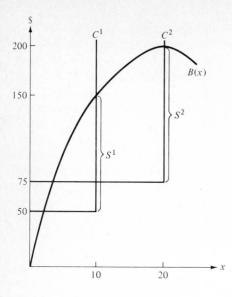

Figure 6-3 Desirable investments may lose money.

We then have the following results:

Capacity	Cost, $	Price per journey, $	No. of journeys	Benefit, $	Benefit − cost. $
10	50	10	10	150	100
20	75	0	20	200	125

The situation is illustrated in Figure 6-3, which is analogous to Figure 6-1c. C^1 is the total cost curve for the smaller bridge, and C^2 for the larger one. For the small bridge the optimal price is the slope of $B(x)$ for $x = 10$, and for the larger bridge it is the (zero) slope of $B(x)$ for $x = 20$. But the social surplus $B - C$ is greater for the larger bridge: $S^2 > S^1$. So with discontinuities, we can only tell whether additional investment should pay for itself financially by a specific investigation of each particular case.

Extracting the Consumers' Surplus

How is it that an activity which is justified cannot be made to pay for itself? Suppose for a moment that there were only a *single user* of the bridge, whose demand curve was the one shown in Figure 6-1. Then we could perfectly well charge him the cost of building the bridge. We should do this in a lump-sum form, charging him for the right to use the bridge but not for any individual journey that he made, since this would lead him to underutilise it. If the all-or-nothing payment he was willing to pay for the bridge exceeded the cost (as in our example), the bridge would be built and not otherwise. This is what is required for efficiency, for the user is being made to compare what he is willing to pay for the bridge with its true cost to society. But when we move to *many users* we cannot do this, for we cannot force each individual to reveal how much he would be willing to pay for being able to use the bridge. If asked, he will tend to understate this, for what he says is unlikely to affect whether the bridge is built, and, if it *is* built, he wants to pay as little as possible towards it. We shall meet this type of problem (sometimes called the *free-rider problem*) again in the theory of externality. In the present case it is of course possible, while charging the marginal cost for each unit that consumers buy, to charge in addition a fixed charge (standing charge) intended to extract some of the consumers' surplus.† However, such two-part tariffs are not fully efficient. For suppose there are some consumers who at a price equal to marginal cost are just willing to consume 1 unit each. It is efficient that they should do so, but any significant standing charge will stop them.

Thus with all goods subject to increasing returns to scale and used by many users there is a problem arising from the fact that users cannot be charged as much as they are willing to pay—not because they cannot be physically excluded from use of the good but because any system of charging that covered costs would be inefficient. A so-called *pure public good* is a special case of such a good, where the marginal cost of providing an extra unit of service to an individual is zero for all units from zero to infinity.‡

To repeat, the difficulty arises because we cannot get consumers to reveal their preferences. If we could, we should be able to charge each consumer his own demand price for each unit of the service. This system, known as *perfect price discrimination*, would be fully efficient: for the bridge problem the price of the *marginal* unit would be zero. But it is not practical.

The problem of deficits arises from the absence of any efficient method of inducing groups of consumers to reveal their preferences. It is most acute in the case of pure public goods, where the marginal cost of a unit of service to an individual is zero for all units from zero to infinity.

Q6-2 Should people be charged for
    (i) Listening to a particular radio programme
    (ii) Having the right to listen to radio programmes in the following cases:
        (a) There is no way of preventing unauthorised listeners.
        (b) It is possible by scramblers to prevent unauthorised listening.

Q6-3 Suppose I live isolated in a remote area outside the transmitting range of the local broadcasting station.

---

† This kind of fixed charge must be distinguished sharply from any charge intended to cover the cost of connecting a particular user to water, electricity, telephone, or other facility. Such charges to the single user of any particular connection present no problem.

‡ This is the definition first developed by P. A. Samuelson in "The Pure Theory of Public Expenditure," *Review of Economics and Statistics*, vol. 36, pp. 387–389, November 1954.

(i) I can be brought within range of broadcasts by building a new transmission tower. Would it be efficient if I was asked to pay for it?

(ii) Suppose instead that I could receive broadcasts if the power of transmission were increased. This would cost $x for each hour of transmission at extra power. What would be an efficient system of operation?

Q6-4 (i) Suppose there is a railroad from A to B. Only one train per day runs from A to B and back, and all passenger trips are round trips. The cost of operating the train for each daily round trip is $500, plus $100 per carriage. Each carriage holds 100 passengers. The daily demand for passenger trips (x) is

$$p = 20 - 0.01x$$

where p is the price per trip ($). What price should be charged per trip? (Hint: Use the rule of maximising benefits minus costs.)

(ii) Suppose railroad pricing and investment was optimal. Would you expect the railroad system of your country to make a financial surplus or deficit?

Joint Costs

The next main issue which arises is therefore how prices are to be set, assuming that there is a limit to the deficits that are acceptable. Before tackling this, however, there is one other special problem about first-best pricing which often arises. This is where a given element of cost automatically makes possible more than one type of output. For example, an electricity generator can provide electricity during peak hours and off-peak hours. Or a lorry that makes a trip from A to B also provides a trip from B to A. Thus peak electricity supply cannot be increased without increasing potential off-peak output, and the number of journeys from A to B cannot be increased without increasing the number of journeys from B to A. In such fixed-proportions cases, how is the cost of an increase in capacity to be allocated between the prices of the two outputs, and how is the optimal capacity to be determined?

The answer is simple and can be illustrated with the lorry example. Suppose that any trip out from A to B also involves a trip back, and the round trip costs $c. The demand for trips out is higher than the demand for trips back, as is shown in Figure 6-4. (This might arise, for example, if A is a coal mining centre and B a steel town.) What are the optimal prices for trips out and trips back?

As usual we find the level of round trips x which maximises $B(x) - C(x)$. In this case the benefits of x round trips are $B_{out}(x)$ and $B_{back}(x)$, so at the efficient output (x^*)

$$B'_{out}(x^*) + B'_{back}(x^*) = C'(x^*) \qquad B'_i \geq 0$$

This is the first case we have met where, as later with externality, a given action produces benefits (positive or negative) in n different ways. In such cases optimality requires in general that

$$\sum_i \mathrm{MRS}^i_{yx}(x^*) = \mathrm{MRT}_{yx}(x^*) \tag{2}$$

subject to the proviso that if consumption is voluntary and $\mathrm{MRS}^i(x^*) < 0$, we replace this figure by zero.

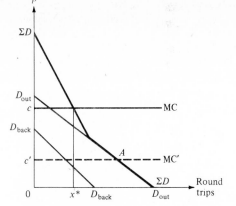

Figure 6-4 Optimal pricing with joint costs.

Diagrammatically we find the optimum by summing the demand curves *vertically* rather than horizontally, since the same unit of x is providing more than one benefit. Optimum output is where the curve of summed demand prices is cut by the curve of marginal cost (see Figure 6-4).

Having determined the optimal scale (x^*), we must price each type of output so that the available facilities are optimally used. For each type of output we therefore read off the relevant demand price:

$$p_{out} = B'_{out}(x^*)$$

$$p_{back} = B'_{back}(x^*)$$

Since the demand for trips out is higher, we find that $p_{out} > p_{back}$.[†]

In fact, if instead the marginal cost were lower at c', the summed demand curve would cut the marginal cost curve at point A. At this level of x some lorries would be coming back empty and the optimal price for trips back would be zero. The whole cost of the marginal round trip would be borne by the demander of the trip out, since it is solely on account of his demand that the round trip is being provided. This provides the basic case for not charging off-peak users a full share of the marginal cost of the plant that provides them with electricity, rail services, and the like.[‡]

Q6-5 Suppose that there are two types of electricity (peak and off-peak). Half the day is peak, and half the day off-peak. To produce 1 unit of electricity per half-day requires a unit of turbine capacity costing 8¢ per day (interest charges on a permanent loan). The cost of a given capacity is the same whether it is used at peak times only or off-peak also. In addition to the costs of the turbine capacity, it costs 6¢ in operating costs (labour and fuel) to produce 1 unit per half-day.

---

† An identical solution would be reached under competitive conditions by free-enterprise operators.
‡ For a detailed solution of optimal price structure under joint costs, the Kuhn-Tucker theorem provides the best approach.

Suppose the demand for electricity per half-day during peak hours is $p = 22 - 10^{-5}x$ and during off-peak hours is $p = 18 - 10^{-5}x$, where x is units of electricity per half-day and p is price in cents ($p \geq 0$).

(i) What is the efficient price for peak and off-peak electricity? (Hint: Ask yourself how much a user who is willing to pay x cents for a unit of electricity is willing to pay for the corresponding generating capacity if he has to pay y cents for the operating cost of the unit of electricity.)

(ii) What if the cost of a unit of capacity were only 3¢ per day?

6-2 SECOND-BEST PROBLEMS AND EFFICIENT COMMODITY TAXES

We have so far assumed that Pareto optimality can be achieved. But the economy is full of distortions (monopolies, irrational subsidies, externalities, and so on). Policy usually has to be made on the assumption that one or more of these distortions is given. Suppose for example that road transport is subsidised in such a way that price is less than marginal cost; it is also politically infeasible to remove the subsidy. Then is it right to price at marginal cost on the railways— or should they too charge less than marginal cost? Clearly the fact of the road subsidy means that the economy cannot be Pareto-optimal with respect to the constraints imposed only by tastes, technology, and endowments. A first-best optimum is ruled out, and the problem is now to do the best we can, subject to the additional constraint imposed by the road subsidy. In other words, we have to find a second-best optimum.

An unthinking person might imagine that it would still be right to equate price to marginal cost in the rest of the economy. But this is not so. Once one of the efficiency conditions is ruled out, the other general efficiency conditions are no longer desirable. This is easy to see. Suppose there are n goods and, for simplicity, assume there is an unambiguous social utility function $u(x_0, \ldots, x_n)$.[†] There is also a transformation surface $T(x_0, \ldots, x_n) = 0$ which defines the frontier of production possibilities. The first-best problem is to maximise u subject to T:[‡]

$$\max u^* = u(x_0, \ldots, x_n) - \lambda T(x_0, \ldots, x_n)$$

Thus
$$u_i = \lambda T_i \qquad (i = 0, \ldots, n)$$

and
$$T(x_0, \ldots, x_n) = 0$$

These $n + 2$ equations can be solved for the $n + 1$ goods and λ. The equations $u_i = \lambda T_i$ are, of course, none other than our standard Chapter 1 conditions: that for any pair of goods i, j the rate of substitution should equal the rate of transformation.[§]

---

† This assumption merely simplifies the exposition. It does not affect the conclusion about the desirable ratios between rates of substitution and transformation.

‡ Alternatively, we could measure all benefits and costs in terms of one good, say x_0, and then maximise $B(x_1, \ldots, x_n) - C(x_1, \ldots, x_n)$.

§ Totally differentiating $T(x_0, \ldots, x_n)$ with respect to x_i and x_j, we get

$$T_i dx_i + T_j dx_j = 0 \qquad \frac{T_i}{T_j} = \frac{-dx_j}{dx_i} = \text{MRT}_{ji}$$

$$\text{MRS}_{ji} = \frac{u_i}{u_j} = \frac{T_i}{T_j} = \text{MRT}_{ji}$$

With the second-best problem we have an additional constraint. Suppose we can express this by saying that for good 1

$$u_1 = \theta T_1$$

where θ is different from λ due to artificial constraints on the pricing of good 1. Our problem is now

$$\max u(x_0, \ldots, x_n) - \lambda T(x_0, \ldots, x_n) - \mu(u_1 - \theta T_1)$$

Hence

$$u_i = \lambda T_i + \mu(u_{1i} - \theta T_{1i})$$

and

$$\frac{u_i}{u_j} = \frac{\lambda T_i + \mu(u_{1i} - \theta T_{1i})}{\lambda T_j + \mu(u_{1j} - \theta T_{1j})}$$

Relative prices should now equal the expression on the right-hand side, and there is no reason why this should equal T_i/T_j. So if efficiency is impossible in one part of the economy, the efficiency conditions are no longer relevant in the rest of the economy. We do not any longer want relative prices to reflect relative marginal costs.

> *Theory of second best. If one of the standard efficiency conditions cannot be satisfied, the other efficiency conditions are no longer desirable.*†

This is a rather shattering discovery after all the trouble we have taken to prove that we do want relative prices to equal relative marginal costs. Is everything lost? When Lipsey and Lancaster formalised the theory of second best, they tended to imply that it was.‡ As they pointed out, there are few a priori propositions that economists can offer to policy makers that are of any real help in a world full of constraints.§ It all depends on the structure of demand and

---

† In other words, the conditions which guarantee Pareto optimality when tastes, technology, and endowments are the only constraints differ from those that guarantee Pareto optimality subject to those constraints *plus* additional constraints. When the additional constraints are as intrinsic to the human situation as the constraints of tastes, technology, and endowments· it is in some ways odd to refer to the problem as second best. The kind of constraint we have in mind is the impossibility of taxing leisure (see page 184).

‡ R. G. Lipsey and K. J. Lancaster, "The General Theory of the Second Best," *Review of Economic Studies*, vol. 24, pp. 11–32, 1956–7.

§ Some important general remarks can still be made about our present example. We do require $\text{MRS}_{ji} = \text{MRT}_{ji}$ if either of the following conditions are satisfied:

(i) $u_{1i} = u_{1j} = T_{1i} = T_{1j} = 0$

(i.e., goods i, j are not closely related as complements or substitutes to good 1 either in consumption or production).

(ii) $u = u[x_1, \ldots, f(x_i, x_j), \ldots, x_n]$
$0 = T[x_1, \ldots, g(x_i, x_j), \ldots, x_n]$

(i.e., goods i, j are separable in consumption and production). Check this proposition. A possible example would occur if electricity and gas had constant marginal costs and there were a demand for "energy," where "energy" = f (electricity, gas) and f is strictly quasi-concave.

supply relationships (u and T). But this is hardly surprising. One could not expect to pronounce about the world without knowing some *facts* about the world. Fortunately, we now know more and more about the structure of these relationships, and this makes the computation of second-best optima a lot more feasible than it was 20 years ago. So the development of positive economics has in its way contributed to a renewed faith in applied welfare economics (now reborn as "public economics"). There has also been a burgeoning of theory, much of it based on the hope that the relevant parameters may one day be estimated.

Thus in principle it is possible to compute a second-best optimum price structure for any number of constraints. Some prices may be constrained to differ from marginal costs due to politically unavoidable subsidies, some due to monopoly, others due to tariffs. However, on top of all this there is one constraint of prime importance, on which we shall henceforth exclusively concentrate: the government must balance its budget and it cannot tax leisure.

Efficient Commodity Taxes

Suppose the government were free to affect all prices. It is still not completely free, for its budget must balance. If there are increasing returns to scale in some industries and these industries charge marginal costs, they will have to be subsidised. This money has to come from somewhere, and in fact the government will also want some resources for its own use. So prices must now be optimised, subject to the government balancing its budget. Unless lump-sum taxes (like poll taxes) are adequate, which they generally are not, some arrangement is needed by which the consumer prices of some commodities exceed their marginal factor cost (evaluated at the prices which the factor owners receive).

Leisure Taxable: Equiproportional Taxes

But which prices should exceed marginal costs? Should all prices be an equiproportional markup over marginal cost? Intuitively it is obvious that if all goods that affect utility can be taxed, they should all be taxed equiproportionately. To illustrate this, we shall assume that all goods are produced by labour, and all units of labour are homogeneous and correspond to leisure foregone. The economy is endowed with T^0 units of time, which can be devoted to leisure x_0 or to the production of the other n private goods. Or it can be surrendered to the government, which requires an amount R^0.†

So, assuming constant marginal costs, the *resource constraint* of the economy is

$$c_0 x_0 + \cdots + c_n x_n + R^0 = T^0 \tag{3}$$

where c_i is the marginal cost of good i in units of time and $c_0 = 1$, since the

---

† We could think of this R^0 as covering the fixed costs of all goods subject to increasing returns to scale.

time-cost of leisure is unity. But the government needs command over R^0 units of labour and acquires this by taxes which raise the prices p_i of private goods, measured in terms of leisure, above their corresponding marginal costs c_i. So the *government's budget constraint* is

$$(p_0 - c_0)x_0 + \cdots + (p_n - c_n)x_n = R^0 \tag{4}$$

From adding Equations (3) and (4) we can confirm that the *household budget constraint* is

$$p_0 x_0 + \cdots + p_n x_n = T^0 \tag{5}$$

The households' endowment of T^0 is not sufficient to buy the total output it produces, which includes the government output corresponding to R^0.

The welfare problem is now to find a set of proportional tax rates $p_i/c_i - 1$ which will lead to the maximisation of u subject to (3) and (5).† But if all goods are taxable, we can make constraint (5) identical to constraint (3). For if we set

$$\frac{p_i}{c_i} = \frac{T^0}{T^0 - R^0} \qquad \text{all } i$$

then (5) becomes

$$c_0 \frac{T^0}{T^0 - R^0} x_0 + \cdots + c_n \frac{T^0}{T^0 - R^0} x_n = T^0$$

which is the same as (3). And, as we saw earlier, if u is maximised subject to (3) we get a first-best optimum in which all rates of substitution equal all rates of transformation. But this is exactly what our assumption about taxes implied, since it required that

$$\frac{p_i}{p_j} = \frac{c_i}{c_j}$$

So equiproportional taxes will lead to a first-best optimum‡

If all goods including leisure can be taxed, they should be taxed equipro-portionately. The solution is a first-best optimum.

The same result could equally be achieved by a proportional tax on the value of the consumer's original endowment.§

---

† Or to (3) and (4). But we want to concentrate here on (3) and (5).

‡ The literature is in places confused on this point. Some writers imply that imposing an equiproportional tax on all goods leaves the household budget constraint unchanged. However, this is only the case if wages are raised by the same multiple as the prices of goods (including leisure). But the whole point is that the wage should remain unchanged and the price of leisure be made to exceed it.

§ This finding is essentially a restatement of that in Sec. 3-2.

This is the line of reasoning behind the value-added tax. But the problem is that there is no way in which leisure can be taxed, because it cannot be accurately observed by the government. Even if hours at work could be recorded in a lie-proof manner, there are other dimensions of work (such as effort) which cannot be truly recorded. As a result leisure, widely interpreted, cannot be measured. This would not matter if we wanted to tax everyone the same amount. We could then have a simple poll tax ($x per person). But, when the English taxmen arrived to collect the poll tax in 1381, the peasants revolted. Like them, we want taxation to be related to the individual's ability to pay. Ideally, we should measure this by the individual's original endowment (say his fundamental abilities) rather than by anything over which he has control, such as his earnings (i.e., his wage rate *times* his hours of work). If, instead, we levy a proportional tax on earnings, this is equivalent to a tax on goods levied at the same rate (assuming no saving). It fails to tax leisure.

Leisure Untaxable and No Cross Effects: The Inverse-Elasticities Rule

The theory of second best tells us that if we cannot tax leisure, we can do better than by taxing all other goods equiproportionately. Intuitively one would suppose that, if leisure cannot be taxed, the next best thing is to concentrate taxes more heavily on goods that are complementary to leisure (sports gear, for example). And so it turns out.

Prices (and thus the tax rates) must be chosen so as to yield the required revenue, specified in (4). But, subject to this, we want to maximise the social surplus of benefits over costs $B - C$, both of which we shall measure in terms of leisure.† Alternatively, we could say that, subject to (4), we want to minimise the excess burden of taxes. The two statements are equivalent, but we shall think in terms of maximising $B - C$, subject always to Equation (4). So we choose prices to

$$\max B(x_1, \ldots, x_n) - \sum_{j=1}^{n} c_j x_j + \phi \left[\sum_{j=1}^{n} (p_j - c_j) x_j - R^0 \right]$$

Let us for the moment assume that there are no cross-effects in demand, i.e., $\partial x_j / \partial p_i = 0$, all $j \neq i$. So, differentiating by p_i, we require

$$\frac{\partial B}{\partial x_i} \frac{\partial x_i}{\partial p_i} - c_i \frac{\partial x_i}{\partial p_i} + \phi \left[(p_i - c_i) \frac{\partial x_i}{\partial p_i} + x_i \right] = 0 \qquad \text{all } i$$

Since consumer choices will ensure that $\partial B / \partial x_i = p_i$ (marginal value equals price, each measured in units of leisure), we require

$$(p_i - c_i) \frac{\partial x_i}{\partial p_i} = -\phi \left[(p_i - c_i) \frac{\partial x_i}{\partial p_i} + x_i \right] \tag{6}$$

The meaning of this can be readily seen from Figure 6-5. The current price

---

† To confirm that this formulation is legitimate, you are asked to derive the results we now derive but using the indirect utility function approach (see Question 6-7).

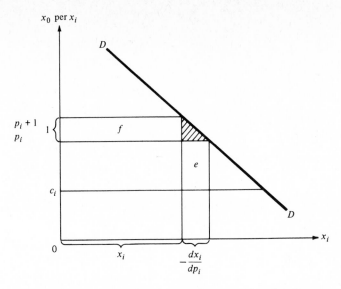

Figure 6-5 Welfare and tax-revenue effects of an increased excise tax.

of good i is p_i. We now consider raising the price by 1 (small) unit. The change in the social surplus is

$$\frac{\partial(B - C)}{\partial p_i} = \text{minus area } e = (p_i - c_i)\frac{\partial x_i}{\partial p_i}$$

(the shaded area can be ignored, being of the second order of smalls). The change in surplus is thus the waste per unit reduction of output $(p_i - c_i)$ times the change in output. At the same time tax revenue R changes by

$$\frac{\partial R}{\partial p_i} = \text{area } f \text{ minus area } e = x_i + (p_i - c_i)\frac{\partial x_i}{\partial p_i}$$

Revenue increases by x_i due to the higher tax on each unit consumed, but against this must be set the loss due to the fall in consumption of the good. For an efficient tax structure, we require that the loss of social surplus per dollar of additional revenue should be the same for every good.

$$\frac{\partial(B - C)}{\partial p_i} \bigg/ \frac{\partial R}{\partial p_i} = -\phi \qquad \text{all } i$$

This confirms that Equation (6) makes sense. Rearranging it, we find that

$$\frac{p_i - c_i}{p_i} = -\frac{\phi}{1 + \phi}\frac{x_i}{p_i}\frac{\partial p_i}{\partial x_i} = \frac{\phi}{1 + \phi}\frac{1}{|\varepsilon_{ii}|} \tag{7}$$

But $(p_i - c_i)/p_i$ is the proportional tax on good i (expressed as a proportion of the after-tax price). And this tax rate should be inversely proportional to the elasticity of demand. Taxes should, for example, be high on food and low on cars.

If leisure is untaxable and there are no cross effects in consumption, the proportional tax rate on a good should be inversely proportional to its elasticity of demand.

This seems in some ways intuitively reasonable. For, if goods in very elastic demand were subjected to the same tax rates as other goods, demand might in extreme cases fall to zero: no tax would be collected, but the social loss would be great. Instead, the inverse-elasticities formula ensures that the consumption of all goods declines by the same proportion, subject to two conditions: (i) there are no cross effects; (ii) demand curves are linear ($\partial x_i/\partial p_i = $ const) over the range from p_i to c_i. Then, if Δ indicates the change from the no-tax position,

$$\Delta x_i = \frac{\partial x_i}{\partial p_i} \Delta p_i = \frac{\partial x_i}{\partial p_i} (p_i - c_i) = \frac{\partial x_i}{\partial p_i} \left(-\frac{\phi}{1+\phi} x_i \frac{\partial p_i}{\partial x_i} \right)$$

$$= -\frac{\phi}{1+\phi} x_i$$

The contrast between the inverse-elasticities rule and our earlier equiproportional rule is striking until one reflects on the key difference in assumptions. We are now in a world where leisure cannot be taxed. We therefore want to tax leisure's complements more highly. Now, if good i is a gross complement to leisure, leisure falls when p_i rises. But how is this connected to the elasticity of demand for the good? Quite simply. If the demand for x_i is inelastic, more is spent on good i when its price rises. But spending means leisure foregone. If there are no cross effects, spending on all other market goods is constant. So when p_i rises, more leisure is foregone. Thus, in the case of zero cross effects, a good in inelastic demand is a gross complement for leisure ($\partial x_0/\partial p_i < 0$). So the inverse-elasticities rule means taxing such complements more highly.

Leisure Untaxable: Tax Complements to Leisure

But the assumption of no cross effects is implausible. If we allow cross effects, the change in social surplus when p_i rises includes the effect of changes in p_i on the social surplus in respect of the other goods.

$$\frac{\partial(B-C)}{\partial p_i} = (p_i - c_i) \frac{\partial x_i}{\partial p_i} + \sum_{j \neq i} (p_j - c_j) \frac{\partial x_j}{\partial p_i}$$

We also need to allow for changes in tax receipts on other goods:

$$\frac{\partial R}{\partial p_i} = x_i + (p_i - c_i) \frac{\partial x_i}{\partial p_i} + \sum_{j \neq i} (p_j - c_j) \frac{\partial x_j}{\partial p_i}$$

Since

$$\frac{\partial(B-C)}{\partial p_i} = -\phi \frac{\partial R}{\partial p_i}$$

we require

$$\frac{p_i - c_i}{p_i} = -\frac{\phi}{1 + \phi} \frac{x_i}{p_i} \frac{\partial p_i}{\partial x_i} - \sum_{j \neq i} \frac{p_j - c_j}{p_i} \frac{\partial x_j}{\partial p_i} \Big/ \frac{\partial x_i}{\partial p_i} \tag{8}$$

The n equations of this form plus the budget constraint can be solved for the n tax rates and ϕ.

It is not easy to see from the formula what pattern of tax rates is implied. However, the following proposition can be demonstrated:[†]

If good i has a higher elasticity of substitution with leisure x_0 than has good j ($\sigma_{i0} > \sigma_{j0}$), it should have a lower tax rate, and vice versa.

We have assumed so far that there is one factor of production and constant marginal costs. And the same propositions can be demonstrated for the many-factor case assuming constant returns to scale in each industry. Suppose, however, that in the single-factor case there were rising marginal costs, so that in Equation (4) c_i is no longer constant but rises with x_i. In this case it is easy to show in the case of small taxes and zero cross effects that the optimal tax rates are

$$\frac{p_i - c_i}{p_i} = \psi \left(\frac{1}{|\varepsilon_{ii}|} + \frac{1}{\eta_{ii}^s} \right)$$

where η_{ii}^s is the elasticity of supply. (To check this, just modify the supply curve in Figure 6-5.) This assumes that the government cannot collect in taxes any profits that arise because marginal costs exceed average costs.

Let us now look, briefly, at the problem as it may face some agency of government rather than the government itself. This agency (say, a nationalised industry) may be required to satisfy a profit constraint:

$$p_1 x_1 + \cdots + p_n x_n - C(x_1, \ldots, x_n) = \pi^0$$

where $C(\quad)$ is the cost function.

This is formally identical to (4) except where marginal costs are nonconstant. Within this constraint the agency is instructed to maximise the social surplus. So its problem is

$$\max B(x_1, \ldots, x_n) - C(x_1, \ldots, x_n) + \phi \left[\sum_j p_j x_j - C(x_1, \ldots, x_n) - \pi^0 \right]$$

It is easy to see that, even if there are not constant marginal costs, this has the solution shown in (7) or (8), depending on one's assumption about cross effects. This is so even if marginal costs are not constant, because the agency collects any profit (or incurs any loss) arising from the difference between marginal and average costs.

Does this section really answer the problem of optimal tax? Unfortunately

[†] For proof see W. J. Corlett and D. C. Hague, "Complementarity and the Excess Burden of Taxation." *Review of Economic Studies*, vol. 21, pp. 21–30, 1953–4.

not. For it altogether ignores the question of equity.† But, if it were not for equity considerations, we should not have commodity taxes at all—we should have lump-sum poll taxes. So how is equity to be handled? Obviously the income tax has a role to play. In Chapter 11 we discuss the problem of how to construct an optimal linear income tax, assuming there are no commodity taxes. But ideally we should simultaneously optimise the income tax and the system of commodity taxes. In this case, we might well find it necessary to incorporate equity as well as efficiency considerations into the pattern of commodity taxes. The possible cases are too complex to be discussed here. Under certain assumptions, we should find that no commodity taxes were needed; under others we should find that commodity taxes could be based solely on efficiency considerations of the kind discussed above; while, under yet other assumptions, commodity taxes need to embody equity as well as efficiency considerations.‡

This is all we shall say about the second best (except in Chapter 11). In the rest of this chapter we shall assume that Pareto optimality prevails in the rest of the economy, but the usual second-best reservations apply to whatever we say.

Q6-6 Suppose a nationalised coal industry sells coal to two markets (domestic and commercial). The demand curves are as follows:

$$\text{Domestic} \qquad x_1 = 1 - \tfrac{1}{2}p_1$$
$$\text{Commercial} \qquad x_2 = 1 - p_2$$

The marginal cost of coal is constant at $\tfrac{1}{3}$ and the agency has fixed (overhead) costs of $\tfrac{11}{32}$.
   (i) Check that the price structure

$$p_1 = \tfrac{3}{4} \qquad p_2 = \tfrac{1}{2}$$

is optimal if costs must be covered.
   (ii) What would the industry charge if it were a profit-maximising monopoly?
   (iii) What is the ratio of marginal social loss to marginal profit for each price in (i)? In (ii)?

*Q6-7 (i) What are the arguments in the indirect utility function for a consumer facing the household budget constraint

$$x_0 + p_1 x_1 + \cdots + p_n x_n = T^0$$

and having the direct utility function $u(x_0, \ldots, x_n)$?
   (ii) Maximise the indirect utility function subject to

$$(p_1 - c_1)x_1 + \cdots + (p_n - c_n)x_n = R^0$$

Confirm that you obtain Equation (7) if

$$\frac{\partial x_j}{\partial p_i} = 0 \qquad \text{all } i \neq j$$

You will need to use Roy's identity. If you want, also confirm Equation (8).

---

† Using the best econometric evidence, we should probably find we needed to place the heaviest tax rates on necessities.
   ‡ See A. B. Atkinson and J. E. Stiglitz, "The Design of Tax Structures: Direct versus Indirect Taxation." *Journal of Public Economics*, vol. 6, pp. 55–76, July/August 1976.

6-3 EXTERNALITY, TRANSACTIONS COSTS, AND PUBLIC GOODS

We turn now to the second main source of market failure. This occurs when the consumption or production decisions of one agent affect the consumption or production opportunities open to another directly, rather than through the prices which he faces.† The price system is only efficient in allocating resources when prices measure marginal opportunity costs. If a household or entrepreneur contracts to acquire a commodity at the stipulated price, the costs then become his legal responsibility and are debited in his accounts. But even the great classical economists realised that there may well be costs which were not so debited. These costs would be imposed on some other, perhaps all, members of the community. Thus the social costs of an action might deviate considerably from the private costs. Similarly, it may well be that there are social benefits in certain actions and that not all such benefits are fully reflected in the wealth of the person generating them. However, as we shall shortly see, the problem can only arise if there are costs of negotiation between the parties concerned.

Let us start from first principles and consider the ideal output of a good x whose output level affects the welfare of n individuals.

If the output of a good affects n individuals (for good or ill), then its output level is efficient if the amount which the n individuals affected are willing to sacrifice for an extra unit equals the amount that has to be sacrificed.‡

$$\sum_{i=1}^{n} \mathrm{MRS}_{yx}^{i} = \mathrm{MRT}_{yx}$$

Or, to put the matter in terms of benefits and costs, we require that the sum of marginal benefits equals marginal costs. Or, yet again, the sum of marginal *net* benefits must be zero.

The price mechanism can often bring about this desirable state of affairs. For example, if x is the number of sheep and $\mathrm{MRS}^{1}(x)$ is the value of the xth sheep's wool and $\mathrm{MRS}^{2}(x)$ the value of its mutton, the price mechanism will ensure

$$\mathrm{MRS}_{yx}^{1}(x) + \mathrm{MRS}_{yx}^{2}(x) = \mathrm{MRT}_{yx}(x)$$

The problem of externality arises when there is not only jointness but a lack of institutions which ensure that individuals pay for the costs of their actions and are paid for the benefits resulting from their actions. To see this consider the standard example of a factory that makes more smoke the more x it produces. This smoke pollutes the environment and increases the laundry costs of the

---

† In the next chapter we discuss the case where one firm's output decisions affect the prices at which other firms can buy inputs and explain why such "pecuniary" external effects are not a source of inefficiency. Only "technological" external effects cause efficiency problems.

‡ See P. A. Samuelson, "The Pure Theory of Public Expenditure," *Review of Economics and Statistics*, vol. 36, pp. 387–389, November 1954.

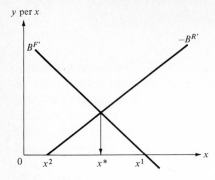

Figure 6-6 Externality.

community. The factory owner sells his output in a competitive market, but his profit varies with the level of output. So his net benefits B^F depend on x. So do the net benefits B^R accruing to the rest of the community. The social optimum requires

$$\max B^F(x) + B^R(x)$$

So if x^* is the efficient output,

$$B^{F'}(x^*) + B^{R'}(x^*) = 0$$

As we have already said, the sum of marginal net benefits must be zero.

This ideal is illustrated in Figure 6-6, where $B^{F'}$ shows the marginal benefits to the factory owner and $-B^{R'}$ the marginal disbenefit to the rest of the world. At the ideal x^*

$$B^{F'}(x^*) = -B^{R'}(x^*) \tag{9}$$

However, since the factory owner decides the level of x, he will, unless induced otherwise, go on producing x till x^1, where

$$B^{F'}(x^1) = 0 \tag{10}$$

Hence it seems that a tax is called for equal to $-B^{R'}(x^*)$, so that the firm will have no incentive to produce beyond the optimal level.

But the analysis should be pursued further. The fact that the factory produces too much smoke will surely have an effect on the rents of residences in the fallout neighbourhood of the factory. The residential rents of dirty areas will be less than those of clean areas, and the difference will, in equilibrium, just reflect the market's valuation of a clean environment.† So, if the houses were owned by the factory owner, there would be no question of the free market producing a misallocation of resources. For the factory-owner-cum-house-owner would be induced to maximise $B^F(x) + B^R(x)$, which would lead to the social optimum.

---

† We suppose that if there are visitors to the area their disbenefit is reflected in the rents in the vicinity.

The factory would produce soot until the marginal advantage in the production process was just equal to the marginal cost of the loss of rents. It would produce the efficient amount of dirt, and the externality would have been "internalised."

Now consider, however, the case where the factory owner does not own the houses. Suppose that the houses are all owned by a single landlord. The fact that the factory owner has the legal right to make as much soot as he wishes does not mean that the landlord must simply sit and suffer. He can negotiate with the factory owner to produce less soot. He will be willing to pay for soot reduction so long as the marginal increase in rents due to soot reduction exceeds this additional payment; and the factory will agree to receive payments to produce less soot if profits fall by less than the receipts from the landlord. Thus output will be reduced until the point where the marginal increase in rents exactly equals the corresponding fall in profits. So there seems no reason why the efficient combination of factory output and cleanliness of the environment should not emerge.

To check this we note that to get output reduced from x^1 to any particular level x the landlord will be willing to pay any amount up to his total gain from this reduction. So in Figure 6-6, the landlord is always willing to pay up to $-B^{R'}$ for a unit reduction in x and the factory owner is always willing to receive anything above $B^{F'}$. Thus so long as

$$-B^{R'} > B^{F'}$$

there is an opportunity for fruitful trade and x will be reduced until $x = x^*$. The exact division of the gains from trade depends on the bargaining skill of the two parties. But output is optimal, and the invisible hand has done it again.

In this argument it has been assumed that the factory owner has the right to produce as much soot as he wishes. Suppose, however, that the legal conditions deny the right to produce soot without compensating the victims, and instead confer the right of residents to clean air. Clearly the relative wealth of the factory owner and landlord will be changed from the case considered in the previous paragraph. But will there be any difference in the allocative outcome? The landlord can now sell the factory owner the privilege of making soot. And agreements will be concluded until the gain in profit due to a small amount of additional soot production is equal to the reduction in landlord's rent generated by that small increment in soot. Any level of output above x^2 hurts the landlord. But so long as

$$-B^{R'} < B^{F'}$$

the factory owner is willing to compensate the landlord for the marginal damage from making soot. So once again we arrive at x^*. The equilibrium bargain is independent of legal liability.

This is the remarkable result put forward by Coase.† Clearly under the

---

† R. H. Coase, "The Problem of Social Cost," *Journal of Law and Economics,* vol. 3, pp. 1–44, October 1960. The primary purpose of Coase's paper was to explore institutional and legal arrangements for enabling private agreements to be concluded.

second arrangement (with the factory liable) the factory owner is worse off, and the rest of the community is better off, than if the factory was not held liable for compensation. This difference in wealth may of course alter the value which the rest of the community places on soot. If this happens, the equilibrium bargain would not be independent of the pattern of legal liability, since the $B^{R'}$ schedule would have shifted. But Coase assumes that redistribution does not affect marginal values. He thus arrives at this remarkable theorem:

> *Coase theorem. If costless negotiation is possible, rights are well-specified, and redistribution does not affect marginal values, then*
> *1. The allocation of resources will be identical, whatever the allocation of legal rights.*
> *2. The allocation will be efficient, so there is no problem of externality.†*
> *Furthermore, if a tax is imposed in such a situation, efficiency will be lost.*

Q6-8 Suppose a tax of $B^{F'}(x^*)$ per unit of x is imposed on F and that F can negotiate with R. What conditions determine the resulting level of x? Is this greater or less than x^*?

The Coase theorem assumes there are no transactions costs. But suppose there are. Then these transactions costs involve the use of real resources, and if they are high enough, they will prevent the arrangement of a bargain which would confer positive benefits in the absence of the transactions costs. That is the argument for state intervention. However, this is obviously only justified if the transactions costs of state activity are lower than the private transactions costs by an amount at least as great as the benefits of the transaction. In cases involving only two private individuals, this is not always likely.

But we have so far assumed that there *are* only two people to come to a bargain—the factory owner and the landlord. However, there may be many landlords and many factory owners. If, for example, there are a large number of house owners, then since, *ex hypothesi*, each cannot negotiate for his own supply of clean air, the contractual arrangements must be concluded through some sort of collective of house owners. Each individual householder may be asked to contribute to the payment to the factory owner to ensure that the soot level is reduced. But each householder will have an incentive to hide his true preferences and contribute little to the collective, in the hope that others will feel sufficiently hurt by the smoke to pay more and ensure that the contract goes through. In other words, each householder has an incentive to be a *free rider* and to disguise his true preferences and enjoy the benefits which are bought by other people's money. (This is once again the *free-rider problem*.) Clearly, under conditions of widespread ownership, the free-rider problem will tend to ensure that there is too much

---

† Proposition 2 holds even if redistribution does affect marginal values. Proposition 1 holds even if there are transactions costs, provided these are independent of the pattern of legal liability.

smoke, too much output, and too low an environmental quality. In the limit we are back to x^1, where $B^{F'}(x) = 0$.

But as always, the *ceteris paribus* must be examined carefully. If it is inefficient for the houses to be owned by many persons, one would surely expect the market arrangements to reflect this fact. The owners would find it advantageous to sell to a single landlord. Since that landlord could negotiate advantageously to increase the value of the properties, he would offer a higher price than that which would obtain if there were many owners. Or the new landlord might be the factory owner himself. Against this, there is the notorious "hold-out" problem. The individual householder realises that, if he waits his time, the landlord will be willing to offer more than the existing market price, and in fact anything up to the capitalised value of the higher, soot-reduced rent. But if many householders hold out for prices this high, it will not be worth the single landlord's going ahead with his plan. This is simply the free-rider problem in a different form. And that again may prevent the optimum arrangement from being reached. There is then a presumption that the state might usefully intervene. It could try to bring about the optimum arrangements either by taxation, as originally suggested, or by regulation. However, one should note the information that the state would need in order to hit on x^* or even to ensure that state intervention increased the social surplus above its unregulated level with $x = x^1$. There are also the administrative costs of state activity that need to be taken into account.

Before leaving the topic, we shall revert to the Coase theorem and ask: Is it really true? It is important to stress the assumption of costless transactions. The implicit notion is that both sides know each other's net-benefit functions and can speedily arrive at some division of the gains from agreeing to an output of x^*. But in fact even when bargains are struck between two people only, there is the possibility of threat and counterthreat, bluff and double-bluff, which might well affect the outcome not merely in terms of the distribution of wealth, but also in the allocation of resources. For example, the factory owner may deliberately make smoke and soot, not as a byproduct of his production process, but in order to extract an even larger payment from the unfortunate landlord. The *threat* to produce bads may have a most profitable payoff, provided that the factory owner is not required to pay for the damage resulting from his production of bads, i.e., he is not liable for the smoke emission. It might be held, however, that the existence of the smoke threat merely adds to the bribe that he can extract from the landlord and will not affect the distribution of resources. But this must be incorrect, since if it is possible to obtain wealth by means of threats, then resources will be diverted into the threat-producing industry; indeed, the factory owner must invest in equipment to produce clouds of black smoke so that the landlord will be aware that the threat is real. Any effective threat requires *some* evidence of its potentiality. And there will be an incentive to invest in knowledge about potential threats, which will again be a waste of resources. These arguments suggest that the nature of the liability law is certainly not a matter of indifference with respect to the allocation of resources.

Nevertheless, Coase's theorem, that with no transaction costs and no legal restrictions on contracts, any misallocation of resources would be put right by bargains in the market, is an important one. Empirically one would expect to observe that those situations where there appear to be unappropriated social costs or benefits would characteristically have high contractual costs. Otherwise, there would be bargains which effectively internalised such externalities.

One of the interesting and much discussed cases of externalities was the "Fable of the Bees." The bee keeper provides pollination services for the surrounding fruit growers and the growers in turn provide nectar for the bees. To many economists this seems to be a clear case of externality. The bee keeper does not collect a price per pollination activity, nor does the bee keeper pay for the nectar extracted from the trees. Such social benefits are not reflected in the price system, or at least so it was thought until Cheung carried out a proper empirical study of the problem.† He discovered that, instead, contractual payments were characteristic of bee keeping and fruit farming. The fruit growers hired hives to provide pollination of those trees which gave little suitable nectar, and the bee keepers paid for the privilege of "grazing" their bees on the superior nectar-producing trees. Furthermore, the values involved in these contractual arrangements were quite consistent with the theoretical prediction of the appropriate rents. Cheung has provided a dramatic and evocative example of the application of Coase's theorem.

Congestion Externalities

With this we conclude our analysis of production externalities in the private sector and turn to some notorious cases of externality in the public or semipublic sector. An important externality arises in congestion from the provision of "free-access" public facilities such as roads, beaches, museums, etc. These congestion externalities arise from the fact that the government does not charge for the scarce services of some facility (e.g., road space) that it provides. Consequently, too many motorists use the road and they get in one another's way, thus driving up the costs of all motorists. The individual will decide on the basis of his own costs whether or not to take a trip, but his own costs do not include the additional congestion cost he imposes on others, and so too many motorists use the road.

In Figure 6-7 we assume that the only cost is time. The average cost per journey rises with the number of journeys. So, when an individual makes an extra journey, he raises the average cost which everyone (including himself) pays. The cost he imposes on *other* people is the externality disbenefit. This external disbenefit is thus the marginal cost to society as a whole minus the average cost (which the traveller pays himself anyway). This is illustrated in Figure 6-7. We assume that the value of time is the same for every traveller.

† S. N. S. Cheung, "The Fable of the Bees: An Economic Investigation," *Journal of Law and Economics*, vol. 16, pp. 11–34, April 1973.

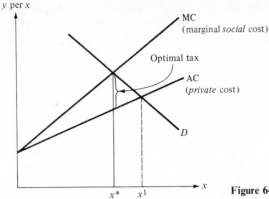

Figure 6-7 Congestion externality.

The marginal social cost (MC) exceeds the average private cost (AC). Without government intervention, the number of journeys is x^1, but the social optimum is at x^*, where

$$\text{Marginal benefit} = \text{marginal cost}$$

To induce private behaviour to bring about this solution, we must make the private cost equal the social cost by imposing a tax equal to MC − AC. (For the exact calculation see Question 6-9 below.)

The same problem may arise with any resource that is freely available. No one owns the halibut in the sea. Fishermen take into account only their own costs in deciding on the level of their fishing activity. But as fish are extracted, the stock is depleted and it becomes increasingly expensive to catch fish. However, an individual fisherman, one among many, will not take into account this depletion cost when deciding how much to fish. Consequently there will be too much fishing, and the halibut stock will be too low—the identical analysis (and diagram) applies.†

Public Goods

Finally, we revert to the case of pure public goods. As we explained on page 177, these are usually defined as goods where, for a given output, additional consumption by one person does not imply reduced consumption by another.‡ This is a satisfactory description of some types of public good (type-1 public goods), where the individual can indeed vary his use of the facility, e.g., television or uncongested parks and museums. But in other cases (type 2), he cannot vary his use—of national defence, clean air, or public health.

---

† The above ignores the intertemporal dimension of the depletable resources problem and assumes the cost curves of Figure 6-7 are constant from period to period.

‡ Impure public goods are those for which MC/AC is low. Thus all goods could be scaled on the private-public–good scale according to the value of MC/AC. The other relevant scale is the "cost of exclusion" (see next page).

Both types of commodity fit neatly into the framework we have already described for handling cases of jointness or externality. Type-2 cases fit the most easily. The individual places a certain value on a certain level of service. And the ideal rule varies the level of service until $\Sigma \, \text{MRS}^i(x) = \text{MRT}(x)$. In type-1 cases, there are two problems to be settled, as we saw in Sec. 6-1. First, we need to charge the optimal price to secure optimum utilisation of any given level of service. This will be zero for a pure public good with zero marginal cost. Next, the right level of service has to be determined. For a small unit addition to the *size* (x) of a park, the ith individual's valuation will consist of the increase in the area under his compensated demand curve for *visits* to that park (say z). And this is the meaning in his case of $\text{MRS}^i(x)$: it is his valuation of the unit change in the size of the park.

For both types of public good there would be no harm in charging $\text{MRS}^i(x)$ to each individual i, if only you could get him to reveal his preferences. But owing to the free-rider problem you cannot get people to reveal their preferences by questionnaire, and charging a price per unit of z will lead to a waste of potential benefit. So "nonrevelation of preference" is the first basic problem in this field.

In addition, in type-2 cases it would be impossible to make access to benefits conditional on payment. So there is a second problem, of "excludability." In type-1 cases it would usually be possible to charge for the right to use the incremental facility, but the direct "cost of exclusion" (scrambler devices, turnstiles, etc.) might be too high.

So we are left with the state paying for pure public goods. To do this efficiently it has to make guesses about individual preferences, just as it must if it wishes to regulate externality.

Q6-9 (i) Suppose that there is a road from A to B. The demand for trips from A to B depends only on the time taken, according to the function $p = 20 - 0.001x$ where x is trips per day and p is the time per trip in hours. The more trips are made in total, the slower they are because one person's extra journey slows down the other drivers. The relation of time taken to trips made is given by $p = 2 + 0.001x$. There are no other costs of travel, and the value of time is \$1 per hour for all trips.

(a) What is the optimal number of trips?

(b) What money tax should be levied on drivers for a trip in order to ensure optimal utilisation? (Hint: The optimal tax equals the optimal price minus the cost the drivers will in any case be facing.)

(ii) The following system of road pricing has been proposed for London: any car travelling in inner London on any particular day must have a licence to do so costing £1. Would such a system be efficient? Discuss the advantages and disadvantages. (Singapore already operates a similar system.)

Q6-10 Two prisoners are locked in separate cells, each accused of the same offence. Each is told that the following sentences await him:

"(A) If the other prisoner confesses, you will get 20 years if you confess and 30 years if you deny guilt."

"(B) If the other prisoner denies guilt, you will get nothing if you confess and 2 years if you deny guilt."

(i) What will each prisoner do, assuming they do not trust each other?

(ii) If a private voice tube linked their two cells, what would they agree on?

(iii) If there were no tube but the prisoners trusted each other, what might they do?

(iv) What conclusion do you draw from the parable of the prisoner's dilemma about the problems of achieving social efficiency in one country, and of achieving international peace?

*Q6-11 Consider the following map:

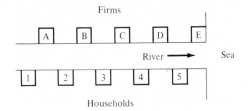

(a) Each firm exudes 12 gallons of detergent (x) per period, which flows downstream.

(b) Each household likes swimming in clean water and is willing to pay $1 for every gallon of detergent less that there is in the water.

(c) Each firm could avoid producing detergent if it put its effluent through a filter costing $25 per period.

(d) Each household could install its own swimming bath (and so provide a swim in clean water) at a cost of $40 per period.

(i) What private arrangements, if any, do you expect to emerge if the firms are not liable?

(ii) What, if anything, do you think the state should do? What more information, if any, is relevant?†

6-4 WELFARE EFFECTS OF NONPRICE ALLOCATION AND PRICE CONTROL

Finally we consider the efficiency implications of allocating private goods by methods other than the price mechanism.‡ This is an important matter since in most economies the free bargaining of the price system has been abrogated in the allocation of some resources and commodities. Examples include imported goods of many kinds (in India) and rented accommodation (in the United Kingdom).

The free bargaining of the price system must be somehow banned by law in order to examine the effects of nonprice allocation systems. (This is easier to implement in law than in practice.) The authorities must then determine how the goods are to be allocated. There are an infinite number of allocation criteria. Perhaps the most common and best known is the queue: first come, first served.

---

† Problem due to M. Polinsky.

‡ A private good is one for which additional consumption by one person means an equivalent reduction in another's consumption of it (all other levels of consumption unchanged).

Queueing

A crucial characteristic of such a rationing system is that the goods are distributed in limited, well-specified bundles. When one gets to the head of the queue one cannot get all the goods one wants. The limited quantity rule is usually "not more than x^0 per customer." Thus the customer has the opportunity of spending a certain time in the queue in order to acquire the right to buy a specific quantity of goods or services.

Suppose, for simplicity, that the money price paid is zero. Then, if there were no queue, the consumer illustrated in Figure 6-8 would want x^1 units. But the

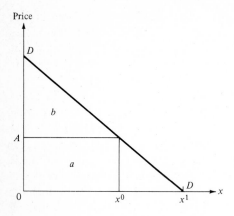

Figure 6-8 Individual demand for x.

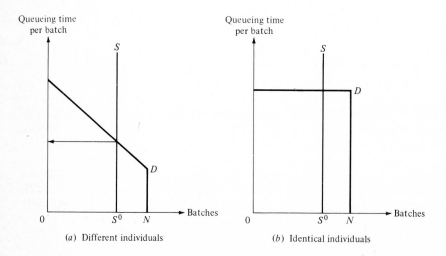

(a) Different individuals

(b) Identical individuals

Figure 6-9 Market demand for batches of x^0 in relation to the queueing time. *Note*: We assume only 1 batch can be bought by each individual. N = total population.

maximum he can get is the ration, x^0. For this quantity he would be willing to pay the areas $a + b$. Thus this measures the number of hours he is willing to spend in the queue times the value of each hour spent queueing. Given the value of his time, we thus know the amount of time he is willing to queue to get x^0.

Arraying these different times for all individuals in the community gives us a market demand curve for batches, each containing x^0 units of the good (see Figure 6-9). In Figure 6-9a we assume consumers vary in the time they are willing to queue. As a result there is a standard downward-sloping demand curve. If the number of available batches is S^0, this determines the time spent in the queue (which is assumed to be the same for all members of the queue). The marginal person as usual gets no rent, but the intramarginal people do.

We can compare the welfare effects of queueing and price rationing directly in the case when all individuals are willing to spend the same time to gain access to a batch (Figure 6-9b). For in this case the equilibrium quantity of queueing time is exactly equal to the time that each individual in the queue is willing to spend in it. So *all consumers surpluses have been dissipated*. It is easy to see how this comes about. The queue ration is an all-or-nothing proposition: either you queue and get x^0, or you do not queue and you get nothing. Thus an individual who would normally pay only area a for a quantity x^0, if it were possible to buy a little more or a little less than x^0 at a fixed price $0A$, ends up instead paying areas $a + b$.† In resource terms, of course, real resources have been expended in the process of allocation, which is not the case in costless exchanges in which money passes between people. In fact the following general theorem holds: given identical demands, all surplus is dissipated by any form of nonprice allocation in which the individual can take action to qualify himself for the ration and the cost of such action is the same for all individuals. Thus allocation on grounds of sex leads to no dissipation of surplus, except in so far as it encourages sex change. But if, to qualify one's children for a certain type of school, one has to live in a particular area, some of the surplus which such schooling might provide is dissipated by the choice of otherwise less preferred locations for residence.

We have so far assumed that the individual is only able to stand in the queue once per period. If instead he could rejoin the queue as many times as he wanted, it would follow that, even if individuals were identical, surpluses would accrue if the number of batches exceeded the number of people. For though the individual gets no surplus on his marginal batch, he gets some on his intra-marginal ones.‡

Q6-12 (i) "A household that would not be willing to buy as much as x^0 on a normal market at any positive price would not be willing to queue for x^0 at a zero money price." True or false?

*(ii) Suppose that in a queueing situation the size of batch was reduced. Would this reduce the loss of surplus? (Assume identical demand curves and identical time values for all individuals.)

† It is worth noting that, if only 1 unit of good would be demanded by each individual under free-market arrangements, there would be no surplus anyway, given identical demands.

‡ For further discussion see Y. Barzel, "A Theory of Rationing by Waiting," *Journal of Law and Economics*, vol. 17, pp. 73–93, April 1974.

*(iii) It is often argued that with single-batch queueing systems the poor (individuals) are more likely to get the good than the rich. Show that, if the income elasticity of demand is higher than the price elasticity of the all-or-nothing demand, this will not be so. Assume that a person's value of time is proportional to his income. (Hint: Try using an individual all-or-nothing demand curve $x = \alpha p^{-\beta} m^{\gamma}$.)

*(iv) If batches are small and rejoining is possible, compare the consumption of the poor
(a) When a given supply is rationed by queue
(b) When the same supply is sold at a market-clearing money price

Administrative Rationing

Another way of allocating a given supply, often used in wartime, is by administrative rationing. The simplest version of this is when an individual is simply allotted a particular quantity of a given good. The allotment may either be equal for all individuals or it may differ according to some administrative assessment of need, as would normally be the case if, say, gasoline were to be rationed. The good may also have a money price, in which case the individual cannot normally be forced to take up his full allotment. For simplicity let us assume the money price is low enough to induce each individual to buy his full quota. Suppose too that, as in Figure 6-10, there is a given supply x^0 to be allocated. Under a freely functioning price mechanism A would get x^{A0} and B would get x^{B0}; the price would be p^0. Now suppose we introduce rationing and allocate $x^{A0} - \lambda$ to A and $x^{B0} + \lambda$ to B; the price is pegged at zero. The welfare changes are now, in terms of areas,

A	$-a + b$
B	$f + e$
Suppliers of x	$-b - f - e - d$
Total	$-a - d$

There would be an efficiency loss under any allocation except one where $\lambda = 0$.

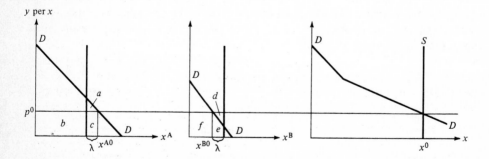

Figure 6-10 Rationing.

However, what would happen if people were able to *sell their ration coupons*? Clearly a market would emerge for coupons. If the money price remained zero, the price of coupons would be p^0 for each 1-unit coupon. Or, more generally, if the money price were p_{money}, we would find

$$p_{coupon} = \text{demand price for } x^0 - p_{money}$$

We are now back to allocation by price, and the welfare cost of rationing has been eliminated. But, equally, what point could there be in such a curious version of rationing? To answer this we need to look at the distribution of income. B gets coupons for $x^{B0} + \lambda$ but sells λ coupons to A in return for λp^0. So the welfare changes as compared with the initial unimpeded price mechanism situation are

A	$+ b$
B	$+ f + e + d$
Suppliers of x	$- b - f - e - d$
Total	$-$

The rationing system has redistributed income, especially towards those who receive a high allocation relative to their demand at free-market prices.

In fact, most rationing schemes have distributional objectives. Rationing is commonly introduced after some sharp economic change in order to prevent the sudden redistribution of income that would otherwise occur. But the problem then is how to replace it with a more efficient system that is also fair.

Price Control

Finally, let us examine the case of price control without rationing. Consider first a maximum price of p^1 for x. This involves two efficiency costs. First, suppose the total supply of x is given at x^0, as in Figure 6-11a. Then the price control has no effect on the supply of x. But it has a profound effect on the allocation of the supply between demanders. Previously the available units only went to buyers who valued them at p^0 or above. But now price has been reduced to p^1, demand has risen to x^1. This exceeds supply. We do not know how suppliers will allocate the available supply between demanders. They may do it on the basis of colour, sex, etc., or they may do it randomly. However the allocation is done, the total value of the available units to consumers will be less than the value under price rationing (in other words, less than the area under the demand curve between $x = 0$ and $x = x^0$).

If we now allow supply to be variable, we get a further efficiency cost, since supply will be altered. This is illustrated in Figure 6-11b. Once again we do not know which demanders will get the available supply. So the shaded triangle is

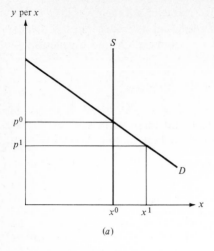
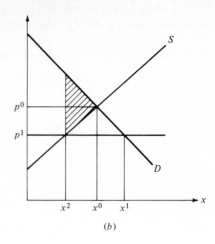

Figure 6-11 A maximum price.

a minimum estimate of the welfare cost of the price control. Exactly analogous principles apply to a minimum price (e.g., a minimum wage).

In every case the group in whose favour a price is controlled are likely to gain from this—when the group is taken as a whole. But the gain will often be uneven, and some members of the group may well lose (tenants who cannot find homes, or workers who cannot find jobs). Thus if governments wish to help particular groups, they should explore other ways of doing so before resorting to price control. Taxes and subsidies do not raise the problem of arbitrary allocation that we have just discussed.

Of course matters would be different if the beneficiaries could negotiate among themselves. For this would ensure the efficient exploitation of given opportunities. But this is exactly the problem we have been studying in this chapter. In large societies there are many fruitful negotiations that simply do not occur because of their high cost. This means that, where there are increasing returns to scale, efficient production will involve the producer in losses—he cannot extract the surplus of his individual customers. Similarly, where there are technological externalities, production will often be inefficient since all effects are not considered when decisions are made. However, policies to deal with these problems must take into account those distortions in the economy which are inevitable (the problem of second best). These constraints include the administrative capacities of the government itself and the nature of politics and bureaucracy.

Q6-13 What assumption has been made about income effects in the analysis in Figure 6-10?

Q6-14 Suppose that the quantity of oil reaching a non-oil-producing country from abroad is suddenly reduced, but the import price remains constant. Compare the efficiency and distributional effects of

(i) Rationing, with sale of coupons illegal, and the maximum retail price controlled at its previous level

(ii) Rationing, with sale of coupons legal and the maximum retail price controlled at its previous level

(iii) No rationing, no price control but an increased tax on oil high enough to keep the net price at which importers sell constant

(iv) No rationing, no price control, no tax increase

What would you do if you were the government?

Q6-15 We have not so far considered the case where all goods are rationed. Suppose there are two goods in given supply and two groups of people with different tastes. A market mechanism is replaced by one where an equal amount of each good is allocated free to each person. Are the following statements true or false?

(i) If both groups had the same money income under the price mechanism, both become worse off.

(ii) Even if both had different incomes, both become worse off.

Q6-16 Now suppose we have a freer system, in which each consumer is given an equal number of "ration points" P^0. To acquire 1 unit of any good an individual must hand over a number of points specified by the government. The goods also have a money price, and the consumer has to satisfy his "money budget constraint" as well as his "points budget constraint." Are the following true?

(i) If both groups have the same income, each will necessarily be better off if points can be bought and sold than if they cannot.

(ii) If both groups have different incomes, each will necessarily be better off if points can be bought and sold than if they cannot.

Q6-17 Suppose the demand curve for x (housing?) is $p = 1 - x$ and the available supply is x^0. The price is controlled below its equilibrium level. Assume that the available supply is rationed out randomly among those who demand it at the going price. Now price control is abolished. Show that

(i) Consumers as a whole lose.

(ii) There is a potential Pareto improvement.

PART
THREE

THE PRODUCT MARKET

COST, SUPPLY, AND COMPETITIVE EQUILIBRIUM

We now revert to positive analysis. In Chapter 5 we saw what determines consumers' demand for a particular product. We now scrutinise the supply side of the market. Our main aim is to see what determines the elasticity of the supply curve, and how this in turn affects the market's stability.

So we start by looking at the individual firm and asking how it will respond to changes in the product price, holding constant the prices of factors and of any other jointly produced goods. The industry supply function is then the sum of the supply functions of all firms that could potentially operate in the industry— subject to various snags. First the industry may face a rising supply price for the factors it employs. At the industry level we therefore want to hold constant the factor supply functions (rather than the factor prices) as we trace out the industry's response to a change in its product price.† It may also happen that the scale of the industry's output affects the production functions of the individual firms. This too needs to be taken into account. When we allow for these influences, we find that the industry's supply price could fall as output expands. This in turn raises important problems for the stability of market equilibrium and for price control. Finally we introduce dynamic elements and look at the problem of periodic fluctuations within a product market. Other important themes we deal with in this chapter are the true nature of cost and the sources of (excess) profits.

---

† In addition, if an industry produces more than one good (e.g., x_1 and x_2), we would normally want to derive the supply of x_1 holding constant the demand function for x_2 rather than its price p_2.

7-1 THE FIRM'S COST AND SUPPLY

One Input

With given inputs a firm can only produce a certain range of outputs. Suppose there is one output (x per period) and one input (L per period). There is then a set of values of (x, L) which is technically feasible. This is called the *production set*, and consists of the shaded area in Figure 7-1. But presumably the firm will want to maximise its output for any given input. This is not necessarily as easy as it sounds, but for the moment we shall assume that this problem of *technical efficiency* has been solved. So we can confine our attention to those feasible points where output has been maximised for given inputs. The equation describing these points is called the *production function*, which here could be written

$$x = x(L)$$

It is clearly the upper boundary of the production set.

We now assume that the firm maximises its profit, subject to the production function and its market opportunities for selling outputs and buying inputs. The profit-maximisation assumption is of course much more sweeping than the corresponding assumption of utility maximisation in consumer theory. However, though one might want to vary it to explain certain specific phenomena, it has proved remarkably successful in explaining and predicting responses to policy changes and other exogenous changes in the economy. Though many other theories exist of the firm's objectives (maximising the utility of managers, etc.), space precludes us from treating them in this book.†

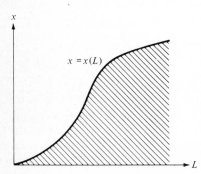

Figure 7-1 Production set and production function.

---

† See for example, O. E. Williamson, *The Economics of Discretionary Behaviour: Managerial Objectives in a Theory of the Firm*, Prentice-Hall, Englewood Cliffs, N.J., 1964. There is also no room for treating the interesting issue of the behaviour of nonprofit organisations and ones whose profit is regulated, see J. P. Newhouse, "Towards a Theory of Nonprofit Institutions: An Economic Model of a Hospital," *American Economic Review*, vol. 60, pp. 64–74, March, 1970, and A. A. Alchian and R. A. Kessel, "Competition, Monopoly, and the Pursuit of Pecuniary Gain," in H. G. Lewis (ed.), *Aspects of Labour Economics*, Princeton University Press for National Bureau of Economic Research, 1962.

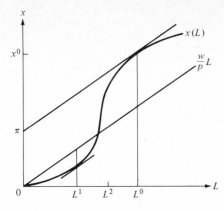

Figure 7-2 Profit maximisation and concavity.

We shall also assume in this chapter that the firm is a price taker in all its markets. It is too small to affect either the price of its output (p) or of its input (w). So the problem is

$$\max \pi = \text{receipts} - \text{costs} = px(L) - wL$$

For a unique local maximum we require

$$\frac{d\pi}{dL} = px_L(L) - w = 0$$

and

$$\frac{d^2\pi}{dL^2} = px_{LL}(L) < 0 \tag{2}$$

In addition, since the firm always has the option of producing nothing, we require

$$\pi \geq 0 \tag{3}$$

A large fraction of the whole theory of production is contained in the implications of this simple exercise. We can begin with the second-order condition (2), which says that at the optimal output the marginal product of labour must be diminishing. In other words the production function must at the optimal output be concave from below (see Figure 7-2).† The reason for this is clear. Suppose we respecify the problem as

$$\max x(L) - \left(\frac{w}{p}\right)L$$

As Figure 7-2 shows, there can be two values of L that satisfy the first-order conditions (L^0 and L^1). But at L^1 profit is minimised. Only where the production function is locally concave is there a local profit maximum. The profit (in units of output) is measured by 0π; the rest of output $[\pi x^0 = (w/p) \cdot 0L^0]$ goes to labour.

---

† For definitions, see Appendix 1. In the language of sets, the production set is locally strictly convex, i.e., if **y** is the vector of inputs and outputs, and if $\mathbf{y}^0$ and $\mathbf{y}^1$ are in the set, then so is the vector $\lambda\mathbf{y}^0 + (1 - \lambda)\mathbf{y}^1$ (and it is not on the boundary).

1. *If there exists a local optimum for a profit-maximising competitive producer, the production function at that point must be concave from below.*

But in addition we have the more important condition (3) that profit be non-negative. This implies that

$$\frac{x(L)}{L} \geq \frac{w}{p}$$

But from the first-order condition (1)

$$\frac{w}{p} = x_L(L)$$

Hence

$$\frac{x(L)}{L} \geq x_L(L)$$

or

$$1 \geq \frac{dx}{dL}\frac{L}{x}$$

This implies nonincreasing returns to scale: the elasticity of output with respect to input must not exceed unity. When returns to scale are increasing and factors are paid their marginal product (in units of output), the product would be "overexhausted" in paying the factors: nothing would be left for profit. This has just been proved in the case of a single input. In the many-input case, if

$$x = f(z_1, \ldots, z_n)$$

and f is homogeneous of degree ρ, then if factors are paid their marginal product,

$$\text{Factor payments} = f_1 z_1 + \cdots + f_n z_n = \rho x$$

(by Euler's theorem, see Appendix 3). But if $\rho > 1$, $\rho x > x$ and the product is overexhausted.

2. *A profit-maximising, price-taking firm will not be found producing where returns to scale are increasing.*

To check on this the reader can ask himself at what value of w/p the firm would employ L^2 in Figure 7-2. Note however that we are *not* saying that there are no ranges of output over which returns to scale are increasing—only that competitive producers do not produce there.

For many purposes it is more useful to think of this proposition in terms of cost, especially in the case of many-input production functions that are not homogeneous.† In our simple case

$$\text{Total cost} = C = wL$$

---

† In this case the measurement of returns to scale depends on the proportions in which the different factors are employed.

$$\text{Average cost} = \frac{C}{x} = \frac{wL}{x}$$

$$\text{Marginal cost} = \frac{dC}{dx} = \frac{dC}{dL}\frac{dL}{dx} = \frac{w}{x_L}$$

Since $x/L \geq x_L$,

$$\text{Marginal cost} \geq \text{average cost}$$

Therefore *average* cost is nondecreasing: if your latest baseball score is at least as good as your average, your average will not fall. In common parlance the word "average" here is often left out and we simply say we have "nondecreasing costs." This is the more general formulation in cost terms of the requirement of nonincreasing returns to scale.

   2′. A profit-maximising, price-taking firm will not be found producing where there are decreasing (average) costs, i.e., where marginal cost is less than average cost.

   We can now focus on the all-important first-order condition (1), which can be written in two interesting ways. One

$$p = \frac{w}{x_L}(L) = \text{marginal cost (MC)}$$

is the *supply function of output*, since for each L there is a corresponding x. The other

$$w = px_L(L) = \text{value of marginal product (VMP)}$$

is the *demand function for the input*. Both relations are homogeneous of degree zero in all prices. From the supply function we find that

$$\frac{\partial L}{\partial p} = -\frac{x_L}{px_{LL}} > 0$$

and from the demand function that

$$\frac{\partial L}{\partial w} = \frac{1}{px_{LL}} < 0$$

Thus the supply of output rises as its price rises, and the demand for an input falls as its price rises. Using this information plus the nonnegative profit condition, we can define the output supply and factor demand curves as follows:

   3. The supply curve is the marginal cost curve over the range where marginal cost is rising and exceeds (or equals) average cost. For lower product prices, supply is zero. The factor demand curve is the value of the marginal product curve, where marginal product is falling and is less than (or equal to) average product. For higher factor prices, demand is zero.

We can now, in Figure 7-3, assemble the whole theory of the single-input firm in one picture. Parts *a* and *b* are total diagrams, and *c* and *d* are the corresponding per-unit diagrams. Part *a* is the production function used in Figure 7-2; up to (L^m, x^m) returns to scale are increasing and costs decreasing. Part *b* is the cost function which, apart from change of units, is the same curve as in part *a*, but with the axes reversed. Part *c* shows the factor demand curve: this is the VMP curve for $L \geq L^m$. Part *d* shows the product supply curve: this is the MC curve for $x \geq x^m$.

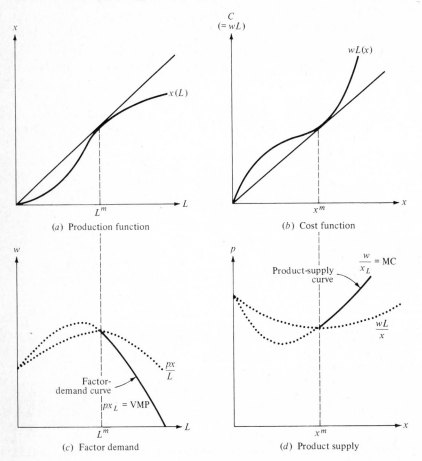

(*a*) Production function   (*b*) Cost function

(*c*) Factor demand   (*d*) Product supply

Figure 7-3 Cost, supply, and factor demand.

Q7-1 Suppose the production function can be written

$$L = x - x^2 + x^3$$

where L is labour per period and x is output per period.

    (i) Derive the firm's supply curve if $w = 1$.
    (ii) How much will it produce per period if $p = 1$? And if $p = \frac{1}{2}$?
    (iii) How much profit is made if $p = 1$?

(iv) What will the firm do if $p = 1$ and a profits tax of 80 percent is imposed on all firms producing the good x?

(v) What will the firm do if $p = 1$ and a levy of \$0.2 per period is made on all firms producing the good x? (You will have noticed that the length of period in this example is rather short, to keep the arithmetic down!)

(vi) For what values of x are returns to scale increasing, decreasing, constant? How does this tie up with your answer to (i)?

(vii) Suppose that $p = \frac{1}{2}$, but the firm is required by law to employ $\frac{1}{3}$ unit of labour at a wage $w = 1$. What output, if any, will it supply?

Fixed and Variable Costs

Now suppose that production requires not only labour but also a factory. Suppose only one size of factory is possible and that, if the factory is in use, the relationship between output x and the labour producing it (L) is given by our original function $x(L)$. What difference does this make to our analysis?

This depends entirely on the contractual arrangement under which the firm uses the factory. Suppose it rents the factory for a rent of \$$f$ per period on a binding lease which has five more years to run. Then the firm's output decision for the next five years will be exactly as we have already described it. No alteration in the level of output (not even closing down altogether) will alter the rent. So, if the rent is inescapable, it is not relevant to the output decision. In fact, it is not a part of the costs of production.

> *No input is a true cost unless it is possible by varying the use of the input to vary the amount paid for it. The only costs that are relevant to economic decisions are those that are escapable.*

But this raises the question: escapable over what time period? In the very long run most inputs involve escapable costs. Even railroad tunnels eventually have to be repaired if the tunnel is to remain in use. Equally, in the short run many inputs, including labour, may be employed on contracts which make the cost inescapable. But, whatever the run, the decision which is made over that run should be influenced only by the costs which can be escaped over that run.

So, reverting to our firm with its factory, what is its long-run supply curve? In the long run the rent for the factory can be escaped by producing nothing. So the firm's problem is

$$\max \pi = px(L) - wL - f$$

subject to $\pi \geq 0$. As before, the firm will only be in equilibrium if marginal cost is at least as high as average cost, but the average cost now includes the rent of the factory. As before, the supply curve is the rising marginal cost curve over the range where $MC \geq AC$. But the minimum price at which production will begin is now higher and so is the minimum scale of output.

Many Inputs, All Variable

So far we have only considered one continuously variable input. Now suppose the production function is $x = x(z_1, z_2)$, when z_1 and z_2 are continuously variable inputs, costing w_1 and w_2. Once again we want to derive the firm's supply function for x. We could of course continue to think of the firm as engaged in a single act of profit maximisation. However it is more convenient to approach the question in two stages and ask

1. What is the minimum cost of producing every possible level of output?
2. Given this and the output price, what is the optimal level of output?

So, for any given output x^0 the first problem is

$$\min C^* = w_1 z_1 + w_2 z_2 + \lambda[x^0 - x(z_1, z_2)]$$

Hence

$$w_1 = \lambda x_1(z_1, z_2)$$
$$w_2 = \lambda x_2(z_1, z_2) \tag{4}$$
$$x^0 = x(z_1, z_2)$$

If the production function is quasi-concave, these three equations will have a unique solution for z_1, z_2, and λ. From (4), $\lambda = w_i/(\partial x/\partial z_i)$, so λ measures marginal cost. This and the demand for the two factors depends on x, w_1, and w_2. So

$$z_1 = f^1(w_1, w_2, x^0)$$
$$z_2 = f^2(w_1, w_2, x^0)$$

these functions being homogeneous of degree 0 in prices.

But once we know z_1 and z_2 we know the cost C, since

$$C = w_1 f^1(w_1, w_2, x^0) + w_2 f^2(w_1, w_2, x^0)$$

Thus, quite generally,

$$C = C(w_1, w_2, x)$$

The supply curve of the firm is then, as before, the rising marginal cost curve over the range where marginal is at least as great as average cost. By staying on its supply curve the firm maximises profits at the prevailing structure of prices.

We can now derive the cost function geometrically in Figure 7-4. In the right-hand panel, we draw a series of isocost lines, showing combinations of z_1 and z_2 which have the same money cost. We then find the cheapest isocost line which can yet purchase sufficient z_1, z_2 to produce x^0. At the relevant tangency point P the rate of substitution between z_2 and z_1 equals the relative price w_1/w_2. This corresponds to the requirement in Equations (4) that

$$\frac{x_1(z_1, z_2)}{x_2(z_1, z_2)} = \frac{w_1}{w_2}$$

As the level of output changes with given factor prices, we trace out an

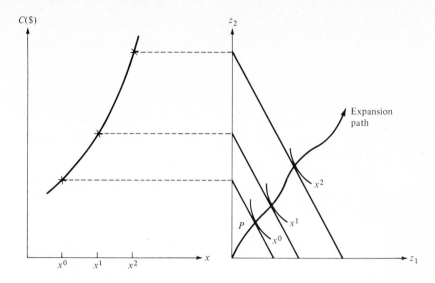

Figure 7-4 Cost-minimisation and cost function: method 1.

"expansion path" in (z_1, z_2) space. (This is straight if the production function is homogeneous.) For each x, the cost (in units of z_2) is measured by the vertical intercept of the isocost line. By suitable choice of scale we can now project the cost (in dollars) into the left-hand panel of the figure and chart it against the corresponding output. As we have drawn it (with $x^1 - x^0 = x^0$ and $x^2 - x^1 = x^0$), the production function has been assumed to exhibit first increasing returns to scale and then decreasing returns: isocost lines corresponding to equal increases in output lie first closer together and then further apart. This generates, in the left-hand panel, first decreasing and then increasing average costs.

The reader will probably have noticed the similarity between the cost function of the firm and the consumer cost function of Chapter 5. In fact they are formally identical except that in one case output is being produced and in the other case utility is. Apart from this, there is no formal difference between the theory of the consumer and of the firm, provided scale (i.e., output or utility) is taken as given. For in each case the decision maker will want to minimise the cost of whatever output or utility is being produced. It follows that *all* the propositions about substitution effects which we derived in Chapter 5 apply equally to the demand for factors of production.† There is no point repeating them in detail here, but this formal similarity between consumer theory and the theory of the firm clearly adds greatly to the simplicity of the subject. In addition, the

---

† They include

$$\left.\frac{\partial z_i}{\partial w_i}\right|_x \le 0 \qquad \left.\frac{\partial z_i}{\partial w_j}\right|_x = \left.\frac{\partial z_j}{\partial w_i}\right|_x \qquad \sum_j \varepsilon^*_{ij} = 0 \qquad \sum_i v_i \varepsilon^*_{ij} = 0$$

Further substitution relationships are introduced in Chapter 9.

second-order condition for cost minimisation is the same as that for utility maximisation: the production function (like the utility function) must be quasi-concave. For profit maximisation, as we have already seen, a stronger condition is required: the production function must be concave.

Short- and Long-Run Costs

If all inputs are variable over the same period, then that is all there is to be said about the theory of profit maximisation. But usually some costs are fixed in the short run while others are variable. In such cases one must be clear about the relation between short-run and long-run cost. Suppose that, in the short run, capital (K) is fixed while labour is variable. Thus, in the short run, total cost (including the irrelevant fixed cost) is

$$\text{Total cost} = \text{fixed cost} + \text{variable cost}$$

This is illustrated in Figure 7-5, which presents exactly the same information as Figure 7-4, but in a different way. The fixed cost is measured by the intercept on the vertical axis: $w_K K^1$ is the fixed cost of the smallest plant. All costs above this level correspond to the variable costs of labour. These short-run curves can be thought of in terms of the curves in Figure 7-3, but with one crucial difference. In Figure 7-3, labour was the only input. Now there is another input, K. This is held *constant* as labour is varied. The effects on output of varying the labour input (capital constant) may be traced by slicing through the production surface parallel to the L axis, holding K constant. This would trace out a

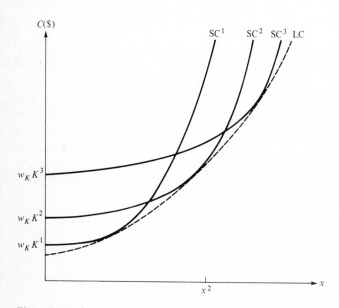

Figure 7-5 Cost-minimisation and the cost function: method 2.

production response analogous to that shown in Figure 7-3a. But the slope of this no longer measures returns to scale: to do this we should need to vary both inputs along the expansion path. The partial response exhibits the so-called law of diminishing *marginal* returns: that eventually the marginal product of any factor falls, as its quantity is increased, other factors held constant. In Figure 7-3c we have allowed the marginal product to fall to zero. It could of course become negative, but no producer paying a positive wage would produce in this "uneconomic region." As before, the short-run variable cost curve is simply the mirror image of the production response.

As K is varied in Figure 7-5, a family of curves is obtained. The curves intersect, with minimum average cost being reached at larger outputs the larger the plant. These curves are called short run because they are only defined once K is established. By contrast, the long-run cost curve shows for each output what the least cost would be if the optimal K for that output could be chosen. It thus consists of the envelope along the underbelly of all the short-run curves.

This diagram brings out the very important relation that exists between short-run and long-run marginal costs. Let us suppose that plants vary in size in a continuous fashion: any size is possible. Then for every output there is a plant size such that its short-run cost curve is tangential to the long-run cost curve at just that output. For example, for x^2 the optimal plant size is K^2. So, in the neighbourhood of x^2 the short-run cost curve for $K = K^2$ is locally *identical* to the long-run cost curve. It follows that if plant size is optimal, short-run marginal cost (SMC) and long-run marginal cost (LMC) are necessarily identical.† However, if the plant size were too large (K^3), there would be so much spare capacity in it that SMC $<$ LMC. Equally, if the plant size were too small (K^1), it would be extremely expensive to produce further units if x^2 were already being produced, and SMC $>$ LMC.

If for a given output, plant size is optimal, SMC = LMC. If plant size is too small, SMC > LMC and vice versa.

The "capacity" of a given plant is sometimes described as that output for which the given plant is optimal, but this does not mean that more than that output cannot be produced from that plant. Figure 7-6 shows the relationship of the various curves, short-run curves being shown only for the plant size K^2.

We can now look at this firm's output decision, bearing in mind the question

---

† C = fixed cost + variable cost $= w_K K + V(x, K)$. If the plant size is optimal,

$$\frac{\partial C}{\partial K} = w_K + V_K = 0$$

So $\qquad$ $\text{LMC} = \dfrac{dC}{dx} = w_K \dfrac{dK}{dx} + V_x + V_K \dfrac{dK}{dx}$

$$= V_x + \frac{dK}{dx}(w_K + V_K) = V_x + \frac{dK}{dx}(0) = V_x = \text{SMC}$$

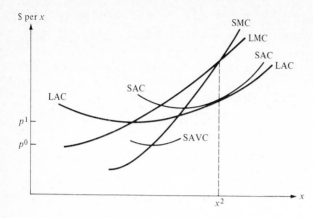

Figure 7-6 Long-run costs per unit, and short-run costs per unit for $K = K^2$. *Note:* L = long; S = short; M = marginal; A = average; V = variable.

of whether costs are escapable. Suppose that it has a given plant size K^2 and the cost of this plant is inescapable in the short period. If the price is high enough to cover the costs it can escape (i.e., above p^0), it will supply the amount indicated by its short-run marginal cost curve. This result is identical to the single-factor case. However, if the cost of plant can be escaped (and over some very long period this must be possible), then the firm will insist on covering its plant costs. It will also of course adjust its plant size. So it will produce nothing at any price below p^1, and at prices above this it will produce along its long-run marginal cost curve.

There are a number of gaps in this approach. Surely, you might say, the businessman, even if he could change plant size, would not simply do so in response to the current price level: he would form some view of the future price level. If there were costs involved in changing plant sizes, he certainly would. In this case the long-run supply curve tells us how much he would supply if the stated price were expected to persist over a long period. But in fact life is lived in a context of change. A more complete theory of supply (and certainly of investment) would require a capital-theoretic approach, including allowance for uncertainty. We take up these questions in Chapters 12 and 13. We should also allow for the obvious fact that costs depend not only on the rate of output per unit time but on the length of the production run. This is discussed in Appendix 6, while Appendix 7 discusses the implications of stochastic variations in product demand and factor supply. But a great deal can be learned from the present simple framework, and for the moment we shall stick to it.

Q7-2 "Long-run marginal costs must be higher than short-run marginal costs since the latter do not include the cost of capital." True or false? (Give reasons.)

Q7-3 Suppose a firm has a production function $x = K^{1/4}L^{1/4}$ and $w_K = w_L = \$1$.

    (i) Derive the long-run supply curve.

    (ii) Suppose K is fixed at 1. Derive the short-run supply curve. Which is more elastic, the short- or long-run supply curve? For what output level is $K = 1$ the optimum plant size?

    (iii) Suppose K is fixed at 2. Compare the short-run cost curve with that in (ii) both for intercept and slope (marginal cost).

(iv) Suppose $p_x = \$4$. A levy of $\$2.5$ per period is levied on all firms producing any x. What will the firm's output be

    (a) In the long-run?

    (b) If it has a fixed $K = 1$ whose cost cannot be escaped?

Q7-4 Quote from the London *Times*: "Some £550 m has been spent on Concorde to-date, £300 m of it by taxpayers in Britain. If there was a point at which a decision to cancel should have been made, it is, with sums like these already committed, long past." Comment.

Q7-5 (A question on joint products.) Suppose a firm produces two outputs (x_1, x_2) jointly, subject to the production relation

$$L = f(x_1, x_2)$$

The firm faces given product and factor prices.

    (i) Find the conditions for maximising revenue, subject to given cost L^0.

    (ii) Find the conditions for maximising profit.

The Nature of the Firm

Before we can proceed to the industry's supply function, we have to deal with one obvious puzzle: why do firms exist? Imagine that each of us owns a certain quantity of factors: property, labour services, and so on. We can hire out these factors, or retain them for our own use. There is no inherent reason in a frictionless world why the marginal productivity of these factors should vary according to whether they are hired out or kept for our own use. Hence there is apparently no way of explaining why some people do keep their own factors and hire other people's as well, while the rest are content to hire out their services.

    What we have overlooked, of course, is the importance of transactions costs. If I were a self-employed steel worker, I could make a contract with the owner of a steel mill to pull such and such a lever at 10 A.M., 12 A.M., and so on and another contract to open such a valve at 11 A.M., 1 P.M., and so on. But this would be very clumsy. The contracts might have to be rewritten every day and would involve heavy costs of transactions. Instead I offer myself to the steel-mill owner as an employee on a fairly general contract and the owner then uses me in what he regards as the most productive way at each moment. My work can be better organised by the internal administrative process of the firm than by the detailed operation of the price system.† Hence the chief rationale of the firm is its organisational role. Moreover, if firms experience diseconomies of scale, it must be because of the difficulty of maintaining efficiency in large organisations. It cannot be due to the laws of physics, since, if for physical reasons output cannot be doubled by doubling the size of a plant, it must be physically possible to double it by building a second plant identical to the first.

    Thus the firm exists to overcome transactions costs.‡ But why are some firms

---

† It is true that firms often operate their own internal price system as between different branches in order to promote efficiency. Why then are the branches under common management? It is largely to overcome uncertainties of supply and demand, and to take advantage of economies of scale in financing.

‡ For a full development of this argument, see R. Coase, "The Nature of the Firm," *Economica*, vol. 4, pp. 386–405, 1937, reprinted in G. J. Stigler and K. E. Boulding (eds.), *Readings in Price Theory*, Irwin, Homewood, Ill., 1952.

successful and others not? In any industry we only observe a certain number of firms operating, and yet there must be many more which, in more favourable circumstances, would have also operated. Moreover, even among those operating, some make more profit than others. We should normally explain this by saying that some firms are more efficient than others. With given inputs they can produce more output: they have better production functions. But why are they more efficient? We cannot say, "They have better managers," for managers can be hired, and better managers are better inputs than worse managers. We might say, "They have a better tradition of organisation and this cannot be automatically introduced into other firms." This is more plausible, but it introduces historical time into our theory, whereas we want our theory to reflect tendencies to long-run equilibrium. So for convenience we resort to a *deus ex machina*, a fudge which does only a little more than giving a name to our ignorance. We have so far assumed that all factors are marketable. However, we now specify *entrepreneurial capacity*, E, as a quality possessed by all of us that is *not* marketable and for which contracts cannot be drawn up. Each person possesses entrepreneurship which he may or may not use. It is a personal attribute and cannot be alienated from a person. So in the x industry each person i has a potential production function which might be written

$$x^i = x(K^i, L^i, E^i) = x^i(K^i, L^i)$$

and similarly in other industries.

Here E^i is a variable measuring the particular capacity of individual i in the x industry. We are assuming he cannot operate as an entrepreneur in more than one industry, and he may not choose to operate as an entrepreneur in any industry. If I do not use my entrepreneurial capacities, I hire out my factor services to someone who is prepared to use his, and who will therefore hire my factor services.

There is one crucial difference between a factor of production and an entrepreneur. Factors are hired on a contractual basis, whereas an entrepreneur receives a residual income, i.e., is paid on a noncontractual basis. The entrepreneur's net reward is the difference between the amount he obtains when organising a firm's activities and the amount he could receive by hiring out his services to some other entrepreneur. A firm comes into existence if this net reward exceeds zero. This net reward can be regarded as the return to a person's "entrepreneurial capacity." When he works as an entrepreneur, his total income is thus composed of two parts: the income he pays himself for hiring himself to himself *plus* the return to his entrepreneurial capacity. Suppose we define pure profit as the difference between a firm's income and the cost of the factors of production it uses. Then, as we shall shortly see, in a world of certainty with perfect competition, pure profit *is* the rent to entrepreneurial capacity (i.e., to whatever makes one firm's production function different from another's).

This approach is well designed to cover some real-world cases, such as small businesses, and less well designed to cover others, like joint-stock companies. However, for the present it is sufficient to say that there are available in each industry an array of different production functions, one for each potential firm. This gives us a sufficient basis for examining the supply curve of the industry. As we have mentioned already, one of our major questions will be: What determines the elasticity of supply?

7-2 INDUSTRY SUPPLY

No External Effects

Each potential firm has its own supply curve for given technology and factor prices (and, where relevant, prices of other joint products). So for the ith firm

$$x^i = x^i(p, w_K, w_L)$$

Figure 7-7 draws the supply curve of firms A and B, A being the more efficient since it produces each output at a lower average cost. The industry supply is simply the sum of the supplies of all potential firms. The drawing is to scale, and you should make sure you understand how it is constructed (by *horizontal* summation of the marginal cost curves). The industry supply function is

$$x = \sum_i x^i(p, w_K, w_L)$$

For competitive supply there must of course be many firms, but we shall not complicate the drawing to allow for this.

We can now introduce demand and determine the price and quantity of output. If demand is given by D^0, the price is p^0. Output is x^{A0} and is produced by firm A only. If firm B were to produce anything at that price, it would make

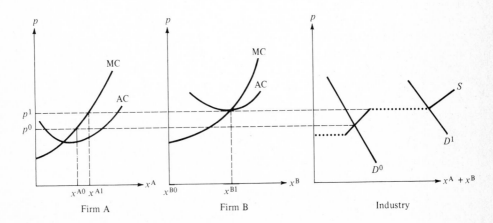

Figure 7-7 Industry supply with different efficiencies.

a loss. However firm A makes a profit of x^{A0} *times* $[p^0 - AC(x^{A0})]$, where AC is average cost. Alternatively, the profit could be measured as $x^{A0} \cdot p^0$ minus the area under the marginal cost curve (assuming there are no fixed costs that have to be incurred before any output is produced). This residual income is a rent since the entrepreneur of firm A would be willing to produce x^{A0} for its average cost.† (A rent is any payment above that just needed to induce an economic agent to do what he does.)

If demand now rises to D^1, price rises to p^1 and firm B finds it just worthwhile to produce x^{B1}. At the same time firm A expands his output to x^{A1}, so industry output is

$$x^1 = x^{A1} + x^{B1}$$

The price mechanism has done its job and called forth greater output in response to greater demand.

If technology and factor prices are independent of industry output, the industry supply curve is the horizontal sum of the supply curves of all potential firms. If firms differ in efficiency, it slopes upward, being less elastic the greater the differences in efficiency.

We can now examine the special case where all potential firms are equally efficient and there is no relevant limit to the number of *potential* firms. This is the assumption we implicitly made in Part I of the book. It is illustrated in Figure 7-8. The left-hand panel shows the supply curve of the "representative firm." The right-hand panel shows the industry. Suppose first that there are 20 firms

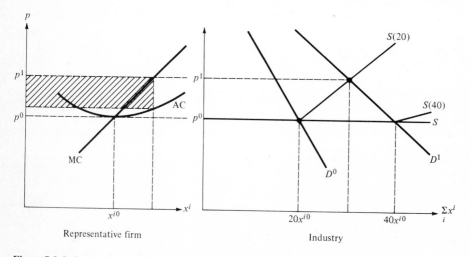

Figure 7-8 Industry supply with identical efficiencies.

† We are assuming that the entrepreneur's cost curves include the market price he could get for hiring out any factors of his own that he uses.

operating. $S(20)$ indicates the aggregate supply curve given this number of firms. If demand is given by D^0, price is p^0 and the existing firms make no profit. So there is no incentive for any of the other potential firms to enter the industry. But suppose demand rises to D^1. With the existing number of firms, price rises to p^1 and output accordingly. Each firm now makes profits indicated by the shaded area. But since each potential firm is as efficient as existing producers, new firms will enter until all profit is eroded and price is back to minimum average cost.† In Figure 7-8 it in fact requires the entry of 20 more firms to do this. Thus at any price above p^0, industry output will in the long run be infinite; and at any price below, it will be zero. The industry supply curve is infinitely elastic. Do not be confused by the fact that for a given number of firms this is not so. For we are concerned with predicting the response of output to a change in price, and this involves the output from all *potential* firms.

In this situation price is determined solely on the supply side, and demand then determines the quantity. So the number of firms is determinate. But all potential firms are identical and are now indifferent between producing x^{i0} and producing nothing. So which of the potential firms will actually be in operation is indeterminate.

Finally note that each firm is producing at the bottom of its minimum average cost curve, where returns to scale are locally constant. This is the crude justification for the constant returns assumption in Part I of this book. However in Part I we did not find (as now) that constant returns to scale imply a constant price of x (in terms of y) whatever the quantity of x. So we seem to have a contradiction. But, no. For in Part I, as x expanded, factor prices changed. But in this chapter we have so far assumed that factor prices are constant. We are now about to relax this assumption.

Q7-6 A competitive industry faces a demand

$$x = 800 - 8p$$

Each firm faces identical cost conditions

$$C^i = 200 + 10\, x^i + 2x^{i^2}$$

where x^i is the output of the firm and C^i its cost. There is free entry and an unlimited number of potential entrants. What is the equilibrium output and price?

Q7-7 The price of a product in a perfectly competitive industry will equal
    (i) The marginal cost of all firms in the industry
    (ii) The average cost of the marginal firm
    (iii) Both
    (iv) Neither

Q7-8 The total equilibrium output of a competitive industry is x^0. A quota system is now introduced. Each of the n firms currently producing in the industry is given a quota of x^0/n coupons, each

---

† In Figure 7-7 of course the rise in demand from D^0 to D^1 would have produced an immediate rise in price to above p^1 until firm B entered. But with differing efficiencies the *final* price p^1 is above p^0.

coupon entitling it to sell 1 unit. Assuming there is no collusion between the firms, what happens to total output of the commodity

(i) If coupons are not transferable.

(ii) If the coupons are transferable and a market develops for coupons (what will the coupon price be?). (Assume no one firm is allowed to buy enough coupons to achieve monopoly power.)

Q7-9 Suppose there are a number of oil wells of varying quality (i.e., with some it is cheaper to produce oil than with others). Assume the oil industry is perfectly competitive and all firms are identical except for the quality of the field that they use.

(i) What determines the rental price of different fields?

(ii) Could any field have a zero rental price?

(iii) If there is an increase in demand for oil, what will happen to the number of fields used and the rental price of fields?

Q7-10 (i) "A firm's output decision is not normally affected by a lump-sum tax on each producer in an industry, so equilibrium industry output cannot be affected by such a tax." True or false?

(ii) Suppose that the government imposes a binding maximum price on a good produced by competitive industry. A penalty of f is imposed on every producer for each unit sold above that price, and his perceived probability of being caught is (small) α. How is the black market price determined? Is it above or below the equilibrium price?

Q7-11 "Since the marginal cost of filling an empty aeroplane seat is virtually zero, competitive behaviour drives the price levels down to zero and explains the widespread bankruptcy in the industry." True or false?

Q7-12 Wool (x) and mutton (y) are jointly produced with

$$\max (x, y) = L$$

The demand curves are

$$p_x = 1 - x$$
$$p_y = 2 - y$$

If the price of labour is $1, what is the supply curve of x?

External Effects of Scale

Changes in the size of an industry can affect firms in it in two ways.

1 Pecuniary effects Factor prices may vary as industry output expands. The wages of computer programmers may rise, the more computing there is (an external diseconomy of scale); this could happen if people who hate programming need to be attracted in. Or wages may possibly fall, the more computing there is (an external economy); this could happen if extra supply reduces the average cost of computer training, due to internal economies of scale in training.

2 Technical effects The output that can be produced with given inputs may vary as industry output expands. As the amount of lorry traffic grows, speeds may fall, raising road hauliers' costs (a technical diseconomy). Or as coal output rises, the water table may fall, reducing pumping costs in each separate mine (a technical

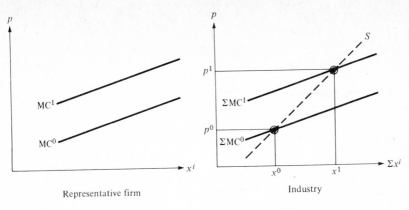

Figure 7-9 Industry supply with external diseconomies of scale.

economy).† All these effects of scale are external in the sense that a change in scale by one firm affects the costs of other firms. If present, these effects must clearly be taken into account in predicting how industry supply will vary with price. For, as we have said, we want our supply curve to be defined holding constant

1. Technology (i.e., the production functions, where industry scale now enters as a variable)
2. Input supply conditions (where factor prices now vary with quantity supplied), and, where relevant,
3. The demand conditions for jointly produced goods

We can begin by considering external pecuniary diseconomies. For simplicity we shall assume that there is a limited number (n) of potential firms all having the same production functions. The representative firm is shown in the left-hand panel of Figure 7-9 and the industry in the right-hand panel (the horizontal scale being $1/n$th of that for the firm). When industry output is x^0, factor prices are such that the marginal cost curve of each firm is MC^0. So ΣMC^0 is a quasi-supply curve—"quasi" in the sense that it only shows the supply response that will prevail at the factor prices associated with x^0. It follows that p^0 must be the price at which x^0 is supplied (it is the MC of x^0 when x^0 is being produced). But if industry output is increased to x^1, factor prices rise, and the firm's marginal cost curve rises to the line marked MC^1. It follows that p^1 must be the price at which x^1 is supplied. Thus the two circled points trace out the industry supply function. Now let us put it to work. Suppose we start with price p^0: x^0 is

† There is another very important external economy of scale. If the market grows, more specialisation (division of labour between firms) becomes possible. If there are increasing returns to specialised activities this will reduce the costs of final output. This may constitute some case for subsidisation.

supplied, each firm producing x^0/n. Now the price rises to p^1. Each firm tries to produce the amount indicated by its MC^0 curve—an amount which is much bigger than x^1/n. But, as all the firms try to expand simultaneously, they find their factor prices rising and so eventually they expand only to x^1/n each—a good deal less than their planned expansion.

The key point is that with external *diseconomies* of scale the supply curve is *less* elastic than the sum of the marginal cost curves for given factor prices. This explains the rising supply curve we found in Part I of the book: as x expands the rise in the y price of the factor in which x is intensive outweighs in importance the fall in the y price of the factor in which y is intensive.

The analysis in Figure 7-9 could equally well apply when the rise in marginal cost curves is due to technical rather than pecuniary diseconomies. So we can turn now to the case of external *economies*. Here the marginal cost curves drop when output expands. So the supply curve is less steep than the sum of the marginal cost curves. It is clearly possible, but not necessary, that it slopes downwards in a forward-falling fashion, and that is how we have drawn it in Figure 7-10.

Before discussing the stability of market equilibrium with a falling supply curve, we must refer to the welfare problems raised by external effects of scale. The problem of technical effects is clear: if they are favourable (economies), the industry should be subsidised; and if unfavourable, taxed. The problem of pecuniary effects is different. Any action I take affects the prices faced by other people and by myself. But so long as the economy is undistorted and the price change is very small, its net effect on the rest of the world is zero. Only transfers occur, and the gainers' gains equal the losers' losses. Thus, so long as my decision moves me to a position that is better for me, it is a potential Pareto improvement. For this reason there is no welfare problem with pecuniary externalities. This is obvious in the case of diseconomies of scale. However if an increase in output *reduces* the price of an input, this must be because of internal economies of scale (in the production function) elsewhere in the economy, e.g.,

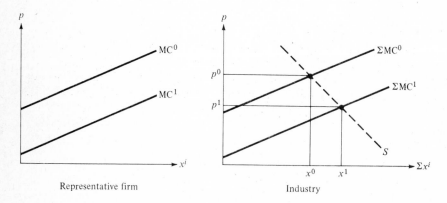

Figure 7-10 Industry supply: a case of external economies of scale.

in the input-producing industry. But these economies should be exploited (if at all) by subsidising the input. So the general principle holds that only externalities that are technical should be considered for government intervention.

Q7-13 (i) "If there are diseconomies of industry scale, there is no reason why the industry supply curve should not bend backwards." True or false? (Give reasons.)

(ii) "If there are diseconomies of industry scale, there is no reason why one particular firm's output should not fall when price rises." True or false? (Give reasons.)

Q7-14 To reduce the price of potatoes, the government imposes a binding maximum price for tractors. Will the policy lower the potato price, raise it, or leave it unchanged?

7-3 STABILITY OF MARKET EQUILIBRIUM

We now turn to the conditions for a stable market equilibrium, especially when the supply curve is downward-sloping. This point has given rise to unnecessary confusion due to a failure to think clearly about what the supply curve means.

The Supply Curve and "Changes in Supply"

It is best viewed as a line in price-quantity space that separates those points that are attainable from those that are not. By an attainable point we mean one at which the supplier would be willing to operate if the alternative were supplying less at the same price. Let us now apply this logic to the three possible types of curve illustrated in Figure 7-11.

1 The forward-rising supply curve This case is simple. All points left and above the curve are attainable. Thus the curve tells us both (i) the *maximum quantity* that will be supplied at each price and (ii) the *minimum price* at which each quantity will be supplied.

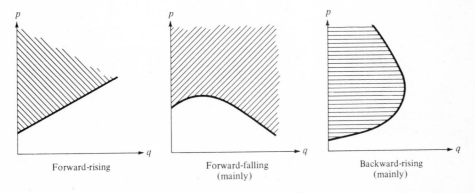

Forward-rising

Forward-falling
(mainly)

Backward-rising
(mainly)

Figure 7-11 Three types of supply curve (attainable areas shaded).

2 The forward-falling supply curve This is not the case with the forward-falling supply curve produced by external economies of scale. Here, once the curve has started falling, there are attainable points to the right of the curve. The curve therefore shows the *minimum price* at which each quantity will be sold, but not the maximum quantity for each price.

3 The backward-rising supply curve The forward-falling supply curve is not the only supply curve that may be negatively sloped. For example it is often said that the supply of labour is backward-rising: the higher the wage, the less work is done.† This curve therefore shows the *maximum quantity* supplied at each price, but not the minimum price for each quantity.

The distinction between 2 and 3 is crucial when identifying an increase (or decrease) in supply. Naturally an increase must mean an increase in the attainable area. For a backward-rising curve it therefore means a rightward shift—a greater quantity is supplied for the same price. But for a forward-falling curve an increase in supply means a downward shift of the curve— the minimum price for a given quantity is lowered.

Q7-15 (i) Suppose the demand curve is

$$p = 1 - x$$

and there is a forward-falling supply curve

$$p = \tfrac{3}{4} - \tfrac{1}{2}x$$

How will an increase in supply affect the quantity supplied?
(ii) Suppose the demand curve is again

$$p = 1 - x$$

and there is a backward-rising supply curve

$$p = \tfrac{3}{2} - 2x$$

How will an increase in supply affect the quantity supplied?

Stability of Equilibrium

The distinction between the two types of negatively sloped supply curves is equally crucial in relation to market equilibrium. As we said in Chapter 2, an equilibrium is stable if any disturbance from it sets in motion forces tending to eliminate the disturbance. In thinking about this we shall assume that prices adjust continuously upwards if excess demand is positive, and downwards if it is negative. A plausible formulation might be to make the speed of adjustment proportional to the degree of excess demand:

$$\frac{dp}{dt} = k \cdot [D(p) - S(p)]$$

---

† The supply curve of a product would be most unlikely to bend back.

The question now is: What conditions must the slopes of the demand and supply curves satisfy for an equilibrium to be stable in this sense? We can begin by stating our conclusion, on the assumption that the demand curve slopes down.

Conditions for a stable equilibrium.
1. *If the supply curve is forward-rising, no further conditions are required.*
2. *If the supply curve is backward-rising, it must be (absolutely) steeper than the demand curve.*
3. *If the supply curve is forward-falling, it must be (absolutely) flatter than the demand curve.*

A moment's thought will confirm that these conditions are highly likely to be satisfied—a backward-rising curve can be thought of as a steeply rising curve that has been "bent back" a bit, and a forward-falling curve is a barely rising curve that has been "bent down" a bit.

To see the rationale for our conditions we can begin with condition 2 (the rationale is essentially the same for condition 1). As Figure 7-12 shows, equilibrium is at (p^0, x^0). Suppose there is a price disturbance and price falls to p^1. This will set up excess demand which will tend to raise the price, thus offsetting the initial disturbance. Or suppose there is a quantity disturbance and quantity rises to x^1. A market clearing price will now be set at p^1 (the demand price). Once the price is established, suppliers will reduce the quantity they supply, again offsetting the disturbance.

The position is more complicated for condition 3, relating to our external-economies forward-falling curve (see Figure 7-13). Suppose that starting from equilibrium at (p^0, x^0) we have a price disturbance and price falls to p^1. A casual look at the supply and demand curves suggests this would produce excess supply, leading to further destabilising downward pressure on prices. But far from it. For producers will tend to react along their quasi-supply curves ($\Sigma\ MC^0$), reducing output. Thus excess demand will result, tending to raise the price towards

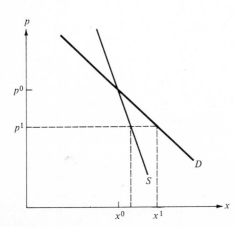

Figure 7-12 Stable equilibrium for a backward-rising supply curve.

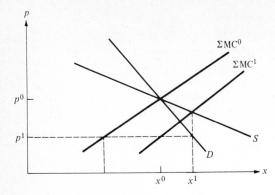

Figure 7-13 Stable equilibrium for a forward-falling supply curve.

its original level. Equally, suppose a quantity disturbance to say, x^1. This will reduce price to the demand price for x^1: i.e., p^1. The Σ MC curve will move down to that corresponding to the output level x^1. So if price is p^1, producers will start reducing output, and the disturbance will be offset. To check your understanding of this analysis examine what would happen after a quantity disturbance, if the supply curve were steeper than the demand curve.

The properties of the forward-falling supply curve are of more than academic interest. For example, suppose the government tried to hold down the price to below its equilibrium level (see Figure 7-14). Then, if output were initially x^0, it would tend to contract along $\Sigma \, MC^0$. But as industry output fell, each firm's marginal cost curve would rise. So Σ MC would rise, leading to further falls in the quantity supplied at $p = p^{max}$. Eventually output would fall to zero. The reason for this is simple. The area which is feasible from the point of view of supply is that above S (try shading it in). The area that is feasible from the point of view of demand is that below D (try shading it in). The intersection of these two areas is the triangle a. There is no point in this area that satisfies the government's edict that $p \leq p^{max}$.

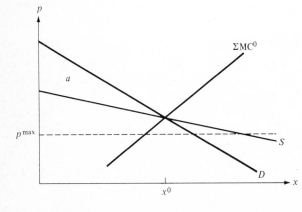

Figure 7-14 Price control with a forward-falling supply curve.

Q7-16 Suppose (as in Question 7-6) that demand is

$$x = 800 - 8p$$

but that each firm has a minimum average cost of \$$(50 - 0.025x)$, where x is industry output. There is free entry and an unlimited number of potential entrants. What are the consequences if the government imposes

(i) A maximum price of \$40?
(ii) A maximum price of \$30?
(iii) A minimum price of \$40?

Q7-17 "Since butter and oleo margarine are substitutes in consumption, a binding quota on butter production will reduce the market price of oleo margarine." True or false? (Give reasons.)

Lagged Adjustment and the Hog Cycle

In our previous analysis of stability we assumed that all adjustment is continuous. But many markets, especially for products with an annual crop cycle, operate period by period. In such cases we have to replace our continuous adjustment formula by a discrete one:

$$p_t - p_{t-1} = k \cdot [D(p_{t-1}) - S(p_{t-1})]$$

If k were very large, there would in theory be a danger, after a price disturbance, of prices oscillating with ever-increasing amplitude around the equilibrium. This could happen even if the stability condition given above were satisfied. However this danger seems relatively implausible.

A much more practical and well-documented problem arises where demand and supply respond to prices in different periods. Suppose for example that the demand for hogs depends on the current price:

$$x_t^D = a_0 - a_1 p_t$$

But the supply depends on the price in the previous period, since it was then that the breeding decisions were made which determine present supply:

$$x_t^S = b_0 + b_1 p_{t-1}$$

Each year's supply is sold, so that

$$x_t^S = x_t^D$$

This is a recursive model. Last year's price determines this year's quantity (the supply relation). This quantity in turn determines this year's price (via the demand relation and assuming market clearance). This price in turn determines next year's supply and so on. The process is illustrated in Figure 7-15a. The equilibrium price and quantity are (p_e, x_e). But suppose that one year there is swine fever and output falls to x_0. This determines p_0 (via the demand relation). This determines x_1, which determines p_1, which determines x_2, and so on. The cycle is sometimes called a *cobweb cycle* because of the pattern of the diagram. There are two crucial points.

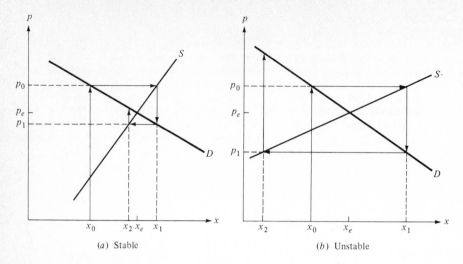

Figure 7-15 The hog cycle.

1. Each period x oscillates from one side of its equilibrium value to the other side, as happened with world beef supplies in the early 1970s. p oscillates likewise. This happens with any cobweb cycle.
2. As we have drawn the curves, output tends to return towards its equilibrium value; x_2 is nearer x_e than x_0 was. However this depends on the way the curves are drawn. Figure 7-15b gives an example where the oscillations become wider each period.

The reader may like to spend a minute trying to work out what determines whether a cycle is converging (i.e., equilibrium is stable) or whether it is diverging (i.e., equilibrium is unstable). Or he can read on.

One's intuition suggests that the more elastic the supply response, the less stable the situation: if suppliers react violently to every price change, a market is unlikely to settle down. Similarly the less elastic the demand, the more any change in supply will change prices. In fact it turns out that so long as supply is more elastic than demand, equilibrium is unstable, and vice versa.

With lagged supply adjustment and instantaneous demand adjustment, equilibrium is unstable if the elasticity of supply exceeds the (absolute) elasticity of demand.

To prove this we revert to our linear demand and supply equations plus the condition $x_t^D = x_t^S$. These tell us that

$$a_0 - a_1 p_t = b_0 + b_1 p_{t-1} \tag{5}$$

Using this, we first evaluate the equilibrium price p_e, and then ask whether, starting from some arbitrary price p_0 that is different from p_e, we get a time path of prices that ultimately leads back to p_e.

If we are in equilibrium, $p_t = p_{t-1} = p_e$.

Hence
$$a_0 - a_1 p_e = b_0 + b_1 p_e$$

giving
$$p_e = \frac{a_0 - b_0}{a_1 + b_1}$$

Now what is the time path of prices, starting at $p = p_0$? To answer this, we take the first-order linear difference equation (5) and find its "solution." This indicates the price in period t as a function of the price in period 0.† The solution is

$$p_t = \frac{a_0 - b_0}{a_1 + b_1} + \left(-\frac{b_1}{a_1}\right)^t \left(p_0 - \frac{a_0 - b_0}{a_1 + b_1}\right)$$

$$= p_e + \left(-\frac{b_1}{a_1}\right)^t (p_0 - p_e)$$

Suppose that, as in our diagram, b_1 is positive (the supply curve slopes up), a_1 is positive (the demand curve slopes down), and $p_0 > p_e$. Then the evolution of this system goes as follows. In the first period

$$p_0 = p_e + \left(-\frac{b_1}{a_1}\right)^0 (p_0 - p_e) = p_e + p_0 - p_e = p_0$$

In the next period

$$p_1 = p_e - \left(\frac{b_1}{a_1}\right)(p_0 - p_e)$$

This is less than p_e, whereas in the previous period we had a price higher than p_e. Thereafter this oscillation proceeds period by period. But will the price converge on p_e? Only if $(-b_1/a_1)^t$ tends to zero as t tends to infinity: in other words, only if the elasticity of supply is less than of demand. Fortunately, and somewhat surprisingly, there are no recorded cases of markets subject to ever-increasing oscillations.

Q7-18 The proportion of first-year students opting for engineering courses shows a clear 8-year cycle (from peak to peak). How would you explain this? Why 8 years?

Q7-19 "The price of beef can be reduced as follows. Initially it is pegged below its equilibrium level. This encourages farmers to produce other types of meat, which so reduces their prices as to knock the bottom out of the controlled beef market." True or false?

Q7-20 (i) Suppose the government wants to guarantee a certain net income (profit) to wheat farmers. It proposes to do this by offering them a $1 billion subsidy on each unit of wheat produced. However a senator points out that the same net income could be guaranteed if the government bought up enough wheat in the market to raise the price sufficiently high. Using the following information, work out which policy would cost the government most, assuming the wheat the government bought up was not resold but destroyed at zero cost.

† On difference equations see, for example, K. Wallis, *Introductory Econometrics*, Gray-Mills, London, 1973, pp. 24–26. For a more detailed treatment see R. G. D. Allen, *Mathematical Economics*, 2d ed., Macmillan, New York, 1963, chap. 6.

Private demand is as follows, where p is in \$ billions per unit,

$$p^D = 4 - x$$

The supply curve is

$$p^S = 1 + x$$

where x is units of output and p the price per unit.

(ii) What is the net income that is being guaranteed by the subsidy of \$1 billion per unit, assuming there are no external effects of scale nor fixed costs involved before any output can be produced. If there were external diseconomies of scale, would the preceding calculation over- or underestimate net income?

EIGHT

IMPERFECT COMPETITION

We now take a step in the direction of realism. Except in markets for financial assets or for "commodities" (like tin), there are very few sellers who do not have some latitude in the prices they can charge. Most sellers can raise their prices without losing all their customers; equally, if they reduced their prices, most could not sell an unlimited output. So the model of perfect competition is only an approximation to reality.

There are at least three other possible situations. The first is the classic case of monopoly. The seller believes that he faces a given downward-sloping demand curve, comprising the demands of many buyers—far too many for them to be able to negotiate with him collectively. The price is then set unilaterally by the seller.

A second situation is where prices are set by bargaining. This may be bargaining between a single seller and a single buyer. Or it may be bargaining between different sellers who know that, if they combine, they will have the same market power as if they merged to create a single monopoly. However, any sellers' combination will always be subject to centrifugal forces, since, to keep up price, output must be restricted more severely than is in the interest of a single seller acting on his own.

Hence we often observe markets in which there is neither one seller nor a seller's collective, but rather a small number of firms engaged in economic warfare with each other. Any one of these firms does not face a predictable demand curve, since if it changes its price, the demand for its product will depend on how its rivals change their prices. The essence of the game is to guess how your rival will react to any move of your own and to conceal from him how you will react to any move of his. There is thus even more scope for "strategic behaviour" than when you are *bargaining* with your rival.

In this chapter we consider these three cases in turn and then see what conclusions can be drawn for antitrust (or antimonopoly) policy. For most of the chapter we are concerned with the product market and with market power concentrated on the seller's idea of the market. But market power may also exist on the buyer's side of the market (monopsony) and we also look at this.

8-1 MONOPOLY AND MONOPSONY

Monopoly

A monopolist, we assume, is as keen on profit as a competitive firm. But, be he the local drugstore or General Motors, he faces a downward-sloping demand curve. He does not negotiate with his customers, who are legion. He just sets the price. But in doing this he notes that his marginal revenue (MR) from an extra unit sold is *less* than the price he charges, because he has to drop the price on the x intramarginal units. This follows from the definition of marginal revenue:

$$\text{MR} = \frac{d}{dx}(px) = p + x\frac{dp}{dx} = p\left(1 + \frac{1}{\varepsilon}\right)$$

where ε is the elasticity of demand and is negative. The firm then equates marginal cost (MC) to marginal revenue, so in equilibrium

$$\text{MC} = p\left(1 - \frac{1}{|\varepsilon|}\right)$$

or

$$\frac{p - \text{MC}}{p} = \frac{1}{|\varepsilon|}$$

The proportional excess of price over marginal cost is inversely proportional to the elasticity of demand. If the firm is a price taker (a perfect competitor), price equals marginal cost because the demand elasticity is infinite. But the lower the elasticity of demand, the greater the divergence of price and marginal cost. Thus:

The market power of a seller is measured by the inverse of the demand elasticity he faces.

If there is an elastic supply of good substitutes for his product, the demand he faces will be fairly elastic, and he will lose much business by raising his price. But if there are no good substitutes, he will have considerable leverage. The best substitute is of course a good identical in quality, time, and place. If, in the neighbourhood of equilibrium, there is a perfectly elastic supply of such products, the individual is a perfect competitor. But if he runs a corner drugstore, there is no one else selling the same goods at the same place. The next seller may be some distance away. This gives the drugstore keeper some market power. But the range over which he can vary his prices may still be small, compared say with a firm like Bell Telephone, which has a legal monopoly on telephone communication over much of the United States.

Notice that we have not defined a monopolist as the sole seller of a product within a given market, for this raises endless problems about defining the boundaries of products and markets. Is not every branded type of candy a separate product? And is not the whole world one market? Instead therefore we have said: "Consider the world market for a given product made by this firm; how elastic is the demand for it?"

There is, however, a lower limit to the elasticity of demand at which any seller will in fact operate. For since marginal cost is positive,

$$1 - \frac{1}{|\varepsilon|} > 0$$

So
$$|\varepsilon| > 1$$

A monopolist always operates where the demand elasticity exceeds unity.

The reason is obvious. If demand is inelastic, revenue can be increased by reducing quantity, and costs can also be saved. So quantity gets reduced until demand has become elastic.

Figure 8-1 illustrates the monopolist's equilibrium. x^* is the output at which MR = MC. To generate demand for this, the monopolist charges p^*. This gives him a profit of FG per unit of output. (The monopolist must, of course, get nonnegative profit to keep him in business.) There is no reason why the monopolist's MC curve should not be downward-sloping. We only require, for a local optimum, that it be less steep than the MR curve. This can be seen by evaluating the second-order conditions for profit maximisation:

$$\max \pi = R(x) - C(x)$$

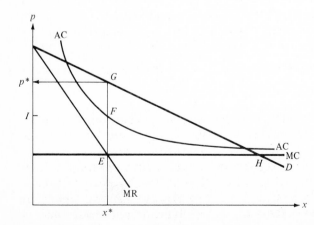

Figure 8-1 Monopolist's equilibrium.

$$\frac{d\pi}{dx} = R'(x) - C'(x) = 0$$

$$\frac{d^2\pi}{dx^2} = R''(x) - C''(x) < 0$$

Monopsony

We turn now to the analogous case of monopsony. This occurs when a buyer, buying from many potential sellers, has latitude in fixing his price, because he faces a rising supply curve. For example, the London School of Economics decides how much to pay its secretaries. If it wants more secretaries, it has to pay more; and once again this involves extra payments to the (x) existing secretaries as well as to additional ones taken on.

$$MC = \frac{d}{dx}(px) = p + x\frac{dp}{dx} = p\left(1 + \frac{1}{\eta}\right)$$

where η is the elasticity of supply and is positive. The buyer equates his demand price or marginal benefit (MB) to the marginal cost. Hence

$$MB = p\left(1 + \frac{1}{\eta}\right)$$

and
$$\frac{MB - p}{p} = \frac{1}{\eta}$$

The unfortunate suppliers are paid less than the marginal benefit they confer upon buyers. This is sometimes termed "exploitation" (see Figure 8-2). Some people may be unwilling to limit this term to the case of imperfect competition, but this usage draws attention to the fact that under perfect competition price is set by impersonal forces and not by people.† In general most buyers tend to

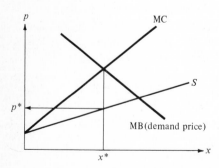

Figure 8-2 Monopsonist's equilibrium.

† A benevolent buyer can always pay more than the market price, but no one can pay less.

pay as little as they can, and most sellers to charge as much as they can. But it is mainly under imperfect competition that one hears complaints that employers are "not paying a penny more than they need to," or sellers are "charging what the market will bear." These complaints may arise because the individuals concerned have substantial latitude in fixing the price.

Q8-1 (i) The London School of Economics has the following demand and supply price schedules for secretaries (in dollars per annum):

$$w^D = 40,000 - 100x$$

$$w^S = 10,000 + 100x$$

What wage will it pay them? What is the supply elasticity at that point?

(ii) Could any supply curve exist such that equilibrium occurred where the supply elasticity was less than unity?

Q8-2 (i) "A binding minimum wage may increase employment." True or false? (Give reasons.)

(ii) "A binding maximum price may increase output." True or false? (Give reasons.)

(iii) "A monopolist may charge a price more than double marginal cost." True or false? (Give reasons.)

(iv) "A monopolist must necessarily make a profit that is significantly different from zero." True or false? (Give reasons.)

Q8-3 In Figure 8-1 what area measures

(i) The welfare cost of the monopoly?

(ii) The monopolist's profit?

Monopoly in the Product Market with Monopsony in the Factor Market

Monopsony can, of course, occur in product markets (for aerospace equipment) as well as in factor markets. And monopoly can occur in factor markets (trade unions) as well as product markets. However, there is a pairing of monopoly and monopsony which must necessarily occur in the following case: if there is a monopoly in a product which employs specialised factors, then this firm must face rising supply prices of those specialised factors. Thus in the two-sector case, unless x and y are equally labour-intensive, x (the labour-intensive good) must face a rising supply price of labour (measured in terms of y) and a falling supply price of capital. This means that, even if there exist constant returns to scale and equally efficient potential firms, the supply price of x (if competitively supplied) will rise as x rises. This supply price is of course both the marginal cost of x (to its individual atomistic producers) and its average cost. But if the x industry is now monopolised (say by legislative process), the new owner will surely notice that his average costs rise as his output expands. He will now calculate a marginal cost curve which takes this into account and fix a price such that this marginal cost = marginal revenue (see Figure 8-3).

Moreover, cost minimisation requires that the rate of substitution between factors should equal the ratio of their marginal costs to the firm. Therefore, the

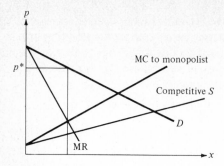

Figure 8-3 Monopoly in the product market with monopsony in the factor market.

unequal supply elasticities of labour and capital will affect the mix of factors he uses. For if $x = x(K, L)$, then

$$\frac{x_K}{x_L} = \frac{\text{MC of } K}{\text{MC of } L} = \frac{w_K(1 + 1/\eta_K)}{w_L(1 + 1/\eta_L)} \neq \frac{w_K}{w_L}$$

So production will not occur on the economy's locus of efficient production, as we defined it in Figure 1-4. This conclusion must apply to any monopoly which does not employ factors of production in the same ratio as the rest of the economy.

Price Discrimination

From now on we shall confine ourselves to the problem of monopoly rather than monopsony. Suppose that a monopolist can sell at different prices in the different submarkets that he faces. It will normally pay him to charge different prices in those different submarkets. The reason is simple. If he is selling in two markets (1 and 2), he will only maximise revenue from a given output if he equates the marginal revenue in the two markets.

$$\text{MR}_1 = \text{MR}_2$$

This gives
$$p_1\left(1 - \frac{1}{|\varepsilon_1|}\right) = p_2\left(1 - \frac{1}{|\varepsilon_2|}\right)$$

If a monopolist is able to charge different prices in different submarkets, he will charge the higher price where the demand is less elastic.†

Thus we might expect, for example, to find higher prices being charged to business travellers than to holiday travellers.

What conditions must exist for price discrimination to be possible? First, the good sold must not be resaleable, since, if it is, people being charged the higher price will simply buy from people who are being charged the lower

---

† Similarly, a monopsonist would pay less to suppliers with less elastic supplies.

price. The main items which are not readily resaleable are personal services (like medical care) and utilities involving expensive connection facilities (gas, water, electricity). But ordinary capital goods can also be made nonresaleable. For the monopolist can refuse to sell the goods as such and only lease out the use of them, making it a condition that no subleasing-out occurs. This may explain the past refusal of the U.S. Shoe Machinery Company to sell its machines.

If the monopolist knew the exact demand curve of each of his customers, he could (for a nonresaleable item) extract from each customer almost the full consumer surplus (or excess profit, if the customer is a producer). He would proceed as follows. First, he would calculate the level of firm output for which the demand price equalled the firm's marginal cost. He would next evaluate each individual consumer's demand at that price. Call it x^i. Each consumer i would then receive an all-or-nothing offer under which he could buy x^i for a fixed sum almost equal to the maximum he would be willing to pay for that quantity. Such a procedure is known as *perfect price discrimination*, for each unit is sold for very nearly its demand price.

However, this brings us to the second difficulty: of identifying each customer's demand curve. The machinery firm might now proceed as follows. For each machine leased out the demand price is presumably related to the number of shoes that will be made with the machine. So one way of extracting the shoe maker's profit would be to charge him on the basis of the number of shoes he made with the machine. An alternative would be to charge the same rent per machine to each shoe maker, but to insist that as a condition of renting the machine he buy all his shoe-working materials from the monopolist. If these materials were then priced at more than they cost the monopolist, he could extract some of the buyer's surplus by means of his profit on the "tie-in sales" of materials.†

It may often happen that different customers demand different qualities of a particular product. This makes it particularly easy to separate the markets, since the products then naturally have different prices. In such cases, if the ratio of price to marginal cost were different for the two qualities of product, we should know that the monopolist was practising price discrimination. A familiar example comes from the book industry. It costs about $0.50 to give a book a hard, rather than paper, back, but the difference in price between hardback and paperback editions of the same book is quite disproportionate to this. For hardbacks sell to libraries, which have less elastic demand curves than students, who are more inclined to buy paperbacks.

In conclusion we should note that nothing definite can be said about whether output is higher or lower under price discrimination than under uniform profit-maximising prices. Under perfect price discrimination output is of course higher.

† Tie-in sales may also be used as a way of extracting consumer's surplus when the tied goods are unrelated. Suppose for example that consumers were allowed to buy as much x as possible at p_x but only on condition that they buy at least y^0 of good y at p_y. Then $y^0(p_y - MC_y)$ is effectively a lump-sum charge for the right to buy x. On tie-in sales see M. Burstein, "Economics of Tie-in Sales," *Review of Economics and Statistics*, vol. 42, pp. 68–73, February 1960.

Q8-4 The IATA cartel permits much lower air fares for flights booked well in advance.
    (i) Why?
    (ii) Could it do this if tickets were transferable?

Q8-5 Suppose a monopolist can sell electricity in two markets. The demand curves are:

$$p_1^D = 3 - \tfrac{1}{2}x_1$$
$$p_2^D = 2 - \tfrac{1}{2}x_2$$

The escapable costs of output are

$$C = 2\tfrac{1}{3} + (x_1 + x_2)$$

    (i) What are profit-maximising prices in each market and what are the corresponding elasticities of demand?
    (ii) What would happen to output if price discrimination was banned?
    (iii) What can you say about the desirability of price discrimination in this case, and in general?

Origins of Monopoly

We have so far taken the existence of monopoly for granted, without discussing how it arises. If the monopoly is making profits, one has to explain why other firms do not set up in the industry. There must be some "barriers to entry." One important form of these is economies of scale (relative to demand). To examine this we shall first assume that there exist any number of firms which can produce the same product with identical cost curves. Monopoly will result if economies of scale within the firm persist up to near the level of output demanded at a price equal to the firm's average cost. To be precise, if the industry demand curve is

$$D = D(p)$$

it is sufficient for monopoly to result that for every value of p the average cost of $\tfrac{1}{2}D(p)$ exceeds p. For in this case (illustrated in Figure 8-4) if the market is split equally between two firms, both will make a loss (AC $> p$). Even though demand is small, this is the source of the corner shop's monopoly position. The classic or "natural" monopolies are those where fixed costs are high relative to demand (e.g., the fixed cost of supplying gas, water, or electricity to a street, or rail services to a town).

It is sometimes said that if one entrepreneur is more efficient than all others at supplying each level of firm's output, this will necessarily lead to monopoly. This is obviously false if marginal costs and average costs are rising. But it could in principle lead to monopoly even if scale economies did not exist.

Private monopolies may also be created by governments. Some rulers (like King James I of England) have sold monopoly franchises as a way of raising money. But a more justifiable case of legally created monopoly arises from the patent system. In order to encourage invention, inventors are given a limited-period monopoly in the right to use the invention. For, otherwise, since the cost of learning about new processes is small, the inventor would be in danger of

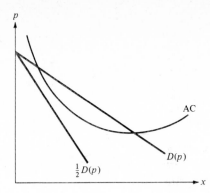

Figure 8-4 A sufficient condition for monopoly.

receiving no return to his often costly efforts. The inventor's monopoly is in the right to use the invention. He can sell this right by licensing a judiciously selected number of other firms, if he thinks that will bring him more profit than by establishing himself as the sole producer.

Finally, monopolies may be created by mergers among firms which would otherwise be competing with each other. But if these firms have no entry barriers to hide behind, they will be very vulnerable to interlopers. We shall be looking more closely at this case (analogous to a cartel) in the next section.

Q8-6 (i) Would a competitive firm be likely to advertise its product?

(ii) Would a competitive industry be likely to advertise its product?

(iii) Would a monopolist be likely to advertise his product? If so, formulate the condition for optimising advertising expenditure.

(iv) "A monopolist would never advertise his product if it made the demand curve more elastic." True or false?

Q8-7 (i) A monopolist has two plants with the following costs:

$$C_1 = 2x_1$$
$$C_2 = \tfrac{1}{4} + x_2 + \tfrac{1}{2}x_2^2$$

His demand curve is

$$p = 4 - \tfrac{1}{2}(x_1 + x_2)$$

How much output (if any) will he produce in each plant? What price will he charge?

*(ii) "If a monopolist has two plants, one of which has rising marginal costs and the other falling marginal costs, he will necessarily concentrate all his output in the plant with declining marginal costs." True or false?

8-2 BARGAINING AND CARTELS

As we saw in the last section, many prices in the economy are not fixed by an impersonal market but by agents having market power, acting on their own. Other noncompetitive prices are determined by a different mechanism: the mechanism of bargaining. Bargaining occurs when both parties to the bargain have market power.

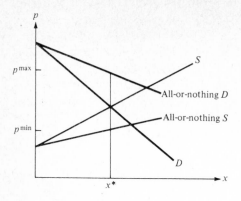

Figure 8-5 Bilateral monopoly.

Bilateral Monopoly

The classic bargaining situation arises where there is a sole seller (a monopolist) facing a sole buyer (a monopsonist). Figure 2-1 (on page 53) was an example of this. We found then that, provided there are no transactions costs, the parties will arrive at a Pareto-optimal solution, i.e., one lying on the contract curve. But the final price was not predictable by our theory, except that it must be high enough to make the seller at least as well off as with no sale and low enough to make the buyer at least as well off also.

The position can be illustrated using the per-unit diagram in Figure 8-5. The demand and supply curves speak for themselves. Lying above the demand curve is the buyer's all-or-nothing demand curve, showing the maximum price per unit he is willing to pay for any given quantity. Lying below the supply curve is the seller's all-or-nothing price, showing the minimum price per unit at which he is willing to sell each quantity. For these latter schedules to be independent of the outcome of the bargain (as we are assuming), there must be no income effect in the demand or supply of x. We can now examine the outcome.

If there are no transactions costs, the parties will arrive at a situation that is Pareto-optimal for them, where one cannot gain by any further negotiation without the other losing. The two parties maximise their joint profit $B(x) - C(x)$, by agreeing that x^* should be the quantity exchanged. But what about the price? This could vary widely depending on who has been the most successful bargainer. The highest possible price is that where the buyer is no better off as a result of the contract than without it. His net benefits are zero:

$$B(x^*) - p^{\max}x^* = 0$$

So
$$p^{\max} = \frac{B(x^*)}{x^*}$$

The lowest possible price is that where the seller is no better off from the contract than without it.

$$p^{\min}x^* - C(x^*) = 0$$

So
$$p^{\min} = \frac{C(x^*)}{x^*}$$

All prices between p^{max} and p^{min} are possible outcomes, lying on the contract curve. Our theory does not enable us to say which one will prevail.†

In fact, it may be too much to expect that x^* will be reached. For if the buyer is using his quantity decision as a weapon to get down the price, x^* would only be reached if both parties knew each other's demand and cost curves. If the cost of repeated negotiations is high, it may often be most profitable for the two sides to merge. There would then be no difficulty in reaching x^*. This may be the reason why bilateral monopoly is relatively uncommon, except in the case of relations between employers and trade unions.

Cartels

Bilateral monopoly involves bargaining between the two opposite sides of a market. If there are no transactions costs, the outcome is efficient.‡ This is not the case when bargaining occurs between agents on the same side of the market.§ It *is* normally in the interest of sellers to combine to raise price, and of buyers to combine to lower it.¶ Let us concentrate on the case where it is the sellers only who combine. One way for them to do this is to merge and form a single enterprise. But another way is less drastic: the sellers might remain independent but agree among themselves about the price and the carve-up of the market. Such arrangements are known as cartels.

If the costs of negotiation were small, the firms in the cartel would presumably choose output so as to maximise their joint profit. The problem is illustrated in Figure 8-6 for a two-firm cartel. It is in fact identical to the problem

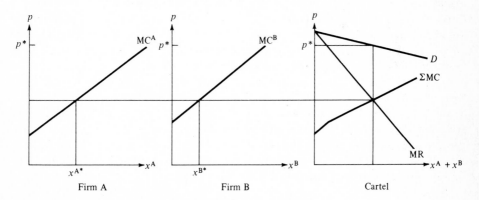

Figure 8-6 Joint profit-maximising output for a cartel.

---

† The chief bargaining model with a determinate outcome is the Nash-Zeuthen model, see R. L. Bishop, "A Zeuthen-Hicks Theory of Bargaining," *Econometrica*, vol. 32, pp. 410–417, July 1964. But it is not easy to apply this to actual situations.

‡ If it is not, this is because of market power which one or other agent possesses in some other related market.

§ Unless they can practise perfect price discrimination.

¶ See Figure 2-8. A buyer's combination is usually called a "ring."

of the two-plant monopolist [see Question 8-7(i)]. In the solution the marginal revenue of the cartel is equated to the marginal cost in each firm (plant). This determines the price to be fixed. But the cartel must do more than fix the price, for at the optimum price the two firms taken together would like to produce more than the output demanded at the optimum price. So the cartel must also fix the outputs to be produced by each firm (x^{A^*}, x^{B^*}). In the simplest form of cartel these outputs will be allocated to each firm as quotas.

Problems Facing Cartels

We can already see why most cartels are short-lived or survive from one crisis to another. The fundamental problem is to stop chiselling (cheating among members) and to keep out interlopers. For the purpose of the cartel is to raise price above marginal cost. Yet if price is above marginal cost, each firm in the cartel has an incentive to produce more.† The cartel does not want it to, since this floods the market and reduces joint profit. But, looking at the matter selfishly, the individual firm wants to have its cake and eat it. It wants to benefit from the existence of the cartel (which raises the price) without being bound by the rules of the cartel. This is another example of the free-rider problem we have met before. In fact, the free rider might even find it worth its while dropping its price a bit below the cartel price so that it could be sure of selling its whole desired output. The cartel, unless it had legal status, would find it difficult to discipline the free rider. Moreover, even if the members of the cartel can discipline themselves, there may well be other potential firms outside the cartel which would find it worthwhile starting up in the industry to take advantage of the price. If enough potential firms act as free riders, whether they are nominal members of the cartel or interlopers, output will expand so much and price fall so much that the cartel will fall apart. To reduce these pressures, the cartel may deliberately start off by setting a price that is lower than optimal.

What does all this tell us about the conditions for a successful cartel? If it has many members (all with increasing costs), cheating by one member will have a smaller effect on price than if there are few members. On the other hand it will also be more difficult to detect. So more members are likely to cheat. Since transactions costs are higher the more parties there are to an agreement, it follows that a cartel is likely to be found in an industry where there are fairly few potential firms capable of producing at the cartel price. In such a case each firm has a strong incentive to join, since, if it did not, the cartel would be unlikely to be formed at all (and the consequent benefits of high price would be lost).

Apart from problems of free riders, the cartel has two main administrative problems: how to set quotas and how to carve up the profit. Figure 8-6 shows the optimal quotas. But these will leave the less efficient firm B with relatively little profit. It may therefore urge that quotas should be more equally distributed.

---

† This is why an informal cartel, where one firm is a price leader but where there are no quotas, cannot be fully "efficient." There will be continual excess supply.

But any move towards greater equality would reduce total profit. A better approach would be to stick to the unequal quotas (x^{A*}, x^{B*}) but for firm A to make a "side payment" to firm B.

However, this adds to the complexity of the rules of the cartel. It is much easier if there are no side payments and quotas are allocated in some simple way, say in proportion to precartel output or in proportion to capacity. The latter rule has been quite common. But it has the obvious defect of encouraging investment, at the same time as output is being discouraged. And the greater capacity is relative to optimum output, the stronger the pressures to chisel. So pause for a moment to see if you can think of better approaches to the quota problem.

Economic theory suggests two, both of which have in fact been tried. One is to have, say, equal original quotas but to allow members to sell some of their quotas to other members who are marginally more efficient. An alternative approach is not to have any quotas, but instead to restrict output by levying an *ad valorem* tax on all members of the cartel. The proceeds of the tax are then handed out in lump-sum payments to members. This is called *revenue pooling* and is quite common in transport.† Firms turn over to the pool a fraction of their gross revenue. If the price and the fraction of the price (i.e., of receipts) handed over are both set correctly, the effects are of course identical to optimally determined quotas. But, given the difficulty of getting accurate knowledge about costs, the pooling arrangement is probably more efficient from the firms' point of view.

At this point one might well ask: What is the difference between a cartel and the equivalent merger? If the merger leaves the relevant cost curves unaffected (e.g., if there are no economies of scale), there is no essential difference, except that the merger eliminates all problems of discipline and of renegotiation of the terms of the cartel. The merger is thus the more stable form of organisation. It will, however, be as vulnerable to interlopers as the cartel and, like the cartel, is only likely to be successful if there are effective "barriers to entry." As we saw in considering monopoly, the main barriers to entry are economies of scale or legal privileges. The latter are common, as the numerous instances of licensing (e.g. taxicabs) indicate. It is remarkable that governments often issue such licenses free even though they convey market power. Where no legal barriers exist, cartels are likely to be unstable. We may then observe a third form of non-competitive market organisation: oligopoly.

Q8-8 Suppose there are a large number of potential firms, all of which can provide arsenic (x) with the following cost (in \$10m):

$$C^i = 1 + x^i + x^{i^2}$$

† See E. Bennathan and A. A. Walters, "Revenue Pooling and Cartels," *Oxford Economic Papers*, vol. 21, pp. 161–176, July 1969, for examples from international airlines and steamship conferences.

The competitive demand for arsenic is

$$p = 5 - \frac{x}{12}$$

(i) What would be the competitive equilibrium of this industry? In particular, what is the equilibrium number of firms (call it n^e).

(ii) Suppose these n^e firms now form a cartel. What price will they set, and what quotas?

(iii) Under this arrangement what profit is each member of the cartel making? How much would an interloper expect to make if he did not join the cartel but assumed he could sell as much as he wanted at the cartel price?

(iv) Suppose the cartel is now given legal rights to force any firm in the industry into the cartel, but there is free entry into the cartel. How many more firms will eventually join it?

(v) Suppose the government now changes its mind about the cartel and forbids all restrictive practices. What happens, assuming the fixed cost of $10m cannot be escaped, once incurred? What is the new price? What is the fate of the original n^e firms? What moral, if any, do you draw?

Q8-9 Suppose that in the previous question, part (ii), the cartel wished not to use quotas but instead to use revenue pooling as a method of restricting output. What fraction of revenue would they require firms to put into the pool?

Q8-10 (For discussion.) How long do you expect the Organisation of Petroleum Exporting Countries cartel to survive, if it still exists when you read this?

8-3 OLIGOPOLY

Suppose that there are important economies of scale in producing a product, but not sufficient for one firm to have become the sole producer.† If the various firms have failed to form a cartel (or have been prevented by law), then we are likely to observe them in a state of economic warfare. Each knows that if it varies its own behaviour, then the others will respond in some way. For example, if it cuts its prices, it may expect some reaction from its competitors. To make the best decisions, you must make the best possible guess about how your rival will react. But equally you want your own decisions to be as unpredictable as possible to your rivals.

The situation is thus totally different from that facing a perfect competitor or a monopolist. For the perfect competitor faces a known product price, while the monopolist faces a known demand curve for his product, after allowing for all the predictable changes that will occur when he varies his price. But the oligopolist faces a demand curve he can only guess at. This makes the oligopoly case very difficult for economists to analyse. For we have to make some assumptions about how producers expect their rivals to react.

The first person to analyse the problem at all rigorously was Cournot in the 1830s. He assumed that each agent expected *no* reaction from the others, in response to a change in his own behaviour. The particular problem he took was the case of a homogeneous product produced by two producers (duopolists). Being homogeneous, the products of the two producers must sell at the same

---

† It is impossible to think about oligopoly (as opposed to monopoly), without some concept of an industry producing a product.

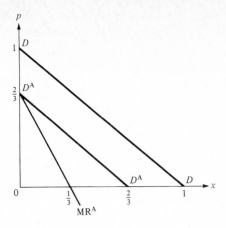

Figure 8-7 Duopoly: the Cournot solution.

price. Cournot considered the case of two mineral springs each with zero costs of production. The market demand for the mineral water is

$$p = 1 - x$$

and is shown by DD in Figure 8-7. The question is: What output will the two springs produce?

Cournot postulated that firm A will expect *no* reaction from firm B, when firm A changes its output. In this sense he expected firm A to behave as if it were an isolated individual in a purely passive environment. So suppose that firm B were producing an output of $\frac{1}{3}$ unit. Firm A then makes its output choice as follows. It assumes $x^B = \frac{1}{3}$. Hence its own demand curve is

$$p = 1 - x^A - x^B = \tfrac{2}{3} - x^A$$

and its marginal revenue is

$$MR = \tfrac{2}{3} - 2x^A$$

Given zero marginal cost, optimal output is given by

$$x^A = \tfrac{1}{3}$$

where A's marginal revenue crosses the horizontal axis. We now turn to firm B. It takes firm A's output as given, and is therefore happy to remain at $x^B = \frac{1}{3}$. So we have an equilibrium. The reader is asked to check that, whatever initial value was assumed for x^B, we should end up at this equilibrium if the adjustment occurred by a sequence of moves by A and B, one after the other (see Question 8-11).

More generally, the Cournot solution could be expressed as follows:

$$p = p(x^A + x^B) \qquad C^A = C^A(x^A) \qquad C^B = C^B(x^B)$$

So
$$R^A = x^A \cdot p(x^A + x^B)$$

$$R^B = x^B \cdot p(x^A + x^B)$$

Hence
$$\frac{\partial R^A}{\partial x^A} = p(x^A + x^B) + x^A p'(x^A + x^B) = C^{A'}(x^A) \tag{1}$$

and
$$\frac{\partial R^B}{\partial x^B} = p(x^A + x^B) + x^B p'(x^A + x^B) = C^{B'}(x^B) \tag{2}$$

The two equations on the right-hand side can be solved for equilibrium values of x^A and x^B. Equation (1) is sometimes called A's "reaction function" and Equation (2) B's "reaction function." See if you can formulate the conditions for these two functions to give a stable equilibrium (see Question 8-12).

The Cournot solution can be criticised on two possible grounds. First someone might say: Why not assume that the rival's price, rather than output, is held constant? The answer is of course simple. If the two products are the same, if A sets a price below B, he will get the whole market. But B will then drop his price to undercut A. And so a price-cutting war would develop until the price had fallen to zero. This is exactly the same output as would prevail under competition, and seems an even less plausible outcome than the Cournot solution.

But a more fundamental question is this: Why would a firm continue to expect its rival not to react when it continually found it was reacting? One's credulity is strained by such an assumption, and in practice economists have hardly found the Cournot model useful for analysing real-world cases of duopoly. An alternative assumption might be that firm A expects firm B to react in the way in which in fact it always does react, and similarly for B. We could then have an equilibrium (x^A, x^B), where x^A was such that B had no reason to change x^B and vice versa. However it is unlikely that it would be in either firm's interest to react in a stable fashion—the way to win a game is by surprising your opponent. The "theory of games" has something to say about this, but has not proved particularly successful in explaining actual behaviour.

As one passes to the case where there are more than two suppliers to a market (but still so few that each of them has an appreciable effect on the market) the problems multiply. The additional difficulties arise from the fact that there are more reactions and strategies to take into account. And each reaction interacts with all the others. But beyond a certain point, as the number of oligopolists increases, the relevance of any particular oligopolist to the behaviour of any other becomes increasingly small, and the situation approaches that of perfect competition, where the behaviour of any market participant has such a small effect on the behaviour of the others that it can be ignored.

The analytical problems are probably fiercest when there are three or four participants in an oligopolistic market, and solutions are few. One could proceed as we did above in the duopoly case to analyse what would happen if each participant assumed passive behaviour on the part of all other oligopolists in the market. But little new would be added to the duopoly case already analysed.

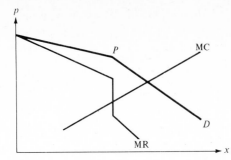

Figure 8-8 The kinked oligopoly demand curve.

It is sometimes alleged that imperfect competitors (call them oligopolists) are less prone than competitive industries to change their prices when cost or demand conditions change.† This has been explained by the following theory. The oligopolist believes that, if he raises his price, competitors will rapidly steal his market. For they will keep their prices where they are now, and the oligopolist's product will therefore become uncompetitive with other close substitutes. On the other hand if the oligopolist were to lower his price, he would not expect to gain much business because he believes his competitors would match his price cuts. Thus his demand curve, as he sees it, is kinked at the point where he is currently operating—at point P in Figure 8-8. This means that his marginal revenue curve is discontinuous. As x increases, marginal revenue suddenly falls when P is reached, and the demand curve becomes less elastic. The firm is in equilibrium so long as the marginal cost curve cuts the marginal revenue curve somewhere in the discontinuous interval. So the marginal cost can shift a lot with no change in equilibrium output or price. Similarly the demand curve could shift out horizontally a good distance with no change in equilibrium price, since the kink occurs at the same price. However, the reader will note that the theory does not explain the existing price, but only why it stays put. It is thus an incomplete theory.

This is, alas, true of the theory of oligopoly in general. Because of the difficulties of developing testable propositions where strategic behaviour is involved, some writers have suggested that it is better to regard oligopolists as firms which are trying to form a cartel but are only being partially successful.‡ This gives rise

---

† The evidence on this point varies. E. Bennathan and A. A. Walters (*The Economics of Ocean Freight Rates*, Praeger, New York, 1969) show that ocean shipping cartels maintain much more stable rates than their fellow steamship owners in the highly competitive bulk cargo and tramp operations. For a different view, see G. J. Stigler, "The Kinky Oligopoly Demand Curve and Rigid Prices," in G. J. Stigler and K. E. Boulding (eds.), *Readings in Price Theory*, American Economic Association, G. Allen and Unwin, London, 1953, and G. J. Stigler and J. K. Kindahl (eds.), *The Behavior of Industrial Prices*, National Bureau of Economic Research, General Series No. 90, New York, 1970.

‡ G. J. Stigler, "A Theory of Oligopoly," *Journal of Political Economy*, vol. 72, no. 1, pp. 44–61, February 1964.

to some specific propositions about the conditions favouring high profits and high concentration ratios in an industry. But which approach will ultimately prove most fruitful remains unsettled.

Q8-11 Suppose that $p = 1 - x^A - x^B$ and both firms A and B have zero costs. Firm B starts with $x^B = b$. Prove that if x^A and x^B are determined alternately using the Cournot assumption, x^B will tend to $\frac{1}{3}$ as the number of periods tends to infinity. The solution to the relevant difference equation was given on page 233.

Q8-12 Suppose that $p = p(x^A + x^B), C^A = C^A(x^A)$, and $C^B = C^B(x^B)$. What condition must the reaction functions satisfy for a stable equilibrium?

Q8-13 (i) Suppose that $p = 1 - x^A - x^B$ and both firms A and B have zero costs. Each believes that whatever price it sets will be matched exactly by the other firm and that it will then get a constant, one-half, share of the market. What is the equilibrium output of the industry? Any comment?

(ii) Suppose now that firm A believes it will get a share k and firm B believes it will get $1 - k$. What happens?

Q8-14 Suppose two firms A and B produce nonidentical products which are close substitutes. Do not assume zero costs.

(i) Formulate the first-order conditions for the Cournot equilibrium.

(ii) Formulate the first-order conditions for an equilibrum if each firm believed that the other's price (rather than output) would not be altered in response to any change in its own behaviour.

8-4 ANTITRUST POLICY

In the light of all this, what can be said about government policy towards industrial concentration? A typical issue is whether two or more firms shall be allowed to merge, or, alternatively whether one large firm shall be forced to reduce its size by selling off some of its assets.

The conventional analysis of this is based on the case where the monopolist would have a marginal cost curve equal to the horizontal sum of the marginal cost curves of the potential constituent firms. If there were unfettered competition, each producer would equate marginal cost to the market price he faces. This is Pareto-efficient. If a monopoly is formed, it fixes price such that marginal revenue equals marginal cost. This leads to too little being produced, and that output being produced inefficiently if the monopolist is also a monopsonist in the factor market. In addition income is redistributed towards the monopolist and away from consumers and from owners of factors in which the industry is intensive. This redistribution is likely to arouse much more public concern than the loss of the usual welfare triangle.

So far, all the arguments seem to be against monopoly. But matters are very different if we consider instead the case where the monopoly arises from economies of scale. If the monopoly is banned (say by forbidding any firm to produce more than one-fifth of industry output), we shall have many firms incurring the fixed costs, instead of one. Moreover, if marginal costs fall with firm size, it is even possible that, under monopoly, output will be higher than under the modified form of competition which would otherwise replace it. However let us

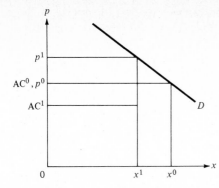

Figure 8-9 Efficiency effects of monopoly and off-setting cost savings.

ignore this possibility. Assume instead that if monopoly is permitted, output falls from a "competitive" output, produced at an average cost AC^0 with zero excess profit, to a monopoly level produced at a lower average cost AC^1, but sold at a higher price, p^1 (see Figure 8-9).† The change in output when monopoly comes into force is

$$\Delta x = \frac{dx}{dp}\,\Delta p = \frac{dx}{dp}\frac{p^1}{x^1}x^1\frac{\Delta p}{p^1} = \varepsilon x^1\frac{\Delta p}{p^1}$$

where ε is the elasticity of demand at (x^1, p^1). The change of consumers' surplus is

$$-x^1\Delta p + \tfrac{1}{2}\Delta x\,\Delta p = -x^1\Delta p + \tfrac{1}{2}\varepsilon x^1\frac{(\Delta p)^2}{p^1}$$

The monopolist's profit is

$$x^1\Delta p + x^1(AC^0 - AC^1)$$

So the change in social welfare, if we treat each person's dollar as of equal value, is

$$\frac{\varepsilon x^1}{2}\frac{(\Delta p)^2}{p^1} + x^1(AC^0 - AC^1) = x^1 p^1\left[\frac{\varepsilon}{2}\left(\frac{\Delta p}{p^1}\right)^2 - \frac{\Delta AC}{AC^0}\left(1 - \frac{\Delta p}{p^1}\right)\right]$$

Thus, for example $\varepsilon = -2$, and $\Delta p/p^1 = 0.1$, social welfare increases if $|\Delta AC/AC^0| > 0.011$.‡ So quite small gains in productive efficiency may outweigh

---

† We assume the demand curve linear.

‡ The reader may wonder how we can have both $\Delta p/p^1 = 0.1$ and $\varepsilon = -2$, when

$$\frac{p^1 - MC^1}{p^1} = \frac{1}{|\varepsilon_1|}$$

But $p^1 - MC^1 > p^1 - p^0$. On the classic measurement of the cost of monopoly, see A. C. Harberger, "Monopoly and Resource Allocation," *American Economic Review*, vol. 44, pp. 77–87, May 1954.

any allocative distortion produced by monopoly, provided $\Delta p/p^1$ is not too high.†

However, there is yet a third issue to be considered. We have so far assumed that cost minimisation is pursued independently of market structure. But Leibenstein has argued that the main difference between monopoly and competition lies in the extent to which firms achieve "x efficiency," i.e., how nearly they maximise output for given inputs.‡ A monopolist is less likely to produce his maximum output with given inputs than a competitive firm threatened with bankruptcy. If this is true, it provides a further argument against unregulated monopoly or merger.

But the x-efficiency issue has another twist to it. Under managerial capitalism it is not easy for owners to ensure that managers are maximising owner's equity. For the cost to a small shareholder of helping to oust a sleepy board of directors may exceed the return to him, even though it is less than the collective return to all shareholders. This externality problem can, however, be overcome if the managers of wide-awake enterprises are free to take over firms whose current managers are generating profits below potential profits and whose firms are consequently underpriced on the stock market. Thus any takeover that does not lead to an increase in market power is likely to improve x efficiency, while one that does increase market power may or may not do so.

The degree of monopoly power generated by a merger depends of course on the market in which the merged firms sell.

1. If the merger is between unrelated firms (a *conglomerate* merger) all the benefits in x efficiency are gained without any increase in market power. Such mergers do not therefore seem objectionable.
2. If the merger is between a supplier (A) and a firm he supplies (B) (a *vertical* merger), market power is only increased if this alliance enables either A or B to secure a greater monopoly position in its own market. If neither A nor B has market power in his own market, the merger certainly cannot confer market power on either. But if one or other already has market power, the merger will in certain cases tend to reinforce it. Suppose for example that A is a monopolist in industry x, which supplies an input to a competitive industry y. Now A buys up firm B in industry y. What effect has this? Previously firm A's ability to make profits was limited by two things: (i) the elasticity of demand for y, (ii) the fact that other inputs would be substituted for x if its price is raised. Now, having bought up firm B, A refuses to sell to any other firm in the y industry. A's monopoly power is now only limited by item (i), the elasticity of demand for y.§

† See O. E. Williamson, "Economics as an Antitrust Defense: The Welfare Trade-offs," *American Economic Review*, vol. 58, pp. 18–36, March 1968.

‡ H. Leibenstein, "Allocative Efficiency Versus x-Efficiency," *American Economic Review*, vol. 56, pp. 392–416, June 1966.

§ Other cases are also possible. For example, A may buy up B in order to practice price discrimination. He can now "sell" at a different price to B from that at which he sells to the outside world. This will increase A's profits if B produces a product with a different elasticity of demand from the products produced by other buyers of A's output.

3. Finally there is the *horizontal* merger between firms supplying the same market. This is a real source of increased market power. The allocative and income distributional case against such mergers is strong, though it is always important to check whether the market power is being exercised (fear of the law may be sufficient to tame the monopolist). In addition there is the x-efficiency argument against such mergers. The only argument in favour of monopolistic giants is the economies of elephantine scale, where these exist.

This chapter has, we hope brought out the range of noncompetitive forms of behaviour that can exist. But in each case the theory remains to some degree incomplete. The theory of monopoly, though well developed, is obviously incomplete since it does not take into account rivals' reactions. Theories which attempt to do this are many, but none have been found to have much predictive value. If one wishes to study a particular noncompetitive sector of the economy, one must therefore proceed in a fairly *ad hoc* way, interpreting the strategies of those concerned as best one may. If one is concerned with the configuration of the economy as a whole, one often finds that the predictions of competitive theory are well borne out, even though noncompetitive elements in the economy abound. It is a pity that noncompetitive theory is in such a primitive state as regards tested propositions, and this is why the rest of the book is concerned with competitive markets.

PART

FOUR

PRODUCTION AND
FACTOR DEMAND

THE DERIVED DEMAND FOR FACTORS

We turn now to the market for factors of production. If this is competitive, the income of each factor will be determined by supply and demand. Each firm's demand price for a factor will equal the firm's return from employing more of the factor, i.e., the marginal revenue product of the factor. And if the product market is perfectly competitive, the marginal revenue product of a factor is its physical marginal product times the product price. This is usually called the *value of the marginal product*. So, with perfect competition in factor and product markets, each factor is paid the value of its marginal product. This is the *marginal productivity theory of distribution*.

Notice that the marginal product does not *determine* the factor income. This is determined by the supply of the factor as well as its demand. But if some given quantity is supplied, the income of the factor is then the value of the marginal product of that quantity.

We have already derived this equality of wage to value of marginal product in Chapter 7. But what is really interesting is how factor incomes change in response to altered circumstances. How much, for example, are graduates' wages likely to fall as their supply increases? Obviously this depends on the elasticity of demand for graduates. Or we might ask: What determines the power of a trade union to raise wages by reducing supply, assuming it faces a competitive demand curve? The answer again lies in the elasticity of demand for the factor.

So we shall spend most of the chapter examining the own-price elasticity of demand for a factor within an industry. Marshall first identified the four main influences governing this. His rules can be stated as follows for the two-factor case, given constant returns to scale.†

---

† We have for convenience varied the order of the four influences from that used by Marshall.

Marshall's rules. Within an industry, the (absolute) elasticity of demand for a factor i ($|\varepsilon_{ii}|$) varies directly with[†]

1. *The (absolute) elasticity of demand for the product the factor produces ($|\eta^p|$)*
2. *The share of the factor in the cost of production (v_i)*
3. *The elasticity of supply of the other factor (η^s)*
4. *The elasticity of substitution between the factor in question and the other factor (s_{ij})*

Time has shown the usefulness of these rules, and only rule 2 has needed modification (see below).

We shall spend much of the chapter deriving and expanding on these rules. But this all assumes only two factors. So we then move on to the three-factor case and ask, for example: How will the increased supply of graduates affect the wages of unskilled workers? This requires us to investigate the pattern of complementarity and substitution between factors. Finally we apply all these ideas using a particular form of production function, having constant elasticity of substitution. The whole discussion of substitution relationships in this chapter is equally applicable to the consumer's demand for products.

9-1 OUTPUT EFFECT AND SUBSTITUTION EFFECT

To investigate Marshall's rules, we need to start with demand at the level of the firm. If returns to scale are constant, the firm's demand curve for a factor has a very simple form. For the average product of a factor depends only on the ratios in which the factors are employed (see Appendix 3). So if z_1 and z_2 are the two factors that produce x,

$$\frac{x}{z_i} = f^i\left(\frac{z_2}{z_1}\right)$$

By the same token, the factor input per unit of output (i.e., the input coefficient) depends only on the factor proportions and is independent of scale:

$$\frac{z_i}{x} = g^i\left(\frac{z_2}{z_1}\right)$$

But the relative factor quantities are also uniquely related to relative marginal products and thus depend only on relative factor prices:

$$\frac{z_i}{x} = h^i\left(\frac{w_1}{w_2}\right)$$

or

$$z_i = x \cdot h^i\left(\frac{w_1}{w_2}\right)$$

---

† I.e., the two variables rise together and fall together.

Hence
$$\log z_i = \log x + \log h^i\left(\frac{w_1}{w_2}\right)$$

and
$$\frac{\partial \log z_i}{\partial \log w_j} = \frac{\partial \log x}{\partial \log w_j} + \frac{\partial \log h^i(w_1/w_2)}{\partial \log w_j}$$

The elasticity of demand can be decomposed into an *output effect* and a *substitution effect* (holding output constant). Quite generally,

$$\frac{\partial \log z_i}{\partial \log w_j} = \text{output effect} + \text{substitution effect}$$

This is extremely useful.

1. *The output effect is the change which would occur if factor proportions were held constant, but output changed in response to changes in its price.*
2. *The substitution effect is the change which would occur if output was held constant, but factor proportions changed in response to the factor price change.*

These two effects are illustrated in Figure 9-1.

At this point we turn from the firm to the industry. How, we ask, *will* the output of an industry change when there is a rise in the price of a factor it employs? Clearly this will raise the price of the product.† And this in turn will reduce the demand for output. This accounts for the output effect, which affects all factors equally. On top of this, the demand for the factor whose price has risen will fall

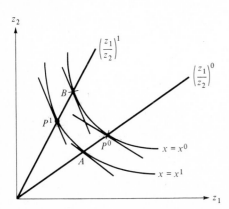

Figure 9-1 Output effect and substitution effect of a rise in w_1 (w_2 constant). *Note:* The move from P^0 to P^1 can be considered as a move from P^0 to A (output effect) and from A to P^1 (substitution effect). For small moves an identical breakdown would consist of the move P^0 to B (substitution effect) and B to P^1 (output effect).

---

† Given constant returns to scale, the price of the product must equal its average cost (or unit cost). This is

$$\frac{C}{x} = w_1\frac{z_1}{x} + w_2\frac{z_2}{x} = w_1 h^1\left(\frac{w_1}{w_2}\right) + w_2 h^2\left(\frac{w_1}{w_2}\right)$$

$$= j(w_1, w_2)$$

This unit cost is homogeneous of degree 1 in prices and independent of scale.

due to its reduced input coefficient (the substitution effect). What is so convenient is that the two effects can be treated as additive. This provides an extremely convenient framework for most of our chapter. First we examine the output effect by considering demand under fixed factor proportions. Then we move on to the substitution effect where factor proportions are variable, and finally bring the two effects together. For most of the time we are assuming that all other factor prices are given, though on occasions we shall relax this assumption to allow for a rising supply price of other factors to the industry.

9-2 DEMAND WITH FIXED FACTOR PROPORTIONS: THE OUTPUT EFFECT

Suppose 1 unit of x requires a units of K and b units of L. Then, under perfect competition the price of x is

$$p = aw_K + bw_L$$

Constant Prices of Other Factors

Now we let w_L rise but assume that the price of the other factor (w_K) is constant. The proportional increase in price is

$$\frac{dp}{p} = \frac{bw_L}{p}\frac{dw_L}{w_L} = v_L\frac{dw_L}{w_L}$$

or

$$d \log p = v_L d \log w_L$$

where v_L is the share of L in costs.

But the price increase reduces output:

$$d \log x = \eta^D d \log p = \eta^D v_L d \log w_L$$

And, since production is by fixed proportions, the proportional fall in each factor is the same as the proportional fall in output.

So

$$d \log L = d \log x$$

Hence

$$\frac{\partial \log L}{\partial \log w_L} = \varepsilon_{LL} = v_L \eta^D$$

Thus if airport services account for one-tenth of the cost of air travel (in fact rather less for European trips) and the elasticity of demand for air travel is about -1.5, the elasticity of demand for airport services is -0.15. Thus the short-run demand elasticity for any airport's service is quite low, though in the longer run, of course, other airports can be substituted, and the number of landings per trip reduced by larger planes, fewer stopovers, and so on. Proportions are likely to be variable in the long run. Thus

For a fixed-proportions production function with other factor prices fixed

$$\varepsilon_{ii} = v_i \eta^D$$

This expression also measures the output effect in ε_{ii} in the case where there is also a substitution effect.

This principle already confirms Marshall's first rule. It would appear to confirm his second rule too (the "importance of being unimportant"). For the lower your share in costs, the less a rise in your price raises the price of the product. However, what Marshall overlooked was that (unlike η^D) v_i also affects the substitution effect.

Variable Supply Price of Other Factors

Before turning to this, however, we can conveniently look at the effect of rising supply prices of other factors. We now suppose that when x falls (due to the rise in w_L), w_K will fall, since less K is now demanded and the supply curve of K is rising. This is illustrated in Figure 9-2. We choose units so that 1 unit of x requires 1 unit of L and 1 unit of K. The top panel shows the demand curve for x and the rising supply curve of K. Since it takes 1 unit each of L and K to produce 1 unit of x, the product price must be

$$p = w_L + w_K$$

So the demand price for L must equal the demand price for x minus the supply price for the corresponding amount of K. This is shown in the bottom panel.

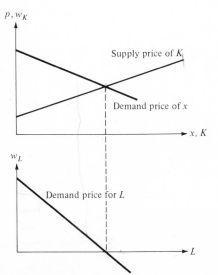

Figure 9-2 The demand for a factor (L) with fixed factor proportions and imperfectly elastic supply of the other factor (K).

Reverting to the more general formulation with no arbitrary choice of units, it must be the case that

$$d \log p = v_K d \log w_K + v_L d \log w_L$$

Thus

$$d \log x = \eta^D d \log p = \eta^D v_K d \log w_K + \eta^D v_L d \log w_L$$

But $d \log L = d \log K = d \log x$ (due to fixed proportions), and $v_K = 1 - v_L$.

Therefore

$$1 = \eta^D (1 - v_L) \frac{d \log w_K}{d \log K} + \eta^D v_L \frac{d \log w_L}{d \log L}$$

where

$$\frac{d \log w_K}{d \log K} \qquad \text{refers to the supply function for } K$$

and

$$\frac{d \log w_L}{d \log L} \qquad \text{refers to the demand function for } L$$

So

$$\frac{1}{\varepsilon_{LL}} = \frac{1}{\eta^D v_L}\left[1 - \frac{\eta^D (1 - v_L)}{\eta^S}\right]$$

Hence

$$\varepsilon_{LL} = \frac{v_L \eta^D}{1 - (1 - v_L)\eta^D/\eta^S}$$

This confirms Marshall's third principle. The term $[-(1 - v_L)\eta^D/\eta^S]$ is positive: and the smaller η^S, the larger this term is, and, consequently, the smaller (absolutely) is ε_{LL}. Note that, as $\eta^S \to \infty$, $\varepsilon_{LL} \to v_L \eta^D$. So, if the industry faces given prices of other factors, our previous formula applies. We shall generally assume this from now on.

Q9-1 Suppose that currently a ton of bananas in Jamaica costs $100 free on board (f.o.b.) and the cost of shipping a ton to New York is $50. The elasticity of demand for Jamaican bananas in New York is -3. What is the elasticity of demand for banana trips from Jamaica to New York if the elasticity of supply of bananas in Jamaica is
  (i) Infinity?
  (ii) 10?

Q9-2 "The market power of the oil-exporting countries is exaggerated if one looks only at the elasticity of demand for refined petroleum products." True or false?

Q9-3 Suppose one derives a demand curve for K in a corresponding manner to the demand curve just derived in Figure 9-2 for L. Can both be valid at the same time?

Q9-4 (A question analogous to that dealt with in Figure 9-2.) Suppose that each sheep (z) produces 1 unit of wool (x_1) and 1 of mutton (x_2). The demand curve for wool is

$$p_1 = 10 - x_1$$

and the supply curve of sheep is

$$w = 1 + z$$

What is the supply curve of mutton? What is the analogy between this question and that discussed in the text?

9-3 DEMAND WITH FIXED OUTPUT: THE SUBSTITUTION EFFECT

We also have to take into account the fact that a rise in the price of one factor is likely to alter factor proportions, as well as to alter output. We are only interested now in the substitution that occurs with output constant. If other prices are constant, the total effect of a (small) unit change in log w_i on the quantity log z_i is simply the sum of this substitution effect and the output effect $(v_i + \eta^D)$.

Needless to say, the size of the substitution effect depends on the elasticity of substitution. However, this concept needs to be carefully defined in order to get the right answer. We shall therefore proceed as follows. First, we shall develop a feel for the quantitative measurement of substitutability by discussing the two-factor case, using the so-called "direct" elasticity of substitution. However, if there are only two factors, each must be a substitute for the other (output constant). The two-factor case thus misses many of the important issues that arise—does a rise in the supply price of unskilled labour raise or lower the demand for skilled labour (it could do either)? We therefore move next to the general (three- or more factor) case and develop the Allen elasticity of substitution, which, though less intuitively simple is in the general case more practically useful than the "direct" elasticity.

Effects of Price on Quantity: Two-Factor Case

Suppose that $x = x(K, L)$. Then the difficulty of substitution is indicated by the sharpness of the curvature of the isoquants. Figure 9-3 illustrates the two polar cases (for the unit isoquant). The first is the fixed-proportions case, envisaged by Marx and analysed in full by Leontief. Here there is no possibility of substitution. If the production function exhibits constant returns, it is written

$$x = \min \left(\frac{K}{a}, \frac{L}{b} \right)$$

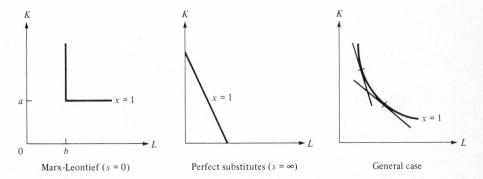

Figure 9-3 Elasticity of substitution.

The other polar case is where the rate at which labour can be substituted for capital is constant, whatever the capital-labour ratio: even if the farm is fully automated, a worker can still be replaced by the same amount of extra capital as when an ox was introduced to pull his plough. The corresponding equation is

$$x = aK + bL$$

But in between is the usual case where the more of one factor you have, relative to the other, the less is its relative marginal product. As the relative factor quantities change, say, towards higher capital intensity, the relative marginal product of labour rises.† So the rate at which one factor can be replaced by another changes. The difficulty of substitution is measured by the rate at which this rate changes as w_L/w_K changes (i.e., by the curvature of the isoquant). If the isoquant is very curved as in the fixed proportions case, substitution is difficult. If the isoquant is almost straight, as in the case of almost perfect substitutes, substitution is easy.

So far, we have looked at this question of substitution in terms of the effect of relative factor quantities (K/L) on relative marginal products. However, for the price-taking firm it is more interesting to look at the effect of relative marginal products on relative quantities, since firms will be equating relative marginal products to relative prices. The question we are now asking is how much substitution will occur when relative prices change. So if $x = f(K, L)$, a natural measure is to define the *direct elasticity of substitution* as the proportional change in K/L associated with a unit proportional change in f_L/f_K, holding output constant.‡

The direct elasticity of substitution between K and L is defined as

$$s_{KL} = \frac{\partial \log (K/L)}{\partial \log (f_L/f_K)} = -\frac{\partial \log (K/L)}{\partial \log (f_K/f_L)}$$

output being held constant. It is positive.

Under constant returns and with two factors of production, the direct elasticity of substitution turns out to be§

$$s_{KL} = \frac{f_K f_L}{x f_{KL}}$$

This makes excellent sense: the more that extra K raises f_L and vice versa, the less the elasticity of substitution.

---

† But it rises continuously and not discontinuously from 0 to ∞, as it does in the Marx-Leontief case when K/L passes from just below a/b to just above it.

‡ The term "direct" is to distinguish it from the Allen elasticity of substitution (see below).

§ For proof see R. G. D. Allen, *Mathematical Analysis for Economists*, Macmillan, London, 1964, chap. 13, p. 343. This formula does not hold with three or more factors.

We expect the elasticity of demand for a factor to be higher the higher the elasticity of substitution, and this is the case. With two factors and holding output constant,[†]

$$\frac{\partial \log L}{\partial \log w_L} = -(1 - v_L)s_{KL}$$

Thus, if we add the substitution and output effects, we find

$$\varepsilon_{LL} = v_L \eta^D - (1 - v_L)s_{KL}$$

or, multiplying through by -1,

$$|\varepsilon_{LL}| = v_L |\eta^D| + (1 - v_L)s_{KL}$$

Thus the (absolute) elasticity of demand for labour is a weighted average of the elasticity of demand for the product and the elasticity of substitution. This confirms Marshall's fourth proposition. But what about the second proposition—the importance of being unimportant? Imagine two alternative equilibria. In the first v_L is higher than in the second and in both η^D and s_{KL} are the same. Then the elasticity of demand will only be higher in the first if $|\eta|^D > s_{KL}$. So Marshall's second proposition only holds if the elasticity of product demand exceeds the elasticity of substitution.

Finally, we may note the general elasticity formula in which the other factor has a rising supply curve ($\eta^S < \infty$). This is[‡]

$$|\varepsilon_{LL}| = \frac{|\eta^D|s_{KL} + \eta^S[v_L|\eta^D| + (1 - v_L)s_{KL}]}{\eta^S + [v_L s_{KL} + (1 - v_L)|\eta^D|]}$$

This unwieldy formula is mainly of interest in giving us another special case, where the other factor is fixed ($\eta^S = 0$). Then

$$\frac{1}{|\varepsilon_{LL}|} = \frac{v_L}{|\eta^D|} + \frac{1 - v_L}{s_{KL}}$$

Once again, we have an expression consisting of two additive components— the first an output effect and the second a substitution effect. And again, Marshall's second proposition only holds if the elasticity of product demand exceeds the elasticity of substitution.

Effect of Price on Quantity: Three-Factor Case

With luck, the preceding discussion will have given the reader some feeling for the issues involved in the substitution between two factors. A rise in w_L (output constant) must lower the demand for L and raise the demand for K. However, in the three- (or more) factor case, this is by no means necessary. We are now interested not only in the size of the elasticities but, as regards the cross elasticities,

[†] This is proved in Appendix 8, which is best read after reaching page 272.
[‡] For proof see J. R. Hicks, *The Theory of Wages*, 2d ed., Macmillan, London, 1963, pp. 243–244.

in their signs. In other words, we want to know for each pair of factors whether they are complements or substitutes.

For the moment, we are interested only in the substitution effect. We therefore derive the relevant demand functions, output being held constant. The firm's problem is to minimise costs, subject to an output constraint. If there are three factors, z_1, z_2, and z_3, we have

$$\min C = w_1 z_1 + w_2 z_2 + w_3 z_3$$

subject to

$$x^0 = f(z_1, z_2, z_3)$$

First-order conditions are

$$\lambda f_1(z_1, z_2, z_3) = w_1$$

$$\lambda f_2(z_1, z_2, z_3) = w_2$$

$$\lambda f_3(z_1, z_2, z_3) = w_3$$

$$f(z_1, z_2, z_3) = x^0$$

These can be solved to give three demand functions (homogeneous of degree 0 in factor prices) of the form

$$z_i = g^i(w_1, w_2, w_3)x^0$$

plus an equation for λ (marginal cost).

If we want to know whether factor i is a Hicks-Allen substitute or complement to factor j, we simply ask:

Is

$$\left(\frac{\partial z_i}{\partial w_j}\right)_x < 0 \qquad i, j \text{ complements}$$

or

$$\left(\frac{\partial z_i}{\partial w_j}\right)_x > 0 \qquad i, j \text{ substitutes}$$

They are complements in the first case, because when w_j rises, z_j falls, and if z_i also falls it is reasonable to call them complements. In the opposite case z_i is being substituted for z_j.

In asking this type of question we need only ask about $\partial z_i / \partial w_j$ since

$$\left(\frac{\partial z_i}{\partial w_j}\right)_x = \left(\frac{\partial z_j}{\partial w_i}\right)_x$$

We have already proved the symmetry of cross-substitution effects on page 145, but it is useful to repeat the proof here. If the cost function is

$$C = C(w_1, w_2, w_3, x)$$

then

$$z_i = \frac{\partial C}{\partial w_i}(w_1, w_2, w_3, x)$$

is the output-constant ("compensated") demand function (see page 145).† It follows that

$$\left(\frac{\partial z_i}{\partial w_j}\right)_x = \frac{\partial^2 C}{\partial w_i \partial w_j} = \left(\frac{\partial z_j}{\partial w_i}\right)_x$$

We shall use the synbol C_{ij} to denote $\partial^2 C/(\partial w_i \partial w_j)$.

Once again, we are as interested in the strengths of effects as in their signs. From our previous equation the output-constant cross elasticity of demand is

$$\left(\frac{\partial \log z_i}{\partial \log w_j}\right)_x = \left(\frac{\partial z_i}{\partial w_j}\right)_x \frac{w_j}{z_i} = C_{ij} \frac{w_j}{z_i} = \varepsilon_{ij}^*$$

We can now introduce a more general concept of the elasticity of substitution. As in Chapter 5 we shall define the "Allen elasticity of substitution" as follows.

> *The Allen elasticity of substitution is defined as $\sigma_{ij} = \varepsilon_{ij}^*/v_j$, where v_j is the share of z_j in total cost and ε_{ij}^* is the output-constant cross elasticity of demand.*

We can again check that $\sigma_{ij} = \sigma_{ji}$.

$$\sigma_{ij} = \left(\frac{\partial z_i}{\partial w_j}\right)_x \frac{w_j}{z_i} \frac{C}{w_j z_j} = \frac{C_{ij} C}{C_i C_j}$$

where $C_i = \partial C/\partial w_i = z_i$.

Similarly,‡

$$\sigma_{ji} = \left(\frac{\partial z_j}{\partial w_i}\right)_x \frac{w_i}{z_j} \frac{C}{w_i z_i} = \frac{C_{ij} C}{C_i C_j}$$

It is time to revert to our original problem. What determines the market demand for a factor? By definition the output-constant elasticity is

$$\varepsilon_{ij}^* = v_j \sigma_{ij}$$

and the own-price substitution elasticity§ is got by setting $j = i$:

$$\varepsilon_{ii}^* = v_i \sigma_{ii}$$

It follows that the total (gross) elasticities are as follows.

---

† The cost function is of the form $C = h(w_1, w_2, w_3)x$.

‡ An expression for σ_{ij} in terms of the parameters of the production function, rather than the cost function, can be found in Appendix 8.

§ Like other writers, we use the phrase substitution elasticity to refer to ε_{ij}^* and the phrase elasticity of substitution to refer to $\sigma_{ij} = \varepsilon_{ij}^*/v_j$.

The following expressions for own- and cross-price elasticities of demand, other factor prices constant, are totally general:

$$\varepsilon_{ij} = v_j(\eta^D + \sigma_{ij})$$

$$\varepsilon_{ii} = v_i(\eta^D + \sigma_{ii})$$

The own-price elasticity must be negative since both η^D and σ_{ii} are negative (output and substitution effects are negative). But a cross-price effect may be positive if the factors are substitutes ($\sigma_{ij} > 0$) and the positive substitution effect outweighs the negative output effect.

The expression we derived for the own elasticity in the two-factor case was

$$\varepsilon_{ii} = v_i\eta^D - (1 - v_i)s_{ij}$$

This is consistent with the general formulation, since in the two-factor case, as Appendix 8 proves, $v_i\sigma_{ii} = -(1 - v_i)\sigma_{ij}$ and $\sigma_{ij} = s_{ij}$. But the general formulation is clearly preferable.

Effects of Quantity on Marginal Product: Two-Factor Case

Though in this chapter we are primarily interested in tracing the effects of prices on quantities, we may pause briefly to check the remarks made in Chapter 2 about the effect of changes in factor proportions upon relative shares in costs (income shares). In the two-factor case the share of labour relative to capital is

$$\frac{w_L L}{w_K K} = \frac{f_L L}{f_K K}$$

If L/K rises (due say to immigration) the relative share of labour rises if the proportional rise in L/K exceeds the proportional fall in f_L/f_K, i.e., if

$$d \log \left(\frac{L}{K}\right) > -d \log \left(\frac{f_L}{f_K}\right)$$

or

$$\frac{\partial \log (K/L)}{\partial \log (f_L/f_K)} > 1$$

In other words, the elasticity of substitution must exceed unity; labour must not be too difficult to absorb.

What happens to the total *absolute* income of labour, if labour rises with capital constant?

$$\frac{\partial(f_L L)}{\partial L} = L f_{LL} + f_L$$

By the properties of constant returns (Appendix 3)

$$f_{LL} = -\left(\frac{K}{L}\right) f_{LK}$$

Thus
$$\frac{\partial(f_L L)}{\partial L} = -K f_{LK} + f_L$$

$$= \frac{-K f_K f_L}{x s_{KL}} + f_L$$

$$= f_L \left(1 - \frac{f_K K}{x s_{KL}}\right)$$

$$> 0 \qquad \text{if } s_{KL} > \frac{f_K K}{x}$$

So labour's total income may rise (even if its relative share falls) provided the elasticity of substitution exceeds the relative share of the other factor in total income.

Q9-5 In most Western countries the share of labour has been rising in recent years, while capital deepening (a rise in K/L) has also occurred. Similarly, the share of labour is generally higher in richer than poorer countries. What does this suggest about s_{KL}?

Effect of Quantity on Marginal Product: Three-Factor Case

Going on to the three-factor case, we might ask: If we are holding other factor quantities constant, how does an increase in unskilled labour, N, affect the marginal products of skilled labour, S, and capital, K? The answer is simple. If $x = f(K, S, N)$, we need to evaluate the effect of an increase in N on f_S and f_K. So we compute the cross-partial derivatives f_{SN} and f_{KN}. Suppose f_{ij} were positive. It would then seem natural to call factors i and j complements since more of factor j raises the marginal product of factor i. But does $f_{ij} > 0$ imply that the factors are Hicks-Allen complements? Not at all. It is extremely frustrating to find that this is not the case. However, most first-year students have made just such a discovery. If we take the two-factor case, and the cost-minimising second-order conditions are satisfied,† then $f_{ij} > 0$. Yet we know the two factors are Hicks-Allen substitutes:

$$\left(\frac{\partial z_i}{\partial w_j}\right)_x > 0$$

The answer to this apparent paradox is that we have to distinguish, as Hicks has done more recently, between the relationship of factors i and j when we go from price into quantity (the p-into-q relationship) and the relationship when we go from quantity into price (the q-into-p relationship). If there are two factors, they must be p-into-q substitutes ($\sigma_{ij} > 0$) and q-into-p complements ($f_{ij} > 0$). If there are three or more factors, each factor must have at least one p-into-q substitute

---

† These require $f_{11} < 0$. And (from Appendix 3) $f_{12} = -(z_1/z_2)f_{11}$.

and one q-into-p complement. It is also impossible for a pair to be both p-into-q complements and q-into-p substitutes; but otherwise almost anything is possible. However, suppose we define the unit free *elasticity of complementarity* as

$$c_{ij} = \frac{f_{ij}\, f}{f_i\, f_j}$$

It is then likely in a general way that pairs of factors which are more complementary than other pairs in terms of c_{ij} will tend to be more complementary in terms of σ_{ij}, and vice versa.[†]

9-4 THE CES PRODUCTION FUNCTION

These concepts are all very well, but can any of them in practice be measured? We have already seen how important they are both for understanding income distribution, tax incidence, trading patterns, and many other matters. Yet progress in empirical measurement has been inevitably slow. As in demand theory, some of the main advances have come from assuming some particular form of (production) function. Of these perhaps the most commonly used in production theory is one that assumes a constant direct and Allen elasticity of substitution between pairs of factors.[‡] It can be written for any number of factors, but we shall confine ourselves first to two factors (K and L). The function has the following form[§]

$$x = \gamma[\delta K^{-\rho} + (1 - \delta)L^{-\rho}]^{-v/\rho} \qquad \begin{array}{c} -1 < \rho < \infty \\ \rho \neq 0 \\ 0 < \delta < 1 \\ v, \gamma > 0 \end{array}$$

The function is homogeneous of degree v, as can be seen by multiplying K and L by λ. To make the function homogeneous of degree 1, we shall henceforth set $v = 1$. This leaves three parameters:

γ, the efficiency parameter
ρ, the substitution parameter
δ, the distribution parameter

[†] On the relation of the two measures see R. Sato and T. Koizumi, "On the Elasticities of Substitution and Complementarity," *Oxford Economic Papers*, vol. 25, pp. 44–56, March 1973, and J. R. Hicks, "Elasticity of Substitution Again: Substitutes and Complements," *Oxford Economic Papers*, vol. 22, pp. 289–296, November 1970. In the two-factor case $c_{ij} = 1/\sigma_{ij}$.

[‡] It is also increasingly used in the utility analysis of labour supply.

[§] This function was first introduced K. J. Arrow, H. B. Chenery, B. S. Minhas, and R. M. Solow, "Capital-Labour Substitution and Economic Efficiency," *Review of Economics and Statistics*, vol. 43, pp. 228–232, August 1961.

The first of these is easily disposed of. If one firm has a higher γ than another, it produces proportionately more output from given inputs. For any one firm, γ can be eliminated from the function by a suitable choice of units in which to measure x. We shall henceforth assume that units have been chosen such that $\gamma = 1$. This gives us a stripped-down function:

$$x = [\delta K^{-\rho} + (1 - \delta)L^{-\rho}]^{-1/\rho}$$

or

$$x^{-\rho} = \delta K^{-\rho} + (1 - \delta)L^{-\rho}$$

We can now get down to the real business, which is to find the elasticity of substitution. Totally differentiating,

$$-\rho x^{-\rho-1}dx = -\rho\delta K^{-\rho-1}dK - \rho(1 - \delta)L^{-\rho-1}dL \tag{1}$$

Thus writing x_L as f_L, and x_K as f_K,

$$f_L = \frac{\partial x}{\partial L} = (1 - \delta)\left(\frac{x}{L}\right)^{1+\rho} \tag{2}$$

and

$$f_K = \frac{\partial x}{\partial K} = \delta\left(\frac{x}{K}\right)^{1+\rho} \tag{3}$$

Hence

$$\frac{f_L}{f_K} = \frac{1 - \delta}{\delta}\left(\frac{K}{L}\right)^{1+\rho} \tag{4}$$

Thus

$$\frac{K}{L} = \left(\frac{\delta}{1 - \delta}\frac{f_L}{f_K}\right)^{1/(1+\rho)} \tag{5}$$

and

$$s_{KL} = \frac{\partial \log (K/L)}{\partial \log (f_L/f_K)} = \frac{1}{1 + \rho}$$

So ρ deserves its name: the substitution parameter. Assuming profit maximisation (i.e., $f_L = w_L/p_x$ and $f_K = w_K/p_x$), the value of ρ can be estimated empirically from any one of Equations (2) to (5), depending on data availability and the relevant econometric assumptions. The equation is estimated in log-linear form.

The analysis also makes it clear why we restrict ρ such that

$$-1 < \rho < \infty$$

For if the isoquant is to be convex to the origin

$$s_{KL} > 0$$

Thus

$$\frac{1}{1 + \rho} > 0$$

We can now examine what happens as ρ approaches each of these limits and also as it approaches zero. The results can be summarised as follows:

Limiting value of		Production
ρ	s_{KL}	function
∞	0	Marx-Leontief
0	1	Cobb-Douglas
-1	∞	Perfect substitution

The first and last of these are clear. But the second needs some explaining. If we insert $\rho = 0$ into the CES function, it vanishes. However, we can show that as $\rho \to 0$ the function tends to the Cobb-Douglas, as follows.

From Equation (1)

$$\frac{dx}{x^{1+\rho}} = \delta \frac{dK}{K^{1+\rho}} + (1 - \delta) \frac{dL}{L^{1+\rho}}$$

If $\rho = 0$

$$\frac{dx}{x} = \delta \frac{dK}{K} + (1 - \delta) \frac{dL}{L}$$

Thus
$$d \log x = \delta \, d \log K + (1 - \delta) \, d \log L$$

which, if integrated, gives

$$x = \gamma K^{\delta} L^{1 - \delta}$$

where γ is a constant of integration. This is the Cobb-Douglas function. There is no difficulty in checking that it has an elasticity of substitution of unity, since

$$f_L = (1 - \delta) \frac{x}{L}$$

$$f_K = \frac{\delta x}{K}$$

Thus
$$\frac{f_L}{f_K} = \frac{1 - \delta}{\delta} \frac{K}{L}$$

So much for ρ. What of δ? In the Cobb-Douglas function we already know that labour's income share relative to capital's is

$$\frac{w_L L}{w_K K} = \frac{f_L L}{f_K K} = \frac{1 - \delta}{\delta}$$

So δ determines distribution, independent of factor proportions. In the general case, whatever the value of ρ, Equation (4) gives

$$\frac{w_L L}{w_K K} = \frac{f_L L}{f_K K} = \frac{1 - \delta}{\delta} \left(\frac{K}{L}\right)^{\rho}$$

Distribution depends on K/L and ρ as well as on δ.

Q9-6 Suppose that

$$x = (0.2\ K^{-1} + 0.8\ L^{-1})^{-1}$$

(i) What is the elasticity of substitution?
(ii) Suppose $K = \frac{1}{2}$ and $L = 1$. What are absolute and relative income shares?
(iii) What if K now rises to 1? Is this consistent with your finding about s_{KL}?
(iv) Suppose a firm is faced with

$$w_K = w_L = 1$$

What K/L will it use?

Q9-7 Suppose that

$$x = (0.2\ K^{-1} + 0.8\ L^{-1})^{-1}$$

and

$$y = K^{1/3} L^{2/3}$$

Is x or y unambiguously the more K-intensive? If not, at what w_L/w_K does the factor-intensity reversal occur?

Q9-8 An international cross-sectional study has shown that

$$\log \left(\frac{w_S}{w_N} \right) = a_0 - \frac{1}{8} \log \left(\frac{S}{N} \right)$$

where S is the number of workers with eight or more years of schooling, N is the number with less than eight years of schooling, and w_S and w_N are the corresponding wage rates. What, if anything, do you think can be inferred about the validity of basing educational plans on the assumption that more education will have a negligible effect on the wage structure?

Three-Factor Case

There is no difficulty in introducing a third factor, by, say, distinguishing between skilled labour S and unskilled labour N. Now we have

$$x^{-\rho} = \delta_K\ K^{-\rho} + \delta_S\ S^{-\rho} + (1 - \delta_K - \delta_S)N^{-\rho}$$

However, if the function is written in this "symmetrical" way, it implies that $s_{KS} = s_{KN} = s_{SN}$. There is no differential pattern of complementarity. This requirement is often unrealistic. For example, it may be argued that unskilled labour can quite easily be replaced by machinery, whereas skilled labour cannot and in fact is needed to manage the machinery. Thus we might expect that the elasticity of substitution between capital and unskilled labour (s_{KN}) would be higher than between capital and skilled labour (s_{KS}). We might also suppose that the elasticities of complementarity would have the following relationship:

$$c_{KS} > c_{KN}$$

Both these properties could be represented by a two-level CES function in which K and S were "nested" together in a subaggregate input Q using one value of ρ, and then Q and N were entered into the main production function with a different and lower value of ρ. Thus

$$x^{-\rho_2} = \delta Q^{-\rho_2} + (1 - \delta)N^{-\rho_2}$$

where

$$Q^{-\rho_1} = \alpha K^{-\rho_1} + (1 - \alpha)S^{-\rho_1}$$

So long as $\rho_1 > \rho_2$,

$$\frac{1}{1 + \rho_1} < \frac{1}{1 + \rho_2}$$

This means that the direct elasticity of substitution (s_{KS}) between K and S within the nest is lower than the direct elasticity of substitution (s_{QN}) between N and the nested aggregate Q. But we are interested in the relationship between N and one input K within the nest—not with the whole nested aggregate Q. This is easiest to analyse in terms of the elasticity of complementarity. We are interested in the conditions needed for

$$c_{KS} > c_{KN}$$

Thus, writing $x = f(K, S, N)$, we require

$$\frac{f_{KS} x}{f_K f_S} > \frac{f_{KN} x}{f_K f_N}$$

i.e.,

$$\frac{\partial \log f_S}{\partial K} > \frac{\partial \log f_N}{\partial K}$$

In other words, as capital accumulation occurs, this must raise the relative skill differential. It is relatively easy to show that this is implied if $\rho_1 > \rho_2$ (see Question 9-9). It is more laborious to show in addition that $\rho_1 > \rho_2$ also implies $\sigma_{KS} < \sigma_{KN}$. But the point has, we hope, been made.

With the aid of this and other forms of production function, economists are learning more and more about the structure of production. But, as Marshall pointed out, that is not the whole story about factor demand. For, unless there is only one industry, the market demand for a factor is the sum of the demands from the different industries. And each of these demands depends not only on the parameters of the production function, but also on the demand for the industry's product and the supply of other factors of production.

Q9-9 Show that in the production function given above

$$\rho_1 > \rho_2 \quad \text{implies} \quad \frac{\partial \log f_S}{\partial K} > \frac{\partial \log f_N}{\partial K}$$

Q9-10 (i) If the above function is correctly specified and $\rho_1 > \rho_2$, will the international cross-section regression specified in Question 9-8 over- or underestimate the depressing effect of more education on the relative wages of educated people, K being held constant?

(ii) Under what general restrictions on the production function would it be legitimate to run the function specified in Question 9-8, given that K varies between countries?

FURTHER ASPECTS OF PRODUCTION

What does it mean to say that a factor is paid the value of its marginal product? If ten men are working with ten shovels, how much would output rise if an extra man is hired but the number of shovels held constant? Surely the value of the marginal product is zero, if there are fixed proportions in production? To show that this need not be the case, we develop the programming analysis of the firm, which has also proved of great practical use to businessmen. In our treatment we assume that each good can only be produced by one unique fixed-proportions technology.

However, in practice there are few goods which can only be produced by one method of production. In most practical cases, once the technique of production has been chosen, the factor proportions are fixed; but before this there *is* a choice between techniques, each involving different factor proportions. In other words, there is no *ex-post* substitution, but there is *ex-ante* substitution, If there is enough *ex-ante* substitution, we can approximate long-run steady-state choices by the usual continuous production functions.

Having established this, we turn to dynamic aspects of production. We ask: What on the production side leads to economic growth? How can we usefully classify types of technical progress? And, how does this help us to understand the pattern of income distribution at a point in time?

10-1 PROGRAMMING ANALYSIS OF THE FIRM

The economist's theory of production is often criticised on the grounds that it does not help businessmen to make decisions. The criticism has some force: the theory was devised to predict how businessmen would behave rather than to help them decide how to. However, the postwar development of programming methods has made the charge much less valid. For this provides tools that can be applied to detailed decisions in the firm, while at the same time providing the economist with a good framework for predicting business behaviour. Within the firm it has the enormous advantage of providing a common language for engineers, accountants, and economists. We shall concentrate mainly on *linear* programming.

To get a feel for this let us first consider a practical problem. A firm produces two types of metal product, x_1 and x_2, which it can sell at fixed prices. The firm has available a certain fixed quantity of machine hours per period:

$$
\begin{array}{ll}
24 \text{ type-1 machine hours} & (z_1^0 = 24) \\
21 \text{ type-2 machine hours} & (z_2^0 = 21) \\
9 \text{ type-3 machine hours} & (z_3^0 = 9)
\end{array}
$$

In the short run it cannot buy any more equipment, nor can it sell any of its existing equipment on the market. However, the firm can buy any amount of labour and raw materials at the going prices. The distinction between machine hours and other inputs thus corresponds roughly to the accountant's dichotomy between fixed costs and variable costs. There are no stocks, so all output is sold in the period when it is produced. Each output and input is assumed to be infinitely divisible, and the outputs are produced by fixed proportions, constant-returns-to-scale processes.

Since labour and materials are available in unlimited supply, the firm first calculates the gross profit which it makes on each good after deducting labour and material costs. This is not of course the economist's measure of excess profit after deducting capital costs; it *is* the accountant's measure of gross profit, from which "overheads are to be covered leaving a margin of true profit." To make the most gross profit constitutes the firm's short-run "objective function," or more shortly, its objective.

Suppose that the gross profit per unit (or the "price" p) of the two outputs is

$$ p_1 = 2 \qquad p_2 = 5 $$

The firm's problem is then to maximise gross profit

$$ \Pi = p_1 x_1 + p_2 x_2 $$

subject to the physical constraints imposed by the limited availability of machines. Suppose the machine hours input-coefficient matrix is

$$
\begin{pmatrix} a_{11} & a_{12} \\ a_{21} & a_{22} \\ a_{31} & a_{32} \end{pmatrix} = \begin{pmatrix} 4 & 1 \\ 1 & 3 \\ 1 & 1 \end{pmatrix}
$$

where a_{ij} is the input of machine hours i per unit of output j. Then the firm's

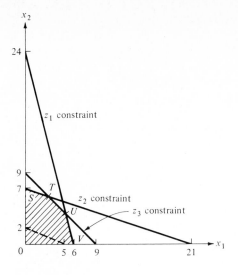

Figure 10-1 The linear programming problem.

problem is

$$\begin{array}{cc}
\textit{General expression} & \textit{Specific expression} \\
\max \Pi = p_1 x_1 + p_2 x_2 & \max \Pi = 2x_1 + 5x_2
\end{array}$$

$$\begin{array}{cc}
\text{such that} \quad a_{11}x_1 + a_{12}x_2 \le z_1^0 & \text{such that} \quad 4x_1 + x_2 \le 24 \\
a_{21}x_1 + a_{22}x_2 \le z_2^0 & x_1 + 3x_2 \le 21 \\
a_{31}x_1 + a_{32}x_2 \le z_3^0 & x_1 + x_2 \le 9 \\
x_1, x_2 \ge 0 & x_1, x_2 \ge 0
\end{array} \quad (1)$$

where the nonnegative constraints at the bottom arise from the fact that negative outputs are impossible.

The constraints are shown graphically in Figure 10-1. They define a "feasible region" indicated by the shaded area. This feasible region must be convex, though not strictly convex.† (Try drawing one that is not convex.) It has five corners (or "extreme points"), at each of which two constraints cross. As we have set up the problem, all the constraints play a role in defining the feasible region, but this is not of course a necessary feature of all problems. However, it is always convenient to eliminate redundant constraints before solving a problem.

The solution to our problem is easy to see. The equation

$$\Pi = 2x_1 + 5x_2$$

is a plane in three-dimensional space, whose equal-Π contours, projected into the (x_1, x_2) plane, are straight lines with a slope of

$$\left| \frac{dx_2}{dx_1} \right| = \frac{2}{5}$$

† See Appendix 1.

One such contour for $\Pi = 10$ is shown by the dotted line in Figure 10-1. As Π increases, the contours move out parallel to each other. Π clearly reaches its constrained maximum where a contour line passes through one or more of the "extreme points" of the feasible region. In our case the solution must be at point T, since at point U both constraints have (absolute) slopes greater than $\frac{2}{3}$, and at point S the z_2 constraint has a slope less than $\frac{2}{3}$. Thus the solution is given by writing the z_2 and z_3 constraints as equalities, and solving for x_1 and x_2. The answer is

$$x_1 = 3 \qquad x_2 = 6 \qquad \Pi = 36$$

The solution illustrates a perfectly general property of the solution of all linear programming (LP) problems.

1. The solution of a linear programming problem (if finite) will be found at one (or more) of the extreme points of the feasible set.†

The logic behind this is clear. The solution (if finite) must lie on the boundary of the feasible set. The boundary consists of linear segments. And the thing to be maximised is a linear form. Therefore there are only two possibilities:

1. The solution may occur only at one extreme point, as in our example.
2. The solution may occur along the whole length of one segment of the boundary, if the slope of the isoprofit contour equals the slope of the relevant constraint. Such a solution will include both extreme points at either end of the segment. [What profit function(s) would give solutions all along the segment TU? The answer is below.‡] The preceding theorem is extremely useful, since it means that to solve an LP problem we need only look at the corners. But before we come to this, there is another important property of the solution to be looked at.

The number of structural constraints that are binding is equal to the number of outputs that have nonzero values. There are two nonzero outputs (x_1 and x_2) and two constraints are binding (z_2 and z_3), while the third (z_1) is slack: some machines are not in use. This again is a perfectly general property of the solution to an LP problem.

2. The number of structural constraints that are binding equals the number of nonzero outputs (or activities).§

To check this, imagine that with our original constraints we had $p_1 = 1$ and

---

† It is sufficient for a finite solution to exist that for each output j, $a_{ij} > 0$ for at least one input i.

‡ Answer: $\Pi = \lambda x_1 + \lambda x_2$, where λ is any positive number.

§ An exception occurs if three or more constraints intersect at the same point and this point is the solution to the problem. In this case the solution is called "degenerate" and the number of binding constraints (i.e., ones without slack) exceeds the number of activities.

$p_2 = 5$. What is the number of nonzero outputs and the number of structural constraints that are binding at the optimum? (The answer is below.†) There is of course nothing mysterious about proposition 2. It follows directly from the fact that, to determine a given number of unknowns, there must be an equal number of equations (i.e., equalities, or binding constraints).

Proposition 1 given above is what makes linear programming problems so readily soluble. A crude method of proceeding is simply to calculate for all the possible "basic feasible solutions," corresponding to all the extreme points of the feasible set, the levels of x_1, x_2, and Π. The optimal solution is then the solution for which Π is largest. However, this may be an unnecessarily elaborate operation. We may not need to visit all corners. If we could find a systematic way of moving from one corner to another, plus a rule that told us when to stop, we might get away with much less work. Suppose we start at the origin $(x_1 = x_2 = 0)$. Now we ask: Should we move to S or V? At S, profit is higher than at V, so let us move there. But can we do better still? The slope of the z_2 constraint is $\frac{1}{3}$, so the marginal cost of x_1 (in terms of x_2) is $\frac{1}{3}$. But the marginal revenue from expanding x_1 (measured in terms of x_2) is $\frac{2}{5}$. So x_1 should be expanded. This takes us to T, from which no further expansion of x_1 is profitable. The type of comparison outlined above is the essence of the simplex method, which can be used to solve linear programming problems of any size.‡

The striking point about the preceding strategy is its close relation to the comparisons implicit in ordinary economic analysis using production functions. The difference is the much richer detail that goes into the linear programming approach. In the production function approach we should write the problem as

$$\max \Pi = p_1 x_1 + p_2 x_2$$

subject to $$0 = f(x_1, x_2, z_1^0, z_2^0, z_3^0)$$

where f is the production function stated in implicit form. Obtaining knowledge about the production function would be regarded as a prior technical problem and the choice of outputs as the economic problem. But in the LP approach the two problems cease to be distinguishable. The engineering decision (of how to maximise x_2 for any given x_1) is made simultaneously with the economic decision regarding the choice of outputs.

Shadow Prices and the Dual

What does all this tell us about the value of the factors of production? The obvious measure of the value of a type-1 machine hour is the increase in revenue which would result if one more such machine hour were available. This is the true "shadow price" of the factor. It measures the scarcity value of the factor

---

† Answer: one nonzero output (x_2) and one structural constraint (z_2).

‡ For a detailed analysis, see any of the basic textbooks, such as G. Hadley, *Linear Programming*, Addison-Wesley, Reading, Mass., 1961.

in the eyes of its owner, since it tells us how much he could advance his own objective by having one more unit of the factor.

LP provides us precisely with the firm's shadow prices. However, since this is not immediately obvious, let us first work out the shadow price of z_2 in a completely explicit way. We know that, at the solution values of x_1 and x_2, only the z_2 and z_3 constraints are binding. So

$$\Pi - p_1 x_1 - p_2 x_2 = 0$$

$$a_{21} x_1 + a_{22} x_2 = z_2^0$$

$$a_{31} x_1 + a_{32} x_2 = z_3^0$$

If we now let z_2 vary, holding z_3 constant, we find

$$\begin{pmatrix} 1 & -p_1 & -p_2 \\ 0 & a_{21} & a_{22} \\ 0 & a_{31} & a_{32} \end{pmatrix} \begin{pmatrix} d\Pi \\ dx_1 \\ dx_2 \end{pmatrix} = \begin{pmatrix} 0 \\ dz_2 \\ 0 \end{pmatrix}$$

So the shadow price of z_2 is what we shall label as w_2, where

$$w_2 = \frac{d\Pi}{dz_2} = \frac{p_1 a_{32} - p_2 a_{31}}{a_{21} a_{32} - a_{31} a_{22}}$$

By holding z_2 constant and varying z_3, we could likewise find the shadow price of z_3. Since z_1 is not a binding constraint, varying it cannot alter profit; so its shadow price is zero.

An alternative approach which gives the same answer argues as follows. If we are making the optimum use of our resources, the price of each output j that is being produced must be exactly equal to its implicit marginal cost. This in turn equals $\Sigma_i a_{ij} w_i$, where a_{ij} is the amount of input i needed per unit of output j, and w_i is that input's shadow price. We know that the shadow price of z_1 is zero. So

$$p_1 = a_{11}(0) + a_{21} w_2 + a_{31} w_3$$

$$p_2 = a_{12}(0) + a_{22} w_2 + a_{32} w_3$$

(2)

So, once again,

$$w_2 = \frac{p_1 a_{32} - p_2 a_{31}}{a_{21} a_{32} - a_{31} a_{22}}$$

and similarly for w_3.

However, both of these approaches require us first to solve the original LP problem. Only after we know which outputs are to be produced and which constraints are binding can we work out the shadow prices. But these can be obtained directly by solving what is known as the "*dual*" of the original (or "primal") programming problem. In the primal problem we solved for the quantities of outputs (x_i), whereas in the dual problem we solve for the shadow prices of inputs (w_j). The constraints are now that the cost of production of each good, when inputs are valued at their shadow prices, shall be at least as large as its price; for, if not, more of it should be produced. The shadow prices are to be nonnegative. And the objective is to minimise the cost of inputs, valued at the shadow prices. Thus the problem is to solve for w_1, w_2, and w_3 in

$$\min C = z_1^0 w_1 + z_2^0 w_2 + z_3^0 w_3$$

such that
$$a_{11}w_1 + a_{21}w_2 + a_{31}w_3 \geq p_1 \tag{3}$$

$$a_{12}w_1 + a_{22}w_2 + a_{32}w_3 \geq p_2$$

$$w_1, w_2, w_3 \geq 0$$

This problem can be solved on its own without solving the primal.† However, to save time, let us use the knowledge we have already obtained; that both goods are being produced. So their cost cannot exceed their price. (If a good is not produced in the primal, its cost in the dual exceeds its price.) It follows in our case that we can write the two structural constraints in (3) as equalities. In addition we also know that $w_1 = 0$, so we are back with the pair of equations (2) which we solved earlier. We thus have as the solution of the dual problem in our example

$$4(0) + w_2 + w_3 = 2$$

$$1(0) + 3w_2 + w_3 = 5$$

So
$$w_2 = \tfrac{3}{2} \qquad w_3 = \tfrac{1}{2} \qquad C = 36$$

This brings out a striking property of the dual: the function being minimised in the dual has the same solution value as the function being maximised in the primal (36 in each case).

While a lot more could be said about the dual, its basic practical importance for economic analysis is that it provides the implicit value attaching to each of the constrained items in the primal problem. In other words, it shows how the maximand could be increased if the constrained quantity was relaxed by 1 unit. So we could think of these values as equivalent to the Lagrangian multipliers of ordinary calculus, with one difference. Since each constraint need not be binding,

---

† Note that the relationship between the dual problem (3) and the primal problem (1), and between any primal and its dual, is that

1. The constraint values of the primal become the coefficients of the objective function in the dual and vice versa.
2. The input coefficient matrix is transposed.
3. The direction of the inequalities in the structural constraints is reversed.
4. The objective function is maximised in the primal and minimised in the dual.

The dual of the dual problem is the primal problem.

the value of the multiplier need not be nonzero; when the constraint is not binding, the multiplier will be zero.†

> 3. *The shadow price of a resource constraint equals the effect which one extra unit of the resource would have upon the objective function. If a resource constraint is not binding, its shadow price is zero.*

So even if factors are employed in fixed proportions in producing each particular good, an additional unit of a factor can add to the value of output. In this sense the value of the marginal product of a factor, holding other factors constant, is not zero. But, in saying this, we have to be very clear about what experiment we are making. If we take the production of one particular good and start with the correct factor proportions, then increasing one of the factors producing that good (while holding the other constant) will have no effect on the output of the good, and thus no value. But if we take the production of, say, two goods, and increase the total amount of one factor producing the two goods (while holding constant the total quantity of other factors producing these same goods), then there *is* an increase in the value of output. This comes about through an increase in the production of the good that is intensive in the augmented factor, and a fall in the production of the other good.‡

Parametric Programming and Factor Demand

We can now trace out, in our example, how the shadow price of a factor varies with its quantity. In other words we can derive the factor demand function. To do this we use *parametric programming*, where one of the parameters of the original problem is continuously altered and the corresponding solution values for quantities and shadow prices traced out. Parametric programming can clearly be used to trace out the demand curve for any factor and the supply curve of any output. We shall confine ourselves to the demand curve for z_1.

For each value of z_1 we need to compute the maximum possible profit Π. The shadow price of z_1 then equals the change in profit per (small) unit change in $z_1 (\Delta\Pi/\Delta z_1)$. So let us revert to Figure 10-1. Start with $z_1 = 0$. Now increase z_1 only. z_1 is the only binding constraint, and given our function only x_2 will be produced. So $\Delta\Pi/\Delta z_1 = p_2/a_{12} = 5$. As z_1 expands, the production point moves along $0S$, until it reaches S. At this point z_2 also becomes binding. As z_1 expands further, the production point slides down along ST to T. Over this range an extra unit of z_1 produces a smaller outward shift of the isoprofit line. So $\Delta\Pi/\Delta z_1 < p_2/a_{12}$. Once T is reached, further increases in z_1 have no effect on

---

† In addition, since we have nonnegativity constraints, it does not follow that $\partial\Pi/\partial x_i = 0$ for all *i*. For any x_i for which optimal $x_i = 0$, $\partial\Pi/\partial x_i < 0$. This point and the one in the text are the essence of the Kuhn-Tucker theorem, which applies also to nonlinear programming.

‡ This is the corollary of the point established in Chapter 2 that, provided there is some substitution in consumption, the real prices of factors are quite well-defined, even if there are fixed proportions in production (see Question 2-11).

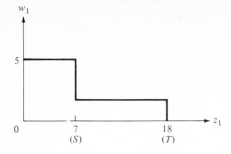

Figure 10-2 The firm's demand for a factor (fixed proportions in production).

profit. z_1 is no longer binding, and its shadow price is zero. Thus the demand function for z_1 (like the other factor demand curves and product supply curves) consists of linear segments (see Figure 10-2). All the standard predictions of comparative static theory about the signs of factor-price response still hold, subject to the qualification that there may be no response at all. Thus we now have

$$\frac{\partial z_1}{\partial w_1} \leq 0 \qquad \text{instead of} \qquad \frac{\partial z_1}{\partial w_1} < 0$$

Needless to say, linear programming methods could be applied to a much wider range of problems than the one we have considered. In addition, many extensions of linear programming are possible. "Dynamic programming" allows for optimisation over more than one period of time, and "integer programming" allows for the possibility that outputs are indivisible and can only be produced in discrete whole numbers. Nonconstant returns to scale can also be allowed for by introducing a set of piecewise linear constraints. A more radical departure is when the objective function also becomes nonlinear (like, for example, a standard utility function)—this requires "nonlinear programming."†

However, the basic approach of all these methods is the same: They throw up both primal values for the quantities and dual values for the shadow prices of the constraints. These dual values make possible a much more decentralised form of corporate management than would otherwise be possible. Two forms of decentralisation are possible. In one, each branch of the firm is made to use the shadow prices in its accounts. If each branch is then instructed to maximise its profit, this will then lead to the maximisation of the firm's total profit. A less drastic approach is to require each branch to use the shadow prices for decision making, undertaking all ventures which would yield a profit using these prices. But in its operational accounts the branch may not actually be charged the shadow prices.

Programming methods can also be used for national planning. In this case, the maximand must, of course, be some social welfare function, and the constraints must include whatever technical and behavioural constraints are present (including, where relevant, any technological external effects). The shadow prices,

---

† For a good introduction to this and to the Kuhn-Tucker theorem, see W. J. Baumol, *Economic Theory and Operations Analysis*, 3d ed., Prentice-Hall, Englewood Cliffs, N.J., 1972, chap. 7.

expressed in terms of some numeraire good, can then again be used for decentralised decision making. One approach would be to charge each separate agency the shadow prices of the resources it uses and then instruct it to maximise its algebraic profit.† Alternatively, the shadow prices can be used as "accounting prices" for purposes of decision making (cost-benefit analysis) but not for purposes of operational accounting. Much academic research is done along these lines in the centrally planned economies. But little practical use is made of programming. Planners prefer to use input-output analysis, where they themselves specify the pattern of final output.

Q10-1 A farmer wants to know how many cattle to raise and how much corn to grow. He has one square mile of land and his own labour (7 man-days per week). A full herd (of 1000 cattle) require 2 square miles of land and 7 man-days per week of labour throughout the year. A unit of corn requires $\frac{2}{3}$ square miles of land and $\frac{7}{2}$ man-days per week of labour for one year, except for 12 weeks in summer when it requires 7 man-days per week. The annual gross profit from a full herd (net of bought-in materials) is \$70,000, and the gross profit per unit of corn is \$50,000.
    (i) What outputs should the farmer produce?
    (ii) What is the shadow price of each resource?
    (iii) Suppose population movements now make it possible for him to hire labour at \$100 per day. Will his cropping pattern change?

Q10-2 In Figure 10-2, what is the shadow price of z_1 for $7 < z_1 < 18$? (The figure is not to scale!)

10-2 *EX-ANTE* AND *EX-POST* SUBSTITUTION

So far in this chapter we have assumed that any one good can only be produced by one fixed-proportions technique. This is very rarely the case. But it *may* often be true that, once the machines have been selected, there is no scope for increasing output, beyond the notional capacity of the machine, by increasing the input of other factors like labour. So we could have no *ex-post* substitution and yet a substantial *ex-ante* range of choice of techniques. This is illustrated in Figure 10-3. This shows the unit isoquant for a machine of size $K = K^2$ (a plough) and the unit isoquant for a less capital-intensive technique (digging sticks) involving a total amount of $K = K^1$ (some digging sticks).‡ Each technology uses fixed proportions. Thus once the investment in K has been made, there are no *ex-post* substitution possibilities at all. But what is the *ex-ante* position? Suppose in the extreme case that there is an infinite number of technologies, none dominated by any other, but each employing a different K/L. Then *ex-ante*, we have a continuous convex isoquant from which any K/L can be selected. But once a selection has been made, no substitution is possible. Capital is thus like the material used by an artist. Before he has given it form, it is as putty in his hands; but, once given form, it hardens as clay. The extreme case of full *ex-ante* and zero *ex-post* substitution is therefore sometimes called the *putty-clay* model.

---

† See page 27.
‡ The problem of measuring capital is treated briefly on pages 346–347.

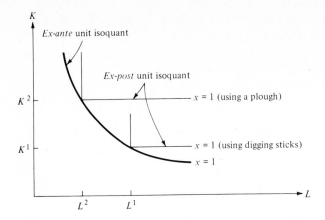

Figure 10-3 *Ex-ante* and *ex-post* production functions (zero *ex-post* substitution).

Let us look at the matter in terms of the relation of x/K to L/K (see Figure 10-4). We shall assume constant returns to scale for each technique. We shall also assume that, once K has been selected, output is proportional to labour up to the point where the machine is working at full capacity. After that, further application of labour has no effect on output. So, for $K = K^1$, the *ex-post* production function is as shown. But suppose we now go back a stage. The technique has not yet been chosen. We can now always increase x/K by increasing L/K.† Only when we have the technique that is appropriate to a given L/K can we achieve the *ex-ante* maximum x/K for our given equipment. This is of course exactly what we would expect: capital in the form of a digging stick is not going to

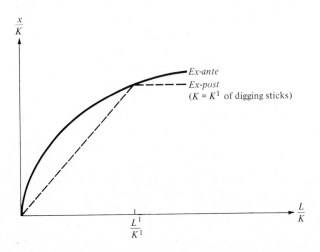

Figure 10-4 *Ex-ante* and *ex-post* production relations (no *ex-post* substitution).

† This assumes no noneconomic region (see page 400).

be very efficient if there is very little labour to work it. Machines do best if designed to fit the labour that is going to be available.

If *ex-ante* and *ex-post* production functions are different, they cannot be summarised by writing a single function $x(K, L)$, since the nature of the *ex-post* relation depends on the form that capital takes. In principle we would like to be able to estimate the *ex-ante* production function. But in a world of change we cannot assume that all the output/input observations we have lie on the *ex-ante* function. This had led a number of economists to advocate an approach to the study of production possibilities that is nearer to the engineers'. Such an approach would clearly be impractical if there were a wide range of undominated technologies available: the research task would be too great. However, it is often argued that for each product there is not really a continuous set of technologies but perhaps only four or five that are not dominated by some others. If we could get information on these, we could infer the firm's production function directly from the engineering data.

For simplicity we shall assume that the firm has two possible ways of producing x, each involving constant returns to scale (see Figure 10-5). Output of x by method 1, is

$$x_1 = \min\left(\frac{K_1}{a_1}, \frac{L_1}{b_1}\right)$$

when K_1 and L_1 are capital and labour employed in method 1. Similarly, using method 2, output of x is

$$x_2 = \min\left(\frac{K_2}{a_2}, \frac{L_2}{b_2}\right)$$

Since $x = x_1 + x_2$, we can get 1 unit of x by manufacturing *either* 1 unit of x_1 (with $K = a_1$ and $L = b_1$) *or* 1 unit of x_2 (with $K = a_2$ and $L = b_2$) *or* λ units of x_1 and $(1 - \lambda)$ units of x_2. In the latter case the factor input requirements are

$$K = \lambda a_1 + (1 - \lambda)a_2 = a_2 - \lambda(a_2 - a_1)$$

and
$$L = \lambda b_1 + (1 - \lambda)b_2 = b_2 - \lambda(b_2 - b_1)$$

So, as λ varies from 0 to 1, the sloping isoquant $P_2 P_1$ is traced out. Thus the *ex-ante* production function with noncontinuous technology is represented by isoquants consisting of linear segments.†

It is possible that our knowledge of production functions would be best advanced by attempting to construct such "engineering production functions." But progress to date has been slight. From now on we shall generally gloss over the problem discussed in this section. We shall assume that there is an infinite spectrum of *ex-ante* technologies. We shall also assume that at any one moment firms are employing the optimal machines for the existing K/L ratio, even if the K/L ratio is growing. This is clearly a simplification of reality.

---

† This is sometimes called the linear programming production function, since for any (K, L) we show that x which corresponds to the maximisation of $x_1 + x_2$.

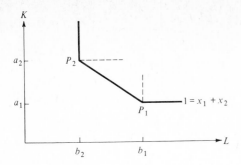

Figure 10-5 The segmented isoquant of linear programming.

10-3 TECHNICAL PROGRESS AND GROWTH

We make this simplification in order to examine one of the main preoccupations of modern man: economic growth. In this section we look at the matter mainly from the production side, taking the amount of saving or the rate of saving as given, depending on our specification. We shall be using an *aggregate* production function for the economy as a whole. Whether it is possible to specify a useful aggregate production function which has similar properties to micro production functions is a large and hotly-debated question, which we leave aside.

Growth Accounting and Productivity Change

Suppose the aggregate production function for the whole economy is†

$$Y = Y(K, L)$$

Thus the growth of national output over time must be due, in an immediate sense, to the growth of the inputs. We shall write

$$\dot{Y} = \frac{dY}{dt} \qquad \dot{K} = \frac{dK}{dt} \qquad \dot{L} = \frac{dL}{dt}$$

Then, differentiating the production function with respect to time, we find that

$$\dot{Y} = Y_K \dot{K} + Y_L \dot{L}$$

Hence
$$\frac{\dot{Y}}{Y} = Y_K \frac{K}{Y} \frac{\dot{K}}{K} + Y_L \frac{L}{Y} \frac{\dot{L}}{L}$$

Thus the rate of growth of output is a weighted average of the rates of growth of the inputs. The weights are the elasticities of output with respect to each input, which in competitive conditions are measured by their factor shares.

   In the later 1950s there developed a "growth accounting" industry in which this formula was applied to explaining the long-term growth of the U.S. economy.

---

† In this section we use capital Y to refer to total output, since in growth theory y is often used to denote output per head.

Unfortunately the early attempts were markedly unsuccessful. One famous study concluded, for example, that of 3 percentage points of growth per year only 1 point could be explained by the growth of capital and labour (measured in man-hours). This left an unexplained "residual" of 2 points.[†] Not surprisingly, this study roused a real hornet's nest. Some claimed that the inputs had not been properly measured, and that, when appropriate (Divisia) indices are constructed to allow for changes in the quality of labour and capital, there is no residual left.[‡] However, by that time a whole "technical progress" industry had developed. The idea of technical progress was not of course new. It is evident that inventions affect the productive possibilities open to men. The problem is to conceptualise these changes in quantifiable form.

Hicks-Neutral and Biased Technical Progress

The simplest concept of technical change is to suppose that it increases the output from given inputs without in any way affecting the way the inputs interact. The production function for period t then becomes

$$Y_t = A(t)f(K_t, L_t)$$

So

$$\frac{\dot{Y}}{Y} = f(K_t, L_t)\frac{\dot{A}}{Y} + Af_K\frac{K}{Y}\frac{\dot{K}}{K} + Af_L\frac{L}{Y}\frac{\dot{L}}{L}$$

$$= \frac{\dot{A}}{A} + Y_K\frac{K}{Y}\frac{\dot{K}}{K} + Y_L\frac{L}{Y}\frac{\dot{L}}{L}$$

The residual is now simply the rate of growth of A, or, if you like, the rate of growth of the economy's efficiency parameter. It is sometimes called the growth in "total factor productivity."

The technical change is "neutral" in the sense that for a given K/L the marginal rate of substitution between factors is unchanged. All that happens is that the isoquants are renumbered (each isoquant gets a higher output index each year), and the marginal product of each factor (for given factor supplies) rises by $\dot{A}/A$ each year. Thus within any one industry relative income distribution is unaffected if relative factor prices are constant.

This neutrality assumption may not strike you as plausible. Alternative assumptions would be that technical progress either (1) raises the relative marginal product of labour for a given K/L or (2) raises the relative marginal product of capital. In either case technical progress is, in the Hicks sense, biased.[§] In case (1), the effect, if factor prices were constant, would be to reduce the optimal

[†] See R. M. Solow, "Technical Change and the Aggregate Production Function," *Review of Economics and Statistics*, vol. 39, pp. 312–320, August 1957.

[‡] See D. W. Jorgenson and Z. Griliches, "The Explanation of Productivity Change," *Review of Economic Studies*, vol. 34, pp. 249–283, July 1967.

[§] For a further discussion of technical progress see R. G. D. Allen, *Macroeconomic Theory*, Macmillan, New York, 1967, chap. 13.

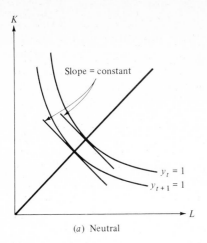
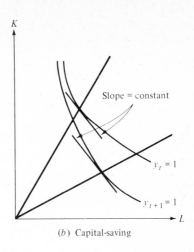

Figure 10-6 Hicks-neutral and Hicks-capital-saving technical progress.

K/L; such progress is therefore called *capital-saving*. In case (2) the effect, if factor prices were constant, would be to raise the optimal K/L; such progress is therefore called *labour-saving*. Figure 10-6 illustrates neutral technical progress and capital-saving technical progress.

> *For a given K/L, Hicks-neutral progress leaves relative marginal products unaffected; capital-saving technical progress raises the relative marginal product of labour, and labour-saving technical progress raises the relative marginal product of capital.*

Harrod-Neutral Technical Progress

A quite different concept of neutrality is that introduced by Harrod. It may seem a strange one, and its rationale will only become clear in a minute. The Harrod-neutral production function is of the form

$$Y_t = Y[K_t, a(t)L_t]$$

Output is a function of capital and of labour measured in efficiency units. The number of efficiency units per worker rises through time, i.e., there is "labour-augmenting" technical progress. Let us call these efficiency units "trogs" (N)

$$N_t = a(t)L_t$$

Hence $$Y_t = Y(K_t, N_t)$$

Suppose that this production function exhibits constant returns to scale. Three properties follow.

1. The marginal product of capital (Y_K) depends on the ratio of capital to trogs (K/N).

2. The ratio of output to capital (Y/K) also depends on K/N.
3. Therefore, if K/N is constant, $Y/K \, Y_K$ is constant so that the relative distribution of income is constant. This is the rather surprising sense in which Harrod-neutral technical progress is neutral. The key relation is often expressed as follows.

> *Harrod-neutral technical progress implies that whenever it happens that Y/K is constant, Y_K is constant and vice versa.*

The relevance of this will become clear shortly.

But first we note an interesting point. It is possible for technical progress to be both Hicks-neutral and Harrod-neutral. However, this requires that the production function be Cobb-Douglas, i.e., of the form

$$Y = bK^{\alpha}[a(t)L]^{1-\alpha} = [a(t)]^{1-\alpha}bK^{\alpha}L^{1-\alpha}$$

This function clearly satisfies both criteria. To see why it is the only one that does, consider the following. Suppose that in the Harrod function the ratio $K_t/a(t)L_t$ were the same in period T and period $T + 1$. Then since $a(T + 1) > a(T)$, the ratio K/L must have risen. But the distribution of income is constant. The only Hicks-neutral function $a(t)f(K, L)$ in which the distribution of income is constant when K/L rises is the Cobb-Douglas (since $\sigma = 1$). The fact that technical progress can be at once labour-augmenting and Hicks-neutral should make it obvious that there is no clear relation between the two systems of classification. A function that is labour-augmenting is not necessarily either Hicks-capital-saving or Hicks-labour-saving.†

Neoclassical Growth Models

So far we have only asked: For given technical progress and given changes in factor supply, how will output change? We have not asked: What determines the rate of investment? This question is the subject of Chapter 12, and can only be properly handled within the context developed there. However, many models of economic growth have been based on the simplifying assumption that the fraction (s) of income that is saved and invested is exogenous.‡ Using this assumption, the models then predict the steady-state growth path of the economy.

---

† If we write $y = Y/L$ and $k = K/L$, then if $Y = aLf(K/aL)$

$$y = af\left(\frac{k}{a}\right) \qquad \frac{\partial Y}{\partial K} = f'\left(\frac{k}{a}\right) \qquad \text{and} \qquad \frac{\partial Y}{\partial L} = af\left(\frac{k}{a}\right) - f'\left(\frac{k}{a}\right)k$$

Thus
$$\frac{\partial Y}{\partial L}\bigg/\frac{\partial Y}{\partial K} = af\left(\frac{k}{a}\right)\bigg/f'\left(\frac{k}{a}\right) - k$$

and
$$\frac{\partial}{\partial a}\left(\frac{\partial Y}{\partial L}\bigg/\frac{\partial Y}{\partial K}\right) = \frac{1}{f'^2 a}\left[f'(y - kf') + ff''k\right]$$

This cannot be signed without further information.

‡ Sometimes the assumption relates to the whole economy, sometimes separately to workers and capitalists, where the latter save more than the former.

Before examining any such model, let us ask what facts it is trying to explain. Economists who are interested in steady-state growth argue that this is a fair approximation to the world around us. They claim that the following stylised facts are roughly true:

1. Y/L has been rising at a constant rate.
2. K/L has also been rising at a constant rate.

These facts could be consistent with a stable constant-returns production function. But from 2 one would then expect a fall in Y/K and Y_K. However,

3. Y/K has been constant.
4. Y_K has been constant. So, from 3 and 4,
5. Y/KY_K has been constant (constant income shares).

Thus we have steady-state growth. It is a steady state in the sense that Y/K, Y_K, and income shares are constant. But it is growth in the sense that the real wage per man is rising. How can these facts (if true) be explained?†

The standard neoclassical growth model argues as follows. Output (Y) is a constant-returns function of capital K and labour, measured in trogs N:

$$Y = Y(K, N)$$

The economy is experiencing Harrod-neutral technical progress at a constant proportional rate m, so

$$N_t = e^{mt} L_t$$

If the growth rate of the labour force is l, the trog growth rate is

$$\frac{\dot{N}}{N} = m + l = n$$

Capital is growing at the same rate:

$$\frac{\dot{K}}{K} = n$$

Therefore Y_K is constant and so is Y/K.

But why should capital grow at this rate? This is where the constant exogenous savings rate comes in. Savings per period are sY. So

$$\text{Savings per trog} = \frac{sY}{N}$$

But Y/N is a function of K/N. So

$$\text{Savings per trog} = s \cdot g\left(\frac{K}{N}\right)$$

† These stylised facts were noted in the 1960s and do not take account of the marked changes that have occurred in the 1970s.

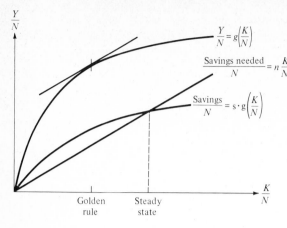

Figure 10-7 The neoclassical growth model.

This function is shown in Figure 10-7. The top curve is the production function relation between Y/N and K/N, and the lower curve is a constant fraction of the upper curve.

But if K/N is to be constant and N is growing at a rate n, to maintain K/N constant we need $\dot{K}/K = n$.

Hence

$$\frac{\dot{K}}{N} = n \frac{K}{N}$$

Therefore

$$\text{Savings needed per trog} = n \frac{K}{N}$$

This linear function is also shown in Figure 10-7. However, if we assume that output and capital consist of the same jellylike substance, output saved is equal to investment. So investment needed is the same as savings needed. And when savings per trog equal savings needed per trog, we have a steady-state equilibrium value of K/N defined by

$$s \cdot g \left(\frac{K}{N}\right) = n \frac{K}{N}$$

But is there any reason to suppose that we shall get there? In other words, is the equilibrium stable? Yes. Suppose trogs start poor (low K/N). Savings per trog are more than are needed to keep K/N constant, so K/N grows. Equally, if trogs start rich (high K/N), there are insufficient savings to maintain so high a K/N, so K/N falls.

This steady-state model is clearly very artificial. We need not criticise it too severely on the grounds of the fixed savings rate—it is possible to derive steady states with constant savings rates from ordinary utility maximisation. More questionable is the assumption of Harrod-neutral technical progress, which is not only sufficient but necessary for a steady state. We have already seen that some economists claim to be able to explain growth without recourse to technical progress. They and others would question the stylised facts the model is meant to explain. In addition, labour force growth is not usually constant.

The Golden Rule

However, for normative economics, it is often difficult, if not impossible, to grapple with problems that have an intertemporal aspect without setting them up in a framework where different steady states are compared for their desirability. The most famous of these exercises asks the question: "Suppose s can be determined by the government once and for all, in the knowledge that this will generate steady-state equilibrium growth. What s maximises welfare, assuming welfare varies directly with consumption per head?" For simplicity, we shall assume now that there is no technical progress ($m = 0$), so that there is no problem of asymmetry between generations and N now indicates population ($=$ labour). There is population growth at rate n. The problem is simple.

$$\text{Consumption per head} = \frac{Y - \dot{K}}{N} = \frac{Y}{N} - \frac{\dot{K}}{N}$$

But in a steady state

$$\frac{\dot{K}}{N} = n\frac{K}{N}$$

Thus

$$\text{Consumption per head} = g\left(\frac{K}{N}\right) - n\frac{K}{N}$$

The optimal capital-labour ratio is thus where

$$g'\left(\frac{K}{N}\right) - n = 0$$

So

$$Y_K = n$$

The marginal product of capital (interest rate) must equal the rate of growth of population (and output) (see Figure 10-7).

This is the so-called *golden rule of accumulation*. It determines the optimal K/N, Y/N, and s. The golden rule rate of saving s may of course be higher or lower than any actual rate of saving. In Figure 10-7 the golden rule gives a lower K/N than the equilibrium ratio, which implies that the "savings" curve needs to be lowered so as to intersect the "savings needed" curve at a lower K/N. The golden rule, is incidentally, satisfied if, as in "classical" growth models, all profits ($Y_K K$) are saved and all wages consumed, since then

$$\dot{K} = Y_K K$$

so that

$$Y_K = \frac{\dot{K}}{K} = n$$

But this condition, although sufficient, is not necessary.

Depreciation

An observant reader will have noticed one obvious omission from all this. Capital is assumed to last for ever. But we know that it wears out. The pattern of wearing out is different for different machines. The simplest assumption is that a machine loses a constant fraction d of its productive potential each year. This assumption (of "radioactive decay") is probably not very realistic. It implies that machines never completely collapse; like old soldiers, they just fade away. It also implies a rather drastic loss of potential in the early years. An alternative, and probably more realistic, assumption is that machines have a finite length of life θ, and that up to this moment of "sudden death" their productivity is unimpaired. Either assumption is relatively simple to embody in a growth model.

If we assume radioactive depreciation, the savings needed to maintain the ratio K/N have to provide not only extra capital for the new trogs $(\dot{N}K/N)$ but also replacement for capital that wears out $(d \cdot K)$

Thus
$$\text{Savings needed per trog} = n\frac{K}{N} + d\frac{K}{N}$$

So equilibrium is given by

$$s \cdot g\left(\frac{K}{N}\right) = (n + d)\frac{K}{N}$$

With "sudden death," matters are slightly less tidy. In steady-state growth both investment and capital are growing at a rate n. As before

$$\text{Investment} = \text{net investment} + \text{depreciation}$$

$$= N\left(\frac{K}{N}\right) + \text{depreciation}$$

But now depreciation equals gross investment θ periods earlier. But, in steady-state growth, investment is growing at a rate n. So

$$\text{Investment}_t = \text{investment}_{t-\theta} \cdot e^{n\theta}$$

So
$$\text{Investment}_t = \dot{N}\left(\frac{K}{N}\right) + \text{investment}_t\, e^{-n\theta}$$

Thus
$$\dot{K} = \dot{N}\left(\frac{K}{N}\right) + \dot{K}e^{-n\theta}$$

Hence
$$\frac{\dot{K}}{N} = \left(\frac{n}{1 - e^{-n\theta}}\right)\frac{K}{N} = \text{savings needed per trog}$$

The story is not fundamentally changed.

However, we have still left out many important dimensions of the problem. For example, machines are often scrapped not because they have worn out (depreciated) but because they are no longer profitable to operate, though they are as physically productive as ever. We now turn to a model which explains such obsolescence, as well as overcoming two other obvious artificialities of our previous model.

Vintage Models of Technical Progress

The first is the assumption that output and capital are the same thing: a sort of jelly, which can be either consumed or used with labour to produce more output. This is obviously unsatisfactory. Second, there is the assumption that technical progress somehow increases output from *given* inputs. This may be possible if organisation is improved and the like. But in most peoples' minds technical progress has to be *embodied* in new inputs. A given person with a given calculating machine cannot suddenly do more sums per hour, but he may be able to do more sums with an electronic calculator costing the same to make as the mechanical calculator. This leads us to think of technical progress as occurring because of improvements in the quality of machines created at a given cost in terms of consumption foregone.

Thus we are no longer assuming that consumption and machines are the same thing. Instead we suppose that in any particular year we can, by sacrificing 1 unit of consumption, get a machine capable of producing b units of consumption next year and for ever.† By giving up more units of consumption, we can have more machines, at the same marginal and average cost; so consumption and capital goods are, as outputs, perfect substitutes.

Each machine needs a certain number of men to work with it, so there is no *ex-post* substitution between men and machines. Once a machine is built, it needs the same number of men to work with it in each future year—there is no disembodied technical progress. But the design of machines improves from year to year. The machines designed in year 0 require b workers, and output per worker is unity (we have chosen our units to make it so). But each year's machines require a fraction a fewer men to work with them while producing the same output (b). So, for a machine built in year v (of vintage v)

$$\text{Men per machine} = be^{-av}$$

$$\text{Output per man} = e^{av}$$

We can now place ourselves in calendar time. What do we see? Since the Creation there has been a sequence of investments, but only some of these machines are still in use. Which ones? Obviously, the most recent. For output per man is higher on these machines.

The income of any machine once it is in being is a rent, since no income is necessary to ensure its existence. But, for politeness, this is normally called a quasi-rent, since the prospect of income was necessary to induce its existence. In our example, the quasi-rent on a machine is (in units of output) the difference between output and wage costs (measured in units of output). So

$$\text{Quasi-rent} = b - be^{-av}w$$

where w is measured in units of output (the "product wage"). The quasi-rents

---

† We could allow b to vary over time; but for simplicity we shall not.

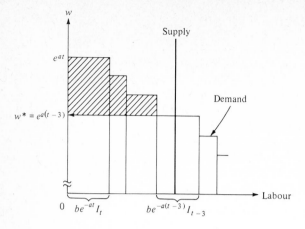

Figure 10-8 The demand for labour in year t in a vintage model. *Note*: No steady-state investment is assumed, but a steady technical progress at rate a per annum is assumed.

are higher the more recent the vintage, and for an old enough vintage they would be negative. Once the quasi-rent becomes negative the machine is scrapped on grounds of obsolescence.

We can fruitfully depict the scene in year t in Figure 10-8. The labour is employed most productively on this year's newly-created machines. If I_t has been invested this year, these machines will employ $be^{-at}I_t$ workers. Output per worker is e^{at}. Having created the machines, employers would be willing to pay up to e^{at} to attract labour onto these machines. However, they are not likely to have to pay that much. For output per man is lower on last year's machines and so on.

How in fact is the wage determined? We know that workers will always be employed on younger rather than older machines. Suppose that, as in Figure 10-8, there are only enough workers to man all the machines created in the last three years plus a fraction of those built the year before. Then the wage will equal the output per worker on three-year-old machines. On these machines there will be no quasi-rent, while on the intramarginal machines quasi-rents will be those indicated by the shaded areas in Figure 10-8.

How does this kind of model, with its greater concreteness and realism, modify the conclusions of our previous growth model? Surprisingly, barely at all, as far as its steady-state properties are concerned. If the rate of population growth plus the rate of labour-augmenting technical change is n and the rate of saving s, this model will converge on a steady-state growth path, with output growing at a rate n and with a constant share of income going in wages. The length of life of machines will be constant, and so will the age structure of the stock of machines in use. Since the number of machines per unit of output is constant, we can say, somewhat loosely, that the capital-output ratio is constant. We state these propositions without proving them,[†] but it is reassuring to know that the results of the neoclassical model can be replicated using a more realistic, but more

---

[†] For proof see R. M. Solow, *Growth Theory: An Exposition*, Oxford University Press, London, 1970, chap. 3.

cumbersome, apparatus. However none of this means that any actual economy is on a steady-state growth path.

Vintage models can also be constructed for the case where *ex-post* substitution *is* possible. Such models can also lead to steady-state solutions. Vintage models are also relevant to the study of non-steady-state economies. But progress in empirical work on technical progress has been slow.

Q10-3 Suppose we revisit the scene of Figure 10-8 in a year's time (year $t + 1$). "Wages will have risen more, *ceteris paribus*,

  (i) The higher investment in year $t + 1$
  (ii) The higher investment in year $t - 4$"
Which statement, if either, is true? (Do not assume steady-state growth.)

FACTOR SUPPLY

ELEVEN

LABOUR SUPPLY AND WAGE STRUCTURE

To have a complete theory of distribution, we need to explain not only the demand for productive factors but also their supply. For the inputs to the economy are not given. The land area of the world may be roughly unalterable but the powers of the soil can be changed, depending on the rewards for doing so. And, even if population is considered exogenous, the supply of labour is not—people decide how much to work and what skills to acquire. In fact, both land and labour are largely man-made, as, of course, is physical capital.

So we need to know on what terms the factors are supplied. This provides us with the right framework for understanding the current distribution of income, and for predicting how it will respond to exogenous changes or to new policies. For example, suppose there were a technical change, like the discovery of the computer, which raised the relative demand for graduates. How much would existing graduates benefit? If the supply of graduates was infinitely elastic, they would not benefit at all. The more inelastic the supply, the more the benefit to graduates. Or suppose that undergraduate education were more highly subsidised. Who would gain? Not students, if the supply of students was infinitely elastic. So a key question in this chapter (on labour) and the next (on capital) is: What forces determine the elasticities of factor supply?

There are many dimensions to a person's labour: his effort per hour, his hours per week, his weeks per year, his length of working life, his skill, the area where he works, the job he chooses, and so on. We shall concentrate first on the supply of hours, showing how simple utility theory illuminates a whole range of behavioural phenomena. We then move to the supply to an occupation, which provides the springboard for analysing the determinants of wage structure and earnings inequality. Finally we come to the normative question: How progressive should the income tax be? As we shall see, this depends crucially on how elastic is the labour supply response. The more inelastic the supply, the more consumer surplus is available for taxation and redistribution.

11-1 THE SUPPLY OF HOURS

We begin by considering how an individual chooses to spend his time in a given period. We shall ignore any long-term considerations that may affect his current behaviour, and ask, first, how a change in the current real wage rate per hour (w) will affect his choice of current working hours. Most people can vary their working hours to some extent. They can either decide whether to work at all, or for how long to work (either by their choice of job or within a given job).

The Simple Theory of Time

In the simplest analysis we suppose a person values only two things: goods y and leisure time T. But goods, let us assume, can only be bought out of wage income, all of which is spent. If the individual faces a given constant real wage per hour (w) and he works H hours a day, his income and expenditure per day are

$$y = wH$$

His hours of work per day are 24 hours minus leisure per day:

$$H = 24 - T$$

So the problem

$$\max u(y, T)$$

becomes

$$\max u(wH, 24 - H)$$

Differentiating by H and setting the result equal to zero, we obtain

$$u_y w + u_T(-1) = 0$$

At the optimum the individual equates the marginal benefit of work ($u_y w$) to the marginal cost due to the leisure foregone (u_T). If we express both benefit and cost in terms of goods, we have

$$w = \frac{u_T(wH, 24 - H)}{u_y(wH, 24 - H)}$$

He equates the rate (w) at which goods can be transformed into leisure to his subjective rate of substitution between goods and leisure.

The preceding equation gives a relation between the wage rate and hours of work. In other words, it represents the supply curve. What shape will this have? Suppose that in Figure 11-1 the wage rises from w^0 to w^1, due say to a cut in a proportional income tax. The worker is subject to two opposing influences:

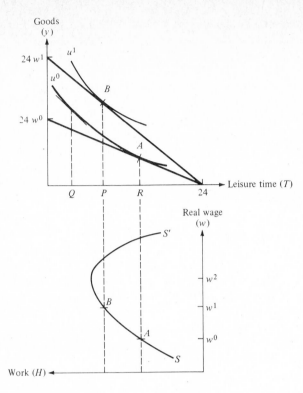

Figure 11-1 Supply of hours.

1. A substitution effect ("it's worth working more now"), measured by RQ.
2. An income effect ("you don't need to work so hard now"), measured by QP. (We are assuming that leisure is a normal good.)

In our example, the substitution effect outweighs the income effect: the person works more. But, as we have drawn the supply curve, there comes a time (for $w > w^2$) when the reverse is true and the supply curve is backward-bending.

   Let us formalise all this. Suppose that we allow the individual to have some unearned income Y as well as his wages. Then

$$y = wH + Y$$

The supply curve obtained from utility maximisation is now

$$H = H(w, Y)$$
$$? \; -$$

where the signs refer to the partial derivatives. Now, if w rises, the total effect on hours can, by the Slutsky decomposition, be written as

$$\frac{\partial H}{\partial w} = \left(\frac{\partial H}{\partial w}\right)_u + H\frac{\partial H}{\partial Y}$$
$$\phantom{\frac{\partial H}{\partial w} =} ? \qquad + \qquad -$$

If w rises by 1 (small) unit, the worker's "income" rises by H and the income effect on his labour supply is a fall, since $\partial H/\partial Y$ is negative (assuming leisure normal).

The size of the substitution effect in labour supply is one of the oldest issues in political economy. Those who worry about incentives tend to imply that the effect is large, while people on the left tend to imply it is small. But evidence is not altogether lacking. As every child knows, male working hours have fallen for the last hundred years. This suggests a backward-bending labour supply curve for "prime-age males," and this is confirmed by cross-sectional and experimental evidence.† In other words, for men the substitution effect is smaller than the absolute size of the income effect. But at the same time as men's hours have fallen, married women's working hours have been rising. This suggests for them a rising supply curve, which is again confirmed by cross-sectional work. This can be rationalised by saying that, given our social institutions, men have two chief uses of time (market-work and leisure), while women have three (market-work, home-work, and leisure). So when the wage rate for women's market-work changes, there is more scope for substitution. And market goods (like dishwashers), which can be paid for out of market earnings, may be quite good substitutes for home-work.‡

What does all this imply for the "problem of incentives?" One might think that if the supply curve is backward-bending, there is no problem: after all, heavier taxes make people work more. But this inference is a fallacy. For suppose that in Figure 11-2a a tax reduces wages from w^0 to $w^0(1 - t)$. The worker's choice point moves from A to B: he works harder. There will be no welfare loss provided the gainers (the taxpayers) can compensate the losers. But can they? To compensate the worker [while keeping his net wage at $w^0(1 - t)$] the taxpayers would need to give him an amount PQ. But if they did this, he would move his choice point to Q and the taxes he paid would be PR. So the taxpayers would only be receiving taxes of PR from which to effect compensation PQ. So the excess burden of the tax is RQ.§ This does not mean the tax is wrong. It may be needed for equity reasons or to finance public goods.

The only case where there is no excess burden occurs when there is no substitution between leisure and goods (see Figure 11-2b). Then, if the worker were compensated, he would consume at the original point A and the compensation needed (PA) would equal the taxes paid. Thus in this special case

---

† See, for example, O. Ashenfelter and J. Heckman, "Estimating Labour Supply Functions," in G. L. Cain and H. W. Watts (eds.), *Income Maintenance and Labour Supply*, Rand-McNally, Chicago, 1973; and C. V. Brown, E. Levin, and D. T. Ulph, "Estimates of Labour Hours Supplied by Married Male Workers in Great Britain," *Scottish Journal of Political Economy*, vol. 23, pp. 261–277, November 1976.

‡ On all this see J. Mincer, "Labour Force Participation of Women," in H. G. Lewis (ed.), *Aspects of Labour Economics*, National Bureau of Economic Research, New York, 1962.

§ The excess burden of a tax is the additional lump-sum income which the gainers from the tax (the government) would need in order to be able to compensate the losers (who are paying the tax). This is only equal to the sum of the compensating variations resulting from the tax when tax receipts are unaffected by the act of hypothetical compensation.

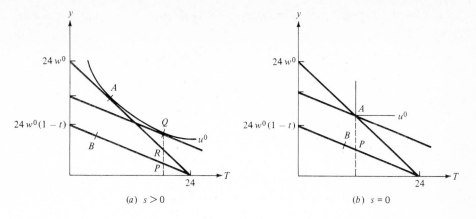

Figure 11-2 The excess burden of an income tax.

an income tax is like a lump-sum tax: the worker can (by virtue of his tastes) take no evasive action. Looking back at Figure 11-2a, it is clear that the greater the elasticity of substitution (i.e., the less curved the indifference curve), the greater the excess burden of the tax.† Consequently, the less the scope for redistribution. If the elasticity of substitution is low, different units of leisure have markedly different values and there is more surplus to be extracted. In our final section we shall find that the elasticity of substitution becomes crucial in affecting the optimal rate of tax.

The supply curve of hours is backward-bending if the negative income effect of a wage increase outweighs the positive substitution effect. But even if it is backward-bending, there may remain a problem of incentives.

The fact that different people work different hours raises serious problems for the measurement of income distribution. Suppose A earns $18 a day and works 6 hours and B earns $20 and works 10 hours. Which is better off? The answer is that we must compare the opportunities for the two people. Both are endowed with 24 hours a day, but A can transform leisure into goods at $3 per hour, while B can only get $2. So A's opportunity set is larger, and, unless we have interpersonally comparable utility functions for A and B, we must consider A better off.

So far we have assumed that leisure is always a good. It may not always be so, as is shown by those people who work for less income than they could get (without working) from the social security authorities. But utility functions such as theirs can easily be handled within our framework.

† This echoes our finding in Chapter 3.

Q11-1 Draw the indifference map and opportunity set of someone who prefers working for a living to receiving the same income as unemployment relief.

Q11-2 Suppose a Negative Income Tax were introduced by which each person was given $30 a week and then taxed at a rate of 25 percent on all of his earnings. Would the following people necessarily reduce their work effort:

    (i) Someone earning $100 a week when there were no taxes

    (ii) Someone earning $160 a week when there were no taxes

(Assume leisure a normal good, both here and henceforth. Before the N.I.T. there were no taxes and no nonlabour income.)

Q11-3 Suppose a person has a utility function

$$u = y + 2T^{1/2}$$

where y is goods and T leisure.

    (i) Derive his labour supply function.

    (ii) What is the minimum wage at which he is willing to work at all?

    (iii) How will his supply of hours respond to a small cut in a proportional income tax?

    (iv) How will his supply of hours respond to an equiproportional cut in a general value added tax?

Q11-4 (i) Suppose a person has a job at n per hour, where maximum hours (but not minimum hours) are fixed by his employer. Would he be willing to take secondary work if it is available at less than n per hour?

    (ii) In many countries the old-age pension is reduced dollar for dollar if the pensioner has earnings. Suppose this rule were abolished. Would the Treasury necessarily lose money? Assume pensioners' only income is from the pension or from earnings. Assume that all earnings, other than those for which the pension is reduced, are subject to a proportional tax t. The pension is tax-free.

    (iii) Suppose an employer has been paying his workers $5 an hour for the first 40 hours per week and $7.50 per hour for voluntary overtime. Average overtime is 10 hours per week. The employer also has to pay $10 a week social security contribution per employee (irrespective of hours worked). The workers now suggest abolishing overtime rates and replacing them by a flat rate system paying $5.50 per hour for each hour from zero upwards. Will the employer agree?

Q11-5 (i) Compare the same family at two points in time. In period 1 the husband can earn £4 per hour and the wife £1 per hour. Now the husband's wage rises to £5. Will the wife work more or less?

    (ii) Suppose now that in periods 1 and 2 the husband can earn £4 per hour but the wife's wage rises from £1 to £2. Will she work more or less?

*Q11-6 If a person's labour supply curve is vertical and he has no unearned income, what does this tell us about his elasticity of substitution between goods and leisure?

Q11-7 (i) "If the supply curve of labour is backward-bending, leisure is a luxury." True or false?

    (ii) "If when his hourly wage rate rises, a man chooses so much more leisure that his earnings fall, earnings are an inferior good." True or false?

Q11-8 "Turning to the market for man-hours, suppose a tax is imposed on labour, the price to the employers must rise and so man-hours must fall." True or false?

A More General Theory of Time

The theory, as presented so far, seems to imply that people have no feelings whatever about work as such. This can easily be remedied by writing

$$u = u(y, T, H)$$

The equilibrium conditions then include

$$w = \frac{u_T}{u_y} - \frac{u_H}{u_y}$$

The wage has to compensate for the (marginal) value of leisure lost minus any value attached to working. This is obviously a more satisfactory approach, since people are never concerned with the value of time as such (unless considering the issues of birth and death); instead they are concerned with the differences in value attaching to using time in different ways. From peoples' behaviour when facing specified alternatives, one should be able to infer the relative marginal valuations which people put on different uses of time. For example, suppose that it is possible to travel to work by two equally comfortable modes of transport, one taking 10 minutes longer than the other but costing \$0.10 less. For the marginal person (the one who is currently indifferent between the two modes of transport) the value of time spent commuting must be \$0.60 per hour less than the value of time spent in some alternative way. All statements about the value of time are of this form. Our first formulation of the work-leisure choice can be regarded as a shorthand for the present approach, $u(y, T, 24 - T)$ having been rewritten as some other function $u(y, T)$.

However, there is a weakness even in our present formulation. It does not enable us to consider the effect on labour supply of changes in the relative price of goods. A more realistic and fruitful theory may be as follows. Utility flows not from goods or leisure, but from activities, each of which involves as inputs the use of market goods and time. For example, going into the countryside involves incurring the cost of transport (a market good) but also involves spending time. Suppose that utility depends only on two activities Z_1 and Z_2. The first (like going into the country) is time-intensive in that the (fixed) time input per unit of output (t_1) is high relative to the money value of the goods input per unit of output $(p_1 a_1)$. The other activity (like eating) is less time-intensive. So

$$\frac{t_1}{p_1 a_1} > \frac{t_2}{p_2 a_2}$$

The individual's budget constraint is

$$p_1 a_1 Z_1 + p_2 a_2 Z_2 = (24 - t_1 Z_1 - t_2 Z_2)w + Y^0$$

In labour supply analysis, it is often convenient to rewrite the budget equation with the value of the individual's endowment on the right-hand side—this is called his *full income*. Doing this, we find

$$(p_1 a_1 + wt_1)Z_1 + (p_2 a_2 + wt_2)Z_2 = 24w + Y^0$$

Here $(p_1 a_1 + wt_1)$ is the full price of Z_1. Suppose now that there is a fall in p_1, compensated by a fall in Y so that welfare is unchanged. There will be a substitution from Z_2 to the time-intensive Z_1, which will increase the amount of time devoted to leisure activities, and reduce work effort. (You are asked to prove this later.) In this connection the fall in the relative price of goods inputs to recreation appears to offer some explanation of the secular decline of working hours in the United States.

Two further extensions of the analysis are worth referring to briefly. First, if substitution is allowed between the time and goods inputs into Z_1, and likewise for Z_2, the above effect could be reduced. A fall in p_1 would lead to less time and more goods being used to "produce" Z_1. Hence labour supply might not fall, depending on the relative elasticities of substitution in "production" and consumption. Second, we need not assume a constant wage rate per hour independent of the number of hours, and we can even allow for a person's consumption to affect his earning power. His optimising solution remains perfectly determinate, and at the same time economic theory becomes more realistic and human.[†] However, for many problems simple theory is adequate.

Q11-9 Suppose that data were collected for a number of north of England towns showing

x, trips to the Lake District National Park per head of population
M, money cost of getting to the edge of the Lake District (£)
T, time spent getting to the edge of the Lake District (minutes)

A regression then showed that

$$x = a + bM + cT$$

(i) What significance would you attach to the magnitude of c/b?

(ii) If a similar analysis was made of journeys to one particular spot in the National Park from other places within the National Park, would you expect c/b to be bigger or smaller?

Q11-10 (i) Queues in barbers' shops are longer in poor areas than in rich areas. Why?

(ii) Indians (in India) are on average more economical in their use of goods than North Americans and less economical in their use of time. Why?

*Q11-11 Prove that in the case described in the text an income-compensated fall in p_1 will induce an increase in leisure $(t_1 Z_1 + t_2 Z_2)$. Hint: Draw the budget lines in the space of Z_1, Z_2 in such a way that the new compensated budget line goes through the original consumption point (where consumption occurred before p_1 fell).

11-2 THE SUPPLY TO AN OCCUPATION

We have so far assumed that the individual will earn the same wage whatever occupation he practises. This is not generally the case. Suppose that there are two occupations A and B requiring the same skill. Hours of work are prescribed by the

---

[†] Those who wish to pursue this should read G. S. Becker, "A Theory of the Allocation of Time," *Economic Journal*, vol. 75, pp. 493–517, September 1965.

employer and are the same in both jobs. The annual real wages are w_A and w_B, respectively. Which job will a person choose? Clearly the one which he finds the more satisfactory. In other words he will weigh up the monetary characteristics w and nonmonetary characteristics $\mathbf{x}$ of each job, and will choose A if

$$u(w_A, \mathbf{x}_A) > u(w_B, \mathbf{x}_B)$$

This is simply the principle of maximising "net advantage."

Another way of describing his choice is to say that he will choose A provided the monetary advantages of A over B more than outweigh any nonmonetary advantages of B over A. Suppose A is, money apart, a lousy job, like being a garbage collector, while B is an office job. Then for any given w_B^0 there will be some value w_A^* which is just sufficient to make a particular individual indifferent between the two jobs:

$$u(w_A^*, \mathbf{x}_A) = u(w_B^0, \mathbf{x}_B)$$

The difference $(w_A^* - w_B^0)$ is then a compensating or "equalising" differential, just sufficient to compensate for the nastiness of job A. This differential might or might not vary with w_B. It seems likely that it would. If the real wage in offices doubled, one would think that the wage needed to induce a person to collect garbage would at least double. For simplicity we shall assume that the absolute differential which a person needs is always a fraction k of w_B. So k is the proportional compensating differential, or what we shall henceforth call, quite simply, the *compensating differential*.† Thus the individual chooses A, provided

$$\frac{w_A - w_B}{w_B} > k$$

or provided

$$\frac{w_A}{w_B} > 1 + k$$

But individuals differ in their attitudes to jobs. Some may even prefer garbage collecting to office work. So we now have a separate compensating differential k_i for each individual i. This measures his supply price to the occupation:

$$\left(\frac{w_A}{w_B}\right)_i = 1 + k_i$$

To obtain the supply curve to occupation A we take people in ascending order of this compensating differential. The array of the ascending supply prices is the supply curve. As we have drawn it in Figure 11-3, there is one person who so likes garbage collecting that he is willing to do it provided $w_A/w_B > 0.8$. In other

---

† In ordinary parlance the word "differential" is more often used to refer to proportional than absolute differentials.

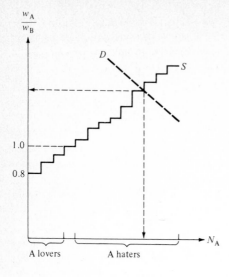

Figure 11-3 The supply curve to occupation A.

words his $k = -0.2$. As its wage rises he will be the first to enter the occupation. There are not many others who prefer A to B, and, if more than four people are to be attracted into garbage collecting, it will have to have a positive differential in its favour.

The more people differ in their attitudes, the more steeply the supply curve will rise. So supply is less elastic, the greater the differences between people. This is a perfectly general principle, and is analogous to the point that the supply of hours is less elastic the more differently an individual values different units of leisure.

> *The supply curve to an occupation is the array of the supply prices of the different individuals, taken in ascending order of price. The more individuals differ, the more inelastic the supply curve.*

The first principle has an important corollary. Market differentials are determined by supply and demand (see Figure 11-3).

> *The market wage differential is therefore the compensating differential of the marginal man.*

If the supply curve is completely elastic, his differential will be the same as the compensating differential of everybody else. But if the supply curve is fairly inelastic, due to big differences between people, many of those in an occupation will be earning substantial rents, which have no allocative function. These could be taxed away with little loss of efficiency, and possibly with some gain in equity. That is why it is so important to know about the elasticities of supply.

But we have so far considered only one dimension along which jobs differ (their intrinsic pleasantness) and one dimension along which people differ (their evaluation of the pleasantness of jobs). We can now extend the analysis to include other factors affecting occupational choice and thus affecting wage structure.

Q11-12 "If everybody agreed about the desirability of occupation A relative to B, the pay differential would necessarily be greater than with the present diversity of views." True or false?

11-3 WAGE STRUCTURE AND HUMAN CAPITAL

The differences in income between people in different jobs arise partly from differences between jobs, and partly from differences between people. There are many ways in which jobs differ in their attractions—in pleasantness of work, risk, prospects, and training cost, to name but a few. People differ in tastes, in original abilities, and in educational and other opportunities. If people did not differ, but jobs did, then the long-run (but not short-run) supply curves to each occupation would be infinitely elastic. So long-run differentials would be "supply-determined" in the sense of arising from (uniform) differences in supply price. Figure 11-4a illustrates the source of wage differentials between two occupations A and B in such a world. There is a given labour force N^0 which allocates itself between the two occupations so that the desired wage differential of A over B (k^0) is maintained. Since this differential is compensating, the rich and the poor, though unequal in income, are equally well off.

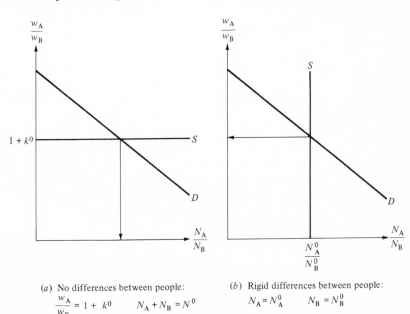

(a) No differences between people:
$$\frac{w_A}{w_B} = 1 + k^0 \qquad N_A + N_B = N^0$$

(b) Rigid differences between people:
$$N_A = N_A^0 \qquad N_B = N_B^0$$

Figure 11-4 Two models of wage differentials.

Real inequality arises from differences between people, especially in abilities and opportunities. To illustrate this, Figure 11-4b gives a possible different account of this same wage differential. In this case people are born so that they are either able to do occupation A (N_A^0 of them) or occupation B (N_B^0 of them). Wages are then "demand-determined" in the sense that they reflect the demand prices for the given inelastic supplies.

Economists vary widely in the importance they attach to "differences between people" as determinants of wage inequality. In America such differences tend to be given less weight than in Europe. If "all men are born equal," then wage inequality can only be due to differences between jobs, and need cause no loss of sleep. But if men are not born equal, then wage inequality may arise in part from interpersonal differences and this, especially if the differences are in abilities or opportunities, may be worrying. Interestingly, those who believe that people are not very dissimilar in abilities or opportunities often stress their differences in tastes. But then differences in tastes are difficult to evaluate in terms of equity, unless we have evidence on interpersonally comparable utilities.

However, despite differences of emphasis, all economists would agree that differences between people do have some influence on wage structure. To see how this works we shall take the various differences between jobs as our framework. For each of these we shall ask what compensation is needed for the difference, and how this compensation varies between people. In this context differences between people come in as factors affecting the elasticity of supply: the more the differences between people, the less elastic the supply. We assume throughout that everyone in a given occupation is paid the same. This is not the case in occupations as conventionally defined. But we can make it so, by defining an occupation so narrowly as to include only those doing similar work with similar skill in a similar place, and consequently paid the same under perfect competition.

Pleasantness of Work, and Risk

Occupations differ, as we have noted, in pleasantness of work. If some people would not do job A at any price and the rest would not do job B, then the supply to each occupation is completely inelastic. By contrast, if tastes are similar, supply curves are highly elastic.

Jobs also differ in riskiness. If job A adds to the income variance of each individual more than B does, then, if the expected wage $\bar{w}_A$ is lower than the expected wage $\bar{w}_B$, only risk lovers will enter occupation A. If most people are risk-averse, the average wage in A will be higher than in B, unless the demand for A is very low (see Figure 11-5).† The more people differ in their attitudes to risk, the less elastic the supply curve.

---

† We continue to keep N_A/N_B on the axis since this is the variable relevant to demand. If A and B are the only occupations, as N_A rises, N_B falls by the same amount. The words written along the axis relate to the characteristics of those individuals who enter occupation A at the corresponding relative wage.

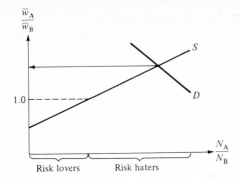

Figure 11-5 Risk-preference and occupational differentials.

Training Costs and Prospective Returns

Some jobs require more training than others. Consider first the case of full-time education. Suppose job A needs one more year of education than job B, and that everybody in job A earns the same, irrespective of age, and will continue to do so in future. Likewise for job B. There are no tuition fees. Then people will only be willing to supply themselves in job A if they are compensated for the earnings (w_B) which they lose during their last year of education. If the capital market is perfect, the compensation must be such that the present value of the lifetime income a person can obtain in each occupation is the same. If he enters occupation B, he is paid a (virtual) perpetuity of w_B; if he enters occupation A, he gets a perpetuity of w_A but starting one year later (see Figure 11-6). So if the jobs are equally pleasant and risky, he will only enter A if

$$\text{PV (occupation A)} \geq \text{PV (occupation B)}$$

Thus

$$\frac{w_A}{i}\frac{1}{1+i} \geq \frac{w_B}{i}$$

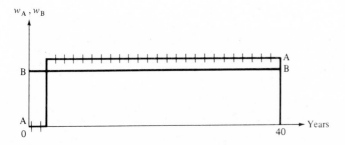

Figure 11-6 Lifetime income profile of occupations A and B.

where i is the interest rate.† Assuming that everyone is equally capable of training for A, people will move from B into A until the present values are equalised. So in equilibrium

$$w_A - w_B = i\, w_B$$

The absolute differential $(w_A - w_B)$ is just enough to pay the interest on the cost (w_B) of gaining access to it. In terms of relative differentials

$$\frac{w_A}{w_B} = 1 + i$$

So i is the compensating differential.‡

Thus if everybody is equally capable of training for job A, capital markets are perfect and jobs A and B are considered equally pleasant and risky, the wage differential between the two jobs is completely supply-determined, as in Figure 11-4a. Viewed from the side of supply, it is a compensating differential, but viewed from the side of demand it reflects the greater productivity of the worker with more "human capital."

The analysis of on-the-job training proceeds in exactly the same way. Suppose two jobs A and B require the same education, followed by a year's apprenticeship before full professional competence is achieved. In job A (say accountancy) the apprentice, though learning a lot, contributes little to current output. But in job B (say brick laying), the apprentices are quite productively employed. Assuming that the apprentices are paid their marginal products (w_A^* and w_B^*, respectively, with $w_A^* < w_B^*$), a compensating differential will be required between the adult wages w_A and w_B such that

$$w_A - w_B = i(w_B^* - w_A^*)$$

The compensating differential again equates the present value of lifetime incomes in the occupations.

The same analysis can be used to compare the supply prices to the two apprenticeships, each of which open up different prospects (w_A and w_B). Someone is only willing to enter apprenticeship in A so long as the current earnings he foregoes by not doing an apprenticeship in B are not greater than the present

---

† $1 now has the same value as $i per year for ever. So $1/i$ now has the same value as $1 per year for ever, and w_B/i now has the same value as w_B per year for ever.

‡ If there were tuition fees F, we should require

$$w_A - w_B = i(w_B + F)$$

$$\frac{w_A}{w_B} = 1 + i\left(1 + \frac{F}{w_B}\right)$$

value of the earnings differential $(w_A - w_B)$. So in equilibrium,[†] we have

$$w_B^* - w_A^* = \left(\frac{w_A - w_B}{i}\right)$$

So long as a person's training affects his marginal product equally whatever employer he works for, his wage will always equal his marginal product (assuming perfect capital and insurance markets). The employer has no incentive to finance the training. For once trained, the worker will leave if he is paid less than his marginal product, since he could earn that elsewhere. There is therefore no inducement for the employer to pay *more* than the marginal product during the period of training. This type of training has been called "general," as opposed to "specific" training, which raises a person's productivity more if he works for his present employer than for another.[‡]

Specific training may or may not be financed by employers. The employer may be willing to finance it, since, once the training is done, he will only have to pay the worker his marginal product as it would have been without the training. He can thus trap the returns to training by paying the trained worker less than his actual marginal product. There is, however, the danger that the trained man may leave, which could lead his employer to make the worker finance the training (as in general training). On the other hand, the worker faces the danger that the employer may sack him, in which case he could not reap the returns to his training, since these returns are specific to the work done in the firm. Exactly who bears the costs of specific training remains an unsettled issue, but, insofar as employees do so, workers will not be paid their current marginal product—an important exception to the general presumption that they are, and one which we shall ignore from now on.

[†] We might appear to have reached a circular result here: adult wages are determined by apprenticeship wages and vice versa. But we are not saying this. For we have not so far determined the absolute level of the wages—only their ratio. To determine the absolute wages we would have to bring in demand. Suppose for simplicity a production function

$$y = f(N_A^*, N_B^*, N_A, N_B)$$

where * indicates apprentice, and also that

$$N_A^* + N_B^* = N_0^*$$

$$N_A + N_B = N_0$$

and

$$\frac{N_A^*}{N_A} = \frac{N_B^*}{N_B}$$

Then if

$$f_{N_A} - f_{N_B} = i(f_{N_B^*} - f_{N_A^*})$$

all real wages are determined.

[‡] G. S. Becker, *Human Capital*, National Bureau of Economic Research, New York, 1964, chap. 2.

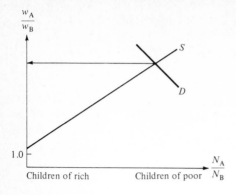

Figure 11-7 "Opportunities" and occupational differentials.

Opportunity and Ability

So far we have made the artificial assumption that everybody has the same opportunities and is equally able. A key source of unequal opportunity is capital-market imperfections. Not everybody can borrow at the same rate and some cannot borrow at all. (Those who cannot borrow at all will be using their subjective rate of discount to derive their equalising differences, while those sufficiently affluent to be lenders will finance their human capital by lending less and so will use their lending rate, see Chapter 12.) So the children of the rich, who can borrow cheaply or finance themselves from diverted family investments, will use a low discount rate to compute their equalising differences, while the children of the poor, other things equal, will use a higher discount rate. So, taking the case where job A requires one more year of education, the supply price of individual i to occupation A is given by

$$\left(\frac{w_A}{w_B}\right)_i = 1 + r_i$$

where r_i is his marginal discount rate. The higher r_i, the higher the supply price. If workers are arrayed in order of their supply prices, this gives us a rising supply price (see Figure 11-7). The more the variation in r, the less elastic the supply curve. Capital-market imperfections clearly help to explain why, despite the supposed nonmonetary returns to education, real private financial rates of return to education have been higher than the real rates of interest at which most people can lend.

    People also differ in their abilities. Those who are less able will have to undertake more training to be able to perform a given job. Suppose for simplicity that once people have qualified for occupation B they need to spend different lengths of time in training to fit themselves for occupation A. The ith individual needs to spend n_i years training. Provided n_i is small, the cost to him of his training is $n_i w_B$. So his supply price is given by

$$\left(\frac{w_A}{w_B}\right)_i = 1 + r \cdot n_i$$

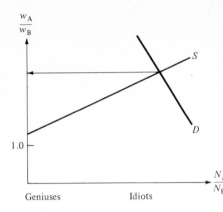

Figure 11-8 Ability and occupational differentials.

The supply is again less elastic the more ability varies (see Figure 11-8). In equilibrium the able will be earning rents. If ability could be directly measured, it could be taxed without producing misallocation of resources. But any tax on *earnings* will have some allocative effect, as well as extracting rents.

In an older book the limited supply of persons for many skilled occupations would have been treated under the heading "noncompeting groups." However this is not altogether satisfactory, since there is *some* price at which a person from a very poor home may be attracted to, say, medicine, and *some* price at which a quite stupid person may be able to acquire skills. However, the old distinction between "equalising differences" and "noncompeting groups" is in a sense preserved in our distinction between differences between jobs and differences between people in the terms on which they are willing to do the jobs. The whole complex of wage structure cannot be explained without attending to both of these aspects, as well as to demand.

In addition, of course, there are many labour markets which are not in long-run equilibrium, and many where rates are determined by nonmarket forces. Some rates are kept up by restricted entry to these professions. Others are raised by union activity. It is estimated, for example, that in the United States unionisation raises the relative wages in the unionised sector by, on average, about 15 percent. This, however, is a fairly small differential compared to the full spread of differentials in the labour force. To explain this latter, the preceding framework is the most fruitful we have.

Q11-13 "As employers only have to pay unskilled people low wages and pay no more than they need to pay, this shows that low pay has nothing to do with low productivity." True, false, or uncertain? Give reasons.

Q11-14 Suppose there was a perfect capital market with a 10 percent interest rate, all people were equally able, education was free of tuition charges and had no psychic value, and all people with a given education were paid the same, irrespective of age and calendar time.

(i) Suppose we observe graduates from a two-year course earning, after tax, $2100 per annum more than nongraduates. How much must nongraduates be earning (after tax)?

(ii) Suppose there is a permanent increase in the relative demand for graduates. Will this increase graduate earnings in the short run? In the long run?

(iii) Now allow for differences in opportunity or ability. Will increased demand for graduates increase graduate earnings in the short run? In the long run?

Q11-15 "Since university education generates socially productive human capital and student time is an important input to university education, students should be paid a wage." True, false, or uncertain?

Q11-16 Suppose all public subsidies to education beyond age 18 were abolished; what would be the effect on the inequality of personal incomes?

The Interpersonal Distribution of Earnings

We have so far concentrated on how the pattern of occupational wages is determined. But the interpersonal distribution of earnings depend also on how many people there are in each occupation, i.e., earning each wage. To think about this we move to a slightly different, though related, framework.

In equilibrium each individual will have a set of productive characteristics which have been priced by the market (by the operation of supply and demand). But if two individuals with identical productive characteristics are working in different occupations, the one in the occupation that is less desirable (to the marginal person) will be more highly paid. So job characteristics also get priced in the market. Thus the wage of the ith individual will depend on his own productive characteristics ($\mathbf{q}_i$) and on the nonmonetary attributes of his job ($\mathbf{x}_i$).

$$w_i = f(\mathbf{q}_i, \mathbf{x}_i)$$

This relation is known as a wage function. It is fundamentally a descriptive relation, since it is the reduced form of the system of supply and demand functions and does not enable us to identify either of them.

However, the theory of occupational supply does give us some clues to the appropriate form for the wage function. For suppose we take the simple schooling model developed above. This indicates that in a perfect capital market, where relative wages are determined entirely on the supply side,

$$w_1 = w_0(1 + r)$$

where w_i is the wage of someone with i years of education and r is the interest rate. So, for someone with s years of schooling,

$$w_s = w_0(1 + r)^s \simeq w_0\, e^{rs}$$

Thus
$$\log w = \log w_0 + rs$$

Taking variances on both sides and assuming w_0 and r constant, we find that

$$\text{var}\,(\log w) = r^2\, \text{var}(s)$$

The proportional inequality of wages (measured by the variance of the logs) is r^2 times the variance of years of schooling. This simple model has been found to explain a part of the interstate and intercountry variation in inequality. But within any one country it explains only a small proportion of wage inequality. Obviously some of the other factors we have mentioned need to be brought in: ability, family background, and, of course, work experience. Much research is now in progress on these questions, but clearly if we knew the function $f(\mathbf{q}_i, \mathbf{x}_i)$ together with the joint distribution of $\mathbf{q}_i$ and $\mathbf{x}_i$, we should have a complete description of the sources of wage inequality. Theory provides important clues in this work.†

Q11-17 "If log $w_i = a + bs_i$ (for all i) and there is a perfect capital market with interest rate $r = b$, there is no inequality between people in the present value of their lifetime earnings." True or false?

11-4 THE OPTIMAL INCOME TAX

People have always been interested in labour supply, because they have always been interested in poor relief. Those who were against liberal relief argued that handouts would discourage the poor from working, while the taxes needed to finance the handouts would discourage the better-off from working. Those in favour of liberal relief believed these fears were exaggerated. The arguments, though vociferous, were not always very precisely formulated. But much effort has been devoted recently to developing a systematic approach to the question of the optimal degree of redistribution, taking into account labour supply responses.‡

In thinking about this we shall confine ourselves to the effects of redistribution on the supply of hours, though similar lines of argument apply to the effects upon effort, skill acquisition, and so on.§ We take each individual's gross hourly wage w_i as given. This implies that his marginal product is independent of the labour supplied by others: there is perfect substitution in production. So, assuming the individual has no private unearned income, his gross income is $w_i H_i$.

The equity problem is that people differ in their productivities w_i: productivity has a frequency distribution $f(w)$. To deal with this problem and to raise money for its own expenditure on public goods, the government introduces a tax-subsidy scheme which specifies the net income y for each level of gross income wH. For simplicity we shall assume that this function is linear:¶

$$y_i = w_i H_i(1 - t) + Y \tag{1}$$

The individual pays taxes at a rate t on all his income, but receives a tax-free handout Y. This scheme is equivalent to an income tax with a constant marginal

---

† For example, it points to problems that may arise if ability and family background are included simultaneously in f; see G. S. Becker, *Human Capital*, 2d ed. National Bureau of Economic Research, New York, 1975, pp. 117–146.

‡ The seminal, though difficult, article is that of J. A. Mirrlees: "An Exploration in the Theory of Optimum Income Taxation," *Review of Economic Studies*, vol. 38, pp. 175–208, April 1971.

§ For an analysis that concentrates on effects on educational choices see A. B. Atkinson, "How Progressive Should Income Tax Be?," in M. Parkin (ed.), *Essays in Modern Economics*, Longman, London, 1973.

¶ Mirrlees found that his optimal unconstrained tax schedule was approximately linear.

tax rate levied on all income above an exemption limit (Y/t) and a corresponding subsidy (Negative Income Tax) paid to those with incomes below the exemption limit.

The government's problem is to find the optimal t and Y. Obviously the citizens would like as low a t and as high a Y as possible. But the government is constrained by the need to balance the books. So, if R is expenditure on public goods, and there are Q members of society, then

$$\sum_{i=1}^{Q} tw_i H_i = QY + R \tag{2}$$

The government is also constrained by the fact that the tax-subsidy scheme will affect hours of work. If all individuals have the same utility function

$$u_i = u(y_i, H_i) \tag{3}$$

they will have the same labour supply function

$$H_i = H[w_i(1 - t), Y] \tag{4}$$

Given these four constraints (1) to (4), the government then selects t and Y to maximise its welfare function:

$$W = W(u_1, \ldots, u_i, \ldots, u_Q) \tag{5}$$

The solution to this problem clearly depends on the structure of the utility and welfare functions, as well as on the degree of underlying inequality in abilities and on the government revenue needed. Calculations by Stern† confirm one's intuitions that the marginal tax rate should generally be higher:

1. The less elastic the labour supply response (i.e., the lower the elasticity of substitution in the utility function)
2. The stronger one's inequality aversion (i.e., the lower the elasticity of substitution in the welfare function)
3. The wider the dispersion of abilities, and
4. The higher the government's revenue requirements

Let us look at these features more closely. We shall suppose that the (cardinal) utility function is of the constant-elasticity-of-substitution variety:

$$u = [\delta y^{-\rho} + (1 - \delta)(24 - H)^{-\rho}]^{-v/\rho} \qquad v > 0 \qquad \rho > -1 \qquad \rho \neq 0$$

Here v measures returns to scale in producing utility. The elasticity of substitution is $1/(1 + \rho)$. The lower the elasticity of substitution, the less elastic the supply of labour. United States estimates of male labour supply imply an elasticity of substitution of about 0.4.

† N. H. Stern, "On the Specification of Models of Optimum Taxation," *Journal of Public Economics*, vol. 6, pp. 123–162, 1976; and N. H. Stern, "Welfare Weights and the Elasticity of the Marginal Valuation of Income," in M. Artis and R. Nobay (eds.) *Studies in Modern Economic Analysis*, Blackwell, Oxford, 1977, pp. 209–258.

Next we need to make a value judgment about the social welfare function. Suppose it has the form†

$$W = \frac{1}{\alpha} \, [u_1^\alpha + \cdots + u_Q^\alpha] \qquad \alpha \leq 1 \qquad \alpha \neq 0$$

Clearly α is a measure of inequality aversion: the smaller it is, the more the aversion to inequality. It is commonly assumed that the product $\alpha v = -1$. Using these parameter values (for ρ and αv) together with reasonable estimates of $f(w)$ and R for the U.K., Stern calculates, for illustration, an optimal marginal tax rate of just over 50 percent and a minimum income guarantee Y equal to one-third of average income. These figures are not offered as prescriptions, but as contributions to the developing attempt to incorporate equity considerations in a consistent way into economic policy discussion.

The figures have an important corollary. Even when the optimal income tax is levied, a great deal of inequality is left. Suppose we calculate the marginal social value of a lump-sum \$1 given to people at different levels of net income; i.e., we compute for a person i at each income level

$$\frac{\partial W}{\partial u_i} \frac{\partial u}{\partial y} (y_i, H_i)$$

If we take a person at the 15th percentile of ability (i.e., a fairly poor person), his dollar is worth about $2\frac{1}{2}$ times the dollar of a person at the 85th percentile. So difficult is it to achieve equality, when taxes induce unfavourable labour supply responses (even with an elasticity of substitution as low a 0.4).

Even if our welfare function were of the Rawlsian maximin variety, it would not be in the interests of the poorest man that complete equality were brought about: higher taxes would so reduce the total available for distribution. Only in one case would complete equality be desirable: when the elasticity of substitution in the (CES) utility function is zero.

This can be shown by taking the case of two workers with different productivities ($w_A < w_B$). If we assume $v = 1$ and zero elasticity of substitution, the CES function becomes, in the limit,

$$u = \min \left(\frac{y}{a}, \frac{T}{b} \right)$$

So consumption will always occur along a ray from the origin. Suppose that initially there is a marginal tax rate less than 100 percent. So A is less well off than B; their utilities are marked as u^{A0} and u^{B0} at the corresponding consumption points in Figure 11-9. Now suppose the marginal tax rate was raised and so was the handout, in such a way that u^A was raised to

$$u^{A1} = \tfrac{1}{2}(u^{A0} + u^{B0})$$

As before, A and B together consume the whole national product. So where must B be consuming? Suppose he too was consuming at u^{A1}. Then his consumption

† See page 48.

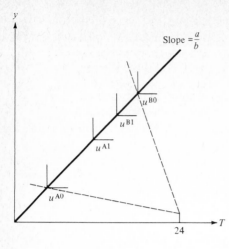

y

Slope $=\dfrac{a}{b}$

u^{B0}

u^{B1}

u^{A1}

u^{A0}

24

T

Figure 11-9 Redistribution with zero elasticity of substitution.

of y would have fallen by the same amount that A's consumption had risen. So national output must be the same as before. But this cannot be so. For B is more productive than A and has increased his hours by as much as A has reduced his. So total output must have gone up. Therefore B cannot consume at u^{A1}. He must consume more, e.g., at u^{B1} as we have marked it. Does (u^{A1}, u^{B1}) give more welfare than (u^{A0}, u^{B0})? Yes, using any symmetrical quasi-concave welfare function. For if both were consuming at u^{A1}, this must be at least as good as (u^{A0}, u^{B0}). And (u^{A1}, u^{B1}) is better.

So, by raising the tax rate and the handout once, we have improved things. It follows that we can do so again and again, until eventually we reach a marginal tax rate that approaches 100 percent in the limit. And at that limit we reach a state of complete equality. The argument clearly does not depend on having a linear tax schedule, and generalises to an economy of more than two people.†

However, unfortunately there *is* a substitution response. Some of this problem can of course be overcome by partially relying on commodity taxes, and taxing more heavily those goods which are complements to leisure (see Chapter 6). But a system in which all taxes were levied on commodities at a rate independent of the customer's means would be unlikely to satisfy one's equity objectives. So there remains a crucial role for income taxation, and in principle the rates of all taxes should be simultaneously determined.

Within any framework, empirical estimates of labour supply are of central importance to the makers of tax policy. They are needed not only for men, who

† For a more rigorous proof, see N. H. Stern, "On the Specification of Models of Optimum Taxation," *Journal of Public Economics*, vol. 6, pp. 123–162, 1976. Note also that if utility is "produced" at decreasing returns to scale ($v < 1$), the result referred to is strengthened.

as usual receive most attention, but for women. And we want them not only in relation to the supply of hours but in relation to effort, occupational choice, migration, and all the other dimensions of labour supply. Where other policies (as on education) have labour supply effects, they too should be analysed in the light of these. If this is not done, statements about gains and losses from government policy can be grossly misleading.

TWELVE

CAPITAL AND INTEREST

The capital assets of any economy, including its human capital, depend on its past pattern of savings and investment. In each period every individual decides how much to save and how much productive investment to make. If the capital market (loans market) is perfect, everyone can borrow and lend unlimited amounts at a given rate of interest. So the individual's plan for saving and investment will depend on the rate of interest, his productive investment opportunities, and his preferences. Once he has decided how much to save and invest, he must (assuming no change in his holding of money) lend out any excess of savings over investment or borrow to finance any excess of investment over savings. The market supply and demand for loans are thus a function of the rate of interest, and the rate is determined so as to equate supply and demand. Thus we need first to look at individual behaviour (in Secs. 12-1 to 12-3) before coming to the market (in Sec. 12-4).

This in essence is the neoclassical theory of the rate of interest, pioneered by Irving Fisher, which is the centrepiece of this chapter.† It is in fact, extremely similar to the single-period model of general equilibrium, with only two modifications: (1) all commodities are dated, and (2) there is a market for inter-temporal claims. For convenience, we shall generally assume there is only one consumption commodity in each period, but the theory can easily be generalised to more than one.

The assumption of perfect capital markets is obviously artificial. In practice people cannot borrow unlimited amounts at a given rate of interest, because the

---

† Sections 12-1 to 12-3 draw heavily on J. Hirshleifer, "On the Theory of Optimal Investment Decisions," *Journal of Political Economy*, vol. 66, pp. 329–351, August 1958.

more they borrow the greater the risk of default. So in Secs. 12-1 to 12-3, which concern individual choice, we allow for the possibility of capital-market imperfections. But in Sec. 12-4, where we move to the market, we confine ourselves to the determinants of "the" rate of interest, rather than of a schedule of opportunities facing each individual.

Neoclassical capital theory has been much criticised, especially from Cambridge, England. In the final section we examine these criticisms and attempt to show which points in the critique are valid.

12-1 THE INDIVIDUAL: TWO-PERIOD CASE, CONVEX PRODUCTION SET

We begin by considering a person who lives only two periods (periods 0 and 1) and has to choose from a number of mutually "independent" investment projects. (If two projects are *independent*, this means that one of them can be done, whether or not the other one is.) There are three elements involved in any person's choices over time:

1. His productive investment opportunities
2. His borrowing-lending opportunities
3. His preferences

To simplify matters we shall first consider a hermit (Robinson Crusoe?) for whom there are no borrowing-lending opportunities (2), and then a ne'er-do-well for whom there are no production opportunities (1), before bringing all three elements together.

No Borrowing-Lending Opportunities

The individual's investment opportunities consist of a set of projects, each of which involves a sacrifice of current consumption (c_0) and an increase in future consumption (c_1). So a project can be represented by a vector $(\Delta c_0, \Delta c_1)$ which when charted in consumption space corresponds to a move northwest from, say, E to E' (Figure 12-1).

The rate of return (ρ) on the project corresponds to the ratio of the return to the cost and is given by

$$\frac{\Delta c_1}{-\Delta c_0} = \frac{\text{return}}{\text{cost}} = \frac{\text{return} - \text{cost}}{\text{cost}} + 1 = \rho + 1$$

Having calculated ρ for each project, and provided projects are not only independent but small, Crusoe resolves to consider projects in order of their rate of return. Suppose that if he did no projects (just gathered berries), his output of consumption goods would be at E, the endowment point in Figure 12-2. If he did the project with the highest ρ (planting seeds?), he could produce at E''. And so

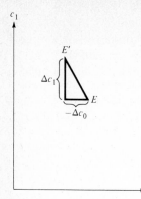

Figure 12-1 An investment project.

on. By adding in more and more projects in order of their rates of return, he traces out a convex production frontier reaching northwest from E. The slope of the curve at any point is $1 + \rho$, where ρ is now the rate of return on the marginal project.

Since Crusoe is isolated from the capital market, his production frontier is also his consumption frontier. His problem is thus:

$$\max u(c_0, c_1)$$

such that
$$f(c_0 - c_0^E, c_1 - c_1^E) = 0 \qquad \text{(production constraint)}$$

where (c_0^E, c_1^E) is the consumption vector at E and f represents his investment opportunities. At his optimum, using our usual notation for derivatives,

$$\frac{f_0}{f_1} = \frac{u_0}{u_1}$$

In geometrical terms, his optimum is at a tangency between his production frontier and an indifference curve. The absolute slope of the production frontier is $f_0/f_1 = \rho + 1$, as we have already seen. The absolute slope of the indifference

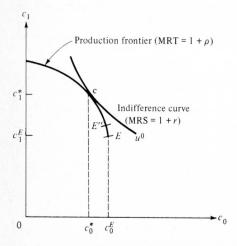

Figure 12-2 The isolated individual.

curve is

$$-\frac{dc_1}{dc_0} = \frac{u_0}{u_1} = \frac{u_0 - u_1}{u_1} + 1 = r + 1$$

where r is the "rate of time preference," since it measures the proportion by which the value of consumption today exceeds that of consumption tomorrow. In equilibrium therefore $r = \rho$. At less investment than the optimum, we have $\rho > r$, but as more investment is done ρ falls and r rises till equality is reached. (The reader could represent this by charting ρ and r against accumulated investment.)

At the optimal production and consumption point **c**, Crusoe has determined not only his rate of saving and investment ($c_0^E - c_0^*$, as a fraction of his total income of c_0^E), but also the rate of growth of his economy $[(c_1^*/c_0^E) - 1]$ and his equilibrium rate of time preference ($r^* =$ the absolute slope of the indifference curve at **c**, minus 1). Once we know the (*ex-post*) discount rate (r^*) we could equally well describe Crusoe's problem as being to undertake all projects which have positive present values when future flows are discounted at r^*. The "present value (PV) rule" is then: do all projects for which

$$\text{PV} = \Delta c_0 + \frac{\Delta c_1}{1 + r^*} > 0$$

A little manipulation will show that this "present value rule" is equivalent to the "rate of return rule": do all projects for which

$$\rho > r^*$$

where
$$\rho = \frac{\Delta c_1}{-\Delta c_0} - 1$$

However, we shall shortly show the inadequacy of the rate of return rule when production frontiers are nonconvex or when consumption in more than two periods is at stake.

> *Except when there are capital-market imperfections, the present value rule is invariably correct; though the rate of return rule gives the same answer in the two-period convex-production possibilities case, it has no general validity.*

Q12-1 If Crusoe does no project, he produces 110 units in each year. His utility function is $u = c_0 c_1$. How much will he invest/save in the first year, and how fast will his economy grow
    (i) If he has a very large number of projects open to him, all with 10 percent rates of return?
    (ii) If the available projects have the following costs and returns?

Project	Δc_0	Δc_1
A	-1	1
B	-5	10
C	-1	1.11

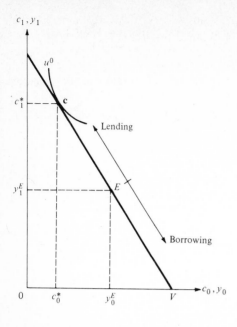

Figure 12-3 Perfect capital markets: consumption loans only.

No Productive Investment Opportunities

Now consider a person with no opportunities for productive investment, but with opportunities for borrowing and lending at a constant interest rate (i). (Note that the acquisition of financial assets is not an investment.) The individual earns his income (y_0^E, y_1^E) at E in Figure 12-3, but he may wish to exploit his market opportunities to choose a different consumption point. Any loans he makes in period 0 must be repaid with interest in period 1 (borrowing being merely negative lending, and repayment to others being negative repayment by others). So his *capital-market constraint* is

$$\text{Lending} \times (1 + i) = \text{repayment by others}$$

Hence
$$(y_0^E - c_0)(1 + i) = c_1 - y_1^E$$

So
$$y_0^E + \frac{y_1^E}{1 + i} = c_0 + \frac{c_1}{1 + i}$$

Thus
$$\text{PV of income} = \text{PV of consumption} = \text{distance } 0V$$

This is the equation of his market opportunity line. Its absolute slope is $1 + i$ and it passes through both E and V. The crucial point for what follows, however, is that a person's consumption possibility frontier can, in a perfect capital market, be defined simply by its slope i and its intercept on the horizontal axis; in other words, by the interest rate and the person's present value (see Figure 12-3).

The individual now maximises utility subject to his capital-market constraint, by again equating his rate of subjective time preference to the objective rate of transformation available to him, in this case the interest rate. Hence $r = i$. In the illustration he chooses to consume at point **c**, and lends $(y_0^E - c_0^*)$ (a pure consumption loan) in period 0 and is repaid $(y_0^E - c_0^*)(1 + i)$ in period 1.

Q12-2 Suppose the individual has an income 110 in each period and can borrow/lend at 10 percent and $u = c_0 c_1$.
  (i) What will he consume in the two periods?
  (ii) How much will he borrow/lend in the first period and repay/be repaid in the second?
  (iii) What is the PV of his income? Of his consumption?

Productive Investment Opportunities and Borrowing-Lending Opportunities

We now bring together opportunities for productive investment and for borrowing and lending. In a perfect capital market, such as we have assumed, the individual's problem can be solved in two sequential steps (in Figure 12-4).†

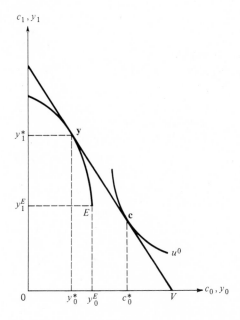

Figure 12-4 Perfect capital markets, with variable production.

---

† This can also be seen from a glance at the mathematical structure of the problem:

$$\max u(c_0, c_1)$$

such that $\qquad c_0 + \dfrac{c_1}{1 + i} = y_0 + \dfrac{y_1}{1 + i} \qquad$ capital-market constraint

and $\qquad f(y_0 - y_0^E, y_1 - y_1^E) = 0 \qquad$ production constraint

The problem is clearly recursive and can be solved by maximising $y_0 + y_1/(1 + i)$ subject to the second equation, and then u subject to the first, rewritten to include y_0^* and y_1^*, where these are the solutions to the previous problem.

1. Choose the production point (**y**) which maximises the present value of the stream of income (net of investment outlays)(i.e., maximise $0V$). This guarantees that the consumption frontier is pushed as far to the right as possible. It is done by undertaking all projects with positive present values when discounted at the market rate of interest (i). The rule is thus: Do all projects for which

$$PV = \Delta y_0 + \frac{\Delta y_i}{1+i} > 0$$

Equivalently, we could do all projects for which

$$\rho = \frac{\Delta y_1}{-\Delta y_0} - 1 > i$$

So, in equilibrium, $i = \rho$.

2. Having expanded the consumption set to its maximum, choose the preferred consumption point (**c**). At this point, if r^* is the *ex-post* discount rate, we have $r^* = i = \rho$.

The individual borrows $c_0^* - y_0^*$ in period 0 and repays $(c_0^* - y_0^*)(1 + i)$ in period 1, but we cannot say how much of the loan is a consumption loan, unless we arbitrarily assert that $y_0^E - y_0^*$ (which equals the investment) is an investment loan. Note that the collection of investments which the person undertakes raises his present value from the present value of the vector at E to the present value of the vector at **y**, i.e., by an amount equal to

$$\left(y_0^* + \frac{y_1^*}{1+i} \right) - \left(y_0^E + \frac{y_1^E}{1+i} \right)$$

or

$$y_0^* - y_0^E + \frac{y_1^* - y_1^E}{1+i} = \Delta y_0 + \frac{\Delta y_1}{1+i}$$

Q12-3 Suppose an individual can borrow and lend at 10 percent .His utility is $u = c_0 c_1$ and, if he does no investing or borrowing/lending, his income is 110 in each period. Calculate c_0, c_1 as well as his borrowing/lending in period 0 and repayment in period 1. Assume the available projects are those listed in Question 12-1(ii).

Imperfect Capital Markets

Once we allow for imperfect capital markets, the recursive procedure just described breaks down. Suppose the borrowing rate (i_B) to an individual exceeds his lending rate (i_L), even though both are constant. It is then no good telling him to maximise his present value, until we know whether he is a lender or a borrower. This depends on his production possibilities and his preferences. To find the answer we must start with his production frontier and then, using i_B

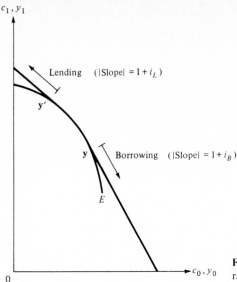

c_1, y_1

Lending ($|\text{Slope}| = 1 + i_L$)

$\mathbf{y'}$

$\mathbf{y}$ Borrowing ($|\text{Slope}| = 1 + i_B$)

E

c_0, y_0

0

Figure 12-5 Unequal borrowing and lending rates for the same person.

and i_L, construct his consumption frontier (see Figure 12-5). He may then choose to

1. Produce at $\mathbf{y}$ and consume on the borrowing line (he does this if at $\mathbf{y}$, $r > i_B$)
2. Produce at $\mathbf{y'}$ and consume on the lending line (he does this if at $\mathbf{y'}$, $r < i_L$), or
3. Produce and consume somewhere between $\mathbf{y}$ and $\mathbf{y'}$ (a direct tangency solution like Robinson Crusoe's)

When we know which of these cases maximises his utility, we can then characterise his production decision as maximising the present value of his income at the *ex-post* discount rate. If two people have the same i_B, i_L, the same tastes, and the same endowment E, but one has good production opportunities and the other bad ones, the former will tend to be a borrower and the latter a lender.

Some borrowers do not face constant borrowing rates but rates that rise with the amount being borrowed, the reason being that the marginal risk of default rises with the amount borrowed and the creditor therefore requires a premium for lending more. In this case we trace out the investor's overall consumption frontier by taking each possible production point, drawing from it the corresponding conditional consumption frontier, and then finally taking the envelope of all such frontiers. For example, if up to x can be borrowed at an interest rate i and thereafter nothing, the envelope reproduces the shape of the production frontier (see Figure 12-6). At a regular optimum, such as that shown at $\mathbf{c}$, the rate of time preference equals the rate of return on the marginal project. In fact the same holds even if the marginal borrowing rate rises continuously, rather than discontinuously from i to infinity as in Figure 12-6.

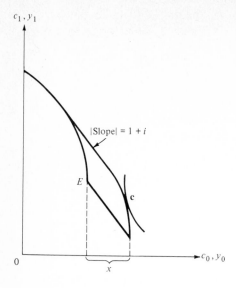

Figure 12-6 Limited borrowing opportunities.

However, where projects are not small or divisible, the optimum may well involve a corner solution.

> *With imperfect capital markets the only safe rule is the general one of maximising $u(c_0, c_1)$ subject to the production and capital-market constraints.*

This requires the investor to estimate his utility for all feasible points (c_0, c_1) that are not obviously dominated.

For example, suppose a person can borrow and lend at a constant rate but cannot borrow more than x. He has to decide whether to do a certain indivisible project. He first determines what he would consume in each period if he did the project, assuming he could borrow and lend without constraint. He then checks whether this point is feasible, given the borrowing constraint. If it is not, then, if he did the project, he would have to consume at

$$c_0 = y_0^E + \Delta y_0 + x$$

$$c_1 = y_1^E + \Delta y_1 - x(1 + i)$$

The utility given by this point must now be compared with that he could obtain if he did not do the project. (For the case where he does *not* do the project, he must also determine the regular optimum and then check whether it is feasible and if not determine his constrained consumption point.)

Borrowing rates may of course vary between individuals, from something near zero up to infinity. For people who have no security to offer as collateral, borrowing rates are often very high. If they cannot borrow, the borrowing rate is infinite and their investment decision occurs at a direct tangency, as in the case of Robinson Crusoe. Except in a society where slavery is permitted, human capital cannot often be used as collateral, so that in poor families the private cost of human capital investment is often met by an equal reduction in consumption.

Q12-4 (i) Suppose there is a project (A):

Δy_0	Δy_1
-600	1111

If he does not do the project, the investor receives 110 per period. He can borrow and lend at 10 percent but cannot borrow more than 500. $u = c_0 c_1$. Will he do the project?

(ii) Would he do the project (B) below if the alternative was again no project?

Δy_0	Δy_1
-500	1111

12-5 Suppose two individuals have the same tastes, endowments, and abilities to profit from investment in human capital, but A has a higher borrowing rate than B. Both borrow to finance their education.

(i) Which will invest most?

(ii) Suppose the present value of the lifetime income of each is evaluated using A's discount rate, which individual has the higher present value?

(iii) Which is better off?

(iv) What conclusion do you draw?

12-2 THE INDIVIDUAL: TWO-PERIOD CASE, NONCONVEX PRODUCTION SET

Perfect Capital Market

We now allow for interdependence between projects. If projects are mutually exclusive or if one project can only be done if another intrinsically less productive project has been done first, then the production frontier cannot be constructed by simply arranging all projects in order of their rates of return. Instead we seek that frontier that maximises y_1 for each y_0, after allowing for which combinations of projects are permissible.

For example, suppose all projects are small and independent, except for two large mutually exclusive projects A and B, each of which is more productive than any of the small independent projects. Then if project A is done rather than B, we have a permissible production frontier EAA'; if project B is done rather than A, we have a permissible production frontier, EBB' (see Figure 12-7). Since each of these frontiers is permissible, the overall frontier must be the envelope of the two, which is EDB'. This is nonconvex.

If nonconvexity is present, it may be right to prefer a project with a lower rate of return to a project with a higher one. The only correct rule is to maximise the present value of income. For example, in Figure 12-7 the optimal

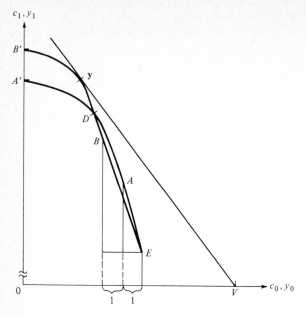

Figure 12-7 Nonconvex production frontier.

production point is $\mathbf{y}$ assuming a perfect capital market with interest rate equal to the slope of $\mathbf{y}V$. But selecting $\mathbf{y}$ means selecting project B and rejecting project A, which has a higher rate of return. The reason is simply that project B has a higher present value. In order to maximise his total present value the investor chooses among mutually exclusive projects those that have the highest present values. For $0V$ is nothing other than the present value of his original endowment plus that of all his projects.

In the two-period case a project with a lower rate of return can only have a higher present value than some other project if it is larger, as in the following example:

Project	Δy_0	Δy_1	ρ	PV (approx.)†	
				$i = 0.01$	$i = 0.08$
A	-1	1.1	0.10	0.09	0.02
B	-2	2.16	0.08	0.14	0.00

† Note that for small a, i, $(1 + a)/(1 + i)$ is approximately equal to $1 + a - i$.

If the interest rate is 1 percent, B has the larger present value. However, as interest rates rise, the difference in present value falls, and there must be some critical rate of interest less than 8 percent at which A becomes more profitable (see Figure 12-8). At any interest rate above this level, A should be done rather

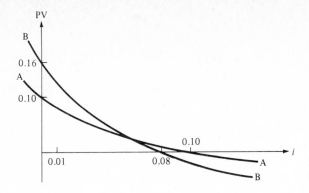

Figure 12-8 Present values at different interest rates.

than B. A glance at Figure 12-7 confirms that, as interest rates rise, a switch to project A is necessary if the consumption frontier is to be kept as far to the right as possible.

Nonconvexity also occurs if a more productive project R can only be done if an intrinsically less productive project S has been done already. In order to maximise his present value the investor must evaluate the present value of each project that can be done on its own (such as S) and the present value of joint projects (such as $R + S$). There is no point in his evaluating a project like R on its own (unless he has already decided to do S).

Imperfect Capital Markets

If interdependent projects have to be evaluated in imperfect capital markets, the rule of maximising present values does not help until we know whether a person is a borrower, lender, or neither. The only safe approach is the general one of maximising utility subject to the production and capital-market constraints. However, we shall henceforth revert to perfect capital markets.

Q12-6 An investor has the following projects available:

Project	Δy_0	Δy_1
A	-2	2.02
B (conditional on A)	-2	2.28
C	-1	1.14
D (conditional on C)	-1	1.01

All projects are independent, except that B can only be done if A has been done, and D can only be done if C has been done. Which projects should he do if
 (i) $i = 0.05$?
 (ii) $i = 0.10$?
Which projects should he do if
 (iii) $i = 0.05$ and, in addition to the above restrictions, it is impossible to do both A and C?

12-3 THE INDIVIDUAL: n-PERIOD CASE

Permanent Income Streams

Most investments last more than two periods, but we can preserve the essentials of the two-period analysis if we confine ourselves to projects involving costs in the first year and a permanent stream of constant returns thereafter. The reason is that we thereby continue to rule out any possibilities of substitution between future periods. We simply modify the two-period model by relabelling the vertical axis as permanent consumption (c_p) and permanent income (y_p). The slopes of the curves become ρ, r, and i rather than $(1 + \rho)$, $(1 + r)$, and $(1 + i)$, since

$$\rho = \frac{\Delta y_p}{-\Delta y_0}$$

$$i = \frac{\Delta y_p}{-\Delta y_0}$$

and the utility function is defined as $u(c_0, c_p)$. The present value of a project is given by

$$PV = \Delta y_0 + \frac{\Delta y_p}{i}$$

Q12-7 Suppose there are the following two mutually-exclusive projects for supplying a given quantity of electricity (the real-life dilemma is roughly as indicated).

Project	Δy_0	Δy_p
Thermal	-50	15
Nuclear	-100	22

Which method should be adopted if
   (i) $i = 0.10$?
   (ii) $i = 0.20$?

The General Case

Most choices are not between permanent income streams, nor need the interest rate be the same between one pair of adjacent years and another pair. Given perfect capital markets, the only generally correct investment rule is

$$\max PV = y_0 + \frac{y_1}{1 + i_1} + \frac{y_2}{(1 + i_1)(1 + i_2)} + \cdots + \frac{y_n}{\prod_{t=1}^{n}(1 + i_t)}$$

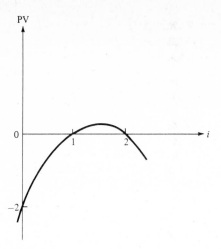

Figure 12-9 Present value of $-1, 5, -6$.

where i_t is the interest rate between periods $t - 1$ and t—subject always to the production constraint.

From this it is at once obvious why the rate of return rule cannot be used in the many-period case. The rate of return on a project is got by solving for ρ in

$$\text{PV} = \Delta y_0 + \frac{\Delta y_1}{1 + \rho} + \frac{\Delta y_2}{(1 + \rho)^2} + \cdots + \frac{\Delta y_n}{(1 + \rho)^n} = 0$$

Now, suppose we obtained a single solution for ρ. Which interest rate, out of i_1 to i_n, should we compare it with? On top of this, the polynomial in which we solve for ρ may either have no real roots (if $\Sigma \Delta y_t < 0$) or multiple roots. The maximum number of roots having economic significance (i.e., greater than -1) equals the number of sign changes in the stream of net returns. Thus a mining project that had to be filled in when it was finished could easily have two rates of return. An example of multiple roots would be the project $(-1, 5, -6)$. This has roots of 1 and 2, but as Figure 12-9 shows, should only be done if the interest rate is between 100 and 200 percent.

The deficiency of the rate of return approach is that it does not ask the key question: If the project is done, can the investor maintain his planned pattern of consumption (as it would be without the project) and add something to it?† However, the rate of return concept can be saved (after a fashion) if we confine it to the two-period case and treat n-period projects as aggregations of two-period projects, each of which is judged by the rate of return rule. If we can decompose

---

† This assumes we have a perfect capital market. If there were no capital market, we make our production decisions to maximise $u(c_0, \ldots, c_n)$. This is formally equivalent to maximising

$$\text{PV} = \sum_i c_i \frac{u_i}{u_0}$$

where the u_i/u_0 are evaluated at the optimum.

the n-period project into $(n-1)$ two-period projects each of which pass the rule, then the total project should be passed. Thus, suppose $i = 0.05$. If we take the project $(-1, 1, 1)$ this can be decomposed into two projects:

$$
\begin{array}{llll}
\text{A: periods 0 and 1} & -1, 1.05 & \rho = 0.05 = i \\
\text{B: periods 1 and 2} & -0.05, 1 & \rho = 19 & > i
\end{array}
$$

The first project just passes, and the second passes with flying colours, so the overall project passes. Project A has no adverse effect on the individual's ability to pay for his original consumption plan, while if he sticks to his plan he will be left at the end of period 2 with a surplus of $1 - 1.05$ (0.05) to spend on consumption then, or when suitably discounted, in some earlier period.

In the case of projects ending with negative returns, the rate of return language has to be modified somewhat. Reverting to the project $(-1, 5, -6)$, we can decompose this into

$$
\begin{array}{lll}
\text{A: periods 0 and 1} & -1, 1.05 & \rho = 0.05 = i \\
\text{B: periods 1 and 2} & 3.95, -6 &
\end{array}
$$

The first project passes the rate of return test. Of the second we ask: If the investor lent out the 3.95 he gets in period 1, could he earn enough to repay 6 in period 2. The answer is a resounding no. But had the interest rate been 100, the answer to the comparable question would have been a bare yes, for the subprojects would have been

$$
\begin{array}{lll}
\text{A: periods 0 and 1} & -1, 2 & \rho = 1 = i \\
\text{B: periods 1 and 2} & 3, -6 & \rho = 1 = i
\end{array}
$$

However, this face-saving operation has little point, other than to remind us of the underlying rationale of the present value rule.

From a substantive point of view, the main change which enters when we move to the many-period case is that the length of life of different projects affects the way their relative present values change when interest rates change. The lower the interest rate, the better the relative performance of long-lived projects, as can be seen by comparing projects A and B below. Thus more durable machines are likely to be built in periods when real interest rates are low. By the same token, if two projects are the same length, lower interest rates favour projects whose returns are concentrated later in the period (see example below).

Project	Stream of net returns	PV (approx.)	
		$i = 0.01$	$i = 0.10$
A	$-1, 1.1, 0, 0, 0$ (forever)	0.09	0
B	$-1, 0.1, 0.1, 0.1, 0.1$ (forever)	9	0

Low interest rates favour more long-lived and (as shown earlier) larger projects.

Q12-8 (i) At what interest rate do the following projects have the same present value?

A: −1, 1, 1.1
B: −1, 1.1, 0.99

(ii) Which has higher PV at interest rates lower than that?

12-4 CAPITAL-MARKET EQUILIBRIUM

We have so far seen how the individual's demand for borrowing will depend on his preferences, his production possibilities, and assuming perfect capital markets, on the real interest rate. Given this, it is easy to see how the interest rate is determined in a two-period model (see Figure 12-10).

Consider first the world of Figure 12-3, where there is no productive investment. When the interest rate rises, borrowers will naturally want to borrow less, as present consumption is more expensive in terms of future consumption; and, being poorer, they will anyway tend to consume less in both periods. The case of lenders is less clear. The higher interest rate increases the rewards to lending, but against this it raises lenders' real income, making them tend to consume more in both periods. Thus the supply curve of funds may be rising or backward-bending. There may thus be multiple equilibria, of which alternating equilibria will be stable.

If we now introduce productive investment, the probability of multiple equilibria is reduced. When the interest rate rises, borrowers' demands for borrowing are further cut by the fact that fewer projects are worth doing, so the demand curve for funds becomes flatter. At the same time lenders are more willing to lend, as fewer of their own projects are worth doing; so the supply curve bends back less sharply. However multiple equilibria may still exist.

Figures 12-3 and 12-4 have been drawn to illustrate an interest rate which produces equilibrium in the loans market, assuming there are the same large

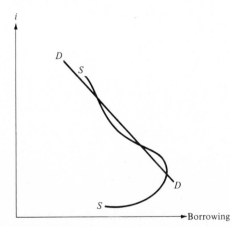

Figure 12-10 The equilibrium of the capital market.

number of people characterised by Figures 12-3 and 12-4. Total lending (in Figure 12-3) equals total borrowing (in Figure 12-4). Moreover, for each individual his total inflow of funds must equal his total disposal of funds. So

$$\text{Income} + \text{borrowing} = \text{consumption} + \text{investment} + \text{lending}$$
$$+ \text{ net hoarding of cash}$$

The same is true when summed over individuals. Thus if in the whole community total borrowing equals total lending and there is no net hoarding, it follows that for the community

$$\text{Investment} = \text{income} - \text{consumption} = \text{saving}$$

How would a change in the nation's investment opportunities affect the interest rate? This clearly depends on the elasticity of substitution in the intertemporal utility function. If the elasticity of substitution is infinite, the interest rate is determined entirely on the supply side—by the supply price of funds. But, more realistically, we must think of the interest rate as determined by both the supply and demand for funds.

We have so far dealt with a world in which there is only one consumption good in each period. Suppose there are many. The individual will then face a capital-market constraint in which each dated commodity has a price relative to one of the dated commodities, taken as a numeraire. Thus, by giving up a claim over a specified form of consumption today, he can acquire a claim to some specified form of consumption tomorrow. He will maximise utility subject to his production opportunities and this capital-market constraint. This will determine his excess demand in the market for each commodity, and the market will determine the relative prices, such that the excess demands for each good, summed over all individuals, add to zero. There will be no such thing as the money rate of interest unless we introduce money as a commodity. There is simply a set of relative prices between all dated commodities; and the rate at which, say, butter, in year t, can be substituted for butter in year $t + 1$ is not necessarily the same as the rate at which butter in year $t + 1$ can be substituted for butter in year $t + 2$. The strength of the whole theory is that it is not linked to any notional steady state.

12-5 AGGREGATE CAPITAL AND THE CAPITAL CONTROVERSY

The reader may have noticed that we have not so far mentioned the concept of capital. This is because there be dragons here. Joan Robinson and her colleagues have made their attack on the concept of aggregate capital the centrepiece of their attack on neoclassical theory.† But the concept is unnecessary

---

† For a useful collection of articles on both sides of the controversy see G. C. Harcourt and N. F. Laing (eds.), *Capital and Growth*, Penguin, Harmondsworth, 1971.

for theoretical purposes. At no point in this chapter have we needed a measure of the aggregate capital stock at a point in time. All we have assumed is that at any moment, producers believe they can add to future output by the use of current resources, according to some determinate relationship. However, for empirical work it is often convenient to use measures of aggregate capital, and we must therefore be aware of the dangers of doing this.

To understand Joan Robinson's objection, we can refer to J. B. Clark's one-sector model of the distribution of income. Here there is only one kind of good which serves both for consumption and as a capital good. Then if output is produced by capital and homogeneous labour, we have

$$y = f(K, L)$$

The rate of profit is determined by the stocks of labour and capital, at a level equal to the marginal product of capital. Since output and capital are measured in the same units, the marginal product of capital is a pure number. If there are constant returns to scale, it also follows that as capital per man (K/L) increases, the rate of profit (i) falls, and the real wage (w) rises.

This approach to the rate of profit is obviously wrong, since consumption and capital goods are not the same. Supposing there were only one capital good, and one additional unit of investment (now) yielded a permanent increase in the output of consumption goods of Δc_p. If the value of the capital good in units of current consumption were ΔK, one might still be tempted to say that the marginal product of capital was $\Delta c_p/\Delta K$ and that this explained the interest rate. This unidirectional analysis would however be completely misleading, since, viewed from another angle, the value of the machine is determined such that it equals the present value of its output. In that case

$$\Delta K = \frac{\Delta c_p}{i}$$

In fact, of course, the interest rate and the quantity of machines are simultaneously determined by intertemporal preferences and the possible combinations of present and future consumption implied in the physical productivities of machines and labour. In this sense Figure 12-4 is a partial analysis for the individual, since the amount of future consumption output he can produce by giving up different amounts of current income to buy capital goods depends on the final equilibrium set of prices. However, on reasonable assumptions there would be such an equilibrium, whether there is one or many capital goods.

Even so, as the Cambridge (England) school points out, it does not follow that, if different steady-state equilibria are compared, the rate of profit necessarily falls as the value of capital per man (measured in consumption goods) rises. To get a feel for the argument, consider the case where the consumption good can be produced by two possible technologies.

Using technology A, 1 unit of output can be produced in year t by applying 7 units of labour in year $t - 2$. Using technology B, 1 unit of output can be produced by applying 2 units of labour in year $t - 3$ and 6 units in year $t - 1$.†

	Labour requirement per unit of output in year t		
Technique	$t - 3$	$t - 2$	$t - 1$
A	...	7	...
B	2	...	6

It is simplest to think of all the labour being used to improve the quality of the raw materials, so that all capital is working capital. But the example is chosen for simplicity only, and the result which follows could equally occur when all capital is in the form of durable machines.

We now examine the different possible steady states in which such an economy could operate if it had a constant labour force. (A steady state is one in which output per unit of capital is constant.) To do this it is convenient to start by positing the interest rate i and then find what real wage w and value of capital per man (K/L) would be consistent with it. Now, producers will always choose that technique which minimises the cost of producing a unit of output, cost being measured by its present value measured in the year of sale. Unit cost using technology A is

$$C^A = w[7(1 + i)^2]$$

and unit cost using technology B is

$$C^B = w[2(1 + i)^3 + 6(1 + i)]$$

So technology A is used whenever

$$2(1 + i)^2 - 7(1 + i) + 6 > 0$$

and when that expression equals zero, producers are indifferent between A and B. Since the expression is a polynomial, it may have more than one root (as we saw in the case of the rates of return on n-period projects). If this happens, there may be more than one interest rate at which producers switch between techniques A and B. In fact in the example given the position is as follows:

$i > 1$	A cheaper
$1 > i > 0.5$	B cheaper
$0.5 > i$	A cheaper

This is the so-called phenomenon of "reswitching" or "double-switching." As the interest rate falls, a given technique can be found profitable, then unprofitable again. This, if it happens in the real world, has devastating implications for the conclusions usually drawn from the one-sector model of distribution. To see this,

---

† This example is taken from P. Samuelson, "A Summing Up," *Quarterly Journal of Economics*, vol. 80, pp. 568–583, November 1966.

we first compute the wage levels at the "switching" rates of interest. If technique A is used, the real wage is given by equating the sale value of output to the present value of its costs at the moment of sale. So

$$w[7(1 + i)^2] = 1$$

Similarly for technique B,

$$w[2(1 + i)^3 + 6(1 + i)] = 1$$

At the switching rate of interest $i = 1$, the wage is the same irrespective of technique and is $\frac{1}{28}$ in units of output. Similarly at $i = 0.5$, the wage using both techniques is $1/15.75$. Thus far, the one-sector model's results survive: given constant returns, wages rise if interest rates fall. But unfortunately it is not necessarily true that the value of capital per man also rises (capital being valued in units of consumption).

If technique A is used, the value of capital in year t is the capital value of work-in-progress done in year $t - 2$ plus that done in year $t - 1$. If there are L workers and K is the value of capital in units of output then

$$\left(\frac{K}{L}\right)^A \left(\frac{1}{L}\right)[Lw(1 + i)^2 + Lw(1 + i)] = w[(1 + i)^2 + 1 + i]$$

Since, if technique A is used

$$w = \frac{1}{7(1 + i)^2}$$

$$\left(\frac{K}{L}\right)^A = \frac{1}{7}\left(1 + \frac{1}{1 + i}\right)$$

As the interest falls, K/L rises, as in the one-sector model. The same is true using technique B. The problem arises when we switch from one technique to the other.

Consider the switch at $i = 1$. The value of capital per worker using technique A is

$$\left(\frac{K}{L}\right)^A = \tfrac{1}{7}(1 + \tfrac{1}{2}) = \tfrac{6}{28}$$

But, using technique B, the value of capital is the value of work-in-progress done in year $t - 3$ plus that done in year $t - 2$ plus that done in year $t - 1$. If there are L workers of whom $2L/8$ work at the first stage of production and $6L/8$ at the second stage, then

$$\left(\frac{K}{L}\right)^B = \frac{1}{L}\left\{\frac{2Lw}{8}[(1 + i)^3 + (1 + i)^2 + (1 + i)] + \frac{6Lw}{8}(1 + i)\right\}$$

$$= w\{\tfrac{2}{8}[(1 + i)^3 + (1 + i)^2] + 1 + i\}$$

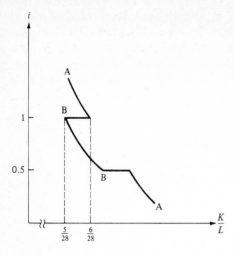

Figure 12-11 The reswitching of techniques.

At $i = 1$, using our earlier calculation that $w = \frac{1}{28}$, we find

$$\left(\frac{K}{L}\right)^{\text{B}} = \frac{1}{28}(\frac{2}{8} \cdot 12 + 2) = \frac{5}{28} < \frac{6}{28}$$

Thus when i falls to 1, the value of capital per worker falls, as shown in Figure 12-11. It then rises steadily until $i = 0.5$, when it rises discontinuously as technique A comes back into use.

Looking at the matter from the more traditional angle, a given value of capital per man is consistent with more than one rate of profit, depending on what technique is being used. This contradicts the story of the Austrian economists like Bohm-Bawerk, according to which as production becomes more "roundabout" and takes place over a longer period of time, interest rates must fall and capital per man increase. The reason is, of course, that when one compares techniques A and B, it is quite unclear which of them *is* the more roundabout. If, instead, we had a point-input point-output case, there would be no ambiguity, nor would there be if, for a given technique, labour was always applied uniformly over time. The importance of reswitching as an empirical phenomenon has been little investigated by those who stress its importance, but it must be more important the less easy it is to tell unambiguously whether a process is roundabout and mechanised, or unroundabout and unmechanised.

What the reswitching debate has done is to counsel caution in the use of simplified models. It in no way undermines the generalised neoclassical theory outlined in Section 12-4, which is not concerned with any artificial steady-state situation. However, in empirical work there remains the problem of aggregation. This is an acute problem whether one is measuring capital services, labour services, or output. In general, aggregation is only possible where the items to be aggregated are either perfect complements or perfect substitutes. Otherwise, there is normally a danger of estimation bias. The danger is reduced if the relative weights which are used in aggregating any two items correspond to their "shadow prices" (i.e., to the relative effects which an additional unit of each would have on output or utility). The special problem with capital equipment is that, because once installed it is less readily marketable than labour or current output, the prices available for aggregating capital are less relevant than those for aggregating labour or current output. In a world of economic change, the annual value of the historic costs of a machine (even after adjusting for inflation) may bear little relation to the value of its current services. And due to the costs of resale, second-hand markets often provide no further guidance. This poses real problems for econometricians. But the neoclassical theorists emerge unscathed, provided they state their theory in sufficiently general terms.†

Q12-9 Suppose output can be produced automatically by two machines (there are no others). Each machine is built in one year by one worker. They yield the following flows of output:

Machine	$t + 1$	$t + 2$
A	2	0
B	1	2

If the value of capital per man increases, must the interest rate fall?

† See, for example, K. J. Arrow and F. H. Hahn, *General Competitive Analysis*, Holden-Day, San Francisco, 1971. For a simplified exposition see C. R. S. Dougherty, "On the Rate of Return and the Rate of Profit," *Economic Journal*, vol. 82, pp. 1324–1350, December 1972.

PART
SIX

UNCERTAINTY

THIRTEEN
UNCERTAINTY

Unfortunately, life is uncertain, and this uncertainty makes much of what we have said so far unrealistic. People do not know whether they are going to be sick or burgled or even employed. So how do people behave in the face of uncertainty, and what difference does uncertainty make to the various propositions we have been putting forward about capitalist economies? In this chapter we first develop a theory of how individuals choose in the face of risk, and show what this implies for insurance behaviour and portfolio selection. We then move to the level of the market, showing how it reallocates risk between people. Under certain assumptions, *laissez-faire* capitalism still produces Pareto-efficient outcomes, even in the presence of uncertainty. But the assumptions are unrealistic: they imply, for example, that all risks can be insured against. We therefore explore the implications of the failure of insurance markets and conclude with a brief analysis of the economics of information.†

13-1 INDIVIDUAL BEHAVIOUR TOWARDS RISK

We start with the individual. Suppose that a Punjab farmer is debating whether to buy fertiliser to put on his land. His decision will, as usual, depend on his opportunities, as he sees them, and his preferences.

† This chapter assumes some knowledge of elementary probability and statistics, such as is provided by J. C. Hodges and E. C. Lehmann, *Basic Concepts of Probability and Statistics*, Part I, Holden-Day, San Francisco, 1964, or any similar textbook.

The Structure of Uncertainty

Consider first his opportunities. The net return to fertiliser will depend on whether there is a favourable rainfall. If the rains fail, the net return may be negative, with the cost outweighing the benefits. But if the rains come, there will be a fine return. So the first ingredient in his opportunities is his evaluation of his own net income in each of the possible *states of the world* (rain or no rain), as a result of each possible *plan* (fertiliser or no fertiliser). This information, sometimes called the *payoff matrix*, is assembled below.

Farmer's net income (*y*)

Plan		State of the world	
		1 Rain	2 No rain
A	Fertiliser	50	10
B	No fertiliser	30	30
(Probability)		( )	( )

Ignore the probabilities (in parentheses) for the moment, and note that the 'payoff' in this matrix is not the net return to fertiliser use but the farmer's net income, conditional on a given plan and a given state of the world. In terms of symbols we shall represent it by

Farmer's net income

Plan	State 1	State 2
A	y_{A1}	y_{A2}
B	y_{B1}	y_{B2}
(Probability)	( )	( )

The second ingredient in the farmer's perception of his opportunities is the *subjective probability* he attaches to each of the possible states of the world. People often object if you tell them they decide on the basis of subjective probabilities. They say they have no idea how likely it is that state 1 will happen rather than state 2.[†] At this point you say, "Oh, you mean they are equally

---

[†] In this case they are faced with what Knight called "uncertainty," rather than "risk," where subjective probabilities do exist. We shall describe what Knight called risk as either "risk" or "uncertainty" and ignore the case which he called uncertainty. For various theories of how people behave in the latter case, see R. Dorfman, in A. Maass *et al.* (eds.), *Design of Water Resource Systems*, Harvard, Cambridge, Mass., 1962, pp. 129–58; reprinted in R. Layard (ed.), *Cost-Benefit Analysis*, Penguin, 1972.

likely?" to which they normally reply, "Oh, no, state 1 (or 2) is definitely more likely." So we shall assume that people always operate on the basis of probabilities, however vague and ill-specified. Suppose then that the farmer thinks there is a 50-50 chance of rain.

$$\pi_1 = .5 \qquad \pi_2 = .5$$

You may find it convenient to write in the probabilities below each payoff matrix. Note that π_1 and π_2 must sum to unity.

The farmer's opportunities now consist of two alternative *prospects*. The first prospect, if he takes action A, is a .5 chance of 50 and a .5 chance of 10. We can conveniently write this as

$$\text{Prospect A} = (50, 10; .5, .5)$$

where the outcomes precede the semicolon, and the corresponding probabilities follow it in the same order. Similarly, prospect B consists of the certainty of 30, which can be written

$$\text{Prospect B} = (30, 30; .5, .5)$$

The two prospects are partially depicted in Figure 13-1. The horizontal axis measures income-if-the-rains-come and the vertical axis measures income-if-the-rains-fail. The diagram does not record the probabilities of rain and no rain.

The farmer's choice will depend on his preferences. We assume he is able to order all feasible prospects, including prospects A and B. Let us represent this ordering by an *ex-ante* utility index V. Then if there are only two possible states of nature, it follows that

$$V = V(y_1, y_2; \pi_1, \pi_2)$$

For given probabilities, this becomes of course just a function of y_1 and y_2, which can be represented by a set of indifference curves in Figure 13-1.

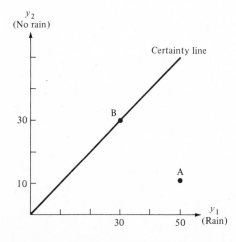

Figure 13-1 A risky prospect (A) and a safe one (B).

So what can be said about the farmer's decision? To set this in context, let us first compute the *expected value* of each alternative (i.e., the income which can be expected to result on average from an infinitely long sequence of repetitions of the same action). The expected value is the probability of each state of nature times the resulting income, summed over all states of nature. So the expected value of income if plan A is adopted is

$$E(y|A) = \pi_1 y_{A1} + \pi_2 y_{A2} = .5(50) + .5(10) = 30$$

If action B is taken the expected value is equal to its certain value, namely, 30.

If the farmer made his decision on the basis of expected values, he would be indifferent between the two actions. To put the matter another way, choosing A in preference to B is like taking on a "fair gamble" (i.e., one with zero expected value). On average he will neither win nor lose, so if he maximises expected income he is indifferent between the two actions.

However, most people are influenced by the spread of possible outcomes, as well as by the average outcome to be expected. In other words, they care about risk. If a person is averse to risk, he will not be willing to give up the certainty of 30 for a 50-50 chance of 50 and 10, even though this is a fair gamble. By contrast a person who positively likes risk will be willing to take a fair gamble, and even an unfair one, provided it is not too unfair.

A risk-averse person will not take a fair gamble, while a risk lover will.

Note that in this discussion we have been assuming that the individual has the same needs in all the possible situations being considered. This may not be right. The farmer's needs may not be the same in sunshine and in rain. Punjab houses often get washed away in rain, and a cautious farmer may be glad to have more income if it rains in order to repair his house. However, we can deal with this problem by assuming that the payoff matrix measures net income in some sense, so that needs are now the same in both states of the world.†

Given this, what are the indifference curves in Figure 13-1 going to look like? If a person's needs are the same in each state and he thinks each state to be equally likely, his indifference curves must be symmetric about the 45° line. It follows that, if the person is risk-averse, his indifference curves must be convex to the origin, for only this guarantees that he will not take a fair gamble. (Check that in this case B is preferred to A.) So convexity of the indifference curves is equivalent to risk aversion. And what if state 1 and state 2 have different probabilities? Then, if the indifference curves are convex, they must also cross the certainty line with a slope equal to π_1/π_2: for only thus can we be sure that the individual will never take a fair gamble.‡ This condition makes sense: if state

---

† In the fully general approach, people are assumed to have preferences between states as well as between incomes. Hence the term "state-preference theory."

‡ The slope of a line joining a point on the 45° line to a risky point of equal expected value is π_1/π_2, since

$$E(y) = \pi_1 y_1 + \pi_2 y_2$$

1 is more likely than state 2, income-in-state-1 is more valuable than income-in-state-2.

Q13-1 Suppose the payoff matrix were, more realistically,

Plan	Rain	No rain
Fertiliser	50	10
No fertiliser	30	20
(Probability)	(.5)	(.5)

What would a farmer do, if he were
    (i) A risk lover?
    (ii) Risk-neutral?
    (iii) Risk-averse?

The Expected-Utility Approach

The utility function we have used so far is totally general. For many purposes this is enough to obtain powerful results—particularly in welfare economic problems, as we shall see later. However, for some purposes a more specific utility function yields further insights. We shall first state the existence of the function as a hypothesis and explore its implications, before showing much later how the existence of the function follows from certain axioms.

According to the "expected utility hypothesis," alternative prospects are ranked according to the expected utility they provide. If $u^i(y_i)$ is the utility which arises in state i from income y_i and there are two possible outcomes, expected utility is $\pi_1 u^1(y_1) + \pi_2 u^2(y_2)$. Thus our previously general function is now assumed to be of the expected-utility form

$$V(y_1, y_2 ; \pi_1, \pi_2) = \pi_1 u^1(y_1) + \pi_2 u^2(y_2)$$

Assuming henceforth that needs are the same in all states, we have the same *ex-post* utility function in each state, so that

$$V(y_1, y_2 ; \pi_1, \pi_2) = \pi_1 u(y_1) + \pi_2 u(y_2)$$

What light does this throw on our Punjab farmer's behaviour? His expected utility if he does the fertiliser project (A) is

$$E(u|A) = \pi_1 u(y_{A1}) + \pi_2 u(y_{A2})$$
$$= .5u(50) + .5u(10)$$

His expected utility if he does not do the project is

$$E(u|B) = u(30)$$

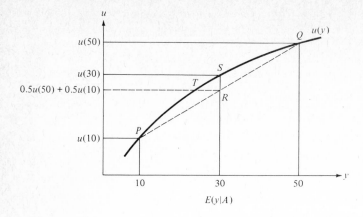

Figure 13-2 Expected utility: a risk-averse utility function.

He selects A if

$$E(u|A) > E(u|B)$$

Whether this is so depends on the shape of the utility function. If it is concave from below, this means by definition that

$$u(\lambda y_1 + (1 - \lambda)y_2) > \lambda u(y_1) + (1 - \lambda)u(y_2)$$

for all $0 < \lambda < 1$. Thus setting $\lambda = .5$, we have $u(30) > .5u(50) + .5u(10)$. In other words, we can represent the psychological characteristic of risk aversion by the expected-utility hypothesis plus the assumption of a concave utility function.

To get a feel for this, ask yourself why a farmer would prefer a certain income to an equal chance of winning or losing 20 units? One natural answer is that the gain in utility from winning 20 is less than the loss of utility from losing 20. In other words, there is diminishing marginal utility of income. We shall return later to the philosophical basis for this interpretation, but it does at any rate help one to remember the basic structure of the argument.

This is illustrated in Figure 13-2. The farmer's (expected) utility if he buys no fertiliser is $u(30)$. If he buys fertiliser, his expected utility is $.5u(50) + .5u(10)$. To measure this, note that the height of P measures $u(10)$ and the height of Q measures $u(50)$. So, if we bisect the line PQ at R, the height of R measures the average of the two (with weights .5 to each). But, since R bisects PQ, it also stands directly above $E(y|A) = .5(10) + .5(50) = 30$. Therefore the height $u(30)$ is registered by a point S on the utility function and lying on a vertical line through R. Since $u(y)$ is concave, $u(y)$ lies above any chord, such as PQ. But R lies in PQ. Therefore S lies above R.

By contrast, if the farmer was a risk lover, he would prefer the uncertain prospect to the certain one with the same expected value. This could be represented by a utility function that is convex downwards (see Figure 13-3).

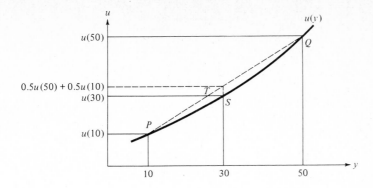

Figure 13-3 Expected utility: a risk-loving utility function.

If a person maximises expected utility and the utility function is the same in all states of nature, risk aversion implies a concave (downwards) utility function, risk loving a convex function, and risk neutrality a linear function.

Q13-2 Suppose the following payoff matrix and probabilities.

Plan	State 1	State 2
A	100	100
B	200	50
Probability	.33	.67

(i) Confirm that the expected value of income is the same for both decisions.
(ii) Draw a diagram to confirm that if $u(y)$ is concave (downwards), then $E(u|A) > E(u|B)$.

Insurance and Gambling

If a person is risk-averse, he will be willing to pay to avoid risk. This is the basis of insurance. For example, suppose in Figure 13-2 that I currently have an income of 50 but will lose 40 if my house burns down, and I think there is a 50-50 chance of this happening. If I do not insure, my expected utility is measured by the height of R. If, instead, someone offered me a guaranteed income of $(30 - TR)$, I should be equally happy. So I am willing to pay the insurance company each period a premium of up to

$$50 - (30 - TR) = 20 + TR$$

provided they will pay the bill when the house burns down. For, if I do this, I will have transformed the uncertain prospect

$$\text{Prospect A} = (50, 10; .5, .5)$$

into the new prospect

$$\text{Prospect C} = (30 - TR, 30 - TR; .5, .5)$$

which has the same expected utility. On average, of course, the company will pay me 20 each year; so their expected profit is TR.

Turning to the gambler, we have seen that he would be willing to enter into a fair gamble. But he is unlikely to be offered many, at Las Vegas at any rate. However, he may, of course, be willing to take an unfair gamble, provided it is not too unfair. For example, suppose his income is 30 and he is offered a bet of 20 units on the famous filly Mae West at even odds. He will be willing to take it, according to Figure 13-3, provided he believes the probability of a win for Mae West exceeds or is equal to PT/PQ. For suppose he thinks the probability is PT/PQ. He will then, by taking the bet, transform the certain prospect

$$\text{Prospect B} = (30, 30; .5, .5)$$

into the uncertain prospect

$$\text{Prospect D} = (50, 10; PT/PQ, TQ/PQ)$$

But the expected utility of prospect D is

$$E(u|D) = \frac{PT}{PQ} u(50) + \frac{TQ}{PQ} u(10)$$

This is represented by the height of point T and equals the utility of 30 for sure, measured by the height of S. So if he rates Mae West's chances any better than PT/PQ, he will be only too willing to have a go.

In a famous article,[†] Friedman and Savage asked why the same person often both insures *and* gambles. (Don't you?) To explain this, they postulated a utility of income function that was concave at low incomes, convex at middle incomes, and concave again at high incomes (see Figure 13-4). Consider a person with income y^0. Suppose he faces a small risk ($\pi = .3$) of a large loss (L). If he is offered a fair insurance, he will take it since

$$u(y^0 - .3L) > .7u(y^0) + .3u(y^0 - L)$$

(Check this by completing Figure 13-4.) But this does not mean that he will not also take a fair gamble. If the probability of gain is less than a half and the bet is fair, the winnings, if successful, must be larger than the losses, if unsuccessful. Thus suppose he is offered a bet at $3:1$ on a stake S. If he wins he gains $3S$, and if he loses, he loses S. He considers the odds fair: the probability of winning is $\pi = .25$. He is willing to take this gamble since

$$u(y_0) < .75u(y_0 - S) + .25u(y_0 + 3S)$$

[†] M. Friedman and L. J. Savage, "The Utility Analysis of Choices Involving Risk," *Journal of Political Economy*, vol. 56, pp. 279–304, August 1948.

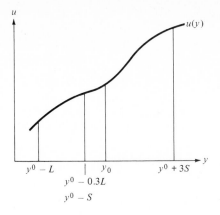

Figure 13-4 Explaining gambling and insurance.

(Check this too by completing Figure 13-4.)

However, does this really explain the behaviour in question? If we assume that all individuals have the same utility function, it implies that gambling will be concentrated in the middle income groups, except that upper middle groups will also be willing to place bets at very short odds (on favourites) and lower middle groups will be willing to place bets at very long odds (on outsiders). The facts do not seem to support those predictions.

One might alternatively suppose that individuals differ in their utility functions, but each individual has a function that is first concave, then convex, and then concave, with the convex section beginning at about the level of his current income (y^0). Then every individual would both insure and gamble. But there is still a snag. If the convex section extended for any distance, individuals would bet for large stakes in order to have a chance of changing their incomes substantially. Yet, typically, people have a sequence of small flutters.

So how else can we explain gambling? There are two obvious possibilities. First, people may overestimate the probabilities of success. Second, they may (in the right atmosphere) enjoy the sensation of gambling for its own sake, as well as for the outcomes to which it gives rise. These explanations seem quite sufficient, and we shall henceforth assume that, in their evaluation of *outcomes*, people are invariably risk-averse. It is, of course, perfectly possible that in normal situations people are averse to a risky alternative not only because of their evaluation of its possible outcomes, but because they dislike not knowing how well off they are going to be. In fact, people probably do insure partly because for most of the time they want certainty for its own sake, just as in the gambling den they want uncertainty for its own sake. But in insuring themselves, people must be mainly influenced by the nasty thought of how they would feel after the event if a disaster struck. From now on we shall assume, as before, that risk aversion stems solely from the evaluation of the outcomes of different decisions in different states of the world. We shall also assume that people are risk-averse.

Q13-3 "Suppose $y_1 > y_2 > y_3 > y_4$ and $u(y_1) + u(y_4) = u(y_2) + u(y_3)$. A risk-averse individual who maximises expected utility will prefer a 50-50 chance of y_2 and y_3 to a 50-50 chance of y_1 and y_4, since the latter implies a higher variance of utility." True or false?

Q13-4 If a particular offence is detected the criminal will be fined. Suppose that social science research has shown that a 1 percent increase in the fine has a smaller deterrent effect than a 1 percent increase in the probability of detection. Does this imply that criminals are risk lovers or risk haters?

Q13-5 Suppose a project offers the following prospect:

$$\text{prob}(\Delta y = 100) = p$$
$$\text{prob}(\Delta y = -90) = 1 - p$$

Any individual considering the project will evaluate it on the basis of his resulting total wealth $(y^0 + \Delta y)$. Suppose the utility function is

$$u = k - e^{-\alpha y}$$

Will a person's decision to do the project or not be affected by the level of his initial wealth y^0?

*Q13-6 Suppose you were offered the following option. A coin is to be tossed until it comes down heads. If n is the number of tosses up to and including the first head, you will be paid 2^n dollars.

    (i) What is the expected money return on this option?
    (ii) How much would you be willing to pay for the option?
    (iii) If $(i) > (ii)$, explain why, using the expected-utility hypothesis.

The Cost of Risk

Delving deeper, we may usefully ask: What is the cost of risk? For example, in evaluating a risky investment project, like using fertiliser, we may want to know how much to deduct from its expected return in order to allow for risk and have a "certainty-equivalent" measure of the return. Or we may want to know how much of his expected income a person faced with a risky prospect would be willing to sacrifice to an insurance company in order to achieve certainty. These two problems are formally identical. They require us to find the certainty-equivalent income, i.e. that certain income which gives the same utility as the expected utility of the uncertain prospect.

    The cost of risk is the difference between the expected value of a risky prospect and its certainty-equivalent income.

Turning back to Figure 13-2, the cost of the risk involved in

$$\text{Prospect A} = (50, 10; .5, .5)$$

is clearly the distance TR. The more curved the utility function, the greater the cost of risk.

    To see this it is useful to develop an appropriate measure of the cost of risk (C). It is defined by

$$u(\bar{y} - C) = \sum_{i=1}^{N} \pi_i u(y_i) \tag{1}$$

where there are N possible states of nature, $\bar{y}$ is expected income, and $\bar{y} - C$ is the certain income giving utility equal to the expected utility of the risky prospect. To get a measure of C we need approximations for both sides of this equation. Provided C is reasonably small, we can approximate the left-hand side by a Taylor's series expansion around $\bar{y}$, ignoring second- and higher-order terms:

$$u(\bar{y} - C) \simeq u(\bar{y}) - u'(\bar{y}) \cdot C \tag{2}$$

We thus use a linear approximation to the utility function. On the right-hand side, however, we need to allow for the possibility that y may on occasion take values that differ quite widely from $\bar{y}$. We therefore introduce the second-order term in the Taylor's series expansion. This gives

$$u(y) \simeq u(\bar{y}) + u'(\bar{y}) \cdot (y - \bar{y}) + \tfrac{1}{2}u''(\bar{y}) \cdot (y - \bar{y})^2$$

So
$$\sum \pi_i u(y_i) \simeq u(\bar{y}) + u'(\bar{y}) \sum \pi_i(y_i - \bar{y}) + \tfrac{1}{2}u''(\bar{y}) \sum \pi_i(y_i - \bar{y})^2$$
$$= u(\bar{y}) + u'(\bar{y})0 + \tfrac{1}{2}u''(\bar{y}) \cdot \text{var}(y) \tag{3}$$

So from Equations (1), (2), and (3) we find that

$$C \simeq - \frac{u''}{2u'} \text{var}(y) \tag{4}$$

The cost is proportional to the variance of income. This is only an approximation and does not hold for large variances. But, this apart, the cost of risk is proportional to the variance of income.

Alternatively, we may prefer to look at the *risk premium* i.e., the fraction of his expected income that a person would be willing to sacrifice for the sake of certainty. This is given by

$$\frac{C}{\bar{y}} \simeq - \frac{u''\bar{y}}{2u'} \frac{\text{var}(y)}{\bar{y}^2}$$

For small variances the cost of risk is proportional to the variance of income, and the risk premium is proportional to its coefficient of variation squared.

Given this, we may call $-u''/u'$ the degree of *absolute risk aversion* and $-u''\bar{y}/u'$ the degree of *relative risk aversion*. To get a feel for the latter, it is helpful to write it out more fully:

$$\text{Relative risk aversion} = \frac{du'}{dy} \frac{\bar{y}}{u'}$$

So the degree of relative risk aversion is the elasticity of the marginal utility of income with respect to income: the faster marginal utility falls, the more risk aversion. If an individual's utility function exhibits constant absolute risk aversion, he will rank projects the same way, however wealthy he is. If, by contrast, he has constant relative risk aversion, he will be less averse to risky projects, the richer he is.

13-7 Consider the following functions
 (i) $u(y) = k - e^{-\alpha y}$ $\alpha > 0$
 (ii) $u(y) = -1/\alpha + y^{\alpha}/\alpha$ $\alpha < 1, x \neq 0$
One of these is the only function exhibiting constant absolute risk aversion, and the other is the only one exhibiting constant relative risk aversion. Which is which?

Risk-Pooling and Risk-Spreading

We can now examine two major mechanisms, by which the cost of risk is reduced in modern economies: risk-pooling and risk-spreading. The gains from risk-pooling can be shown without using formal utility theory and can be dealt with quite quickly. Suppose there is a large number (n) of individuals, all of whom face the same risky prospect. Each person's income is a random variable y with a given distribution, including mean and variance, which is the same for all individuals. Assume the distribution of each person's income is independent of the distribution of each other person's income. (This might well be the case where the risk arises from, say, fire hazard—except in densely populated areas with wooden buildings.) If each individual depends entirely on his own income, there is a risk attached to this which has to be offset against the expected value of his income.

But suppose the n individuals get together and pool their incomes, agreeing that each shall draw the average income out of the pool. The variance in the total of their incomes is of course the same whether the incomes are pooled or not. It is

$$\text{var}\,(y_1 + y_2 + \cdots + y_n) = n\,\text{var}\,(y)$$

since all the incomes are independent and have the same variance. But clearly the variation in individual incomes is greatly reduced. Originally the individual received y and his variance was var (y). But now he receives $(1/n)(y_1 + \cdots + y_n)$, and the variance of this is

$$\text{var}\left(\frac{y_1}{n} + \frac{y_2}{n} + \cdots + \frac{y_n}{n}\right) = n\,\text{var}\left(\frac{y}{n}\right) = \frac{n}{n^2}\,\text{var}\,(y) = \frac{\text{var}\,(y)}{n}$$

which tends to zero as n tends to infinity.

> *The Law of Large Numbers. If n identically distributed and independent incomes are pooled, the variance of average income tends to zero as n tends to infinity.*

So the cost of risk to the individual also tends to zero.† Thus the more people join the pool, the better off the individual is. For his expected income is the same whether in the pool or out, but the cost of risk is reduced in the pool. Classic cases of risk-pooling include friendly societies, business mergers, and so on.

A different process is the spreading of one given risky income over more than one person. Suppose, for example, that everyone in the Punjab had the same

---

† If n is finite, the cost of risk to each individual is $(-u''/2u')$ var $(y)/n$.

certain income, but that in addition there was a fertiliser project yielding returns y with a 50-50 chance of $(+30)$ and (-10). If the project is undertaken by one person, the variance in his income is var (y). The cost of risk is then

$$C^0 = -\frac{u''}{2u'} \text{var} (y)$$

But suppose the same single project is undertaken jointly by a group of n farmers who agree to divide the proceeds equally. Each will receive y/n, where y is the project income in the state of nature which comes about. So the variance of each farmer's income is $(1/n^2)$ var (y). The cost of risk to each farmer is thus $-(u''/n^2 2u')$ var (y). Since there are n farmers, the total cost of risk is n times the cost to each farmer:†

$$C^1 = -\frac{nu''}{n^2 2u'} \text{var} (y) = -\frac{u''}{2u'} \frac{\text{var} (y)}{n}$$

Thus if a *single* project is spread over a large enough number of people, the cost of the risk goes to zero. However, for reasons that will become clear in a moment, this is so only if the returns to the project are independent of the incomes which the participants get from other sources.

> *If the net returns to a given project are independent of the incomes which those concerned derive from other sources, the cost of the risk associated with the project tends to zero as the number of participants in the return tends to infinity.‡*

This is, of course, the basis of the joint-stock company. It is also the basis of an important argument put forward by Arrow and Lind. According to them, the net benefits of most public sector projects can be spread over a large enough number of people for the cost of risk to be negligible. They should therefore be assessed on the basis of their expected value, using a discount rate that is free of any risk premium, provided the returns to the project are independent of the other sources of income of those concerned.

† The formula is related to the formula for risk-pooling as follows. Risk-pooling of the type described above is no more than the spreading of n identical and independent risks over n people. If one of these risks is spread over n people, its cost of risk falls from $(-u''/2u')$ var y to $(-u''/2u')$ var $(y)/n$. So, if n of these risks is spread, their total cost falls from $n(-u''/2u')$ var (y) to $(-u''/2u')$ var (y), and the cost to each of the n individuals falls from $(-u''/2u')$ var (y) to $(-u''/2u')$ var $(y)/n$, which is the result derived earlier (footnote to page 362). The reason for discussing risk-pooling independently of risk-spreading is that because of the independence assumption the gains from risk-pooling are evident without recourse to utility theory: as n goes to infinity, income becomes virtually certain, while expected income remains unchanged. By contrast, risk-spreading would have no benefits if the cost of risk were, say, proportional to the standard deviation of income; to show the benefits, utility theory is needed.

‡ For a proof not involving use of our approximation, see K. J. Arrow and R. C. Lind, "Uncertainty and the Evaluation of Public Investment Decisions," *American Economic Review*, vol. 60, pp. 364–378, 1970, reprinted in R. Layard (ed.), *Cost-Benefit Analysis*, Penguin, 1972. If our approximation holds, it is easy to show that the cost tends to zero, as n tends to infinity, even if people differ in their certain incomes and in their degree of risk aversion.

Q13-8 "If A and B have the same income and tastes and there is a project which neither is willing to do on his own, they will not be willing to do it on a 50-50 basis, since halving the project merely halves the returns to each person and halves his cost of risk." True or false?

Q13-9 Suppose:

(i) The net annual returns to a channel tunnel between Britain and France are £50 m if the European Economic Community survives and −£40 m if it disintegrates.

(ii) Both events are equally likely.

(iii) All other components of national income are fixed.

(iv) The net returns to the project will be spread over about one million households. If household utility is given by $u_i = k - 1/y_i$, would you conclude (as would Arrow and Lind) that the project's cost of risk is negligible?

The Cost of Covariant Risk

So far we have assumed that the individual only has one possible source of uncertainty. For example, we assumed that the Punjab farmer would have a certain income unless he used fertiliser. However, a more realistic picture of his opportunities might be the following.

Plan	State 1: Rain	State 2: No rain
A: Fertiliser	50	10
B: No fertiliser	30	20

How does this affect the cost of risk associated with the fertiliser project?

The farmer's income y can be thought of as consisting of two parts: x, his income without the fertiliser project, and z, the returns to the fertiliser project:

$$y = x + z$$

We can now readily compute the project's cost of risk, following the same procedure as before. The cost C is defined by finding what certain return to the project $(\bar{z} - C)$ would give the same expected utility as the actual project.

$$\sum \pi_i u(x_i + \bar{z} - C) = \sum \pi_i u(x_i + z_i)$$

So

$$u(\bar{x} + \bar{z} - C) + \tfrac{1}{2}u'' \text{ var }(x) \simeq u(\bar{x} + \bar{z}) + \tfrac{1}{2}u'' \text{ var }(x + z) \qquad \text{[by analogy with (3)]}$$

Hence

$$u(\bar{x} + \bar{z}) - u'C + \tfrac{1}{2}u'' \text{ var }(x) \simeq u(\bar{x} + \bar{z}) + \tfrac{1}{2}u'' [\text{var }(x) + \text{var }(z) + 2 \text{ cov }(x, z)]$$

Thus

$$C \simeq -\frac{u''}{2u'} [\text{var }(z) + 2 \text{ cov }(x, z)] \qquad (5)$$

If the covariance between x and z were zero, we would be back to (4). But, if not, we have another important element to take into account. In our case the fertiliser project is less desirable than it would otherwise be, because it pays off best in years when income is high in any case.

To reinforce this point let us introduce a third possible project—a tube well that would be used only when the rains failed (but would still involve capital charges even if not used):

Plan	State 1: Rain	State 2: No rain
A: Fertiliser	50	10
C: Tube well	20	40
B: Neither	30	20
(Probability)	(.5)	(.5)

As compared with doing nothing, the returns to the two projects are

Option	State 1	State 2
A	+20	−10
C	−10	+20

So they both have the same mean (+5) and variance (225). If the farmer can only do one of them, which will he do? Clearly the tube well project, since the returns to this are negatively correlated with the farmer's underlying income if he does neither project.† The importance of covariance has only recently become fully recognised in development planning, though, as we shall see, it has been well appreciated for some time in portfolio selection.

The cost of risk of a project depends on its contribution to the variance of total income, and hence not only on its own variance but on its covariance with the other elements of income.

Q13-10 "If n identical individuals pool n identical risky incomes that are perfectly correlated with each other, there is no reduction in the cost of risk." True or false?

Mean-Variance Analysis and Portfolio Selection

The stock market is an institution that greatly facilitates the pooling and spreading of risks. We shall return to the equilibrium of this market later. For the present we are concerned only with a single investor's choice of optimum portfolio.

---

† It would obviously be possible for the negative covariance to be so large in absolute size that the tube well project was no longer preferred. This reminds us that expression (5) is only an approximation.

Traditionally this has been analysed on the assumption that the investor only cares about the mean and variance of his income. The assumption is thus

$$V = V[\bar{y}, \text{var}(y)] \tag{6}$$

This can be justified as an approximation, following the line we have adopted so far, which implies that we can write [from (3)]

$$V = E(u) \simeq f[\bar{y}, \text{var}(y)]$$

However, for an exact reconciliation of (6) with the expected-utility hypothesis, one or both of the following conditions must hold.

1 The utility function is quadratic

$$u(y) = a + by - cy^2 \qquad b, c > 0$$

So

$$E[u(y)] = a + bE(y) - cE(y^2)$$
$$= a + b\bar{y} - c[\bar{y}^2 + \text{var}(y)]$$

since

$$\text{var}(y) = E(y - \bar{y})^2 = E(y^2) - \bar{y}^2$$

There are two drawbacks to a quadratic utility function. First, for sufficiently high incomes utility falls as income rises. This is not a real disadvantage since we can assume that this occurs outside the relevant range of incomes. More seriously, the quadratic utility function implies that, if there is one risky asset (or income source) and one safe one, the investor will hold less of the risky one as he gets richer. (Try formulating this problem and proving the proposition, see Question 13-11.) Common observation does not suggest that risk is inferior: the rich tend to hold riskier and higher yielding portfolios than the poor. So the quadratic utility function may not be a useful justification for mean-variance analysis.

2 Each security in the portfolio has a normal distribution†

Suppose the ith security has a normal distribution of income with mean μ_i and variance $\sigma_{ii}(= \sigma_i^2)$, and its covariance with the jth security is σ_{ij}. Then if a_i is the number of securities held of type i, the mean total income the investor can expect is

$$\mu = \sum_i a_i \mu_i$$

---

† This is because if each security y_i has a normal distribution, differing only in mean and variance from that of each other security, then a portfolio $\sum a_i y_i$ will also have a normal distribution which can be compared for mean and variance with any other portfolio, including one consisting of only one security (which is also normal). However, there is no other two-parameter distribution with finite variance for which it is true that $\sum a_i y_i$ has the same form of distribution function as each y_i taken on its own (i.e., which is a so-called "stable" distribution). In his original exposition Tobin overlooked this difference between normal and other two-parameter distributions ("Liquidity Preference as Behaviour Towards Risk," *Review of Economic Studies*, vol. 25, pp. 65–86 February 1958). He was corrected by Feldstein ("Mean-Variance Analysis in the Theory of Liquidity Preference and Portfolio Selection," *Review of Economic Studies*, vol. 36, pp. 5–12 January 1969).

and the variance of his total income is

$$\sigma^2 = \sum_i \sum_j a_i a_j \sigma_{ij}$$

and the distribution of his total income is normal. Choosing a different portfolio means choosing a different set of a_i s. But whatever set is chosen, the resulting distribution will be normal. Thus all possible distributions have the same shape, differing only in mean μ and variance σ^2. It follows that the investor only need be concerned with the mean and variance of the distribution. To repeat, this depends on the factual assumption that all securities are normally distributed, which is not very realistic. So we must inevitably think of the mean-variance approach as an approximation. But we shall continue to use it.

Its convenience derives from the relative ease with which it is possible to compute the investor's opportunity set in a manner relevant to choice. As we have seen, each vector **a** determines unique μ and σ^2. Of two portfolios with the same σ^2, a risk-averse investor will always prefer the portfolio with the higher μ. So, to define his opportunity set, the investor needs to know for each σ^2, the maximum μ available. This will define a frontier in the space (μ, σ^2) or, more conveniently, in the space (μ, σ). IBM and other firms now have a programme that will do this for him (on the basis of past experience of the incomes given by different shares). What will this frontier look like?

Suppose there are only two available securities x and z. Each is perfectly divisible, but 1 unit of each will cost the investor his whole wealth. We can expect the market to ensure that the riskier security has a higher mean return. In Figure 13-5, the points x and z show the investor's mean income and standard deviation if he puts all his wealth into x or z, respectively. Now suppose he puts half his wealth into each.

His mean income is now

$$\hat{\mu} = \tfrac{1}{2}\mu_x + \tfrac{1}{2}\mu_z$$

The variance of his income is

$$\hat{\sigma}^2 = \tfrac{1}{2}^2\sigma_x^2 + \tfrac{1}{2}^2\sigma_z^2 + 2\tfrac{1}{2}\tfrac{1}{2}\sigma_{xz}$$

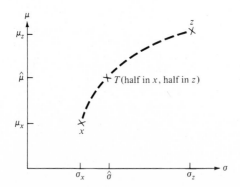

Figure 13-5 The mean-variance frontier: two assets.

Provided x and z are not perfectly (and positively) correlated, we have

$$r_{xz} = \frac{\sigma_{xz}}{\sigma_x \sigma_z} < 1$$

Thus $\qquad \hat{\sigma}^2 < \tfrac{1}{2}^2 \sigma_x^2 + \tfrac{1}{2}^2 \sigma_z^2 + 2\tfrac{1}{2}\tfrac{1}{2}\sigma_x \sigma_z = (\tfrac{1}{2}\sigma_x + \tfrac{1}{2}\sigma_z)^2$

So $\qquad\qquad\qquad\qquad \hat{\sigma} < \tfrac{1}{2}(\sigma_x + \sigma_z)$

We can now chart $(\hat{\mu}, \hat{\sigma})$ at T in Figure 13-5. It lies above the straight line joining x and z. By analogy, if we form a new portfolio consisting half of x and half of the mixture found at T, the (μ, σ) for this new portfolio will lie above the straight line xT, and so on. So the frontier of the opportunity set is concave from below. However many more linearly independent risky securities are introduced, this finding will be repeated. So we can draw an overall opportunity set composed of risky assets as shown in Figure 13-6.

Now suppose that in addition there is one riskless asset R yielding an income $0R$ for sure if all the investor's wealth is placed in that asset. The investor can of course combine the riskless asset with some risky ones. For example, he could put half his wealth into the riskless asset and a half into that risky mix which, if he put his whole wealth into it, would yield him the (μ, σ) indicated at P. The resulting (μ, σ) is that indicated at Q. (Check that you know why.) Alternatively he could mix R with some other point inside the set of risky portfolios. However, it is clear that he would never in fact mix R with any other portfolio than that represented by P. For mixing P with R expands his overall opportunity by the whole dotted area, which is more than he could achieve in any other way. But what about the area in Figure 13-6 to the right of point P? As the investor moves along RP towards P, the fraction of his wealth invested in the risky asset increases from 0 to 1. Beyond P he is borrowing at the riskless rate. So the chequered area is also part of his opportunity set.

What do we learn from this? First, let us establish the generality of the opportunity set we have discovered. We have constructed it for someone whose whole wealth would buy 1 unit of any of the available securities. If we consider a person with double that wealth, his opportunity set is identical to that of

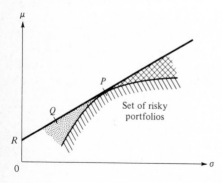

Figure 13-6 Mean-variance analysis.

Figure 13-6 except that every point is twice as far out along a ray from the origin. Next let us revert to the preference ordering. A point on the straight line through R and P is preferred to any point below it. It follows that the investor will always choose a point on that line. In other words, he will put a fraction of his wealth into the riskless asset and a fraction into that bundle of risky assets, which if he put all his wealth into it would yield him the portfolio indicated by point P. So, whatever his utility function, he will always mix his risky assets in the unique ratios $(a_1 : a_2 :$ etc.$)$ indicated by point P. And these ratios will be independent of his wealth. His utility function and wealth will, of course, affect what fraction of his wealth he puts into the riskless asset.

> *Separation theorem. If there is a riskless asset and conditions 1 and/or 2 are satisfied and all investors have the same subjective probability distributions, then investors will differ in the amount of wealth they hold in risky assets, but they will not differ in the fraction of that "risky" wealth devoted to each particular risky asset.*

Experience does not support this assertion. This may be because people guess differently about the μ_i's and σ_i's, or because they start from different historically determined portfolios and are locked in by transactions costs or tax problems, or because different assets offer different tax advantages to different people. Or it may be because of the defects of the mean-variance approach, as compared to a more general approach.

*Q13-11 Prove that, if there is one risky asset and one safe one, and the investor has a quadratic utility function, he will, as he becomes richer, hold less of the risky asset.

Q13-12 Suppose a riskless asset exists. If the utility function is quadratic, would you expect to find an investor holding only riskless assets. (Hint: Determine the shape of an indifference curve, giving constant expected utility.)

The Expected-Utility Theorem

So far, we have assumed that people maximise expected utility, and have treated this as a hypothesis to be confirmed or disproved on the basis of the evidence.† An alternative approach, from which the idea in fact arose, is to deduce this type of behaviour from a set of axioms. If the axioms are correct, the theory must be correct. The axioms were developed by Neumann and Morgenstern in the 1940s and earlier by Ramsey.‡ We shall confine ourselves to the essence of the argument. It is quite simple.

† For a discussion of the experiments that have been done to test the theory, see K. H. Borch, *The Economics of Uncertainty*, Princeton, 1968, Chap. 6.

‡ J. von Neumann and O. Morgenstern, *Theory of Games and Economic Behaviour*, 2d ed., Princeton, 1947, especially Appendix.

We begin with a slight change of notation. We have so far described a prospect by listing its outcomes in each relevant state of nature and then listing the probabilities of each state of nature. For example

$$\text{Prospect } A = (50, 10; .5, .5)$$
$$\text{Prospect } B = (30, 30; .5, .5)$$

In this particular case there are three possible outcomes (50, 30, 10), though the probability of 30 is zero in prospect A, and the probabilities of 50 and 10 are zero in prospect B. It is now more convenient to adopt a different notation. For each prospect we set out the probability of *every* possible outcome, even if the probability is zero. Thus, for example,

$$\text{Prospect } A = (50, 30, 10; .5, 0, .5)$$
$$\text{Prospect } B = (50, 30, 10; 0, 1, 0)$$

More generally we could write

$$\text{Prospect } A = (y_1, y_2, y_3 ; \pi_1^A, \pi_2^A, \pi_3^A)$$

where y_i represents a complete description of one particular outcome i (including, if relevant, the state of the world in which it occurs). Since for every prospect we have the same list of outcomes, we can, for short, write

$$\text{Prospect } A = (\pi_1^A, \pi_2^A, \pi_3^A)$$

We can now begin, with two pretty standard assumptions.

1. *There is a preference ordering among all* outcomes (*and this is complete and transitive*). *Here* y_1 *is preferred to* y_2, *which is preferred to* y_3.
2. *There is also a preference ordering among all* prospects (*and this is complete and transitive*). *Since prospects differ only in their vectors of probabilities, we can write*

$$V = V(\pi_1, \pi_2, \pi_3)$$

The question we are investigating is the structure of this V function. Our aim is to prove that it can be written as some function of a weighted average of the probabilities, i.e.,

$$V = V(\pi_1 u_1 + \pi_2 u_2 + \pi_3 u_3)$$

where u_i could be called the utility of outcome i but can also be interpreted as a probability.

The approach involves only two steps.

(a) We take the best and worst possible outcomes (here y_1 and y_3) and ask for each outcome (y_i) the following question: "At what probability u_i would we be indifferent between y_i for certain and a lottery offering a probability u_i of y_1 and a probability $(1 - u_i)$ of y_3?" Thus, for example, y_2 is equivalent to a lottery (L_2) with a probability u_2 of y_1 and a probability $(1 - u_2)$ of y_3.

(b) We then say: "If this is so, then a probability π_2 of y_2 must be equivalent to a probability π_2 of lottery L_2. But this in turn is equivalent to a probability $\pi_2 u_2$ of y_1 and a probability $\pi_2(1 - u_2)$ of y_3."†

So welfare would be unaffected if π_2 were reduced to zero but at the same time the probability of y_1 were raised by $\pi_2 u_2$ and the probability of y_3 raised by $\pi_2(1 - u_2)$. So

$$V(\pi_1, \pi_2, \pi_3) = V[\pi_1 + \pi_2 u_2, 0, \pi_3 + \pi_2(1 - u_2)]$$

If there were other outcomes lying between y_1 and y_3, we should proceed likewise to reduce their probabilities to zero while raising the probabilitites of y_1 and y_3.

Finally, we can do the same with y_1 and y_3 themselves. Clearly $u_1 = 1$ and $u_3 = 0$.‡ So we can write

$$V(\pi_1, \pi_2, \pi_3) = V(\pi_1 u_1 + \pi_2 u_2 + \pi_3 u_3, 0, 1 - \pi_1 u_1 - \pi_2 u_2 - \pi_3 u_3)$$

We then end with a welfare function in which all the probabilities are zero except for the "equivalent probabilities" of y_1 and y_3. The equivalent probability of y_3 equals unity minus the equivalent probability of y_1. So clearly the equivalent probability of y_1 is sufficient to determine the welfare ranking of a prospect. Thus, suppressing all arguments except the first as redundant, we can write

$$V = V(\pi_1 u_1 + \pi_2 u_2 + \pi_3 u_3)$$

where V is any strictly increasing function.

We are nearly home and dry. But what, again, are these u measures? u_2 is a measure of the sure value of the outcome y_2. So prospects are ranked according to the probability of each outcome times its value (if sure), summed over all outcomes: in other words, according to expected utility.

This is the structure of the proof. However, we need to make rather more explicit the assumptions that have been made. We have already made two unexceptionable ones. We now add another:

3. *If y_i is preferred to y_j, a prospect offering a higher probability of y_i and a lower one of y_j will, other things equal, be preferred.*

Finally, come the two key assumptions, corresponding to the two steps in the proof.

---

† This is due to the ordinary law of compound probabilities, which tells us that if lottery L is a prize in some other lottery, the total probability of getting a given prize in lottery L is the probability of winning access to lottery L *times* the probability of winning the specified prize in lottery L, given that one is participating in lottery L.

‡ y_1 for certain has the same value as a lottery in which the probability of y_1 is 1 and the probability of y_3 is 0. y_3 for certain has the same value as a lottery in which the probability of y_1 is 0, and the probability of y_3 is 1.

4. Assumption of continuity. For any particular y_1 preferred to y_2, preferred to y_3, there is one unique probability u_2 at which the sure outcome y_2 is indifferent to the lottery with probability u_2 of y_1 and $(1 - u_2)$ of y_3.

This is certainly very plausible. If u_2 were very low (almost zero), y_2 would clearly be a better bet than the risky prospect with little hope of getting y_1. But equally, if u_2 were nearly unity, the risky prospect would be preferable. Assuming elementary properties of continuity, there must be some u_2 in between at which indifference occurs. This assumption has two implications. First it asserts that for every probability distribution involving two outcomes there is a certainty equivalent. We got used to this some pages back. But more important for our present proof is the idea that for every certain prospect (for example, of y_2) there exists an equivalent probability distribution involving y_1 and y_3.

The other key assumption is this:

5. Assumption of independence. The evaluation of a prospect is not affected if some element in it is replaced by another element which is indifferent to it. In particular, any certain element can be replaced by an uncertain prospect of equal value.

Thus if y_2 is indifferent to the lottery just mentioned, that indifference holds irrespective of the context within which the comparison is being made. This assumption has often been criticised. For example, it is said, it may require a high probability (u_2) of y_1 to induce a person to sacrifice y_2, if y_2 is really certain. But if y_2 is not certain anyway, a smaller probability u_2 might be sufficient to compensate him. This argument seems to imply that people are averse to risk not just because of their concern about the outcomes of the various alternatives but because they dislike the condition of uncertainty as such. If this is so, it is indeed unlikely that individual behaviour can be represented by the maximisation of expected utility.

Now let us take a closer look at the utility index. Clearly it can be subjected to any increasing linear transformation. For the ranking of projects according to $\sum_i \pi_i(a + bu_i)$ will be the same as according to $\sum_i \pi_i u_i$. Equally, the utility indicator cannot be subjected to *any* nonlinear increasing transformation without running the risk that projects will be ranked differently before and after the transformation. (Try putting $u_i^* = u_i^2$.) So we can now summarise our findings.

Expected-utility theorem. Given assumptions 1 to 5, an individual chooses among risky prospects according to $\sum \pi_i u_i$, where π_i is the probability of outcome i, and u_i (a utility index for the outcome) is invariant between prospects and is unique up to a linear transformation.†

† The proof of this given above is based on the case where the number of possible outcomes is finite, but it can be generalised to the infinite case.

Does this mean that we have found the philosopher's stone—a cardinal measure of utility, albeit one relating to a particular individual? The answer, alas, is no. For behaviour is predicted by $V(\Sigma \pi_i u_i)$, where V is *any* increasing function. True, the u_i can only be subjected to linear transformations. But suppose we ask: What is the ratio of the utility interval between y_1 and y_2, both obtained with certainty, to the utility interval between y_2 and y_3, both obtained with certainty? The answer is

$$\frac{V(u_3) - V(u_2)}{V(u_2) - V(u_1)}$$

which can be varied at will by any nonlinear transformation of V.

Finally, it is worth asking why a linear utility function $V(\Sigma u_i \pi_i)$ *is* a plausible way of representing choice between risky bundles of probabilities while a linear utility function $V(\Sigma u_i x_i)$ is *not* a plausible way of representing choice between bundles of commodities obtained with certainty (see Chapter 5). The answer is that in the latter case when some of one commodity is bought, so is some of another, and these two commodities may be complements or substitutes. By contrast, if a given probability of y_1 is bought together with a given probability of y_2, y_1 and y_2 will never be consumed together. Thus the problem of complementarity does not arise. For the essence of uncertainty is that one and only one state of nature will actually happen. That is what makes life so difficult.

Q13-13 "Suppose $y_1 > y_2 > y_3 > y_4$ and a person is offered a choice between the following prospects:

Prospect	y_1	y_2	y_3	y_4
A	$\frac{1}{4}$	$\frac{1}{4}$	$\frac{1}{4}$	$\frac{1}{4}$
B	$\frac{1}{2}$			$\frac{1}{2}$
C		$\frac{1}{2}$	$\frac{1}{2}$	

The person cannot consistently choose A." True or false?

*Q13-14 Suppose the following prospects:

Prospect	$5 m	$1 m	0
A		1.00	
B	0.10	0.89	0.01
C		0.11	0.89
D	0.10		0.90

Offered the choice of A or B, the individual chooses A. If offered the choice between C and D, how will he choose?

13-2 MARKET EQUILIBRIUM AND WELFARE ECONOMICS

Turning to the market we can show, with the aid of one simple trick, that even under uncertainty it can produce an efficient outcome.

Efficient Allocation

We confine ourselves initially to the case where output is given, so we only have a problem of efficient consumption. Suppose there is one good (corn), two possible states of the world, and the output of corn in each state is as follows:

The example	General notation
Output of corn	Output (y)
Rain No rain	State 1 State 2
100 50	$\bar{y}_1$ $\bar{y}_2$

There are two individuals, A and B, who can each rank all possible prospects affecting them. For A, a prospect specifies how much corn he will receive in state 1 (y_1^A) and how much in state 2 (y_2^A). So his *ex-ante* utility function is

$$V^A = V^A(y_1^A, y_2^A)$$

where the function of course depends on his subjective probabilities of the states of the world. Similarly

$$V^B = V^B(y_1^B, y_2^B)$$

Efficient consumption requires that *ex ante* V^A is maximised for any given V^B, subject to the availability constraints:

$$y_1^A + y_1^B = \bar{y}_1$$
$$y_2^A + y_2^B = \bar{y}_2$$

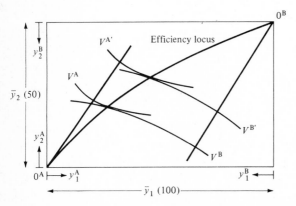

Figure 13-7 Allocation of claims to corn.

This is the standard efficiency problem of Chapter 1, with only one modification. Corn as such is no longer a "good"; corn-in-state-1 is now one good and corn-in-state-2 is another good. So the trick is that goods now become *state-contingent commodities*, or *contingent commodities*, for short.† Every good is, in fact, a claim to a commodity in a given state of nature. Since these goods are the only objects that enter into the utility function, it follows that, if there is a market in them, a Pareto-efficient allocation will result. This was essentially the argument introduced by Arrow in his pioneering discussion of the subject and subsequently refined by Debreu.‡

Before going any further, we should point out a major drawback of this approach. Social welfare is judged entirely in terms of individual preferences as they are *before* the state of nature is known. Suppose someone thinks that a hurricane is most unlikely and buys no food for himself in the event of a hurricane. If the hurricane comes, should we allow him to starve? In other words, should we be concerned only with *ex-ante* utility, or also with *ex-post* utility? Most people would say that *ex-post* utility is at least as important. If people systematically underestimate a probability, such as the probability of long life, the state might then force them to insure more than they otherwise would against the event in question. However, from now on we shall continue to consider only *ex-ante* utility.§

The efficiency problem is shown diagramatically in Figure 13-7. We suppose that both A and B consider the chance of rain to be 50-50. So the absolute slope of A's indifference curves for $y_1^A = y_2^A$ is unity, and similarly for B. Both are risk-averse, so the indifference curves are convex to the origin. But A is more risk-averse than B, so his indifference curves are more sharply bent than B's (he has a lower elasticity of substitution). Thus the efficiency locus is concave-downwards. The meaning of this is clear. If the locus were straight, this would mean

$$\frac{y_2^A}{y_1^A} = \frac{y_2^B}{y_1^B} = \frac{50}{100}$$

Both A and B would receive half as much in a bad year as in a good year. But because the efficiency locus is concave-downwards,

$$\frac{y_2^A}{y_1^A} > \frac{50}{100} \qquad \frac{y_2^B}{y_1^B} < \frac{50}{100}$$

† Note that for intertemporal economics we performed a similar trick in Chapter 12: goods became entities like corn-in-period-1, corn-in-period-2, or "dated commodities."

‡ K. J. Arrow, "The Role of Securities in the Optimal Allocation of Risk-Bearing," *Review of Economic Studies*, vol. 31, pp. 91–96, April 1964, and first published in French in 1953; G. Debreu, *Theory of Value*, Wiley, New York, 1959, Chap. 7 (the discussion uses topological methods and includes an analysis of production, rather than pure exchange only).

§ The *ex-post* problem raised above was one involving social justice as well as efficiency. There are also *ex-post* problems connected only with efficiency. It can, for example, be shown that the *ex-post* outcome is only Pareto-efficient if *ex ante* all economic agents attached the same probability to the actual state of nature which occurred.

So A, who is more risk-averse than B, is in an efficient allocation nearer to a situation of certainty than B is. And B carries more risk.

Q13-15 Suppose that in the preceding example A and B were equally risk-averse.
  (i) What is the efficient ratio y_1/y_2 for A, and for B?
  (ii) Suppose the initial allocation were

Person	State 1	State 2
A	35	10
B	65	40

Is it possible to achieve a Pareto improvement on this?

Market for Contingent Commodities

How will the market bring about the efficient allocation? The simplest procedure is to postulate a market in these contingent commodities. Then individuals like A and B will have an initial endowment of money m which they can spend on state-contingent claims. A claim to 1 unit of corn-in-state-1 will have a price p_{y_1} and a claim to 1 unit of corn-in-state-2 will have a price p_{y_2}. Individual A will maximise $V^A(y_1^A, y_2^A)$ subject to

$$p_{y_1} y_1^A + p_{y_2} y_2^A = m^A$$

and this will define his demands for y_1 and y_2. B will do the same. And the set of equilibrium prices is that for which the demand for corn-in-state-1 is just equal to the supply of corn that will be available in that state. This leads to a Pareto-optimal allocation.

> *If there is a full set of contingent commodities markets, a free-market allocation (with no externalities or increasing returns) is Pareto-efficient.*

Diagramatically, we can represent the endowment point in Figure 13-7 by finding that point P lying on $0^A 0^B$ for which

$$\frac{0^A P}{0^A 0^B} = \frac{m^A}{m^A + m^B}$$

The market equilibrium requires that the common budget line through P crosses the efficiency locus at a point where it is tangential to both indifference curves. Suppose $m^A = m^B$. Try drawing in the equilibrium budget line in Figure 13-7. Note that

$$\frac{p_{y_1}}{p_{y_2}} < 1$$

This of course makes sense. Since states 1 and 2 are equally likely but more corn will be around in state 1, corn-in-state-1 is less scarce and commands a lower price.† So the market works.

But, one might say, this is all very well, but do these state-contingent commodities markets exist? They are not very common.‡ However, there *are* many markets for state-contingent deliveries of money rather than of goods. Insurance is one example, stock markets another. So does it make any difference if there are no state-contingent commodities markets? Is it just as good if people receive sums of money income depending on which state occurs and then maximise their current utility, spending their current income at the spot prices currently ruling?§

To examine this question we need to abandon the one-commodity world we have used so far. Suppose there are two goods, milk x and honey y, and the total output of each is as follows:

Commodity	State 1	State 2
x	$\bar{x}_1$	$\bar{x}_2$
y	$\bar{y}_1$	$\bar{y}_2$

Then, assuming expected-utility maximisation, the preferences of A are represented by¶

$$V^A = \pi_1 u_1^A(x_1^A, y_1^A) + \pi_2 u_2^A(x_2^A, y_2^A)$$

and similarly for B. The efficiency problem, as before, is to maximise V^A for any given V^B, subject to the four availability constraints of the four state-contingent commodities.

This could clearly be done via contingent commodities markets. But, equally, it *could* in theory be done using securities markets only. For we can easily imagine two equivalent procedures which would lead a person to consume the same bundle of contingent commodities. Under one scheme, he is faced with four prices for contingent commodities $(p_{x_1}, p_{y_1}, p_{x_2}, p_{y_2})$. Under the other scheme he is faced initially with

---

† This would be so even if A and B were equally risk-averse and the efficiency locus were along the diagonal of the Edgeworth box. Notice that prices are not proportional to probabilities. They would only be so in the case of a risk independent of the rest of GNP and given sufficient economic agents for full risk-spreading to be possible.

‡ Most insurance policies (e.g., fire insurance) pay out money rather than commodities if disaster strikes. But some (e.g., medical insurance) only pay bills for specific commodities. Crop-sharing arrangements also effectively allow for purchases of contingent commodities. Note also that ordinary futures markets are not state-contingent: you pay now for a *certain* future delivery.

§ A spot price is a price currently quoted for a current delivery; in other words, it is what is normally meant by a price.

¶ Actually, there is no real need for additive separability; the argument would be unaffected if $V^A = V^A[u_1^A(x_1^A, y_1^A), u_2^A(x_2^A, y_2^A)]$, where u_i^A relates to utility actually achieved in state i.

1. A price today for a dollar to be delivered in state 1 (p_1) and another price today for a dollar to be delivered in state 2 (p_2), plus
2. Correct forecasts of four future spot prices, for milk and honey in each of the two states of the world

$$(p^*_{x_1}, p^*_{y_1}, p^*_{x_2}, p^*_{y_2})$$

Let us explore the second scheme. He first allocates his initial wealth between the two "securities," buying q_1 of the first and q_2 of the second. So

$$p_1 q_1 + p_2 q_2 = m$$

In doing this he, of course, is already planning how he will spend q_1, if state 1 occurs, or q_2, if state 2 occurs. Time now moves on and state 1 or 2 does occur. Suppose state 1 comes about. Individual A will now of course maximise $u^A_1(x^A_1, y^A_1)$ subject to

$$p^*_{x_1} x^A_1 + p^*_{y_1} y^A_1 = q_1$$

Provided his original forecast of the spot prices is correct, as we have assumed, he will in fact consume the same bundle that he had already *planned* to consume if state 1 occurred.

Under what circumstances will the actual bundle consumed be the same under both schemes? Clearly the implied contingent-commodity prices in the second scheme must be the same as the actual ones in the first. For example, we need

$$p^*_{x_1} p_1 = p_{x_1}$$

In other words, the dollars paid in state 1 for one pint of milk *times* the dollars paid initially for a dollar in state 1 must *equal* the dollars paid initially for a pint-of-milk-in-state-1.

None of this seems very likely. First, there is no obvious mechanism by which individuals would forecast just those spot prices which would actually come about in the given state, given the securities purchased by every other individual. And only if everyone did forecast correctly would it turn out that $p^*_{x_1} p_1$ was equal to the price p_{x_1} which would have originated in a contingent-commodities market. So we can conclude that a securities market is not in practice sufficient for Pareto optimality in the face of uncertainty.[†] The same goes *a fortiori* for insurance markets, where there is normally some limit to a person's money claim in any one state of nature.

Pareto efficiency is achieved if there is a perfect market for state-contingent money payments, provided individuals correctly foresee the structure of product prices.

However, let us not be too perfectionist. Suppose we forget the diversity of commodities and assume that utility depends only on income (or corn) in each

---

† See R. Radner's useful survey of the Arrow-Debreu model, "Problems in the Theory of Markets Under Uncertainty," *American Economic Review*, vol. 60, no. 2, pp. 454–460, May 1970.

state of nature. Then clearly securities markets can do the same job as contingent-commodities markets. But we need securities markets that can provide each individual with whatever income he chooses (subject to his means) in each possible state of nature. What kinds of securities markets can do this? Will ordinary common stocks in productive enterprises do the trick? Or are insurance markets also needed?

Production Decisions and the Stock Market

To examine this further, we need to introduce production as well as consumption.†
How will a productive enterprise (firm) in fact behave so as to maximise the welfare of its owners? Let us suppose that for a firm there exist a number of possible projects, and each combination yields the following net income for the firm.

	Net return	
Prospects	State 1	State 2
A	50	10
A + B	60	12
...	...	...

How will the firm decide which projects to do? Since the firm maximises the owners' utility, let us see what individual utility depends on. The ith individual, we assume, maximises his expected utility:

$$\max \sum_k \pi_{ik} u^i(y_{ik}) \tag{7}$$

where k is an index for the state of the world. His income equals his share of the income of each firm in which he owns shares. Now the income of the jth company in the kth state of the world is R_{jk}. So if the ith individual owns a fraction S_{ij} of the shares in the jth firm, his income from his ownership of the firm is $S_{ij} R_{jk}$. So his total income in state k is

$$y_{ik} = \sum_j S_{ij} R_{jk} \qquad \text{each } k \tag{8}$$

The individual then allocates his wealth between the different shares available so as to maximise (7) subject to (8) and to his budget constraint. If he now holds a fraction S_{ij}^0 of the shares of the jth company, his budget constraint is

---

† If we insert production into the (unrealistic) contingent-commodities model, it makes no important difference. Firms pay now for state-contingent inputs and are paid now for state-contingent outputs. They must, of course, buy enough inputs-in-each-state to enable them to deliver their promised outputs. But their problem is simply to maximise profit now, and this profit is known with certainty. All risk is thus borne by consumers and none by the owners of firms.

$$\sum_j S_{ij} M_j = \sum_j S_{ij}^0 M_j \qquad (9)$$

where M_j is the market value of all the shares of the jth company.

This formulation shows that the shareholders of a firm will gain in welfare from an increase in the market value M_j of the firm. For this increases their initial wealth, thus expanding their consumption possibilities.† So how can a firm decide whether a given investment will raise its market value?‡ The answer is quite simple, on one assumption which can be illustrated using the data for our hypothetical firm and its possible projects:

Prospect	Net return	
	State 1	State 2
A	50	10
A + B	60	12

It will be noted from these data that, whatever projects the firm does, its incomes in the two states of the world are in the ratio $5:1$. Doubtless for many other firms the ratio will be different. But if there are enough other firms for which the ratio is $5:1$, there will be a determinate market price for an income prospect $(5, 1)$ which will not change if our firm invests in prospect B. Thus the firm can use this price as the basis for its evaluation of the project. For example, the price of a perpetuity $(5, 1)$ might be 10.§ The firm would then invest provided the cost of the investment was less than 10. If everyone agreed that states 1 and 2 were equally likely, we could say that the relevant discount rate to apply to the mean return (3) of a prospect with this distribution of returns was $\frac{3}{10}$ or 30 percent. Unless the pattern of returns were strongly negatively correlated with the rest of national income, we would expect this discount rate for a risky prospect to exceed the riskless rate of interest.

In cases where a pattern of returns is common enough in the economy to have

† The shareholders cannot together buy more than the existing shares of a firm since they own all the shares that exist. They can, however, sell some of the shares if they wish. So a rise in the share price is unambiguously in their collective interest.

‡ The answer we give ignores the possibility that the firm's investment may be partially financed by borrowing. However, Modigliani and Miller have shown that this question of "gearing" will not affect firms' decisions if (*inter alia*) there is a perfect capital market, no taxes, no transactions costs in issuing debt, and full information about payoffs to investment in each state of nature. See F. Modigliani and M. H. Miller, "The Cost of Capital, Corporation Finance and the Theory of Investment," *American Economic Review*, vol. 48, pp. 261–297, June 1958. For wider discussions of the issues discussed in this section see P. A. Diamond, "The Role of a Stock Market in a General Equilibrium Model with Technological Uncertainty," *American Economic Review*, 57, pp. 759–776, September 1967; and S. J. Nickell, *The Investment Decisions of Firms*, Cambridge University Press, 1977, Chap. 8.

§ Here we are assuming that the project does well every year or badly every year.

a well-determined price, independent of the firm's decision, we say that the firm belongs to a *risk class.*†

> *If a firm belongs to a risk class, it maximises the total value of the firm's business by evaluating prospects at the price relevant to their risk class.*

This is, in essence Proposition 3 of Modigliani-Miller. Only if it applies can we consider that the necessary conditions for a Pareto-optimal competitive equilibrium exist: the firm is then behaving as a price taker. When one considers the number of possible states of nature and the different possible patterns of returns, it seems unlikely that the condition would be generally satisfied.

More seriously, even if they were, the states of nature relevant to the individual might well not give different net returns to any productive enterprise. For example, if my house burns down, there is no productive enterprise that experiences an increase in profit. So I cannot insure myself against fire by any pattern of share purchases.

Let us pursue this for a moment. For the share market to be a fully efficient instrument for the allocation of risk, it must be possible for me to assemble a prospect of whatever proportions is optimal for me, given my initial wealth. This requires that, if there are n states of nature, there are at least n firms whose incomes are linearly independent.‡ To prove this, assume that I wish to buy the following particular vector of incomes in each state of nature: $(y_1^0, \ldots, y_n^0)$. R_{jk} is the net income of the jth firm in the kth state of nature. If there are n firms, and there are n states of nature, this gives us an $n \times n$ matrix whose elements R_{jk} show the income of each firm in each state of nature. If this matrix is nonsingular, there must exist a vector of shareholdings $(S_1, \ldots, S_n)$, where S_j is the fraction of the jth firm owned by me, such that I guarantee myself the specified income in each state of nature. This pattern of shareholdings is got by solving for $(S_1, \ldots, S_n)$ in

$$(y_1^0, \ldots, y_n^0) = (S_1, \ldots, S_n) \begin{pmatrix} R_{11} & \cdots & R_{1n} \\ \vdots & & \vdots \\ R_{n1} & \cdots & R_{nn} \end{pmatrix}$$

If there are more than n firms, my task is easier and I have an infinite number of satisfactory portfolios. However, as we have said, it is essential that at least n

---

† If the pattern of marginal returns is different from the average (see illustration below), then the value of the firm has to be evaluated using different discount rates for the two income prospects A and B where these have the following values:

Prospect A: 50, 10
Prospect A + B: 60, 14

‡ Shares A and B are linearly independent if the vector $\mathbf{R}_A$ is not a scalar multiple of $\mathbf{R}_B$, and n shares are linearly independent if there is no prospect $\mathbf{R}_A$ equal to a weighted sum of the other prospects. In other words, the income matrix is nonsingular.

firms have linearly independent income vectors. If all productive enterprises have the same income in any two of the relevant states of the world (e.g., whether or not my house burns down), then this condition is not satisfied.† It seems most unlikely that it would be satisfied. For this reason insurance against personal misadventure cannot be achieved fully through the stock market, because the stock market is limited by the requirement that each individual gets the *same* fraction of a given firm's income in every state of nature.

The insurance market is free of this constraint. So perfect insurance markets will do the trick: they will allow us to ensure for ourselves (subject to our means) any income in any state of nature.

13-3 THE ECONOMICS OF INFORMATION

The Insurance Market and Moral Hazard

But perfect insurance markets are like all perfect markets, an ideal state which is never fully realised. Insurance, however, raises special problems. In a perfect insurance market a given individual would be able to bet to an unlimited extent at fixed odds on any particular state of nature coming to pass. For example, he might wish to have a large sum of money (y) if he were ill, partly to pay his medical bills but partly to pay for a Caribbean cruise. He would then find an insurance company which would pay him y if he turned out to be ill, while he would pay them p if he were not. Here p is, if you like, the stake in a bet that he will be ill, the odds offered by the insurance company being $y : p$ against.‡

However, if you looked for an option of this kind, you would be unlikely to find any insurance company that would offer to take a bet of unlimited size at fixed odds $y : p$. Most probably you would be told that you could insure only for the cost of your medical bills, and there would usually be a maximum cover. Similarly if you wanted fire insurance, no company would cover you for more than the cost of the building. Why? There are two basic reasons why perfect insurance markets do not exist, which in the jargon are referred to as the problems of *moral hazard* and *adverse selection*. Underlying both is the fact that one lot of people (the insurance companies) have less of the relevant information than another lot of people (their customers). The economics of information is concerned with all situations of this kind, but we can learn a good deal about the economics of information by continuing to concentrate on these two insurance problems: of moral hazard and adverse selection.

Putting it crudely, moral hazard arises when the customers of an insurance company can affect the liabilities of the company without the company knowing it. Thus whether you are ill or have a fire may depend in part on your own

---

† Nor is it satisfied if all firms earn an income in one state of nature that is a multiple of their earnings in some other state; e.g., they all earn 1 percent more if the economy grows 1 percent faster.

‡ Because we are using the language of gambling it does not mean that the individual is a risk lover.

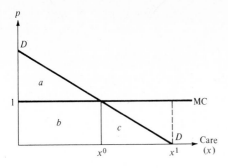

Figure 13-8 Moral hazard: the demand for medical care.

actions and not only on the state of nature. If you are heavily insured, you may take less trouble to keep well or to look after your house. In the case of illness, there could even be arguments as to how ill you were or how much treatment you needed.

> *There is a problem of moral hazard whenever the liability of the insurance company is affected by actions of the insured party about which the insurance company has incomplete information; the state of nature is thus unobservable by the insurance company.*

There are two main types of case. First, there is the case where the specified event, broadly defined, is exogenous (e.g., being ill), but the exact extent and nature of the illness is not observable by the insurance company. If the company has undertaken to cover all medical costs, the effective price of medical care to the individual is zero. So he will demand too much medical care, because it is now free. Suppose, for example, that my demand curve for medical care conditional on my having some particular illness is shown in Figure 13-8 (my demand is free of any income effects). Medical care is measured in units whose marginal cost is unity. So if there were no insurance, I would demand x^0; but, if I have unlimited insurance cover, I will demand x^1. The ideal arrangement would be to insure me for x^0 to be paid conditionally on my having this particular disease. But this is not general. Instead we observe insurance policies which pay any medical bill arising from a wide range of illnesses, though payment may be subject to a maximum. All this may lead to overconsumption of medical care among the insured.

To see this, assume for the moment that every insurance policy provides unlimited cover. For every individual the probability of being sick is π. Premiums are only paid when one is well, and the premium is $x^1\pi/(1 - \pi)$. (No profit is made.) Suppose too that utility if sick (u^S) depends on money spent on other goods plus the value of medicare (measured by the area under the demand curve in Figure 13-8). Utility if not sick (u^N) depends simply on money spent on other goods. Gross income is m. Then under insurance

$$E(u) = \pi u^S(m + a + b + c) + (1 - \pi)u^N\left(m - x^1\frac{\pi}{1 - \pi}\right)$$

With no insurance

$$E(u) = \pi u^S(m + a) + (1 - \pi)u^N(m)$$

There is no reason why the first need always exceed the second.† If it does not, no insurance contract will come about. This may be one reason why insurance markets are incomplete. It also means that many of those that do exist are inefficient.

To overcome moral hazard, insurance companies often practise *coinsurance*, whereby the insured party has to pay a fraction of any loss. Also common are *deductions*, where insurance is only paid on the excess of loss over some fixed sum; this is partly intended to discourage frivolous claims. In practise insurance companies also rely on individuals to moderate their claims, and on doctors to practise nonprice rationing.

Thus a more efficient outcome will result if people behave responsibly than if they maximise their own welfare as isolated individuals. For such private welfare maximisation involves externalities. By demanding more than the efficient amount of care, I force the insurance companies to raise their premiums to all their customers. All customers can be made better off if all restrain their claims. This problem arises whether insurance is provided by private or public agencies. Some would argue that in a bureaucratically operated system like the British National Health Service, nonprice rationing can be more effectively pursued, while others point to the tendency of such systems to be too unresponsive to individual preferences. One crucial point must be repeated at this stage, though it applies throughout our discussions. To show that actual free markets are subject to market failure, when compared with idealised free markets, is not the same as showing that state intervention will do better than actual free markets. That is a separate question which can only be answered by investigating the actual behaviour of the state.‡

The second type of moral hazard problem arises where the insurance company now faces a well-defined cost if the event occurs, but the individual customer can affect the probability of the event occurring and the company cannot monitor what he is doing about this. For example, my car accident insurance may affect how hard I try to avoid minor damage to my car. This again is an externality problem. If I buy more insurance, I at the same time increase the probability of my having an accident. Insurance companies react by charging higher premium rates per dollar of cover, the larger the amount of insurance demanded. However, if all individuals could get together and agree not to let their degree of cover affect their preventive policies, all could be better off.

---

† An approximate condition for it to do so is $b + c > x^1 u^{N'}/u^{S'}$. Since $b + c < x^1$, this necessarily requires $u^{N'} < u^{S'}$, which is likely. This condition is not, however, sufficient.

‡ This point is forcibly made by H. Demsetz, "Information and Efficiency: Another Viewpoint," *Journal of Law and Economics*, vol. 12, pp. 1–22, April 1969.

For example, consider this case. d is the loss in the event of a disaster. π is the probability of the disaster and this depends on the efforts e made to prevent the disaster

$$\pi = \pi(e) \qquad \pi' < 0$$

Suppose identical individuals got together to set up a cooperative insurance scheme. If this paid out y to an individual struck by disaster, and individuals paid in p in other years, then for the scheme to balance

$$p = \frac{\pi y}{1 - \pi}$$

The individuals then agree collectively on the amount of preventive effort e they will make.

So if utility in state i is u^i and e is measured in utils, their problem is

$$\max_{y,\, e} E(u) = \pi u^1(m - d + y) + (1 - \pi)u^2(m - \pi y/1 - \pi) - e$$

For the present argument, it is sufficient to focus on one first-order condition. If $u^{i'}$ is marginal utility in state i, then

$$\frac{\partial}{\partial y} E(u) = \pi u^{1'} + (1 - \pi)u^{2'}\left(-\frac{\pi}{1 - \pi}\right) = 0$$

So

$$\pi u^{1'} = \pi u^{2'}$$

Thus if the utility function is independent of the state of nature, income in each state of nature should be equal, so as to equalise the marginal utilities. The community prefers certainty, and it prescribes the effort to be made to prevent disaster.

However, the cooperative insurance company now breaks up. A private insurance company may feel unable to prescribe the level of preventive effort because it cannot police it. So, allowing for the fact that people with higher cover have higher probabilities of disaster, it offers a schedule where the premium per dollar is a rising function of the cover y

$$p = yf(y) \qquad f' > 0$$

Individuals now maximise their welfare with respect to cover and effort. So their private problem is

$$\max_{y,\, e} E(u) = \pi u^1(m - d + y) + (1 - \pi)u^2[m - yf(y)] - e$$

$$\frac{\partial}{\partial y} E(u) = \pi u^{1'} + (1 - \pi)u^{2'}(-f - yf') = 0$$

But for the insurance companies' books to balance, they will be charging premiums such that

$$yf(y) = \frac{\pi y}{1 - \pi}$$

where π is evaluated for the corresponding y. Thus

$$\pi u^{1'} = \pi u^{2'} \left(1 + \frac{yf'}{f}\right) > \pi u^{2'}$$

Consequently people do not achieve the certainty that they would choose if they could agree on a common plan—or if the insurance companies could issue insurance policies in which the premium rate depended on the preventive effort the individual made. Once again there is an externality problem, and once again some believe that state action to overcome it would improve things, while others believe it would introduce fresh problems.

The Insurance Market and Adverse Selection

We turn now to the second problem affecting insurance markets: the problem of adverse selection. Imagine there are two groups in the population, a high risk group (H of them) and a low risk group (L of them). Suppose both groups risk a disaster costing d but the probabilities are π_H and π_L, where

$$\pi_H > \pi_L$$

Then if both groups participate in the insurance policy and the company cannot distinguish between them, the premium for a full-coverage insurance must be

$$p = d\left(\pi_H \frac{H}{H + L} + \pi_L \frac{L}{H + L}\right)$$

However the expected loss of the low risks is only

$$d\pi_L < d\left(\pi_H \frac{H}{H + L} + \pi_L \frac{L}{H + L}\right)$$

So, if individuals know their own risks, those with low risks may not be willing to take out the policy. The company will try to discover ways of getting the low-risk people to reveal themselves by offering some coinsurance or deduction scheme which may appeal more to them. But, if this fails, the basic policy will obviously be most attractive to the high-risk people. This will drive up the premium. Eventually only the high-risk people will be left in and there will be no insurance policies for the low-risk people. If there were many classes of risk, one can imagine situations in which the only surviving market would attract the very worst class of risks.

In some cases no market at all may exist, as for mental health insurance or chronic disease. In such cases the state might be able to improve welfare by compulsory insurance. However, what equilibria are likely in insurance markets is still a matter of debate, and overinsurance is possible as well as underinsurance. The most we can say with certainty is this:

The problem of adverse selection arises if individuals know their own riskiness but insurance companies do not; the policies that are offered are then less efficient than would exist if individually tailored policies could be offered.

This is one of a whole class of economic problems which arise if one lot of people have different information from another. In the case of insurance policies the buyers know their own personal characteristics better than the sellers of policies do. But the opposite is equally common. The sellers of labour or of bonds or of used cars generally know more about what they are selling than the buyers do. This leads to what is sometimes called the imperfection of these markets. But in these circumstances none of the standard propositions about competitive equilibrium or welfare economics necessarily holds. This is a new area of economics and an important one. But few general propositions have so far been developed.

Q13-16 Why do brand new cars resold on the second-hand market fetch less than their price as new?

Unproductive Screening

To gain a flavour of the kind of thing which is possible, consider the following. There are two kinds of people, geniuses (G of them) and idiots (I of them). Each person has an intrinsic productivity, which is independent of the other factors with which he is employed (he is a perfect substitute for them). The productivity of a genius is P_G, which exceeds the productivity of the idiot P_I. So $P_G > P_I$. The only way employers can discriminate between geniuses and idiots is on the basis of external characteristics visible before the contract of employment is made. If they can see no differentiating characteristics, they will pay each group the same, so that everyone is paid

$$W = P_G \frac{G}{G+I} + P_I \frac{I}{G+I} = \bar{P}$$

However, one way in which geniuses may be able to differentiate themselves is by acquiring a signal, such as education. We might then have a competitive equilibrium in which all geniuses were educated and no idiots were. Such an equilibrium would then be self-sustaining if employers kept on finding that the productivity of educated people was P_G and that of uneducated people P_I. In this case they would pay all educated people P_G and all uneducated people P_I.

Under what conditions could such an equilibrium exist? Clearly it must not be privately worthwhile for an idiot to become educated. So if C_I is the cost of education to an idiot, then

$$P_G - P_I < C_I$$

Equally it must be privately worthwhile for a genius to become educated:

$$P_G - P_I > C_G$$

So the cost of the signal must be higher for the idiot than for the genius, and in fact high enough for the signal not to be worthwhile for the idiot.

But, though the signal is privately worthwhile for the genius, is it socially worthwhile? Certainly not. His education adds not a whit to his wits. So it is a deadweight social loss. All that education does is to raise the wage of the genius by separating him out from the mass of people. At the same time it lowers the wages of those with whom his productivity was previously averaged. And it lowers their wages by more than it raises his own wage net of education costs. This must be so, since the resource cost of education is now being borne by somebody.

We have described one possible equilibrium: a "separating" equilibrium. But there might be another equilibrium as well. Suppose that we start with no one being educated. It is quite possible that this is another equilibrium. If a small group of geniuses separated themselves off and got educated, they would get paid P_G, and otherwise they would only get $\bar{P}$. But nothing said so far implies that the following is impossible:

$$P_G - \bar{P} < C_G$$

In this case, if no geniuses were getting educated, it would not be worth any small group of them attempting to do so. So there also exists a "pooling" equilibrium, where no one gets educated.

Q13-17 Which is socially preferable, the pooling or the separating equilibrium?

Once differential information exists, multiple equilibria become possible, and often one equilibrium is a Pareto improvement over another. In the previous example, the government ought obviously to forbid education. But the result is very sensitive to the assumptions made.†

Productive Screening

In the preceding example information had no social value. Individuals could use resources to transmit information about themselves that was privately valuable to them but did not increase the social product. This was because it did not matter who did which job. But in reality some people have comparative advantage in some jobs. We have probably all gained because Newton was made a fellow

---

† For a discussion of the previous model and other approaches to the problem, see J. E. Stiglitz, "The Theory of 'Screening,' Education and the Distribution of Income," *American Economic Review*, vol. 65, pp. 283–300, June 1975. For empirical evidence casting doubt on the screening model, see R. Layard and G. Psacharopoulos, "The Screening Hypothesis and the Social Returns to Education," *Journal of Political Economy*, vol. 82, pp. 985–998, October 1974.

of Trinity College, Cambridge. Likewise some people would enjoy some jobs more than others. So up to a point resources ought to be devoted to the process by which employers learn about workers and workers learn about jobs. It is this productive role of information that has been stressed particularly by writers of the Chicago school like Stigler and by many of those who believe that the "natural" rate of unemployment is also optimal, since it leads to just the right amount of labour-market search.†

Information About the Natural World

However, it ought to be clear by now that this is a difficult subject and that each particular instance needs empirical analysis and cannot be settled on a priori grounds. This applies not only to processes which transmit information about commodities being marketed but also to those which generate information about the natural world. For example, consider the returns to weather forecasting. This activity may be highly productive: farmers may be warned of a deluge and harvest their crops a few days earlier. But equally, there may be cases where knowing the weather makes no difference to the social product. For example, an individual, by using resources, may learn that a hurricane is going to devastate his apple crop and that nothing can be done about it. The information is socially valueless. But the individual can make money from it by selling his crop forward to someone who knows nothing of the hurricane. Thus again it is perfectly possible that too many resources will be devoted to the production of information.

When one turns to basic research, matters are even more complicated. Clearly the Arrow-Debreu framework has little meaning in this context. Those who paid for 19th century science were not wondering whether or not it would lead to the hydrogen bomb: the bomb was simply not thought of. It is unclear whether free enterprise would lead to too much money or too little being spent on research. There are two problems here. First, information about the natural world is a public good. Once it has been discovered, it can be transmitted relatively cheaply. However, if it is sold at the marginal cost of distributing it, those who produce the research get no return and therefore produce no research. So patent laws exist to ensure that there are incentives to generate knowledge. As a result research is done in secret, and duplication may occur. However, by definition discovery cannot be systematically planned and there may or may not be social losses resulting from duplication. Equally, since patents have a limited lifespan and antitrust laws limit the profits to which they give rise, there may be under-investment in research. If so, this could in principle be remedied by public subsidy, but it is not at all easy to know on what principles the subsidy should be allocated.

---

† G. J. Stigler, "Information in the Labour Market," *Journal of Political Economy*, vol. 70, Suppl., pp. 94–105, October 1962; and A. Alchian, in E. Phelps (ed.), *The Microeconomic Foundations of Employment and Inflation Theory*, Norton, New York, 1970.

This last section has been brief because settled results are few and we are on the frontiers of our subject. Some general conclusions emerge. The justifications for capitalism developed in Chapter 1 were always qualified by provisos about increasing returns and externality. In a world of differential information these provisos become even more important. But it is an empirical question as to whether bureaucratic systems can handle these difficulties any better. Sticking to the free-enterprise framework, the uninhibited quest for private advantage is not always efficient. Trust between persons is a great saver of resources, and *caveat emptor* (buyer beware) is not the last word.

Q13-18 Should there be laws regulating
   (i) The information about weights and measures of packaged foods?
   (ii) Fire precautions in hotels?
   (iii) Fire precautions in private houses?
   (iv) Other building standards in private houses?

Q13-19 Should there be
   (i) Compulsory minimum state health insurance?
   (ii) State management of the production of medical care?

CONCAVITY AND QUASI-CONCAVITY

These concepts are of central importance in economics.

CONCAVITY

We can begin with a function of one variable $f(x)$. This function is concave if, looking at it from below, it "looks" concave. A concave function is illustrated in Figure A1-1. Think of it as a section through a concave dome. If the dome is strictly concave, straight beams can be inserted joining any two points on the

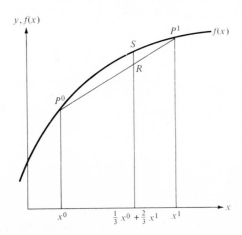

Figure A1-1 A concave $f(x)$.

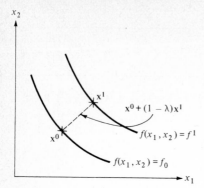

Figure A1-2 A concave $f(x_1, x_2)$.

dome, such as points P^0 and P^1. Clearly, any point on the beam (or chord) lies below that point on the dome that is vertically in line with it. For example, point R lies below point S. But both these points lie above the point on the horizontal axis corresponding to $x = \frac{1}{3}x^0 + \frac{2}{3}x^1$. Therefore

1. The height of S is

$$f\left(\tfrac{1}{3}x^0 + \tfrac{2}{3}x^1\right)$$

2. The height of R is

$$f(x^0) + \frac{P^0 R}{P^0 P^1}\left[f(x^1) - f(x^0)\right] = f(x^0) + \tfrac{2}{3}f(x^1) - \tfrac{2}{3}f(x^0)$$
$$= \tfrac{1}{3}f(x^0) + \tfrac{2}{3}f(x^1)$$

So

$$f\left(\tfrac{1}{3}x^0 + \tfrac{2}{3}x^1\right) > \tfrac{1}{3}f(x^0) + \tfrac{2}{3}f(x^1)$$

The function value of the (weighted) average exceeds the average of the function values. Replacing $\frac{1}{3}$ by λ, we can write the general definition of concavity as follows.

$f(\mathbf{x})$ is concave if $f[\lambda\mathbf{x}^0 + (1 - \lambda)\mathbf{x}^1] \geq \lambda f(\mathbf{x}^0) + (1 - \lambda)f(\mathbf{x}^1)$ for any $\mathbf{x}^0$, $\mathbf{x}^1$, and λ (between 0 and 1). Strict concavity requires the strict inequality ($>$) to hold.

This definition holds whether x is single-valued or a vector in two dimensions (x_1, x_2) or in n dimensions. In the case of two dimensions, suppose we have $\mathbf{x}^0$ and $\mathbf{x}^1$ as shown in Figure A1-2. Then the function value above the spot $\lambda\mathbf{x}^0 + (1 - \lambda)\mathbf{x}^1$ exceeds the weighted average of the heights at $\mathbf{x}^0$ and $\mathbf{x}^1$: the dome is indeed concave. Clearly, if a strictly concave function has a local maximum, this is also a global maximum.

QUASI-CONCAVITY

By contrast we cannot think in terms of domes in relation to quasi-concavity.

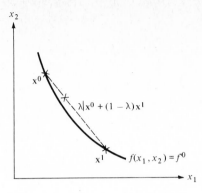

Figure A1-3 A quasi-concave $f(x_1, x_2)$.

We can only consider the effect of averaging in relation to two vectors $\mathbf{x}^0$ and $\mathbf{x}^1$ whose function values are the same. Suppose we require in Figure A1-3 that

$$f[\lambda\mathbf{x}^0 + (1 - \lambda)\mathbf{x}^1] \geq \lambda f(\mathbf{x}^0) + (1 - \lambda)f(\mathbf{x}^1)$$

Since $\mathbf{x}^0$ and $\mathbf{x}^1$ have the same function value, all that we learn from the inequality is that the iso-f curve for $f(x_1, x_2)$ is convex to the origin. We learn nothing about the overall surface of the function, since we are told nothing about the effect of *unrestricted* averaging. The definition of quasi-concavity is thus as follows.

> $f(\mathbf{x})$ is quasi-concave if $f[\lambda\mathbf{x}^0 + (1 - \lambda)\mathbf{x}^1] \geq f(\mathbf{x}^0)$ for all λ between 0 and 1 and all $\mathbf{x}^0, \mathbf{x}^1$ for which $f(\mathbf{x}^0) = f(\mathbf{x}^1)$. Strict quasi-concavity requires the strict inequality $(>)$ to hold.

The concept has clearly no meaning for a function of a single variable only, since if $f(x^0) = f(x^1)$, then $x^0 = x^1$. Clearly a two-or-more-variable function that is concave and increasing is also quasi-concave. If a function is strictly quasi-concave and is maximised subject to a linear constraint, any local maximum is also a global maximum.

CALCULUS INTERPRETATION

The definitions that have been given above are perfectly general. If the function f has well-defined first and second derivatives (i.e., is twice differentiable), we can define concavity and quasi-concavity in terms of the second derivatives of the function. Assume we have a function of n variables $f(x_1, x_2, \ldots, x_n)$.

1. Strict concavity requires that if we start at a certain point on the function, say at $f(x_1^0, x_2^0, \ldots, x_n^0)$ and move along the function surface by increasing any or all of the x_i's, we find this surface is curved from below; i.e., the slope falls the further we go. For a function of a single variable it is clear what this implies. The first derivative f' must fall as x increases. So we require $f'' < 0$ (diminishing returns to scale). For the n-variable case we need to perform the

following experiment. First we raise all the x_i's by a given small vector $\mathbf{dx}$ and record the increase in f. Then, starting from the new point, we raise the x_i's again by the same small vector $\mathbf{dx}$ and record the increase in f. The second increase must be less than the first. The change in f is

$$df = \sum_i f_i \, dx_i$$

and the change in the change is

$$d^2f = \sum_i \sum_j f_{ij} \, dx_i \, dx_j < 0 \qquad \text{all } dx_i, dx_j \neq 0 \text{ together}$$

where

$$f_{ij} = \frac{\partial^2 f}{\partial x_i \, \partial x_j}$$

For this quadratic form to be negative definite we require the appropriate signs on the cofactors of the matrix of second-order partial derivatives. For a function of two variables, $f(x_1, x_2)$, we require $f_{11} < 0, f_{22} < 0, f_{11}f_{22} > f_{12}^2$. [In the case of a constant returns to scale function, $f_{12} = -(x_1/x_2)\,f_{11} > 0$ (see Appendix 3).]

2. Strict quasi-concavity requires that the function be curved *only* so long as we remain on an iso-f contour of the function. So for strict quasi-concavity we need

$$\sum_{i=1}^{n} \sum_{j=1}^{n} f_{ij} \, dx_i \, dx_j < 0$$

for all dx_i, dx_j ($\neq 0$ together) satisfying the relation

$$\sum_{i=1}^{n} f_i \, dx_i = 0$$

This requires the appropriate signs on the cofactors of the relevant *bordered* Hessian matrix. For an example in the two-variable case see page 134. The answer to Question 5-10 proves that this is equivalent to iso-f curves that are convex to the origin.

THE CONCEPT OF A CONVEX SET

Finally we need to relate these concepts to the concept of a convex set. Suppose each element of a set can be described by a vector $\mathbf{z}$.

A set is convex if and only if, for any two elements $\mathbf{z}^i$ and $\mathbf{z}^j$ belonging to the set, every point on a line joining $\mathbf{z}^i$ and $\mathbf{z}^j$ also lies in the set. In other words, $\lambda\mathbf{z}^i + (1 - \lambda)\mathbf{z}^j$ lies in the set (for all i, j, and $0 < \lambda < 1$).

Now refer to Figure A1-1. Consider all the points lying on or beneath the line $f(x)$, i.e., all the points for which $y \leq f(x)$. The line joining any two such points must lie wholly below $f(x)$, since $f(x)$ is concave from below. So the set of the points (y, x) for which $y \le f(x)$ is convex. Turning to the $(n + 1)$-dimensional case where

$$y = f(x_1, x_2, \ldots, x_n)$$

the following holds:

> If $f(x_1, x_2, \ldots, x_n)$ is concave, all elements $(y, x_1, x_2, \ldots, x_n)$ for which $y \le f(x_1, x_2, \ldots, x_n)$ form a convex set.

Strict convexity requires that every point on a line joining two elements of the set lies inside rather than on the boundary. If $f(\ )$ is strictly concave, all elements for which $y \le f(\ )$ form a strictly convex set.

In the case of quasi-concavity, if we take a particular value of the function $f(x_1, x_2, \ldots, x_n)$ such as f^0, a convex set is formed by all points $(x_1, x_2, \ldots, x_n)$ for which $f(x_1, x_2, \ldots, x_n) \ge f^0$.

QA1-1 Which of the following functions

$$y = K^{2/3} L^{2/3} \qquad \underline{\hspace{1cm}} IRS \quad \text{(not convave)}$$
$$y = K^{1/3} L^{1/3} \qquad \underline{\hspace{1cm}} DRS \quad \text{(convave)}$$

(i) Are concave?
(ii) Are quasi-concave?

TWO

WELFARE MAXIMISATION

The result given on page 6 is obtained as follows:

$$\max W^* = W[u^A(x^A, y^A), u^B(x^B, y^B)]$$
$$+ \lambda_1(\overline{K} - K^x - K^y) + \lambda_2(\overline{L} - L^x - L^y)$$
$$+ \lambda_3[x^A + x^B - x(K^x, L^x)] + \lambda_4[y^A + y^B - y(K^y, L^y)]$$

$$\frac{\partial W^*}{\partial K^x} = -\lambda_1 - \lambda_3 x_K = 0 \tag{1}$$

$$\frac{\partial W^*}{\partial K^y} = -\lambda_1 - \lambda_4 y_K = 0 \tag{2}$$

$$\frac{\partial W^*}{\partial L^x} = -\lambda_2 - \lambda_3 x_L = 0 \tag{3}$$

$$\frac{\partial W^*}{\partial L^y} = -\lambda_2 - \lambda_4 y_L = 0 \tag{4}$$

$$\frac{\partial W^*}{\partial x^A} = W_{u^A} u_x^A + \lambda_3 = 0 \tag{5}$$

$$\frac{\partial W^*}{\partial x^B} = W_{u^B} u_x^B + \lambda_3 = 0 \tag{6}$$

$$\frac{\partial W^*}{\partial y^A} = W_{u^A} u_y^A + \lambda_4 = 0 \tag{7}$$

$$\frac{\partial W^*}{\partial y^B} = W_{u^B} u_y^B + \lambda_4 = 0 \tag{8}$$

From (1)–(4)

$$\frac{x_L}{x_K} = \frac{y_L}{y_K}$$

From (5)–(8)

$$\frac{u_y^A}{u_y^B} = \frac{u_x^A}{u_x^B}$$

From (1), (2), (5), and (7)

$$\frac{u_x^A}{u_y^A} = \frac{y_K}{x_K}$$

From (5) and (6)

$$\frac{u_x^A}{u_x^B} = \frac{W_{u^B}}{W_{u^A}}$$

THREE

HOMOGENEOUS FUNCTIONS

CONSTANT RETURNS TO SCALE

The function $y = f(K, L)$ is homogeneous of degree 1 if

$$f(\lambda K, \lambda L) = \lambda y$$

i.e., doubling K and L doubles y.

Setting $\lambda = 1/L$, we find that

$$\frac{y}{L} = f\left(\frac{K}{L}, 1\right) = g\left(\frac{K}{L}\right) \tag{1}$$

Output per head depends only on capital per head. Rewriting the relation, we obtain

$$y = Lg\left(\frac{K}{L}\right)$$

So

$$y_K = Lg'\left(\frac{K}{L}\right)\frac{1}{L} = g'\left(\frac{K}{L}\right) \tag{2}$$

The mariginal product of capital depends only on the capital-labour ratio. The same is true of the marginal product of labour:

$$y_L = g\left(\frac{K}{L}\right) + Lg'\left(\frac{K}{L}\right)\left(-\frac{K}{L^2}\right) = g\left(\frac{K}{L}\right) - \frac{K}{L}g'\left(\frac{K}{L}\right)$$

We can now prove Euler's theorem.

$$y_K K + y_L L = g'\left(\frac{K}{L}\right) K + g\left(\frac{K}{L}\right) L - Kg'\left(\frac{K}{L}\right)$$

$$= Lg\left(\frac{K}{L}\right)$$

Thus $\qquad\qquad\qquad y_K K + y_L L = y \qquad\qquad\qquad (3)$

i.e., the product is exhausted if factors are paid their real marginal product. Differentiating Euler's theorem by K, we obtain

$$y_K + Ky_{KK} + Ly_{LK} = y_K$$

So $\qquad\qquad\qquad y_{KK} = -\frac{L}{K} y_{LK} \qquad\qquad\qquad (4)$

Also by symmetry

$$y_{LL} = -\frac{K}{L} y_{LK}$$

The preceding results, obtained for the two-variable case, can be generalised to the n-variable case:

$$f = f(x_1, \ldots, x_n)$$

$$\lambda f = f(\lambda x_1, \ldots, \lambda x_n)$$

$$\frac{f}{x_1} = g^1\left(\frac{x_2}{x_1}, \ldots, \frac{x_n}{x_1}\right) \qquad\qquad (1')$$

$$f_1 = h^1\left(\frac{x_2}{x_1}, \ldots, \frac{x_n}{x_1}\right) \qquad\qquad (2')$$

$$f = f_1 x_1 + \cdots + f_n x_n \qquad\qquad (3')$$

$$f_{11} = -\left(\frac{x_2}{x_1} f_{12} + \cdots + \frac{x_n}{x_1} f_{1n}\right) \qquad\qquad (4')$$

These propositions can be proved by following the same strategy as was used in the two-variable case.

NONCONSTANT RETURNS TO SCALE

If a function is homogeneous but with nonconstant returns to scale, this means that the proportional change in the function following on a (small) equiproportional increase in all variables is constant but is not unity. In other words, the general definition of homogeneity is

$$f(\lambda x_1, \ldots, \lambda x_n) = f \lambda^p$$

where ρ is a constant. Setting $\lambda = 1/x_1$, we find

$$\frac{f}{x_1} = x_1^{\rho-1} g^1\left(\frac{x_2}{x_1}, \ldots, \frac{x_n}{x_1}\right) \tag{1''}$$

$$f_1 = x_1^{\rho-1} h^1\left(\frac{x_2}{x_1}, \ldots, \frac{x_n}{x_1}\right) \tag{2''}$$

$$\rho f = f_1 x_1 + \cdots + f_n x_n \tag{3''}$$

These relations can again be obtained by the same strategy as was followed earlier. As they imply, scale affects marginal and average products. Also, by Euler's theorem $(3'')$, if factors are paid their marginal products and returns to scale are increasing $(\rho > 1)$, then the factor payments will overexhaust the product (i.e., will equal more than the product f).

HOMOTHETICITY

A *homothetic function* is some transformation of a homogeneous function. Its isofunction surfaces have exactly the same shapes as those of the original function; but the function values need not exhibit any particular pattern. Thus, whereas an increasing homogeneous function has a constant elasticity, an increasing $(\rho > 1)$, then the factor payments will overexhaust the product (i.e., less rapidly and then more rapidly again. For example, a U-shaped cost curve cannot be obtained from a homogeneous function but could be obtained from a homothetic one. The only mathematical property that holds of homothetic functions is that the ratios of derivatives depend only on the ratios of quantities, e.g.,

$$\frac{f_1}{f_2} = j^{12}\left(\frac{x_2}{x_1}, \ldots, \frac{x_n}{x_1}\right)$$

This corresponds to the property that all iso-f surfaces are parallel along a ray from the origin.

THE NONECONOMIC REGION

Finally, we return to constant returns and the two-variable case. If returns to scale are constant, this does not imply that marginal products are everywhere positive. It may well be that beyond a certain K/L ratio, y_K falls below zero. Such a possibility is illustrated in Figure A3-1. The areas where $y_K < 0$ or $y_L < 0$ are called the noneconomic regions.† Clearly production will not occur there, so long as both factors have positive prices.

† See O. P. Tangri, "Omissions in the Treatment of the Law of Variable Proportions," *American Economic Review*, vol. 56, pp. 484–492, June 1966.

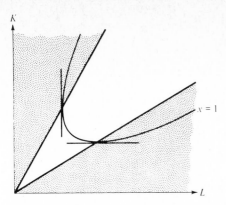

Figure A3-1 The noneconomic region.

THE GEOMETRY OF DISTRIBUTION

An alternative analysis of distribution to that offered in Chapter 2 is shown in Figure A3-2. Suppose an economy endowed with $\overline{K}/\overline{L}$. This tells us y/L. We now rely on relation (2). Since

$$g'\left(\frac{K}{L}\right) = y_K$$

$$\frac{PQ}{\overline{K}/\overline{L}} = g'\left(\frac{K}{L}\right) = y_K$$

So

$$PQ = y_K \frac{\overline{K}}{\overline{L}}$$

But

$$OQ = \frac{y}{\overline{L}}$$

Thus

$$\frac{PQ}{OQ} = \frac{y_K \overline{K}}{y} = \text{capital's relative share}$$

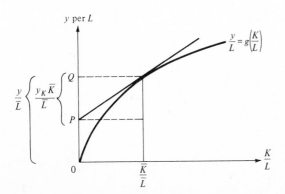

Figure A3-2 Distribution in the one-sector model.

QA3-1 Consider the production function

$$x = K^2L^2(aK^3 + bL^3)^{-1}$$

(i) Does it exhibit constant returns to scale?

(ii) What is the maximum K/L at which production will be observed at any positive price of capital?

FOUR

THE PARETO-OPTIMALITY OF COMPETITIVE EQUILIBRIUM

Chapter 1 offers a proof that depends on the special assumption that all goods are perfectly divisible and are also *indispensable*, so that some of every good is always purchased by every consumer. The following proof does not depend on either of these assumptions. It may be best read after reading Chapter 5.

EFFICIENT CONSUMPTION

The economy is endowed with a vector of goods $\bar{x}$. If x^h is the consumption vector of the hth household, then

$$\sum_h x^h = \bar{x}$$

Now suppose there is an alternative allocation (denoted $\hat{\ }$) in which at least some people are better off and no one is worse off. So

$$u^h(\hat{x}^h) > u^h(x^h) \qquad \text{some } h \tag{1}$$

$$u^h(\hat{x}^h) \geq u^h(x^h) \qquad \text{all } h \tag{2}$$

From (1) it follows that if p^* is the equilibrium vector of prices, then

$$p^*\hat{x}^h > p^*x^h \qquad \text{some } h \tag{3}$$

since if $\hat{x}^h$ makes the household better off than x^h, it would have been purchased instead of x^h, unless it was more expensive. For another household, indifferent between its $\hat{x}^h$ and x^h, $\hat{x}^h$ must cost at least as much as x^h since if it cost less it would have been bought in order to save money. So

$$p^*\hat{x}^h \geq p^*x^h \qquad \text{all } h \tag{4}$$

Taking (3) and (4) together and summing over all households, we find that

$$p^* \sum_h \hat{x}^h > p^* \sum_h x^h$$

or
$$p^*\hat{x} > p^*\bar{x} \tag{5}$$

So the only vector of goods which can make some better off and none worse off is one in which more of some goods are available. With the existing supply of goods, no Pareto improvement is possible.

OVERALL EFFICIENCY

If firms are profit-maximising price takers and there are no externalities nor information problems, the existing output vector ($\bar{x}$) is that, from all technically feasible vectors, which maximises the value of output at current prices. So, for any other technically feasible output vector $\hat{x}$

$$p^*\hat{x} < p^*\bar{x} \tag{6}$$

But we have seen from (5) that to generate a Pareto improvement over the equilibrium vector we need a vector $\hat{x}$ for which

$$p^*\hat{x} > p^*\bar{x}$$

So there is no technically feasible output vector which can produce a Pareto improvement over the present one.

THE EQUATIONS OF
GENERAL EQUILIBRIUM

Chapter 2 offers a verbal-plus-geometrical proof of the determinacy of general equilibrium with two goods and two factors. It is also useful to set out the equilibrium conditions in a general mathematical form and to check that there are just sufficient equations to determine the system of relative prices, when there are more than two goods and factors.

PURE EXCHANGE

We begin with the case of pure exchange. We shall suppose there are three goods, since moving from that to the n-good case is simple. The goods are x_1, x_2, and x_3 ; and the economy as a whole is endowed with them in the following quantities: $\bar{x}_1$, $\bar{x}_2$, and $\bar{x}_3$. Individual i has the endowment $\bar{x}_1^i$, $\bar{x}_2^i$, $\bar{x}_3^i$.

We shall take the third good as the numeraire, setting its price to unity. The budget constraint of the ith individual is now

$$p_1(x_1^i - \bar{x}_1^i) + p_2(x_2^i - \bar{x}_2^i) + (x_3^i - \bar{x}_3^i) = 0$$

He maximises $u^i(x_1^i, x_2^i, x_3^i)$ subject to this constraint. So, given his utility function and his endowments, his demand for good 1 is a function (personal to him) of p_1 and p_2:

$$x_1^i = f^{1i}(p_1, p_2)$$

Similar equations hold for the other goods

$$x_2^i = f^{2i}(p_1, p_2)$$
$$x_3^i = f^{3i}(p_1, p_2)$$

Turning now to the market for each good, the sum of demands for each good must depend on p_1 and p_2. And for each good the sum of these demands must equal the total supply. Thus

$$\sum_i f^{1i}(p_1, p_2) = \bar{x}_1$$

$$\sum_i f^{2i}(p_1, p_2) = \bar{x}_2 \qquad (1)$$

$$\sum_i f^{3i}(p_1, p_2) = \bar{x}_3$$

This appears to provide three equations to be solved for only two unknowns. However, we know by Walras' Law that if any two markets are in equilibrium, the third must be. So we can drop any one of the previous equations, leaving us with two equations to solve for two unknowns.

AN ECONOMY WITH PRODUCTION

We now assume that some goods may be produced. In terms of the productive process there are now three classes of goods. Some, like cake, only figure as outputs of a productive process. Others, like electricity, figure as outputs of some processes and inputs into others. And yet others, like labour time, only figure as inputs. We use the symbol $\hat{x}_i^j$ to measure the net output of x_i by firm j. If the item is only an input, this will be a negative quantity. So for labour time $\hat{x}_i^j$ will always be negative; for cake it will always be positive; and for electricity it will be positive or negative depending on whether or not j is a power station. The jth producer's operating profit is now

$$\pi = p_1 \hat{x}_1^j + p_2 \hat{x}_2^j + \hat{x}_3^j$$

He maximises this subject to his implicit production function:

$$T^j(\hat{x}_1^j, \hat{x}_2^j, \hat{x}_3^j) = 0$$

He thus has net output functions

$$\hat{x}_1^j = g^{1j}(p_1, p_2)$$
$$\hat{x}_2^j = g^{2j}(p_1, p_2) \qquad (2)$$
$$\hat{x}_3^j = g^{3j}(p_1, p_2)$$

and a profit function,

$$\pi^j = \pi^j(p_1, p_2)$$

Turning to the household, its budget constraint is as before, plus any profit income accruing to the household (which depends on p_1 and p_2). We therefore continue to have household demand functions, of the form shown on the left-hand side of (1).

Market equilibrium requires that

$$\text{Household demand} = \text{endowments} + \text{net outputs}$$

So

$$\sum_i f^{1i}(p_1, p_2) = \bar{x}_1 + \sum_j g^{1j}(p_1, p_2)$$

$$\sum_i f^{2i}(p_1, p_2) = \bar{x}_2 + \sum_j g^{2j}(p_1, p_2)$$

As before, Walras' Law requires us to leave out the market equation for the third market. So once again we have two equations and two unknowns. If we had n goods, we should have $n - 1$ equations and $n - 1$ relative prices to solve for.

SIX

THE SIZE OF THE PRODUCTION RUN

We generally think of the production function as a relationship between the rate of output at time t and the rate of inputs at time t. This may ignore some important aspects of the production process. For example, the average cost of a particular model of Ford (say a Cortina) depends not only on the number of Cortinas produced in one particular year but also on the number of Cortinas ever produced. The reason is that many of the fixed costs of making Cortinas are once-for-all costs of design and tooling-up rather than fixed costs per annum. If more Cortinas are eventually produced, this means that these once-for-all costs are spread over more units of output. We shall denote the size of the production run (or the total volume of output) as V.

Let us analyse the role of the production run in relation to costs. Since production occurs in more than one period, total costs C are defined as the present value of the total stream of costs incurred in producing the complete production run. Let us suppose that production occurs at a rate of x Cortinas per year. If V Cortinas are produced in total, production must go on for V/x years. The total discounted cost of the run (C) then depends on V, x, and the interest rate i:

$$C = C(V, x, i)$$

But what interests us is the effect of V and x on the cost of Cortinas evaluated at the time when they are being produced. To calculate this we need to know the annual payment R which, if paid out over the period of production, has a present value equal to the total discounted cost C:

$$R = C \bigg/ \sum_{t=1}^{V/x} (1 + i)^{-t} = R(V, x, i)$$

First let us examine the effect of changing the time-rate of output (x) holding volume constant. There seems no reason to modify our previous conclusions that an increase in the time-rate of output raises costs and that beyond a certain point it raises them at an increasing rate. So, beyond that point marginal and average costs are rising:

$$\frac{\partial}{\partial x} \left(\frac{R}{x} \right) > 0$$

The selling price needed to cover costs rises.

However, if we look at the effect of increasing the volume V of production, a different pattern emerges. What happens when V is increased by extending the number of years for which Cortinas are produced, while holding annual output (x) constant? There are now more units of output over which the total tooling-up costs can be spread. So the annual cost R falls, and, since annual output is constant, average costs fall without limit:

$$\frac{\partial}{\partial V} \left(\frac{R}{x} \right) < 0$$

The selling price needed to cover costs falls.

Thus, whereas it seems likely that beyond some level of output (which may be very high), average costs will tend to rise with the level of annual output, there seems no reason why this should ever be the case in relation to the size of production run. The effect of a simultaneous and equiproportional increase in V and x is indeterminate; it depends on the strength of the two opposing elements involved. But whatever the outcome, in much detailed economic analysis the concept of production run is crucial, and we only approximate reality if we ignore it.†

---

† For a fuller argument see A. Alchian, "Costs and Outputs," in M. Abramovitz (ed.), *The Allocation of Economic Resources*, Stanford University Press, Palo Alto, Cal., 1959. We have modified the argument so as to focus more sharply on the average cost at which sales could take place.

SEVEN

THE INFLUENCE OF RANDOM VARIATION ON COST AND PRODUCTION FUNCTIONS

Another dimension often ignored in the theory of the firm is the role of randomness. However, some of the established models of production are now being developed to take account of these elements. Consider the total cost curve of a firm in Figure A7-1. Normally we think of the producer selecting an output and we then read off costs from the total cost curve. Suppose, however, the firm has not the choice of producing a *particular* output. Such a situation occurs when a firm, producing to order, is obliged to respond to demand. A common example is that of a transport firm which supplies services on demand at, usually, a fixed price. To simplify matters, let us suppose that the firm must produce either x^0 or x^1. In order to find out which output will be produced, we must find the probability attached to each level of demand. Suppose each level is equally probable. Then we can find the expected cost $E(C)$, which will be different from the actual cost of producing x^0 or x^1. We find the expected cost by dividing the chord joining $C(x^0)$ and $C(x^1)$ in the proportion of the probabilities assigned: in this case in half. In the region where the total cost curve is bending downwards (declining marginal cost), expected cost will be below the level of costs that would occur if we were required to produce the mean output each period. The cost of the certain output $(x^0 + x^1)/2$ exceeds the expected cost of the probability distribution of outputs. Further up the total cost curve, as we have drawn it, $E(C)$ will exceed the cost of producing the mean output with certainty.

To compare the expected cost with the ordinary nonstochastic cost, one must decide what we mean by the "distribution" of output. Probably the simplest way of defining the distribution in our example is to take the same difference in output between the high and the low outputs, over the entire range of output levels. Then if we construct the expected cost curve, we find that it will look much

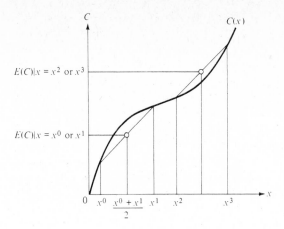

Figure A7-1 Expected cost.

straighter than the ordinary cost curve. At low outputs $E(C)$ is below C, while at higher outputs $E(C)$ is above C as we have drawn it. That is, marginal cost does not vary nearly as much for the $E(C)$ curve as it does for the actual cost curve. We have then the surprising result that marginal cost is subject to less variation under probability conditions than in the certainty case.

Now, suppose we have a special type of total cost function consisting of *fixed* costs (which are really costs which must be incurred to produce anything) plus constant marginal cost up to an absolute capacity constraint (Figure A7-2). There will be difficulties now about defining the distribution of outputs about the mean output. But if the distribution is of the kind used already, as you move in the direction of greater output there is an increasing probability of hitting capacity costs. This is so even though mean output is below capacity. If the firm is not able to supply the amount demanded, then we can attribute a "penalty cost" to this. In practise this may appear in a decline in the "quality of service"— "you cannot always get it when you want it." The probability of incurring

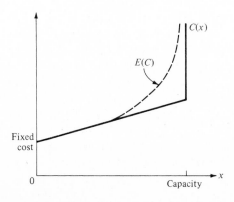

Figure A7-2 Expected cost with a capacity constraint.

these large penalty costs increases as mean output rises. Therefore the $E(C)$ curve will rise in advance of the capacity limitation. It is characteristic then of the $E(C)$ curve not only to moderate variations in marginal costs, but also to smooth out discontinuities.

This concept of an expected cost curve naturally has the analytical attributes of ordinary cost curves. We can get marginal expected cost $ME(C)$ by simply taking the first derivative of the $E(C)$ curve. This is distinct from the expected marginal cost which is found from the ordinary marginal cost curve by considerng the probability of each marginal cost being incurred. It is useful in many applications to think of entrepreneurs deciding on their output mix by taking into account $ME(C)$, that is, the change in the expected costs of various uncertain prospects.

This concept has an application to factor relationships also. Take the relationship typical of the Leontief-Marx type of production function, that is, fixed technical coefficients. What would happen if the producer did not know, when he hired an extra quantity of labour, whether he would actually obtain the labour services he expected? The worker might be ill, there might be a strike, or, on the other hand, the labour might turn out to be very efficient. There are all sorts of chance elements involved, and what actually happens is in the lap of the gods. We can think of a distribution of labour services, and another of capital services, which we would get as a consequence of hiring given inputs. If we do this, then we find that the expected-output isoquants are smoothed out and we are right back in a neoclassical world with rounded corners to our isoquants. So, even if we have a fixed proportions production function relating certain inputs to certain output, we have a smooth neoclassical function relating inputs purchased to expected output.†

---

† See A. A. Walters, "Marginal Productivity and Probability Distributions of Factor Services," *Economic Journal*, vol. 70, pp. 325–330, June 1960 and N. Liviathan, "The Marginalist Principle in a Discrete Production Model Under Uncertain Demand," *Quarterly Journal of Economics*, vol. 85, pp. 684–703, November 1971.

THE ELASTICITY OF SUBSTITUTION

In this Appendix we show the relation between the elasticity of substitution and the parameters of the production function (rather than the cost function). This then enables us to derive the equation given at the top of page 267.

For the sake of economy we shall confine ourselves to the two-factor case, but our results up to Equation (1) below apply equally to the n-factor case. The cost minimising conditions are

$$\lambda f_1(z_1, z_2) = w_1$$
$$\lambda f_2(z_1, z_2) = w_2$$
$$f(z_1, z_2) = x^0$$

Totally differentiating for λ, z_1, z_2, and w_1, we obtain

$$\begin{pmatrix} f_{11} & f_{12} & f_1 \\ f_{21} & f_{22} & f_2 \\ f_1 & f_2 & 0 \end{pmatrix} \begin{pmatrix} \lambda dz_1 \\ \lambda dz_2 \\ d\lambda \end{pmatrix} = \begin{pmatrix} dw_1 \\ 0 \\ 0 \end{pmatrix}$$

So if F is the determinant of the whole matrix and F_{12} the cofactor of the element f_{12}, by Cramer's Rule we have

$$\lambda dz_2 = dw_1 \frac{F_{12}}{F}$$

So
$$\frac{\partial z_2}{\partial w_1} = \frac{1}{\lambda} \frac{F_{12}}{F}$$

413

or, totally generally,

$$\frac{\partial z_i}{\partial w_j} = \frac{1}{\lambda}\frac{F_{ji}}{F} = \frac{1}{\lambda}\frac{F_{ij}}{F} = \frac{\partial z_j}{\partial w_i}$$

This confirms the symmetry of the cross-substitution effects (also proved from the cost function on pages 268–269).

As explained on page 269, by definition

$$\sigma_{ij} = \frac{\partial \log z_i}{\partial \log w_j}\frac{1}{v_j} = \frac{1}{\lambda}\frac{F_{ij}}{F}\frac{w_j}{z_i}\frac{x}{f_j z_j}$$

But

$$\lambda = \text{marginal cost} = \frac{w_j}{f_j}$$

So

$$\sigma_{ij} = \frac{F_{ij}}{F}\frac{x}{z_i z_j} \tag{1}$$

It remains to be proved that in the two-factor case, the equation given on page 267 holds, i.e., that

$$\frac{\partial \log z_1}{\partial \log w_1} = -(1 - v_1)s_{12} = -v_2 s_{12}$$

The demand function

$$z_1 = h(w_1, w_2, x)$$

is homogeneous of degree zero in factor prices, so that

$$\frac{\partial \log z_1}{\partial \log w_1} + \frac{\partial \log z_1}{\partial \log w_2} = 0$$

Hence

$$v_1 \sigma_{11} + v_2 \sigma_{12} = 0$$

and

$$\frac{\partial \log z_1}{\partial \log w_1} = v_1 \sigma_{11} = -v_2 \sigma_{12}$$

So we only need to show that $\sigma_{12} = s_{12}$.

From (1),

$$\sigma_{12} = \frac{F_{12}}{F}\frac{x}{z_1 z_2}$$

$$= \frac{-f_1 f_2 (f_1 z_1 + f_2 z_2)}{(f_{11} f_2^2 - 2f_{12} f_1 f_2 + f_{22} f_1^2) z_1 z_2}$$

Using the properties of constant returns to scale set out on page 399, this reduces to

$$\sigma_{12} = \frac{f_1 f_2}{x f_{12}} = s_{12} \qquad \text{(see footnote to page 266)}$$

FURTHER READING

This list may be supplemented by references in the text. Items marked ** go beyond the material discussed in the book in interesting and sometimes controversial ways. Items marked * provide good alternative presentations of material covered in the book.†

1 WELFARE ECONOMICS

* Bator, F. M., "The Simple Analytics of Welfare Maximisation," *American Economic Review*, vol. 47, pp. 22–59, March, 1957.

Mishan, E. J., "A Survey of Welfare Economics," *Economic Journal*, vol. 70, pp. 197–256, June, 1960; reprinted in Mishan, E. J., *Welfare Economics*, Part 1, Chap. 1, Random House, New York, 1964.

** Sen, A. K., *On Economic Inequality*, Chaps. 1 and 2, Oxford University Press, London, 1973.

** Harberger, A. C., "Three Basic Postulates for Applied Welfare Economics," *Journal of Economic Literature*, vol. 9, pp. 785–797, September, 1971.

Graaf, J. deV., *Theoretical Welfare Economics*, Cambridge University Press, London, 1957.

2 GENERAL EQUILIBRIUM

* Newman, P., *The Theory of Exchange*, Chaps. 3 and 4, Prentice-Hall, Englewood Cliffs, N.J., 1965.

** Koopmans, T., *Three Essays on the State of Economic Science*, Lecture 1, McGraw-Hill, New York, 1957.

---

† For a useful collection of some of these readings, see W. Breit and H. Hochman (eds.), *Readings in Microeconomics*, Holt, New York, 1968. For a more abstract treatment of many issues raised in this book, see E. Malinvaud, *Lectures on Microeconomic Theory*, North Holland, Amsterdam, 1972.

3 APPLICATIONS TO PUBLIC FINANCE

** Harberger, A. C., "Taxation, Resource Allocation and Welfare," in his *Taxation and Welfare*, Little, Brown, Boston, 1974.

Harberger, A. C., "The Incidence of the Corporation Income Tax," *Journal of Political Economy*, vol. 70, pp. 215–271, June, 1962, and in *Taxation and Welfare*, Little, Brown, Boston, 1974.

Little, I. M. D., "Direct Versus Indirect Taxes," *Economic Journal*, vol. 61, pp. 577–584, September, 1951.

* Johnson, H. G., *The Two-Sector Model of General Equilibrium*, Chaps. 1 and 2 and Appendices A and B, G. Allen and Unwin, London, 1971.

4 APPLICATIONS TO INTERNATIONAL TRADE

Samuelson, P. A., "International Factor Price Equalisation Once Again," *Economic Journal*, vol. 59, pp. 181–197, June, 1949.

** Caves, R. E. and Jones, R. W., *World Trade and Payments*, Chaps. 8–10 and 12–13 (including supplements), Little, Brown, Boston, 1973.

Hindley, B., *The Theory of International Trade*, Gray-Mills, London, 1974.

5 UTILITY AND CONSUMER DEMAND

* Friedman, M., *Price Theory*, Chaps. 2 and 3, Aldine, Chicago, 1962.

Friedman, M., "The Marshallian Demand Curve," *Journal of Political Economy*, vol. 57, pp. 463–495, December, 1949.

Hicks, J. R., *A Revision of Demand Theory*, Oxford University Press, London, 1956, and *Value and Capital*, Chaps. 1–3, Oxford University Press, London, 1939.

* Machlup, F., "Professor Hicks' Revision of Demand Theory," *American Economic Review*, vol. 47, pp. 119–135, March, 1957.

Harberger, A. C., "The Measurement of Waste," *American Economic Review*, vol. 54, pp. 58–76, May, 1964.

Brown, A. and Deaton, A., "Models of Consumer Behaviour: A Survey," *Economic Journal*, vol. 82, pp. 1145–1228, December, 1972.

** Phlips, L., *Applied Consumption Analysis*, Chaps. 1–5, North Holland, Amsterdam, 1974.

6 EFFICIENT PRICING WITH INCREASING RETURNS TO SCALE AND EXTERNALITY

Turvey, R., *Economic Analysis and Public Enterprises*, G. Allen and Unwin, London, 1971.

** Walters, A. A., *The Economics of Road User Charges*, Chaps. 2–4, John Hopkins, Baltimore, 1968.

* Lerner, A. P., "On Optimal Taxes with an Untaxable Sector," *American Economic Review*, vol. 60, pp. 284–294, June, 1970

Baumol, W. J. and Bradford, D., "Optimal Departures from Marginal Cost Pricing," *American Economic Review*, vol. 60, pp. 265–283, June, 1970.

Dixit, A. K., "On the Optimum Structure of Commodity Taxes," *American Economic Review*, vol. 60, pp. 295–301, June, 1970.

Mohring, H., "The Peak Load Problem with Increasing Returns and Pricing Constraints," *American Economic Review*, vol. 60, pp. 693–705, September, 1970.

** Samuelson, P. A., "The Pure Theory of Public Expenditure," *Review of Economics and Statistics*, vol. 36, pp. 387–389, November 1954.
** Coase, R. H., "The Problem of the Social Cost," *Journal of Law and Economics*, vol. 3, pp. 1–44, October, 1960.
Demsetz, H., "Exchange and Enforcement of Property Rights," *Journal of Law and Economics*, vol. 7, pp. 11–26, October, 1964.
Cheung, S., "The Fable of the Bees," *Journal of Law and Economics*, vol. 16, pp. 11–33, April, 1973.

7 COST, SUPPLY, AND COMPETITIVE EQUILIBRIUM

** Alchian, A., "Cost," *International Encyclopaedia of Social Sciences*, vol. 3, pp. 404–415, 1968.
* Friedman, M., *Price Theory*, Chap. 5, Aldine, Chicago, 1962.
** Alchian, A., "Costs and Outputs," in M. Abramovitz (ed.), *The Allocation of Economic Resources*, Stanford, 1959.

8 IMPERFECT COMPETITION

Lerner, A. P., "The Concept of Monopoly and the Measurement of Monopoly Power," *Review of Economic Studies*, vol. 1, pp. 157–175, 1934.
Leibenstein, H., "Allocative Efficiency v. X-Efficiency," *American Economic Review*, vol. 56, pp. 392–415, June, 1966.
** Patinkin, D., "Multiple-Plant Firms, Cartels, and Imperfect Competition," *Quarterly Journal of Economics*, vol. 61, pp. 173–205, February 1947.
Stigler, G., "A Theory of Oligopoly," *Journal of Political Economy*, vol. 72, pp. 44–61, February, 1964.

9 THE DERIVED DEMAND FOR FACTORS

** Friedman, M., *Price Theory*, Chaps. 7 and 9, Aldine, Chicago, 1962.
Hicks, J. R., *The Theory of Wages*, Chap. 6 and Appendix, Macmillan, London, 1932.
Allen, R. G. D., *Mathematical Analysis for Economists*, Chaps. 11.8, 12.7, 12.8, 12.9, and 13.7. Macmillan, London, 1938.
* Walters, A. A., "A Survey of Cost and Production Functions," *Econometrica*, vol. 31, pp. 1–66, January, 1963.
Allen, R. G. D., *Macroeconomic Theory*, Sec. 3.8 (on the CES function), Macmillan, London, 1967.
Brown, M. (ed.), *The Theory and Empirical Analysis of Production*, National Bureau of Economic Research, New York, 1967 (especially paper by Solow).

10 FURTHER ASPECTS OF PRODUCTION

Johansen, L., *Production Functions*, Chap. 2, North Holland, Amsterdam, 1972.
Hahn, F. H. and Matthews, R. C. O., "The Theory of Economic Growth: A Survey," *Economic Journal*, vol. 74, pp. 779–902 (first two sections), December, 1964.
** Solow, R. M., *Growth Theory*, Chaps. 1–3, Oxford, 1970.

11 LABOUR SUPPLY AND WAGE STRUCTURE

* Friedman, M., *Price Theory*, Chap. 11, Aldine, Chicago, 1962.
** Becker, G. S., *Economic Theory*, Chaps. 34–36, Knopf, New York, 1971, or *Human Capital*, Chaps. 2 and 3, National Bureau of Economic Research, New York, 1964.
Stern, N., "On the Specification of Models of Optimum Income Taxation," *Journal of Public Economics*, vol. 6, pp. 123–162, July, 1976.

12 CAPITAL AND INTEREST

* Hirshliefer, J., "On the Theory of Optimal Investment Decisions," *Journal of Political Economy*, vol. 66, pp. 329–351, August, 1958; reprinted in Solomon, E., *Management of Corporate Capital*, Free Press, New York, 1959.
Stigler, G., *The Theory of Price*, Chap. 17, 3d ed., Macmillan, New York, 1966.

13 UNCERTAINTY

** Friedman, M. and Savage, L. J., "The Utility Analysis of Choices Involving Risk," *Journal of Political Economy*, vol. 56, pp. 279–304, August, 1948; reprinted in American Economic Association, *Readings in Price Theory*, Irwin, Homewood, Ill., 1952.
** Arrow, K. J., *Essays in the Theory of Risk Bearing*, North Holland, 1970: Chap. 3, "The Theory of Risk Aversion," Chap. 4, "The Role of Securities in the Optimal Allocation of Risk Bearing," Chap. 5, "Insurance, Risk and Resource Allocation," Chap. 8, "Uncertainty and the Welfare Economics of Medical Care," Chap. 11, "Uncertainty and the Evaluation of Public Investments," (with R. C. Lind). Other sources of these chapters are as follows: Chaps. 3, 5: *Aspects of the Theory of Risk Bearing*, Yrjö Jahnssonin säätio, Helsinki, 1965; Chap. 4: *Review of Economic Studies*, vol. 31, pp. 91–96, 1963–4, originally published in French, 1953; Chap. 8: *American Economic Review*, vol. 53, pp. 941–973, 1963, reprinted in A. Culyer, *Health Economics*, Penguin, 1973; Chap. 11: *American Economic Review*, vol. 60, pp. 364–378, 1970, reprinted in R. Layard (ed.), *Cost-Benefit Analysis*, Penguin, 1972.
Luce, R. D. and Raiffa, H., *Games and Decisions*, Chap. 2, Wiley, New York, 1957.
* Alchian, A., "The Meaning of Utility Measurement," *American Economic Review*, vol. 43, pp. 26–50, March, 1953.
Tobin, J., "Liquidity Preference as Behaviour Towards Risk," *Review of Economic Studies*, vol. 25, pp. 65–86, February, 1958.
Hirshliefer, J., "The Investment Decision Under Uncertainty: Choice-Theoretic Approaches," *Quarterly Journal of Economics*, vol. 79, pp. 509–536, November, 1965; and "The Investment Decision Under Uncertainty: Applications of the State Preference Approach," *Quarterly Journal of Economics*, vol. 80, pp. 252–277, May, 1966. (These are summarised in H. A. J. Green, *Consumer Theory*, Part V, Penguin, 1971.)
Akerlof, G. A., "The Market for 'Lemons': Qualitative Uncertainty and the Market Mechanism," *Quarterly Journal of Economics*, vol. 84, pp. 488–500, August, 1970.
Demsetz, H., "Information and Efficiency: Another Viewpoint," *Journal of Law and Economics*, vol. 12, pp. 1–22, April, 1969.

NOTATION

Superscripts are used

1. to refer to an allocation:
   e.g., x^A is the quantity of x allocated to A
2. to refer to a particular value of a variable:
   e.g., w^0 is a particular wage level (sometimes that occurring in state 0)
3. to index certain variables:
   e.g., u^A is the utility of A

Subscripts are used

1. to denote derivatives:

   $$\text{e.g., } x_L = \frac{\partial x}{\partial L}$$

2. to index goods and factors:
   e.g., x_1 = quantity of good 1
   p_1 = price of good 1
   t_1 = tax on good 1

It would be tedious to list every symbol used in the book since we attempt to make their meanings clear in the context. However, some of the main symbols are listed below.

x, y	Particular product (generally y is the numeraire good, and sometimes the only good)
K, L	Capital, labour
x_i	A typical product
z_i	A typical factor
p_i	A product price
w_i	A factor price
u	Utility
V	*Ex-ante* utility
W	Social welfare
B	Benefit
C	Cost
c	Consumption
m	Money income
ε_{ij}	Elasticity of ith item with respect to jth price
η_{im}	Elasticity of ith item with respect to money income
s_{ij}	Direct elasticity of substitution
σ_{ij}	Allen elasticity of substitution
e_{ij}	Elasticity of complementarity
t	Proportional tax rate
T	Per-unit tax *or* time
v_i	Share of item i in total expenditure

These are not "model" answers but outline answers to help the reader check his or her own.

Q1-1

$$\left(-\frac{dy}{dx}\right)^C = \frac{1}{3} \qquad \left(-\frac{dy}{dx}\right)^F = \frac{2}{4} = \frac{1}{2}$$

where y = manna, x = quails. Thus Friday values x more highly (u_x/u_y is higher for him). So x (quails) should go from Crusoe to Friday, and y (manna) from Friday to Crusoe.

Q1-2 At this allocation

$$\frac{x_L}{x_K} = 2\frac{\overline{K}}{\overline{L}} \qquad \frac{y_L}{y_K} = \frac{1}{2}\frac{\overline{K}}{\overline{L}}$$

Therefore L should be shifted into L-intensive x and/or K into K-intensive y.

Q1-3 $u_x/u_y = 2$. To obtain the marginal cost, totally differentiate the transformation function:

$$2x\,dx + 2y\,dy = 0$$

$$MC = -\frac{dy}{dx} = \frac{x}{y} = \frac{1}{2}$$

Therefore x should rise.

Q1-4 There is no problem of efficient consumption. The relevant equations are therefore Equations (2) and (3) of Chapter 1.

$$\frac{x_L}{x_K} = \frac{y_L}{y_K} \tag{2}$$

Hence

$$\frac{2}{3}\frac{x}{L^x}\bigg/\frac{1}{3}\frac{x}{K^x} = \frac{1}{3}\frac{y}{\overline{L} - L^x}\bigg/\frac{2}{3}\frac{y}{\overline{K} - K^x}$$

Thus

$$2\frac{K^x}{L^x} = \frac{1}{2}\frac{\overline{K} - K^x}{\overline{L} - L^x}$$

Also

$$\frac{u_x}{u_y} = \frac{y_K}{x_K} \tag{3}$$

421

So

$$\frac{y}{x} = \frac{2}{3} \frac{y}{\bar{K} - K^x} \bigg/ \frac{1}{3} \frac{x}{K^x}$$

Hence

$$1 = \frac{2K^x}{\bar{K} - K^x} \qquad K^x = \frac{1}{3}\bar{K}$$

Thus, substituting in (2),

$$L^x = \tfrac{2}{3}\bar{L}$$

He spends two-thirds of his time on the time-intensive output. (The question can be answered more quickly by substituting for x and y in $u = xy$ and maximising with respect to L^x and K^x.)

Q1-5 The production functions are

$$x = 1.5K^x + 5L^x$$

$$y = K^y + 2L^y$$

The relative marginal products are different in the two industries, and efficient production can only be characterised by the more general condition that x should be maximised for any given y. Production occurs along the edges of the Edgeworth box. The maximum output of y is $1(100) + 2(100) = 300$. The first units of x will be produced by L alone since this has comparative advantage in x (the y-cost of x is 0.4, as against 0.66 in the hilly field). When all L is employed producing x we have

$$x = 500 \qquad y = 100$$

The maximum output of x is $1.5(100) + 5(100) = 650$. The transformation curve is thus as follows:

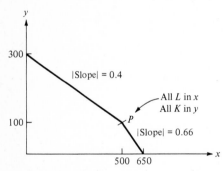

Suppose equilibrium is at point P:

$$\frac{u_x}{u_y} = \frac{y}{x} = \frac{100}{500} = 0.2$$

The value of x here is well below the rate at which it can be transformed into y. Therefore we have to

$$\max xy$$

such that

$$y = 300 - 0.4x$$

So

$$\max 300x - 0.4x^2$$

$$\frac{dy}{dx} = 300 - 0.8x = 0$$

This gives

$$x = \tfrac{3000}{8}$$

Thus all K is employed in y. 75 acres of L produce x and the rest y.

Q1-6

$$\frac{a^3}{a^3 + b^3} \quad \text{in A}$$

He spends over half his time in the more productive field. [Method: max $aL^{A^{2/3}} + b(\bar{L} - L^A)^{2/3}$].

Q1-7

	x	y
Crusoe	2.5	2.5
Friday	2.5	2.5
Both	5	5

Q1-8 False

Q1-9 For an optimum

$$MRT = MRS$$

So

$$b - 2cx^* = e - fx^*$$

Thus

$$x^* = \frac{e - b}{f - 2c}$$

Under free enterprise

$$MRT = \text{marginal revenue}$$

Hence

$$b - 2cx = \frac{d}{dx}(e - fx)x = e - 2fx$$

Thus

$$x = \frac{e - b}{2f - 2c} < x^*$$

Q1-10 (i) We require that

$$MRS \text{ of driver} + MRS \text{ of nondriver} = MRT$$

So

$$e - fx^* - g = b$$

This gives

$$x^* = \frac{e - g - b}{f}$$

(ii) The private optimum is

$$e - fx = b$$

Therefore

$$x = \frac{e - b}{f} > x^*$$

(iii) If they can negotiate, Friday will offer Crusoe up to g for each journey he agrees to forego. Every journey he makes, Crusoe foregoes this amount g. So he travels up to the point where

$$e - fx - g = b$$

So

$$x = x^*$$

(iv) g.

Q1-11 Two-thirds. The optimal allocation of factors is as in Question 1-4. We now require that Friday's factor income will enable him to buy half the national product. Since for each individual $u = xy$, half their expenditure will go on each product. (Check this by maximising u subject to a budget constraint.) Similarly $\frac{1}{3}$ of the expenditure on x will be spent in payments to K and $\frac{2}{3}$ in payments to L. (Check this by minimising costs subject to an output constraint.) By contrast, $\frac{2}{3}$ of the expenditure on y will be spent in payments to K and $\frac{1}{3}$ in payments to L. So half the national income goes to K and half to L. Since Friday receives $\frac{1}{3}$ of L income, he needs $\frac{2}{3}$ of K income.

Q1-12 Utilities are as follows:

State	A	B
0	100	100
1	117	117
2	81	169

1 is Pareto-superior to 0; 2 is Kaldor-superior to 0; 2 and 1 are identical in Kaldor terms. Distinctions between 2 and 0, and 2 and 1 require an ethical social welfare function.

Q1-13

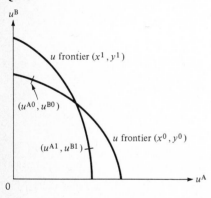

With x^1, y^1 it is possible to produce a Pareto improvement on u^{A0}, u^{B0}; and ditto in reverse. Your answer is of course satisfactory if it is identical to this with 0 and 1 interchanged throughout.

Q1-14 Yes. If u^A is held constant at $9 \times 9 = 81$ and u^B is maximised subject to that constraint and to the new endowments, $(x = 16, y = 36)$, we find

x^A	x^B	x	y^A	y^B	y	u^B
6	10	16	13.5	22.5	36	225

B is better off. A short-cut approach is as follows. The utility functions specified imply that both consumers will consume the same proportions of x and y and that these proportions determine the MRS_{yx} (see Appendix 3). So there is a unique community indifference map representable by $u = xy$. Since $16(36) > 23^2$, we have a potential Pareto improvement. Note that if A's pattern of consumption had not been reduced to allow for the new scarcity of x, we should not have been able to improve B's welfare.

Q1-15 (i)

$$\text{Welfare cost} = \tfrac{1}{2}t(x^0 - x^1)$$

Before tax

$$MRS = MRT$$

$$e - fx^0 = b + 2cx^0$$

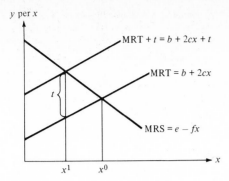

This gives

$$x^0 = \frac{e - b}{2c + f}$$

After tax

$$\text{MRS} = \text{MRT} + t$$

Therefore

$$x^1 = \frac{e - b - t}{2c + f}$$

Therefore

$$x^0 - x^1 = \frac{t}{2c + f}$$

Thus

$$\text{Welfare cost} = \frac{1}{2} \frac{t^2}{2c + f}$$

(ii) The same.

Q1-16 Ignoring income distribution, we can make the following calculation, which suggests that the dam should not be built. Grain is valued by the area under the demand curve (assuming the income elasticity of demand for grain is low). This area is 1m tons times the average demand price (= 950 rupees per ton).

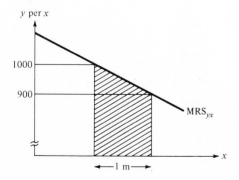

	Rs per year
Value of extra grain (1 m tons × 950 rupees per ton)	950 m
− Cost of inputs (1 m tons × 500 rupees per ton)	−500 m
− Cost of foreign loan	−500 m
	− 50 m

The water charges are a transfer payment from farmers to taxpayers and can be ignored, if the same value attaches to income accruing to each group. If income distribution were to be taken into account, we should need to know more about the effect of the dam on wages, land rentals, etc.

Q1-17 The utilitarians would have preferred state 1. By contrast if

$$W = \frac{1}{\alpha} u^{A^\alpha} + \frac{1}{\alpha} u^{B^\alpha} \qquad \alpha < 1$$

state 2 would be preferred if α was sufficiently low. For example if $\alpha = -1$, then

$$W^2 = -1 > -\tfrac{6}{5} = W^1$$

Q1-18 State 3 is more equal than 2 since it can be reached from 2 by transfers from richer to poorer. Similarly 1 is more equal than 2. As between 1 and 3, it depends on your welfare function. If the Atkinson index is used with

$$W = \frac{1}{\alpha} y^{A^\alpha} + \frac{1}{\alpha} y^{B^\alpha} \qquad \alpha < 1$$

1 is more unequal for high α and 3 for low α. For example, the inequality measures are as follows for $\alpha = \tfrac{1}{2}$ and $\alpha = -1$, together with Gini coefficients in brackets:

| State | Atkinson inequality index | | (Gini) |
	$\alpha = \tfrac{1}{2}$	$\alpha = -1$	
1	0.11	0.34	(0.33)
3	0.10	0.45	(0.28)

Q1-19 Suppose $\alpha = -1$; $W^2 = -1 > -\tfrac{6}{5} = W^1$. Breaking this into efficiency and equity aspects, the move from 1 to 2 raises E by $\tfrac{4}{5}$ and lowers $\bar{y}$ by less ($\tfrac{1}{3}$). For large enough α, 1 would be preferred.

Q1-20 $y^A = y^B = \tfrac{1}{2}\bar{y}$. Do you consider this a practical argument in favour of equality?

Q2-1 In equilibrium the sum of excess demands for x must be zero. B's excess demand is got by maximising $u^B = x^B y^B$ such that

$$\left(\frac{p_x}{p_y}\right) x^B + (y^B - \bar{y}) = 0$$

Thus

$$ED^{x^B} = x^B = \frac{1}{2} \frac{\bar{y}}{p_x/p_y}$$

Similarly A's excess demand is got by maximising $u^A = x^A y^A$ such that

$$\frac{p^x}{p_y}(x^A - \bar{x}) + y^A = 0$$

Thus

$$ED^{x^A} = x^A - \bar{x} = -\tfrac{1}{2}\bar{x}$$

Market equilibrium requires that $ED^{x^A} + ED^{x^B} = 0$. Therefore,

$$\frac{p_x}{p_y} = \frac{\bar{y}}{\bar{x}}$$

As excess demand decreases monotonically with price, the equilibrium is unique and stable (assuming Walras' adjustment mechanism). (You may have noticed by now that if a function $x_1^{\alpha_1} x_2^{\alpha_2}$ is maximised subjected to

$$p_1 x_1 + p_2 x_2 = Q^0$$

the solution is always

$$p_i x_i = \frac{\alpha_i}{\alpha_1 + \alpha_2} Q^0 \qquad \alpha i = 1, 2)$$

Q2-2 Virtually infinite. B's offer curve is horizontal at $\frac{1}{2}\bar{y}$ and A need offer barely any x in return for y in order to induce B to supply $\frac{1}{2}\bar{y}$. Therefore any positive price is sufficient to induce this supply.

Q2-3

Country	$\dfrac{K}{L}$	$\dfrac{w_L}{p_y} = 50 \sqrt{\dfrac{K}{L}}$	$\dfrac{y}{L} = 100 \sqrt{\dfrac{K}{L}}$
1	90,000	15,000	30,000
2	10,000	5,000	10,000
3	25	250	500

Actually intercountry differences in output per head cannot be fully explained by differences in factor inputs, see P. R. Fallon and P. R. G. Layard, "Capital-Skill Complementarity, Income Distribution, and Output Accounting," *Journal of Political Economy*, vol. 83, pp. 279–302, April 1975.

Q2-4 (i) Any increase in K/L raises the real wage y_L and lowers the real capital rental y_K.
(ii) Relative shares are constant:

$$y_L = \tfrac{3}{4} y L^{-1} \qquad y_K = \tfrac{1}{4} y K^{-1}$$

So relative shares are

$$\frac{y_L}{y_K} \frac{L}{K} = \frac{\tfrac{3}{4}}{\tfrac{1}{4}} = 3$$

This holds independently of K/L. So s must be unity.
(iii) Since s is unity, $s > y_L L/y$. So the absolute share of capital must rise. To check this, $y_K K = \tfrac{1}{4} y$. This rises as K rises.

Q2-5 (i)

State	$\dfrac{w_L}{p_x}$	$\dfrac{w_L}{p_y}$
1	1	1
2	$\tfrac{2}{3}$	$\tfrac{2}{3}$
3	2	$\tfrac{1}{2}$

1 is preferred to 2 since 2's budget line lies wholly inside 1's. But we cannot discriminate between 1 and 3, nor between 2 and 3, since in each case the budget lines cross.

(ii) We first need to find the indirect utility function which specifies the maximum utility of a worker (call it u^*) as a function of the prices tabulated. So

$$\max u = xy \quad \text{such that} \quad p_x x + p_y y = w_L$$

Hence $\qquad x = \dfrac{w_L}{2p_x} \qquad y = \dfrac{w_L}{2p_y}$ (see answer to Question 2-1 above)

This gives

$$u^* = \frac{1}{4}\left(\frac{w_L}{p_x}\right)\left(\frac{w_L}{p_y}\right)$$

$$u^{*1} = \frac{1(1)(1)}{4} = \frac{1}{4} \qquad u^{*2} = \frac{1}{4}\frac{2}{3}\frac{2}{3} = \frac{1}{9} \qquad u^{*3} = \frac{1}{4}$$

So 1 and 3 are equally desirable, but 3 is preferred to 2.

Q2-6 Yes. Such tariffs would raise the price of the labour-intensive good and so raise real wages (see Chapter 4).

Q2-7 (i) For productive efficiency

$$\frac{x_L}{x_K} = \frac{y_L}{y_K}$$

Thus

$$\frac{1}{3}\frac{x}{L^x}\bigg/\frac{2}{3}\frac{x}{K^x} = \frac{2}{3}\frac{y}{L^y}\bigg/\frac{1}{3}\frac{y}{K^y}$$

This gives

$$\frac{1}{2}\frac{K^x}{L^x} = \frac{2(\bar{K} - K^x)}{\bar{L} - L^x}$$

So (a) $\qquad\qquad K^x = 0.5 \qquad\qquad K^y = 0.5$

$\qquad\qquad\qquad\qquad L^x = 0.2 \qquad\qquad L^y = 0.8$

$\qquad\qquad\qquad\qquad x = (0.05)^{1/3} \qquad y = (0.32)^{1/3}$

(b) $\qquad\qquad K^x = 0.8 \qquad\qquad K^y = 0.2$

$\qquad\qquad\qquad\qquad L^x = 0.5 \qquad\qquad L^y = 0.5$

$\qquad\qquad\qquad\qquad x = (0.32)^{1/3} \qquad y = (0.05)^{1/3}$

(ii)

$\dfrac{w_K}{p_x}$	$\dfrac{w_K}{p_y}$	$\dfrac{w_L}{p_x}$	$\dfrac{w_L}{p_y}$	$\dfrac{w_L}{w_K}$	$\dfrac{p_x}{p_y}$
x_K	y_K	x_L	y_L	$\dfrac{x_L}{x_K}$	$\dfrac{y_K}{x_K}$
$\dfrac{2}{3}\left(\dfrac{K^x}{L^x}\right)^{-1/3}$	$\dfrac{1}{3}\left(\dfrac{K^y}{L^y}\right)^{2/3}$	$\dfrac{1}{3}\left(\dfrac{K^x}{L^x}\right)^{2/3}$	$\dfrac{2}{3}\left(\dfrac{K^y}{L^y}\right)^{1/3}$		
(a) $\dfrac{2}{3}(0.4)^{1/3}$	$\dfrac{1}{3}(1.6)^{2/3}$	$\dfrac{1}{3}\left(\dfrac{1}{0.4}\right)^{2/3}$	$\dfrac{2}{3}\left(\dfrac{1}{1.6}\right)^{1/3}$	$\dfrac{1}{0.8}$	$\dfrac{1}{2}(6.4)^{1/3}$
(b) $\dfrac{2}{3}\left(\dfrac{1}{1.6}\right)^{1/3}$	$\dfrac{1}{3}\left(\dfrac{1}{0.4}\right)^{2/3}$	$\dfrac{1}{3}(1.6)^{2/3}$	$\dfrac{2}{3}(0.4)^{1/3}$	0.8	$\dfrac{1}{2}(10)^{1/3}$

Labour is better off at (a), where production of labour-intensive y is higher. Note the relation of relative factor prices and relative product prices.

Q2-8 (i) Both goods are equally capital-intensive. The efficiency locus in input space is straight, so that at all points we have

$$\frac{K^x}{L^x} = \frac{K^y}{L^y}$$

and points (a) and (b) are identical.

$$K^x = \tfrac{1}{2} \qquad K^y = \tfrac{1}{2}$$
$$L^x = \tfrac{1}{2} \qquad L^y = \tfrac{1}{2}$$
$$x = \tfrac{1}{2} \qquad y = 1$$

So the transformation curve is straight. For distributional purposes we are in effect back with the one-sector model but with output measured by $x + \tfrac{1}{2}y$: the output mix will not affect relative prices of goods or factors.

(ii)

$\dfrac{w_K}{p_x}$	$\dfrac{w_K}{p_y}$	$\dfrac{w_L}{p_x}$	$\dfrac{w_L}{p_y}$	$\dfrac{w_L}{w_K}$	$\dfrac{p_x}{p_y}$
$\tfrac{2}{3}$	$\tfrac{4}{3}$	$\tfrac{1}{3}$	$\tfrac{2}{3}$	$\tfrac{1}{2}$	2

Q2-9 (i)

$$K^x = \tfrac{1}{3} \qquad K^y = \tfrac{2}{3}$$
$$L^x = \tfrac{1}{3} \qquad L^y = \tfrac{2}{3}$$
$$x = \tfrac{1}{3} \qquad y = \tfrac{4}{3}$$

(ii) No change from Question 2-8. Since the efficiency locus is straight, real factor prices are independent of output and so are relative product prices.

Q2-10 The structure of this question is identical to Question 1-5. The two inputs are "perfect substitutes" in producing x and likewise in producing y, as shown by the fact that the isoquants are straight. The efficiency locus in input space lies along the bottom and right-hand edges of the Edgeworth box.

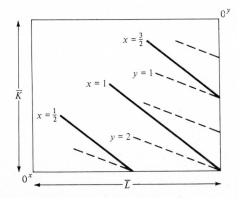

As x expands from zero it initially uses only L, in which it is relatively intense, until all L is employed in x. Up to this point the slope of the transformation curve is

$$-\frac{dy}{dx} = 1$$

Beyond this point x expands by shifts of K out of y. Hence the slope becomes steeper and

$$-\frac{dy}{dx} = 2$$

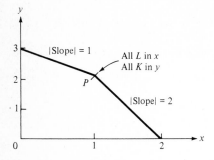

To compute the general equilibrium, it is convenient to start by assuming it lies at point P, where all L is in x and all K in y. If the demand price for these outputs is

$$1 \leq \frac{p_x}{p_y} \leq 2$$

then this is the correct solution. If not, we move off along the appropriate linear segment of the transformation curve till $u_x/u_y = \mathrm{MRT}_{yx}$.

(i) At P, $u_x/u_y = \frac{3}{4}\, y/x = \frac{3}{2}$. Therefore P is an equilibrium. Relative product prices are determined by demand

$$\frac{p_x}{p_y} = \frac{3}{2}$$

Factor prices are determined by this and by their marginal products in the industries where they are employed:

So
$$\frac{w_K}{p_y} = 2 \qquad \frac{w_L}{p_x} = 1$$

Thus

$\dfrac{w_K}{p_x}$	$\dfrac{w_K}{p_y}$	$\dfrac{w_L}{p_x}$	$\dfrac{w_L}{p_y}$
$\frac{4}{3}$	2	1	$\frac{3}{2}$

(ii) At P, $u_x/u_y = \frac{4}{3}$, $y/x = \frac{8}{3}$. Therefore P is not an equilibrium. More x has to be produced. So relative product prices are given by relative production costs (in terms of K).

$$\frac{p_x}{p_y} = 2$$

Factor prices are determined by this and by their marginal productivities in the industries where they are employed.

$\dfrac{w_K}{p_x}$	$\dfrac{w_K}{p_y}$	$\dfrac{w_L}{p_x}$	$\dfrac{w_L}{p_y}$
1	2	1	2

(The reader, if worried, can work out the equilibrium quantities of x, y, K^x, and K^y and check that these quantities satisfy the product exhaustion conditions.)

Q2-11 The production frontier (transformation curve) is defined by two linear constraints, a capital constraint and a labour constraint:

$$\bar{K} \geq 2x + y \qquad \bar{L} \geq x + y$$

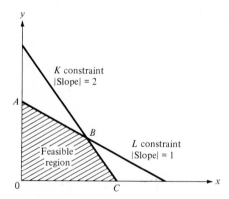

Production may occur on either linear segment or at apices A, B, or C, depending on demand. If production occurs at B, there is full employment—both constraints are binding. If it occurs northwest of B, there is unemployed K, and if southeast of B, unemployed L. Production will occur at B if at that point

$$1 \leq \frac{u_x}{u_y} \leq 2$$

(i) At B,

$$1.8 = 2x + y$$

$$1 = x + y$$

$$x = 0.8 \qquad y = 0.2$$

$$\frac{u_x}{u_y} = \frac{y}{x} = \frac{1}{4}$$

Too much x is being produced, since the marginal cost of x is 1. Production therefore occurs along the labour constraint with unemployed capital. Relative product prices are determined by relative costs.

$$\frac{p_x}{p_y} = 1$$

Real factor prices are determined by this and by the product exhaustion equations:

$$\frac{p_x}{p_y} = 2\frac{w_K}{p_y} + 1\frac{w_L}{p_y} \qquad \text{for } x$$

$$\frac{p_y}{p_y} = 1\frac{w_K}{p_y} + \frac{w_L}{p_y} \qquad \text{for } y$$

$\dfrac{w_K}{p_x}$	$\dfrac{w_K}{p_y}$	$\dfrac{w_L}{p_x}$	$\dfrac{w_L}{p_y}$
0	0	1	1

(ii) At B,

$$1.4 = 2x + y$$

$$1 = x + y$$

$$x = 0.4 \qquad y = 0.6$$

$$\frac{u_x}{u_y} = \frac{y}{x} = \frac{3}{2}$$

B is an equilibrium.

Relative product prices are determined by demand at point B.

$$\frac{p_x}{p_y} = \frac{3}{2}$$

Factor prices are determined by this and by the product exhaustion equations.

$\dfrac{w_K}{p_x}$	$\dfrac{w_K}{p_y}$	$\dfrac{w_L}{p_x}$	$\dfrac{w_L}{p_y}$
$\frac{1}{3}$	$\frac{1}{2}$	$\frac{1}{3}$	$\frac{1}{2}$

(iii) At B, x is negative. The capital constraint dominates the labour constraint; even if no x is produced, y is constrained by K and there is unemployed L. As in (i) relative product prices are determined by relative costs:

$$\frac{p_x}{p_y} = 2$$

and

$\dfrac{w_K}{p_x}$	$\dfrac{w_K}{p_y}$	$\dfrac{w_L}{p_x}$	$\dfrac{w_L}{p_y}$
$\frac{1}{2}$	1	0	0

Readers interested in pursuing this approach to unemployment in poor countries can read R. S. Eckaus, "The Factor Proportions Problem in Underdeveloped Areas," *American Economic Review,* vol. 45, pp. 539–565, September 1955.

Q2-12 No. Suppose that x were capital-intensive. If the increase in p_x/p_y caused by the minimum wage raised the quantity of y demanded sufficiently, this could raise the welfare of workers in y. To see this consider the Edgeworth box below. If x_L is fixed, this fixes $(K/L)^x$, given by the slope of $0^x R^x$. Since the constraint is binding, the previous equilibrium allocation must lie to the right of this, at, say, P. Equally the new equilibrium cannot lie on the straight-line section $0^x P'$ since the wage would be higher on the curved efficiency locus $0^x P'$ [where $(K/L)^x$ is higher]. So the new equilibrium is on the straight-line section $P'R^x$. If it lies on $P''R^x$, $(K/L)^y$ has fallen and y_L has therefore fallen and labour in y is worse off. On the other hand, at higher outputs of y (along $P'P''$), y_L will have risen and may have risen enough to raise

$$u\left(\frac{w_L}{p_x}, \frac{w_L}{p_y}\right)$$

where w_L is the wage of workers in the y industry.

By contrast, if x were labour-intensive, no such result is possible, since the rise in the price of x raises the demand for K-intensive y.

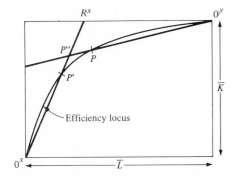

Q3-1 (i) The market price (which is the seller's price) falls to less than the equilibrium level of the seller's price.

(ii) The market price rises to less than the equilibrium level of the buyer's price. Therefore the seller's price, which is market price minus tax, is below its equilibrium level.

Workers do better under (i).

Q3-2 Most—salt; least—hotel rooms in Miami. The world supply of salt is fairly elastic and demand fairly inelastic. (This is why the French kings taxed it.) The demand for holidays in Miami is fairly elastic (good substitutes elsewhere), while supply is inelastic. For yellow shirts demand and supply are both quite elastic.

Q3-3 (i) Miami hotel rooms (on the preceding assumptions).

(ii)

Tax
$$\frac{dp^D}{dx}\Delta x = \frac{dp^S}{dx}\Delta x + \Delta T$$

So
$$-\Delta x = \frac{T}{dp^S/dx - dp^D/dx} = \frac{Tx}{p}\frac{1}{1/\eta^S - 1/|\varepsilon^D|}$$

where η^S = elasticity of supply, ε^D = elasticity of demand

Thus
$$-\frac{1}{2}T\,\Delta x = \frac{T^2x}{2p}\frac{1}{1/\eta^S - 1/|\varepsilon^D|} = \left(\frac{T}{p}\right)^2\frac{xp}{2}\frac{1}{1/\eta^S - 1/|\varepsilon^D|}$$

The excess burden depends on the proportional tax rate, expenditure on the good, and η^S and $|\varepsilon^D|$. Going on, we find that

$$-\frac{1}{2}\frac{T}{Tx}\frac{\Delta x}{} = \frac{1}{2}\frac{T}{p}\left(\frac{1}{1/\eta^S - 1/|\varepsilon^D|}\right)$$

For a given T/p, excess burden per dollar of tax revenue is larger, the larger η^S and $|\varepsilon^D|$. (We shall revert to this result in Chapter 6.)

    (iii) (a) $y_{max} + a + b + c + d$
        (b) $y_{max} + b + c + d$
        (c) $y_{max} + d$

Q3-4 (i)

$$\frac{t}{1+t} = \frac{1}{10} \quad \text{so} \quad t = \frac{1}{9}$$

    (ii)
$$\frac{w_K}{p_y}\overline{K}t = \frac{y_K}{1+t}\overline{K}t = \left(\frac{1}{4}\frac{y}{K}\right)\frac{1}{1+t}\overline{K}t = \frac{1}{10}y$$

Hence
$$t = \tfrac{2}{3}$$

    (iii)
$$t = \tfrac{1}{9} \quad \text{[as in (i)]}$$

Q3-5 False, unless there are income effects on the composition of demand for products, or on the supply of other factors.

Q3-6 (i) Mainly landlords. (The tenants are willing to pay less to the landlords for the stock of property, which is inelastically supplied.)
    (ii) Tenants.

Q3-7 The production of x must rise since the government spends the tax proceeds on x and there is a substitution effect of private spending towards x (since p_x/p_y has fallen). Since x is capital-intensive, the capital intensity of production falls and the marginal product of labour falls in both industries. In addition, labour cannot buy its marginal product in the y industry. So L necessarily loses, even though the relative price of the good x for which it has a relatively strong preference has fallen. Since K has a relatively strong preference for the good y whose price has risen, it is likely (but not certain) that it too has lost.

3-8 (i) A tax on all factor incomes is equivalent to an equiproportional tax on both goods. So, if this is combined with a subsidy on food, the total package is equivalent to a tax on manufactures and a (smaller) subsidy on food. Assuming food output increases, the marginal product of labour in both industries falls. But its purchasing power over subsidised food may rise. So, if it spends a very high share of its income on food, it could gain. (If labour gained, landlords must lose, since the original state was Pareto-optimal.)
    (ii) The two assumptions are not necessarily inconsistent. If factors are in given supply and all industries have equal factor intensities, the transformation curve is straight and the MRT constant. With taxes on one or more products, relative factor prices are unaltered, and the tax is borne by factory owners in relation to their preferences for the goods. A factor tax, by contrast, is borne chiefly by the taxed factor.

Q3-9 Assume that the production of x falls. Therefore production occurs on the new locus between 0^x and P'. Therefore $(K/L)^x$ falls, x_K rises and x_L falls. In the y industry we have two possible cases:
    Case (a). x falls only a little and production occurs in the range RP'. $(K/L)^y$ rises, y_K falls, and y_L rises. Since w_K/p_y has fallen and p_x/p_y has risen, w_K/p_x has fallen and capital is worse off. Labour may or may not be worse off.
    Case (b). x falls a lot and production occurs along 0^xR. $(K/L)^y$ falls, y_K rises, and y_L falls. So labour loses from the tax on the product in which it is intensive, and capital may or may not lose.
    The overall conclusion is thus

$\dfrac{w_K}{p_x}$	$\dfrac{w_K}{p_y}$	u^K	$\dfrac{w_L}{p_x}$	$\dfrac{w_L}{p_y}$	u^L
?	?	?	↓	?	?

J. B. Shoven and J. Whalley ("A General Equilibrium Calculation of the Effects of Differential Taxation of Income from Capital in the U.S.," *Journal of Public Economics*, vol. 1, pp. 281–321, November 1972) discuss the U.S. Corporation Income Tax, which is a tax on capital in the labour-intensive sector. They estimate that the effect fell in class (a). Capital lost from the tax, and labour barely lost at all.

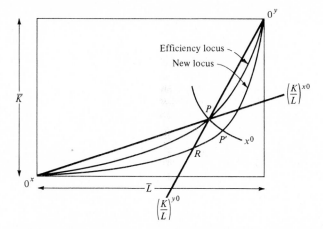

Q3-10 (i) This is just like t_{Lx}. Nonunionised labour (which gets wages net of "tax") loses. Unionised labour gains in case 1 on pages 97–98 since x_L rises and p_x/p_y rises; it may lose in case 2.

(ii) This is just like t_{Kx}, but where K is taken to mean labour and x is taken to be capital-intensive. Unionised labour gains since its marginal product in the unionised industry rises and so does the relative price of the unionised product. Nonunionised labour may gain in case (b) of Question 3-9, since the rise in the unionised product's price so greatly increases the quantity of the nonunionised product demanded; it loses in case (a).

H. G. Johnson and P. Mieszkowski ("The Effects of Unionisation on the Distribution of Income: A General Equilibrium Approach," *Quarterly Journal of Economics*, vol. 84, pp. 539–561, November 1970) point out that in the U.S. the unionised sector is relatively labour-intensive and unionisation may not even benefit union members.

Q3-11 Step 1. To compute t_{Lx} proceed as follows. If $u = xy$, expenditure on x is always one-half of money national product (henceforth N), see Question 1-11. Therefore if $t_x = \frac{1}{10}$, the government get $\frac{1}{11}\frac{1}{2}N$. But if there is a tax on labour in x, $x = (K^x)^{1/3}(L^x)^{2/3}$, so L^x always costs $\frac{2}{3}$ of x and therefore $\frac{2}{3}\frac{1}{2}N\ (=\frac{1}{3}N)$. So

$$\frac{t_{Lx}}{1 + t_{Lx}}\frac{1}{3}N = \frac{1}{22}N$$

and

$$t_{Lx} = \tfrac{3}{19}$$

Step 2. Note that each consumer spends half his income on each product. Hence

$$x^L = \frac{1}{2}\frac{w_L}{p_x} \qquad y^L = \frac{1}{2}\frac{w_L}{p_y}$$

Thus
$$u^L = \frac{1}{4}\frac{w_L}{p_x}\frac{w_L}{p_y} \qquad u^K = \frac{1}{4}\frac{w_K}{p_x}\frac{w_K}{p_y}$$

Step 3. Now use the five-equation model of Sec. 3-4 to determine K^x, K^y, L^x, L^y, and the equations of Table 3-1 to determine the prices, and hence the utilities. These are shown in the following table. The conclusion is that K is better off with a tax on L in x than with a tax on x, while L is worse off.

	K^x	K^y	L^x	L^y	$\dfrac{w_K}{p_x}$	$\dfrac{w_K}{p_y}$	u^K	$\dfrac{w_L}{p_x}$	$\dfrac{w_L}{p_y}$	u^L
No tax	$\dfrac{1}{3}$	$\dfrac{2}{3}$	$\dfrac{2}{3}$	$\dfrac{1}{3}$	$\dfrac{1}{3}(2)^{2/3}$	$\dfrac{1}{3}(2)^{2/3}$	0.0703	$\dfrac{1}{3}(2)^{2/3}$	$\dfrac{1}{3}(2)^{2/3}$	0.0703
$t_x = \dfrac{1}{10}$	$\dfrac{1.0}{3.2}$	$\dfrac{2.2}{3.2}$	$\dfrac{2.0}{3.1}$	$\dfrac{1.1}{3.1}$	$\dfrac{1}{3.3}2^{2/3}\left(\dfrac{3.1}{3.2}\right)^{-2/3}$	$\dfrac{1}{3}2^{2/3}\left(\dfrac{3.1}{3.2}\right)^{-1/3}$	0.0657	$\dfrac{1}{3.3}2^{2/3}\left(\dfrac{3.1}{3.2}\right)^{1/3}$	$\dfrac{1}{3}2^{2/3}\left(\dfrac{3.1}{3.2}\right)^{2/3}$	0.0617
$t_{Lx} = \dfrac{3}{19}$	$\dfrac{1}{3}$	$\dfrac{2}{3}$	$\dfrac{19}{30}$	$\dfrac{11}{30}$	$\dfrac{1}{3}(1.9)^{2/3}$	$\dfrac{1}{3}(2)^{2/3}(1.1)^{1/3}$	0.0697	$\dfrac{1}{3.3}(1.9)^{2/3}$	$\dfrac{1}{3}(2)^{2/3}(1.1)^{-2/3}$	0.0576

Q3-12 (i) Regressive, unless the subsidised good is strongly intensive in factors owned by the poor.

(ii) Mildly progressive, provided we can legitimately treat everyone in a given income group as having the same income. For the debate about the actual situation in California, see R. W. Hartman, "A Comment on the Pechman-Hansen-Weisbrod Controversy," *The Journal of Human Resources*, vol. V, pp. 519–522, Fall 1970.

Q3-13 Not necessarily true. The policy is progressive if the handout raises the average income of the poor proportionately more than that of the rich.

If p_P is the proportion of the poor who are white and p_R is the proportion of the rich who are white, $(p_P < p_R)$, the condition for progressivity is

$$\frac{p_P(1) + (1 - p_P)(0)}{y_P} > \frac{p_R(1) + (1 - p_R)(0)}{y_R}$$

i.e.,
$$\frac{p_P}{p_R} > \frac{y_P}{y_R}$$

The relative income of the poor must be less than the fraction of poor who are white relative to the fraction of rich who are white. (The proportional tax of course leaves inequality unaffected.)

Q4-1 False. There will be a gain only if foreign prices are different, but the relative price (of x?) can be higher or lower.

Q4-2 (i) Suppose two factors, land T and labour L, and two goods, food F and clothing C. The opening of the U.S. prairies reduced p_F/p_C facing Britain, which reduced w_T/w_L, w_T/p_F, and w_T/p_C.

(ii) Let L denote all factors other than land T. The abolition of the tariff lowered p_F/p_C and raised w_L/w_T, w_L/p_F, and w_L/p_C; i.e., it benefitted the newly enfranchised classes.

Q4-3 The loss from the consumption tax (area d in Figure 4-3) is greater than the loss from the production tax (of equal size to area b) if the demand curve has a flatter slope than the domestic supply curve.

Q4-4 False. The tariff will eliminate the distortion in consumption. Since $t_x = t_y$, the consumption of both goods is taxed equally and

$$\text{MRS} = \frac{p_x}{p_y} = \frac{\pi_x}{\pi_y}\frac{1 + t_x}{1 + t_y} = \text{MRT}^f$$

But the tariff introduces a new production distortion since

$$MRT = MRT^f(1 + t_x) > MRT^f$$

An equal tax on the consumption of x (rather than a tariff) would have eliminated the distortion.

Q4-5 False. If world prices are given, the export subsidy raises the domestic price of the export good until producers are indifferent between exporting and supplying home consumers.

Q4-6 If the government is determined to maintain the tariff, it should build the mill, since the cost of steel is less than consumers' valuation of steel. But it would be better to drop the tariff and import more steel than to build the mill. For the controversy over this issue, provoked by I. M. D. Little and J. A. Mirrlees, *Manual of Industrial Project Analysis in Developing Countries, Vol. II, Social Cost Benefit Analysis*, Organisation for Economic Cooperation and Development, Paris, 1969 (which recommends the use of world prices), see R. Layard (ed.), *Cost-Benefit Analysis*, Penguin, 1972. (For a restatement of the Little-Mirrlees case, see their *Project Appraisal and Planning for Developing Countries*, Heinemann, London, 1974.)

Q4-7 False. A prohibitive tariff leaves the economy at its no-trade production point.

Q4-8 (i) Under no circumstances will country A produce any x. In the initial state it imports x^0 from country B (the cost per unit is 4 and the consumer price 7). In the customs union it imports x^1 from country C (the cost per unit is 5 and so is the consumer price). The country gains if area r exceeds area q: in other words, if the gains from "trade creation" exceeds the losses of "trade diversion" from lower- to higher-cost producers.

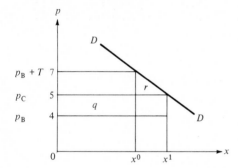

In other words

$$(p_C - p_B)x^0 < \tfrac{1}{2}(T + p_B - p_C)(x^1 - x^0)$$

So

$$\frac{p_C - p_B}{p_C} < \frac{1}{2}\frac{(T + p_B - p_C)^2}{p_C^2}\frac{(x^1 - x^0)}{(T + p_B - p_C)}\frac{p_C}{x^0}$$

Hence

$$\Delta \log (\text{unit cost}) < \tfrac{1}{2}(-\Delta \log \text{price})^2 |\varepsilon|$$

Gain is more likely the less the cost difference and the larger the elasticity of demand and the tariff.
    (ii) No.

Q4-9 (i) The country maximises its utility by a recursive procedure. First it maximises the value of output at world prices subject to the transformation curve. Let

$$\frac{p_x}{p_y} = p$$

So

$$-\frac{dy_P}{dx_P} = \frac{x_P}{y_P} = p \quad \text{and} \quad x_P = py_P$$

Hence
$$p^2 y_P^2 + y_P^2 = k^2$$

Therefore
$$y_P = \frac{k}{\sqrt{1 + p^2}} \qquad x_P = \frac{kp}{\sqrt{1 + p^2}}$$

Next maximise utility subject to the trading budget constraint, which is

$$px_C + y_C = px_P + y_P = \frac{kp^2 + k}{\sqrt{1 + p^2}} = k\sqrt{1 + p^2}$$

Therefore
$$\frac{u_x}{u_y} = \frac{y_C}{x_C} = p \qquad \text{and} \qquad y_C = px_C$$

So
$$2y_C = k\sqrt{1 + p^2}$$

Therefore
$$y_C = \frac{1}{2} k\sqrt{1 + p^2} \qquad x_C = \frac{1}{2p} k\sqrt{1 + p^2}$$

Thus if x and y are quantities traded,

$$y = y_P - y_C = \frac{k}{2} \frac{1 - p^2}{\sqrt{1 + p^2}}$$

$$x = x_C - x_P = \frac{k}{2p} \frac{1 - p^2}{\sqrt{1 + p^2}}$$

(Note that the identity of exchange, $y/x = p$, is satisfied.) If $p < 1$, exports of y and imports of x are positive. If $p > 1$, the reverse. The offer curve is as follows:

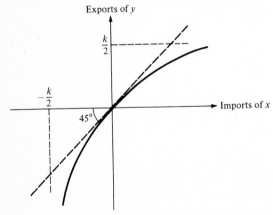

(ii) No. The offer curve of B (using x to mean its exports of x, and y to mean its imports) would be the mirror image of A's, touching it tangentially at zero exports and imports.

(iii) Country B now has a greater y intercept than country A and a lower x intercept. For a given y/x the relative cost of x is increased. So the country will export y. (The perceptive reader will have noticed that the transformation curve is not convex-outwards throughout, but it is convex over the relevant range if b is small.)

Q4-10 (i) From the budget identity

$$p_x x = p_y y$$

So
$$\frac{p_x}{p_y} = \frac{y}{x} = Ax^{\alpha - 1} \qquad \text{in country A}$$

$$= Bx^{\beta - 1} \qquad \text{in country B}$$

Country A is the importer of x since, when p_x/p_y rises, x falls ($\alpha < 1$). The reverse is true of y.

(ii) $Ax^{\alpha-1} = Bx^{\beta-1}$

So $\qquad x = \left(\dfrac{A}{B}\right)^{(\beta-\alpha)^{-1}} \qquad \dfrac{p_x}{p_y} = A\left(\dfrac{A}{B}\right)^{(\beta-\alpha)^{-1}(\alpha-1)} \qquad y = A\left(\dfrac{A}{B}\right)^{(\beta-\alpha)^{-1}\alpha}$

Q4-11

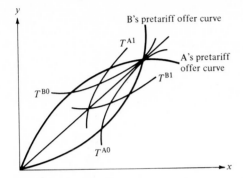

Q4-12 False. Suppose the quota is $0x^1$ in Figure 4-6. The quota drives up the domestic price of imports and drives down the supply price. But the crucial question is: Who collects the profit corresponding to those tax proceeds which would have resulted if the restriction had been achieved by a tariff? If the import quotas (licenses) are auctioned by the government, the country can collect the proceeds and the quota is formally identical to a tariff. But, if not, the profits are likely to go to foreigners, and the country imposing the quota will lose.

Q4-13 Britain is more or less a price taker for the bulk of its agricultural imports. So the production subsidy system was preferable to the tariff.

Q4-14 $\qquad\qquad\qquad\qquad \dfrac{p_x}{p_y} = (1+t)\dfrac{\pi_x}{\pi_y}$

Measuring p_x/p_y on the vertical axis, the foreign supply curve shifts up, since a given quantity is supplied at the same π_x/π_y and a higher p_x/p_y. The tariff therefore lowers p_x/p_y, π_x/π_y, and the welfare of labour.

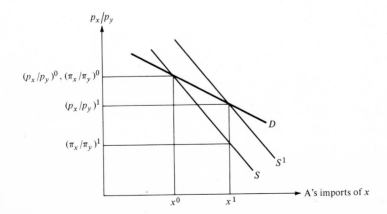

Q4-15 (i) y.
 (ii) y.
 (iii) x.
 (iv) x.
 (v) y.

(v) is the most complicated case, since A has comparative advantage in x but also has a relative preference for x. To resolve the problem, first construct the world transformation curve TT'' by combining the transformation curves of A and B. The maximum of y is $2\frac{1}{2}$ (at T). The first unit of x is then produced by A, leading us to point T'. The next two units of x are produced by B, leading us to T''.

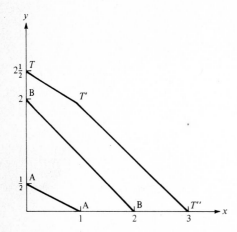

What will the price p_x/p_y be? Suppose $p_x/p_y = 1$ (i.e., production is on the segment $T'T''$). Country A would buy more x than y, and B would buy the same amount of each. So p_x/p_y is the equilibrium price. Therefore A specialises entirely in producing x. But it consumes $\frac{2}{3}$ units of x ($\frac{2}{3}$ of its expenditure is on x, see Question 1-11). So it does export x and import y. The point could equally well be made using offer curves.

Q4-16 (i) The labour-intensive good must be a necessity, i.e., form a higher proportion of the expenditure of poor than of rich, i.e., have an income elasticity less than unity.

(ii) Directly (both higher, the more K/L). Generally speaking, the opposite is observed, which tends to support the relevance of closed-economy models of distribution.

Q5-1 No. Assumptions 1 and 2 together rule it out. For in the following diagram $\mathbf{x}^0$ and $\mathbf{x}^1$ are equally desirable, and $\mathbf{x}^1$ and $\mathbf{x}^2$ are equally desirable.

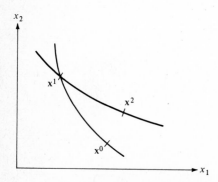

Therefore from the basic properties of an ordering (assumption 1) $\mathbf{x}^0$ and $\mathbf{x}^2$ must be equally desirable. But from assumption 2, $\mathbf{x}^2$ must be preferred to $\mathbf{x}^0$. Therefore intersecting indifference curves are inadmissible.

Q5-2 (i) No. In B he chooses a point that lies inside the budget line from case A. (Try drawing the diagram).

(ii) He is consistent. He is better off in case B since he can still buy his original consumption bundle and have something left over.

Q5-3 The following corner solution is possible.

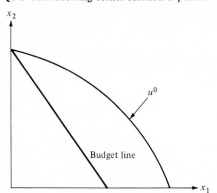

Q5-4 (i).

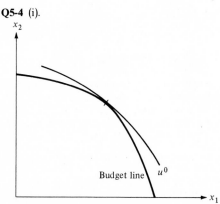

(ii) The second-order condition is that the curvature of the budget line must exceed that of the indifference curve (for a local maximum rather than a minimum). In terms of the per-unit analysis, the MRS rises less fast than the MC, as x_1 increases.

(iii) Monopsony.

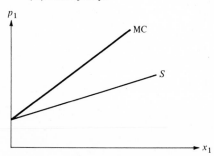

A monopsonist faces a rising supply price and hence his marginal cost rises.

Q5-5 (i) A.

(ii) B.

Q5-6 (i)

$$\max x_1 x_2 + \lambda(m - p_1 x_1 - p_2 x_2)$$

$$x_2 = \lambda p_1$$

$$x_1 = \lambda p_2$$

$$p_1 x_1 + p_2 x_2 = m$$

Thus

$$x_1 = \frac{1}{2}\frac{m}{p_1} \qquad x_2 = \frac{1}{2}\frac{m}{p_2}$$

(ii)

$$x_1 = \frac{\alpha_1}{\alpha_1 + \alpha_2}\frac{m}{p_1} \qquad x_2 = \frac{\alpha_2}{\alpha_1 + \alpha_2}\frac{m}{p_2}$$

In each case

$$\varepsilon_{11} = \varepsilon_{22} = -1$$

$$\varepsilon_{12} = \varepsilon_{21} = 0$$

$$\eta_{1m} = \eta_{2m} = 1$$

Q5-7 (i) Conditions for maximising $u(x_1, x_2)$ such that $p_1 x_1 + p_2 x_2 = m$ are

$$\frac{u_1}{u_2} = \frac{p_1}{p_2} \qquad \text{and} \qquad p_1 x_1 + p_2 x_2 = m$$

Now,

$$\max f[u(x_1, x_2)] + \lambda(m - p_1 x_1 - p_2 x_2)$$

$$f'u_1 - \lambda p_1 = 0$$

$$f'u_2 - \lambda p_2 = 0$$

So again the same conditions are required.

(ii) False.

Q5-8 For convex indifference curves we require

$$\frac{d}{dx_1}\left(\frac{dx_2}{dx_1}\right) = \frac{d}{dx_1}\left[-\frac{u_1(x_1, x_2)}{u_2(x_1, x_2)}\right] > 0$$

Hence

$$\frac{-u_2(u_{11} + u_{12}\, dx_2/dx_1) + u_1(u_{21} + u_{22}\, dx_2/dx_1)}{u_2^2} > 0$$

But this is to be evaluated along the budget line so that

$$\frac{dx_2}{dx_1} = -\frac{u_1}{u_2}$$

Therefore

$$-\frac{1}{u_2^3}(u_2^2 u_{11} - 2u_1 u_2 u_{12} + u_1^2 u_{22}) > 0$$

But

$$u_1 = \lambda p_1$$

$$u_2 = \lambda p_2$$

So

$$p_2^2 u_{11} - 2p_1 p_2 u_{12} + p_1^2 u_{22} < 0$$

This satisfies the required sign of the determinant in the text.

Q5-9 (i)

$$\varepsilon_{11} = \alpha_1$$

$$\varepsilon_{12} = \alpha_2$$

$$\eta_{im} = \beta$$

$$\alpha_1 + \alpha_2 + \beta = 0$$

(ii) No. Suppose the income elasticities of x_1 and x_2 are β_1 and β_2, respectively. Then we would require

$$v_1\beta_1 + (1 - v_1)\beta_2 = 1$$

where v_1 is the expenditure share of x_1. This implies a unique value of v_1. But if $\beta_1 \neq \beta_2$, v_1 will vary with m. Therefore we cannot have β_1 and β_2 constant.

Q5-10 (i) The values found by S. J. Prais and H. S. Houthakker, *The Analysis of Family Budgets*, Cambridge University Press, 1955, pp. 106–107, are

Rice	0.3	Normal necessity
Condensed milk	−0.2	Inferior
Butter	0.4	Normal necessity
Margarine	−0.3	Inferior
Tea	0.4	Normal necessity
Coffee	0.7	” ”
Drink (alcoholic and soft)	1.6	Luxury
Carpets	2.4	”
Theatres	2.0	”

(ii) One should subsidise the most inferior good. For the share of the rich in the consumption of the good will be lower, the less consumption rises with income.

(iii) The benefit which a person receives (assuming everyone has the same price elasticity of demand) is proportional to his consumption of the good. Therefore, using the notation of Chapter 3,

$$B = am^\beta$$

$$C = bm \qquad \text{(due to the proportional tax)}$$

So
$$\frac{B - C}{m} = am^{\beta - 1} - b$$

This falls as m rises if $\beta < 1$.

Q5-11 (i) $\varepsilon_{ii}^* = \varepsilon_{ii} + v_i\eta_{im} = -1 + 0.25(2) = -1 + 0.5 = -0.5$

(ii) $\varepsilon_{ij}^* = \varepsilon_{ij} + v_j\eta_{im} = -0.1 + 0.05(3) = 0.05 > 0$

They are substitutes. This is not necessarily impossible. For though scooters use gasoline, so do cars and the demand for cars is not unaffected by the gasoline price rise. If scooters are very good substitutes for cars, they may be substitutes for oil.

$$\varepsilon_{ji} = \varepsilon_{ji}^* - v_i\eta_{jm} = v_i\sigma_{ij} - v_i\eta_{jm} = \frac{v_i\varepsilon_{ij}^*}{v_j} - v_i\eta_{jm} = -0.01$$

Q5-12 False, but true provided x_i is an inferior good.

Q5-13 (i)

$$\sum_i p_i x_i = m$$

Now let p_j change as well as all x's, but not m:

$$\sum_i p_i \frac{\partial x_i}{\partial p_j} + x_j = 0$$

Thus
$$\sum_i \frac{p_i x_i}{m} \frac{\partial x_i}{\partial p_j} \frac{p_j}{x_i} = \frac{-p_j x_j}{m}$$

(ii) Now let p_j change as well as all x's *and* m.

$$\sum_i p_i \frac{\partial x_i}{\partial p_j} + x_j = \frac{\partial m}{\partial p_j}$$

Now require that m changes to hold u constant.

Therefore
$$dm = x_j\, dp_j$$

or
$$\frac{\partial m}{\partial p_j} = x_j$$

So
$$\sum_i \frac{p_i x_i}{m} \left(\frac{\partial x_i}{\partial p_j}\right)_u \frac{p_j}{x_i} = 0$$

(iii)
$$\sum_j \left(\frac{\partial x_i}{\partial p_j}\right)_u \frac{p_j}{x_i} = 0$$

Therefore
$$\sum_j \left(\frac{\partial x_i}{\partial p_j}\right)_u p_j = \sum_j \left(\frac{\partial x_j}{\partial p_i}\right)_u p_j = 0$$

Hence
$$\sum_j \frac{p_j x_j}{m} \left(\frac{\partial x_j}{\partial p_i}\right)_u \frac{p_i}{x_j} = 0$$

i.e.,
$$\sum_j v_j \varepsilon_{ji}^* = 0$$

Q5-14

$$x = \frac{m}{2p} \qquad y = \frac{m}{2} \qquad \text{(ordinary demand curves, given } p_y = 1\text{)}$$

This gives
$$u = xy = \frac{m^2}{4p}$$

So
$$C = m = (4pu)^{1/2}$$

For
$$u = u^0 = \frac{100^2}{4(1)} \qquad C = (4pu^0)^{1/2} = 100p^{1/2}$$

Thus
$$\text{CV} = C(p^0, u^0) - C(p^1, u^0) = 100 - 100(0.25)^{1/2} = 50$$

The price index for $u = u^0$ is
$$\frac{C(p^1, u^0)}{C(p^0, u^0)} = \frac{50}{100} = 0.5$$

Q5-15

$$C(p, u^0) = 100p^{1/2} \qquad \text{given that the price of } y \text{ is unity}$$

So
$$x(p, u^0) = \frac{\partial C}{\partial p} = 50p^{-1/2}$$

This compares with the ordinary demand curve
$$x(p, m^0) = 50p^{-1}$$

i.e., the compensated demand curve is less elastic.
$$\text{CV} = \int_{p^1}^{p^0} 50p^{-1/2}\, dp = [100p^{1/2}]_{0.25}^{1} = 100 - 50 = 50$$

Q5-16

$$x = \frac{m}{2p_x} \qquad y = \frac{m}{2p_y}$$

This gives
$$u = \frac{m^2}{4p_x p_y}$$

So
$$C = m = (4p_x p_y u^0)^{1/2} = 100 p_x^{1/2} p_y^{1/2}$$

Thus
$$CV = C(\mathbf{p}^0, u^0) - C(\mathbf{p}^1, u^0)$$
$$= 100 - 100(0.25)^{1/2}(2.25)^{1/2} = 100 - 75 = 25$$

Price index $= \frac{75}{100} = 0.75$. The rise in the price of y does not cancel out the fall in the price of x; only a rise to $p_y = 4$ would do that.

Q5-17
$$CV = -(e - m) = -\text{EV of opening the market}$$
$$EV = -(m - c) = -\text{CV of opening the market}$$

Q5-18 (i) $-[C(\mathbf{p}^0, 1, u^0) - C(\mathbf{p}^0, 0, u^0)]$. It is minus the CV. It could be infinity.

(ii) (a) A's question assumes that effectively he starts with no daylight and u equals, say, u^i. He is then asked how much he will pay for daylight. If the variable x equals 1 when he has daylight and 0 when he does not, he starts at $(0, m)$ and is willing to pay $m - y^1$ to get daylight, while keeping utility at u^i (see diagram). B's question assumes that he starts with daylight at $(1, m)$ and u equals, say, u^j. He has to be paid $y^2 - m$ to compensate him for loss of daylight. The discontinuous variable x could be considered normal if $(y^2 - m) > (m - y^1)$. Presumably it *is* normal. So B's question would produce a bigger answer. Note that $m - y^1$ must be bounded but $y^2 - m$ could be infinite.

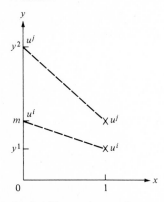

(b) On this question see the text.

Q5-19 $u^1 = 100^2/4(0.25)$

So
$$C(p, u^1) = (4pu^1)^{1/2} = \frac{100}{0.5} p^{1/2} = 200 p^{1/2}$$

Thus
$$EV = C(p^0, u^1) - C(p^1, u^1) = 200 - 200(0.25)^{1/2}$$
$$= 100 > 50 = CV$$

Q5-20 (i)
$$\frac{u_x}{u_y} = 2 - x = p$$

So
$$x = 2 - p, \quad y = m - px = m - p(2 - p)$$
$$u = 2(2 - p) - \tfrac{1}{2}(2 - p)^2 + m - p(2 - p)$$
$$= (2 - p)(2 - 1 + \tfrac{1}{2}p - p) + m$$
$$= 2 - 2p + \tfrac{1}{2}p^2 + m$$

Thus
$$C = u - (2 - 2p + \tfrac{1}{2}p^2)$$
CV and EV are independent of u because
$$\frac{d}{dy}\left(\frac{u_x}{u_y}\right) = 0$$

[A sufficient condition for this is $u = f(x) + y$.]
$$\text{CV} = \text{EV} = 2(1 - \tfrac{1}{4}) - \tfrac{1}{2}[1 - (\tfrac{1}{4})^2]$$
$$= \tfrac{33}{32}$$

(ii) The money cost of the subsidy is
$$\tfrac{3}{4}x = \tfrac{3}{4}(2 - \tfrac{1}{4})$$
$$= \tfrac{3}{4}\tfrac{7}{4} = \tfrac{21}{16}$$

So the welfare cost of the subsidy
$$= \text{taxpayers' loss} - \text{consumers' gain}$$
$$= \tfrac{21}{16} - \tfrac{33}{32} = \tfrac{9}{32}$$

(iii) The all-or-nothing demand curve is got by first computing u^0 for $x = 0$, $y = m$. Thus $u^0 = m$. Along the indifference curve for $u = u^0$
$$y = m - 2x + \tfrac{1}{2}x^2$$

Therefore the amount of y surrendered for given x is
$$m - y = m - m + 2x - \tfrac{1}{2}x^2$$

Hence if $p^*(x)$ is the average price of x he is just willing to pay
$$p^*(x) = \frac{2x - \tfrac{1}{2}x^2}{x} = 2 - \frac{1}{2}x$$

This compares with the ordinary demand curve
$$p(x) = 2 - x$$

Q5-21

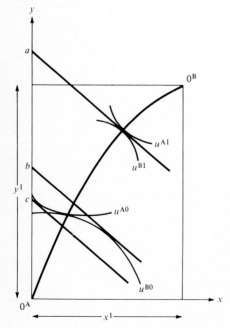

$$CV^A = a - c$$
$$CV^B = -(a - b)$$

Thus
$$CV^A + CV^B = b - c > 0$$

Thus $\sum CV > 0$ does not imply that the Kaldor criterion is satisfied, but satisfaction of the Kaldor criterion implies that $\sum CV > 0$.

Q5-22 (i) False (see the reverse of Figure 5-14).

(ii) $6 billion. It is not an approximate measure in the sense in which we have been talking. For the consumer's price is (presumably) unaffected and there is no substitution towards oil. There is simply a profit of $6 per barrel.

Q5-23 Suppose p falls from p_0 to p_1.

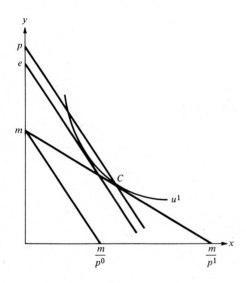

(i) $P = p - m > e - m = EV$. If given $p - m$, one would buy less x and improve one's welfare beyond u^1.

(ii) No. We are only concerned with substitution effects in this comparison.

(iii)
$$EV = \int_{p_1}^{p_0} x(p, u^1)\, dp$$

Q5-24 This is Questions 5-14 and 5-19 in reverse.

$$EV = -50$$
$$CV = -100$$
$$L = -0.75x^0 = -0.75\frac{100}{2(0.25)} = -150$$
$$P = -0.75x^1 = -0.75\frac{100}{2(1)} = -37.5$$

Thus
$$L < CV < EV < P$$

Q5-25 True. For income in 1971 was $110, and the cost of the 1965 bundle at 1971 prices was (in dollars)

$$25(1.3) + 50(1.1) = 87.5$$

Another approach is the following. Calculate $\mathbf{L}$ and compare this with the ratio of 1971 income to 1965 income. Since we know that $\mathbf{L}$ exaggerates the price rise, it follows that if

$$\mathbf{L} < \frac{m^1}{m^0}$$

welfare has improved.

$$\mathbf{L} = \frac{\sum p^1 x^0}{\sum p^0 x^0} = \frac{87.5}{75} < \frac{110}{75} = \frac{m^1}{m^0}$$

Q5-26 They are end-year (Paasche) price weights. If y is the index of real income ($y^0 = 1$), then

$$y^1 = \frac{m^1}{m^0} \bigg/ \mathbf{L} = \frac{\sum p^1 x^1 \sum p^0 x^0}{\sum p^0 x^0 \sum p^1 x^0} = \frac{\sum p^1 x^1}{\sum p^1 x^0}$$

Q5-27 (i) No. Each individual k's own price index is

$$\mathbf{L}^k = \frac{\sum p^1 x^k}{\sum p^0 x^k}$$

where x_i^k is consumption of good x_i in period 0. The "group-$\mathbf{L}$" for a two-person group, consisting of person A and person B, is

$$\mathbf{L} = \frac{\sum p^1 x}{\sum p^0 x} = \frac{\sum p^1 x^A}{\sum p^0 x^A} \frac{\sum p^0 x^A}{\sum p^0 (x^A + x^B)} + \frac{\sum p^1 x^B}{\sum p^0 x^B} \frac{\sum p^0 x^B}{\sum p^0 (x^A + x^B)}$$

The individual indices are weighted by the shares of the individuals in total national income.

(ii) The price changes of luxuries are more heavily represented than if rich and poor were weighted equally.

(iii) No, for the prices of luxuries might be rising faster than those of necessities.

(iv) We need to discover what is the income m^k of the individual k who spends the same proportion of his income on each good i as the community as a whole. First we find the share spent on good i by the community of n people as a whole. For the individual

$$p_i x_i^k = p_i \gamma_i + \beta m_i - \beta \sum p_j \gamma_j$$

Therefore, summing over individuals

$$\sum p_i x_i = n(p_i \gamma_i - \beta \sum p_j \gamma_j) + \beta \sum m_i$$

So

$$\text{Overall share} = \frac{\sum p_i x_i}{\sum m_i} = \frac{p_i \gamma_i - \beta \sum p_j \gamma_j}{\overline{m}} + \beta$$

$$\text{Individual share} = \frac{p_i x_i^k}{m^k} = \frac{p_i \gamma_i - \beta \sum p_j \gamma_j}{m^k} + \beta$$

If individual share equals overall share, $m^k = \overline{m}$. The representative individual's income is the average, which is usually well above the median.

Q5-28 (i) No. $\alpha_i > 0$.

(ii) For necessities the intercept of the Engel curve is negative; i.e., at hypothetical zero income, consumption would be positive, so that $p_i x_i / m$ falls as m rises.

So

$$\gamma_i - \alpha_i \frac{\sum p_j \gamma_j}{p_i} > 0$$

(iii) Inelastic.

$$x_i = \gamma_i + \alpha_i\left(\frac{m}{p_i} - \gamma_i - \sum_{j \neq i} \frac{p_j \gamma_j}{p_i}\right)$$

$$\frac{\partial x_i}{\partial p_i} = \frac{-\alpha_i\left(m - \sum_{j \neq i} p_j \gamma_j\right)}{p_i^2}$$

Hence

$$\frac{\partial x_i}{\partial p_i}\frac{p_i}{x_i} = \frac{1}{x_i}\left[\frac{-\alpha_i\left(m - \sum_{j \neq i} p_j \gamma_j - p_i \gamma_i\right)}{p_i} - \alpha_i \gamma_i + \gamma_i - \gamma_i\right]$$

$$= \frac{1}{x_i}\left[-x_i + \gamma_i(1 - \alpha_i)\right]$$

$$= -\frac{1}{x_i}\left[x_i - \gamma_i(1 - \alpha_i)\right]$$

Thus

$$|\varepsilon_{ii}| < 1$$

(iv) Yes, all goods.

$$\frac{\partial x_i}{\partial p_j} = \frac{-\alpha_i \gamma_j}{p_i}$$

A rise in p_j reduces supernumerary income. Since the share of supernumerary income spent on each good is constant, independent of prices, the quantity of each other good consumed falls.

Q5-29 (i) That all other goods are separable from it.

(ii) Write

$$\frac{\partial \log x_i}{\partial \log p_j} = \varepsilon_{ij} \qquad \frac{\partial \log x_i}{\partial \log m} = \eta_{im} \qquad \text{and} \quad \frac{\partial \log \lambda}{\partial \log m} = f$$

From Equations (5) and (7) on page 164 we get:

$$f \varepsilon_{ii} = \left(\frac{\partial \log \lambda}{\partial \log p_i} + 1\right)\eta_{im} \tag{i}$$

And from (6) and (7) we get:

$$f \varepsilon_{ij} = \frac{\partial \log \lambda}{\partial \log p_j} \eta_{im} \qquad i \neq j \tag{ii}$$

Getting ε_{ij}, $i \neq j$, from (ii) and ε_{jj} from (i), form the sum

$$f\left(\sum_i v_i \varepsilon_{ij}\right) = \frac{\partial \log \lambda}{\partial \log p_j}\left(\sum_i v_i \eta_{im}\right) + v_j \eta_{jm}$$

Using (E-2) and (E-4), we find

$$\frac{\partial \log \lambda}{\partial \log p_j} = -f v_j - v_j \eta_{jm}$$

Substituting this into (i) for $j = i$ gives our first result:

$$f \varepsilon_{ii} = (-f v_i - v_i \eta_{im} + 1)\eta_{im}$$

or

$$f(\varepsilon_{ii} + v_i \eta_{im}) = (1 - v_i \eta_{im})\eta_{im}$$

or
$$\frac{\varepsilon_{ii}^*}{\eta_{im}} = \frac{1 - v_i \eta_{im}}{f}$$

From (ii) comes our second result, in exactly the same way:

$$\frac{\varepsilon_{ij}^*}{\eta_{im}} = \frac{-v_j \eta_{jm}}{f}$$

We see that for small values of the v_i, the result is the same as that on page 164.

Q5-30 The following estimates are based on L. D. McClements, "Equivalence Scales for Children," Department of Health and Social Security, London, mimeo, 1975. They are based on a quadratic form of the Engel curve and on the assumption that there are different equivalence scales for different goods, of which these are weighted averages.

Single adult	1.00
Child 0–1 years	0.15
2–4	0.30
5–7	0.34
8–10	0.38
11–12	0.41
13–15	0.44
16–18	0.59
Additional adult	0.64

Q5-31 Since $h = 1$ for a single adult, the general Engel curve for households of any size h must be

$$\frac{x_i}{h} = c_{i1}\left(\frac{m}{h}\right)^{b_i}$$

Therefore for households of size h_k, we have

$$x_i = h_k c_{i1}\left(\frac{m}{h_k}\right)^{b_i} = h_k^{1-b_i} c_{i1} m^{b_i}$$

But we also know that for these households

$$x_i = c_{ik} m^{b_i}$$

Thus
$$c_{ik} m^{b_i} = h_k^{1-b_i} c_{i1} m^{b_i}$$

So
$$h_k = \left(\frac{c_{ik}}{c_{i1}}\right)^{1/(1-b_i)}$$

Since $h_k > 1$, $c_{ik} > c_{i1}$ if $b_i < 1$ (i.e., x_i is a necessity). At given m, large families consume more necessities than small ones, and fewer luxuries.

Q6-1 (i) Zero.
(ii) Yes. At zero price the CV of consumers is $1000 > $800.
(iii) max $px = 2000p - 2000p^2$. So $p = \frac{1}{2}$.
(iv) No. Profit-maximising revenue is $\frac{1}{2}[2000 - 2000(\frac{1}{2})] = 500$.
(v) No. Benefits are now $750.
(vi) Charge the demand price given by $1500 = 2000 - 2000p$.

Q6-2 No, in all cases. Radio is a pure public good.

Q6-3 (i) Yes.

(ii) I should say when I want transmissions at extra power and pay $x for each such hour.

Q6-4 For any given number of carriages the price should be just sufficient to fill the marginal carriage. We therefore first find the optimal number of carriages and then the price that will fill them. Thus we maximise $B(x) - C(x)$ subject to x being a multiple of 100. As a first step, treat x as a continuous variable:

$$\frac{d(B - C)}{dx} = \frac{d(20x - 0.005x^2 - 500 - x)}{dx}$$

$$= 19 - 0.01x = 0$$

Therefore $x = 1900$. This (conveniently) *is* a multiple of 100. It is easy to check that the net benefit of the 19th carriage is positive and of the 20th carriage negative. To fill the 19th carriage (just) we need a price of $1. Note that this equals the cost per carriage divided by the number of passengers per carriage. This is to be expected, given that carriages can be added at constant returns to scale (try drawing a diagram analogous to Figure 6-3). But the price is justified by its equality with "short-run marginal cost" given the correct investment decision.

(ii) Obviously no general answer is possible. Influences tending to produce a deficit are the fixed costs, consisting of track and station costs and certain fixed cost elements per train [see (i) above]. But, if the demand for rail services is high enough, some of the track may be being used at capacity levels and the prices (rents) charged on this account may be high enough to cover fixed costs. This could be so if the capacity bottlenecks occurred in densely populated areas where there are increasing costs of expanding capacity.

Q6-5

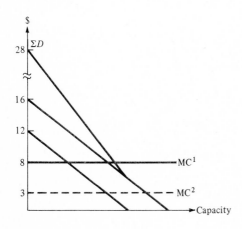

(i) Total demand price for capacity to produce x units per half-day is the demand price for a unit minus the operating cost per unit.

So

$$\sum \text{MRS} = (22 - 10^{-5}x - 6) + (18 - 10^{-5}x - 6)$$

$$= 28 - (2)10^{-5}x$$

Hence optimal capacity is given by

$$28 - (2)10^{-5}x = \text{MRT} = 8$$

Therefore

$$10^{-5}x = 10 \qquad x = 10^6$$

Thus peak electricity is charged the demand price for capacity of $x = 10^6$ *plus* the operating cost (and similarly for off-peak).

So
$$p_{\text{peak}} = 16 - 10^{-5+6} + 6 = 12$$

$$p_{\text{off-peak}} = 12 - 10^{-5+6} + 6 = 8$$

Note that the full cost of capacity is covered ($12 - 6 + 8 - 6 = 8$).

(ii) If the marginal cost of capacity is 3¢ per day, the off-peak should not be charged for any increments to capacity (see diagram above). Therefore

$$p_{\text{peak}} = 9$$

$$p_{\text{off-peak}} = 6$$

Q6-6 (i) Optimality requires

$$\frac{p_1 - c_1}{p_1} \Big/ \frac{p_2 - c_2}{c_2} = \frac{|\varepsilon_{22}|}{|\varepsilon_{11}|}$$

Now
$$\varepsilon_{11} = \frac{dx_1}{dp_1} \frac{p_1}{x_1} = -\frac{1}{2} \left[\frac{3}{4 \left(1 - \frac{1}{2} \cdot \frac{3}{4}\right)} \right] = -\frac{3}{5}$$

$$\varepsilon_{22} = \frac{dx_2}{dp_2} \frac{p_2}{x_2} = -1 \left(\frac{\frac{1}{2}}{\frac{1}{2}} \right) = -1$$

So
$$\frac{p_1 - c_1}{p_1} \Big/ \frac{p_2 - c_2}{p_2} = \frac{\frac{3}{4} - \frac{1}{3}}{\frac{3}{4}} \Big/ \frac{\frac{1}{2} - \frac{1}{3}}{\frac{1}{2}} = \frac{5}{3} = \frac{\varepsilon_{22}}{\varepsilon_{11}}$$

To balance the budget we need

$$(p_1 - c_1)x_1 + (p_2 - c_2)x_2 = \text{fixed cost}$$

But
$$(p_1 - c_1)x_1 + (p_2 - c_2)x_2 = (\tfrac{3}{4} - \tfrac{1}{3})[1 - \tfrac{1}{2}(\tfrac{3}{4})] + (\tfrac{1}{2} - \tfrac{1}{3})\tfrac{1}{2}$$

$$= \tfrac{5}{12} \cdot \tfrac{5}{8} + \tfrac{1}{6} \cdot \tfrac{1}{2} = \tfrac{25}{96} + \tfrac{8}{96} = \tfrac{33}{96} = \tfrac{11}{32}$$

(ii)
$$\max p_1 x_1 + p_2 x_2 - (c_1 x_1 + c_2 x_2 + \tfrac{11}{32})$$

Since marginal costs are constant, this is two separate questions.

First
$$\max (p_1 - c_1)(1 - \tfrac{1}{2}p_1)$$

So
$$(1 - \tfrac{1}{2}p_1) + (p_1 - c_1)(-\tfrac{1}{2}) = 0$$

This gives
$$1 - \tfrac{1}{2}p_1 - \tfrac{1}{2}p_1 + \tfrac{1}{2}c_1 = 0$$

Hence
$$p_1 = 1 + \tfrac{1}{2} \cdot \tfrac{1}{3} = \tfrac{7}{6}$$

Second
$$\max (p_2 - c_2)(1 - p_2)$$

So
$$1 - p_2 - p_2 + c_2 = 0$$

This gives
$$p_2 = \frac{1 + \tfrac{1}{3}}{2} = \tfrac{2}{3}$$

Note that the price of the less elastic good is higher than of the more elastic good. But both prices are higher than is socially optimal given the requirement that the books balance.

(iii) In (i)
$$\frac{(B - C)}{p_1} = (p_1 - c_1)\frac{dx_1}{dp_1} = \left(\frac{3}{4} - \frac{1}{3} \right)\left(-\frac{1}{2} \right) = -\frac{5}{24}$$

$$\frac{\partial \pi}{\partial p_1} = x_1 + (p_1 - c_1)\frac{\partial x_1}{\partial p_1}$$

$$= \tfrac{5}{8} - \tfrac{5}{24} = \tfrac{10}{24}$$

Therefore

$$-\frac{\partial(B - C)}{\partial p_1} \bigg/ \frac{\partial \pi}{\partial p_1} = \frac{1}{2}$$

Check that

$$-\frac{\partial(B - C)}{\partial p_2} \bigg/ \frac{\partial \pi}{\partial p_2}$$

equals the same.

In (ii)

$$\frac{\partial \pi}{\partial p_1} = \frac{\partial \pi}{\partial p_2} = 0$$

So

$$-\frac{\partial(B - C)}{\partial p_i} \bigg/ \frac{\partial \pi}{\partial p_i} = \infty$$

Q6-7 (i) $u(p_1, \ldots, p_n, T^0)$ since p_0 is fixed at unity

(ii) $\max u(p_1, \ldots, p_n, T^0) + \mu\left[\sum_j (p_j - c_j)x_j - R^0\right]$

Assume

$$\frac{\partial x_j}{\partial p_i} = 0 \quad i \neq j$$

So

$$\frac{\partial u}{\partial p_i} + \mu\left[(p_i - c_i)\frac{\partial x_i}{\partial p_i} + x_i\right] = 0 \quad \text{all i}$$

By Roy's Identity

$$x_i = \frac{\partial u}{\partial p_i} \bigg/ \frac{\partial u}{\partial T} = \frac{\partial u}{\partial p_i}\frac{1}{\lambda}$$

where λ is the marginal utility of time:

Thus

$$\mu(p_i - c_i)\frac{\partial x_i}{\partial p_i} = -\lambda x_i - \mu x_i$$

Hence

$$\frac{p_i - c_i}{p_i} = -\frac{\lambda + \mu}{\mu}\left(\frac{x_i}{p_i} \bigg/ \frac{\partial x_i}{\partial p_i}\right)$$

Q6-8 When x is increased, the factory gains $B^{F'}(x) - B^{F'}(x^*)$. So we have the equilibrium condition

$$B^{F'}(x) - B^{F'}(x^*) = -B^{R'}(x)$$

Therefore $x < x^*$.

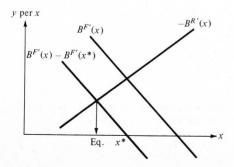

Q6-9 (i) (a) Optimality requires that we max $B(x) - C(x)$, both being measured in hours.

$$B(x) = 20x - 0.0005x^2$$

$$C(x) = x \text{ times the cost per trip}$$

$$= 2x + 0.001x^2$$

So
$$\frac{d(B - C)}{dx} = 20 - 0.001x - 2 - 0.002x = 0$$

Thus
$$x = \frac{18}{0.003} = 6000$$

(b) Drivers must be charged the price which makes them demand this quantity. This is

$$p = 20 - 6 = 14$$

But at the optimum the private cost (net of tax) is

$$p = 2 + 6 = 8$$

So they must be taxed $\$(14 - 8)$.

(ii) The advantage is that some attempt is made to charge a car for the congestion which it causes. The disadvantage is that the charge is not proportional to the congestion. It is the same whether the car travels 1 mile off-peak or 10 miles at peak hours. Thus, once inside inner London, there is no discouragement to unlimited travel, while some drivers who could obtain surpluses of less than £1 while causing small congestion costs are discouraged from travelling at all.

Q6-10 The outcome for any one individual in each possible contingency is as follows.

		Self	
		Confess	Deny
Other	Confess	20	30
	Deny	0	2

(i) If the individual decides on the basis of what is best for himself, taking the other's action as given, he will confess. The result is that both prisoners get 20 years.

(ii) If the individuals can agree at all, they will agree to a plan which has the same effect on each of them. They will prefer both getting 2 years to both getting 20. So both will deny guilt. But note that each could do best for himself by confessing while the other denied guilt (i.e., by behaving as a free rider).

(iii) If they trusted each other, they might work out that solution (ii) was better for both than solution (i) and therefore deny guilt on the assumption that the other would do the same.

(iv) The "contractarian" reasoning in (iii) may be quite widespread within society. So people may in fact follow rules of self-restraint, even though it is not in their self-interest as a free rider (see A. K. Sen, "Behaviour and the Concept of Preference," *Economica*, vol. 40, pp. 241–259, August, 1973). To this extent the economic approach to explaining behaviour outlined on page 3 needs to be given a wider construction than might at first appear. In international relations the same may apply, though there is perhaps less evidence of this. The lower the costs of negotiation (e.g., the clearer the Hot Line), the better, according to this theory.

Q6-11 If no filters are fitted and no swimming baths built, the following is the damage caused by each firm to each household (in \$).

		By					
		A	B	C	D	E	Total
To	1	0	0	0	0	0	0
	2	12	0	0	0	0	12
	3	12	12	0	0	0	24
	4	12	12	12	0	0	36
	5	12	12	12	12	0	48
Total		48	36	24	12	0	120

(i) It would therefore be worthwhile for households 3, 4, and 5 to pay B for a filter, and for households 2, 3, 4, and 5 to pay A for a filter. But would they do so? Household 5 might consider building a swimming pool instead (only *it* would consider this, since $48 > 40$, but $36 < 40$). The "swimming pool project" would be worth $48 - 40 (=8)$ to household 5. If instead, it joined in the filter project, paying its share of the costs, this would be worth to it $24 - (\frac{1}{3} + \frac{1}{4})25 =$ about 10. So it would prefer to join in the negotiations for the filters. But it is unlikely that the filter negotiations would be successful. There is strong psychological resistance among self-perceived pollutees to paying polluters.

(ii) The state, if it had the available information, could coerce the two firms to install filters. Or it could enforce taxes on them equal to the damage caused. This might, of course, drive some of the firms out of business, but if so this would not be inefficient: whether an outcome is efficient or not may quite well depend on the distribution of rights. The state could also force the householders to pay for the installation of the filters, but this would not normally be considered equitable. The state should perhaps be influenced by the relative wealth of house owners and the owners of the firms.

Q6-12 (i) False.

(ii) Only if this led some individuals to obtain more batches than previously.

(iii) If $x = \alpha p^{-\beta} m^{\gamma}$ and price is time T multiplied by a fraction of income (km), $x = \alpha (kT)^{-\beta} m^{\gamma - \beta}$. So for any value of T those who want any given x, and are willing to pay the highest all-or-nothing price for it, are those for whom $m^{\gamma - \beta}$ is highest. If $\gamma > \beta$ these are the rich; otherwise, the poor.

(iv) The poor will consume a higher fraction of any given supply under queueing, for the effective income elasticity across persons has been reduced—in the previous example, from γ to $\gamma - \beta$.

Q6-13 That they are zero.

Q6-14 We make the comparisons with the pre-oil-crisis situation.

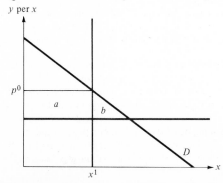

(i) Inefficient. Everyone whose allotment is less than his previous quantity of x purchased loses. Taxpayers are unaffected.

(ii) Efficient. Everyone whose allocation is less than his previous quantity of x purchased loses. Others gain. Taxpayers are unaffected.

(iii) Efficient. Everyone using x loses ($a + b$ in total). Taxpayers gain a.

(iv) Efficient. Everyone using x loses. Importers gain a.

Q6-15 (i) True (use box diagram). Strictly they are as well off or worse off.

(ii) False.

Q6-16 (i) True. It is likely that relative points prices and money prices will diverge. In this case the two budget lines cross. These lines are

$$m = p_x x + p_y y$$
$$P = P_x x + P_y y$$

where P is total points and P_x is the points price of x.

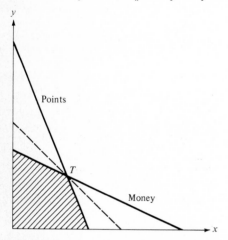

If points are saleable at a money price p, we get a unified budget line.

$$m + pP^0 = (p_x + pP_x)x + (p_y + pP_y)y$$

Since this is a linear combination of the equations above, it must pass through the (x, y) pair that satisfies those equations. It therefore passes through T and lies between the two previous constraints. It is indicated by the dotted line. This extends the feasible region beyond the shaded area. No one is worse off.

(ii) False. The preceding analysis assumed the money prices p_x and p_y fixed, since with no income difference there is no reason why money prices should change when points become saleable. But if there are income differences, the pattern of demand will be drastically altered if the rich can use money to release their points constraint. If money prices change, the poor who are bound by their money constraint may be worse off.

Q6-17 (See diagram opposite.)

(i) Under price control

$$\text{Consumer's surplus} = x^0 \tfrac{1}{2}(1 - p^0)$$

Under free-market prices

$$\text{Consumer's surplus} = x^0 \tfrac{1}{2}(1 - p^1)$$

Therefore $\qquad\qquad \text{Consumer's gain} = x^0 \tfrac{1}{2}(p^0 - p^1) < 0$

(ii) Producer's gain $x^0(p^1 - p^0)$

So
$$\text{Producer's gain} + \text{consumer's gain} = \tfrac{1}{2}x^0(p^1 - p^0) > 0$$

(One should note in passing that with a perfectly general demand curve one could not show that consumers necessarily gain from price control if allocation is random.)

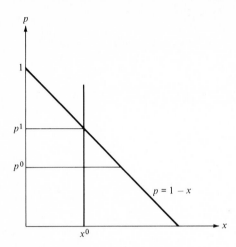

Q7-1 (i) $C(x) = wL = x - x^2 + x^3$

So
$$\text{MC} = C'(x) = 1 - 2x + 3x^2$$

$$\text{AC} = \frac{C(x)}{x} = 1 - x + x^2$$

Therefore min AC is where

$$\frac{d}{dx}\left(\frac{C(x)}{x}\right) = -1 + 2x = 0 \quad \text{and} \quad x = \tfrac{1}{2}$$

Thus
$$\text{min AC} = 1 - \tfrac{1}{2} + \tfrac{1}{2}^2 = \tfrac{3}{4}$$

Hence supply curve is

$$p = 1 - 2x + 3x^2 \quad p \geq \tfrac{3}{4}$$

For
$$p < \tfrac{3}{4} \quad x = 0$$

(ii) If $p = 1$, $1 = 1 - 2x + 3x^2$ and $x = \tfrac{2}{3}$. If $p = \tfrac{1}{2}$, $x = 0$.

(iii)
$$\pi = px - wL = x - (x - x^2 + x^3) = x^2 - x^3$$
$$= (\tfrac{2}{3})^2 - (\tfrac{2}{3})^3$$
$$= (\tfrac{2}{3})^2 \tfrac{1}{3} = \tfrac{4}{27}$$

(iv) Same as before. A profits tax has no effect unless prices change, since if $\pi > 0$, any fraction of π is also positive.

(v) Close down.

(vi) Returns to scale increase if MC < AC.

Hence
$$1 - 2x + 3x^2 < 1 - x + x^2$$

This gives
$$2x^2 < x \quad \text{and} \quad x < \tfrac{1}{2}$$

At $x = \frac{1}{2}$, returns to scale are constant and minimum AC is reached. At $x > \frac{1}{2}$, returns to scale decrease.

(vii) Since it has to pay the $\frac{1}{3}$ unit of labour, whatever output it produces, it will set the labour to work, producing whatever output they will produce ($\frac{1}{3} = x - x^2 + x^3$). But it will not employ any extra labour since the marginal returns would be less than the marginal cost.

Q7-2 False. For any particular output LMC > SMC only if existing plant is larger than optimal for that output: the relatively large plant reduces SMC.

Q7-3 (i) min $K + L - \lambda (K^{1/4}L^{1/4} - x)$

So

$$K = L$$

$$K^{1/4}L^{1/4} = x$$

So

$$K = L = x^2$$

Thus

$$C = K + L = 2x^2$$

And

$$p = \frac{\partial C}{\partial x} = 4x$$

(ii) From the production function $x = L^{1/4}$

Therefore

$$C = 1 + L = 1 + x^4$$

And

$$p = \frac{\partial C}{\partial x} = 4x^3$$

Hence $x = 4^{-1/3}p^{1/3}$. SRS has lower elasticity than LRS ($\frac{1}{3}$ against 1).

If $K = 1$ is optimal, LRC = SRC.

So

$$2x^2 = 1 + x^4$$

This gives

$$(x^2 - 1)(x^2 - 1) = 0$$

Thus

$$x = 1$$

(iii)

$$x = 2^{1/4}L^{1/4} \qquad \text{so} \qquad L = \frac{x^4}{2}$$

Thus

$$C = K + L = 2 + \frac{x^4}{2}$$

Intercept is higher and slope lower.

(iv) (a) If any output is produced,

$$p = 4x^3 = 4$$

So

$$x = 1$$

and

$$\pi = px - (1 + x^4) - 2.5$$

$$= 4(1) - (1 + 1) - 2.5$$

$$= -0.5$$

Therefore no output will be produced.

(b) If any output is produced,

$$p = 4x = 4$$

So

$$x = 1$$

and
$$\pi = px - 2x^2 - 2.5$$
$$= 4(1) - 2(1)^2 - 2.5$$
$$= -0.5$$

If no output is produced, K has to be paid for.

So
$$\pi = -1$$

and output *is* produced, with $x = 1$.

Q7-4 Sunk "costs" are never relevant to any economic decision. True costs are only those that can be escaped by decisions taken now. (Quotation due to S. Nickell.)

Q7-5 (i) max $L = p_1 x_1 + p_2 x_2 + \lambda[L^0 - f(x_1, x_2)]$

   First-order conditions

$$\frac{p_1}{f_1} = \frac{p_2}{f_2} = \lambda$$

$$L^0 - f(x_1, x_2) = 0$$

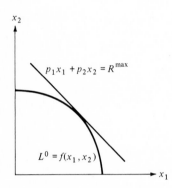

Second-order conditions. The product transformation curve $f(x_1, x_2) = L^0$ must be concave to the origin. Hence

$$f_2^2 f_{11} - 2 f_1 f_2 f_{12} + f_1^2 f_{22} > 0$$

(The proof of this is as in Question 5-8, but with the signs reversed—in that case we had indifference curves *convex* to the origin.)

   (ii)   max $\pi = p_1 x_1 + p_2 x_2 - w_L f(x_1, x_2)$

   First-order conditions

$$\frac{p_1}{f_1} = \frac{p_2}{f_2} = w_L$$

   Second-order conditions

Since
$$d\pi = (p_1 - w_L f_1) dx_1 + (p_2 - w_L f_2) dx_2$$

$$d^2\pi = -w_L f_{11} dx_1^2 - 2w_L f_{12} dx_1 dx_2 - w_L f_{22} dx_2^2 < 0 \qquad \text{for all } dx_i$$

Thus
$$f_{11} dx_1^2 + 2 f_{12} dx_1 dx_2 + f_{22} dx_2^2 > 0$$

This implies that the cost function

$$L = f(x_1, x_2)$$

is not concave (see Appendix 1), i.e., there is rising marginal cost. Specifically we require

$$f_{11}, f_{22} > 0$$

$$f_{11}f_{22} - f_{12}^2 > 0$$

Q7-6 min AC $= 200/x^i + 10 + 2x^i$

$$\frac{dAC}{dx^i} = -\frac{200}{x^{i2}} + 2 = 0$$

So $$x^i = 10$$

and $$AC = 20 + 10 + 20 = 50 = p$$

Therefore $$x = 800 - 400 = 400$$

Q7-7 (iii).

Q7-8 (i) Assuming that firms have different production functions, firms previously producing more than x^0/n units produce less than before. This induces a rise in price so that firms previously producing less than x^0/n units increase output. However, output will never reach its former level since the supply curve is now shifted upwards, each firm's supply becoming infinitely inelastic at x^0/n units.

(ii) If coupons are transferable, firms previously producing more than x^0/n units will find it worthwhile to bid for extra coupons, and other firms will be happy to sell them. Suppose for convenience that output price is unchanged. Then a firm previously producing more than x^0/n will have a demand curve for coupons as shown below.

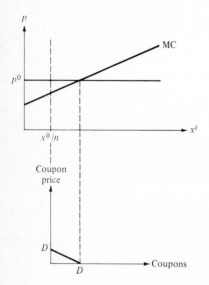

Firms previously producing x^{i0} less than x^0/n will be willing to sell for any nonnegative price any amount of coupons up to $x^0/n - x^{i0}$. At a coupon price of zero the demand for coupons from those previously producing more than x^0/n will exactly equal the maximum supply from those previously producing less. So equilibrium coupon price is practically zero and output quantity x^0.

Q7-9 (i) Rental = operating profit = revenue − cost = shaded area

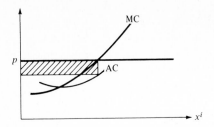

(ii) Yes—the marginal field (if there is one) and all fields not worth operating. The marginal field has the following AC curve.

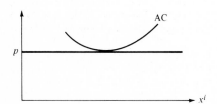

(iii) If originally not all fields were used, the number of fields used will increase, as marginal fields become profitable. Existing fields will increase output and acquire higher rental values.

Q7-10 (i) False. The tax will raise the minimum price at which each firm is willing to produce anything and thus raise the industry supply curve. (Try drawing this.)

(ii) Unless special assumptions are made, all output will be sold on the black market. The supply price in the black market is the normal supply price plus $\$\alpha f$, so the black market price is greater than p^0.

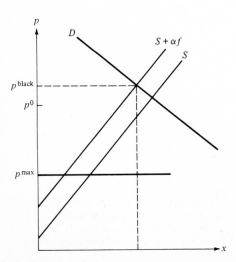

Q7-11 False. Assume that demand is large relative to the capacity of any one plane and that demand does not fluctuate. Then extra planes will be supplied so long as the cost per plane is less than the price of seats times the capacity of a plane, but not beyond. Thus the marginal plane makes neither profit nor loss and intramarginal planes make profits if the supply of planes is upward sloping. If demand fluctuates, it will pay to have some spare capacity on the average, but planes will not be supplied if they are not on average expected to make a profit.

Q7-12 The supply price of a unit of x is the supply price of a unit of sheep (defined to provide 1 unit of x) minus the demand price for the corresponding unit of y. Hence

$$p_x^S = 1 - (2 - x) = -1 + x$$

This holds so long as $x < 2$. At that point p_y has fallen to zero and will fall no further. For $x > 2$, $p_x^S = 1$. All marginal costs are charged to x.

Q7-13 (i) False. Only if there is an increase in industry output does the diseconomy come about.

(ii) True. If firms have different production functions, one firm may be more than usually intensive in a factor whose price rises. Thus, when price rises and industry output expands, its MC curve rises so much that output falls.

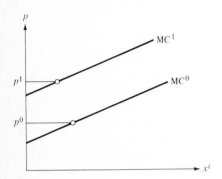

But this analysis can only apply to some firms, not to the generality, for the reason given in (i) above.

Q7-14 Raise it. (i) If the supply of tractors to the industry were infinitely elastic, a binding constraint would mean that no tractors could be used, since none are supplied. In effect the price of tractors has been *raised* to infinity! So the supply price of potatoes must rise for each quantity. Market price will consequently rise.

(ii) If the supply curve of tractors is rising, we first ask: Assuming no price control, at what level of potato output (x^0) would the price of tractors have reached the maximum permitted price? For the constraint to be binding, it follows that the original quantity of potatoes exceeded x^0. We now ask: What happens to the marginal cost of potatoes for quantities of potatoes greater than x^0? The answer is that no further tractors can be used beyond those used when output is x^0, so once again the supply price of potatoes must have risen.

Q7-15 (i) Increase.

(ii) Increase.

Q7-16 The industry supply curve is

$$p = 50 - 0.025x$$

Demand is

$$p = 100 - 0.125x$$

Therefore with no intervention (at equilibrium)

$$0.1x = 50$$

So

$$x = 500$$

$$p = 37.5$$

(i) A maximum price of \$40 makes no difference.
(ii) Output falls to zero.
(iii) Output is limited by the demand curve. Thus

$$40 = 100 - 0.125x$$

$$x = 480$$

At this position there is downward pressure on the legal minimum price as the diagram below shows.

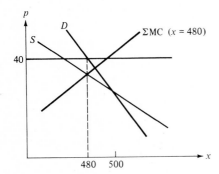

[Note that under external economies producing forward-falling supply curves, the general rule that quantity traded at price p is the minimum of $D(p)$ and $S(p)$ does not apply.]

Q7-17 False, unless the supply curve of oleo margarine is forward-falling. For the butter quota will raise the price of butter, thus raising the demand for oleo margarine.

Q7-18 Freshmen take four years to graduate. If in one year wages are high, many students enter engineering. This floods the market for new engineers four years later, which depresses new engineers' wages and reduces freshman intake into engineering in that year. This raises wages four years later, and we are back where we started.

Q7-19 False. If there is a unique stable equilibrium for the system, no disturbance from the equilibrium can generate a new equilibrium.

Q7-20 (i) If a subsidy of \$1 b per unit is paid

$$4 - x = 1 + x - 1$$

So

$$x = 2$$

$$\text{Seller's price} = 1 + x = 3$$

$$\text{Net income} = \text{quantity} \times \text{seller's price} - \text{cost of quantity}$$

If the same net income is to be guaranteed by government buying, the same sellers' price and quantity have to be achieved by a shift of the demand curve. But the sellers' price is now the same as the buyers' price of \$3 b. The private sector will only buy 1 unit ($3 = 4 - x$). So the government must buy 1 unit. The cost to the government will be \$3 b, higher than for the subsidy programme (\$2 b).

(ii) If there are no external effects of scale, costs are measured by the area under the supply curve

$$= 1x + \tfrac{1}{2}x^2$$

$$= 1(2) + \tfrac{1}{2}2^2 = 4$$

Thus   Net income $= 2$

If there are external diseconomies of scale, the area under the supply curve underestimates the area under the $\sum$ MC curve for current output.

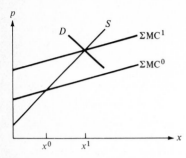

Therefore the calculation exaggerates net income.

Q8-1 (i) $w^D = 40{,}000 - 100x$

$$\text{MC} = 10{,}000 + 200x$$

Therefore $x = 100$

$$w^S = 20{,}000$$

$$\eta = \frac{dx}{dw^S}\frac{w^S}{x} = \frac{1}{100}\frac{20{,}000}{100} = 2$$

(ii) Yes. If the supply were completely inelastic, the monopsonist would be happy to pay an infinitely small price.

Q8-2 (i) True. Take a case where $w^* < w^{\min} < w'$. The marginal cost curve is indicated by the dashed line. This cuts the MB curve at $x > x^*$.

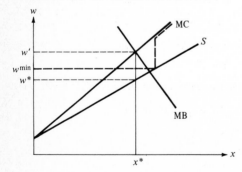

Check also that optimum $x > x^*$ when $w^e > w^{\min} > w^*$, where w^e corresponds to the intersection of MB and S.

(ii) True. Try drawing the analogous diagram to prove it.

(iii) True. For example, if MC was only just positive and the demand curve was linear, p/MC could be nearly infinite.

(iv) False. The following monopolist does not. In this case (of increasing returns) a competitive solution is impossible. Chamberlin maintains that this position is commonly found among monopolists producing goods for which there are a large number of sellers of similar but slightly

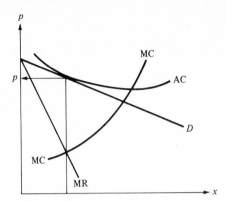

differentiated products (e.g., branded goods) (see E. H. Chamberlin, *The Theory of Monopolistic Competition*, 5th ed., Harvard University Press, Cambridge, Mass., 1946). The details of his theory have the drawback that they depend upon our being able to group products into groups within which there is a high elasticity of substitution between products, and between which groups there is a much lower elasticity of substitution. In fact the real world may exhibit more of a continuum.

Q8-3 (i) *EHG* (assuming *D* is the compensated demand curve).

(ii) *p*I*FG*.

Q8-4 (i) Flights booked well ahead tend to be holiday trips; and those at short notice, business trips, with lower demand elasticities. It is also of course cheaper to provide a seat booked well ahead, but this cost difference is much less than the price difference.

(ii) No. Agents would buy ahead and resell at short notice.

Q8-5 In each case, first work out the interior solution, assuming it is globally optimal. Then check whether it is. Watch out.

(i) $MR_1 = MC$ and $MR_2 = MC$. Thus

$$3 - x_1 = 1 \qquad x_1 = 2 \qquad p_1 = 3 - 1 = 2 \qquad \varepsilon_1 = 2$$

$$2 - x_2 = 1 \qquad x_2 = 1 \qquad p_2 = 2 - \tfrac{1}{2} = \tfrac{3}{2} \qquad \varepsilon_2 = 3$$

$$R = p_1 x_1 + p_2 x_2 = 5\tfrac{1}{2}$$

$$C = 2\tfrac{1}{3} + x_1 + x_2 = 5\tfrac{1}{3} < R$$

(ii) If price discrimination were banned, the aggregate demand curve in the relevant neighbourhood is

$$x_1 + x_2 = 2(3 - p) + 2(2 - p) = 10 - 4p$$

Hence
$$p = \tfrac{10}{4} - \tfrac{1}{4}(x_1 + x_2)$$

$$MR = \tfrac{10}{4} - \tfrac{1}{2}(x_1 + x_2) = MC = 1$$

So
$$x_1 + x_2 = (\tfrac{10}{4} - 1)2 = 3 \qquad p = \tfrac{10}{4} - \tfrac{3}{4} = \tfrac{7}{4}$$

Therefore
$$R = \tfrac{21}{4} = 5\tfrac{1}{4}$$

$$C = 5\tfrac{1}{3} > R$$

Nothing would be produced. Price discrimination is a condition for the firm's existence.

(iii) In this case it is desirable: without it the consumer's surplus would be lost. In general it is an inefficient way of distributing a given quantity, but since the effect on quantity may be positive or negative, no general conclusion follows. (With perfect price discrimination, of course, quantity increases and so does welfare.)

Q8-6 (i) No. The benefit from a given change in price would be too small to warrant the cost of generating it.

(ii) Yes, if firms differed in efficiency. The collective benefit would be large enough to warrant the cost of some advertising.

(iii) Yes (if they differed in efficiency). Suppose the demand curve is $p = p(x, A)$, where A is advertising expenditure. Costs are $C(x) + A$.

$$\pi = xp(x, A) - C(x) - A$$

$$\frac{\partial \pi}{\partial A} = xp_A(x, A) - 1 = 0$$

$$\frac{\partial \pi}{\partial x} = p(x, A) + xp_x(x, A) - C'(x) = 0$$

Solve for x, A. (Second-order conditions and also total conditions must be satisfied.)

(iv) False. A firm welcomes *any* upward shift in its demand curve, for it can sell a given output at a higher price.

Q8-7 (i) First construct the firm's marginal cost curve: this is the horizontal sum of the MC curves of the two plants, provided it is optimal to use them both. $MC_1 = 2$, $MC_2 = 1 + x_2$. If the first unit were produced in plant 1 it would cost 2, whereas if produced in plant 2, it would only cost $1\frac{3}{4}$. So the first units of production do occur in plant 2 up to $x = 1$. For $x > 1$, $MC = 2$. Assume provisionally that both plants are used. Then

$$MR = 4 - x = MC = 2$$

Hence
$$x = 2 \qquad x_1 = 1 \qquad x_2 = 1$$

So
$$p = 4 - 1 = 3$$

This is satisfactory.

(ii) False. Consider a given output x^0. Suppose costs are $C_1 = F(x_1)$ in the *falling* marginal cost plant and $C_2 = R(x_2)$ in the *rising* marginal cost plant. The problem is

$$\min C = C_1 + C_2 = F(x_1) + R(x^0 - x_1)$$

If there is an interior solution, then

$$\frac{dC}{dx_1} = F'(x_1) - R'(x^0 - x_1) = 0 \qquad \text{(marginal costs equal)}$$

$$\frac{d^2C}{dx_1^2} = F''(x_1) + R''(x^0 - x_1) > 0$$

The second-order condition requires that the rate at which R' rises with x_2 must exceed the rate at which F' falls with x_1 (see diagram). If these conditions are satisfied, production will occur in both plants so long as it is not better to concentrate production in one plant only; i.e., provided

$$F(x_1^*) + R(x^0 - x_1^*) < F(x^0)$$

and
$$F(x_1^*) + R(x^0 - x_1^*) < R(x^0)$$

If diversification is not optimal, production will only occur in the falling marginal cost plant if

$$F(x^0) < R(x^0)$$

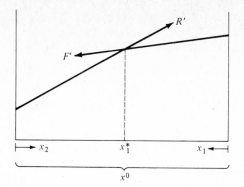

Q8-8 (i) Assume that each firm is producing at minimum AC and then check that this is feasible:

$$AC^i = \frac{1}{x^i} + 1 + x^i$$

$$\frac{d(AC^i)}{dx^i} = -\frac{1}{x^{i2}} + 1 = 0$$

So

$$x^i = 1$$

Hence

$$AC = 3 = p$$

And demand is

$$3 = 5 - \tfrac{1}{12}x$$

Hence

$$x = 24$$

$$n^e = \frac{x}{x_i} = 24$$

Since this is an integer, it is consistent with each firm producing at min AC.

(ii)

$$MC^i = \frac{d}{dx^i}\left(1 + x^i + x^{i2}\right) = 1 + 2x^i$$

$$MR = 5 - \frac{x}{6} = 5 - \frac{24x^i}{6}$$

So

$$5 - 4x^i = 1 + 2x^i$$

Thus

$$x^i = \tfrac{2}{3}$$

Hence

$$p = 5 - \tfrac{16}{12} = \tfrac{11}{3}$$

(iii) For a member

$$\pi^i = px^i - C(x^i) = \tfrac{11}{3}\tfrac{2}{3} - 1 - \tfrac{2}{3} - \tfrac{4}{9}$$

$$= \tfrac{3}{9} = \tfrac{1}{3}$$

For an interloper, first find his optimum output

$$1 + 2x^i = \tfrac{11}{3}$$

Therefore

$$x^i = \tfrac{4}{3}$$

Hence

$$\pi^i = \tfrac{11}{3}\tfrac{4}{3} - 1 - \tfrac{4}{3} - \tfrac{16}{9} = \tfrac{7}{9}$$

(iv) In equilibrium $\pi^i = 0$, so

$$px^i = 1 + x^i + x^{i2} \tag{1}$$

Let the equilibrium number be n:

$$p = 5 - \tfrac{1}{12}nx^i \tag{2}$$

The cartel's marginal revenue must equal marginal cost. Hence

$$5 - \tfrac{1}{6}nx^i = 1 + 2x^i \tag{3}$$

From (1) and (2)

$$n = \left(\frac{4}{x^i} - \frac{1}{x^{i2}} - 1\right)0.12 \tag{4}$$

From (4) and (3)

$$x^i = \tfrac{1}{2}$$

Thus

$$n = (8 - 4 - 1)0.12 = 36$$

(v) If protection was withdrawn, price would be determined by the intersection of demand with supply from 36 firms.

Therefore

$$5 - \frac{36x^i}{12} = 1 + 2x^i$$

So

$$x^i = \tfrac{4}{5}$$

$$p = \tfrac{13}{5}$$

$$\pi^i = px^i - 1 - x^i - x^{i2} = -\tfrac{9}{25}$$

The original firms would have done better not to have founded the cartel. The moral is that nowadays political forecasting is an important element in business success.

Q8-9 The aim is to induce firms voluntarily to choose $x^i = \tfrac{2}{3}$ when the market price is $\tfrac{11}{3}$. If α is the fraction of revenue pooled, the firm's marginal revenue will be $\tfrac{11}{3}(1 - \alpha)$.

Thus

$$\tfrac{11}{3}(1 - \alpha) = \{MC^i \,|\, x^i = \tfrac{2}{3}\} = 1 + 2(\tfrac{2}{3}) = \tfrac{7}{3}$$

This gives

$$\alpha = \tfrac{4}{11}$$

Q8-10 No answer available.

8-11 In period 0, $x^{B0} = b$
In period 1, $MR^A = 1 - 2x^A - b = MC^A = 0$

Hence

$$x^A = \frac{1 - b}{2}$$

So

$$MR^B = 1 - x^A - 2x^B = 1 - \frac{1 - b}{2} - 2x^B = 0$$

Thus

$$x^{B1} = \frac{2 - 1 + b}{2^2} = \frac{1}{4} + \frac{b}{4}$$

$$= \frac{1}{4} + \frac{x^{B0}}{4}$$

The solution of this difference equation is

$$x^{Bt} = \tfrac{1}{3} + (\tfrac{1}{4})^t(b - \tfrac{1}{3})$$

This tends to $\tfrac{1}{3}$ as $t \to \infty$, approaching it continuously from b without oscillation.

Q8-12 The reaction functions can be written

$$f(x^A, x^B) = 0 \qquad \text{A's function}$$

$$g(x^A, x^B) = 0 \qquad \text{B's function}$$

Provided that the absolute slope

$$\left| \frac{dx^B}{dx^A} \right|_{g=0} < \left| \frac{dx^B}{dx^A} \right|_{f=0}$$

equilibrium is stable. The diagram indicates why. If we start with $x^A = x^{A0}$, this induces x^{B0}, which induces x^{A1}. Try swopping the functions and repeating the exercise to show that instability would result.

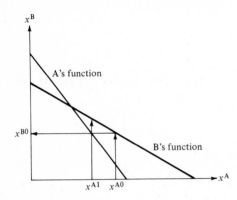

Q8-13 (i) The firm knows that, whatever the price, it will get one-half market demand

Hence
$$p = 1 - 2x^i \qquad i = \text{A, B}$$

So
$$MR^i = 1 - 4x^i$$

$$MR^i = MC^i = 0$$

Thus
$$x^i = \tfrac{1}{4}$$

$$x = \tfrac{1}{2}$$

This is the monopoly solution.
  (ii) The same.

$$p = 1 - \frac{1}{k} x^A$$

So
$$1 - \frac{2}{k} x^A = 0$$

Hence
$$x^A = \frac{k}{2} \qquad x^B = \frac{1-k}{2} \qquad x = \frac{1}{2}$$

Q8-14

$$x^A = x^A(p^A, p^B) \tag{1}$$

$$x^B = x^B(p^A, p^B) \tag{2}$$

(i) From (1) and (2) we can find a function

$$x^A = f^A(p^A, x^B)$$

Therefore A's revenue is

$$R^A = g^A(x^A, x^B)$$

And

$$\frac{\partial \pi^A}{\partial x^A} = \frac{\partial g^A}{\partial x^A}(x^A, x^B) - C^{A'}(x^A) = 0 \tag{3}$$

Similarly

$$\frac{\partial \pi^B}{\partial x^B} = \frac{\partial g^B}{\partial x^B}(x^A, x^B) - C^{B'}(x^B) = 0 \tag{4}$$

Equations (3) and (4) give the Cournot equilibrium values of x^A and x^B (and hence of p^A and p^B).

(ii) From (1)

$$R^A = h^A(p^A, p^B)$$

Therefore

$$\pi^A = h^A(p^A, p^B) - C^A[x^A(p^A, p^B)]$$

Thus

$$\frac{\partial \pi^A}{\partial p^A} = \frac{\partial h^A}{\partial p^A}(p^A, p^B) - C^{A'}\frac{\partial x^A}{\partial p^A}(p^A, p^B) = 0$$

Similarly

$$\frac{\partial \pi^B}{\partial p^B} = \frac{\partial h^B}{\partial p^B}(p^A, p^B) - C^{B'}\frac{\partial x^B}{\partial p^B}(p^A, p^B) = 0$$

The last two equations give the equilibrium values of p^A and p^B (and hence of x^A and x^B).

Q9-1 (i)
$$v_i \eta^D = \tfrac{1}{3}(-3) = -1$$

(ii)
$$\frac{v_i \eta^D}{1 - (1 - v_i)\eta^D/\eta^S} = \frac{-1}{1 - \tfrac{2}{3}\tfrac{1}{10}(-3)} = -\frac{30}{30 + 6} = -\frac{5}{6}$$

Q9-2 False. $|\varepsilon_{ii}| \approx |v_i \eta^D| < |\eta^D|$. Market power is understated.

Q9-3 No. The demand curve for K assumes that one is moving along the supply curve of L, not along its demand curve.

Q9-4 The analogy is the basic idea that one price must equal a weighted average of two others with fixed weights. Here

$$p_1 + p_2 = w$$

So
$$p_2 = w - p_1 = 1 + z - (10 - x_1) = 2z - 9$$

Thus
$$p_2 = 2x_2 - 9 \qquad (x_2 > \tfrac{9}{2})$$

Q9-5 $s_{KL} < 1$ provided

(i) There has been no nonneutral technical progress (see Chapter 10)
(ii) There are no nonneutral technical differences between countries, and
(iii) It is legitimate to think in terms of an aggregate production function.

Q9-6 (i)

$$s_{KL} = \frac{1}{1 + \rho} = \frac{1}{2}$$

(ii)

$$x = [0.2(2) + 0.8]^{-1} = \frac{1}{1.2}$$

$$x_L L = 0.8 \left(\frac{x}{L}\right)^2 L = 0.8 \left(\frac{1}{1.2}\right)^2$$

$$x_K K = 0.2 \left(\frac{y}{K}\right)^2 K = 0.2 \left(\frac{1}{1.2}\right)^2 2$$

Hence

$$\frac{x_L L}{x_K K} = 2$$

(iii)

$$x = (0.2 + 0.8)^{-1} = 1$$

$x_L L = 0.8$ it has risen

$x_K K = 0.2$ it has fallen, since $s_{KL} < x_L L/x$

$\dfrac{x_L L}{x_K K} = 4$ it has risen, since $s_{KL} < 1$

(iv)

$$\frac{x_L}{x_K} = \frac{0.8}{0.2} \left(\frac{K}{L}\right)^2 = 1$$

Thus

$$\left(\frac{K}{L}\right)^2 = \frac{1}{4} \qquad \frac{K}{L} = \frac{1}{2}$$

Q9-7 Find K/L as a function of w_L/w_K:

$$\frac{x_L}{x_K} = \frac{0.8}{0.2} \left(\frac{K}{L}\right)^{x 2}$$

So

$$\left(\frac{K}{L}\right)^x = 0.5 \left(\frac{w_L}{w_K}\right)^{1/2}$$

$$\frac{y_L}{y_K} = 2 \left(\frac{K}{L}\right)^y$$

So

$$\left(\frac{K}{L}\right)^y = 0.5 \frac{w_L}{w_K}$$

For low w_L/w_K,

$$\left(\frac{K}{L}\right)^x > \left(\frac{K}{L}\right)^y$$

For high w_L/w_K,

$$\left(\frac{K}{L}\right)^x < \left(\frac{K}{L}\right)^y$$

Factor intensities are equal at

$$0.5 \frac{w_L}{w_K} = 0.5 \left(\frac{w_L}{w_K}\right)^{1/2}$$

Hence

$$\frac{w_L}{w_K} = 1$$

To remind yourself of the relevance of this, glance at Figures 2-13 and 2-14.

Q9-8 The author of the study (S. Bowles, *Planning Educational Systems for Economic Growth*, Harvard Economic Studies, Vol. 133, Cambridge, Mass., 1969, Chap. 3) claimed that this supported an approach in which relative wages were taken as constant. We disagree for reasons about to be given.

Q9-9

$$f_S = \delta\left(\frac{x}{Q}\right)^{1+\rho_2}(1-\alpha)\left(\frac{Q}{S}\right)^{1+\rho_1}$$

$$f_N = (1-\delta)\left(\frac{x}{N}\right)^{1+\rho_2}$$

Thus

$$\log f_S = \log \delta + (1+\rho_2)\log x - (1+\rho_2)\log Q$$
$$+ \log(1-\alpha) + (1+\rho_1)\log Q - (1+\rho_1)\log S$$

So

$$\frac{\partial \log f_S}{\partial K} = (1+\rho_2)\frac{\partial \log x}{\partial K} + (\rho_1-\rho_2)\frac{\partial \log Q}{\partial K}$$

$$\log f_N = \log(1-\delta) + (1+\rho_2)\log x - (1+\rho_2)\log N$$

Hence

$$\frac{\partial \log f_N}{\partial K} = (1+\rho_2)\frac{\partial \log x}{\partial K}$$

Therefore

$$\frac{\partial \log f_S}{\partial K} > \frac{\partial \log f_N}{\partial K} \text{ if } \rho_1 - \rho_2 > 0$$

Q9-10 (i) Underestimate. For the countries with more educated people relative to uneducated (higher S/N) also have higher K/N. The extra capital raises the relative skill differential in the more educated countries above the level that would prevail if they had the same K/N as the less educated countries. So if K/N were constant, f_S/f_N would fall more (as S/N rises) than it does as we move across countries letting K/N vary. The evidence suggests that $\rho_1 > \rho_2$ (see P. Fallon and R. Layard, "Capital-Skill Complementarity, Income Distribution and Output Accounting," *Journal of Political Economy*, vol. 83, no. 2, pp. 279-301, April 1975).

(ii) S and N would need to be separable from K (see Chapter 5), i.e., $x = f[K, g(S, N)]$. In the two-level CES case this would mean putting S and N in the nest.

Q10-1 (i) Let x_1 be cattle (herds) and x_2 be corn (units) (see diagram opposite)

$$\max \pi = 70{,}000x_1 + 50{,}000x_2$$

such that

$$2x_1 + \tfrac{2}{3}x_2 \leq 1 \qquad \text{(land)} \qquad\qquad (z_1)$$

$$7x_1 + \tfrac{7}{2}x_2 \leq 7 \qquad \text{(nonsummer labour)} \qquad (z_2)$$

$$7x_1 + 7x_2 \leq 7 \qquad \text{(summer labour)} \qquad (z_3)$$

The solution is at P since on a equal-revenue contour

$$\left|\frac{dX_2}{dX_1}\right| = \frac{7}{5}$$

and this lies between the slopes of the two constraints that cross at P (land, summer labour). So these constraints are binding.

Thus

$$2x_1 + \tfrac{2}{3}x_2 = 1$$

$$x_1 + x_2 = 1$$

So

$$\tfrac{4}{3}x_2 = 1$$

This gives

$$x_2 = \tfrac{3}{4}$$

$$x_1 = \tfrac{1}{4}$$

$$\pi = \tfrac{1}{4}(70{,}000) + \tfrac{3}{4}(50{,}000) = 55{,}000$$

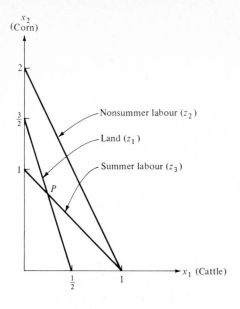

(ii)

$$70,000 = 2w_1 + 7(12)w_3$$

$$50,000 = \tfrac{2}{3}w_1 + 7(12)w_3$$

where w_3 is the shadow price per man day during summer, and w_1 is the shadow price per square mile per year.

Hence

$$\tfrac{4}{3}w_1 = 20,000$$

$$w_1 = 15,000$$

$$w_3 = \frac{40,000}{12(7)} \simeq 470 \qquad w_2 = 0$$

(iii) Yes, since the market price of summer labour ($100) is less than its shadow price at P ($470). (Nonsummer labour is of no interest since it is dominated by the land constraint.) Thus, if we move to R by hiring summer labour, we do better than by staying at P with no hired summer labour. (We would never find an optimal solution between P and R.) The corn output at R is $\tfrac{3}{2}$ units requiring $7(\tfrac{3}{2})$ man days per week in summer and thus $7(\tfrac{1}{2})$ hired man days per week for 12 weeks.

So

$$\pi = \tfrac{3}{2}(50,000) - \tfrac{7}{2}(12)100 \simeq 70,800 > 55,000$$

Therefore, plough up all land.†

Q10-2 The z_1 and z_2 constraints are binding. Thus

$$4x_1 + x_2 = z_1$$

Also

$$x_1 + 3x_2 = 21$$

---

† We could handle the possibility of hiring summer labour by introducing a third activity (x_3) called buying summer labour. This would have a coefficient of -100 in the profit function and of 1 in the summer labour constraint.

or, equivalently,
$$4x_1 + 12x_2 = 84$$

Hence
$$11x_2 = 84 - z_1$$

Thus
$$x_2 = \frac{84 - z_1}{11}$$

and
$$x_1 = 21 - \frac{252 - 3z_1}{11} = \frac{3z_1}{11} - \frac{21}{11}$$

Hence
$$\frac{dx_2}{dz_1} = -\frac{1}{11} \qquad \frac{dx_1}{dz_1} = \frac{3}{11}$$

But
$$\pi = 2x_1 + 5x_2$$

So
$$\frac{d\pi}{dz_1} = 2\frac{3}{11} - \frac{5}{11} = \frac{1}{11}$$

Q10-3 (i) but not (ii).

Q11-1

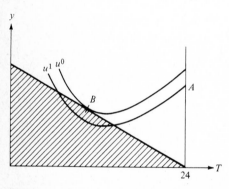

His opportunity set consists of the shaded area plus point A. He prefers point B to point A.

Q11-2 (i) Yes. New budget line lies outside old choice position. So real income rises. Income effect is towards leisure, as is substitution effect.

(ii) Not necessarily. New budget line lies inside old choice position. Now either (a) real income rises and work effort falls, or (b) real income falls and work effort rises or falls, depending on relative strength of income and substitution effects.

Q11-3 (i)

$$\frac{u_T}{u_y} = T^{-1/2} = w$$

So
$$T = 24 - H = w^{-2}$$

Thus
$$H = 24 - w^{-2}$$

(ii) If $H = 0$, $w^{-2} = 24$

Hence
$$w \simeq 0.2$$

(iii)
$$\frac{dH}{dw} = 2w^{-3} > 0$$

Therefore hours increase.

The supply function is

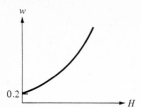

(iv) A change in the real wage has the same effect, however produced, if the theory is right. For some evidence that it is see M. Abbott and O. Ashenfelter, "Labour Supply, Commodity Demand, and the Allocation of Time," *Review of Economic Studies*, vol. 43, pp. 389–412, October 1976.

Q11-4 (i) Yes. With his main employer his opportunity set is the shaded area. He might well prefer a point such as *B* to *A*.

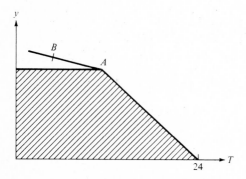

(ii) No. The budget constraint is as follows

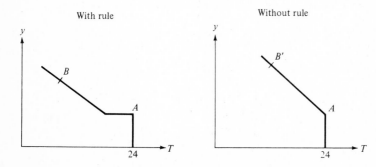

Under the rule, if leisure is a good, pensioners will either not work (i.e., consume at *A*) or work enough to receive no pension (e.g., consume at *B*). Without the rule, the position is as follows.

    (a) Pensioners who do not work with the rule, because *A* is preferred to any other feasible point, may prefer to work when the feasible region is extended. They will then pay tax, which is a gain to the treasury. The gain arises because a discontinuity in the opportunity set has been eliminated.

(b) Pensioners who work under the rule will work less if it is abolished (e.g., consume at B'), assuming leisure is not inferior. Their tax payments were previously

$$t(wH^0 - P) = twH^0 - tP$$

where P is the pension. Now their net payments to the treasury are

$$twH^1 - P$$

Since $H^1 < H^0$, their net payments have fallen. The relative size of the two effects [(a) and (b)] is an empirical question.

(iii) At \$5.5 per hour workers will work fewer hours (income and substitution effects work the same way). So, if the employer was previously obtaining $50n$ man hours by employing n men at a cost of \$$(275n + 10n)$, he would now have to hire more men (say m) to get $50n$ man hours, and the cost would be \$$(275n + 10m)$, where $m > n$. The employer refuses, if he has studied economic theory.

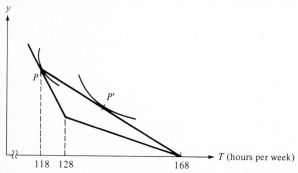

T (hours per week)

Q11-5 (i) Less. The earnings foregone per hour of wife's leisure is the same (i.e., the price is the same). But the family is richer and demands more leisure. In addition the husband's wage has risen, so there may be a cross-substitution effect in which her leisure is raised assuming the two types of leisure are p-substitutes.

(ii) We cannot say for certain, as the income effect and substitution effect work in opposite directions.

Q11-6 It equals unity. He spends a constant fraction of his endowment on leisure.

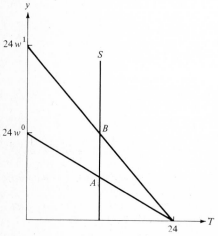

If $s = 1$, S is backward-bending. If $s > 1$, S is forward-rising.

Q11-7 (i) False. If leisure is a luxury, T/y rises as unearned income rises (w constant). This is not necessary for the supply curve to be backward-bending—see this example.

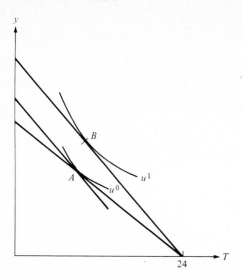

(ii) True. Only a negative income effect could offset the substitution effect toward more earnings. (The example requires earnings to be a Giffen good.)

Q11-8 True, if the supply curve is rising. False, if the supply curve is backward-bending, in which case we have (assuming market stability):

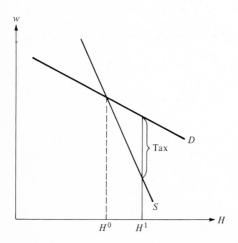

Q11-9 (i) c/b indicates the money value which people place on time in its best alternative use *minus* the value they place on travelling to the Lake District.

(ii) People may well like travelling inside the Lake District more than travelling to it, in which case c/b would be smaller.

Q11-10 (i) The value of poor people's time relative to goods is less than the value of rich people's time. They are, therefore, less willing to pay barbers a higher (goods) price to ensure the ready availability of a barber.

(ii) Time is relatively cheaper in India and goods are more expensive.

Q11-11

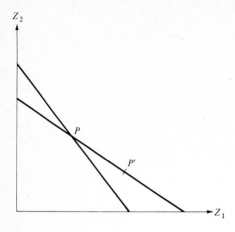

Original consumption point is P; new point is P'. Slope of the budget line through P and P' is the full price of Z_1 divided by the full price of Z_2. So

$$-\frac{dZ_2}{dZ_1} = \frac{a_1 p'_1 + t_1 w}{a_2 p_2 + t_2 w}$$

We wish to find the effect on leisure time $(t_1 Z_1 + t_2 Z_2)$ of an increase in Z_1 along this compensated budget line.

$$\frac{d}{dZ_1}(t_1 Z_1 + t_2 Z_2) = t_1 + t_2 \frac{dZ_2}{dZ_1} = t_1 - t_2 \frac{a_1 p'_1 + t_1 w}{a_2 p_2 + t_2 w}$$

$$= \frac{t_1 a_2 p_2 - t_2 a_1 p'_1}{a_2 p_2 + t_2 w}$$

But

$$\frac{t_1}{a_1 p'_1} > \frac{t_1}{a_1 p_1} > \frac{t_2}{a_2 p_2}$$

Thus leisure rises.

Q11-12 False. It all depends what differential they agreed on. The supply curve is infinitely elastic at their agreed differential. As Figure 11-3 shows, the differential would be greatest if everyone disliked A as much as the most passionate A-hater, but smaller (and of opposite sign) if everyone liked A as much as the most passionate A-lover.

Q11-13 False. In competitive equilibrium every price is a demand price as well as a supply price.

Q11-14 (i) The present value of the benefits and costs must be equal. Suppose we evaluate these in present values measured at the end of the course. Thus

$$\frac{2100}{0.1} = w_B + w_B(1.1) = w_B(2.1)$$

So

$$w_B = \frac{2100}{0.21} = 10,000$$

(ii) Yes, in the short run; no, in the long run.
(iii) Yes in both.

Q11-15 It depends who owns the human capital. If the student owns it, there is (in a world of certainty) no reason why the costs of his education should be subsidised beyond the value of any external benefits which his education confers on the rest of society (higher net tax receipts, unrequited social work, etc.). But if the state acquires a title to a further share of the human capital rental (by, for example, a tax surcharge on graduates), then further subsidy is justified. This might be desirable on the grounds that the returns to education are uncertain, and sharing the costs and returns is an efficient way of reducing the cost of risk (see Chapter 13). Against this is the efficiency loss from high tax rates.

If students are known to underestimate the returns to education, this could constitute a further case for subsidy.

Q11-16 This question involves empirical issues. However, those who get higher education are on average abler and endowed with better capital-market opportunities and inherited nonhuman wealth than the average citizen. There is then an a priori expectation that, if higher education subsidies and the corresponding taxes were reduced, inequality would be reduced. But, given the imperfection of the capital market, some able people from poor families will be excluded from higher education. There could therefore be an efficiency loss.

Q11-17 True.

Q12-1 (i) Slope of $PF = -1.1$

$$\text{Slope of } IC = \frac{dc_1}{dc_0} = \frac{-u_0}{u_1} = \frac{-c_1}{c_0}$$

So
$$c_1 = 1.1c_0$$

This optimum must lie on the PF, which has the equation

$$c_1 = 110 + 1.1(110 - c_0) \qquad (c_0 \leq 110)$$

$$= 231 - 1.1c_0$$

Thus
$$c_0 = \frac{231}{2.2} = 105 \qquad c_1 = 115.5$$

Hence
$$\text{Investment} = 5$$

$$\text{Growth rate} = 5 \text{ percent}$$

(ii) Project A is not worth doing, even if no other projects are done, since $(110 - 1)(110 + 1) < 110^2$. Project B will be considered before project C, as its rate of return is larger (and it is bigger). It will be done since $(110 - 5)(110 + 10) = 12{,}600 > 110^2$. Project C will not be done, since, if B is done, the marginal rate of substitution is

$$-\frac{dc_1}{dc_0} = \frac{c_1}{c_0} = \frac{110 + 10}{110 - 5} \simeq 1.15 > \frac{1.11}{1}$$

Q12-2 (i) $c_0 = 105$, $c_1 = 115.5$ (The borrowing/lending line is the same as the production frontier in Question 12-1.)

(ii) He will lend 5 in the first period and be repaid 5.5 in the second.

(iii)
$$\text{PV of consumption} = \text{PV of income} = 110 + \frac{110}{1.1} = 210$$

Q12-3 Projects B and C have positive present values.

Thus
$$\text{PV} = y_0 + \frac{y_1}{1 + i} = 110 - 5 - 1 + \frac{110 + 10 + 1.11}{1.1} = 214.1$$

So
$$c_0 + \frac{c_1}{1.1} = 214.1 \qquad c_1 = 1.1c_0$$

So
$$c_0 = 107.05 \qquad y_0 = 104 \qquad \text{borrowing} = 3.05$$
$$c_1 = 117.75 \qquad y_1 = 121.11 \qquad \text{repayment} = 3.36$$

Q12-4 (i) *First* suppose project A is done. Suppose the borrowing constraint is not binding.

$$\frac{u_0}{u_1} = \frac{c_1}{c_0} = 1.1$$

$$c_0 + \frac{c_1}{1.1} = y_0 + \frac{y_1}{1.1} = 110 - 600 + \frac{110 + 1111}{1.1} = 620$$

Thus
$$c_0 = 310 \qquad c_1 = 310(1.1)$$

This requires him to borrow 800 in period 1, which is infeasible. Thus borrowing constraint is binding. So

$$c_0 = 110 - 600 + 500 = 10$$
$$c_1 = 110 + 1111 - 550 = 671$$
$$u = 10\,(671)$$

Now suppose project A is not done. Suppose the borrowing constraint is not binding:

$$c_0 = 105 \qquad c_1 = 115.5 \qquad \text{(see Question 12-2)}$$

This requires him to lend 5, which is feasible.

$$u = 105\,(115.5) > 10\,(671)$$

Thus project A is not done.

(ii) Suppose project B is done. Since the individual is richer than if project A is done, he will want to consume more and therefore to borrow $360 - (110 - 500) = 750$. Therefore the borrowing constraint is binding:

$$c_0 = 110 \qquad c_1 = 671$$
$$u = 110(671) > 105(115.5)$$

Thus project B is done.

Q12-5 (i) B.
   (ii) A.

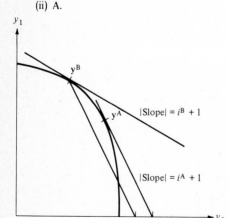

(iii) B.

(iv) If there are imperfect capital markets, great care is needed in making welfare comparisons based on present values (see R. Layard, "On Measuring the Redistribution of Lifetime Income," in M. S. Feldstein and R. P. Inman (eds.), *The Economics of Public Services*, Macmillan, New York, 1976).

Q12-6 (i) A + B, C.

$$PV \text{ of A and B} = -4 + \frac{4.30}{1.05} = 4 \quad -1 + \frac{1.075}{1.05}$$

$$\simeq 4(-1 + 1.025) = 0.1$$

$$PV \text{ of C} = -1 + \frac{1.14}{1.05} \simeq 0.09$$

(ii) C.

(iii) A + B.

Q12-7 Assuming social and private costs and benefits are the same

(i) Nuclear. PV (Nuclear) = 120; PV (Thermal) = 100.

(ii) Thermal. PV (Nuclear) = 10; PV (Thermal) = 25.

Q12-8 (i) Solve for i in

$$1 + \frac{1.1}{1+i} = 1.1 + \frac{0.99}{1+i}$$

$$i = 0.10$$

(ii) A, since its returns come later. Note that at $i = 0$, $PV_A > PV_B$.

Q12-9 Yes. There is only one interest rate at which the two machines have equal present value.

$$\frac{2}{1+i} = \frac{1}{1+i} + \frac{2}{(1+i)^2}$$

Therefore $\qquad\qquad i = 1$

Q13-1 (i) Fertilise.

(ii) Fertilise.

(iii) It depends on the curvature of his indifference curves.

Q13-2 (i) $E(y|A) = 100$; $E(y|B) = \frac{1}{3}(200) + \frac{2}{3}(50) = 100$.

(ii)

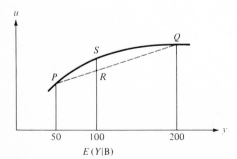

$PR/PQ = \frac{1}{3}$. R lies above $E(y|B)$. Once again S lies above R.

Q13-3 False.

Q13-4 Risk-lovers. Let f_0 be the original fine and p_0 the original probability of being caught. With increased fine or increased chance of being caught, expected income is the same $[E(y) = y_0 - p_0 f_0\ 1.01]$; but when the *fine* is increased, the income loss *if* caught is greater $(y_0 - 1.01\ f_0)$. Since this case is preferred, the utility function must be convex. The diagram illustrates.

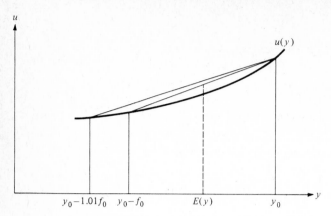

Q13-5 No. Do project if $E(u) > u(y^0)$. This requires

$$-pe^{-\alpha(y^0 + 100)} - (1 - p)e^{-\alpha(y^0 - 90)} > -e^{-\alpha y^0}$$

Hence, multiplying by $e^{\alpha y^0}$, we obtain

$$-pe^{-\alpha 100} - (1 - p)e^{\alpha 90} > -1$$

So y^0 does not matter.

Q13-6 (i) The probability that it will take n tosses up to and including the first head is the probability of getting tails in the first $n - 1$ tosses $(= \frac{1}{2}^{n-1})$ times the probability of getting a head on the nth toss $(\frac{1}{2}) = \frac{1}{2}^n$. If it takes n tosses, you receive 2^n dollars. So your expected receipts are

$$\sum_{n=1}^{\infty} \tfrac{1}{2}^n 2^n = \infty$$

[Your expected return arising from each possible number of tosses (n) is 1, but there is an infinite number of possible n's.]

(ii) I would be willing to pay less than an infinite number of dollars.

(iii) Because I maximise expected utility and my marginal utility of incomes falls with income. This is the answer given by Bernouilli in the 1730s to resolve this paradox, called the St. Petersburg paradox since Bernouilli was teaching there (his paper was reprinted in English in *Econometrica*, vol. 22, pp. 23–36, January 1954). [To guarantee that a person is only willing to pay a finite sum for *any* coin-tossing option, where for each n there is a finite prize $p(n)$, we need to assume a utility function that is bounded above, i.e., for which $du/dy = 0$ for all y greater than some finite number. Bernouilli assumed $u = \log y$, which is not bounded, but guarantees a finite certainty-equivalent income for the particular set of prizes $p(n) = 2^n$.]

Q13-7 (i) Constant absolute risk aversion: $k - e^{-\alpha y}$

$$u' = \alpha e^{-\alpha y}$$

$$u'' = -\alpha^2 e^{-\alpha y}$$

$$\frac{-u''}{u'} = \alpha$$

(ii) Constant relative risk aversion: $-1/\alpha + y^\alpha/\alpha$

$$u' = y^{\alpha - 1}$$

$$u'' = (\alpha - 1)y^{\alpha - 2}$$

$$\frac{-u''}{u'}\,y = 1 - \alpha$$

The formula cannot be used for $\alpha = 0$. Instead use

$$u(y) = \log y$$

This is the limit of $-1/\alpha + y^\alpha/\alpha$ as $\alpha \to 0$.

Q13-8 False. When the project is split in two, the expected return to the individual is multiplied by $\frac{1}{2}$ and the cost of risk by $\frac{1}{4}$.

Q13-9 It is fairly small compared with the mean return.

$$E(y) = 5(10)^6$$

$$\text{var }(y) = [\tfrac{1}{2}(45)^2 + \tfrac{1}{2}(45)^2]10^{12} = 2025(10)^{12}$$

The average household income in Britain is about £5000. Therefore

$$\frac{-u''}{2u'} = \frac{2y^2}{2y^3} = \frac{1}{5000}$$

Hence

$$C = \frac{-u''}{2u'}\frac{\text{var }(y)}{n} = \frac{1}{5000}\frac{2025(10)^{12}}{10^6} \simeq (0.4)10^6$$

This is fairly small compared with the expected return of $5(10)^6$.

Q13-10 True. Suppose, for example, each income pays y_1 in state 1 and y_2 in state 2. Whether incomes are pooled or not, each individual gets y_1 in state 1 and y_2 in state 2.

Q13-11 Suppose there are two assets each costing \$1 per unit and the income yielded by each (per unit) is as follows (\$)

Asset A: y_A sure

Asset B: y_B, with mean $\bar{y}_B$ and variance var (y_B)

The individual has wealth \$W and spends \$B on the risky asset and \$(W − B) on the safe asset.
    The individual's problem is

$$\max E(u) = a + b\bar{y} - c[\bar{y}^2 + \text{var }(y)]$$

$$= a + b(W - B)\bar{y}_A + bB\bar{y}_B - c[(W - B)\bar{y}_A + B\bar{y}_B]^2 - cB^2 \text{ var }(y_B)$$

Thus

$$\frac{dE(u)}{dB} = -b(\bar{y}_A - \bar{y}_B) - 2c[(W - B)\bar{y}_A + B\bar{y}_B](-\bar{y}_A + \bar{y}_B) - 2cB \text{ var }(y_B) = 0$$

Since B is risky, $\bar{y}_B - \bar{y}_A > 0$. Call this Δ. Hence

$$W\bar{y}_A \Delta + B\Delta^2 = -B \text{ var }(y_B) + \text{const}$$

$$\frac{dB}{dW} = -\frac{\bar{y}_A \Delta}{\text{var }(y_B) + \Delta^2} < 0$$

Q13-12 No.

$$E(u) = a + b\mu - c\mu^2 - c\sigma^2 = \text{const}$$

Hence
$$(b - 2c\mu)\, d\mu = 2c\sigma\, d\sigma$$

$$\frac{d\mu}{d\sigma} = \frac{2c\sigma}{b - 2c\mu}$$

This is zero when $\sigma = 0$. As σ rises, μ rises to hold $E(u)$ constant, so $d\mu/d\sigma$ rises with σ, holding $E(u)$ constant.

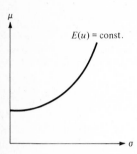

Since risky assets have higher expected returns than safe ones, the opportunity locus is rising. Therefore the equilibrium cannot be on the vertical axis.

Q13-13 True. If A is preferred to B and A is preferred to C, they give two inequality relations which, when added, yield an absurdity.

Q13-14 $u(1) > 0.10u(5) + 0.89u(1) + 0.01u(0)$. Thus, adding $0.89u(0)$ to both sides and rearranging, we have

$$u(1) - 0.89u(1) + 0.89u(0) > 0.10u(5) + 0.01u(0) + 0.89u(0)$$

Hence
$$0.11u(1) + 0.89u(0) > 0.10u(5) + 0.90u(0)$$

Thus C is preferred to D

Q13-15 (i) $\frac{2}{1}$ for each. The efficiency locus is the diagonal.
(ii) Yes.

Q13-16 When I buy a car there is a probability p that it is a dud. Once I have bought it I know whether it is a dud or not. I am more likely to sell it if it is a dud. Potential buyers know this and are willing to pay less than for a new car. For an interesting discussion of this question see G. A. Akerlof, "The Market for Lemons: Quality Uncertainty and the Market Mechanism," *Quarterly Journal of Economics*, vol. 84, pp. 488–500, August 1970.

Q13-17 The pooling is unambiguously better, since it is a Pareto improvement.

$$P_G - C_G < \bar{P} \quad \text{and} \quad P_I < \bar{P}$$

Q13-18
Q13-19 Your answers are, we hope better than ours.

QA1-1 (i) Only $K^{1/3}L^{1/3}$ is concave, for $K^{2/3}L^{2/3}$ implies that an equiproportional increase in both factors leads to a more than equiproportional increase in output, thus:

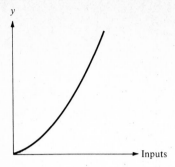

Increasing returns to scale functions are not concave, decreasing returns to scale functions are concave.

(ii) Both. For the isoquants of both functions are convex to the origin (and asymptotic to the axes).

QA3-1 (i)' Yes.

(ii) $x = K^2L^2(aK^3 + bL^3)^{-1}$

Thus
$$\frac{\partial x}{\partial K} = 2KL^2(aK^3 + bL^3)^{-1} - K^2L^2(aK^3 + bL^3)^{-2}3aK^2$$
$$= KL(aK^3 + bL^3)^{-1}[2L - KL(aK^3 + bL^3)^{-1}3aK^2]$$

So long as $w_K \geq 0$

$$\frac{\partial x}{\partial K} \geq 0$$

Therefore
$$\frac{2}{3} \geq aK^3(aK^3 + bL^3)^{-1} = \frac{aK^3}{aK^3 + bL^3} = \frac{a}{a + b(L/K)^3}$$

Hence
$$\tfrac{2}{3}a + \tfrac{2}{3}b\left(\frac{L}{K}\right)^3 \geq a$$

So
$$\left(\frac{L}{K}\right)^3 \geq \frac{a}{2b}$$

INDEX

INDEX

This index is also designed to serve as a glossary. Page numbers in **boldface** indicate places where concepts are defined.